Lecture Notes in Computer Science　　13299

More information about this series at https://link.springer.com/bookseries/558

Yamine Aït-Ameur · Florin Crăciun (Eds.)

Theoretical Aspects of Software Engineering

16th International Symposium, TASE 2022
Cluj-Napoca, Romania, July 8–10, 2022
Proceedings

 Springer

Editors
Yamine Aït-Ameur ⓘ
IRIT
Toulouse, France

Florin Crăciun ⓘ
Babeș-Bolyai University
Cluj-Napoca, Romania

ISSN 0302-9743   ISSN 1611-3349 (electronic)
Lecture Notes in Computer Science
ISBN 978-3-031-10362-9   ISBN 978-3-031-10363-6 (eBook)
https://doi.org/10.1007/978-3-031-10363-6

This Springer imprint is published by the registered company Springer Nature Switzerland AG
The registered company address is: Gewerbestrasse 11, 6330 Cham, Switzerland

Preface

The International Symposium on Theoretical Aspects of Software Engineering (TASE) gathers researchers and practitioners interested by the new results on innovative advances in software engineering. It records the latest developments in formal and theoretical software engineering methods and techniques.

The 16th edition of TASE was held in the beautiful city of Cluj-Napoca in Romania during July 8–10, 2022. TASE 2022 received 71 submissions covering different areas of theoretical software engineering. Each paper was reviewed by at least three reviewers and the Program Committee accepted 21 long papers and five short papers leading to an attractive scientific program.

This edition of TASE was enhanced by the presence of four keynote speakers. The first talk, given by Erika Àbrahàm from RWTH Aachen University in Germany, entitled "SMT Solving: Historical Roots, Recent Developments and Future Directions" dealt with SMT-based formal verification techniques and provided a technical view on the progress in SMT solving. In the second talk entitled "Practical Theory of Computation on Structures", Klaus-Dieter Schewe, from the ZJU-UIUC Institute in China, sketched a theory of computation centered around the notion of algorithmic systems. The two other talks dealt with formal software engineering and artificial intelligence. The talk of Sun Jun, from the Singapore Management University in Singapore, entitled "Neural Network Discrimination: Evaluation, Mitigation and Certification" addressed certification of fairness of neural networks using formal verification techniques. The last talk entitled "Rigorous system design for AI software" given by Saddek Bensalem, from Verimag at the University of Grenoble Alpes in France, presented the results of the FOCETA European project in rigorous verification and validation of critical systems.

TASE 2022 would not have succeeded without the deep investment and involvement of the Program Committee members and the external reviewers who evaluated (with more than 215 reviews) and selected the best contributions. This event would not exist without the authors and contributors who submitted their proposals. We address our thanks to everyone—reviewers, authors, Program Committee members, and organization committee members—involved in the success of TASE 2022.

The EasyChair system was set up for the management of TASE 2022, supporting submission, review, and volume preparation processes. It proved to be a powerful framework.

TASE 2022 had one affiliated workshop, the International Workshop on Formal Engineering of Cyber-Physical Systems, which brought additional participants to the symposium and helped make it an interesting and successful event. We thank all the workshop chairs, organizers, and authors for their hard work on this.

TASE 2022 was hosted and sponsored by Babeș-Bolyai University, Cluj-Napoca, Romania. The local organization committee offered all the facilities to run the event in a lovely and friendly atmosphere. Many thanks to all the local organizers.

Lastly, we wish to express our special thanks to the steering committee members, in particular Shengchao Qin and Huibiao Zhu, for their valuable support.

July 2022

Yamine Aït-Ameur
Florin Crăciun

Organization

Program Committee

Erika Abraham	RWTH Aachen University, Germany
Yamine Ait Ameur (Chair)	IRIT, INPT-ENSEEIHT, France
Étienne André	Loria, Université de Lorraine, France
Toshiaki Aoki	JAIST, Japan
Christian Attiogbe	LS2N, Université de Nantes, France
Guangdong Bai	University of Queensland, Australia
Richard Banach	University of Manchester, UK
Luís Soares Barbosa	University of Minho, Portugal
Marcello Bonsangue	Leiden University, The Netherlands
Marius Bozga	Verimag, Université Grenoble Alpes, France
Liqian Chen	National University of Defense Technology, China
Wei-Ngan Chin	National University of Singapore, Singapore
Horatiu Cirstea	Loria, France
Florin Craciun (Chair)	Babeş-Bolyai University, Romania
Guillaume Dupont	Institut de Recherche en Informatique de Toulouse, France
Flavio Ferrarotti	Software Competence Centre Hagenberg, Austria
Simon Foster	University of York, UK
Marc Frappier	Université de Sherbrooke, Canada
Radu Grosu	Stony Brook University, USA
Kim Guldstrand Larsen	Aalborg University, Denmark
Thai Son Hoang	University of Southampton, UK
Zoltán Horváth	Eotvos Lorand University, Budapest
Zhe Hou	Griffith University, Australia
Fuyuki Ishikawa	National Institute of Informatics, Japan
Andreas Katis	KBR Inc., NASA Ames Research Center, USA
Olga Kouchnarenko	University of Franche-Comté, France
Regine Laleau	Paris-East Créteil University, France
Guoqiang Li	Shanghai Jiao Tong University, China
Qin Li	East China Normal University, China
Dorel Lucanu	Alexandru Ioan Cuza University, Romania
Frederic Mallet	Université Nice Sophia-Antipolis, France
Amel Mammar	Telecom SudParis, France
Dominique Mery	Loria, Université de Lorraine, France
Simona Motogna	Babeş-Bolyai University, Romania

Kazuhiro Ogata	JAIST, Japan
Jun Pang	University of Luxembourg, Luxembourg
Shengchao Qin	Teesside University, UK
Adrian Riesco	Universidad Complutense de Madrid, Spain
Cristina Seceleanu	Mälardalen University, Sweden
Neeraj Singh	IRIT, INPT-ENSEEIHT, University of Toulouse, France
Meng Sun	Peking University, China
Rob van Glabbeek	Data61, CSIRO, Australia
Naijun Zhan	Institute of Software, Chinese Academy of Sciences, China
Huibiao Zhu	East China Normal University, China
Xue-Yang Zhu	Institute of Software, Chinese Academy of Sciences, China

Additional Reviewers

An, Jie
Ardourel, Gilles
Chen, Mingshuai
Cheng, Zheng
Chouali, Samir
Dubois, Catherine
Ehrlinger, Lisa
Enoiu, Eduard Paul
Fan, Guangsheng
Fehnker, Ansgar
Gervais, Frédéric
Gibson, J. Paul
Guo, Xiaoyun
Guok, Ernest
Hajder, Levente
Halder, Raju
He, Mengda
Ishii, Daisuke
Jérôme, Rocheteau
Kobayashi, Tsutomu
Kölbl, Martin
Ligeti, Peter
Lin, Bo
Lin, Shang-Wei
Liu, Ai

Liu, Zengyu
Marinho, Dylan
Masson, Pierre-Alain
McClurg, Jedidiah
Merz, Stephan
Nguyen, Thuy
Pardillo Laursen, Christian
Pintér, Balázs
Seceleanu, Tiberiu
Shi, Ling
Sochor, Hannes
Sun, Weidi
Tejfel, Máté
Tomita, Takashi
Truscan, Dragos
Wang, Shuling
Wen, Cheng
Xue, Bai
Yan, Fang
Zhan, Bohua
Zhang, Haitao
Zhang, Miaomiao
Zhao, Ying
Zhao, Yongxin

Keynotes

Neural Network Discrimination: Evaluation, Mitigation and Certification

Jun Sun

Singapore Management University

Abstract. In recent years, neural network based machine learning has found its way into various aspects of people's daily life, such as face recognition, personal credit rating, and medical diagnose. One desirable property of neural networks for applications with societal impact is fairness. Since there are often societal biases in the training data, the resultant neural networks might be discriminative as well. Recently, there have been multiple attempts on improving fairness of neural networks, with a focus on fairness testing.

In this line of research, we develop a series of approaches and associated software tool-kits to evaluate a given neural network's fairness by systematically generating discriminatory instance (published at ICSE'20), to mitigate discrimination in the neural network by fining tuning a small number of guilty neurons (published at ICSE'22), and to certify the neural network's fairness through formal verification (published at FM'21). We demonstrate that with our approaches are both effective and efficiency using real-world applications.

SMT Solving: Historical Roots, Recent Developments and Future Directions

Erika Ábrahám

RWTH Aachen University, Germany

The development of decision procedures for checking the satisfiability of logical formulas has a long history in mathematical logic and symbolic computation. Besides theoretical interest, their automation in the 60's raised their practical importance and increased the intensity of research in this area. Besides computer algebra systems on the mathematical side, in the 90's another line of developments has been initiated in computer science. Unified under the name *satisfiability checking*, powerful SAT and SAT-modulo-theories (SMT) solvers have been developed that are nowadays at the heart of many techniques for the synthesis and analysis of software and hardware systems with probabilistic, timed, discrete, dynamical or discrete-continuous components, and in general for all types of large combinatorial problems like complex planning and scheduling tasks.

In this talk we give a historical overview of this development, describe our own solver SMT-RAT, discuss some fascinating new developments for checking the satisfiability of real-arithmetic formulas, and conclude with some challenges for potential future research directions.

Rigorous System Design for AI Software

Saddek Bensalem

University Grenoble Alpes, VERIMAG, Grenoble, France
Saddek.Bensalem@univ-grenoble-alpes.fr

Abstract. The convergence of scientific and technological developments in computing and networking with the physical side and Artificial Intelligence (AI) will impact the forthcoming period concerning several system aspects and disciplines. Learning-enabled Systems represent an example of that convergence, which embraces engineering and technological products. The learning-enabled system technologies are expected to bring large-scale improvements through new products and services across various applications ranging from healthcare to logistics through manufacturing, transport, and more. Software is inarguably the enabling factor for realizing such systems. Unfortunately, we still encounter deployment limitations in the safety-critical application (transportation, healthcare, etc.) due to a lack of trust, behavioral uncertainty, and technology compatibility with safe and secure system development methods. I will first provide an overview of the project FOCETA1 (FOundations for Continuous Engineering of Trustworthy Autonomy) and discuss its strategic goal and its challenges. In the second part of my talk, I will present the problem of the verification and validation methods considered in the project and discuss future research directions.

Supported by the European project Horizon 2020 research and innovation programme under grant agreement No. 956123.

Contents

Practical Theory of Computation
on Structures

Klaus-Dieter Schewe$^{(\boxtimes)}$

Zhejiang University, UIUC Institute, 718 East Haizhou Road, Haining 314400,
Zhejiang, China
`kd.schewe@intl.zju.edu.cn`

Abstract. There are hardly two fields in Computer Science that are
further apart than Software Engineering and Theoretical Computer Science.
The lack of theoretical foundations in the field of Software Engineering has a counterpart, as the theoretical foundations have not caught
up with the development of practical software systems. This raises the
question how a theory of computation should look like that modernises
the classical theory and at the same time is suitable for practical systems
development. This article is dedicated to a sketch of a theory of computation centred around the notion of algorithmic systems. I will argue
that behavioural theories are key to the understanding, i.e. we require
language-independent axiomatic definitions of classes of algorithmic systems that are accompanied by abstract machine models provably capturing the class under consideration. The machine models give further rise
to tailored logics through which properties of systems in the considered
class can be formalised and verified, and to fine-tuned classifications on
the grounds of complexity restrictions. All extensions are conservative in
the sense that the classical theory of computation is preserved, universal
in the sense that all practical developments are captured uniformly, and
practical in the sense that languages associated with the abstract machine
models can be used for rigorous high-level systems design and development, and the logics can be exploited for rigorous verification of desirable
properties of systems.

Keywords: Theory of computation · Behavioural theory ·
Computation on structures · Abstract State Machines · Algorithmic
system · Software engineering

1 Introduction

Computer Science has many origins, the most important ones in Mathematics
and in Electrical Engineering. As described in detail in Egon Börger's 1985
influential monograph on computability, complexity and logic (see the English
translation in [2]) it took decades to solve the key problem phrased by Alan
Turing to capture in a mathematically precise way the notion of *algorithm* (or at
least a specific class of algorithms) and to provide formalisms that can then be

© Springer Nature Switzerland AG 2022
Y. Aït-Ameur and F. Crăciun (Eds.): TASE 2022, LNCS 13299, pp. 1–14, 2022.
https://doi.org/10.1007/978-3-031-10363-6_1

used to specify and reason about them. Börger's monograph was at that time the most advanced text summarising the "classical" theory of computation centred around the links between computation theory, logic and complexity theory.

Throughout the centuries the research on the mathematical foundations of a universal computation theory was always coupled with the construction of machines that can be used to do practical computations. With the advent of transistors it became possible to create large computers, which enabled the practical realisation of many computation problems. This example of the *engineering* of practically useful machines was deeply grounded in the development in the mathematical *science*, which provided first the understanding of computing.

While the hardware had become available and the foundational theory existed, the bridge between an understanding of what a computation is to a practical development of algorithmic software systems did not exist. This led to an increasing number of fatal software errors caused by a reduction of software development to "quick and dirty" programming. In order to address these problems leading computer scientists came together in a conference dedicated to analyse the problems and find ways out of the "software crisis". The lengthy discussions were summarised in a report [18].

In a nutshell, while there were differing opinions, the conference participants agreed on the need to establish an engineering discipline addressing the systematic development of software systems. *Software Engineering* was supposed to work as any other engineering discipline: deeply grounded in scientific knowledge, focussed on problems arising in practice, and universal in the sense that software systems of all kinds are to be supported. More than 50 years have passed since this conference, but "Software Engineering" is still far away from the rigour in other engineering disciplines.

Let us take an example from civil engineering, the construction of a large bridge with multiple pillars and long swinging segments. He would most likely start with an idea of the architecture: what type of bridge it should be, how long, how wide, how many pillars would be required, etc. He would investigate the feasibility, whether the bridge could be built at the designated location. He would proceed calculating the statics and dynamics of the construction: which forces are expected, which environmental and weather conditions are to be expected, how the bridge will swing etc. to ensure the stability of the construction under all foreseeable conditions. He would verify, which materials would be required to satisfy all requirements and proceed with a detailed construction plan. Throughout the process all design decisions and all verification would be carefully documented.

These principles of engineering should also apply to the engineering of software systems. In a recent article Börger analyses the role of executable abstract programs for software development and documentation [4]. The intuitive understanding of those programs fits the computational mindset of software system engineers and can be supported by a simple but precise behavioural definition. They can be used in the practitioner's daily work to rigorously formulate every design or implementation decision taken on the path from the application view of the system that is to be developed system. The executable abstract programs of the resulting system documentation represent definitions of implementation steps one can check and justify by validation (due to their executable character) or by reasoning (due to the mathematical definition of their behaviour). For complex systems the implementation obviously involves multiple refinement steps. As such the development process produces as side effect a documentation that facilitates the understandability of the final software and improves its reliability. It also enhances the maintenance process (including reuse and change) and reduces enormously its cost. However, most common methods on Software Engineering lack this grounding in mathematical foundations.

On the other hand, also more than 35 years have passed since the publication of Börger's monograph on the theory of computation, complexity and logic. Over this period the practice of computing has changed a lot, but it seems that also the theoretical foundations have not caught up with the practical challenges.

In this article I will first sketch in Sect. 2 how a theory of computation centred around the notion of algorithmic systems could look like. I will argue that behavioural theories are key to the understanding, i.e. we require language-independent axiomatic definitions of classes of algorithmic systems that are accompanied by abstract machine models provably capturing the class under consideration. The machine models give further rise to tailored logics through which properties of systems in the considered class can be formalised and verified, and to fine-tuned classifications on the grounds of complexity restrictions. I will briefly discuss the practical consequences a precise classification of software systems according to their complexity has. In Sect. 3 as an example I will address Gurevich's conjecture that there is no logic capturing PTIME.

2   Towards a Theory of Computation on Structures

In the introduction we stated that software systems have significantly changed over the last decades. We are now dealing with systems of systems that operate in parallel exploiting synchronously multiple processor cores and asynchronously computing resources distributed over networks, interact with their environment, adapt their own behaviour, integrate reasoning about themselves and their environment, and support random choices.

All these developments require scientific foundations centred around computation theory, complexity and logic:

- Is there a theory of computation that faithfully covers all the aspects of systems of computing systems that occur in practice?
- Is there a methodology grounded in such a theory of computation that permits the definition and classification of complex systems and the provision of means for specification, systematic development, validation and verification?
- Is there a methodology that permits reasoning about problems and their solutions in terms of correctness and complexity?

A first answer was given in 1985 by Gurevich's "new thesis" [14], which was further elaborated in the 1995 Lipari guide [16]. The new theory emphasises

Tarski structures (aka universal algebras) to capture abstract states of systems and evolving algebras, now known as Abstract State Machines (ASMs), as the abstract machines capturing the algorithms on arbitrary levels of abstraction. Egon Börger realised that these ideas do not only create a new paradigm for the foundations of computing subsuming the classical theory, but at the same can be exploited for rigorous systems engineering in practice thereby fulfilling the criteria of a "software engineering" discipline that deserves this name as envisioned in the 1968 conference in Garmisch [18].

A remarkable success story started leading to proofs of compiler correctness for the Warren Abstract Machine for Prolog [7], the translation from Occam to transputers [5], the compilation of Java and the bytecode verifier [23], the development of the sophisticated theory of ASM refinements [3], and much more. The state of the theory and practice of ASMs is well summarised in Egon Börger's and Robert Stärk's monograph on ASMs [9]. More recent examples are found in the modelling companion by Börger and Raschke [6].

While the development proved that ASMs can take over the role of the formal languages in computation theory, it took until 2000 to develop the celebrated "sequential ASM thesis" [17]'. On one hand the thesis provided a language-independent definition of the notion of *sequential algorithm* giving for the first time in history a precise axiomatic definition of the notion of "algorithm" (though restricted to sequential algorithms). On the other hand it contained the proof that all algorithms as stipulated by the defining postulates are faithfully captured by sequential ASMs. This justified further to establish another new notion: a *behavioural theory* comprises a machine-independent axiomatic definition of a class of algorithms (or more generally: algorithmic systems), an abstract machine model, and a proof that the machine model captures the class of computations.

Starting from the first behavioural theory, the theory of sequential algorithms, another behavioural theory of parallel algorithms was developed in [11] closing the case of synchronous parallel algorithms. A convincing behavioural theory for asynchronous algorithmic systems was developed in [8] with *concurrent ASMs* as the machine model capturing concurrent algorithms, i.e. families of sequential or parallel algorithms associated with agents that are oblivious to the actions of each other apart from recognising changes to shared locations. Recently, a behavioural theory of reflective algorithms was developed addressing the question how to capture algorithmic systems that can adapt their own behaviour [20].

The behavioural theories yield variants of Abstract State Machines that can be used for rigorous systems development. Furthermore, Stärk and Nanchen developed a logic for the reasoning about deterministic ASMs [22], which was extended to non-deterministic ASMs in [12] by making update sets first-class objects in the theory and proving completeness with respect to Henkin semantics. It was also shown how the logic can be adapted to reason about concurrent ASMs [13]. An extension to reflective ASMs was approached in [21].

Complexity theory provides means for fine-tuned classification. One of the few studies trying to bring complexity theory to the theory of ASMs is the theory of *choiceless polynomial time* (CPT) [1], which studies the choiceless fragment of PTIME using PTIME bounded deterministic Abstract State Machines. Though it was possible to show that CPT subsumes other models of computation on structures, it is strictly included in PTIME, so Gurevich posted his conjecture that there is no logic capturing PTIME [15].

What is the impact of such fine-tuned classification on the field of Software Engineering? Consider the complexity class NP, which is captured by the existential fragment of second-order logic. That is, if a decision problem can be formulated in this logic, a solution is always possible by a backtracking algorithm, which explores in a depth-first approach an exponentially sized search space. Disregarding the "forgetfull" backtracking all other steps can be captured by deterministic PTIME ASMs. In this way the class the problem is in already determines the structure of the solution algorithm, which adds further support to the rigorous development method. If likewise we have a characterisation of problems in PTIME, we should obtain a different class of algorithms corresponding to ASMs of a certain type. In the next section I will outline that non-deterministic PTIME ASMs with a restricted choice operator will suffice.

Certainly, NP and PTIME provide only a very coarse classification, but this only reflects the state of the theory. It illustrates, however, how the mutual interaction between theory of computation on structures and practical engineering works. Same as the civil engineer whose methods are grounded in mathematical theories, the computation theory must provide the templates for the various problems of software engineers.

3   Insignificant Non-determinism

As an example we will now explore PTIME deeper addressing the problem, whether there exists a computation model over structures that captures the complexity class PTIME rather than Turing machines that operate over finite strings. This problem was raised in 1982 by Chandra and Harel [10].

3.1   Abstract State Machines

An ASM is defined by a signature, i.e. a finite set of function (and relation) symbols, a background, and a rule [9]. The signature defines states as structures, out of which a set of initial states is defined. The sets of states and initial states are closed under isomorphisms. The background defines domains and fixed operations on them that appear in every state, and the rule defines a relation between states and successor states and thus also runs. Here we follow the development for CPT [1] using hereditarily finite sets.

The *background* of an ASM, as we use them here, comprises logic names and set-theoretic names. *Logic names* comprise the binary equality =, nullary function names **true** and **false** and the usual Boolean operations. All logic names are relational. *Set-theoretic names* comprise the binary predicate $\in$, nullary function names $\emptyset$ and *Atoms*, unary function names $\bigcup$ and *TheUnique*, and the binary function name *Pair*.

The signature Υ of an ASM, as we use them here, comprises input names, dynamic and static names. *Input names* are given by a finite set of relation symbols, each with a fixed arity. Input names will be considered being static, i.e. locations defined by them will never be updated by the ASM. *Dynamic names* are given by a finite set of function symbols, each with a fixed arity, including *Output* and a nullary function symbol *Halt*. Some of the dynamic names may be relational. *Static names* are given by a finite set K of nullary function symbols c_f for all dynamic function symbols f.

States S are defined as structures over the signature Υ plus the background signature, for which we assume specific base sets. A *base set* B comprises three parts: a finite set A of *atoms*, which are not sets, the collection $B = HF(A)$ of hereditarily finite sets built over A, and a set K of constants $c_f \notin B$ for all static names c_f. Each element $x \in HF(A)$ has a well-defined *rank* $rk(x)$. We have $rk(x) = 0$, if $x = \emptyset$ or x is an atom. If x is a non-empty set, we define its rank as the smallest ordinal α such that $rk(y) < \alpha$ holds for all $y \in x$. The atoms in A and the sets in $HF(A)$ are the *objects* of the base set $B = HF(A) \cup K$. A set X is called *transitive* iff $x \in X$ and $y \in x$ implies $y \in X$. If x is an object, then $TC(x)$ denotes the least transitive set X with $x \in X$. If $TC(x)$ is finite, the object x is called *hereditarily finite*.

The logic names are interpreted in the usual way, i.e. **true** and **false** are interpreted by 1 and 0, respectively (i.e. by $\{\emptyset\}$ and $\emptyset$). Boolean operations are undefined, i.e. give rise to the value 0, if at least one of the arguments is not Boolean. An *isomorphism* is a permutation σ of the set A of atoms that is extended to sets in B by $\sigma(\{b_1, \ldots, b_k\}) = \{\sigma(b_1), \ldots, \sigma(b_k)\}$ and to the constants c_f by $\sigma(c_f) = c_f$. Then every isomorphism σ will map the truth values $\emptyset$ and $\{\emptyset\}$ to themselves. The set-theoretic names $\in$ and $\emptyset$ are interpreted in the obvious way, and *Atoms* is interpreted by the set of atoms of the base set. If $a_1, \ldots, a_k$ are atoms and $b_1, \ldots, b_\ell$ are sets, then $\bigcup\{a_1, \ldots, a_k, b_1, \ldots, b_\ell\} = b_1 \cup \cdots \cup b_\ell$. For $b = \{a\}$ we have $TheUnique(b) = a$, otherwise it is undefined. Furthermore, we have $Pair(a, b) = \{a, b\}$.

An input name p is interpreted by a Boolean-valued function. If the arity is n and $p(a_1, \ldots, a_n)$ holds, then each a_i must be an atom. Finally, a dynamic function symbol f of arity n is interpreted by a function $f_S : B^n \to B$ (or by $f_S : B^n \to \{0, 1\}$, if f is relational). The domain $\{(a_1, \ldots, a_n) \mid f(a_1, \ldots, a_n) \neq 0\}$ is required to be finite. For the static function symbols we have the interpretation $(c_f)_S = c_f$. With such an interpretation we obtain the set of states over the signature Υ and the given background.

An *input structure* is a finite structure I over the subsignature comprising only the input names. Without loss of generality it can be assumed that only atoms appear in I. If the finite set of atoms in the input structure is A, then $|A|$ is referred to as the *size* of the input. An *initial state* S_0 is a state over the base set $B = HF(A) \cup K$ which extends I such that the domain of each dynamic function is empty. We call $S_0 = State(I)$ the *initial state generated by* I. To emphasise the dependence on I, we also write $HF(I)$ instead of B.

Terms and *Boolean terms* are defined in the usual way assuming a given set of variables V. The set $fr(t)$ of *free variables* in a term t is defined as usual, in particular $fr(\{t(v) \mid v \in s \wedge g(v)\}) = (fr(t(v)) \cup fr(s) \cup fr(g(v))) - \{v\}$. Also the interpretation of terms in a state S is standard. *ASM rules* as we use them are defined as follows:

skip. skip is a rule.

assignment. If f is a dynamic function symbol in Υ of arity n and $t_0, \ldots, t_n$ are terms, then $f(t_1, \ldots, t_n) := t_0$ is a rule.

branching. If φ is a Boolean term and r_1, r_2 are rules, then also **if** φ **then** r_1 **else** r_2 **endif** is a rule. We also use the shortcut **if** φ **then** r_1 **endif** for **if** φ **then** r_1 **else skip endif**.

parallelism. If v is a variable, t is a term with $v \notin fr(t)$, and $r(v)$ is a rule, then also **forall** $v \in t$ **do** $r(v)$ **enddo** is a rule. We use the shortcut **par** $r_1 \ldots r_k$ **endpar** for **forall** $i \in \{1, \ldots, k\}$ **do if** $i = 1$ **then** r_1 **else if** $i = 2$ **then** r_2 **else** $\ldots$ **if** $i = k$ **then** r_k **endif** $\ldots$ **endif enddo**.

choice. If v is a variable, t is a term with $v \notin fr(t)$, and $r(v)$ is a rule, then also **choose** $v \in \{x \mid x \in Atoms \wedge x \in t\}$ **do** $r(v)$ **enddo** is a rule.

In the sequel we further use the shortcut **let** $x = t$ **in** $r(x)$ for **choose** $x \in Pair(t, t)$ **do** $r(x)$ **enddo**. The rule associated with an ASM must be closed. The semantics of ASM rules is defined via update sets that are built for the states of the machine. Applying an update set to a state defines a successor state.

If f is dynamic function symbol in Υ of arity n, and $a_1, \ldots, a_n$ are objects of the base set B of a state S, then the pair $(f, (a_1, \ldots, a_n))$ is a *location* of the state S. We use the abbreviation $\bar{a}$ for tuples $(a_1, \ldots, a_n)$, whenever the arity is known from the context. For a location $\ell = (f, \bar{a})$ we write $val_S(\ell) = b$ iff $f_S(a_1, \ldots, a_n) = b$; we call b the value of the location ℓ in the state S. An *update* is a pair (ℓ, a) consisting of a location ℓ and an object $a \in B$, and an *update set* (for a state S) is a set of updates with locations of S and objects a in the base set of S.

Now let S be a state with base set B, and let $\zeta : V \to B$ be a variable assignment. Let r be an ASM rule. Then we define a set of update sets $\mathbf{\Delta}_{r,\zeta}(S)$ on state S for the rule r depending on ζ i the common way [9].

3.2   Polynomial-Time-Bounded ASMs

An update set Δ is *consistent* iff for any two updates $(\ell, a_1), (\ell, a_2) \in \Delta$ with the same location we have $a_1 = a_2$. This defines the notion of *successor state* $S' = S + \Delta$ of a state S. For a consistent update set $\Delta \in \mathbf{\Delta}_{r,\zeta}(S)$ and a location ℓ we have $val_{S'}(\ell) = a$ for $(\ell, a) \in \Delta$ and $val_{S'}(\ell) = val_S(\ell)$ else. In addition, let $S + \Delta = S$ for inconsistent update sets Δ.

Then the (closed) rule r of an ASM defines a set of successor states for each state S. We write $\Delta_r(S, S')$ for an update set in $\mathbf{\Delta}_r(S)$ with $S' = S + \Delta_r(S, S')$.

A *run* of an ASM M with rule r is a finite or infinite sequence of states $S_0, S_1, \ldots$ such that S_0 is an initial state and $S_{i+1} = S_i + \Delta$ holds for some update set $\Delta \in \mathbf{\Delta}_r(S_i)$. Furthermore, if k is the length of a run ($k = \omega$ for an infinite run), then *Halt* must fail on all states S_i with $i < k$.

Let S be a state with base set B. An object $a \in B$ is called *critical* iff a is an atom or $a \in \{0, 1\}$ or a is the value of a location ℓ of S or there is a location $\ell = (f, \bar{a})$ with $\mathrm{val}_S(\ell) \neq \emptyset$ and a appears in $\bar{a}$. An object $a \in B$ is called *active* in S iff there exists a critical object a' with $a \in TC(a')$. In addition, if $R = S_0, S_1, \ldots$ is a run of an ASM, then we call an object $a \in B$ *active* in R iff a is active in at least one state S_i of R.

A *PTIME (bounded) ASM* is a triple $\tilde{M} = (M, p(n), q(n))$ comprising an ASM M and two integer polynomials $p(n)$ and $q(n)$. A *run* of $\tilde{M}$ is an initial segment of a run of M of length at most $p(n)$ with a total number of at most $q(n)$ active objects, where n is the size of the input in the initial state of the run.

We say that a PTIME ASM $\tilde{M}$ *accepts* the input structure I iff there is a run of $\tilde{M}$ with initial state generated by I and ending in a state, in which *Halt* holds and the value of *Output* is 1. Analogously, a PTIME ASM $\tilde{M}$ *rejects* the input structure I iff there is a run of $\tilde{M}$ with initial state generated by I and ending in a state, in which *Halt* holds and the value of *Output* is 0.

3.3   Insignificant Choice ASMs

Choice rules in the ASMs defined in the previous section are already restricted, as only choices among atoms are permitted. We now introduce two further restrictions. An *insignificant choice ASM* (for short: icASM) is an ASM (as defined above) that satisfies the following two conditions:

local insignificance condition. For every state S any two update sets $\Delta, \Delta' \in \mathbf{\Delta}(S)$ are isomorphic, and we can write $\mathbf{\Delta}(S) = \{\sigma \Delta \mid \sigma \in G\}$ with a set of isomorphisms $G \subseteq \mathcal{I}so$ and $\Delta \in \mathbf{\Delta}(S)$.

branching condition. For isomorphic update sets $\Delta \in \mathbf{\Delta}(S)$ and $\Delta' = \sigma(\Delta) \in \mathbf{\Delta}(S')$ we have $\sigma(\mathbf{\Delta}(S + \Delta)) = \mathbf{\Delta}(S' + \Delta')$, i.e. σ defines an isomorphism between the sets of update sets in the corresponding successor states.

A *PTIME (bounded) icASM* is a PTIME ASM $\tilde{M} = (M, p(n), q(n))$ with an ic-ASM M. The name "branching condition" is due to the fact that this condition mainly depends on branching rules, as we shall see later. The name "local insignificance condition" refers to the fact that condition only refers to update sets in a state. We can also define a "global insignificance condition".

An ASM M is *globally insignificant* iff for every run $S_0, \ldots, S_k$ of length k such that *Halt* holds in S_k, every $i \in \{0, \ldots, k-1\}$ and every update set $\Delta \in \mathbf{\Delta}(S_i)$ there exists a run $S_0, \ldots, S_i, S'_{i+1}, \ldots, S'_m$ such that $S'_{i+1} = S_i + \Delta$, *Halt* holds in S'_m, and *Output* = **true** (or **false**, respectively) holds in S_k iff *Output* = **true** (or **false**, respectively) holds in S'_m. A *PTIME (bounded) globally insignificant ASM* is a PTIME ASM $\tilde{M} = (M, p(n), q(n))$ with a globally insignificant ASM M.

Proposition 3.1. *Every ic-ASM is globally insignificant.*

The complexity class *insignificant choice polynomial time* (ICPT) is the collection of pairs (K_1, K_2), where K_1 and K_2 are disjoint classes of finite structures of the same signature, such that there exists a PTIME icASM that accepts all structures in K_1 and rejects all structures in K_2.

We also say that a pair $(K_1, K_2) \in$ ICPT is *ICPT-separable*. As for the analogous definition of CPT a PTIME icASM may accept structures not in K_1 and reject structures not in K_2. Therefore, we also say that a class K of finite structures is in ICPT, if $(K, K') \in$ ICPT holds for the complement K' of structures over the same signature.

3.4 PTIME Logics

Let us link the definition of ICPT to PTIME logics as defined in [1]. In general, a logic $\mathcal{L}$ can be defined by a pair (*Sen,Sat*) of functions satisfying the following conditions: *Sen* assigns to every signature Υ a recursive set $Sen(\Upsilon)$, the set of $\mathcal{L}$-*sentences of signature* Υ. *Sat* assigns to every signature Υ a recursive binary relation Sat_Υ over structures S over Υ and sentences $\varphi \in Sen(\Upsilon)$. We assume that $Sat_\Upsilon(S, \varphi) \Leftrightarrow Sat_\Upsilon(S', \varphi)$ holds, whenever S and S' are isomorphic. We say that a structure S over Υ *satisfies* $\varphi \in Sen(\Upsilon)$ (notation: $S \models \varphi$) iff $Sat_\Upsilon(S, \varphi)$ holds.

If $\mathcal{L}$ is a logic in this general sense, then for each signature Υ and each sentence $\varphi \in Sen(\Upsilon)$ let $K(\Upsilon, \varphi)$ be the class of structures S with $S \models \varphi$. We then say that $\mathcal{L}$ is a *PTIME logic*, if every class $K(\Upsilon, \varphi)$ is PTIME in the sense that it is closed under isomorphisms and there exists a Turing machine that maps φ to a PTIME Turing machine M_φ that accepts exactly the standard encodings of ordered versions of the structures in the class. We further say that a logic $\mathcal{L}$ *captures PTIME* iff it is a PTIME logic and for every signature Υ every PTIME class of Υ-structures conincides with some class $K(\Upsilon, \varphi)$.

These definitions of PTIME logics can be generalised to three-valued logics, in which case $Sat_\Upsilon(S, \varphi)$ may be true, false or unknown. For these possibilities we say that φ *accepts* S or φ *rejects* S or neither, respectively. Then two disjoint classes K_1 and K_2 of structures over Υ are called $\mathcal{L}$-*separable* iff there exists a sentence φ accepting all structures in K_1 and rejecting all those in K_2.

In this sense, ICPT is to define a three-valued PTIME logic that separates pairs of structures in ICPT. The idea is that sentences of this logic are PTIME icASMs, for which Υ is the signature of the input structure. By abuse of terminology we also denote this logic as ICPT. We therefore have to show that these PTIME icASMs over Υ form a recursive set. We also have to show that every PTIME icASM M can be simulated by a PTIME Turing machine M' such that M produces *Output* = **true** iff M' accepts the standard encoding of an ordered version of the input structure for M.

3.5   Recursive Syntax

We defined icASMs by three restrictions. Choices are only permitted among atoms, which is already covered by the syntactic restriction of choice rules, in which the condition $x \in Atoms$ is required.

Using the logic of non-deterministic ASMs [13] without meta-finite states, multiset functions and update multisets, we will show that the local insignificance and the branching conditions can be expressed in this logic. We then modify the semantics of choice and the semantics of ASM rules by integrating these conditions, which allows us to define icASMs syntactically in the same way as the ASMs in the preceding section. In this way we obtain the required recursive set of "sentences".

Local Insignificance Condition. First we show how to express that X represents an update set, or is consistent. For these we have

$$\text{isUSet}(X) \equiv \forall x_1, x_2, x_3.X(x_1, x_2, x_3) \rightarrow$$

$$\bigvee_{f \in \Upsilon_{dyn}} (x_1 = c_f \wedge \exists y_1, \ldots, y_{ar(f)}.x_2 = (y_1, \ldots, y_{ar(f)}))$$

using $ar(f)$ to denote the arity of f and Υ_{dyn} to denote the set of dynamic function symbols and

$$\text{conUSet}(X) \equiv \text{isUSet}(X) \wedge \forall x_1, x_2, x_3, x_4.$$
$$(X(x_1, x_2, x_3) \wedge X(x_1, x_2, x_4) \rightarrow x_3 = x_4).$$

For local insignificance we need that all update sets in $\boldsymbol{\Delta}_r(S)$ are isomorphic, so we express that X is an isomorphism by

$$\text{iso}(X) \equiv \forall x, y_1, y_2.(X(x, y_1) \wedge X(x, y_2) \rightarrow y_1 = y_2) \wedge \bigwedge_{f \in \Upsilon_{dyn}} X(c_f, c_f) \wedge$$
$$\forall x_1, x_2, y.(X(x_1, y) \wedge X(x_2, y) \rightarrow x_1 = x_2) \wedge \forall x \exists y.X(x, y) \wedge \forall y \exists x.X(x, y) \wedge$$
$$\forall x, y.[X(x, y) \rightarrow (x \in Atoms \leftrightarrow y \in Atoms)$$
$$\wedge \forall u.(u \in x \rightarrow \exists v.v \in y \wedge X(u, v)) \wedge \forall v.(v \in y \rightarrow \exists u.u \in x \wedge X(u, v))]$$

This leads to the following constraint for a rule r expressing that any two update sets yielded by r are isomorphic:

$$\forall X_1, X_2.\, \text{upd}_r(X_1) \wedge \text{upd}_r(X_2) \rightarrow \exists X.(\text{iso}(X) \wedge \text{updIso}(X_1, X_2, X))$$

with

$$\text{updIso}(X_1, X_2, X) \equiv$$
$$\bigwedge_{f \in \Upsilon_{dyn}} [\forall \bar{x}_1, x_2, \bar{y}_1, y_2.(X_1(c_f, \bar{x}_1, x_2) \wedge \bigwedge_{1 \le i \le ar(f)} X(x_{1i}, y_{1i}) \wedge X(x_2, y_2)$$
$$\rightarrow X_2(c_f, \bar{y}_1, y_2))$$

$$\wedge \, \forall \bar{x}_1, x_2, \bar{y}_1, y_2. (X_2(c_f, \bar{x}_1, x_2) \wedge \bigwedge_{1 \leq i \leq ar(f)} X(x_{1i}, y_{1i}) \wedge X(x_2, y_2)$$

$$\rightarrow X_1(c_f, \bar{y}_1, y_2))]$$

We can use this characterisation of insignificant choice to modify the logic in such a way that a choice rule will either become an insignificant choice or there is no update set at all. In order to express local insignificance we modify the definition of formulae $\mathrm{upd}_r(X)$ expressing that the rule r yields an update set X (for details see [13]) by introducing new formulae of the form $\mathrm{upd}_r^{ic}(X)$. If r is not a choice rule, we simply keep the definitions of upd_r (i.e. we replace upd_r everywhere by $\mathrm{upd}_r^{ic}(X)$), but for a choice rule r of the form **choose** $v \in \{x \mid x \in Atoms \wedge x \in t\}$ **do** $r'(v)$ **enddo** we define

$$\mathrm{upd}_r^{ic}(X) \leftrightarrow \exists v. v \in Atoms \wedge v \in t \wedge \mathrm{upd}_{r'(v)}^{ic}(X) \wedge$$

$$\forall Y. (\exists x. x \in Atoms \wedge x \in t \wedge \mathrm{upd}_{r'(x)}^{ic}(Y)) \rightarrow \exists Z. (\mathrm{iso}(Z) \wedge \mathrm{updIso}(X, Y, Z))$$

Syntactically, rules of icASMs are the same as arbitrary ASM rules, but the semantics of choice is changed to enforce semantically the satisfaction of the local insignificance condition.

Branching Condition. For the branching condition two states S and S' have to be considered. However, given a state S of an icASM we only need to consider states S', for which there exists update sets $\Delta' \in \boldsymbol{\Delta}_r(S')$ isomorphic to some $\Delta \in \boldsymbol{\Delta}_r(S)$. We can therefore assume that there exists an ASM rule r_{ini} such that $S' = S + \Delta_{ini}$ for some $\Delta_{ini} \in \boldsymbol{\Delta}_{r_{ini}}(S)$—we will investigate this rule further in the next section. Then the following constraint expresses that the branching condition is satisfied, more precisely: if the condition holds in state S, then the branching condition holds for state pairs S, S', where S' results from S by the rule r_{ini}.

$$\forall X_1, X_2, Z. \mathrm{isUSet}(X_1) \wedge \mathrm{isUSet}(X_2) \wedge \mathrm{isUSet}(Z) \wedge \mathrm{upd}_r^{ic}(X_1) \wedge \mathrm{upd}_{r_{ini}}^{ic}(Z) \wedge$$

$$[Z]\mathrm{upd}_r^{ic}(X_2) \wedge \exists X. \mathrm{iso}(X) \wedge \mathrm{updIso}(X_1, X_2, X) \rightarrow \mathrm{updIsoSet}(X_1, X_2, X, Z)$$

using the definition

$$\mathrm{updIsoSet}(X_1, X_2, X, Z) \equiv \forall Y_1, Y_2. (\mathrm{isUSet}(Y_1) \wedge \mathrm{isUSet}(Y_2) \wedge$$

$$\mathrm{updIso}(Y_1, Y_2, X)) \rightarrow ([X_1]\mathrm{upd}_r(Y_1) \leftrightarrow [Z][X_2]\mathrm{upd}_r(Y_2))$$

Now we can modify the semantics of icASM rules by enforcing that update sets are only yielded in states S that satisfy the condition (??) above. Otherwise no update set will be yielded, which implies the computation of the machine to get stuck. We therefore define

$$\mathrm{Upd}_r(X) \equiv \mathrm{upd}_r^{ic}(X) \wedge \forall Y, Z. (\mathrm{isUSet}(Y) \wedge \mathrm{isUSet}(Z) \wedge \mathrm{upd}_{r_{ini}}^{ic}(Z) \wedge$$

$$[Z]\mathrm{upd}_r^{ic}(Y) \wedge \exists U. \mathrm{iso}(U) \wedge \mathrm{updIso}(X, Y, U) \rightarrow \mathrm{updIsoSet}(X, Y, U, Z))$$

Syntactically, rules of icASMs are still the same as arbitrary ASM rules, but their semantics is changed to enforce semantically the satisfaction of the branching condition.

3.6 PTIME Verification

We want to show that ICPT captures PTIME, so we need to show that (1) for every PTIME problem expressed by a Boolean query φ on a structure I there exists a PTIME icASM that halts on the input structure I with $Output = \textbf{true}$ iff I satisfies φ, and (2) any PTIME icASM M can be simulated by a PTIME Turing machine. More precisely, we need to translate M into a TM $\mathcal{T}$ such that M halts on an input structure I with a result $Output = \textbf{true}$ iff $\mathcal{T}$ accepts the standard encoding of an ordered version of I.

While (1) is rather straightforward, there are several problems associated with (2). We need to simulate a non-deterministic ASM by a deterministic Turing machine. However, according to Lemma 3.1 icASMs are globally insignificant, so a choice can always be replaced by the selection of the smallest atom satisfying the required condition. The translation must be effective, so we consider the direct simulation of every rule construct by a Turing machine. This is straightforward, as we know how to combine Turing machines to realise branching, multiple parallel branches and choices. The simulating Turing machine must work in polynomial time. As the bounds in set terms appearing in **forall**-rules ensure that the number of parallel branches is polynomially bounded by the number of active elements, the crucial problem is to ensure that checking the branching condition in every step as well as checking the local insignificance condition for every execution of a **choice**-rule can be done in polynomial time.

For the local insignificance condition a simulating Turing machine can produce encodings of all update sets in $\boldsymbol{\Delta}(S)$ and write them onto some tape. Any object appearing in an update set must be active, and there is a polynomial bound $q(n)$ on the number of active objects. Furthermore, as choices are only among atoms there are at most n such update sets, and it suffices to explore at most $n-1$ isomorphisms defined by transpositions of two atoms. Applying such an isomorphism to an update set requires time linear in the size of the update set, and a follow-on check of set equality is again possible in polynomial time. Hence checking the local insignificance condition can be simulated by a Turing machine in polynomial time.

Checking the branching condition in PTIME will be more difficult. In the following let S be a fixed state. We then say that a state S' *satisfies BC* iff the pair (S, S') the branching condition.

Lemma 3.1. *It can be checked in polynomial time, if S satisfies BC.*

Next we show that BC satisfaction extends to isomorphic states.

Lemma 3.2. *If S_1 satisfies BC and S_2 is isomorphic to S_1, then also S_2 satisfies BC.*

In order to further reduce the states, for which BC satisfaction needs to be checked, we exploit bounded exploration witnesses, which are generalised from parallel ASMs [11] to non-deterministic ASMs. We use the notation $\langle t \mid \varphi \rangle_V$ for multiset comprehension terms, where t is a term defined over the signature of an ASM, φ is a Boolean term, and V is the set of free variables in the multiset comprehension term. As we deal also with choice, we consider multiset comprehension terms, in which the term t itself is a multiset comprehension term. Call such terms *access terms*. Clearly, the evaluation of an access term in a state S yields a multiset of multisets of objects. A *bounded exploration witness* for an ASM M with rule r is a finite set W of access terms such that for any two states S_1, S_2 of M that coincide on W we have $\Delta_r(S_1) = \Delta_r(S_2)$.

Then we show that BC satisfaction only depends on the W-similarity class. For a bounded exploration witness W and a state S define an equivalence relation $\sim_S$ on W by $t \sim_S t'$ iff $val_S(t) = val_S(t')$. Then we call states S and S' W-*similar* iff $\sim_S = \sim_{S'}$.

Lemma 3.3. *If S_1 satisfies BC and S_1, S_2 are W-similar, then also S_2 satisfies BC.*

Lemma 3.3 shows that we only need to consider representatives S' of W-similarity classes in order to check the branching condition. As W is finite, there are only finitely many equivalence relations on W, so we get only finitely many W-similarity classes, and this number only depends on the ASM M and not on the fixed state S. In order to avoid isomorphism checking for update sets, we may further restrict the states that need to be considered by constructing representatives of the W-similarity classes that yield an update set isomorphic to an update set on S from the given state S.

Theorem 3.1. *ICPT captures PTIME on arbitrary finite structures, i.e. ICPT = PTIME.*

With this theorem we obtain the desired syntactic characterisation of algorithm solving problems in PTIME. Instead of exploiting search with backtracking it is always possible to make a locally insignificant choice, so the algorithm will obtain a solution without ever looking back.

References

1. Blass, A., Gurevich, Y., Shelah, S.: Choiceless polynomial time. Ann. Pure Appl. Logic **100**, 141–187 (1999)
2. Börger, E.: Computability, Complexity, Logic, Studies in Logic and the Foundations of Mathematics, vol. 128. North-Holland (1989)
3. Börger, E.: The ASM refinement method. Formal Aspects Comput. **15**(2–3), 237–257 (2003). https://doi.org/10.1007/s00165-003-0012-7
4. Börger, E.: The role of executable abstract programs for software development and documentation (2022, personal communication, to be published)
5. Börger, E., Durdanovic, I.: Correctness of compiling Occam to Transputer code. Comput. J. **39**(1), 52–92 (1996). https://doi.org/10.1093/comjnl/39.1.52
6. Börger, E., Raschke, A.: Modeling Companion for Software Practitioners. Springer, Cham (2018). https://doi.org/10.1007/978-3-662-56641-1
7. Börger, E., Rosenzweig, D.: A mathematical definition of full Prolog. Sci. Comput. Program. **24**(3), 249–286 (1995). https://doi.org/10.1016/0167-6423(95)00006-E

8. Börger, E., Schewe, K.-D.: Concurrent abstract state machines. Acta Informatica **53**(5), 469–492 (2015). https://doi.org/10.1007/s00236-015-0249-7
9. Börger, E., Stärk, R.: Abstract State Machines. Springer, Heidelberg (2003)
10. Chandra, A.K., Harel, D.: Structure and complexity of relational queries. J. Comput. Syst. Sci. **25**(1), 99–128 (1982). https://doi.org/10.1016/0022-0000(82)90012-5
11. Ferrarotti, F., Schewe, K.D., Tec, L., Wang, Q.: A new thesis concerning synchronised parallel computing - simplified parallel ASM thesis. Theor. Comput. Sci. **649**, 25–53 (2016). https://doi.org/10.1016/j.tcs.2016.08.013
12. Ferrarotti, F., Schewe, K.D., Tec, L., Wang, Q.: A complete logic for Database Abstract State Machines. Logic J. IGPL **25**(5), 700–740 (2017)
13. Ferrarotti, F., Schewe, K.D., Tec, L., Wang, Q.: A new thesis concerning synchronised parallel computing – simplified parallel ASM thesis. Theor. Comput. Sci. **649**, 25–53 (2016). https://doi.org/10.1016/j.tcs.2016.08.013
14. Gurevich, Y.: A new thesis (abstract). Am. Math. Soc. **6**(4), 317 (1985)
15. Gurevich, Y.: Logic and the challenge of computer science. In: Börger, E. (ed.) Current Trends in Theoretical Computer Science, pp. 1–57. Computer Science Press (1988)
16. Gurevich, Y.: Evolving algebras 1993: Lipari guide. In: Börger, E. (ed.) Specification and Validation Methods, pp. 9–36. Oxford University Press (1995)
17. Gurevich, Y.: Sequential abstract state machines capture sequential algorithms. ACM Trans. Comput. Logic **1**(1), 77–111 (2000)
18. Naur, P., Randell, B.: Software Engineering, Report on a conference sponsored by the NATO Science Committee (1968)
19. Schewe, K.-D.: Computation on structures. In: Raschke, A., Riccobene, E., Schewe, K.-D. (eds.) Logic, Computation and Rigorous Methods. LNCS, vol. 12750, pp. 266–282. Springer, Cham (2021). https://doi.org/10.1007/978-3-030-76020-5_15
20. Schewe, K.D., Ferrarotti, F.: Behavioural theory of reflective algorithms I: reflective sequential algorithms. CoRR abs/2001.01873 (2020). http://arxiv.org/abs/2001.01873
21. Schewe, K.-D., Ferrarotti, F.: A logic for reflective ASMs. In: Raschke, A., Méry, D., Houdek, F. (eds.) ABZ 2020. LNCS, vol. 12071, pp. 93–106. Springer, Cham (2020). https://doi.org/10.1007/978-3-030-48077-6_7
22. Stärk, R., Nanchen, S.: A logic for abstract state machines. J. Univ. Comput. Sci. **7**(11) (2001)
23. Stärk, R.F., Schmid, J., Börger, E.: Java and the Java Virtual Machine: Definition, Verification, Validation. Springer, Cham (2001)

Complexity of Distributed Petri Net Synthesis

Raymond Devillers[1] and Ronny Tredup[2(✉)]

[1] Département d'Informatique, Université Libre de Bruxelles,
Boulevard du Triomphe, 1050 Brussels, Belgium
rdevil@ulb.ac.be
[2] Institut Für Informatik, Universität Rostock,
Albert-Einstein-Straße 22, 18059 Rostock, Germany
ronny.tredup@uni-rostock.de

Abstract. *Distributed Petri Net Synthesis* corresponds to the task to decide, for a transition system A (with event set E) and a natural number κ, whether there exists a surjective location map $\lambda : E \rightarrow \{1, \ldots, \kappa\}$ and a Petri net N (with transition set E) such that, if two transitions $e, e' \in E$ share a common pre-place, then they have the same location ($\lambda(e) = \lambda(e')$), whose reachability graph is isomorphic to A (in which case such a solution should be produced as well). In this paper, we show that this problem is NP-complete.

1 Introduction

Labeled transition systems, TS for short, are a widely used tool for describing the potential sequential behaviors of discrete-state event-driven systems such as, for example, Petri nets.

Petri net synthesis consists in deciding, for a given transition system A, whether there exists a Petri net N whose reachability graph A_N is isomorphic to A, i.e., whether the TS indeed describes the behavior of a Petri net. In case of a positive decision, a possible solution N should be constructed as well. In this case, many solutions may usually be exhibited, sometimes with very different structures, and we may try to find solutions in a structural subclass of Petri nets with a particular interest.

Petri net synthesis has numerous practical applications, for example, in the field of process discovery to reconstruct a model from its execution traces [1], in supervisory control for discrete event systems [8], and in the design and synthesis of speed-independent circuits [5].

One of the most important applications of Petri net synthesis is the extraction of concurrency and distributability data from the sequential behavior given for instance by a TS [3]: Although TS are used in particular to describe the behavior of concurrent systems like Petri nets [10], they reflect concurrency only implicitly by the non-deterministic interleaving of sequential sequences of events.

© Springer Nature Switzerland AG 2022
Y. Aït-Ameur and F. Crăciun (Eds.): TASE 2022, LNCS 13299, pp. 15–28, 2022.
https://doi.org/10.1007/978-3-031-10363-6_2

In a Petri net whose reachability graph is isomorphic to a TS, the events of the TS correspond to the transitions of the Petri net, and the pre-places of a transition (an event in the TS) model the resources necessary for the firing of the transition (the occurrence of the event in the TS). Accordingly, the pre-places of a transition control the executability of the latter and, following Starke [11], transitions may be considered to be potentially concurrent if the intersection of their presets is empty, i.e., if they do not require the same resources. The concurrency of events (of the TS) thus becomes explicitly visible through the empty intersection of the presets of their corresponding transitions (in a synthesized net).

The question whether a TS having the event set E allows a distributed implementation not only asks about the concurrency of events, but goes a step further and asks whether concurrent events can actually be implemented at different physical locations. More exactly, for a set $\mathcal{L}$ of locations, one wonders if there is a surjective mapping $\lambda : E \to \mathcal{L}$ that assigns a (physical) location to each event $e \in E$ of the TS such that no two events sent to different locations share an input place.

In particular, it should be emphasized that concurrency and distributability are not equivalent properties: As elaborated in [4], transitions can be concurrent, but still not distributable. This phenomenon occurs, for example, in the context of the problem known as *confusion*: Although two transitions, say a and b, do not share any pre-places (do not require the same resources), there is a third transition, say c, that requires both resources from a and resources from b, so that a, b, and c must always be assigned to the same physical location.

The distributability of a transition system can thus be reduced to the distributability of Petri nets [3]. Note however that a TS may have various kinds of synthesized nets, some of which may be more or less highly distributed, while other ones are not at all. If λ is a distribution over E (in the sense just described), we may then say that a TS is λ-distributable if it has a λ-distributable Petri net synthesis. It is known that the question whether, for a TS A with event set E and a location map $\lambda : E \to \mathcal{L}$, a corresponding λ-distributable Petri net exists can be decided in polynomial time if λ is fixed in advance [3]. However, it is not clear a priori how a set of locations, and a location map can be chosen such that they describe an optimal distributed implementation of A, i.e., such that they imply a solution of the following optimization problem:

Given a TS A with event set E, find the maximum number κ of locations, and a (surjective) location map $\lambda : E \to \{1, \ldots, \kappa\}$ that allow a distributed implementation of A, i.e., such that there exists a λ-distributable Petri net N whose reachability graph is isomorphic to A.

Since location maps are surjective, $\kappa \leq |E|$, and sending all transitions to a single location is always valid so that $\kappa \geq 1$. Moreover, if we have a distribution over κ locations, by grouping some of them we can get location maps to any subset of them. Hence, we can reduce by dichotomy the previous problem to the following:

Given a TS A with event set E, and a natural number κ between 1 and $|E|$, decide whether there exists a (surjective) location map $\lambda : E \to \{1, \ldots, \kappa\}$ allowing a λ-distributable Petri net N whose reachability graph is isomorphic to A.

In this paper, we shall show that the latter problem is NP-complete, hence also the optimal one (so that these problems most probably cannot be solved efficiently in all generality).

The remainder of this paper is organized as follows: The following Sect. 2 introduces the definitions, and some basic results used throughout the paper, and provides them with examples. After that, Sect. 3 analyzes the distribution problem and Sect. 4 provides the announced NP-completeness result. Finally, Sect. 5 briefly closes the paper. The appendix contains some figures to help the reader understand some of the proofs.

2   Preliminaries

In this paper, we consider only finite objects, i.e., sets of events, states, places, etc. are always assumed to be finite.

Definition 1 (Transition System). *A (deterministic, labeled) transition system, TS for short, $A = (S, E, \delta, \iota)$ consists of two disjoint sets of states S and events E and a partial transition function $\delta : S \times E \longrightarrow S$ and an initial state $\iota \in S$.*

An event e occurs at state s, denoted by $s \overset{e}{\longrightarrow}$, if $\delta(s, e)$ is defined. By $\overset{\neg e}{\longrightarrow}$ we denote that $\delta(s, e)$ is not defined. We abridge $\delta(s, e) = s'$ by $s \overset{e}{\longrightarrow} s'$ and call the latter an edge with source s and target s'. By $s \overset{e}{\longrightarrow} s' \in A$, we denote that the edge $s \overset{e}{\longrightarrow} s'$ is present in A. A sequence $s_0 \overset{e_1}{\longrightarrow} s_1, s_1 \overset{e_2}{\longrightarrow} s_2, \ldots, s_{n-1} \overset{e_n}{\longrightarrow} s_n$ of edges is called a (directed labeled) path (from s_0 to s_n in A), denoted by $s_0 \overset{e_1}{\longrightarrow} s_1 \overset{e_2}{\longrightarrow} \ldots \overset{e_n}{\longrightarrow} s_n$.

We assume that A is reachable: there is a path from ι to s for every state $s \in S \setminus \{\iota\}$.

Two transition systems $A_1 = (S_1, E, \delta_1, \iota_1)$ and $A_2 = (S_2, E, \delta_2, \iota_2)$ on the event set E are said isomorphic (denoted $A_1 \cong A_2$) if there is a bijection $\beta : S_1 \to S_2$ such that $\beta(\iota_1) = \iota_2$ and $s_1 \overset{e}{\longrightarrow} s_2 \in A_1$ iff $\beta(s_1) \overset{e}{\longrightarrow} \beta(s_2) \in A_2$ for any $s_1, s_2 \in S_1$, and $e \in E$.

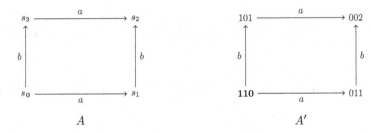

Fig. 1. Two isomorphic TS A and A'; the initial states are indicated in bold.

Definition 2 (Petri net). *A (weighted) Petri net $N = (P, E, f, \mathfrak{m}_0)$ consists of finite and disjoint sets of* places *P and* transitions *E, a (total)* flow *$f :$ $((P \times E) \cup (E \times P)) \to \mathbb{N}$ and an initial* marking *$\mathfrak{m}_0 : P \to \mathbb{N}$ (more generally, a marking is any function $P \to \mathbb{N}$, interpreted as giving a number of tokens present in each place).*
The preset *of a transition is the set $^\bullet e = \{p \in P \mid f(p, e) > 0\}$ of its pre-places. The same may be defined for places, as well as postsets.*
A transition $e \in E$ can fire *or* occur *in a marking $\mathfrak{m} : P \to \mathbb{N}$, denoted by $\mathfrak{m} \xrightarrow{e}$, if $\mathfrak{m}(p) \geq f(p, e)$ for all places $p \in P$. The firing of e in marking $\mathfrak{m}$ leads to the marking $\mathfrak{m}'(p) = \mathfrak{m}(p) - f(p, e) + f(e, p)$ for all $p \in P$, denoted by $\mathfrak{m} \xrightarrow{e} \mathfrak{m}'$. This notation extends to sequences $w \in E^*$ and the* reachability set *$RS(N) = \{\mathfrak{m} \mid \exists w \in E^* : \mathfrak{m}_0 \xrightarrow{w} \mathfrak{m}\}$ contains all of N's reachable markings. The* reachability graph *of N is the TS $A_N = (RS(N), E, \delta, \mathfrak{m}_0)$, where, for every reachable marking $\mathfrak{m}$ of N and transition $e \in E$ with $\mathfrak{m} \xrightarrow{e} \mathfrak{m}'$, the transition function δ of A_N is defined by $\delta(\mathfrak{m}, e) = \mathfrak{m}'$ ($\delta(\mathfrak{m}, e)$ is undefined if e cannot fire in $\mathfrak{m}$).*

Many subclasses of Petri nets may be defined, and we shall consider some examples in the next section.

Definition 3 (Petri net synthesis). *Petri net synthesis consists in deciding, for a given transition system A, whether there exists a Petri net N whose reachability graph A_N is isomorphic to A, i.e., whether the TS indeed describes the behavior of a Petri net.*
In the positive case, one usually wants to also build such a net, called a solution *of the synthesis problem. In the negative case, it may be useful to exhibit one or more reasons of the failure.*
It is also possible to restrict the target to some specific subclass of nets.

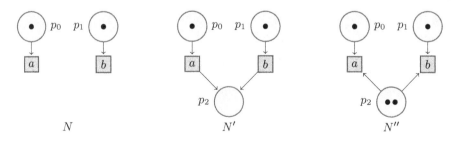

Fig. 2. Three different solutions of the TS A and A' in Fig. 1. A' is the reachability graph of N'.

Classical synthesis procedures are linked to the notion of regions and to the solution of separation properties.

Definition 4 (Region). *Let $A = (S, E, \delta, \iota)$ be a TS. A region $R = (sup, con, pro)$ of A consists of three mappings* support $sup : S \to \mathbb{N}$, *as well as* consume *and* produce $con, pro : E \to \mathbb{N}$, *such that if $s \xrightarrow{e} s'$ is an edge of A, then $con(e) \leq sup(s)$ and $sup(s') = sup(s) - con(e) + pro(e)$.*

A region may be seen as a place of a Petri net with transition set E, with sup giving the marking of the place at each reachable state as specified by A, $con(e)$ giving the number of tokens needed (and thus consumed when firing) by e in that place, and $pro(e)$ giving the number of tokens produced by e in that place when firing.

The *state separation property* ensures that different states may be differentiated by a region, i.e., be associated with different markings:

Definition 5 (State Separation Property). *Two distinct states $s, s' \in S$ define the* state separation atom, *SSA for short, (s, s') of A. A region $R = (sup, con, pro)$ solves (s, s') if $sup(s) \neq sup(s')$. A state $s \in S$ is called* solvable *if, for every $s' \in S \setminus \{s\}$, there is a region that solves the SSA (s, s'). If every state of A is solvable, then A has the* state separation property, *SSP for short.*

The *event state separation property* ensures that if an event e does not occur at a state s in A, that is $s \xrightarrow{\neg e}$, then the transition e cannot fire in the marking associated to s in some region:

Definition 6 (Event State Separation Property). *An event $e \in E$, and a state $s \in S$ of A such that $s \xrightarrow{\neg e}$ define the* event state separation atom, *ESSA for short, (e, s) of A. A region $R = (sup, con, pro)$ solves (e, s) if $con(e) > sup(s)$. An event $e \in E$ is called* solvable *if, for every state $s \in S$ such that $s \xrightarrow{\neg e}$, there is a region of A that solves the ESSA (e, s). If all events of A are solvable, then A has the* event state separation property, *ESSP for short.*

Definition 7 (Admissible Set). *Let $A = (S, E, \delta, \iota)$ be a TS. A set $\mathcal{R}$ of regions of A is called an* admissible set *if it witnesses the SSP and the ESSP of A, i.e., for every SSA, and for every ESSA of A, there is a region in $\mathcal{R}$ that solves it.*
If $\mathcal{R}$ is an (admissible) set of regions of A, $N_A^{\mathcal{R}}$ is the Petri net where E is the set of transitions, $\mathcal{R}$ is the set of places and, for each place $R = (sup, con, pro) \in \mathcal{R}$, the initial marking is $sup(\iota)$ and, for each transition $e \in E$, $f(R, e) = con(e)$ and $f(e, R) = pro(e)$.

A classical result about Petri net synthesis is then:

Theorem 1 ([6]). *A labeled transition system A has a weighted Petri net solution iff it has an admissible set $\mathcal{R}$ of regions. A possible solution is then $N_A^{\mathcal{R}}$.*

3   Distributability

The idea here is to bind the events of a transition system or a Petri net to certain (physical) locations.

Definition 8 (Location Map). *Let E be a set, and $\mathcal{L}$ a set of* locations. *A* location map *(over E and $\mathcal{L}$) is a surjective mapping $\lambda : E \to \mathcal{L}$.*

In the case of a Petri net, the intent is to separate the pre-sets of transitions sent to different locations:

Definition 9 (Distributable Petri net). *Let $N = (P, E, f, \mathfrak{m}_0)$ be a Petri net, $\mathcal{L}$ a set of locations, and $\lambda : E \to \mathcal{L}$ a location map. N will be called λ-distributable if the following condition is satisfied: for all transitions $e, e' \in E$ and every place $p \in P$, if $f(p, e) > 0$ and $f(p, e') > 0$, then $\lambda(e) = \lambda(e')$.*
Let $\kappa \in \mathbb{N}$; N will be called κ-distributable (with $1 \leq \kappa \leq |E|$) if it is λ-distributable for some location map λ such that $|\mathcal{L}| = \kappa$.

The last definition results from the observation that the exact identity of the locations is not important: what really matters is the partition of the transition set defined by λ, i.e., $\{\lambda^{-1}(e) \mid e \in \mathcal{L}\}$. Hence we may always choose $\mathcal{L} = \{1, \ldots, |\mathcal{L}|\}$. Moreover, if π is a permutation of $\mathcal{L}$, we may use equivalently $\pi \circ \lambda$ instead of λ.
For instance, the nets N and N' in Fig. 2 are λ-distributable with $\lambda(a) = 1$ and $\lambda(b) = 2$, hence also 2-distributable. On the contrary, N'' is only 1-distributable.
We may then consider the synthesis problems where the target is the class of λ-distributable Petri nets, for some location map λ, or the class of κ-distributable Petri nets, for some $\kappa \in \{1, \ldots, |E|\}$.

Definition 10 (Localized Region). *Let $A = (S, E, \delta, \iota)$ be a TS, $\mathcal{L}$ a set of locations and $\lambda : E \to \mathcal{L}$ a location map. A λ-localized region is a region $R = (sup, con, pro)$ of A such that, if $con(e) > 0$, and $con(e') > 0$, then $\lambda(e) = \lambda(e')$.*

In other words, if $\lambda(e) \neq \lambda(e')$, then either $con(e) = 0$ or $con(e') = 0$ (or both).

Definition 11 (Localized admissible Set). *Let $A = (S, E, \delta, \iota)$ be a TS, $\mathcal{L}$ a set of locations, and $\lambda : E \to \mathcal{L}$ a location map. An admissible set $\mathcal{R}$ of regions of A will be said λ-localized if all its members are λ-localized. It will be said κ-localizable (for some $\kappa \in \{1, \ldots, |E|\}$) if it is λ-localized for some location map λ with $|\lambda(E)| = \kappa$.*

The following result extends Theorem 1 to the localized context. It states that the question whether there is a λ-distributable (or a κ-distributable) Petri net whose reachability graph is isomorphic to A is equivalent to the question whether there is a λ-localized (or a κ-localizable) admissible set of regions of A:

Theorem 2 ([2]). *Let $A = (S, E, \delta, \iota)$ be a TS, $\mathcal{L}$ a set of locations, $\lambda : E \to \mathcal{L}$ a location map, and $\kappa \in \{1, \ldots, |E|\}$ a degree of distribution. A has a λ-distributed (or a κ-distributed) Petri net solution iff it has an admissible λ-localized (or κ-localizable) set $\mathcal{R}$ of regions. A possible solution is then $N_A^{\mathcal{R}}$.*

If a TS A allows a λ-distributed (hence also a κ-distributed) Petri net solution N, it is possible to extend the location map to the places: if $p \in {}^\bullet e$, we may coherently state $\lambda(p) = \lambda(e)$. If a place p has an empty post-set, we may arbitrarily associate it to any location, for instance to $\lambda(e)$ if $e \in {}^\bullet p$ (if any), but here the location may rely on the particular choice of e. If we add the initial marking and the arcs between the connected places and transitions in each location, we shall then get $|\mathcal{L}|$ subnets $N_1, \ldots, N_{|\mathcal{L}|}$.

If these subnets are well separated, $N = \bigoplus_{i=1}^{|\mathcal{L}|} N_i$ is the disjoint sum of its various localized components, in the sense of [7], and then its reachability graph is isomorphic to the disjoint product of the reachability graphs of those components: if $A_i = RG(A_i)$ for each $i \in \{1, \ldots, |\mathcal{L}|\}$, $A \cong RG(N) \cong \bigotimes_{i=1}^{|\mathcal{L}|} RG(N_i)$. This is the case for example for the net N in Fig. 2, but not for N' while both nets are 2-distributable and solutions of the same TS A.

In general, however, each component N_i still has to send tokens to places belonging to other components, and the relationship on the reachability graphs is not so obvious. In [3], the authors show how to get around the difficulty. Albeit we shall not need it in the following, we sketch here their procedure. When components have to exchange tokens, it is not possible to read it in the corresponding transition systems, since the latter are considered up to isomorphisms, so that the markings disappear. Instead, the idea is to add special transitions materializing the sending or reception of a token to or from another component, but these extra transitions will be considered as invisible from outside. This leads to reachability graphs and transition systems with invisible events, but it is possible to define an equivalence, called branching bisimulation, which generalizes the isomorphism between transition systems without invisible events, and to combine disjoint transition systems with invisible events in such a way that the combination of the reachability graphs of the (extended) components N_i is branching bisimilar to the original TS A. For instance, for net N' in Fig. 2, this leads to the components, reachability graphs and combination illustrated by Figs. 3, 4, and 5.

4 Complexity Analysis

In [3], it is shown that the question whether, for a TS A with event set E and a location map $\lambda : E \to \mathcal{L}$, a corresponding λ-distributable Petri net exists can be decided in polynomial time. But this is only proved when λ is fixed in advance, and it is not clear a priori if this remains true if λ is left unknown, as in the decision problems mentioned in the introduction, which may now be formalized as follows:

OPTIMAL DISTRIBUTABILITY

Input: A TS A with event set E and an integer $\kappa \in \{1, \ldots, |E|\}$.
Question: Is κ the maximal value such that A has a κ-distributable solution?

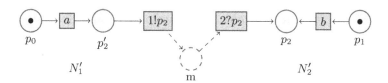

Fig. 3. N_1' and N_2' are the local components of N' associated to locations 1 and 2, respectively; $1!p_2$ is the invisible transition that sends asynchronously a token to p_2 in N_2' from location 1, and $2?p_2$ is the invisible transition that receives asynchronously in N_2' a token for p_2. We can think of this sending/receiving of tokens as follows: There is an additional (message) place m; the firing of $1!p_2$ produces a token on m (message "N_1' sends a token for p_2"); the firing of $2?p_2$ consumes a token from m, and produces a token on p_2 ("message received").

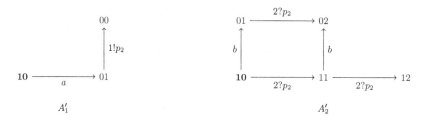

Fig. 4. A_1' and A_2' are the corresponding reachability graph (bounded by the maximal marking 2 of p_2 in N').

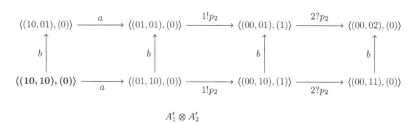

Fig. 5. Finally, $A_1' \otimes A_2'$ is the combination of A_1' and A_2' that is branching bisimilar to A. A state $(\langle (s, s') \rangle, (i))$ of $A_1' \otimes A_2'$ corresponds to the pair (s, s') of states of A_1' and A_2', respectively, and i is the number of messages sent but not yet received.

κ-DISTRIBUTABILITY
Input: A TS A with event set E and an integer $\kappa \in \{1, \ldots, |E|\}$.
Question: Is there a κ-distributable solution?

We shall show in this section that the second problem (hence also the first one) is unfortunately NP-complete. First of all, we argue for the membership in NP: On the one hand, if, for a given TS A, and a natural number κ, there is a location map λ that allows a corresponding λ-admissible set, then a non-deterministic Turing machine can compute λ in polynomial time by simply guessing $\lambda(e) \in \{1, \ldots, \kappa\}$ for all $e \in E$: If $E = \{e_1, \ldots, e_{|E|}\}$, then, for all $i \in \{1, \ldots, |E|\}$, the length of the binary encoding of $\lambda(e_i)$ is bounded by $log_2(|E|) + 1$. Hence, the nondeterministic computation of λ is bounded by $\mathcal{O}(log_2(|E|) \cdot |E|)$. On the other hand, as mentioned above, it is known that once λ is fixed, one can compute in polynomial time a corresponding λ-distributable admissible set $\mathcal{R}$ if it exists (and reject the input otherwise) [2]. Hence, κ-DISTRIBUTABILITY is in NP.

CUBIC MONOTONE 1 IN 3 3SAT (CM1IN33SAT)
Input: A pair $(\mathfrak{U}, M)$ that consists of a set $\mathfrak{U}$ of boolean variables and a set of 3-clauses $M = \{M_0, \ldots, M_{m-1}\}$ such that $M_i = \{X_{i_0}, X_{i_1}, X_{i_2}\} \subseteq \mathfrak{U}$ and $i_0 < i_1 < i_2$ for all $\in \{0, \ldots, m-1\}$. Every variable of $\mathfrak{U}$ occurs in exactly three clauses of M
Question: Does there exist a one-in-three model of $(\mathfrak{U}, M)$, i. e., a subset $\mathfrak{S} \subseteq \mathfrak{U}$ such that $|\mathfrak{S} \cap M_i| = 1$ for all $i \in \{0, \ldots, m-1\}$?

Theorem 3 ([9]). CUBIC MONOTONE 1 IN 3 3SAT *is* NP-*complete.*

Example 1. The instance $(\mathfrak{U}, M)$, where $\mathfrak{U} = \{X_0, X_1, X_2, X_3, X_4, X_5\}$, and $M = \{M_0, \ldots, M_5\}$ such that $M_0 = \{X_0, X_1, X_2\}$, $M_1 = \{X_0, X_1, X_3\}$, $M_2 = \{X_0, X_1, X_5\}$, $M_3 = \{X_2, X_3, X_4\}$, $M_4 = \{X_2, X_4, X_5\}$, and $M_5 = \{X_3, X_4, X_5\}$, allows a positive decision: $\mathfrak{S} = \{X_0, X_4\}$ defines a one-in-three model for $(\mathfrak{U}, M)$.

In the following, until explicitly stated otherwise, let $(\mathfrak{U}, M)$ be an arbitrary but fixed instance of CM1IN33SAT such that $\mathfrak{U} = \{X_0, \ldots, X_{m-1}\}$, and $M = \{M, \ldots, M_{m-1}\}$, where $M_i = \{X_{i_0}, X_{i_1}, X_{i_2}\} \subseteq \mathfrak{U}$, and $i_0 < i_1 < i_2$ for all $i \in \{0, \ldots, m-1\}$. Note that $|\mathfrak{U}| = |M|$ holds by the definition of a valid input.

Lemma 1. *If* $\mathfrak{S} \subseteq \mathfrak{U}$, *then* $\mathfrak{S}$ *is a one-in-three model of* $(\mathfrak{U}, M)$ *if and only if* $\mathfrak{S} \cap M_i \neq \emptyset$ *for all* $i \in \{0, \ldots, m-1\}$, *and* $m = 3 \cdot |\mathfrak{S}|$.

Proof. Every variable of $\mathfrak{U}$ occurs in exactly three distinct clauses. Hence, every set $\mathfrak{S} \subseteq \mathfrak{U}$ intersects with $3|\mathfrak{S}|$ (distinct) clauses $M_{i_0}, \ldots, M_{i_{3|\mathfrak{S}|-1}} \in M$ if and only if $|\mathfrak{S} \cap M_{i_j}| = 1$ for all $j \in \{0, \ldots, 3|\mathfrak{S}| - 1\}$. $\square$

We shall polynomially reduce $(\mathfrak{U}, M)$ to a TS $A = (S, E, \delta, \iota)$ and a number κ such that there is location map $\lambda : E \to \{1, \ldots, \kappa\}$, and a λ-localizable admissible set of A if and only if $(\mathfrak{U}, M)$ has a one-in-three model.

For a start, let $\kappa = \frac{2m}{3} + 3$, and $\mathcal{L} = \{1, \ldots, \frac{2m}{3} + 3\}$. (By Lemma 1, if $m \not\equiv 0 \bmod 3$, then $(\mathfrak{U}, M)$ has no one-in-three model.) We proceed with the construction of A, being the composition of several gadgets that are finally connected by some uniquely labeled edges. First of all, the TS A has the following gadget H that will allow to consider the ESSA $\alpha = (k, h_1)$:

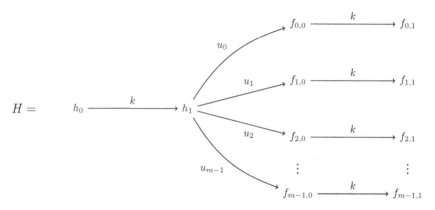

Moreover, for every $i \in \{0, \ldots, m-1\}$, the TS A has the following gadget T_i that represents the clause $M_i = \{X_{i_0}, X_{i_1}, X_{i_2}\}$ by using its variables as events, and uses the event u_i again.

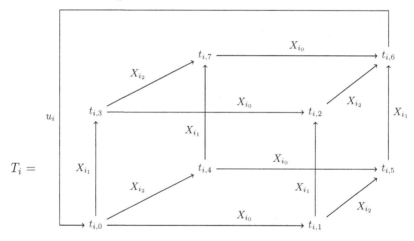

Finally, the TS $A = (S, E, \delta, \iota)$ has the initial state ι from which all introduced gadgets are reachable by unambiguous labeled edges: for every $i \in \{0, \ldots, m-1\}$, the TS A has the edge $\iota \xrightarrow{a_i} t_{i,0}$, and, moreover, it has the edge $\iota \xrightarrow{a_m} h_0$. Note that $E = \mathfrak{U} \cup \{k\} \cup \{a_0, \ldots, a_m\} \cup \{u_0, \ldots, u_{m-1}\}$, and $|E| = 3m + 2$. In the following, for any gadget G, we shall denote by $S(G)$ the set of all its states.

Lemma 2. *If there is a location map $\lambda : E \to \mathcal{L}$ and a λ-localizable admissible set $\mathcal{R}$ of A, i.e., for all $e \neq e' \in E$ and all $R = (sup, con, pro) \in \mathcal{R}$, if $con(e) > 0$ and $con(e') > 0$, then $\lambda(e) = \lambda(e')$, then there is a one-in-three model for $(\mathfrak{U}, M)$.*

Proof. We show that if $R = (sup, con, pro)$ is a λ-distributable region of $\mathcal{R}$ that solves (k, h_1), then the set $\mathfrak{S} = \{X \in \mathfrak{U} \mid con(X) > 0\}$ defines a one-in-three model of $(\mathfrak{U}, M)$.

We first argue that $\lambda(a_i) = \lambda(a_j)$ for all $i \neq j \in \{0, \ldots, m\}$: Since $\mathcal{R}$ witnesses the ESSP of A, and $t_{j,0} \xrightarrow{\neg a_i}$, there is a region $R = (sup, con, pro) \in \mathcal{R}$ that solves the ESSA $(a_i, t_{j,0})$. By $\iota \xrightarrow{a_i}$, we have $con(a_i) \leq sup(\iota)$, and, since R solves $(a_i, t_{j,0})$, we have $con(a_i) > sup(t_{j,0}) \geq 0$. Together this implies $sup(\iota) > sup(t_{j,0})$, and thus $con(a_j) > pro(a_j) \geq 0$, since $sup(t_{j,0}) = sup(\iota) - con(a_j) + pro(a_j)$. Hence, by $con(a_i) > 0$, and $con(a_j) > 0$, we obtain $\lambda(a_i) = \lambda(a_j)$.

Similarly, one argues that if $i \neq j \in \{0, \ldots, m-1\}$ are arbitrary but fixed, then $\lambda(u_i) = \lambda(u_j)$, which results from a region that solves $(u_i, f_{j,0})$. Hence, $\lambda(u_i) = \lambda(u_j)$ for all $i \neq j \in \{0, \ldots, m\}$.

Let $R = (sup, con, pro)$ be a region of $\mathcal{R}$ that solves (k, h_1). (Note that R exists, since $\mathcal{R}$ is an admissible set.) We first show now that the set $\mathfrak{S} = \{X \in \mathfrak{U} \mid con(X) > 0\}$ contains at least $\frac{m}{3}$ elements (which thus have all the same location as k): Let $i \in \{0, \ldots, m-1\}$ be arbitrary but fixed. By $h_0 \xrightarrow{k}$, we have $con(k) \leq sup(h_0)$, and since R solves (k, h_1), we have $con(k) > sup(h_1)$. On the other hand, by $f_{i,0} \xrightarrow{k}$, we have $con(k) \leq sup(f_{i,0})$, which implies $sup(h_1) < sup(f_{i,0})$, and thus $con(u_i) < pro(u_i)$. By $t_{i,6} \xrightarrow{u_i} t_{i,0}$, and $con(u_i) < pro(u_i)$, we have that $sup(t_{i,0}) > sup(t_{i,6})$. This implies that there is an event $X \in \{X_{i_0}, X_{i_1}, X_{i_2}\}$ on the path $t_{i,0} \xrightarrow{X_{i_0}} t_{i,1} \xrightarrow{X_{i_1}} t_{i,2} \xrightarrow{X_{i_2}} t_{i,6}$ that satisfies $con(X) > 0$. This is due to the fact that $sup(t_{i,6}) = sup(t_{i,0}) - (\sum_{j=0}^{2} con(X_{i_j})) + (\sum_{j=0}^{2} pro(X_{i_j}))$. Since i was arbitrary, this is simultaneously true for all $i \in \{0, \ldots, m-1\}$. Hence, as every $X \in \mathfrak{U}$ occurs in exactly three distinct clauses, say M_i, M_j, M_ℓ (corresponding to T_i, T_j, T_ℓ), we have $3|\mathfrak{S}| \geq m$, and thus $|\mathfrak{S}| \geq \frac{m}{3}$. Moreover, for all $X \in \mathfrak{S}$, it holds $\lambda(k) = \lambda(X)$.

Finally, we argue that $\mathfrak{S}$ contains exactly $\frac{m}{3}$ elements: Since λ is a surjective mapping, and $|\{1, \ldots, \frac{2m}{3} + 3\} \setminus \{\lambda(k), \lambda(a_0), \lambda(u_0)\}| \geq \frac{2m}{3}$, and $\lambda(a_0) = \cdots = \lambda(a_m)$, and $\lambda(u_0) = \cdots = \lambda(u_{m-1})$, there have to be $\frac{2m}{3}$ pairwise distinct events left that correspond to the remaining locations, i.e., we have that $|E \setminus (\{k, a_0, \ldots, a_m, u_0, \ldots, u_{m-1}\} \cup \mathfrak{S})| = |(\mathfrak{U} \setminus \mathfrak{S})| \geq \frac{2m}{3}$. By $|\mathfrak{U}| = m$, and $|\mathfrak{S}| \geq \frac{m}{3}$, this implies $|\mathfrak{S}| = \frac{m}{3}$. In particular, by Lemma 1, we obtain that $\mathfrak{S}$ defines a one-in-three model of $(\mathfrak{U}, M)$. This proves the lemma. $\square$

In order to complete the proof of the adequacy of our reduction, we now show that the existence of a one-in-three model for $(\mathfrak{U}, M)$ implies the existence of a location map $\lambda : E \to \{1, \ldots, \frac{2m}{3} + 3\}$ such that there is a λ-localizable admissible set $\mathcal{R}$ of A. So let $\mathfrak{S}$ be a one-in-three model of $(\mathfrak{U}, M)$, and let $\mathfrak{U} \setminus \mathfrak{S} = \{X_{j_1}, \ldots, X_{j_{\frac{2m}{3}}}\}$ be set of all variable events, which do not participate at the model. For all $e \in E$, we define λ as follows:

$$\lambda(e) = \begin{cases} 1, & \text{if } e \in \{k\} \cup \mathfrak{S} \\ 2, & \text{if } e \in \{a_0, \dots, a_m\} \\ 3, & \text{if } e \in \{u_0, \dots, u_{m-1}\} \\ \ell + 3, & \text{if } e = X_{j_\ell} \text{ for some } \ell \in \{1, \dots, \frac{2m}{3}\} \end{cases}$$

The following facts show that A's events are solvable by λ-localizable regions. Due to space restrictions, we present regions $R = (sup, con, pro)$ only implicitly by $sup(\iota)$, and con, and pro; it will be easy to check that the definitions are coherent, i.e., no support is negative and two different paths to a same state do not lead to different supports. We summarize events by $\mathcal{E}_{c,p}^R = \{e \in E \mid con(e) = c \text{ and } pro(e) = p\}$. If $e \in E$ is not explicitly mentioned in a set $E_{c,p}$, where $c \neq 0$ or $p \neq 0$, then $e \in \mathcal{E}_{0,0}^R = E \setminus \{e \in E \mid con(e) \neq 0 \text{ or } pro(e) \neq 0\}$, and we leave this set implicitly defined in the obvious way.

In order to help the reader understand the regions presented in Fact 1 to Fact 4, and Lemma 3, we gathered in an Appendix several figures illustrating the gadgets $H, T_0, \dots, T_5$ of the TS A that would be the result of the reduction applied on the instance of Example 1. For every figure, the coloring of the states corresponds to the support of the states according to the region addressed by the figure: red colored states have support 1, green colored states have support 2, blue colored states have support 3, and states without color have support 0. These figures are intended to be withdrawed in a ready to publish version, to cope with length constraints.

Fact 1. *The event k is solvable by λ-localizable regions.*

Proof. The following region $R_1 = (sup_1, con_1, pro_1)$ solves (k, s) for all $s \in \{h_1\} \cup \bigcup_{i=0}^{m-1}\{f_{i,1}\}$: $sup_1(\iota) = 1$, and $\mathcal{E}_{1,0}^{R_1} = \{k\} \cup \mathfrak{S}$, and $\mathcal{E}_{0,1}^{R_1} = \{u_0, \dots, u_{m-1}\}$.
    The following region $R_2 = (sup_2, con_2, pro_2)$ solves (k, s) for all states $S \setminus S(H)$: $sup_2(\iota) = 0$, and $\mathcal{E}_{1,1}^{R_2} = \{k\}$, and $\mathcal{E}_{0,1}^{R_2} = \{a_m\}$.   □

Fact 2. *If $e \in \{a_0, \dots, a_m\}$, then e is solvable by λ-localizable regions.*

Proof. The following region $R_3 = (sup_3, con_3, pro_3)$ solves (e, s) for all $e \in \{a_0, \dots, a_m\}$ and all $s \in S \setminus \{\iota\}$: $sup_3(\iota) = 1$, and $\mathcal{E}_{1,0}^{R_3} = \{a_0, \dots, a_m\}$.   □

Fact 3. *If $e \in \{u_0, \dots, u_{m-1}\}$, then e is solvable by λ-localizable regions.*

Proof. The following region $R_4 = (sup_4, con_4, pro_4)$ solves (u, s) for all $u \in \{u_0, \dots, u_{m-1}\}$, and all $s \in S \setminus (\{h_1\} \cup \bigcup_{i=0}^{m-1}\{t_{i,6}\})$: $sup_4(\iota) = 0$, and $\mathcal{E}_{3,0}^{R_4} = \{u_0, \dots, u_{m-1}\}$, and $\mathcal{E}_{0,2}^{R_4} = \{k\}$, and $\mathcal{E}_{0,1}^{R_4} = \{a_m\} \cup \mathfrak{U}$.

    Let $j \in \{0, \dots, m-1\}$ be arbitrary but fixed. The following region $R_5^j = (sup_5^j, con_5^j.pro_5^j)$ solves (u_j, s) for all $s \in (\bigcup_{i=0}^{m-1}\{t_{i,6}\}) \setminus \{t_{j,6}\}$: $sup_5^j(\iota) = 0$, and $\mathcal{E}_{1,1}^{R_5^j} = \{u_j\}$, and $\mathcal{E}_{0,1}^{R_5^j} = \{a_j, a_m\}$.   □

Fact 4. *For every $e \in \mathfrak{U}$, the event e is solvable by λ-localizable regions.*

Proof. Let $i \in \{0, \ldots, m-1\}$ be arbitrary but fixed, and let $i_0, i_1, i_2 \in \{0, \ldots, m-1\}$ be the three pairwise distinct indices such that $X_i \in M_{i_j}$ for all $j \in \{0, 1, 2\}$. The following region $R_6^i = (sup_6^i, con_6^i, pro_6^i)$ solves (X_i, s) for all $s \in S \setminus (\{s \in S \mid s \xrightarrow{X_i}\} \cup S(H))$: $sup_6^i(\iota) = 0$, and $\mathcal{E}_{1,0}^{R_6^i} = \{X_i\}$, and $\mathcal{E}_{0,1}^{R_6^i} = \{a_{i_0}, a_{i_1}, a_{i_2}, u_{i_0}, u_{i_1}, u_{i_2}\}$.

The following region $R_7^i = (sup_7^i, con_7^i, pro_7^i)$ solves (X_i, s) for all $s \in S(H)$: $sup_7^i(\iota) = 0$, and $\mathcal{E}_{1,1}^{R_7^i} = \{X_i\}$, and $\mathcal{E}_{0,1}^{R_7^i} = \{a_{i_0}, a_{i_1}, a_{i_2}\}$. Since i was arbitrary, this proves the lemma. □

The following lemma completes the proof of Theorem 4:

Lemma 3. *If there is a one-in-three model for $(\mathfrak{U}, M)$, then there is a location map $\lambda : E \to \{1, \ldots, \frac{2m}{3} + 3\}$, and a λ-localizable admissible set $\mathcal{R}$ of A.*

Proof. By Fact 1 to Fact 4, there are enough λ-localizable regions of A that witness the ESSP of A. Moreover, the region R_3 of Fact 2 solves (ι, s) for all $s \in S \setminus \{\iota\}$. Furthermore, if $i \in \{0, \ldots, m-1\}$ is arbitrary but fixed, then the following region $R_8^i = (sup_8^i, con_8^i, pro_8^i)$, which is defined by $sup_8^i(\iota) = 0$, and $\mathcal{E}_{0,1}^{R_8^i} = \{a_i\}$, solves (s, s') for all $s \in S(T_i)$ and all $S \setminus S(T_i)$. Hence, it remains to argue for the solvability of the SSA (s, s') such that s and s' belong to the same gadget of A.

Let $i \in \{0, \ldots, m-1\}$ be arbitrary but fixed. One finds out that the regions $R_6^{i_0}$, and $R_6^{i_1}$, and $R_6^{i_2}$ that are defined in Fact 4 in order to solve the events X_{i_0}, and X_{i_1}, and X_{i_2}, respectively, altogether solve all SSA of T_i.

Hence, it remains to consider the SSA of H. Let $i \neq j \in \{0, \ldots, m-1\}$ be arbitrary but fixed. The region R_1 of Fact 1 solves (h_0, h_1), and $(f_{i,0}, f_{i,1})$, and the region $R_6^{i_0}$ of Fact 4 solves (s, s') for all $s \in \{h_0, h_1\}$, and all $s' \in \{f_{i,0}, f_{i,1}\}$.

It remains to show that (s, s') is solvable for all $s \in \{f_{i,0}, f_{i,1}\}$, and all $s' \in \{f_{j,0}, f_{j,1}\}$. In order to do that, we observe that there is a $\ell \in \{0, 1, 2\}$, such that $X_{i_\ell} \notin M_j$, since M_i, and M_j would be equal otherwise. Hence, the region $R_6^{i_\ell}$ of Fact 4 solves (s, s'). By the arbitrariness of i, and j, we have finally argued that there is a witness of λ-localizable regions for the SSP of A. □

Combining the various results of this section, we thus get our main result:

Theorem 4. κ-DISTRIBUTABILITY *is NP-complete.*

5 Conclusion

In this paper, we show that the problem of finding an optimal distributed implementation of a given TS A is a computationally hard problem by showing that the corresponding decision problem is NP-complete. The presented reduction is crucially based on the fact that the transitions of λ-distributed Petri nets may simultaneously consume and produce from the same place. Future work could therefore investigate the complexity of the problem restricted to pure Petri nets. Also, one may investigate whether the parameterized version of the problem is fixed parameter tractable when κ is chosen as the parameter.

Acknowledgements. We would like to thank the anonymous reviewers for their detailed comments and valuable suggestions.

References

1. van der Aalst, W.M.P.: Process Mining - Discovery, Conformance and Enhancement of Business Processes. Springer, Cham (2011). https://doi.org/10.1007/978-3-642-19345-3
2. Badouel, E., Bernardinello, L., Darondeau, P.: Petri Net Synthesis. TTCSAES, Springer, Heidelberg (2015). https://doi.org/10.1007/978-3-662-47967-4
3. Badouel, E., Caillaud, B., Darondeau, P.: Distributing finite automata through Petri net synthesis. Formal Asp. Comput. **13**(6), 447–470 (2002). https://doi.org/10.1007/s001650200022
4. Best, E., Darondeau, P.: Petri net distributability. In: Clarke, E., Virbitskaite, I., Voronkov, A. (eds.) PSI 2011. LNCS, vol. 7162, pp. 1–18. Springer, Heidelberg (2012). https://doi.org/10.1007/978-3-642-29709-0_1
5. Cortadella, J., Kishinevsky, M., Kondratyev, A., Lavagno, L., Yakovlev, A.: A region-based theory for state assignment in speed-independent circuits. IEEE Trans. CAD Integr. Circuits Syst. **16**(8), 793–812 (1997). https://doi.org/10.1109/43.644602
6. Desel, J., Reisig, W.: The synthesis problem of Petri nets. Acta Inf. **33**(4), 297–315 (1996). https://doi.org/10.1007/s002360050046
7. Devillers, R.: Factorisation of transition systems. Acta Informatica **55**(4), 339–362 (2017). https://doi.org/10.1007/s00236-017-0300-y
8. Holloway, L.E., Krogh, B.H., Giua, A.: A survey of Petri net methods for controlled discrete event systems. Discret. Event Dyn. Syst. **7**(2), 151–190 (1997). https://doi.org/10.1023/A:1008271916548
9. Moore, C., Robson, J.M.: Hard tiling problems with simple tiles. Discret. Comput. Geom. **26**(4), 573–590 (2001). https://doi.org/10.1007/s00454-001-0047-6
10. Mukund, M.: Transition system models for concurrency. DAIMI Report Series **21**(399) (1992). https://doi.org/10.7146/dpb.v21i399.6633. https://tidsskrift.dk/daimipb/article/view/6633
11. Starke, P.H.: Analyse von Petri-Netz-Modellen. Teubner, Leitfäden und Monographien der Informatik (1990)

Repairing Adversarial Texts Through Perturbation

Guoliang Dong[1], Jingyi Wang[1(✉)], Jun Sun[2], Sudipta Chattopadhyay[3],

Xinyu Wang[1(✉)], Ting Dai[4], Jie Shi[4], and Jin Song Dong[5]

[1] Zhejiang University, Hangzhou, China
{dgl-prc,wangjyee,wangxinyu}@zju.edu.cn
[2] Singapore Management University, Singapore, Singapore
junsun@smu.edu.sg
[3] Singapore University of Technology and Design, Singapore, Singapore
sudipta_chattopadhyay@sutd.edu.sg
[4] Huawei International Pte. Ltd., Singapore, Singapore
{daiting2,SHI.JIE1}@huawei.com
[5] National University of Singapore, Singapore, Singapore
dongjs@comp.nus.edu.sg

Abstract. It is known that neural networks are subject to attacks through adversarial perturbations. Worse yet, such attacks are impossible to eliminate, i.e., the adversarial perturbation is still possible after applying mitigation methods such as adversarial training. Multiple approaches have been developed to detect and reject such adversarial inputs. Rejecting suspicious inputs however may not be always feasible or ideal. First, normal inputs may be rejected due to false alarms generated by the detection algorithm. Second, denial-of-service attacks may be conducted by feeding such systems with adversarial inputs. To address this, in this work, we focus on the text domain and propose an approach to automatically repair adversarial texts at runtime. Given a text which is suspected to be adversarial, we novelly apply multiple adversarial perturbation methods in a positive way to identify a repair, i.e., a slightly mutated but semantically equivalent text that the neural network correctly classifies. Experimental results show that our approach effectively repairs about 80% of adversarial texts. Furthermore, depending on the applied perturbation method, an adversarial text could be repaired about one second on average.

Keywords: Adversarial text · Detection · Repair · Perturbation

1 Introduction

Neural networks (NNs) have achieved state-of-the-art performance in many tasks, such as classification, regression and planning [31,36]. For instance, text classification is one of the fundamental tasks in natural language processing (NLP) and has broad applications including sentiment analysis [10,41], spam detection [19,32] and topic labeling [50]. NNs have been shown to be effective for many text classification tasks [52].

© Springer Nature Switzerland AG 2022
Y. Aït-Ameur and F. Crăciun (Eds.): TASE 2022, LNCS 13299, pp. 29–48, 2022.
https://doi.org/10.1007/978-3-031-10363-6_3

At the same time, NNs are found to be vulnerable to various attacks, which raise many security concerns especially when they are applied in safety-critical applications. In particular, it is now known that NNs are subject to adversarial perturbations [40], i.e., a slightly modified input may cause an NN to predict wrongly. Many attacking methods have been proposed to compromise NNs designed and trained for a variety of application domains, including images [6], audio [7] and texts [29]. Multiple approaches like HotFlip [12] and TEXTBUGGER [22] have been proposed to attack NNs trained for text classification. TEXTBUGGER attacks by identifying and changing certain important characters (or words) in the text to cause a change in the classification result. For example, given the text *"Unfortunately, I thought the movie was terrible"* which is classified as 'negative' by an NN for sentiment analysis, TEXTBUGGER produces an adversarial text *"Unf0rtunately, I thought the movie was terrib1e"* which is classified as 'positive'. While the above perturbation is detectable with a spell checker, there are attacking methods like SEAs [33] that generate hard-to-detect adversarial texts.

Efforts on defending against adversarial attacks fall into two categories. One is to train a robust classifier which either improves the accuracy on such examples, e.g., adversarial training [25,37] and training models with pre-processing samples generated by dimensionality reduction or JPEG compression [8,49], or decreases the success rate for attackers on generating adversarial samples, e.g., obfuscated gradients [9]. None of these approaches, however, can eliminate adversarial samples completely [4] as the adversarial samples may not be a flaw of the model but features in data [17]. Alternative mitigation approaches alleviate the effects of such samples by detecting adversarial samples [23,45,48,53].

Although most of the detecting approaches have focused on the image domain, simple approaches have been proposed to detect adversarial texts as well. One example is to apply a character/word checker, i.e., Gao *et al.* [13], to detect adversarial texts generated by HotFlip and TEXTBUGGER. Detecting adversarial samples is however not the end of the story. The natural follow-up question is then: what do we do when a sample is deemed adversarial? Some approaches simply reject those adversarial samples [24,27,45]. Rejection is however not always feasible or ideal. First, existing detection algorithms often generate a non-negligible amount of false alarms [45,48], particularly so for the simple detection algorithms proposed for adversarial texts [34]. Second, rejection may not be an option for certain applications. For example, it is not a good idea to reject an edit in public platforms (e.g., Wikipedia, Twitter and GitHub) even if the edit is suspected to be maliciously crafted (e.g., toxic) [16]. Rather, it would be much better to suggest a minor "correction" on the edit so that it is no longer malicious. Lastly, rejecting all suspicious samples would easily lead to deny-of-service attacks.

Beyond rejection, a variety of techniques in the image domain are proposed to mitigate the effect of the adversarial samples after these samples are identified. For example, Pixeldefend [39] rectified the suspicious images by changing them slightly towards the training distribution. Akhtar *et al.* [2] attached a network to the first layer of the target NN to reconstruct clean images from the suspicious ones. Agarwal *et al.* [1] proposed to use wavelet transformation and inverse wavelet to remove the adversarial noise.

However, to the best of our knowledge, the question that whether we can effectively repair adversarial *texts* has been largely overlooked so far. Even worse, the aforementioned mitigation approaches cannot be easily extended to the text domain due to several fundamental new challenges. To address the gap, in this work, we aim to develop a framework that automatically repairs adversarial texts. That is, given an input text, we first check whether it is adversarial or not. If it is deemed to be adversarial, we identify a slightly mutated but semantically equivalent text which the neural network correctly classifies as the suggested repair.

Two non-trivial technical questions must be answered in order to achieve our goal. *First, how do we generate slightly mutated but semantically equivalent texts?* Our answer is to novelly apply adversarial perturbation methods in a positive way. One of such methods is the SEAs attacking method which generates semantically 'equivalent' texts by applying neural machine translation (NMT) twice (i.e., translate the given text into a different language and back). Another example is a perturbation method which is developed based on TEXTBUGGER, i.e., identifying and replacing important words in a sentence with their synonyms. *Second, how do we know what is the correct label, in the presence of adversarial texts?* Our answer is differential testing combined with majority voting. Given two or more NNs trained for the same task, our intuition is that if there is a disagreement between the NNs, the labels generated by the NNs are not reliable. Due to the transferability of adversarial samples [14], a label agreed upon by the NNs may still not be reliable. We thus propose to compare the outputs of the models (in the form of probability vectors) based on KL divergence [42] to identify the correct label. Furthermore, we apply the sequential probability ratio test (SPRT) algorithm to systematically evaluate the confidence of each possible label and output the most-likely-correct label based on majority voting only if it reaches certain level of statistical confidence.

We implemented our approach as a self-contained toolkit targeting NNs trained for text classification tasks. Our experiments on multiple real-world tasks (e.g., for sentiment analysis and topic labeling) show that our approach can effectively and efficiently repair adversarial texts generated using two state-of-the-art attacking methods. In particular, we successfully repair about 80% of the adversarial texts, and depending on the applied perturbation method, an adversarial text could be repaired in as few as 1 second.

2   Background

In this section, we present the background that is relevant to this work, including a brief introduction of text classification and several state-of-the-art approaches to generate adversarial texts for NNs.

Text classification is one of the most common tasks in NLP. The objective is to assign one or several pre-defined labels to a text. Text classification is widely applied in many applications such as sentiment analysis [10,41], topic detection [50] and spam detection [19,32]. Neural networks (NNs) have been widely adopted in solving text classification tasks. In particular, Recurrent Neural Networks (RNNs), designed to deal with sequential data, are commonly applied in many NLP tasks. In addition, Convolutional Neural Networks (CNNs) are shown to achieve similar results on text classification tasks [21]. In this work, we focus on RNNs and CNNs.

TEXTBUGGER is a general framework for crafting adversarial texts [22], which has a similar mechanism as HotFlip [12], but is more efficient and scalable. Given an input text, it first identifies the most important sentence and then the most important word. A

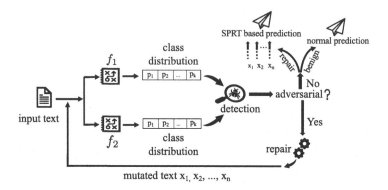

Fig. 1. Overview of our approach.

word is most important if removing it leads to the biggest decrease in the classification confidence. After a word is selected, five operations are applied to generate adversarial texts. Four of the five operations are character-level operations which aim to generate "human-imperceptible" texts, i.e., deleting a character. Similarly, adversarial texts generated by these operations are easily detected by a spell-checker. The last operation is to substitute the selected word with a synonym (hereafter *Sub-W*), which is hard to detect and likely semantic-preserving.

TEXTFOOLER is another recent method to generate adversarial texts [20]. Instead of sorting sentences by importance at first, TEXTFOOLER directly performs word importance ranking, and then replaces the words in the ranking list one by one with a synonym until the prediction of the target model is changed. Compared with TEXTBUGGER, TEXTFOOLER is more likely to generate more natural adversarial texts since it takes the part of speech into account when selecting synonyms.

SEAs aims to generate semantic-equivalent adversarial texts by paraphrasing [33] based on Neural Machine Translation (NMT). SEAs applies NMT to generating semantic-preserving texts as adversarial texts, i.e., SEAs translates an input sentence into multiple foreign languages and then translates them back to the source language using NMT. Next, SEAs selects an adversarial text among those according to a semantic score, which measures how semantic-preserving the text is compared to the original input.

3 Our Repair Approach

Our aim is to automatically repair adversarial texts. We define our problem as follows. *Given a text input x and a pair of different NNs (f_1, f_2) which are trained for the same task, how to automatically check whether x is likely adversarial and generate a repair of x if x is deemed adversarial?* Note that we assume the availability of two models f_1 and f_2. In practice, multiple models can be easily obtained by training with slightly different architectures, or different training sets, or through model mutation [45]. Figure 1 shows the overall workflow of our approach. Given an input text x and two models (f_1, f_2), we first check whether x is likely adversarial. If the answer is positive, we apply adversarial perturbation to generate a set of texts X^* such that each $x \in X^*$ is slightly different from x and likely semantically equivalent to x. Afterwards, we apply a statistical testing method to identify the most-likely correct label of x (with a guaranteed level of confidence) based on X^* and output a text in X^* which is slightly different from x as the repair. In the following paragraphs, we present the details of each step.

3.1 Adversarial Text Detection

Given an input text x, we first check whether it is adversarial. There are multiple methods for detecting adversarial perturbations in the image domain [45,53], but the topic is relatively less studied in the text domain [48]. In this work, we propose an alternative approach to detect adversarial texts by differential testing [26]. We remark that the objective of this work is to propose a framework for automatically repairing an adversarial text and the detection part can be flexibly replaced by other detection method.

Algo 1: $TbPerturb(x, g, f_1, f_2)$	**Algo 2:** $hypTest(c_i, X^*, f_1, \alpha, \beta, \sigma, \rho)$
1 Let C_s be the importance scores for each sentence in x;	1 Let k be the size of X^*;
2 **for** $s_i \in x$ **do**	2 Let z be the size of $\{y \mid y \in X^* \wedge f_1(y) = c\}$;
3 $\quad$ $C_s(i) = D_{KL}(s_i)$;	3 Let $\alpha, \beta, \sigma, \rho$ be the parameter of hypothesis testing;
4 $S \leftarrow$ sort the sentences in x according to C_s;	4 $p_0 = \rho + \sigma$;
5 **for** $s_i \in S_{ordered}$ **do**	5 $p_1 = \rho - \sigma$;
6 $\quad$ Let C_w be the importance scores for each word in s_i;	6 $sprt\_ratio \leftarrow Pr(z, k, p_0, p_1)$;
7 $\quad$ **for** $w_j \in s_i$ **do**	7 **if** $sprt\_ratio \le \frac{\beta}{1-\alpha}$ **then**
8 $\quad\quad$ Compute $C_w(j)$ according to Eq. 1;	8 $\quad$ Accept the hypothesis that $H(c) \ge p_0$;
9 $\quad$ $W \leftarrow$ sort the words in s_i according to C_w;	9 $\quad$ **return**;
10 $\Gamma \leftarrow$ select g words according to S and W;	10 **if** $sprt\_ratio \ge \frac{1-\beta}{\alpha}$ **then**
11 $x' \leftarrow$ replace word $w \in \Gamma$ in x with synonyms;	11 $\quad$ Accept the hypothesis that $H(c) \le p_1$;
12 **return** x';	12 $\quad$ **return**;
	13 **return** *Inconclusive*;

Applying differential testing naively in our context is however problematic because of the transferability of adversarial samples, i.e., f_1 and f_2 may generate the same wrong label given the same input. We thus need a more reliable way to check whether x is adversarial. Our remedy is to further measure the difference between the prediction distributions of the two models. Concretely, the output of a neural network for multi-class classification is a probability vector $f(x) = [p_0, p_1, \cdots, p_K]$, where f is a model and p_i is the probability of the input being class i and K is the total number of classes. We enhance differential testing by comparing the difference of two models' probability vectors. That is, the input x is regarded adversarial if the difference of the probability vectors is larger than a threshold.

We adopt KL divergence (D_{KL}) [42] to measure the difference between the two probability vectors. Formally, let $f_1(x) = [p_0, p_1, \cdots, p_K]$ and $f_2(x) = [q_0, q_1, \cdots, q_K]$, then we have $D_{KL}(f_1(x), f_2(x)) = -\sum_{i=1}^{K} p_i \ln \frac{q_i}{p_i}$. Hereafter, we write $D_{KL}(x)$ to denote $D_{KL}(f_1(x), f_2(x))$. Intuitively, $D_{KL}(x)$ is smaller if two distributions are more similar. Our hypothesis is that if the input is not adversarial, the probability vectors $f_1(x)$ and $f_2(x)$ should be similar and thus the difference $D_{KL}(x)$ should be small; otherwise it should be large. This is confirmed empirically as we show in Sect. 4. Thus, an input x is considered to be normal only if the labels generated by the two models are the same and the $D_{KL}(x)$ is below the threshold. Otherwise, the input is regarded as adversarial. The remaining question is how to set the threshold value, which we solve using the standard method of golden-section search as we discuss in Sect. 4.

3.2 Semantic-Preserving Perturbation

Once we identify an adversarial text x, the next challenge is how to automatically repair the input. In general, a repaired text x' should satisfy the following conditions: 1) x' is syntactically similar to x and semantically equivalent to x; 2) x' is classified as normal by the adversarial sample detection algorithm; and 3) x' is labeled correctly. In the following, we describe how to systematically generate a set of candidate repairs X^* satisfying 1) and discuss how to identify a repair among the candidates that satisfies all the conditions in Sect. 3.3.

We generate candidate repairs through perturbation, i.e., the same technique for generating adversarial texts except that they are used in a positive way this time. In particular, three different adversarial perturbation methods are applied to generate syntactically similar and semantically equivalent texts.

The first one is random perturbation *(RP)*. Let $x = [w_1, w_2, \cdots, w_n]$ where w_i is a word in the text x. This method randomly selects g words in x and replaces them with their synonyms. Note that to preserve the semantics, g is typically small. In particular, for each selected word w_i, we identify a ranked list $[w_{i1}, \cdots, w_{iL}]$ of its synonyms of size L As a result, we obtain g^L perturbations.

The second one is based on the idea of TEXTBUGGER with the Sub-W *operation (SubW)*. That is, we first identify the important sentences, and replace the important words in the sentence with their synonyms. Note that different from TEXTBUG-GER [22], our goal is to decrease $D_{KL}(x)$ so that the perturbed text passes the enhanced differential testing. Thus, we evaluate the importance of a sentence and a word based on its effect on $D_{KL}(x)$ (instead of the effect on the model prediction as in [22]). Concretely, to obtain the importance of a sentence s_i, we calculate $D_{KL}(f_1(s_i), f_2(s_i))$. A sentence with a larger D_{KL} is considered more important. Within a sentence, we obtain the importance of a word w_j by measuring the D_{KL} of the sentence with/without w_j.

$$D_{KL}(f_1(s_i), f_2(s_i)) - D_{KL}(f_1(s_i \setminus w_j), f_2(s_i \setminus w_j)) \qquad (1)$$

Intuitively, a word causing a larger decrease of D_{KL} is more important. Afterwards, the important words are replaced with their synonyms to generate perturbations. The details are shown in Algorithm 1.

The third one is a paraphrase-based perturbation approach using NMT *(ParaPer)*. Formally, an NMT is a function $T(s, d, x) : X_s \to X_d$, where s is the source language, d is the destination language and x is the input text. The basic idea is to translate the input text into another language and then translate it back, i.e., the new text is $x' = T(d, s, T(s, d, x))$. By varying the target language d, e.g., French and German, we can generate multiple perturbations in this way. Furthermore, it is possible to translate across multiple languages to generate even more perturbations. For instance, with two target languages d_1 and d_2, we can generate $x' = T(d_2, s, T(d_1, d_2, T(s, d_1, x)))$ as perturbations.

3.3 Voting for the Correct Label

After generating a set of texts X^* which are slightly mutated from x and yet are semantically equivalent to x, our next step is to identify a member x' of X^* that satisfies the condition 2) and condition 3) proposed in Sect. 3.2. Satisfying 2) is straightforward. That is, we filter those in X^* which are determined to be adversarial using our detection algorithm. Satisfying 3) requires us to know what the correct label is. Our idea is that we can 'vote' and decide on the correct label. Our hypothesis is that the majority of texts in X^* are likely classified correctly, and thus a democratic decision would be correct. This idea is inspired by the observation made in [45], which shows that adversarial samples (with wrong labels) in the image domain have a high label-change rate when perturbations are applied. In other words, perturbing adversarial samples would often restore the correct label. One interpretation is that adversarial samples are generated by perturbing normal samples just enough to cross the classification boundary, and thus a slight mutation often restores the original label. We evaluate this hypothesis empirically in Sect. 4. Based on the hypothesis, we formulate the problem as a statistical testing problem. That is, we present it with a set of hypotheses (e.g., the correct label of a text is c_i where c_i is one of the labels) and the problem is to identify the hypothesis which is most likely true with statistical confidence.

Concretely, we adopt hypothesis testing [38] to guarantee that the probability of choosing the correct label is beyond a threshold, say ρ. That is, given a label c_i, we systematically test the null hypothesis (H_0) and the alternative hypothesis (H_1) which are defined as follows: $H_0(c_i) : P(f(x) = c_i) \geq \rho$ and $H_1(c_i) : P(f(x) = c_i) < \rho$, where $P(f(x) = c_i)$ is the probability that the true label of x is c_i. Given X^* which contains only texts that are semantically equivalent to x, we estimate $P(f(x) = c_i)$ as $\frac{|y \in X^* \wedge f_1(y) = c_i|}{|X^*|}$. Note that all texts in X^* have the same label. In general, given a limited number of perturbations, it might be possible that none of the $H_0(c_i)$ is accepted. Since there are multiple labels, we maintain a pair of hypotheses for each $c_i \in C$ and perform a hypothesis testing procedure for every pair. There are two ways for performing hypothesis testing. One is the fixed-size sampling test (FSST), which performs the test on a fixed number of samples. FSST requires to determine the minimum number of samples to use such that the error bounds are satisfied. Typically, FSST requires a large number of samples [3]. In general, the more samples used, the more accurate the result would be. However, the more samples required, the more computational overhead there is, which may be problematic if such repairing is to be carried out in an online manner. We thus propose to use the sequential probability ratio test (SPRT) [43], which dynamically determines the number of samples required and is known to be faster than FSST [44]. Central to SPRT is to repeatedly sample until enough evidence is accumulated to make a decision (accepting either hypothesis).

Algorithm 2 shows the details on how SPRT is applied in our work, where α is the probability of the case in which H_0 is rejected while H_0 is true (a.k.a. Type *I* error), β is the probability of the case in which H_1 is rejected while H_1 is true (a.k.a. Type *II* error), ρ is the confidence threshold described before, and σ is the indifference interval used to relax the threshold. We then test hypotheses $H_0(c_i) : P(f(x) = c_i) \geq p_0$ and $H_1(c_i) : P(f(x) = c_i) < p_1$ where $p_0 = \rho + \sigma$ and $p_1 = \rho - \sigma$. At line 6, we compute the likelihood ratio of SPRT [44] which is defined as: $Pr(z, k, p_0, p_1) = \frac{p_1^z (1-p_1)^{k-z}}{p_0^z (1-p_0)^{k-z}}$. At line 7, we check whether the ratio is no larger than $\frac{\beta}{1-\alpha}$. If it is the case, the hypothesis $H_0(c_i) \geq p_0$ is accepted and report the label c_i as the true label with error bounded by β. If the ratio is no less than $\frac{1-\beta}{\alpha}$, we then accept $H_1(c_i) \leq p_1$ at line 11 and report the label c_i is not the true label with error bounded by α. Otherwise, it is inconclusive (i.e., more samples are required).

3.4 Overall Algorithm

Algorithm 3 shows the overall algorithm. The inputs include an input text x, a pair of NNs f_1 and f_2, a threshold ϵ for hypothesis testing, and four parameters $\{\alpha, \beta, \sigma, \rho\}$ for Algorithm 2. We first check whether x is adversarial or not at line 1. If it is normal, x is returned without any modification. If it is adversarial and the labels from the two models are the same, the label is added into D at line 3 since we assume that it is not the correct label. The loop from line 4 to 15 then aims to repair x. We first obtain a semantic-preserving perturbation of x at line 5. Note that function $perturb(x)$ can be implemented using either RP, SubW or ParaPer as we discussed in Sect. 3.2. We then check whether the newly generated text $\hat{x}$ is adversarial at line 6. If it is, we generate another one until a perturbed text $\hat{x}$ which is determined to be normal is generated. If $\hat{x}$ has a label which is never seen before, we add the label to C which is a set of potentially correct labels for x. Afterwards, for each $c_i \in C$, we conduct hypothesis testing using Algorithm 2 at line 11. If $H_0(c_i)$ is accepted, we identify a text in X^*

Algo 3: $Repair(x, f_1, f_2, \epsilon, \alpha, \beta, \sigma, \rho)$

---

1 **if** $isAdversarial(x, f_1, f_2, \epsilon)$ **then**
2   Let X^* be an empty set, $C = \emptyset$ be a set of possible labels, and $D = \emptyset$ be a set of rejected labels;
3   Add $f_1(x)$ into D if $f_1(x) = f_2(x)$;
4   **while** *true* **do**
5   Let $\hat{x} = perturb(x)$;
6   **if** *not* $isAdversarial(\hat{x}, f_1, f_2, \epsilon)$ **then**
7              $c = f_1(\hat{x})$;
8              $X^* = X^* \cup \{\hat{x}\}$;
9   Add label c into C if $c \notin C$ and $c \notin D$;
10   **for** *each* $c_i \in C$ *and* $c_i \notin D$ **do**
11   Let co be $hypTest(c_i, X^*, f_1, \alpha, \beta, \sigma, \rho)$;
12   **if** co *is accepted* **then**
13                     $\llcorner$ **return** $x' \in X^*$ s.t. $f_1(x') = c_i$;
14   **if** co *is rejected* **then**
15                     $\llcorner$ $D = D \cup \{c_i\}$;

16 **return** x;

---

which has the label c_i as the repair of x and return it. If $H_0(c_i)$ is rejected, the label c_i is added into D and we continue with the next iteration. Otherwise, if it is inclusive, we continue with the next iteration. Note that to reduce the computational overhead, we conduct hypothesis testing in a *lazy* way. That is, we maintain a set of witnessed labels C (which is initially empty) and only test those in C. Furthermore, we maintain a set of rejected labels D so that when a label is rejected, it is never tested again. Algorithm 3 always terminates. Given any label c_i, Algorithm 2 always terminates since SPRT is guaranteed to terminate with probability 1 [44]. As there are finitely many labels, and each label is tested by Algorithm 2 once, it follows Algorithm 3 always terminates.

4 Experiments

We have implemented our approach as a prototype[1]. All experiments are carried out on a workstation with 1 Xeon 3.50 GHz CPU and 64 GB system memory.

4.1 Experimental Settings

We conduct our experiments on the following three popular real-world datasets: *1) News Aggregator (NA) Dataset.* [11] This dataset contains 422419 news stories in four categories: business, science and technology, entertainment, and health. For the sake of efficiency, we randomly take 10% of the dataset for our experiment. *2) Rotten Tomatoes Movie Review (RTMR).* This is a movie review dataset collected from Rotten Tomatoes pages [28] for sentiment analysis consisting of 5331 positive and 5331 negative sentences. *3) IMDB.* This dataset is widely used in sentiment analysis classification and contains 25k positive movie reviews and 25k negative movie reviews. Following [22], we randomly select 20% of the training data for training the NNs. We follow the standard splitting to have 80% of the dataset for training and 20% for testing.

We adopt two heterogeneous NNs widely used for text classification as the target models: LSTM [15] and TextCNN [21]. In our case, LSTM is a vanilla one as used in [52] and for the TextCNN we follow the configuration used in [21]. Note that each word is transformed into a 300-dimensions numerical vector using GloVe[2] before training models. The test accuracy of our trained models is 89.21%/87.04%, 79.71%/77.88% and 88.24%/87.24% for TextCNN/LSTM on NA, RTMR and IMDB dataset.

We adopt the three state-of-the-art approaches introduced in Sect. 2 to craft adversarial texts, i.e., TEXTBUGGER with *Sub-W*, TEXTFOOLER and SEAs. For each model, we randomly select 300 texts from the dataset and apply these attacks to generate adversarial texts. To generate perturbations using *RP* and *SubW*, we limit the maximum number of words to be replaced to be 4 so that the resultant text is likely semantic-preserving. To obtain the synonyms of a chosen word, we use *gensim*[3], an open-source library to find the most similar words in the word embedding space. To perform SEAs perturbation, we utilize the NMTs from an online Translation API service[4].

---

[1] https://github.com/dgl-prc/text-repair.

[2] https://nlp.stanford.edu/projects/glove/.

[3] https://radimrehurek.com/gensim/.

[4] http://api.fanyi.baidu.com/api/trans/product/index.

4.2   Research Questions

RQ1: Is KL divergence useful in detecting adversarial samples? To answer the question, we measure the accuracy of detecting adversarial texts using the algorithm depicted in Sect. 3.1 and compare that to the basic differential testing. Note that to apply our detection algorithm, we must first select the threshold ϵ. Ideally, the threshold ϵ should be chosen such that D_{KL} of normal texts are smaller than ϵ and D_{KL} of adversarial texts are larger than ϵ (in which case the accuracy of the detection is 1). We adopt golden-section search [5] to identify ϵ and the results are 0.0288/0.0266, 0.0655/0.111 and 0.1593/0.1806 for TextCNN/LSTM on NA, RTMR and IMDB dataset, respectively.

After setting ϵ, we apply our detection algorithm to a set of texts which mixes all adversarial texts and an equal number of normal texts. For the baseline comparison, we compare our algorithm with the alternative approach which simply checks whether the two models agree on the output labels. The text is regarded as adversarial if the answer is no. Otherwise, the text is regarded as normal. To the best of our knowledge, there are few methods or tools which are available for detecting adversarial texts. Note that the tool mentioned in [34,46] are not available. Results are shown in Table 1.

We observe that our approach detects most of the adversarial texts and significantly outperforms the baseline for all datasets and models, i.e., on average 76.5% of the adversarial texts generated by SEAs are detected, 87% of TEXTBUGGER and 84% of TEXTFOOLER are detected, which are 23.5%, 15% and 21.5% higher than that of the baseline respectively. In particular, the detection rate is 41% higher for the TextCNN model with SEAs as the attacking method on the NA dataset. This shows that our

Table 1. The detection rate ("dr") and false discovery rate ("fdr") of baseline approach ("BL") and our approach ("KL-D").

Attack	Dataset	TextCNN				LSTM			
		BL		KL-D		BL		KL-D	
		dr(%)	fdr(%)	dr(%)	fdr(%)	dr(%)	fdr(%)	dr(%)	fdr(%)
SEAs	NA	47	10	88	19	59	2	92	17
	RTMR	44	19	68	36	44	18	63	29
	IMDB	64	14	76	25	59	7	73	18
	Avg	**52**	**14**	**77**	**27**	**54**	**9**	**76**	**21**
TEXTBUGGER	NA	68	7	93	19	73	1	93	18
	RTMR	54	16	76	33	68	12	79	25
	IMDB	84	12	89	23	85	7	93	17
	Avg	**69**	**12**	**86**	**25**	**75**	**7**	**88**	**20**
TEXTFOOLER	NA	62	9	95	23	65	6	95	17
	RTMR	41	16	67	39	50	13	68	28
	IMDB	77	9	89	19	79	9	90	19
	Avg	**60**	**11**	**84**	**27**	**65**	**9**	**84**	**21**
Avg		**60**	**12**	**82**	**26**	**65**	**8**	**83**	**21**

adversarial detection algorithm effectively addresses the problem caused by the transferability of adversarial texts. We also observe that our approach achieves a higher detection rate in detecting adversarial texts generated by TEXTBUGGER than detecting those generated by SEAs, i.e., 10.5% higher on average. One possible explanation is that the adversarial texts generated by TEXTBUGGER are likely to have a relatively small 'distance' from the original text. In comparison, adversarial texts generated by SEAs may have different structures (after two translations) and thus a relatively large distance to the original text. We also notice that the detection rate of adversarial texts generated by TEXTBUGGER is close to that of adversarial texts generated by TEXTFOOLER, i.e., only about a 3% gap. This is not surprising since the two methods in crafting adversarial text are pretty similar as depicted in Sect. 2. On average, our method has false discovery rate of 26% for the adversarial texts generated by attacking the TextCNN and 21% for those generated by attacking the LSTM, which is higher than the baseline approach. Considering that the baseline approach overlooks many adversarial texts (e.g., almost half of those generated by SEAs), we believe this is acceptable. In addition, our framework aims to automatically repair the "alarms" and thus some false positives can be eliminated by the subsequent repair. Later, we will show the effectiveness of our approach on handling the false positive samples in RQ3.

Effectiveness on a Third Model. In the above experiments, we assume that the adversarial samples are from one of the two models used in detection. A natural question is that if our approach can deal with the adversarial texts from a model which is different from the two models used in detection. To answer this question,

Table 2. Effectiveness of detection and repair when adversarial texts are from a third model.

The third model	Detection rate	Repair accuracy
BiLSTM	89%	60%
LSTM	92%	61.4%
TextCNN	87%	46.1%
Avg	89%	55.83%

we introduce a new model, i.e., BiLSTM [35]. We apply our approach to detect the adversarial texts generated from one model and use the other two for the detection. For every third model, we take 1000 adversarial texts (generated by TEXTBUGGER) and 1000 normal texts for the experiments. The results are summarized in Table 2. We can observe that the average detection rate is 89%, which suggests our approach can effectively identify the adversarial texts from an unseen model. *Thus, the answer to RQ1 is that our approach is effective in detecting adversarial texts with a relatively low false discovery rate.*

RQ2: Is our hypothesis for voting justified? To answer this question, we take all the adversarial texts and apply semantic-preserving perturbations to generate 100 perturbed texts for each of them and measure the percentage of the perturbed texts that are labeled correctly. The results are shown in Fig. 2. We can observe that our hypothesis holds across all models, methods used to generate adversarial texts and perturbation methods, i.e., the percentage of perturbed texts with correct labels is more than 50% in all cases. Comparing the results on different perturbation methods, perturbation using ParaPer restores the correct label significantly more often than the other two. This is expected since the ParaPer is paraphrase-based, which preserves the most semantics when generating adversarial texts among the three methods. Comparing different adversarial texts,

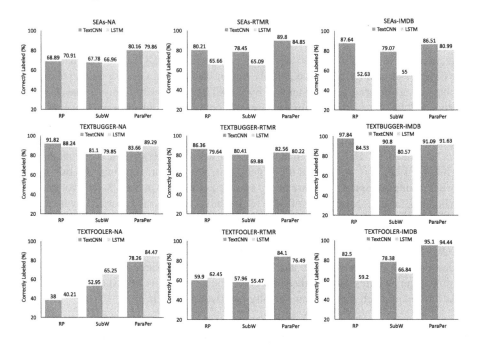

Fig. 2. Results of justifying voting.

adversarial texts generated by TEXTBUGGER, once perturbed, are more likely to have the correct label than those generated by SEAs and TEXTFOOLER. This is reasonable as the adversarial texts generated by SEAs and TEXTFOOLER are more semantically similar to the original texts compared with these texts generated by TEXTBUGGER. *Thus, the answer to RQ2 is that our hypothesis for voting is justified*

RQ3: Is our approach effective in repairing adversarial texts? To answer this question, we systematically apply Algorithm 3 to all the adversarial texts, and measure its overall repair accuracy, which is the percentage of the number of texts which can be correctly predicted after repair in the total number of adversarial texts. The error bounds α and β are both set as 0.1, the confidence threshold ρ is 0.8, and the indifference region σ is to be $0.2 \times \rho$. Note that when we apply ParaPer to generate perturbed texts, we use 25 different target languages for generating 25 semantic-preserving perturbations through two translations. If more is required, we use two target languages each time (and three translations), which provides us additionally 25×25 perturbed texts. To be consistent with ParaPer, we set the perturbation budgets (maximum number of perturbations) for RP and SubW as 650 as well. We compare our approach with two baselines [13,30].

Table 3. Overall repair accuracy (%) comparison between our approach and two baselines.

Attack	Dataset	Model	Our approach			Baselines	
			RP	SubW	ParaPer	Autocorrect	scRNN
SEAs	NA	TextCNN	23.66	42.75	70.23	4.70	27.52
		LSTM	26.71	49.32	67.81	5.66	28.93
	MR	TextCNN	50.00	60.00	76.00	6.76	30.18
		LSTM	50.38	51.13	78.20	5.71	19.05
	IMDB	TextCNN	60.94	53.13	79.69	4.82	38.69
		LSTM	35.25	34.42	75.41	10.12	34.34
	Avg		**41.16**	**48.46**	**74.56**	**6.30**	**29.79**
TEXTBUGGER	NA	TextCNN	64.94	67.53	79.74	18.79	29.09
		LSTM	52.35	58.82	82.84	18.79	36.81
	MR	TextCNN	72.57	67.43	80.01	19.21	29.26
		LSTM	69.40	59.02	79.23	23.81	25.97
	IMDB	TextCNN	87.62	73.27	93.56	27.19	68.86
		LSTM	62.15	56.57	90.44	29.63	64.81
	Avg		**68.17**	**63.77**	**84.30**	**22.90**	**42.47**
TEXTFOOLER	NA	TextCNN	37.37	52.00	70.71	12.00	22.60
		LSTM	38.21	46.21	75.51	12.90	21.60
	MR	TextCNN	40.39	48.21	54.95	20.50	23.30
		LSTM	39.35	41.49	56.99	22.10	23.50
	IMDB	TextCNN	82.35	71.57	90.69	39.30	57.21
		LSTM	53.97	45.63	87.30	36.07	57.14
	Avg		**48.61**	**50.85**	**72.69**	**23.81**	**34.23**
Avg			**52.65**	**54.36**	**77.18**	**17.67**	**35.49**

Both baselines can automatically detect and correct adversarial examples with misspellings. The first baseline [13] used the Python autocorrect package[5] to detect and automatically correct the adversarial texts with misspellings. In the following, we refer this baseline to Autocorrect. The second baseline [30] proposed a word recognition model scRNN for the same task. We first attempt to repair adversarial texts using each baseline and then test the accuracy of the target model on the repaired texts.

The results are summarized in Table 3. On average, we can correctly repair 54.66%, 56.12% and 79.43% of the adversarial texts using RP, SubW and ParaPer respectively, while the two baselines achieve 14.60% and 36.91%. That is, all the three sort of methods in our approach outperform the two baselines and ParaPer achieves the best overall performance among the three. Comparing adversarial texts generated using different methods, we observe that adversarial texts generated by SEAs are harder to repair than those generated by TEXTBUGGER. This is expected as adversarial texts generated

---

[5] https://pypi.org/project/autocorrect/.

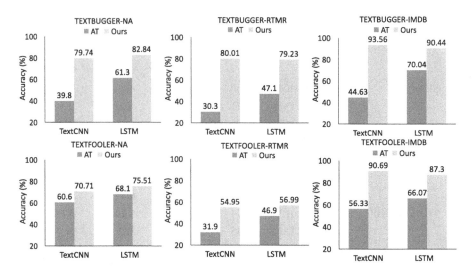

Fig. 3. Accuracy of adversarial-trained models ("AT") and our approach ("Ours") on adversarial texts.

by SEAs (with two translation) are often structurally different from the original normal texts, whereas adversarial texts generated by TEXTBUGGER are very similar to the original normal texts. Comparing different repairing methods, we also observe that ParaPer performs significantly better than the other methods. This is also expected due to the same reason above. The performance of the two baselines is significantly worse than our approaches, which is as expected since the two baselines are to detect the misspellings and thus are not able to handle semantic-preserved adversarial texts.

We also compare our approach with the adversarial training method. We retrained the target model by adding 10% of adversarial texts (half of them are generated by TEXTBUGGER and half by TEXTFOOLER) into the training set. Firstly, we compare the robustness of the models obtained through the two approaches. The results are shown in Fig. 3. We can observe that, respectively, 51.92% and 78.5% of adversarial texts can be predicted correctly by the models from adver-

Table 4. Success rate(%) of attacking different targets.

Dataset	Model	Ori	AT	Ours
NA	TextCNN	53.1	49.4	1.6
	LSTM	63.3	52.8	
RTMR	TextCNN	74.1	71.7	28.4
	LSTM	78.4	77.8	
IMDB	TextCNN	63.9	62.5	6.5
	LSTM	96.3	95	

sarial training and our approach. Secondly, we conducted experiments to evaluate if the model obtained through adversarial training is robust against adversarial attacks (with TEXTBUGGER). The results are shown in Table 4 where "Ori", "AT" and "Ours" denote the original model, the adversarially retrained model and our approach. We can observe that the success rate of attacking indeed decreases, but not significantly, i.e. a 3.3% drop on average. This is consistent with the well-known result that adversarial training easily overfits and has limited effectiveness in defending against unknown

Table 5. The time overhead of our repair approach.

Attack	Dataset	Model	Detect (ms)	Repair (s)		
				RP	SubW	ParaPer
SEAs	NA	TextCNN	7.6	55.1	1.2	181.6
		LSTM	8.2	48.8	1.0	223.2
	RTMR	TextCNN	3.2	46.3	1.4	171.6
		LSTM	3.3	36.5	1.1	144.0
	IMDB	TextCNN	13.4	61.5	1.0	134.8
		LSTM	13.3	92.7	1.1	167.3
	Avg		**8.2**	**56.8**	**1.1**	**170.5**
TEXTBUGGER	NA	TextCNN	6.6	35.0	0.7	157.8
		LSTM	6.4	31.2	0.8	171.5
	RTMR	TextCNN	3.6	39.6	1.4	81.1
		LSTM	3.4	40.0	1.2	67.7
	IMDB	TextCNN	15.2	51.7	0.8	47
		LSTM	17.3	101.0	1.0	76.3
	Avg		**8.8**	**49.7**	**1.0**	**102.8**
TEXTFOOLER	NA	TextCNN	6.7	47.4	0.7	109.0
		LSTM	8.6	54.5	0.7	98.0
	RTMR	TextCNN	4.9	34.2	0.8	85.7
		LSTM	4.8	46.9	1.1	90.3
	IMDB	TextCNN	28.9	141.4	1.5	79.4
		LSTM	32.8	102.6	1.1	99.6
	Avg		**14.5**	**71.2**	**1.0**	**93.7**
Avg			**10.5**	**59.2**	**1.0**	**122.4**

attacks [51], which is also evidenced in [20] where adversarial training only decreases the attack success rate by 7.2% on MR dataset. On the other hand, our approach is resilient under different kinds of attacks with a totally different defense paradigm, i.e. decreasing the attack success rate by 59.4% on average.

Effectiveness on False Positive Samples. Our detection approach may report false positive samples, thus, one question is whether our repair is effective on these samples. To address this concern, we conduct a simple experiment on NA dataset with TextCNN and LSTM. Concretely, we apply our approach to repair randomly selected 1000 samples which are wrongly detected as adversarial. The results show that 81.4% (TextCNN) and 85.2% (LSTM) of samples can be correctly classified after repair, suggesting that our approach can correctly handle most of the false positive samples.

Effectiveness on a Third Model. The column "Repair accuracy" of Table 2 shows the repair results when the adversarial texts from a third model. We can observe that our approach achieves 55.83% repair accuracy on average, which suggests that our approach is still effective in handling this sort of adversarial text. In general, adversarial samples from the third model can be categorized into two groups: 1) adversarial samples which are invalid for both of our models (used for adversarial detection), and 2) adversarial samples which can still fool at least one of our models. In the first case, even if it is wrongly identified as adversarial (because of the large KL divergence), our approach can still produce a right prediction with high probability (see previous paragraph). In the second case, our approach is able to repair the adversarial sample just in the same way with adversarial samples from our own models. *Thus, the answer to RQ3 is our approach can repair about 80% of the adversarial texts and ParaPer performs the best.*

RQ4: What is the time overhead of our approach? The time overhead of our approach mainly consists of two parts: detection and repairing. For detection, measuring the time spent is straightforward. For repairing, precisely measuring the time is a bit complicated. For RP and SubW, the time taken to obtain the synonymy might be different depending on the configuration of *gensim*. For ParaPer, our implementation uses an online NMT service which often suffers from network delay and as a result, the time measure is inaccurate. To discount the effect of the network delay, we thus count the average number of perturbed texts required for voting, which is then multiplied with the average time needed to obtain a perturbed text using the respective methods. According to our empirical study on 1000 trials, the average time taken for generating one perturbed text is 0.55, 0.09, and 1.44 s for RP, SubW and ParaPer respectively.

The results are summarized in Table 5 where column 'Detect' is the average detection time and column "Repair" is the average repair time. The results show that detection is very efficient, i.e., the average time across all datasets are 8.2 ms, 8.8 ms and 14.5 ms for SEAs, TEXTBUGGER and TEXTFOOLER generated adversarial texts respectively. For repairing, RP needs 59.2 s on average (maximum 141 s); SubW needs 1 s on average (maximum 1.5 s); ParaPer needs 122.4 s on average (maximum 223.2 s). Repairing using SubW takes much less time as SubW is designed to generate perturbed texts under the guidance of D_{KL} and the resulting texts thus have a much higher probability to be detected as normal. Besides, we observe that repairing adversarial texts generated by SEAs and TEXTFOOLER are more difficult (consistent with the above). On average, the time needed for repairing adversarial texts generated by the three methods are 76.13 s, 51.16 s and 55.3 s respectively. The results show that adversarial texts generated by TEXTFOOLER are relatively time-consuming to be repaired compared with that of TEXTBUGGER. This is reasonable since the adversarial texts generated by TEXTFOOLER are more nature compared with that of TEXTBUGGER. If our approach is to be used in an online setting, we thus would recommend repairing with SubW which repairs 77% of the adversarial texts with a total time overhead of 1.1 s. We remark that we can easily parallelize the generation of perturbed texts to reduce the time overhead for all three methods. *Thus, the answer to RQ4 is that our approach has the potential to detect and repair adversarial texts at runtime.*

4.3   Threats to Validity

Quality of NMTs. Our ParaPer perturbation method requires the availability of multiple NMTs. In this work, we utilize the online industrial NMTs. The quality of NMTs will influence the performance of our repair algorithm, i.e., we might need more perturbations for a successful repair with worse NMTs.

Word substitution. Random perturbation and Algorithm 1 work by replacing selected words with their synonyms. Currently, we look for synonyms by searching the neighborhood of a given text in the embedding space. However, this may not always find the ideal synonyms, i.e., words which cause syntactical or grammar errors may be returned. Besides, finding better synonyms usually takes more time, which can be time-consuming.

Limited datasets and adversarial texts. Our experiments results are subject to the selected datasets and generated adversarial texts, which have a limited number of labels. In general, it is difficult to vote for the correct label if there are many candidate labels, i.e., more perturbations are needed. Besides, we evaluate our approach on three existing attacks, it is not clear if our algorithm repairs adversarial texts from future attacks.

5   Related Work

This work is related to works on text adversarial attacks, which can be roughly divided into the following categories. One category is adversarial misspelling, which tries to evade the classifier by some "human-imperceptible" misspelling on certain selected characters [12,22]. The core idea is to design a strategy to identify the important positions and afterwards some standard character-level operations like insertion, deletion, substitution and swap can be applied. Another is adversarial paraphrasing. Compared to misspelling, paraphrasing aims to generate semantics-preserving adversarial samples either by replacing certain words with their synonyms or paraphrasing the whole sentence [18,33]. Our work uses paraphrasing as a way of generating repairs instead.

This work is related to the detection of adversarial inputs. Existing detection methods for adversarial perturbation mainly focuses on the image domain [23,45,48,53]. Recently, Rosenberg *et al.* devised a method to detect adversarial texts for Recurrent Neural Networks [34]. The idea is to compare the confidence scores of the original input and its squeezed variant. Wang *et al.* [46] detect adversarial texts by comparing the label of the input given by the target model with the label given by simply quantifying the impact of positive words and negative words of the input text in sentiment analysis. However, this method is not easy to extend to other text classification tasks since obtaining the label of an input text by simply analyzing individual words' polarity is not always attainable.

This work is related to work on defending adversarial perturbation in the text domain. Rosenberg *et al.* [34] presented several defense methods for adversarial texts, like adversarial training in the text domain or training ensemble models. Pruthi *et al.* [30] proposed to place an auxiliary model before the classifier. The auxiliary model is separately trained to recognize and correct the adversarial spelling mistakes. In [47], Wang *et al.* proposed *Synonyms Encoding Method* to defend adversarial texts in the word level, which maps all the semantically similar words into a single word randomly selected from the synonyms. By contrast, our approach can resist attacks of sentence level, i.e., SEAs. Li *et al.* proposed a robust text classification to resist adversarial attacks, but it is specially designed for Chinese-based text classification models.

6 Conclusion

In this work, we propose an approach to automatically detect and repair adversarial texts for neural network models. Given an input text to a pair of neural networks, we first identify whether the input is adversarial or normal. Afterwards, we automatically repair the adversarial inputs by generating semantic-preserving perturbations which collectively vote for the correct label until a consensus is reached (with certain error bounds). Experiments on multiple real-world datasets show the effectiveness of our approach.

Acknowledgements. This research is supported by the Key-Area Research and Development Program of Guangdong Province (Grant No.2020B0101100005), Key R&D Program of Zhejiang (2022C01018) and the NSFC Program (62102359). This research is also supported by the National Research Foundation, Singapore under its AI Singapore Programme (AISG Award No: AISG-RP-2019-012).

References

1. Agarwal, A., Singh, R., Vatsa, M., Ratha, N.K.: Image transformation based defense against adversarial perturbation on deep learning models. IEEE Trans. Dependable Secure Comput. **15**(5), 2106–2121 (2021)
2. Akhtar, N., Liu, J., Mian, A.: Defense against universal adversarial perturbations. In: Proceedings of the 2018 IEEE/CVF Conference on Computer Vision and Pattern Recognition, pp. 3389–3398 (2018)
3. Anscombe, F.J.: Fixed-sample-size analysis of sequential observations. Biometrics **10**(1), 89–100 (1954)
4. Athalye, A., Carlini, N., Wagner, D.A.: Obfuscated gradients give a false sense of security: circumventing defenses to adversarial examples. In: Proceedings of the 35th International Conference on Machine Learning, pp. 274–283 (2018)
5. Avriel, M., Wilde, D.J.: Optimally proof for the symmetric Fibonacci search technique. Fibonacci Q. J. (1966)
6. Carlini, N., Wagner, D.: Towards evaluating the robustness of neural networks. In: Proceedings of the 38th IEEE Symposium on Security and Privacy, pp. 39–57 (2017)
7. Carlini, N., Wagner, D.A.: Audio adversarial examples: targeted attacks on speech-to-text. In: Proceedings of the 39th IEEE Symposium on Security and Privacy Workshops, pp. 1–7 (2018)
8. Das, N., et al.: Keeping the bad guys out: protecting and vaccinating deep learning with JPEG compression. CoRR abs/1705.02900 (2017)
9. Dhillon, G.S., et al.: Stochastic activation pruning for robust adversarial defense. In: Proceedings of the 6th International Conference on Learning Representations (2018)
10. Dos Santos, C., Gatti, M.: Deep convolutional neural networks for sentiment analysis of short texts. In: Proceedings of the 25th International Conference on Computational Linguistics: Technical Papers, pp. 69–78 (2014)
11. Dua, D., Graff, C.: UCI machine learning repository (2017)
12. Ebrahimi, J., Rao, A., Lowd, D., Dou, D.: HotFlip: white-box adversarial examples for text classification. In: Proceedings of the 56th Annual Meeting of the Association for Computational Linguistics, pp. 31–36 (2018)
13. Gao, J., Lanchantin, J., Soffa, M.L., Qi, Y.: Black-box generation of adversarial text sequences to evade deep learning classifiers. In: Proceedings of the 39th IEEE Symposium on Security and Privacy Workshops, pp. 50–56 (2018)

14. Goodfellow, I.J., Shlens, J., Szegedy, C.: Explaining and harnessing adversarial examples (2015)
15. Hochreiter, S., Schmidhuber, J.: Long short-term memory. Neural Comput. **9**(8), 1735–1780 (1997)
16. Hosseini, H., Kannan, S., Zhang, B., Poovendran, R.: Deceiving Google's perspective API built for detecting toxic comments. arXiv preprint arXiv:1702.08138 (2017)
17. Ilyas, A., Santurkar, S., Tsipras, D., Engstrom, L., Tran, B., Madry, A.: Adversarial examples are not bugs, they are features. In: Proceedings of the 33rd Annual Conference on Neural Information Processing Systems, pp. 125–136 (2019)
18. Iyyer, M., Wieting, J., Gimpel, K., Zettlemoyer, L.: Adversarial example generation with syntactically controlled paraphrase networks. arXiv preprint arXiv:1804.06059 (2018)
19. Jain, G., Sharma, M., Agarwal, B.: Spam detection in social media using convolutional and long short term memory neural network. Ann. Math. Artif. Intell. **85**(1), 21–44 (2019)
20. Jin, D., Jin, Z., Zhou, J.T., Szolovits, P.: Is BERT really robust? A strong baseline for natural language attack on text classification and entailment. In: Proceedings of the 34th AAAI Conference on Artificial Intelligence, pp. 8018–8025 (2020)
21. Kim, Y.: Convolutional neural networks for sentence classification. In: Proceedings of the 2014 Conference on Empirical Methods in Natural Language Processing, pp. 1746–1751 (2014)
22. Li, J., Ji, S., Du, T., Li, B., Wang, T.: TextBugger: generating adversarial text against real-world applications. In: Proceedings of the 26th Annual Network and Distributed System Security Symposium (2019)
23. Liu, J., et al.: Detection based defense against adversarial examples from the steganalysis point of view. In: Proceedings of the 2019 IEEE/CVF Conference on Computer Vision and Pattern Recognition, pp. 4825–4834 (2019)
24. Lu, J., Issaranon, T., Forsyth, D.: SafetyNet: detecting and rejecting adversarial examples robustly. In: Proceedings of the IEEE International Conference on Computer Vision, pp. 446–454 (2017)
25. Madry, A., Makelov, A., Schmidt, L., Tsipras, D., Vladu, A.: Towards deep learning models resistant to adversarial attacks. In: Proceedings of the 6th International Conference on Learning Representations (2018)
26. McKeeman, W.M.: Differential testing for software. Digit. Tech. J. **10**(1), 100–107 (1998)
27. Meng, D., Chen, H.: MagNet: a two-pronged defense against adversarial examples. In: Proceedings of the 2017 ACM SIGSAC Conference on Computer and Communications Security, pp. 135–147 (2017)
28. Pang, B., Lee, L.: Seeing stars: exploiting class relationships for sentiment categorization with respect to rating scales. In: Proceedings of the 43rd Annual Meeting on Association for Computational Linguistics, pp. 115–124. Association for Computational Linguistics (2005)
29. Papernot, N., McDaniel, P., Swami, A., Harang, R.: Crafting adversarial input sequences for recurrent neural networks. In: Proceedings of the 2016 IEEE Military Communications Conference, pp. 49–54 (2016)
30. Pruthi, D., Dhingra, B., Lipton, Z.C.: Combating adversarial misspellings with robust word recognition, pp. 5582–5591 (2019)
31. Rastegari, M., Ordonez, V., Redmon, J., Farhadi, A.: XNOR-Net: ImageNet classification using binary convolutional neural networks. In: Leibe, B., Matas, J., Sebe, N., Welling, M. (eds.) ECCV 2016. LNCS, vol. 9908, pp. 525–542. Springer, Cham (2016). https://doi.org/10.1007/978-3-319-46493-0_32
32. Ren, Y., Ji, D.: Neural networks for deceptive opinion spam detection: an empirical study. Inf. Sci. **385**, 213–224 (2017)

33. Ribeiro, M.T., Singh, S., Guestrin, C.: Semantically equivalent adversarial rules for debugging NLP models. In: Proceedings of the 56th Annual Meeting of the Association for Computational Linguistics (Volume 1: Long Papers), pp. 856–865 (2018)

34. Rosenberg, I., Shabtai, A., Elovici, Y., Rokach, L.: Defense methods against adversarial examples for recurrent neural networks. arXiv preprint arXiv:1901.09963 (2019)

35. Schuster, M., Paliwal, K.K.: Bidirectional recurrent neural networks. IEEE Trans. Signal Process. **45**(11), 2673–2681 (1997)

36. Segler, M.H., Preuss, M., Waller, M.P.: Planning chemical syntheses with deep neural networks and symbolic AI. Nature **555**(7698), 604 (2018)

37. Shafahi, A., et al.: Adversarial training for free! In: Proceedings of the 33rd Annual Conference on Neural Information Processing Systems, pp. 3353–3364 (2019)

38. Shaffer, J.P.: Multiple hypothesis testing. Annu. Rev. Psychol. **46**(1), 561–584 (1995)

39. Song, Y., Kim, T., Nowozin, S., Ermon, S., Kushman, N.: PixelDefend: leveraging generative models to understand and defend against adversarial examples. In: Proceedings of the 6th International Conference on Learning Representations (2018)

40. Szegedy, C., et al.: Intriguing properties of neural networks. In: Proceedings of the 2nd International Conference on Learning Representations (2014)

41. Tang, D., Qin, B., Liu, T.: Document modeling with gated recurrent neural network for sentiment classification. In: Proceedings of the 2015 Conference on Empirical Methods in Natural Language Processing, pp. 1422–1432 (2015)

42. Van Erven, T., Harremos, P.: Rényi divergence and Kullback-Leibler divergence. IEEE Trans. Inf. Theory **60**(7), 3797–3820 (2014)

43. Wald, A.: Sequential tests of statistical hypotheses. Ann. Math. Stat. **16**(2), 117–186 (1945)

44. Wald, A.: Sequential Analysis, 1st edn. Wiley, Hoboken (1947)

45. Wang, J., Dong, G., Sun, J., Wang, X., Zhang, P.: Adversarial sample detection for deep neural network through model mutation testing. In: Proceedings of the 41st International Conference on Software Engineering, pp. 1245–1256. IEEE Press (2019)

46. Wang, W., Wang, R., Ke, J., Wang, L.: TextFirewall: omni-defending against adversarial texts in sentiment classification. IEEE Access **9**, 27467–27475 (2021)

47. Wang, X., Jin, H., He, K.: Natural language adversarial attacks and defenses in word level. arXiv preprint arXiv:1909.06723 (2019)

48. Xu, H., et al.: Adversarial attacks and defenses in images, graphs and text: a review. Int. J. Autom. Comput. **17**(2), 151–178 (2020)

49. Yang, J., Wu, M., Liu, X.Z.: Defense against adversarial attack using PCA. In: Proceedings of the 6th International Conference on Artificial Intelligence and Security, pp. 627–636 (2020)

50. Yang, Z., Yang, D., Dyer, C., He, X., Smola, A., Hovy, E.: Hierarchical attention networks for document classification. In: Proceedings of the 2016 Conference of the North American Chapter of the Association for Computational Linguistics: Human Language Technologies, pp. 1480–1489 (2016)

51. Zhang, H., Chen, H., Song, Z., Boning, D., Dhillon, I.S., Hsieh, C.J.: The limitations of adversarial training and the blind-spot attack. arXiv preprint arXiv:1901.04684 (2019)

52. Zhang, X., Zhao, J., LeCun, Y.: Character-level convolutional networks for text classification. In: Proceedings of the 29th Annual Conference on Neural Information Processing Systems, pp. 649–657 (2015)

53. Zheng, Z., Hong, P.: Robust detection of adversarial attacks by modeling the intrinsic properties of deep neural networks. In: Proceedings of the 32nd Annual Conference on Neural Information Processing Systems, pp. 7913–7922 (2018)

Formal Verification of a Keystore

Jaap Boender[✉][ID] and Goran Badevic[ID]

Hensoldt Cyber GmbH, Taufkirchen, Germany
{jacob.boender,goran.badevic}@hensoldt.net

Abstract. This paper is an experience report concerning the verification of a component of our operating system using Isabelle. The component allows for the secure storage of cryptographic key material. We will discuss the method used, describe the connection we created between the component and a standard library, identify lessons learned (both for the verification itself as to the process followed to write and adapt the software to be verified), and discuss possible avenues for further research.

Keywords: Formal verification · Software verification · C language · Experience report · Isabelle · Key store

1 Introduction

Formal verification of software is a concept that has been around for decades. Yet despite continuous advances, it has not been widely adopted in the software industry. Using formal verification in an industrial setting is still an onerous process which, to boot, can only be executed by specialists.

In this paper, we present the work done at Hensoldt Cyber GmbH on verifying a component (a keystore) in the TRENTOS operating system. This keystore, though written specifically to be easy to verify, and therefore not as complex as it might have been, is nonetheless a nontrivial piece of code that is fully integrated within the operating system.

The specific contributions of this paper are a real-world verification project that uses the AutoCorres tool [3], as well as a way to use AutoCorres' heap abstraction mechanism with non-heap abstracted functions (in Sect. 3). More generally, it contributes a description of this verification project that can serve as a guideline to similar verification efforts.

1.1 Related Work

Using proof assistants, by now, is a well established approach for program verification. This development was driven by two landmark verification projects: the CompCert optimising C compiler [7] and the seL4 microkernel [5]. Both of these are software projects of considerable scale and are highly relevant for real world applications.

© Springer Nature Switzerland AG 2022
Y. Aït-Ameur and F. Crăciun (Eds.): TASE 2022, LNCS 13299, pp. 49–64, 2022.
https://doi.org/10.1007/978-3-031-10363-6_4

The CompCert project specified, implemented, and proved correctness of an optimising C compiler. It compiles essentially the whole ISO C99 language and targets several architectures. seL4 is a microkernel of the L4 family. Its verification includes functional correctness as well as the proof of security properties. seL4 is implemented in C and was formally verified using a C verification framework including Isabelle/HOL. Functional correctness was demonstrated down to formal ISA specifications of the ARM and RISC-V architecture [5,10].

AutoCorres was developed to aid in the verification of the seL4 microkernel, but has not been used there so far (our understanding is that this would involve a large redevelopment of the existing proofs, and the team prefers to focus on extending the verification). However, it is increasingly being picked up as a tool for program verification: SABLE [2] is a trustworthy secure loader with close to 4000 lines of code which was partly formally verified. The same team also verified a heap allocator [8] using AutoCorres. More details on AutoCorres can be found throughout the paper, especially in Sect. 2.3.

1.2   The Keystore

The component to be verified is the secure keystore from our operating system TRENTOS. This is a component that allows for the storage of cryptographic keys so that applications can encrypt or decrypt data (through a crypto server) without having access to the keys themselves. The keystore should be accessed only through this crypto server, which will take care of things like access control and privileges.

Every component has an ID (the app ID), and the keystore is partitioned by app IDs, so that components do not have access to keys stored for another component.

It is possible to initialise the keystore with an initial list of keys, for example stored in ROM. Furthermore, there are functions to add and remove keys, to retrieve a given key (either by name or by an index number that uniquely identifies it), and to wipe the keystore entirely.

It should be noted that to the keystore, the key data, as well as the key names, are simply binary blobs. It should not be difficult to adapt it into a generic key-value store by adding some marshalling capability (which could be verified as well).

1.3   Verification Objectives

We will discuss the properties that we intend to verify here; more details about how specifically these properties are verified will then follow in Sect. 2.

First, there are the general properties that pertain to any program, such as memory safety and termination. The semantic model of the tools allows for reasoning about these properties, for example by inserting guards around each C statement that accesses memory.

Second, there is the functional correctness of the program, i.e. that it correctly implements its specification. This is achieved by implementing an abstract specification in Isabelle, and then showing that the C implementation refines this abstract specification. We also verify some properties of the abstract specification, in order to validate that this abstract specification reflects our informal ideas of what the keystore should be.

Third, we want to specifically verify that the keystore is indeed partitioned by app ID. Since we have already proven that the C implementation refines the abstract specification, we can prove this property on the abstract specification, for example showing that retrieving a key using app ID a will only ever result in a key with app ID a.

Since the keystore will only be accessed through the crypto server, we assume that the app ID given is legitimate (checking this is within the purview of the crypto server); dealing with components that present with a false app ID is therefore outside the scope of this verification effort.

In short, the properties we have verified are safety properties; for ensuring security we rely on the general security properties of the seL4 kernel, as well as (on a higher level) the CAmkES component model [6], and the fact that the keystore is not supposed to be accessed otherwise than through the crypto server.

2   Methodology

In this section, we present the methodology used for verifying the keystore, both the process followed in writing the code and keeping it integrated with the proofs, as well as the more technical details of the specifications and proofs themselves. This process is very similar to the verification of the seL4 kernel as described in [5]. The main difference is that we use the AutoCorres tool [3].

The general method of proof is by refinement. We show that the C implementation refines the abstract specification; the formal model of C semantics that we base this on is described in [1]. We use the same refinement framework that is used for the verification of seL4.

The process followed is standard, but described in a relatively detailed way to present a good overview of the keystore and the properties verified, and so that it can serve as a guideline for other verification efforts.

We have followed the same steps as in the seL4 proof, with the exception that we have not used an executable specification to bridge the gap between the abstract specification and the C implementation; instead, we have used Auto-Corres to generate a simplified version of the C code, on which more below.

A basic diagram of the verification steps and how they depend on each other can be found in Fig. 1.

2.1   The Code

After agreeing on an informal specification, we wrote the C code for the keystore. There already was an existing keystore in TRENTOS, but we decided to reimplement the keystore from the ground up. Experience from the seL4 project

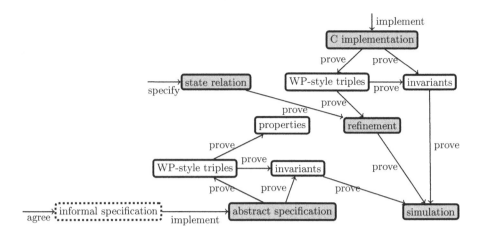

Fig. 1. Schematic overview of the verification components

has shown that code that is not written with verification in mind is very hard, even impossible to verify [4], and in any case the existing keystore had some features that made it unnecessarily complex, such as extensive use of preprocessor macros to simulate a form of polymorphism.

Thus, we wrote a new keystore version that consisted of roughly 250 lines of C, containing the description of the keystore data structure and the implementation of its interface functions. Initially, this code did not depend on external functions of any kind, so as to make it as easy as possible to verify.

The main data structure of the implementation is a simple C array. The canonical solution here would be to use a hash table, but verifying this would have been significantly more effort. Since the number of keys stored in the keystore is likely to be very small, this should not impact performance too much. Moreover, to increase performance, we included a function to retrieve a key based on its index in the array, which did complicate verification, as we will see in the next subsection.

Initially, all keystore functions were set up to pass their parameters by value (in practical terms, this was realised by using nested **structs**). This makes verification significantly easier, as there is no need to prove that the pointers being passed around are correct—this is all taken care of by the verification tools.

During the time needed to write the code, we verified a few standard library functions that were used in the existing version of the keystore[1]. We decided to slightly adapt the new keystore implementation to use these functions, both for efficiency and to find out whether it was possible to do this without complicating the proofs too much. We will discuss this in more detail in Sect. 3.

For the code, this had the effect that the nested structs were removed from the keystore, and the keystore name and data elements became simple char arrays and the parameters to the keystore functions were passed by name.

---

[1] The functions verified are memcmp, memcpy, memset, strncmp, strncpy and strlen.

We used the unit tests as inspiration for the desired properties to validate the abstract specification. In general, it is not possible to validate a specification, but unit tests give some properties that the implementation should have (for example, checking that trying to retrieve a deleted key results in an error, or that a key cannot be added to an already full keystore). If we can prove that these properties also hold (mutatis mutandis) for the abstract specification, we can be more confident that the specification is indeed what we intend it to be—even though it is never possible to be 100% confident.

We also decided during verification to have the add and get functions return a result struct consisting of the actual return value and a possible error code; idiomatic C usage is to return a negative value in case of errors, but this would have made verification much more complex due to either having to deal with signed integers, or (when keeping the return type as an unsigned integer) having to deal with -1 as a special value.

2.2 Abstract Specification

As noted, the verification of the keystore is by showing that the C implementation refines the specification.

The abstract specification of the keystore was written in Isabelle itself, using the same state monad that will later be used to model the C implementation in Isabelle, though at a much higher level of abstraction, using Isabelle datatypes. The Isabelle specification of the keystore data type is shown in Fig. 2.

```
record keystore_state =
  freeSlots :: nat
  maxElements :: nat
  elementStore :: "(app_id_t × key_name_t) ⇀ (nat × bool × key_data_t)"
```

Fig. 2. The abstract keystore datatype

We see that, essentially, the keystore is a map from key name to key data, partitioned by app ID. The freeSlots field is not strictly necessary (its value can be derived from the contents of elementStore), but it is included on the C side for efficiency reasons, and it then makes the refinement proofs simpler if it is included on the abstract side as well.

There are two extra fields in the key data tuple. One (of type nat) is the index of the key, which corresponds to the index of the key in the keystore on the C side; this information is superfluous on the Isabelle side, but it is needed in order to be able to verify functions that use the index (as discussed in the previous subsection). The other (of type bool) indicates whether the key is read-only.

An example function on this abstract specification (in this case, the function to retrieve a key) is shown in Fig. 3. This uses the state monad referred to earlier. We first check whether the parameter a is greater than the maximum allowed app ID (using condition). If this is the case, we terminate with an error condition (`throwError`); otherwise we execute a monad (between `doE` and `odE`) that executes the `getsE` function to retrieve the desired element from the state, and depending on the result we either terminate with an error condition, or terminate normally and return the desired element (`returnOk`).

```
definition Keystore_get :: "app_id_t ⇒ key_name_t ⇒
(keystore_state, unit + (nat × bool × key_data_t)) nondet_monad" where
  "Keystore_get a kn ≡
      condition (λst. a > MAX_APP_ID) (throwError ())
      (doE e <- getsE (λst. elementStore st (a, kn));
        case e of
          None ⇒ throwError ()
        | Some x ⇒ returnOk x
      odE)"
```

Fig. 3. The `Keystore_get` function

The next step was to create Hoare triples that exactly describe the effect of these functions. An example for `key_store_get` is shown in Fig. 4. We can see that this Hoare triple closely reflects the conditions in the implementation of `key_store_get`. There are two possible options: either everything is all right (the app ID is within range and the key exists in the keystore), in which case the generic success postcondition Q should hold (in the same state as before, since retrieving a key does not change the state), or there is some error, in which case the generic error postcondition E should hold in the unchanged state.

```
lemma Keystore_get_wp [wp]: "
  ⦃ λst. (∀ i kd. ((a > MAX_APP_ID ∨ elementStore st (a, kn) = None) ⟶ E () st) ∧
  ((a ≤ MAX_APP_ID ∧ elementStore st (a, kn) = Some (i, kd)) ⟶ Q (i, kd) st)) ⦄
  Keystore_get a kn
  ⦃ Q ⦄, ⦃ E ⦄!"
```

Fig. 4. Hoare triple with weakest precondition for `key_store_get`

These Hoare triples are written in weakest precondition style, i.e. they specify the weakest precondition that must hold for a generic success condition (Q) and a generic error condition (E) to hold. The exclamation point at the end signifies that we are specifying total correctness, i.e. not only that the properties specified hold after execution, but also that the execution terminates.

We also specify some invariant properties over the abstract keystore, shown in Fig. 5.

```
definition store_invariants where
  "store_invariants st ≡
    finite (dom (elementStore st)) ∧
    freeSlots st ≤ maxElements st ∧
    inj_on (λx. fst (the (elementStore st x))) (dom (elementStore st)) ∧
    maxElements st - freeSlots st = card (dom (elementStore st)) ∧
    (∀ x i d. elementStore st x = Some (i, d) ⟶ i < maxElements st)"
```

Fig. 5. Abstract keystore invariants

These are invariants that are needed to prove refinement, such as the invariant specifying that the fields keeping track of the number of elements in the keystore and the maximum keystore size are always kept current with the actual contents of the keystore.

We also verified several more general properties that were inspired by the unit tests, for example showing that adding a key and then retrieving it will return the same key; this is shown in Fig. 6. In this way, we validated the specification to the furthest possible extent.

```
lemma key_add_get: "
  ⦃ λst. a ≤ MAX_APP_ID ∧ freeSlots st > 0 ∧ elementStore st (a, kn) = None ⦄
doE Keystore_add a kn kd;
    (i, r, kd') <- Keystore_get a kn;
    returnOk kd'
odE
⦃ λr st. r = kd ⦄, ⦃ λr st. False ⦄! "
```

Fig. 6. Hoare triple showing the result of adding and retrieving a key

This Hoare triple expresses that this program terminates (the exclamation point at the end), and that after termination we must be in a state where no error occurred, and the return value r of the program must be equal to the parameter kd. The program adds a key with app ID a and key name kn, then immediately retrieves the same key and finally returns the result, so this shows that adding a key and retrieving it afterwards works as expected. The False in the second part of the postcondition indicates that an error condition does not occur.

2.3   C Code

In order to reason about the C code, we must somehow obtain a representation in Isabelle. For this we use the C parser developed for the seL4 project, as well as the AutoCorres tool.

The C parser [11], which is also used in the verification of seL4, reads a C file and generates a representation in the SIMPL language [9]. This representation can be used in Isabelle, though not easily, since the representation is very low-level and close to the original C code. This is a deliberate design choice made for the C parser: given that it is not verified, its functionality has deliberately been kept to a minimum so as to reduce the chances of introducing bugs. Indeed, the C parser must be trusted, since any semantic model it might be verified against would itself be untrusted, creating something of a Catch-22 situation. The way around this is binary verification [10], where the binary code produced by a compiler can be verified against binary code that is proven to refine from the Isabelle representation. This removes the compiler from the trusted computing base, at the cost of needing to trust the formal ISA description used; this description is much simpler than the compiler and therefore easier to trust. This approach has been used for seL4, and should work on the keystore as well, given that we have used the same tools, but we have not attempted binary verification as yet.

Concerning the proof itself, the use of AutoCorres is a key difference between the verification of seL4 and the keystore verification: in the seL4 verification, there is an intermediate layer (the executable specification) between the abstract specification and the SIMPL representation of the C implementation, and refinement is proven by hand.

In the keystore verification, instead of writing an executable specification by hand, and then manually proving refinement, we have used AutoCorres to not only generate a simplified version of the SIMPL representation which is much more easy to work with, but also to generate a proof that this simplified representation is a refinement of the original SIMPL representation.

2.4 Refinement

For the keystore, we show that each of the functions of the C implementation refines its equivalent from the specification.

First, we need to establish a state relation that associates the state of the abstract specification with the state of the C implementation. For the keystore, states are equivalent if and only if the maximum number of keys is the same, and the keys contained in the keystore are the same. There is a similar mechanism to relate the return values of functions. The exact specification of the state relation in Isabelle is shown in Fig. 7.

```
definition state_relation where
  "state_relation ks ≡ {
    (s_a, s_c). maxElements s_a = unat (ks_maxElements s_c ks) ∧
    (∀ a kn idx r kd. (elementStore s_a) (a, kn) = Some (idx, r, kd) ⟷
       (∃ i. i<unat (ks_maxElements s_c ks) ∧
         ks_isFree s_c ks (int i) = 0 ∧
         ks_appId s_c ks (int i) = a ∧
         unat (ks_index s_c (int i)) = idx ∧
         (ks_readOnly s_c ks (int i) ≠ 0 ⟷ r) ∧
         ks_name s_c ks (int i) = kn ∧
         ks_data s_c ks (int i) = kd))}"
```

Fig. 7. State relation

We also need to prove some invariants over the C implementation of the keystore, for example that the C data structures in memory that hold the keystore are valid at all times. We also need the C equivalents of the invariants for the abstract specification. The Isabelle specification of the invariants is shown in Fig. 8.

```
definition conc_store_invariants where
  "conc_store_invariants st ks ≡
     unat (ks_maxElements st ks) * size_of TYPE(KeystoreRamFV_ElementRecord_C) < ADDR_MAX ∧
     is_valid_KeystoreRamFV_C st ks ∧
     (∀ i<unat (ks_maxElements st ks).
       is_valid_KeystoreRamFV_ElementRecord_C st (ks_elementRecord_p st ks (int i))) ∧
     card {i. i < unat (ks_maxElements st ks) ∧ ks_isFree st ks (int i) ≠ 0} =
       unat (ks_freeSlots st ks) ∧
     (∀ x<unat (ks_maxElements st ks).
      ∀ y<unat (ks_maxElements st ks).
         ks_isFree st ks (int x) = 0 ∧ ks_isFree st ks (int y) = 0 ∧
         ks_appId st ks (int x) = ks_appId st ks (int y) ∧
         ks_name st ks (int x) = ks_name st ks (int y) ⟶ x = y)"
```

Fig. 8. Concrete keystore invariants

We then prove that each C function in the keystore implementation refines its equivalent in the abstract specification.

The refinement relation is specified by the **corres_underlying** predicate. This predicate states in essence that the function g (concrete) refines function f (abstract) if and only if given two related states s and s' that satisfy preconditions G and G' respectively, for every state t and return value r that are the result of executing f, there are a state t' and a return value r' that are the result of executing g, such that t and t' are related, as well as r and r'.

The statement of the lemma that shows refinement between **key_store_add** and its C implementation **key_store_add'** is shown in Fig. 9.

The **corres_underlying** predicate takes as parameters the state relation, two parameters determining whether we are reasoning about total correctness (in practice these are almost always True), the return value relation (in this case translating between the option type returned by the abstract function and the C struct returned by the C function), the preconditions, and finally the two functions.

The return relation specifies the fact that on the abstract side, the state is an option type with has value **Inl** in case of an error condition, and **Inr** (with a return value) if there is no error. The equivalent C conditions are shown by the **error** and **index** members of the returned struct, access to which is modelled in Isabelle by the **error_C** and **index_C** functions.

We will explain the preconditions for the concrete function in some more detail below, since they use some specific notation.

- First, we show that the invariants on the concrete side must hold;
- Then, we specify that the **kn** parameter on the abstract side must be equal to the **name** member of the struct **k** on the concrete side. Since **k** is a pointer, we first dereference it (in state **s**) and then use the **name_C** function to model struct access;

– We do the same for the **kd** parameter and the **data** member of k;
– Then we specify that **k** cannot be the NULL pointer;
– We specify that the **name** member of struct **k** cannot be a NULL pointer either, using a short-hand notation that is akin to the arrow operator in plain C;
– And finally, we specify that the pointer **k** in state **s** must point to a valid instance in memory of a KeystoreRamFV_KeyRecord datatype.

```
theorem Keystore_add_refine:
  "corres_underlying (state_relation ks) True True
    (λrₐ rₑ.
      case rₐ of Inl () ⇒ error_C rₑ ≠ 0 | Inr i ⇒ error_C rₑ = 0 ∧
      index_C rₑ = of_nat i)
    (λs. store_invariants s)
    (λs. conc_store_invariants s ks ∧ name_C s[k] = kn ∧ data_C s[k] = kd ∧
      k ≠ NULL ∧ &(k→[''name_C'']) ≠ 0 ∧ is_valid_KeystoreRamFV_KeyRecord_C s k)
    (Keystore_add a kn kd) (KeystoreRamFV_add' ks a k)"
```

Fig. 9. Refinement for key_store_add

During verification, minor changes to the code were made. The largest change (unrelated to the verification effort) was the addition of a new feature: the possibility of initialising the keystore with a predetermined list of keys. The only actual bug discovered during verification was in the code implementing this new feature.

There is an auxiliary function in the keystore that searches the keystore array for a key with a certain app ID and name. Originally, this function would just iterate over all possible elements of the array, and simply skip free elements. The code added for the initialisation feature used this function to check for possible duplicates in the list of given keys, which could result in checking for duplicates in uninitialised memory.

Discovering bugs during formal verification in this way is not straightforward—if there is a bug in the implementation, it means that refinement cannot be proven, but there is no indication of why this is the case[2]. Figuring out what exactly causes refinement to be unprovable can be difficult.

The verification-related changes were simpler. One change involved semantics: we realised that the key names only had to be unique in combination with an app ID domain rather than across the entire keystore, which was a helpful improvement with regards to the keystore functionality.

2.5   Simulation

After proving refinement for each of the functions of the keystore, what remains is to tie everything together. To this end, we define two state machines (one on the abstract side, one on the C side) where the transitions are the different functions

---

[2] In fact, if refinement cannot be proven, one cannot even be sure if this is due to user incompetence or due to bugs in the code...

of the keystore. We then show that there is a forward simulation relation between these two state machines.

In this step, we also need to show that the invariants shown in Figs. 5 and 8 hold across functions; i.e. that they are preserved by every transition in the automaton.

This step serves to show that there is also a refinement relation between arbitrary sequences of function calls.

2.6 Integration

After verification was completed, several changes to the code were requested for integration into TRENTOS. Adapting the proofs to these changes was not entirely trivial, but did not require major changes to the structure of the proofs. The adaptations took about a month of work for one person. This shows that in order to avoid duplication of work, it is important to make sure that such integration efforts must be completed before starting formal verification (or at least before the parts that actually involve the code, i.e. the refinement proofs).

3   Standard Library Connection

The main innovation in the verification of the keystore is its use of standard library functions that have been verified separately without using AutoCorres' heap abstraction mechanism (explained below) and then lifted to the level of the keystore verification, which does use the heap abstraction mechanism. There are some examples in the AutoCorres distribution which do this on a small scale, but as far as we are aware, using this for struct types had not been attempted before.

In this section, we will describe this development in more detail.

3.1 Heap Abstraction

AutoCorres has a heap abstraction mechanism. This mechanism ensures heap separation by providing a separate virtual heap for each different datatype, guaranteeing that there is no memory overlap between different types. This guarantee comes with a price: each struct type will be assigned its own virtual heap, and the only way to access the members of the struct is through predefined access functions; it is not possible, for example, to access members of a struct through the virtual heap corresponding to the type of the member.

This creates difficulties when using standard library functions such as strncpy, for example when trying to copy a string that is a member of a struct to another string that is on its own. The heap abstraction mechanism does not offer the possibility of showing that two places in two different heaps refer to the same thing.

In order to circumvent this limitation, we have written a connecting layer (inspired by some of the examples included with the AutoCorres distribution) that makes it possible to combine standard-library functions that do not use the heap abstraction mechanism with functions that do.

3.2 The Connector

In a nutshell, the connector works by defining a Hoare triple for the non-heap-abstracted standard library function, and then using this Hoare triple to prove another Hoare triple, which can be used in the heap-abstracted calling functions. It is necessary to define versions of this second Hoare triple for each possible permutation of argument types, as we shall see below.

As an example, the non-heap-abstracted Hoare triple for memcpy_fv is shown in Fig. 10. We see that src and dst have to be valid pointers (well aligned and not NULL), that src and dst should be more than sz bytes before the end of memory, that the first sz bytes of memory after src and dst should not overlap, and that there has to be a block bs of bytes of size sz such that the first sz bytes in memory after src are equal to bs.

This Hoare triple only has one postcondition, like all Hoare triples on the concrete side; this is due to the fact that in the C state, there is no general way to indicate an error condition as there was on the abstract side.

```
theorem memcpy_wp:
  fixes src :: "unit ptr"
    and dst :: "unit ptr"
  shows "⦃λs. c_guard src ∧ c_guard dst ∧
             no_wrap src (unat sz) ∧ no_wrap dst (unat sz) ∧ no_overlap src dst (unat sz) ∧
             (∃ bs.
               sz = of_nat (length bs) ∧ bytes_at s src bs ∧
               Q dst (update_bytes s dst bs))⦄
         memcpy_fv' dst src sz
         ⦃ Q ⦄!"
```

Fig. 10. Hoare triple for memcpy_fv

In a heap-abstracted keystore function, memcpy_fv is used as follows:

```
memcpy_fv(key_store->element_store[result.index].key.name, key->name, KEY_NAME_SIZE)}
memcpy_fv(key_store->element_store[result.index].key.data, key->data, KEY_DATA_SIZE)}
```

The AutoCorres translation of this C code is:

```
p <- gets (λs. PTR(unit) &(PTR(int_key_record_C)
    (&s[key_store]→element_store
      uint (index_C result)→[''key_C''])→[''name_C'']));
r <- exec_concrete lift_global_heap (memcpy_fv' p
    (PTR(unit) &(key→[''name_C''])) 0x20);
p <- gets (λs. PTR(unit) &(PTR(int_key_record_C)
    (&s[key_store]→element_store +_p
      uint (index_C result)→[''key_C''])→[''data_C'']));
r <- exec_concrete lift_global_heap (memcpy_fv' p
    (PTR(unit) &(key→[''data_C''])) 0x400);
```

AutoCorres detects the presence of a non-heap-abstracted version of memcpy_fv and uses the exec_concrete and lift_global_heap functions to lift this so that it can be called from the heap-abstracted key_store_add function.

We will now need to define two Hoare triples, one for each invocation of memcpy_fv. One of these is shown in Fig. 11. The other is identical except for the fact that every instance of **name** is replaced by **data**. The two Hoare triples are similar to memcpy_wp, though the different pointer validity preconditions have been replaced by one heap-abstracted predicate per type (the is_valid predicates). The proofs of these heap-abstracted Hoare triples use the proof of the earlier non-heap-abstracted Hoare triple for memcpy_fv. The proofs are rather cumbersome and technical, but they are also very similar and it is very likely that they can be automatically generated to a large extent. We will discuss this further in Sect. 4.

```
lemma memcpy_key_name_C_name_C [simplified]: "
{| λs. is_valid_KeystoreRamFV_ElementRecord_C s (e s) ∧
  e' = (PTR(unit) &(PTR(KeystoreRamFV_KeyRecord_C) &(e s→[''key_C''])→[''name_C'']))) ∧
  is_valid_KeystoreRamFV_KeyRecord_C s k ∧
  (Q (PTR(unit) &(PTR(KeystoreRamFV_KeyRecord_C) &(e s→[''key_C''])→[''name_C''])))
    (verification_code.update_KeystoreRamFV_ElementRecord_key s (e s)
      (name_C_update (λ_. name_C (heap_KeystoreRamFV_KeyRecord_C s k))
      (key_C (heap_KeystoreRamFV_KeyRecord_C s (e s))))))) |}
exec_concrete lift_global_heap
  (memcpy_fv' e' (PTR(unit) &(k→[''name_C''])) (of_nat LENGTH(KEY_NAME_SIZE)))
{| Q |}!"
```

Fig. 11. Heap-abstracted Hoare triple for memcpy_fv with the name field

4   Discussion

In this section, we will reflect on the verification process and identify research directions that could make this kind of verification effort easier in the future.

4.1   Verification

Let us first have a look at the size of the proof effort, both in lines of code and in terms of effort spent. The final, integrated version of the verified code consists of 353 lines of C; Fig. 12 shows the size and effort involved in creating the several proofs – for the keystore as well as for the standard library.

If we combine the figures from Fig. 12, it emerges that we have spent 1.4 person-years per kLOC of C code in verification of the keystore; this is only slightly less than the 1.5 py/kLOC spent in the seL4 proof effort.

Task	Lines of Isabelle	Effort [person days]
Standard library (51 lines of C):		
verification	2489	30 pd
connector	1479	15 pd
Keystore (353 lines of C):		
abstract specification	679	8 pd
refinement proofs	2926	79 pd
simulation	364	20 pd

Fig. 12. Size and effort of verification tasks

A more significant gain could have been expected because of the use of Auto-Corres, which reduced the proof effort necessary (basically, it provided the executable specification for free).

Part of this discrepancy can be explained by the time spent familiarising ourselves with new technologies (this was our first large project using Isabelle and AutoCorres). This had an impact on the cost of the refinement proofs especially.

4.2 Lessons Learned

Looking back on the verification process, the main lesson is that we should have integrated the code into TRENTOS at the beginning of the verification effort rather than at the end. The changes introduced by verification (once the use of standard library functions was decided on) were minor and could have been integrated in TRENTOS relatively easily, while integrating the changes required for integration post-facto took much more time.

We should also have written the abstract specification before the C implementation. This is the proper order, so that the abstract specification can guide the implementation in C; for the keystore, we first agreed on an informal specification and then implemented this directly. Since the keystore is a relatively simple piece of software, this reversed order did not cause problems, but for more complex developments, it might result in dissociation between the different specifications.

Especially during the latter phases, we spent a lot of time adjusting the statements of the different proofs (most notably refinement and simulation) to fit everything together (there were several instances of refinement preconditions not quite matching up across functions, for example). It would be beneficial to write the proof statements first, without actually proving them, and making sure that everything fits together before starting the proofs; this saves effort in reworking the proofs later.

A basic step-by-step plan to verify a TRENTOS component (or any other piece of software) would then be:

0. Agree on an informal specification;
1. Write an abstract specification for the component to be verified;
2. Prove weakest-precondition style Hoare triples for the functions in this specification;
3. Prove specific properties of this specification we are interested in (including invariants);
4. Implement the specification in C;
5. Specify a state relation and return relations for the separate functions;
6. Write proof skeletons for refinement and simulation;
7. Prove weakest-precondition style Hoare triples for the C functions;
8. Prove invariants over the C specification;
9. Prove refinement between the abstract functions and their C equivalents;
10. Specify the abstract and C state machine;
11. Prove simulation between the abstract state machine and the C state machine.

This process can not be completely sequential, since there will still be some need to revise earlier steps in light of results in later steps (for example adjusting the abstract specification if needed to conform to the concrete implementation).

The weakest-precondition style Hoare triples in steps 2 and 7 are meant to avoid duplication of effort. We have noticed that there were a lot of commonalities between the proofs in steps 8 and 9; we suspect that if we first prove a Hoare triple that very strictly specifies the behaviour of each function, we can use these later on, both for proving invariants and for proving refinement. In essence, we will be using these Hoare triples to factor out the common elements between the invariant proofs and the refinement proofs.

4.3   Future Research

The basic techniques used for verifying these components can be refined, extended and integrated. In this subsection, we will offer suggestions for future improvements and research.

At current, the proofs of the lemmas that connect the standard library to the keystore are written by hand, which is a very cumbersome process. As these proofs resemble each other to a large extent, it should be possible to generate these proofs based on the datatype descriptions. We have already started work on this for the simplest of the connecting lemmas, but much more can be done here.

Another avenue of improvement would be permanent storage: at the moment, the keystore stores its contents only in memory, without having recourse to a file system or other type of permanent storage. Having a formally verified file system (that can be adapted to fit to the keystore proofs) would greatly improve the usability of the keystore.

4.4   Conclusion

In this paper, we have presented the formal verification of a keystore component from our TRENTOS operating system. We have shown the process used, and presented a way to use functions that do not use AutoCorres' heap abstraction with functions that do. And finally, we have identified possible improvements to the process and suggested avenues for future research.

We have verified the safety properties of the keystore; for security properties we rely on the trusted code base of the seL4 kernel, the CAmkES system and the crypto server (the latter two as yet unverified). Even though the process is very labour-intensive, it is worth the time and effort because the properties proven are very extensive; other methods may be quicker, but are less complete.

Our experience shows that the methodology used to verify seL4 transfers to other software projects. It shows that using formal verification in an industrial setting is possible, if the code to be verified is critical enough and resources are available. With enough automation and further integration, it is foreseeable that formal verification can be a part of the software engineer's standard toolkit for writing critical software.

References

1. Cock, D., Klein, G., Sewell, T.: Secure microkernels, state monads and scalable refinement. In: Mohamed, O.A., Muñoz, C., Tahar, S. (eds.) TPHOLs 2008. LNCS, vol. 5170, pp. 167–182. Springer, Heidelberg (2008). https://doi.org/10.1007/978-3-540-71067-7_16

2. Constable, S., Sutton, R., Sahebolamri, A., Chapin, S.: Formal Verification of a Modern Boot Loader. Electrical Engineering and Computer Science - Technical Reports, August 2018. https://surface.syr.edu/eecs_techreports/183

3. Greenaway, D., Lim, J., Andronick, J., Klein, G.: Don't sweat the small stuff: formal verification of C code without the pain. In: Proceedings of the 35th ACM SIGPLAN Conference on Programming Language Design and Implementation, PLDI 2014, Edinburgh, UK, pp. 429–439. ACM Press (2013). https://doi.org/10.1145/2594291.2594296

4. Klein, G., Derrin, P., Elphinstone, K.: Experience report: seL4: formally verifying a high-performance microkernel. In: Proceedings of the 14th ACM SIGPLAN International Conference on Functional Programming, ICFP 2009, Edinburgh, Scotland, p. 91. ACM Press (2009). https://doi.org/10.1145/1596550.1596566

5. Klein, G., et al.: seL4: formal verification of an OS kernel. In: Proceedings of the ACM SIGOPS 22nd Symposium on Operating Systems Principles, SOSP 2009, Big Sky, Montana, USA, pp. 207–220. Association for Computing Machinery, October 2009. https://doi.org/10.1145/1629575.1629596

6. Kuz, I., Liu, Y., Gorton, I., Heiser, G.: CAmkES: a component model for secure microkernel-based embedded systems. J. Syst. Softw. **80**(5), 687–699 (2007). https://doi.org/10.1016/j.jss.2006.08.039. https://www.sciencedirect.com/science/article/pii/016412120600224X. Component-Based Software Engineering of Trustworthy Embedded Systems

7. Leroy, X.: Formal verification of a realistic compiler. Commun. ACM **52**(7), 107–115 (2009). https://doi.org/10.1145/1538788.1538814

8. Sahebolamri, A., Constable, S., Chapin, S.: A Formally Verified Heap Allocator. Electrical Engineering and Computer Science - Technical Reports, January 2018. https://surface.syr.edu/eecs_techreports/182

9. Schirmer, N.: Verification of Sequential Imperative Programs in Isabelle/HOL. Dissertation, Technische Universität München, München (2006)

10. Sewell, T.A.L., Myreen, M.O., Klein, G.: Translation validation for a verified OS kernel. In: Proceedings of the 34th ACM SIGPLAN Conference on Programming Language Design and Implementation, PLDI 2013, Seattle, Washington, USA, p. 471. ACM Press (2013). https://doi.org/10.1145/2491956.2462183

11. Tuch, H., Klein, G., Norrish, M.: Types, bytes, and separation logic. In: Hofmann, M., Felleisen, M. (eds.) ACM SIGPLAN-SIGACT Symposium on Principles of Programming Languages, Nice, France, pp. 97–108. ACM, January 2007

A Case Study in the Automated Translation of BSV Hardware to PVS Formal Logic with Subsequent Verification

Nicholas Moore[✉] and Mark Lawford

McMaster Centre for Software Certification, McMaster University,
Hamilton, ON, Canada
{moorenc,lawford}@mcmaster.ca

Abstract. We previously developed a method of formal hardware verification that automatically translates hardware descriptions encoded in Bluespec SystemVerilog (BSV) into the formal logic of Prototype Verification System (PVS) to allow verification of system properties. This paper reports on an extension of our translation tool, BAPIP, that refines the semantic model to cover more Bluespec language constructs and optimizes the translation to PVS to address scalability to allow applicability of the method to real-world hardware examples as demonstrated by a case study of the Shakti RISC-V project's implementation of the RapidIO data packet passing communication protocol. In particular we verify the encoding of byte masks in outgoing memory read requests.

1 Introduction

HDLs are similar to software languages, in that they offer the hardware designer modularizing abstractions that improve productivity, reliability, and manageability of large designs. This paper presents a novel translation algorithm which embeds an expanded subset of the HDL Bluespec SystemVerilog (BSV) in the higher order logic of Prototype Verification System (PVS). We then use PVS's theorem prover to prove formal properties. While originally based on work by Richards and Lester [14], most of this work has been superseded. Our methodology, which previously automated the above work with some extensions, has been further extended to handle some real-world hardware designs. In particular, this is the first algorithm embedding of the full clock cycle semantics of BSV in a formal logical system. Whereas in [9] the case studies we presented were toy examples, the case study presented here was derived from a RISC-V processor design. We also present some optimizations addressing the scalability of our technique which may be of more general interest.

Our proof methodology is a general-purpose mechanism for encoding BSV designs in PVS, and is outlined in Fig. 1.

© Springer Nature Switzerland AG 2022
Y. Aït-Ameur and F. Crăciun (Eds.): TASE 2022, LNCS 13299, pp. 65–72, 2022.
https://doi.org/10.1007/978-3-031-10363-6_5

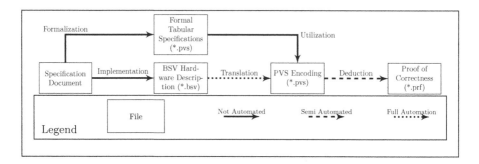

Fig. 1. BAPIP - BSV2PVS mode tool chain

In Sect. 2, we discuss the languages used in the translation process, and provide an overview of the source of our case study. In Sect. 3 we discuss our semantic model of BSV. Section 4 discusses optimization techniques employed by the translator. Our case study is presented in Sect. 5, followed by related works in Sect. 6 and our conclusion in Sect. 7.

2 Preliminaries

Bluespec System Verilog. Bluespec SystemVerilog originated as a library of the functional programming language Haskell [10] as a high-level alternative to Verilog, SystemVerilog and VHDL. Bluespec Inc., was founded in 2003 by Dr. Arvind of MIT. Bluespec Inc. has itself recently pivoted towards being a supplier of RISC-V technologies [1].

A Bluespec design is a hierarchical collection of hardware **modules**. Bluespec designs are analogous to state machines, where state is held by the circuit's sequential components (registers, flip-flops, etc.), and is transformed via **guarded actions**. These atomically executed actions are comprised of a Boolean **guard** expression, and a set of register writes and submodule method invocations. Actions can either be **rules**, which are considered for execution each clock cycle, or **methods**, which must be invoked by the supermodule. Input and output occurs via method calls.

Each clock cycle, those actions which are permitted to execute, or "fire", must be arbitrated to prevent race conditions, as actions may write to non-disjoint sets of memory. Conflicts are resolved via scheduling, and the use of implicit and explicit precedence ordering, as discussed in Sect. 3. In BSV, if conflicts go unresolved, the hardware scheduler makes a "arbitrary but deterministic" decision as to which actions fire [3]. Our translation will fail on such cases to avoid reverse-engineering this arbitrary algorithm, and because designs with conflicts are generally bad practice.

Prototype Verification System. The Prototype Verification System (PVS) is an interactive specification and proof environment, providing a high degree of mechanization and the expressive power of higher order logic [11]. This free tool, developed by SRI International, receives specifications encoded in the PVS specification language, and provides an interactive proof environment in which the user may apply proof tactics to theorems in an effort to prove them. In the past, PVS has been used to successfully verify safety critical embedded systems, such as the shutdown systems for the Darlington nuclear power plant [15].

RISC-V, Shakti and RapidIO. RISC-V is an open-source specification for the design of computer processors [12]. RISC stands for Reduced Instruction Set Computer, and RISC-V is an open-source hardware initiative led by the RISC-V foundation [2]. The Shakti project is a family of implementations of RISC-V by [7], and the RISE group at IIT Madras. The Shakti family of processors have been designed and implemented in Bluespec SystemVerilog, citing a higher level of abstraction, "superior behavioural semantics," architectural transparency and parameterizability as justification. The complexity and open source nature of the Shakti processor [8], and the RapidIO specification [13] make it an ideal case study.

3   Computational Model

Two actions must write to at least one common state element, and have non-disjoint guard expressions in order to be in conflict. Our translation tool uses SMT (Satisfiability Modulo Theory) analysis, via Haskell's SBV library [6] and Yices [5] to evaluate the disjointness of guard expressions. A conflict relation from actions to actions is thereby derived.

To resolve conflicts, actions of higher priority are permitted to pre-empt those of lower priority. Priority is established by explicit declaration, or by implicit language semantics. Methods are prioritized over rules, and actions which write to "wires" (state elements which permit inter-action communication within a single clock cycle) are given precedence over those which read from the same. This applies two partial orders over the set of actions. If any conflict exists which has no priority ordering to resolve it, the translation fails.

The goal of arbitration is to construct a binary decision tree which describes all valid action execution sequences. The decisions of this decision tree are whether or not the guard condition of the action is true, and the action therefore fires. Actions are scheduled in order of maximality with respect to the priority poset. If multiple actions are maximal, an arbitrary decision selects one of them. There is no loss of semantic integrity here, as such actions cannot conflict, or else a priority ordering must exist between them at this stage. In hardware, these actions would execute concurrently. If, along the decision tree, some action is selected to fire which conflicts with others, the actions conflicted with are removed from further consideration along that branch.

Once the universal schedule has been created, a decision tree for each state element must be extracted through traversal. Only those statements which write to the indicated state element, and guard expressions, are retained in the state-specific tree. Subsequently, these state-specific trees generate branching if conditionals, which are inserted to a record update predicate in PVS which encodes state transition for each state element.

4   Optimizations Addressing Scalability

One of the largest problems with the algorithm above is the generation of at most two subtrees (true and false) at each node of the universal scheduling tree. This yields an algorithmic complexity of $O(2^d)$, where d is the depth of the tree (maximally the number of actions to be scheduled). To address these limitations, several algorithmic techniques were applied.

Universal and Specific Tree Pruning. Consider the following simple substitutions.

$$\text{if } True \text{ then } p \text{ else } q \mapsto p \qquad \text{if } False \text{ then } p \text{ else } q \mapsto q$$

$$\text{if } b \text{ then } p \text{ else } p \mapsto p$$

When translating the entire RapidIO library, generated files had hundreds of thousands of lines of code prior to these substitutions. These files were so large PVS could not load them. These optimizations reduced the size of the generated files by two orders of magnitude.

Module Hierarchy Action Set Refinement. As the designs being translated grew, so too did their module hierarchy. We observe, however, that the state elements of any particular module may only be written to by the module itself (through statements), or by any of the module's supermodules (via method calls). As such, a state specific schedule in any particular module need only concern itself with the actions in the above specified modules. Essentially, sibling modules can be safely ignored. Each module, therefore, may have it's own schedule, which takes only itself and supermodules into account, and state-specific trees are calculated from the scheduling tree specific to their module of residence.

Over the whole Shakti RapidIO implementation, this observation reduced maximum scheduling tree depth from 84 to 42 actions. The effect was maximized on those areas of RapidIO with a wide and shallow module hierarchy.

Action Merger via Schedule Independence Checking. Consider a set of actions with identical guard expressions, which take priority over, and are of lower priority than the same sets of other actions (excluding themselves). Such actions would be adjacent in the universal scheduling, yet the order of their execution is immaterial. Such actions may be safely merged to form one "super-action", with no loss of semantic integrity.

By only processing composed actions with unique scheduling properties, we tie run-time complexity to the path complexity of the state element calculations, rather than to the modularization of the designer. This optimization, combined with those listed above, reduced the universal scheduling tree depth to 9 nodes.

5 Case Study: RapidIO Encoder

The objective of this case study is to verify the output values of the Sha-kti RapidIO implementation module RapidIO_InitEncoder_WdPtr_Size.bsv, specifically reg_Size and reg_WdPointer. Behaviour of these outputs is given in [13] in tabular format. Table 1 gives an excerpt. In RapidIO, memory is addressed in 64 bit words, but smaller contiguous chunks are accessible via byte masking, written "byte lanes" below. These byte lanes are encoded in data packets using the wdptr and rdsize fields. In operations on up to 8 bytes, wdptr and rdsize are uniquely determined by the byte lane pattern. This format also supports multi-word operations, where the "number of bytes" field alone determines wdptr and rdsize.

Table 1. Excerpt of Table 4-3 from [13]

Number of bytes	Byte lanes	wdptr	rdsize
2	0b00110000	0b0	0b0110
5	0b11111000	0b0	0b0111
2	0b00001100	0b1	0b0100
⋮	⋮	⋮	⋮

This table is disjoint, in that each row represents unique, non-overlapping inputs, but not complete, as not all combinations of input values are represented. In hardware design, such cases are commonly labelled "don't care" or "reserved" values. Since a default value is not specified, a predicate is used to constrain the inputs during proof construction. We specify that Byte Lanes, for example, may only have those values specified in the table.

The following theorem verifies wdptr functionality. This theorem states that, if we take our generated transition predicate, as well as our input constraint predicates as premises, this should imply that the output of our requirements table (req_word_pointer) should equal the output as received via the module's access method (outputs_WdPointer_).

```
1   correctness_1 : theorem
2     forall(x1 : ByteEn , x2 : ByteCount , x3 : bool) :
3       x3 = True
4       and valid_bytemask(x1)
5       and valid_bytecount(x2)
6         and transition(1, s(0),s(1), x1, x2, x3)
7       implies req_word_pointer(x1, x2) = outputs_WdPointer_(1,s(1),s(1),
              x1,x2,x3)
```

In the above, s is our module's state record. Antecedents include both our input validity predicates and our transition predicate. Since this module arrives at its output in one clock cycle, only one transition predicate is necessary. As consequent, we call the appropriate output method and test its return value against the output of the requirements table.

Proving the Sequent. The following methodology was used to discharge all proof obligations in PVS.

1. At the top-level, our overall correctness theorem is the conjunction of the correctness theorems addressing for the word pointer and read size registers (correctness_1 and correctness_2 respectively). The proof is immediately divided into two sub-proofs for these two sub-theorems using (split). The following steps apply to both.
2. The theorem is expanded using (expand correctness_1) or (expand correctness_2)
3. Skolemization is performed over the universal quantifier, using (skolem!).
4. The top level implication and conjunctions are applied as antecedents and consequents using (flatten).
5. The definition of the valid_bytemask predicate is expanded using (expand valid_bytemask)
6. The proof is then split into 25 sub-proofs (for correctness_1), along the disjunctions of the newly expanded predicate using (split).
7. The general-purpose strategy (grind) is applied to each sub-proof, discharging of all proof obligations.

Using the above strategy, the proof of correctness_total is discharged with an average execution time of 40.546s. The module under test is in compliance with revision 4.1 of the RapidIO Interconnect Specification [13].

6   Related Work

Similarly to BAPIP and the original work of Richards and Lester [14], Kami [4] models individual action semantics, but stops short of action arbitration. The expected workflow in Kami starts with composing the hardware design inside of Kami (and therefore COQ), where individual rules can have their behaviour verified. From there, Kami code is **de-sugared** into Bluespec code.

Many of the issues with the Richards and Lester embedding in PVS recur in Kami. While certain classes of properties can be demonstrated via proof over individual actions, more complex, multi-action behaviours require action scheduling to be modelled. In addition, the only way to verify timing requirements is tying actions to real-world time via whole clock cycles. Kami also explicitly does not a address "constructs that violate one-rule-at-a-time semantics [...] namely "wires," whose behaviour depends on the schedule" [4]. It is only possible to simulate wires in the context of whole clock cycle semantics, so this is an understandable omission in Kami, but not one that is shared by BAPIP.

7   Conclusion

It is our hope that this technique may be used and adapted in further verification projects, so that the immense barrier between formal verification and common practice may be lessened. As future work, the bsv2pvs translation algorithm could be expanded to cover all BSV language constructs.

References

1. Open Source RISC-V Cores and Tools. Bluespec Inc. (2019). https://bluespec. com/. Accessed 29 Mar 2022
2. RISC-V Foundation—Instruction Set Architecture (ISA) (2020). https://riscv. org/. Accessed 29 Mar 2022
3. Bluespec Inc.: Bluespec^{TM}SystemVerilog Reference Guide (2012). http://csg. csail.mit.edu/6.S078/6_S078_2012_www/resources/reference-guide.pdf.   Accessed 29 Mar 2022
4. Choi, J., Vijayaraghavan, M., Sherman, B., Chlipala, A., et al.: Kami: a platform for high-level parametric hardware specification and its modular verification. In: Proceedings of the ACM on Programming Languages, vol. 1(ICFP), p. 24 (2017). https://dspace.mit.edu/handle/1721.1/134865. Accessed 30 Mar 2022
5. Dutertre, B., De Moura, L.: The Yices SMT Solver (2006). http://yices.csl.sri. com/tool-paper.pdf. Accessed 29 Mar 2022
6. Erkok, L.: SBV: SMT Based Verification: Symbolic Haskell Theorem Prover Using SMT Solving (2019). https://hackage.haskell.org/package/sbv. Accessed 29 Mar 2022
7. George, P., Sahoo, A., Menon, A., Kamakoti, V.: SHAKTI: An Open-Source Processor Ecosystem. Advanced Computing and Communications (2018). https:// www.researchgate.net/profile/Neel-Gala-2/publication/330577797_SHAKTI_ An_Open-Source_Processor_Ecosystem/data/5c4969e092851c22a38c2c24/ACCS-SHAKTI-PAPER.pdf. Accessed 30 Mar 2022
8. Madhusudan, G.S.: casl/rapidio/old_src /Logical_Transport/BSV - Bitbucket (2018). https://bitbucket.org/casl/rapidio/src/master/old_src/Logical_Transport/ BSV/. Accessed 29 Mar 2022
9. Moore, N., Lawford, M.: Correct safety critical hardware descriptions via static analysis and theorem proving. In: 2017 IEEE/ACM 5th International FME Workshop on Formal Methods in Software Engineering (FormaliSE), pp. 58–64. IEEE (2017). https://ieeexplore.ieee.org/abstract/document/7967994. Accessed 30 Mar 2022

10. Nikhil, R.: Bluespec System Verilog: efficient, correct RTL from high level specifications. In: Proceedings of the Second ACM and IEEE International Conference on Formal Methods and Models for Co-Design, pp. 69–70. IEEE (2004). https://ieeexplore.ieee.org/abstract/document/1459818. Accessed 30 Mar 2022

11. Owre, S., Rushby, J.M., Shankar, N.: PVS: a prototype verification system. In: Kapur, D. (ed.) CADE 1992. LNCS, vol. 607, pp. 748–752. Springer, Heidelberg (1992). https://doi.org/10.1007/3-540-55602-8_217. Accessed 30 Mar 2022

12. Porter, H.H., III.: RISC-V: An Overview of the Instruction Set Architecture (2018). https://web.cecs.pdx.edu/~harry/riscv/RISCV-Summary.pdf. Accessed 29 Mar 2022

13. RapidIO.org: RapidIO TM Interconnect Specification - Part 1: Input/Output Logical Specification, 4.1 edn., June 2017. https://rapidio.org/files/IO_logical.pdf. Accessed 30 Mar 2022

14. Richards, D., Lester, D.: A monadic approach to automated reasoning for Bluespec System Verilog. Innov. Syst. Softw. Eng. **7**(2), 85–95 (2011). https://doi.org/10.1007/s11334-011-0149-0. Accessed 30 Mar 2022

15. Wassyng, A., Lawford, M.S., Maibaum, T.S.: Software certification experience in the Canadian nuclear industry: lessons for the future. In: Proceedings of the Ninth ACM International Conference on Embedded Software, pp. 219–226. ACM (2011). https://dl.acm.org/doi/abs/10.1145/2038642.2038676. Accessed 30 Mar 2022

Sound Static Analysis of Regular Expressions for Vulnerabilities to Denial of Service Attacks

Francesco Parolini[✉] and Antoine Miné

Sorbonne Université, CNRS, LIP6, 75005 Paris, France
{francesco.parolini,antoine.mine}@lip6.fr

Abstract. Modern programming languages often provide functions to manipulate regular expressions in standard libraries. If they offer support for advanced features, the matching algorithm has an exponential worst-case time complexity: for some so-called *vulnerable regular expressions*, an attacker can craft ad hoc strings to force the matcher to exhibit an exponential behaviour and perform a *Regular Expression Denial of Service* (ReDoS) attack. In this paper, we introduce a framework based on a tree semantics to statically identify ReDoS vulnerabilities. In particular, we put forward an algorithm to extract an *overapproximation* of the set of words that are dangerous for a regular expression, effectively catching all possible attacks. We have implemented the analysis in a tool called **rat**, and testing it on a dataset of 74,670 regular expressions, we observed that in 99.47% of the instances the analysis terminates in less than one second. We compared **rat** to four other ReDoS detectors, and we found that our tool is faster, often by orders of magnitude, than most other tools. While raising a low number of false positives, **rat** is the only ReDoS detector that does not report false negatives.

Keywords: Regular expressions · Denial of Service · Algorithmic complexity attacks · Static analysis · Security and privacy

1 Introduction

Regular expressions (regexes) are often used to verify that strings in programs match a given pattern. Modern programming languages offer support to regexes in standard libraries, and this encourages programmers to take advantage of them. However, matching engines of languages such as Python, JavaScript, and Java employ algorithms with exponential worst-case time complexity in the length of the string. This is because advanced features such as *backreferences* extend the expressiveness of regular expressions. This comes at the cost of exponential matching in the worst case, even for regexes that do not exploit such features. An attacker can craft a string to force the matcher to exhibit the exponential behaviour to perform a *Regular Expression Denial of Service* (ReDoS) attack, a particular type of *algorithmic complexity attack* [13].

© Springer Nature Switzerland AG 2022
Y. Aït-Ameur and F. Crǎciun (Eds.): TASE 2022, LNCS 13299, pp. 73–91, 2022.
https://doi.org/10.1007/978-3-031-10363-6_6

ReDoS attacks are vastly underestimated Denial of Service (DoS) attacks. In a recent study of regexes usage, in nearly 4,000 Python projects on Github, the authors find that over 42% of them contain regexes [11], while in [30] the authors found that 10% of the Node.js-based web services they examined are vulnerable to ReDoS. In this already harsh scenario, in [18] the authors find that only 38% of the developers that they surveyed knew about the *existence* of ReDoS attacks. Many well-known platforms observed such vulnerabilities in their systems: among them, we find Stack Overflow [3], Cloudflare [4], and iCloud [5]. Since it is difficult to detect ReDoS vulnerabilities with manual inspection, it is necessary to automate this critical process. However, for now, there is no practical and widely adopted solution to detect ReDoS vulnerabilities.

There are many different approaches to static semantics-based ReDoS detection [19,28,32,33], and they are all based on automata frameworks. Due to the difficulties to precisely model matching engines with automata, static analyzers often report both false positives and false negatives. In contrast, dynamic approaches to ReDoS detection [29] can hardly be used in practice, since performing dynamic testing on exponential algorithms can be excessively costly.

In this paper, we put forward a novel approach to statically detect ReDoS vulnerabilities. We get rid of the complexities to represent the behaviour of matching engines with automata by defining a *tree semantics* of the matching process. Next, we leverage it to introduce an analysis that determines whether a regex may be vulnerable or not. In particular, the analysis returns an *over-approximation* of the language of words that can cause exponential matching, being effectively *sound* but *not complete*. Nevertheless, our experiments show that our approach reports a low number of false positives.

In this work, we focus on the most dangerous type of ReDoS vulnerability, namely when the matching is exponential. To successfully perform an attack that exploits superlinear but non-exponential matching, a malicious user must be allowed to insert very large strings. Such attacks are considerably less dangerous than the case that we consider.

Our approach not only eliminates the complexities related to using automata, but also opens the possibility to easily introduce optimizations. We implemented our algorithm in a tool called `rat` [25], and we found it to be on average one to two orders of magnitude faster than most existing detectors, while being proved to be sound and raising only 50 false alarms over 74,670 regexes. Furthermore, `rat` can extract the language of possibly dangerous words, being strictly more expressive than most other tools. This expressiveness can be useful in different scenarios: for example, existing matching engines can use our algorithm to filter-out dangerous input strings. It is also possible to use the language of dangerous words by combining our framework with a string analysis in order to prove the absence of ReDoS vulnerabilities in real-world applications.

```
1  import re
2  email_regex = r'^([0-9a-zA-Z]([-.\w]*[0-9a-zA-Z])*@(([0-9
      a-zA-Z])+([-\w]*[0-9a-zA-Z])*\.)+[a-zA-Z]{2,9})$'
3  attack = 'a' * 50
4  re.match(email_regex, attack)
```

Fig. 1. Python program that matches a dangerous string against a vulnerable regex

2 Background

2.1 ReDoS Vulnerabilities

The majority of programming languages that offer support for regexes in standard libraries are vulnerable to ReDoS attacks. Among them, we find Python, Java, JavaScript, PHP, and Ruby. Figure 1 shows an example of a Python program that matches a string with a vulnerable regex that validates email addresses. The regex is taken from the Regexlib [2] database, and possibly many programmers used it. Executing the program on a modern computer with a 4GHz Intel Core i7-4790K CPU takes more than 24 h. In Sect. 4, we give in-depth description of ReDoS vulnerabilities, but here we informally introduce why this behaviour arises. Consider the input string a^{50} and the subexpression ([-.\w]*[0-9a-zA-Z])*: a can be matched in [-.\w]* or in [0-9a-zA-Z]. This implies that in ([-.\w]*[0-9a-zA-Z])* there are four paths to match aa, eight for aaa and in general 2^n for a^n. Normally, the matching engine accepts the first match, but here, as @ does not appear in the string, it exhaustively explores all 2^{50} paths before concluding that no match is possible for a^{50} in the full regex.

Usually programming languages employ matching engines with exponential worst-time complexity to support advanced features such as *backreferences* and *lookarounds* [16,22]. We, like most other analyzers, do not support such features. Nevertheless, our approach is sufficient to analyze the great majority of regexes in real-world applications: in [11] the authors found that in nearly 4000 Python projects, only 4% of the regexes use lookarounds and up to 0.4% use backreferences. Yet, recent surveys determined that up to the 10% of the web services they considered present ReDoS vulnerabilities [30]. This highlights how programmers use vulnerable matching engines while only occasionally taking advantage of advanced features, and motivates the need for a sound ReDoS analyzer even limited to regular constructs.

2.2 ReDoS Detection

There are two main approaches to ReDoS detection:

1. *Semantics-based static detection.* There are many different approaches to semantics-based static ReDoS detection [19,27,28,32,33], and they all rely on automata. In those frameworks, regexes are first transformed into automata, which are then analyzed to determine whether they are vulnerable or not.

The main problem is that transforming regexes to automata can remove or inject vulnerabilities. This is often a source of both false positives and false negatives. We discuss semantics-based static analyzers based on automata in detail in Sect. 6, and we compare them to our approach that is also semantics-based, but operates on regexes instead of automata.

2. *Dynamic detection.* A dynamic analyzer generates strings that are fed to the matching engine. Then, the tool measures the time for the matching and determines whether a regex is vulnerable or not. These tools are sensibly slower than static analyzers, because performing testing on exponential algorithms can be excessively time-consuming. While it is possible to configure generic fuzzers, such as SlowFuzz [26], to detect ReDoS vulnerabilities, in [29] the authors present ReScue: a more precise gray-box approach which leverages a genetic algorithm to efficiently generate input strings.

2.3   Regexes Basics

We now define the regexes that we use for the rest of the paper. Let $\Sigma = \{a_1, a_2, \ldots, a_n\}$ be a finite set of symbols. A *word* is an element of Σ^*, while a *language* is a set of words. We denote the empty word as ε and the concatenation of two languages L_1, L_2 as $L_1 L_2$. Let $a \in \Sigma$.

$$\mathcal{R} \in \mathbb{R} \qquad\qquad\qquad\qquad\qquad\qquad\qquad\qquad \text{Regexes}$$
$$\mathcal{R} := \varepsilon \mid a \mid \mathcal{R}_1 | \mathcal{R}_2 \mid \mathcal{R}_1 \cdot \mathcal{R}_2 \text{ (or } \mathcal{R}_1 \mathcal{R}_2) \mid \mathcal{R}_1^*$$

We assume that regexes automatically remove ε in the concatenation (this is known as a *smart-constructor* [23]), so that $\mathcal{R} \cdot \varepsilon$ and $\varepsilon \cdot \mathcal{R}$ are always simplified to $\mathcal{R}$. This allows representing regexes as they are implemented in programming languages, where ε cannot be inserted by the user in the concatenation. We define two functions to deconstruct the concatenation of a regex $\mathcal{R}$.

$$\text{hd}(\mathcal{R}) \triangleq \begin{cases} \text{hd}(\mathcal{R}_1) & \text{if } \mathcal{R} = \mathcal{R}_1 \mathcal{R}_2 \\ \mathcal{R} & \text{otherwise} \end{cases} \qquad \text{tl}(\mathcal{R}) \triangleq \begin{cases} \text{tl}(\mathcal{R}_1) \cdot \mathcal{R}_2 & \text{if } \mathcal{R} = \mathcal{R}_1 \mathcal{R}_2 \\ \varepsilon & \text{otherwise} \end{cases}$$

Observe that since we assume that the concatenation simplifies ε, if $\text{hd}(\mathcal{R}) = \varepsilon$, then $\text{tl}(\mathcal{R}) = \varepsilon$. We extend the regexes with the possibility to recognize the *empty language*, namely the empty set of words, as follows.

$$\mathcal{R} \in \mathbb{R}^\perp \qquad\qquad\qquad\qquad\qquad\qquad\qquad \text{Empty Regexes}$$
$$\mathcal{R} := \varepsilon \mid a \mid \mathcal{R}_1 | \mathcal{R}_2 \mid \mathcal{R}_1 \cdot \mathcal{R}_2 \mid \mathcal{R}_1^* \mid \perp$$

Observe that $\mathbb{R} \subset \mathbb{R}^\perp$. Let $a \in \Sigma$. The *language recognized by a regex* $\mathcal{R} \in \mathbb{R}^\perp$ is defined as follows.

$$\mathcal{L}(\perp) \triangleq \varnothing \qquad \mathcal{L}(a) \triangleq \{a\} \qquad \mathcal{L}(\mathcal{R}_1 \mathcal{R}_2) \triangleq \mathcal{L}(\mathcal{R}_1)\mathcal{L}(\mathcal{R}_2)$$
$$\mathcal{L}(\varepsilon) \triangleq \{\varepsilon\} \qquad \mathcal{L}(\mathcal{R}_1 | \mathcal{R}_2) \triangleq \mathcal{L}(\mathcal{R}_1) \cup \mathcal{L}(\mathcal{R}_2) \qquad \mathcal{L}(\mathcal{R}_1^*) \triangleq \bigcup_{i \geq 0} \mathcal{L}(\mathcal{R}_1)^i$$

Algorithm 1: Matching algorithm pseudocode

---

1 **fun** Match $(\mathcal{R} : \mathbb{R}, w : \Sigma^*, C : \wp(\mathbb{R})) \to$ bool
2   **if** $\mathcal{R} \in C$ **then**
3   **return** false
4   **switch** $\langle \mathrm{hd}(\mathcal{R}), \mathrm{tl}(\mathcal{R}) \rangle$ **do**
5   **case** $\langle \varepsilon, \varepsilon \rangle$ **do**
6   **return** $w = \varepsilon$
7   **case** $\langle a, \mathcal{R}_1 \rangle$ **do**
8   **if** $w = aw_1$ **then return** Match$(\mathcal{R}_1, w_1, \varnothing)$
9   **else return** false
10   **case** $\langle \mathcal{R}_1 | \mathcal{R}_2, \mathcal{R}_3 \rangle$ **do**
11   **return** Match$(\mathcal{R}_1\mathcal{R}_3, w, C) \vee$ Match$(\mathcal{R}_2\mathcal{R}_3, w, C)$
12   **case** $\langle \mathcal{R}_1^*, \mathcal{R}_2 \rangle$ **do**
13   **return** Match$(\mathcal{R}_1\mathcal{R}_1^*\mathcal{R}_2, w, C \cup \{\mathcal{R}_1^*\mathcal{R}_2\}) \vee$ Match$(\mathcal{R}_2, w, C)$

If $\mathcal{L}(\mathcal{R}_1) = \mathcal{L}(\mathcal{R}_2)$ we write $\mathcal{R}_1 =_{\mathcal{L}} \mathcal{R}_2$. Furthermore, the *union, intersection* and *complement* operations on regexes have respectively type $\mathbb{R}^{\perp} \times \mathbb{R}^{\perp} \to \mathbb{R}^{\perp}$, $\mathbb{R}^{\perp} \times \mathbb{R}^{\perp} \to \mathbb{R}^{\perp}$ and $\mathbb{R}^{\perp} \to \mathbb{R}^{\perp}$. We denote them by $\mathcal{R}_1 \cup^r \mathcal{R}_2$, $\mathcal{R}_1 \cap^r \mathcal{R}_2$ and $\overline{\mathcal{R}_1}^r$. Observe that if $\mathcal{R}_1, \mathcal{R}_2 \in \mathbb{R}$, then $\mathcal{R}_1 \cup^r \mathcal{R}_2 \in \mathbb{R}$.

2.4   Regex Matching

In this section, we provide the pseudocode of the matching procedure. While it is simple and concise, it models the concrete behaviour of realistic matching engines. The pseudocode ignores details specific to a particular implementation, giving a high-level description of the procedure. Our algorithm is a trivial adaptation of the one presented in [9], which models Java's matching engine. Classic textbooks about regexes confirm that matching engines in standard libraries employ a trivial backtracking procedure for the matching [16,22].

In Algorithm 1, we present the matching procedure. The logic operators are short-circuit: as soon as the input word is matched, the unexplored branches of the regex are not considered. The behaviour of function Match depends on the first constructor in the concatenation of the regex, and the remaining portion can possibly be ε. The algorithm is rather trivial, but it models two important aspects of matching engines. First, it implements a *prioritization mechanism* that: (1) tries to expand the left branch before the right branch in alternatives; (2) tries to match as many characters as possible in the body of the stars. Second, the algorithm prevents infinite ε-matching loops. Consider $(\varepsilon|a)^*$: if we remove line 3, the procedure keeps expanding the body of the star forever, never consuming any character of the input string. To prevent this, when a star is expanded, it is inserted in C, that is the set of stars that cannot be expanded again. Initially, C must be instantiated to the empty set. The stars are removed from C only when at least one character is matched. Observe that usually in matching engines the match is successful even if just a prefix of the word matches the regex: we can model this behaviour by appending Σ^* at the end of regexes.

3   Semantics

In this section, we first define a small-step operational semantics as a transition relation between the configurations of the matching engine. We then use it to put forward a tree semantics that precisely describes the steps performed during the matching. Lastly, we use the semantics to formally define ReDoS vulnerabilities.

We extend $\mathbb{R}$ to represent when a star has been expanded and not a single character has been matched yet. The syntax of a regex $\mathcal{R} \in \mathbb{R}^{\mathcal{T}}$ is given by the following grammar.

$$\mathcal{R} \in \mathbb{R}^{\mathcal{T}} \qquad\qquad\qquad \text{Transitional Regexes}$$

$$\mathcal{R} := \varepsilon \mid a \mid \mathcal{R}_1 | \mathcal{R}_2 \mid \mathcal{R}_1 {\cdot} \mathcal{R}_2 \mid \mathcal{R}_1^* \mid \mathcal{R}_1^{\overline{*}}$$

It differs from traditional regexes for the *closed star*, namely $\mathcal{R}^{\overline{*}}$. It is a star that cannot be expanded again in order to prevent infinite ε-matching loops. We will formalize this concept with the transition relation. The closed stars avoid the necessity to keep a separate set of expressions (C in Algorithm 1) during the matching: the information is implicitly included in the regex.

We call a pair in $\mathbb{R}^{\mathcal{T}} \times \Sigma^* \triangleq \mathbb{S}$ a *state*, and it describes the configuration of the matching engine. The first component is the regex that the matcher is expanding, and the second is the suffix of the input word that still has to be matched. We define the function $r : \mathbb{R}^{\mathcal{T}} \to \mathbb{R}$ to transform the closed stars back into regular stars as follows.

$$r(\varepsilon) \triangleq \varepsilon \qquad\qquad r(\mathcal{R}_1|\mathcal{R}_2) \triangleq r(\mathcal{R}_1)|r(\mathcal{R}_2) \qquad\qquad r(\mathcal{R}_1^*) \triangleq r(\mathcal{R}_1)^*$$

$$r(a) \triangleq a \qquad\qquad r(\mathcal{R}_1\mathcal{R}_2) \triangleq r(\mathcal{R}_1)r(\mathcal{R}_2) \qquad\qquad r(\mathcal{R}_1^{\overline{*}}) \triangleq r(\mathcal{R}_1)^*$$

We then define the set of *actions* as $\mathbb{A} \triangleq \{ \oplus, \ominus, \circledast, \bigcirc \} \cup \{ \circleda_a \mid a \in \Sigma \}$. Let $a \in \Sigma$ and $w \in \Sigma^*$. We can finally define the *transition relation* between states. It is not deterministic, but sequences of actions will be ordered later in this section.

$$\langle a, aw \rangle \xrightarrow{\circleda_a} \langle \varepsilon, w \rangle \qquad\qquad\qquad \langle a\mathcal{R}_1, aw \rangle \xrightarrow{\circleda_a} \langle r(\mathcal{R}_1), w \rangle$$

$$\langle \mathcal{R}_1|\mathcal{R}_2, w \rangle \xrightarrow{\oplus} \langle \mathcal{R}_1, w \rangle \qquad\qquad \langle (\mathcal{R}_1|\mathcal{R}_2)\mathcal{R}_3, w \rangle \xrightarrow{\oplus} \langle \mathcal{R}_1\mathcal{R}_3, w \rangle$$

$$\langle \mathcal{R}_1|\mathcal{R}_2, w \rangle \xrightarrow{\ominus} \langle \mathcal{R}_2, w \rangle \qquad\qquad \langle (\mathcal{R}_1|\mathcal{R}_2)\mathcal{R}_3, w \rangle \xrightarrow{\ominus} \langle \mathcal{R}_2\mathcal{R}_3, w \rangle$$

$$\langle \mathcal{R}_1^*, w \rangle \xrightarrow{\circledast} \langle \mathcal{R}_1\mathcal{R}_1^{\overline{*}}, w \rangle \qquad\qquad \langle \mathcal{R}_1^*\mathcal{R}_2, w \rangle \xrightarrow{\circledast} \langle \mathcal{R}_1\mathcal{R}_1^{\overline{*}}\mathcal{R}_2, w \rangle$$

$$\langle \mathcal{R}_1^*, w \rangle \xrightarrow{\bigcirc} \langle \varepsilon, w \rangle \qquad\qquad\qquad \langle \mathcal{R}_1^*\mathcal{R}_2, w \rangle \xrightarrow{\bigcirc} \langle \mathcal{R}_2, w \rangle$$

The transition relation describes all possible choices of the matching engine according to the state. Observe that with the $\circledast$ action the star becomes $\overline{*}$, and it cannot be expanded again until a character is matched. In fact, the transition relation is not defined for $\mathcal{R}^{\overline{*}}$. After consuming a character of the input word, we apply the function r to mark all stars as expandable.

We now leverage the transition relation to define a tree semantics for the matching procedure. Figure 2(a) to 2(d) represent the steps to obtain the semantic matching tree that we define in this section for the initial state $\langle a^*, a \rangle$. We begin by defining the set of *execution traces* for $\langle \mathcal{R}_0, w_0 \rangle \in \mathbb{S}$.

$$\mathcal{T}(\langle \mathcal{R}_0, w_0 \rangle) \triangleq \{ \langle \mathcal{R}_0, w_0 \rangle \xrightarrow{\mathcal{A}_1} \langle \mathcal{R}_1, w_1 \rangle \xrightarrow{\mathcal{A}_2} \cdots \xrightarrow{\mathcal{A}_n} \langle \mathcal{R}_n, w_n \rangle \mid$$
$$\forall i \in [0, n-1] : \mathcal{A}_i \in \mathbb{A} \text{ and } \langle \mathcal{R}_i, w_i \rangle \xrightarrow{\mathcal{A}_{i+1}} \langle \mathcal{R}_{i+1}, w_{i+1} \rangle \}$$

$\{ \langle a^*, a \rangle, \langle a^*, a \rangle \xrightarrow{\circledast} \langle a a^{\overline{*}}, a \rangle,$

$\langle a^*, a \rangle \xrightarrow{\circledast} \langle a a^{\overline{*}}, a \rangle \xrightarrow{@a} \langle a^*, \varepsilon \rangle,$

$\langle a^*, a \rangle \xrightarrow{\circledast} \langle a a^{\overline{*}}, a \rangle \xrightarrow{@a} \langle a^*, \varepsilon \rangle \xrightarrow{\circ} \langle \varepsilon, \varepsilon \rangle,$

$\langle a^*, a \rangle \xrightarrow{\circledast} \langle a a^{\overline{*}}, a \rangle \xrightarrow{@a} \langle a^*, \varepsilon \rangle \xrightarrow{\circledast} \langle a a^{\overline{*}}, \varepsilon \rangle,$

$\langle a^*, a \rangle \xrightarrow{\circ} \langle \varepsilon, a \rangle \}$

$\{ \langle a^*, a \rangle \xrightarrow{\circledast} \langle a a^{\overline{*}}, a \rangle \xrightarrow{@a} \langle a^*, \varepsilon \rangle \xrightarrow{\circ} \langle \varepsilon, \varepsilon \rangle,$

$\langle a^*, a \rangle \xrightarrow{\circledast} \langle a a^{\overline{*}}, a \rangle \xrightarrow{@a} \langle a^*, \varepsilon \rangle \xrightarrow{\circledast} \langle a a^{\overline{*}}, \varepsilon \rangle,$

$\langle a^*, a \rangle \xrightarrow{\circ} \langle \varepsilon, a \rangle \}$

(a) $\mathcal{T}(\langle a^*, a \rangle)$ (b) $\mathcal{T}_c(\langle a^*, a \rangle)$

$\langle a^*, a \rangle \xrightarrow{\circledast} \langle a a^{\overline{*}}, a \rangle \xrightarrow{@a} \langle a^*, \varepsilon \rangle \xrightarrow{\circledast} \langle a a^{\overline{*}}, \varepsilon \rangle,$ $\langle a^*, a \rangle \xrightarrow{\circledast} \langle a a^{\overline{*}}, a \rangle \xrightarrow{@a} \langle a^*, \varepsilon \rangle \xrightarrow{\circledast} \langle a a^{\overline{*}}, \varepsilon \rangle,$

$\langle a^*, a \rangle \xrightarrow{\circledast} \langle a a^{\overline{*}}, a \rangle \xrightarrow{@a} \langle a^*, \varepsilon \rangle \xrightarrow{\circ} \langle \varepsilon, \varepsilon \rangle,$ $\langle a^*, a \rangle \xrightarrow{\circledast} \langle a a^{\overline{*}}, a \rangle \xrightarrow{@a} \langle a^*, \varepsilon \rangle \xrightarrow{\circ} \langle \varepsilon, \varepsilon \rangle$

$\langle a^*, a \rangle \xrightarrow{\circ} \langle \varepsilon, a \rangle$

(c) $(\mathcal{O}_{\sqsubseteq} \circ \mathcal{T}_c)(\langle a^*, a \rangle)$ (d) $(\mathcal{F}_\varepsilon \circ \mathcal{O}_{\sqsubseteq} \circ \mathcal{T}_c)(\langle a^*, a \rangle)$

Fig. 2. Intermediate steps to obtain the matching tree semantics

We denote the last state of a trace t as $\ell(t)$ and we define the set of *complete execution traces* as $\mathcal{T}_c(\langle \mathcal{R}, w \rangle) \triangleq \{ t \in \mathcal{T}(\langle \mathcal{R}, w \rangle) \mid \ell(t) \nrightarrow \}$. Observe that $\mathcal{T}_c(\langle \mathcal{R}, w \rangle)$ represents all possible executions of the matching engine from $\langle \mathcal{R}, w \rangle$ up to a state in which it is not possible to continue. We say that two traces are part of the same matching run if they have the same initial state. To build the matching tree, we need to order the traces from the first that will be explored to the last. Let t_1, t_2 be two complete execution traces in the same matching run, and let $\langle \mathcal{R}_1, w_1 \rangle$ be the last state in the longest common prefix between t_1 and t_2. We impose a lexical order $\sqsubseteq$ such that $t_1 \sqsubseteq t_2$ iff the action chosen by t_1 after $\langle \mathcal{R}_1, w_1 \rangle$ is either $\oplus$ or $\circledast$. This order assigns higher priority to the traces that choose to expand the left branch of the alternative or to expand the body of the star, which is the standard behaviour of matching engines. Let T be a set of complete execution traces such that all of them are part of the same matching run. We denote with $\mathcal{O}_{\sqsubseteq}(T)$ the sequence of traces in T ordered by $\sqsubseteq$.

Observe that $(\mathcal{O}_{\sqsubseteq} \circ \mathcal{T}_c)(\langle \mathcal{R}, w \rangle)$ corresponds to the ordered sequence of *all* complete execution traces. During the concrete execution, some of them will never be explored, because as soon as the state $\langle \varepsilon, \varepsilon \rangle$ is found, the procedure terminates. We want to remove from $(\mathcal{O}_{\sqsubseteq} \circ \mathcal{T}_c)(\langle \mathcal{R}, w \rangle)$ those traces that appear after $\langle \varepsilon, \varepsilon \rangle$. Let $S = t_1, t_2, \ldots, t_n$ be a sequence of complete execution traces. We denote by $\mathcal{F}_\varepsilon(S)$ the sequence $t_1, t_2, \ldots, t_k$ such that t_k is the first trace for which it holds that $\ell(t_k) = \langle \varepsilon, \varepsilon \rangle$. If there is no such trace, then $k = n$ (i.e., there is an exhaustive exploration of all traces before failing).

Let S be a sequence of complete execution traces such that all of them are part of the same matching run. We denote by $\curlyvee(S)$ the tree obtained by merging the common prefixes in S.

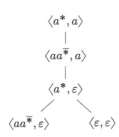

Fig. 3. Representation of $[\![a^*]\!](a)$

Definition 1 (Matching Tree Semantics). *Let* $\mathcal{R} \in \mathbb{R}^{\mathcal{T}}$ *and* $w \in \Sigma^*$. *The matching tree semantics of* $\mathcal{R}$ *with respect to* w *is given by the following tree.*

$$[\![\mathcal{R}]\!](w) \triangleq (\curlyvee \circ \mathcal{F}_\varepsilon \circ \mathcal{O}_\sqsubseteq \circ \mathcal{T}_c)(\langle \mathcal{R}, w \rangle)$$

Figure 3 represents $[\![a^*]\!](a)$. One can reconstruct the steps carried out by the matching engine by doing a depth-first left-to-right traversal of the semantic tree. We denote the number of nodes in a tree t with $|t|$ and its set of leaves as $\mathrm{lvs}(t)$. We define the *language recognized by* $\mathcal{R} \in \mathbb{R}^{\mathcal{T}}$ as $\mathcal{L}(\mathcal{R}) \triangleq \{\, w \in \Sigma^* \mid \langle \varepsilon, \varepsilon \rangle \in \mathrm{lvs}([\![\mathcal{R}]\!](w))\,\}$. We now give the definition of ReDoS vulnerability, using the one that firstly appeared in [32], but adapted to our semantics.

Definition 2 (ReDoS Vulnerability). *Let* $\mathcal{R} \in \mathbb{R}$ *and* $n \in \mathbb{N}$. *We define* $M_\mathcal{R}(n) \triangleq \max\{\, |[\![\mathcal{R}]\!](w)| \mid w \in \Sigma^*, |w| \leqslant n \,\}$. *We say that* $\mathcal{R}$ *has a* ReDoS *vulnerability iff* $M_\mathcal{R} \in \Omega(2^n)$.

4   Detection of ReDoS Vulnerabilities

In this section, we describe a framework to statically detect exponential ReDoS vulnerabilities. The analysis we propose derives from a regex an overapproximation of the set of dangerous words, namely those that can possibly cause an exponential ReDoS attack. The analysis is *sound* but not *complete*: any true vulnerability will be reported, but the algorithm can occasionally raise *false positives* (i.e., harmless regexes can be considered dangerous). Nevertheless, as discussed in Sect. 5, our experiments show that in practice our approach is precise and reports only 50 false positives over 74,670 regexes.

Intuitively, there is an exponential ReDoS vulnerability in a star if it is possible to match a word with at least two different traces. Consider $(a|a)^*$: a is matched in two traces by expanding the left or the right branch of the alternative. This implies that there are four traces to match aa, eight for aaa and in

Algorithm 2: Compute $\mathfrak{M}_2(\mathcal{R})$

1 **fun** $M2(\mathcal{R} : \mathbb{R}) \to \mathbb{R}^\perp$
2   **return** $M2\text{-rec}(\mathcal{R}, \varnothing)$
3 **fun** $M2\text{-rec}(\mathcal{R} : \mathbb{R}^{\mathcal{T}}, E : \wp(\mathbb{R}^{\mathcal{T}})) \to \mathbb{R}^\perp$
4   **if** $\mathcal{R} \in E$ **then**
5   **return** $\perp$
6   **switch** $\langle \text{hd}(\mathcal{R}), \text{tl}(\mathcal{R}) \rangle$ **do**
7   **case** $\langle \varepsilon, \varepsilon \rangle \vee \langle \mathcal{R}_1^{\overline{*}}, \mathcal{R}_2 \rangle$ **do**
8   **return** $\perp$
9   **case** $\langle a, \mathcal{R}_1 \rangle$ **do**
10   **return** $a \cdot M2\text{-rec}(r(\mathcal{R}_1), E)$
11   **case** $\langle \mathcal{R}_1 | \mathcal{R}_2, \mathcal{R}_3 \rangle$ **do**
12       $inter \leftarrow \mathcal{R}_1 \mathcal{R}_3 \cap_{\not{\varepsilon}}^r \mathcal{R}_2 \mathcal{R}_3$
13       $l \leftarrow M2\text{-rec}(\mathcal{R}_1 \mathcal{R}_3, E)$
14       $r \leftarrow M2\text{-rec}(\mathcal{R}_2 \mathcal{R}_3, E)$
15   **return** $inter \cup^r l \cup^r r$
16   **case** $\langle \mathcal{R}_1^*, \mathcal{R}_2 \rangle$ **do**
17       $inter \leftarrow \mathcal{R}_1 \mathcal{R}_1^{\overline{*}} \mathcal{R}_2 \cap_{\not{\varepsilon}}^r \mathcal{R}_2$
18       $l \leftarrow M2\text{-rec}(\mathcal{R}_1 \mathcal{R}_1^{\overline{*}} \mathcal{R}_2, E \cup \{\mathcal{R}\})$
19       $r \leftarrow \mathcal{R}_1^* \cdot M2\text{-rec}(\mathcal{R}_2, E)$
20   **return** $inter \cup^r l \cup^r r$

Algorithm 3: Remove ε from $\mathcal{L}(\mathcal{R})$

1 **fun** $\not{\varepsilon}(\mathcal{R} : \mathbb{R}^{\mathcal{T}}) \to \mathbb{R}^\perp$
2   **switch** $\langle \text{hd}(\mathcal{R}), \text{tl}(\mathcal{R}) \rangle$ **do**
3   **case** $\langle \varepsilon, \varepsilon \rangle \vee \langle \mathcal{R}_1^{\overline{*}}, \mathcal{R}_2 \rangle$ **do**
4   **return** $\perp$
5   **case** $\langle a, \mathcal{R}_1 \rangle$ **do**
6   **return** $a \cdot (r(\mathcal{R}_1))$
7   **case** $\langle \mathcal{R}_1 | \mathcal{R}_2, \mathcal{R}_3 \rangle$ **do**
8   **return** $\not{\varepsilon}(\mathcal{R}_1 \mathcal{R}_3) \cup^r \not{\varepsilon}(\mathcal{R}_2 \mathcal{R}_3)$
9   **case** $\langle \mathcal{R}_1^*, \mathcal{R}_2 \rangle$ **do**
10   **return** $\not{\varepsilon}(\mathcal{R}_1 \mathcal{R}_1^{\overline{*}} \mathcal{R}_2) \cup^r \not{\varepsilon}(\mathcal{R}_2)$

general 2^n for a^n. Nevertheless, $[\![(a|a)^*]\!](a^n)$ is not an exponential tree, because the match succeeds after expanding the left branch of the alternative n times. By appending a character that makes the match fail after a^n, an attacker can force the matching engine to explore all traces, effectively performing a ReDoS attack. This is the reason why $|[\![(a|a)^*]\!](a^n b)| = \Theta(2^n)$.

First, we define a function $\mathfrak{M}_2$ to extract the set of words that are matched in at least two traces in a regex $\mathcal{R}$.

$$\mathfrak{M}_2(\mathcal{R}) \triangleq \{ w \in \Sigma^+ \mid \exists t_1, t_2 \in \mathcal{T}_c(\langle \mathcal{R}, w \rangle) : t_1 \neq t_2 \text{ and } \ell(t_1) = \ell(t_2) = \langle \varepsilon, \varepsilon \rangle \}$$

In the analysis, we use $\mathfrak{M}_2$, and since it is a possibly infinite language we need an algorithm to compute a finite representation of it. The function M2 in Algorithm 2 returns a regular expression $\mathcal{R}_1 \in \mathbb{R}^\perp$ such that $\mathcal{L}(\mathcal{R}_1) = \mathfrak{M}_2(\mathcal{R})$. In Algorithm 2, we compute the intersection of two regexes $\mathcal{R}_1, \mathcal{R}_2 \in \mathbb{R}^{\mathcal{T}}$ that does not include ε, and we denote it by $\mathcal{R}_1 \cap_{\not{\varepsilon}}^r \mathcal{R}_2$. It can be computed as $\not{\varepsilon}(\mathcal{R}_1) \cap^r \not{\varepsilon}(\mathcal{R}_2)$, where $\not{\varepsilon} : \mathbb{R}^{\mathcal{T}} \to \mathbb{R}^\perp$ removes ε from the language of input regexes. The procedure is depicted in Algorithm 3.

The intuition behind M2 is that a word is matched in two different traces if the two branches of a choice[1] recognize some common words, that is, they have a nonempty intersection. Algorithm 2 recursively explores all regexes that can

---

[1] By choice we mean taking the left/right branch of an alternative or expanding/not expanding a star.

be reached from the initial one with the transition relation. When it encounters a choice, it returns the intersection of the two possible branches: the words in it are those that are matched in two different traces. Observe that since the words in $M_2(\mathcal{R})$ are nonempty, we compute the intersections with $\cap_{\slashed{\varepsilon}}^r$.

To ensure termination, we keep track of which stars have already been expanded with the parameter E. When a regex in which the first construct is a star is encountered for the second time, the function returns $\bot$. This guarantees that any star will be expanded exactly once. Observe that the closed stars and the parameter E serve different purposes: the first guarantees termination during the *concrete execution* to avoid infinite ε-matching loops; the second guarantees termination of the M2-rec function.

Example 1. Consider $M2((a|a)^*)$, that initially invokes $\text{M2-rec}((a|a)^*, \varnothing)$. First, $(a|a)(a|a)^{\overline{*}} \cap_{\slashed{\varepsilon}}^r \varepsilon =_{\mathcal{L}} \bot$ is returned; then, the recursive call $\text{M2-rec}(\varepsilon, \varnothing)$ immediately terminates and returns $\bot$ as well. The most interesting recursive call is $\text{M2-rec}((a|a)(a|a)^{\overline{*}}, \{(a|a)^*\})$, where the first construct in the concatenation is an alternative. The function computes and returns the nonempty intersection $a(a|a)^{\overline{*}} \cap_{\slashed{\varepsilon}}^r a(a|a)^{\overline{*}} =_{\mathcal{L}} a^+$. Next, the algorithm invokes $\text{M2-rec}(a(a|a)^{\overline{*}}, \{(a|a)^*\})$, which then calls $\text{M2-rec}(r((a|a)^{\overline{*}}), \{(a|a)^*\})$. Since $r((a|a)^{\overline{*}}) = (a|a)^*$ and $(a|a)^*$ is in E, the algorithm terminates at line 5. To summarize, $M2((a|a)^*)$ recognizes the language a^+, which is exactly $M_2((a|a)^*)$.

To understand how we take advantage of M2, consider a regex $\mathcal{R}^*$ such that $M2(\mathcal{R}^*) \neq_{\mathcal{L}} \varnothing$. In this case, the set of words that are matched with at least two traces in $\mathcal{R}^*$ is not empty. Let $w \in \mathcal{L}(M2(\mathcal{R}^*))$. Since from $\mathcal{R}^*$ there are two traces to match w, then there are four traces to match w^2, eight for w^3, and in general 2^n for w^n. Furthermore, for all $n \geq 1$, $w^n \in \mathcal{L}(M2(\mathcal{R}^*))$. This implies that the words in $M2(\mathcal{R}^*)$ are possibly matched in an exponential number of traces. To have an exponential matching tree, all of them must be explored. Let $\mathcal{S} \in \mathcal{R}$, and consider the case in which w^n is matched with $\mathcal{R}^*\mathcal{S}$. By concatenating w^n with a suffix s that causes the match to fail, it is possible to force the procedure to exhaustively explore all traces, effectively resulting in an exponential matching tree. The language of suffixes that make the match fail is the language of words not accepted by $\mathcal{R}^*\mathcal{S}$, namely $\overline{\mathcal{R}^*\mathcal{S}}^r$. This is the key insight of our analysis, namely that $M2(\mathcal{R}^*) \cdot \overline{\mathcal{R}^*\mathcal{S}}^r$ accepts an overapproximation of the language of words dangerous for $\mathcal{R}^*\mathcal{S}$ that can cause exponential matching in $\mathcal{R}^*$.

With this intuition, we define the analysis $\mathcal{E} : \mathcal{R} \times \mathcal{R} \times \mathcal{R} \rightarrow \mathcal{R}^\bot$ such that $\mathcal{E}(\mathcal{R}, \mathcal{P}, \mathcal{S})$ recognizes an overapproximation of the set of words dangerous for the regex $\mathcal{P} \cdot \mathcal{R} \cdot \mathcal{S}$ that can cause exponential matching in $\mathcal{R}$.

$$\mathcal{E}(\mathcal{R}, \mathcal{P}, \mathcal{S}) \triangleq \begin{cases} \bot & \text{if } \mathcal{R} = \varepsilon \text{ or } \mathcal{R} = a \\ \mathcal{E}(\mathcal{R}_1, \mathcal{P}, \mathcal{S}) \cup^r \mathcal{E}(\mathcal{R}_2, \mathcal{P}, \mathcal{S}) & \text{if } \mathcal{R} = \mathcal{R}_1 | \mathcal{R}_2 \\ \mathcal{E}(\mathcal{R}_1, \mathcal{P}, \mathcal{R}_2 \cdot \mathcal{S}) \cup^r \mathcal{E}(\mathcal{R}_2, \mathcal{P} \cdot \mathcal{R}_1, \mathcal{S}) & \text{if } \mathcal{R} = \mathcal{R}_1 \mathcal{R}_2 \\ \mathcal{P} \cdot \mathcal{R}_1^* \cdot M2(\mathcal{R}_1^*) \cdot \overline{\mathcal{R}_1^* \cdot \mathcal{S}}^r \cup^r \mathcal{E}(\mathcal{R}_1, \mathcal{P} \cdot \mathcal{R}_1^*, \mathcal{R}_1^* \cdot \mathcal{S}) & \text{if } \mathcal{R} = \mathcal{R}_1^* \end{cases}$$

Initially, the analysis must be invoked as $\mathcal{E}(\mathcal{R}, \varepsilon, \varepsilon)$. It recursively explores $\mathcal{R}$, accumulating the prefixes and the suffixes of the portion that it is considering in

$\mathcal{P}$ and $\mathcal{S}$. When $\mathcal{E}$ encounters a star, in addition to calling $\mathcal{E}$ recursively on the regex under the star, it also returns $\mathcal{P} \cdot \mathcal{R}_1^* \cdot M2(\mathcal{R}_1^*) \cdot \overline{\mathcal{R}_1^* \mathcal{S}}^r$. As discussed previously, $M2(\mathcal{R}_1^*)\overline{\mathcal{R}_1^* \mathcal{S}}^r$ recognizes an overapproximation of the language of words dangerous for $\mathcal{R}_1^* \mathcal{S}$ that can cause exponential matching in $\mathcal{R}_1^*$. The first construct $\mathcal{P} \cdot \mathcal{R}_1^*$ in the expression accepts the language of words that the analysis determined to be a prefix of $\mathcal{R}_1^* \mathcal{S}$. Later in this section, we prove that the words in $\mathcal{E}(\mathcal{R}, \varepsilon, \varepsilon)$ are a sound overapproximation of the words that are dangerous for $\mathcal{R}$, and we also provide an example where the analysis loses precision.

We can perform an emptiness check on $\mathcal{E}(\mathcal{R}, \varepsilon, \varepsilon)$ to determine if there are dangerous words. If the language is empty, then $\mathcal{R}$ is not vulnerable; otherwise, we have a sound overapproximation of the words that can lead to ReDoS attacks.

Example 2. Consider $\mathcal{E}((a|a)^*, \varepsilon, \varepsilon)$.

$$\mathcal{E}((a|a)^*, \varepsilon, \varepsilon) = (a|a)^* \cdot M2((a|a)^*) \cdot \overline{(a|a)^*}^r \cup^r \mathcal{E}(a|a, (a|a)^*, (a|a)^*)$$

$$=_\mathcal{L} (a|a)^* a^+ \overline{(a|a)^*}^r \cup^r \bot$$

$$=_\mathcal{L} a^+ \cdot \overline{a^*}^r$$

In this case, the analysis determined that $(a|a)^*$ is vulnerable to arbitrary large sequences of as that are followed by any nonempty word not composed of as only. Observe that, effectively, $|[\![(a|a)^*]\!](a^n b)| = \Theta(2^n)$.

The following soundness theorem provides a strong guarantee that if the analysis of $\mathcal{R}$ returns an empty regex, then the size of any matching tree is at most polynomial in the length of the input word.

Theorem 1 (Soundness). *Let* $\mathcal{R} \in \mathbb{R}$.

$$\mathcal{E}(\mathcal{R}, \varepsilon, \varepsilon) =_\mathcal{L} \bot \implies \exists k \in \mathbb{N} : \forall w \in \Sigma^* : |[\![\mathcal{R}]\!](w)| = O(|w|^k)$$

Some patterns in regexes can cause a loss of precision in the analysis. Consider as example $\Sigma^* |(a|a)^*$ and observe how the matching procedure never explores the right (dangerous) branch of the outermost alternative. However, since the analysis does not consider the order in which the branches are explored (they are merged with $\cup^r$), $\mathcal{E}(\Sigma^* |(a|a)^*, \varepsilon, \varepsilon)$ returns the language $a^+ \overline{a^*}^r$. While our analysis is not complete, our experiments show that over 74,670 regexes taken from real-world use cases, this happens only in 50 instances. This shows that patterns that can make our analysis lose precision rarely occur in practice.

The fact that the analysis returns the language of dangerous words can be useful in different scenarios. For example, it is possible to use our algorithm in a matching engine that tries to match a word only if it is not in the attack language of the input regex. The analysis we put forward can also be integrated with a static analyzer for high-level programming languages: by paring our framework with a sound string analysis, it should be possible to prove the absence of ReDoS vulnerabilities in real-world applications. This is left as future work.

Observe that even though we do not directly support lookaround assertions, it is possible to run the analysis multiple times on each assertion in a regex.

In fact, if none of them is dangerous (i.e., they have empty attack languages), then the initial regex is safe. We also believe that it is possible to automatically overapproximate regexes with backreferences in a sound way (for instance, substituting (a)*\1 with a*a*) to analyze them with our framework, and we would like to explore such extensions in future work.

Table 1. Attributes of the detectors

	Type	Sound	Complete	Language	Deterministic
rat	static	✓	✗	✓	✓
ReScue [29]	dynamic	✗	✓	✗	✗
rexploiter [33]	static	✗	✗	✓	✓
rsa [32]	static	✓	✗	✗	✓
rsa-full [32]	static	✓	✓	✗	✓
rxxr2 [28]	static	✗	✗	✗	✓

5   Experimental Evaluation

To assess the usefulness of the analysis we put forward, we implemented it in the rat [25] tool (**R**eDoS **A**bstract **T**ester) in less than 5000 lines of OCaml code, and we compared it to four other detectors. In our experiments, we wanted to evaluate how rat behaves in terms of precision and performance compared to others. We ran our experiments on a server with 128GB of RAM, with 48 Intel Xeon CPUs E5-2650 v4 @ 2.20GHz and Ubuntu 18.04.5 LTS. We considered the dataset used in [29], composed of: (1) 2,992 patterns from the Regexlib platform [2]; (2) 12,499 patterns from the Snort platform [6]; (3) 13,597 patterns extracted from 3,898 Python projects on Github in [11]. To them, we added 63,352 regexes extracted from modules in the pypi package manager [1] by Davis et al. [15]. From the dataset, we removed the regexes that were not properly sanitized (e.g., that contained non-printable characters) and we removed duplicates, obtaining 74,670 regexes. To the best of our knowledge, it is the first time that such a large dataset of regexes taken from real-world programs is used to compare the precision and performance of ReDoS-detection tools.

In what follows, we say that a detector is *sound* if it identifies as vulnerable all the truly vulnerable regexes, and we say that it is *complete* if all the regexes it identifies as vulnerable are truly vulnerable. Sound detectors forbid *false negatives* and complete detectors forbid *false positives*. The tools we compared rat to are ReScue [29], rexploiter [33], rsa [32] and rxxr2 [28]. In particular, rsa allows the user to improve the precision of the analysis (at the cost of sacrificing some performance) with the "full" mode, that makes it the only sound and complete tool. The only dynamic detector we compare to is ReScue that, due to its nature, never raises false positives. On the other hand, since it relies on a genetic algorithm that generates the input strings with random mutations, the analysis is not deterministic. In Sect. 6, we discuss the details of each approach, and in Table 1 we summarize the characteristics of the tools. While attributes reported in Table 1 summarize the expected behaviour, we found that in practice some detectors do not match the underlying theoretical results. If a detector can extract the language of dangerous words (opposed to a single exploit string) we mark the **Language** column with ✓.

Table 2. Evaluation results

	OK	FP	FN	OOT	RTE	SKIP	TIME
rat	67,049	50	0	181	0	7,390	1:58:29
ReScue	33,541	0	43	32,200	0	8,886	325:54:19
rsa	57,243	190	1	817	242	16,177	19:58:32
rsa-full	54,823	134	1	3,174	399	16,139	39:11:21
rexploiter	53,929	31	180	327	0	20,203	9:42:47
rxxr2	60,792	94	7	11	0	13,766	0:09:37

Precision Comparison. We use the evaluation technique used in [29], which, to the best of our knowledge, is the only article that compares the precision of ReDoS detectors. We analyze each regex with the detectors setting an individual timeout of 30 s, and then we compare the results. If any tool can craft an exploit string of length lesser or equal to 128 characters that makes the Java 8 matching engine perform more than 10^{10} matching steps, we consider the regex to be vulnerable. During our tests, we observed that for the specific matching engine we consider, for strings of length at most 128 characters, 10^{10} matching steps are a sound threshold to clearly distinguish between exponential and non-exponential matching. We cross-reference the results of five different tools (some of which are, at least theoretically, sound) by concretely testing exploit strings on a real-world matching engine, so that we infer with high confidence the number of false positives and false negatives. We classified as vulnerable 313 regexes.

In Table 2, we report the results. The columns correspond to: number of correctly classified regexes (**OK**); false positives (**FP**); false negatives (**FN**); out of time (**OOT**); runtime errors (**RTE**); skipped (**SKIP**) (i.e., not parsed); total runtime displayed as H:MM:SS (**TIME**).

Compared to other static analyzers, rat reports a relatively low number of false positives: 50 over the 67,280 regexes that it parses. The only static analyzer that reports fewer false positives than rat is rexploiter, that on the other hand reports 180 false negatives and skips 20,203 regexes. Interestingly, we observed that in practice rat *is the only detector that does not report false negatives*. This matches our theoretical results, and it gives empirical evidence that our framework performs a sound analysis. We also observe that rat is the detector that parses the highest number of regexes: even more than ReScue, which indeed supports advanced features. This is due to the fact that ReScue does not support some regular patterns such as *named capturing groups* with the syntax (?P<name>pattern), that indeed rat can analyze.

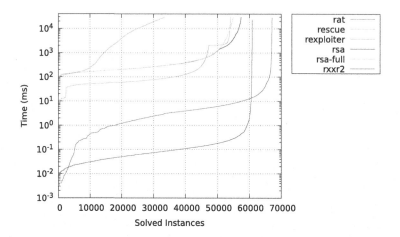

Fig. 4. Survival plot with a logarithmic y axis and linear x axis

Performance Comparison. In case a detector runs out of time for a few regexes, the total runtime in Table 2 grows sharply, not representing precisely the average performance of the tool. For this reason, we use *survival plots* to compare more faithfully the performance of the detectors. On such plot, the y-axis represents the time in milliseconds, and the x-axis is the number of regexes such that each one can be analyzed under the specified time, while the remaining regexes either take longer to analyze or cannot be analyzed by the corresponding detector. No plot for x-axis and detector d means that for $74,670-x$ regexes d did not successfully complete the analysis (i.e., it either ran out of time or it had a parse/runtime error). The plot highlights the relative performance of each tool and how many regexes can be individually analyzed under a time threshold. The survival plot of our experiments is depicted in Fig. 4.

Our experiments showed that `rat` is able to analyze 66,924 regexes over the 67,280 that it parses in less than one second each (∼99.47%). As expected, ReScue is, due to its dynamic nature, significantly slower than static analyzers. After it, we find the cluster composed of `rsa`, `rsa-full` and `rexploiter`. Our detector is on average one to two orders of magnitude faster than them for corresponding points on abscissa x. While `rxxr2` is generally faster than `rat`, we remark that `rat` is performing a strictly more expressive analysis by returning the language of dangerous words. Furthermore, according to Table 2, `rxxr2` is not performing a sound analysis either. We also remark that `rat` analyzes 6,376 more regexes than `rxxr2`.

Discussion. We observed that in practice `rat` is one to two orders of magnitude faster than most detectors, raises a relatively low number of false positives, and it is the only analyzer that does not report false negatives. The approach based on semantic trees significantly improved the analysis' design and the easiness to reason about ReDoS vulnerabilities. It also allowed us to ignore the complexities related to transforming regexes into automata, that for some tools are sources of unsoundness and incompleteness. To the best of our knowledge, our analysis for ReDoS vulnerabilities is the first that operates directly on regexes without having to resort to automata. Regexes also make it easy to implement many performance optimizations. We integrated in `rat` two major performance improvements.

- *Character Classes Representation.* Character classes are features commonly used by programmers. For example, \d is a shortcut for $0|1|\ldots|9$. We extend the regexes to recognize *sets of characters* instead of simple characters. With a slight adjustment to our implementation, regexes containing character classes considerably decreased their size. For example, $0|\ldots|9$ has 19 constructs, while $\{0,\ldots,9\}$ is a regex with a single character set construct.
- *Symbolic Operations.* In our analysis, we perform a large number of intersection and complement operations. Instead of running the algorithm to compute them, we extend again the regexes to support *symbolic intersection* and *symbolic complement*. When a complement or an intersection must be computed, we simply add its symbolic representation to the result.

6   Related Work

Wüstholz et al. [33] put forward an analysis based on automata to detect ReDoS vulnerabilities, and they implement it the `rexploiter` tool. Their approach is the closest to ours, since they can as well extract the language of dangerous words. However, the analysis is not sound nor complete, because transforming a regex into an automaton can introduce or remove vulnerabilities. For example, applying Glushkov's construction [17] to the vulnerable regex $(a^*)^*$ we obtain a non-vulnerable automaton (with respect to [33, Defn. 3]). Since they do not define an algorithm to transform regexes into automata that preserves vulnerabilities, the analysis can report both false positives and false negatives, and our experiments confirmed this.

The `rxxr2` tool is a static analyzer for exponential ReDoS vulnerabilities that infers exploit strings [28]. It is the successor of `rxxr` [19], that turned out to be unsound. Introducing a novel approach based on NFAs with prioritized transitions, `rxxr2` infers strings that can be *pumped* and lead to exponential matching. While the algorithm is sound and complete with respect to automata, transforming regexes to automata can introduce or remove vulnerabilities. Similarly to `rexploiter`, they assume that the input regex has been converted into an automaton following one of the standard constructions, so that the analysis is actually neither sound nor complete.

The framework of *prioritized NFAs* (pNFAs) [9,10] has been leveraged by Weideman et al. [32] to build the `rsa` (**R**egex**S**tatic**A**nalysis) static analyzer.

The authors introduce an algorithm to translate regexes into automata that preserves the ReDoS vulnearbilities. The automata are analyzed with the framework described in [7] to determine the *degree of ambiguity* [31], which allows inferring whether there are ReDoS vulnerabilities or not. The *full* mode performs a sound and complete analysis, while the *simple* mode is only sound, but it usually runs faster. We observe that while the analysis is complete, it is strictly less expressive than ours. In fact, their framework cannot be used to extract the attack language for a regular expression, but only a finite number of exploit strings. For this reason, the two approaches are suitable for different uses: tools that need the specification of dangerous words, such as static analyzers, cannot rely on `rsa` to extract it. Furthermore, our algorithm performs a single *emptyness check* of the attack language, while their analysis performs a *universality check* for each state of the automaton, resulting in a strictly higher complexity. Our experiments confirm that our analysis has a substantial performance advantage over the one proposed in [32].

A radically different approach to ReDoS detection is dynamic analysis. The `ReScue` tool [29] leverages a genetic algorithm to efficiently generate potentially dangerous words, that are then matched by the Java matching engine to determine if they are truly dangerous. For this reason, the tool cannot report false positives. On the other hand, there is no guarantee about the absence of false negatives. The gray-box approach makes it easy to support a wide variety of advanced features, but it has the disadvantage to be several orders of magnitude slower than static analyzers. The analysis is not deterministic, and due to its dynamic nature it is not expressive enough to compute the attack language.

Recently, many techniques have been proposed to mitigate ReDoS attacks. Cody-Kenny et al. [12] use genetic programming to substitute vulnerable regexes with safe ones. Li et al. [20] and Pan et al. [24] put forward techniques for automatic regex repair based on examples. In [14] the authors introduce a matching algorithm that leverages selective memoization to mitigate ReDoS attacks while supporting advanced regex features. Sophisticated techniques based on GPU matching [21,34] and state-merging algorithms [8] have also been proposed to speedup the matching.

7   Conclusions

In this paper, we defined a tree semantics for regular expression matching, which we leveraged to design a sound static analysis that detects ReDoS vulnerabilities. To the best of our knowledge, our ReDoS detection framework is the first one that operates directly on regexes without having to resort to automata. This allowed us to easily reason about the concrete behaviour of complex matching engines, and it opened the possibility to integrate significant performance optimizations.

We implemented our analysis in the `rat` tool, and to assess the effectiveness of our technique, we compared it to four other detectors. We found `rat` to be on average one to two orders of magnitude faster than most tools, while giving strong guarantees about the soundness of the analysis. While raising a relatively low the number of false positives, `rat` is the only ReDoS detector that did not report false negatives.

In future work, would we would like to extend our analysis to support advanced features such as backreferences and lookarounds. We believe that it is possible to automatically overapproximate those features with regular constructs in a sound way. Another interesting extension of this paper would be to integrate our framework in a static analyzer for high-level languages such as Python. We believe that by pairing `rat` with a string analysis, it is possible to prove the absence of ReDoS vulnerabilities in real-world applications.

References

1. The PyPI packet manager. https://pypi.org/. Accessed 09 May 2022
2. Regexlib database. https://regexlib.com/. Accessed 09 May 2022
3. Stack overflow outage postmortem (2016). https://stackstatus.net/post/147710624694/outage-postmortem-july-20-2016. Accessed 09 May 2022
4. Cloudflare's outage postmortem (2019). https://blog.cloudflare.com/details-of-the-cloudflare-outage-on-july-2-2019/. Accessed 09 May 2022
5. National vulnerability database: CVE-2020-3899 (2020). https://nvd.nist.gov/vuln/detail/CVE-2020-3899. Accessed 09 May 2022
6. The snort database (2020). http://www.snort.org/. Accessed 09 May 2022
7. Allauzen, C., Mohri, M., Rastogi, A.: General algorithms for testing the ambiguity of finite automata and the double-tape ambiguity of finite-state transducers. Int. J. Found. Comput. Sci. **22**(04), 883–904 (2011). https://doi.org/10.1142/s0129054111008477
8. Becchi, M., Cadambi, S.: Memory-efficient regular expression search using state merging. In: Joint Conference of the IEEE Computer and Communications Societies, INFOCOM, pp. 1064–1072 (2007). https://doi.org/10.1109/INFCOM.2007.128
9. Berglund, M., Drewes, F., van der Merwe, B.: Analyzing catastrophic backtracking behavior in practical regular expression matching. In: Automata and Formal Languages, AFL. EPTCS, vol. 151, pp. 109–123 (2014). https://doi.org/10.4204/EPTCS.151.7
10. Berglund, M., van der Merwe, B.: On the semantics of regular expression parsing in the wild. Theor. Comput. Sci. **679**, 69–82 (2017). https://doi.org/10.1016/j.tcs.2016.09.006
11. Chapman, C., Stolee, K.T.: Exploring regular expression usage and context in Python. In: International Symposium on Software Testing and Analysis, ISSTA, pp. 282–293. ACM (2016). https://doi.org/10.1145/2931037.2931073
12. Cody-Kenny, B., Fenton, M., Ronayne, A., Considine, E., McGuire, T., O'Neill, M.: A search for improved performance in regular expressions. In: Genetic and Evolutionary Computation Conference, GECCO, pp. 1280–1287 (2017). https://doi.org/10.1145/3071178.3071196
13. Crosby, S.A., Wallach, D.S.: Denial of service via algorithmic complexity attacks. In: USENIX Security Symposium. USENIX Association (2003). https://doi.org/10.1007/11506881_10
14. Davis, J.C., Servant, F., Lee, D.: Using selective memoization to defeat regular expression denial of service (ReDoS). In: IEEE Symposium on Security and Privacy, SP, pp. 543–559. IEEE Computer Society (2021). https://doi.org/10.1109/SP40001.2021.00032

15. Davis, J.C., Coghlan, C.A., Servant, F., Lee, D.: The impact of regular expression denial of service (ReDoS) in practice: an empirical study at the ecosystem scale. In: Joint Meeting on European Software Engineering Conference and Symposium on the Foundations of Software Engineering, ESEC/SIGSOFT FSE, pp. 246–256. ACM (2018). https://doi.org/10.1145/3236024.3236027

16. Friedl, J.E.F.: Mastering Regular Expressions - Understand Your Data and Be More Productive: For Perl, PHP, Java,NET, Ruby, and More, 3rd edn. O'Reilly (2006). https://www.oreilly.com/library/view/mastering-regular-expressions/0596528124/

17. Glushkov, V.M.: The abstract theory of automata. Russ. Math. Surv. **16**(5), 1 (1961)

18. Michael, L.G., Donohue, J., Davis, J.C., Lee, D., Servant, F.: Regexes are hard: decision-making, difficulties, and risks in programming regular expressions. In: International Conference on Automated Software Engineering, ASE, pp. 415–426. IEEE (2019). https://doi.org/10.1109/ASE.2019.00047

19. Kirrage, J., Rathnayake, A., Thielecke, H.: Static analysis for regular expression denial-of-service attacks. In: Lopez, J., Huang, X., Sandhu, R. (eds.) NSS 2013. LNCS, vol. 7873, pp. 135–148. Springer, Heidelberg (2013). https://doi.org/10.1007/978-3-642-38631-2_11

20. Li, Y., et al.: FlashRegex: deducing anti-redos regexes from examples. In: International Conference on Automated Software Engineering, ASE 2020, pp. 659–671 (2020). https://doi.org/10.1145/3324884.3416556

21. Lin, C., Liu, C., Chang, S.: Accelerating regular expression matching using hierarchical parallel machines on GPU. In: Global Communications Conference, GLOBECOM, pp. 1–5 (2011). https://doi.org/10.1109/GLOCOM.2011.6133663

22. López, F., Romero, V.: Mastering Python Regular Expressions. Packt Publishing Ltd. (2014). https://www.packtpub.com/product/mastering-python-regular-expressions/9781783283156

23. Owens, S., Reppy, J., Turon, A.: Regular-expression derivatives re-examined. J. Funct. Program. **19**(2), 173–190 (2009). https://doi.org/10.1017/s0956796808007090

24. Pan, R., Hu, Q., Xu, G., D'Antoni, L.: Automatic repair of regular expressions. Proc. ACM Program. Lang. **3**(OOPSLA), 139:1–139:29 (2019). https://doi.org/10.1145/3360565

25. Parolini, F., Miné, A.: RAT - ReDoS Abstract Tester (2022). https://github.com/parof/rat

26. Petsios, T., Zhao, J., Keromytis, A.D., Jana, S.: SlowFuzz: automated domain-independent detection of algorithmic complexity vulnerabilities. In: Conference on Computer and Communications Security, CCS, pp. 2155–2168. ACM (2017). https://doi.org/10.1145/3133956.3134073

27. Rathnayake, A.: Semantics, analysis and security of backtracking regular expression matchers. Ph.D. thesis, University of Birmingham, UK (2015). http://etheses.bham.ac.uk/6011/

28. Rathnayake, A., Thielecke, H.: Static analysis for regular expression exponential runtime via substructural logics. CoRR abs/1405.7058 (2014)

29. Shen, Y., Jiang, Y., Xu, C., Yu, P., Ma, X., Lu, J.: ReScue: crafting regular expression DoS attacks. In: International Conference on Automated Software Engineering, ASE, pp. 225–235. ACM (2018). https://doi.org/10.1145/3238147.3238159

30. Staicu, C., Pradel, M.: Freezing the web: a study of ReDoS vulnerabilities in JavaScript-based web servers. In: USENIX Security Symposium, pp. 361–376. USENIX Association (2018)

31. Weber, A., Seidl, H.: On the degree of ambiguity of finite automata. Theor. Comput. Sci. **88**(2), 325–349 (1991). https://doi.org/10.1016/0304-3975(91)90381-B
32. Weideman, N., van der Merwe, B., Berglund, M., Watson, B.: Analyzing matching time behavior of backtracking regular expression matchers by using ambiguity of NFA. In: Han, Y.-S., Salomaa, K. (eds.) CIAA 2016. LNCS, vol. 9705, pp. 322–334. Springer, Cham (2016). https://doi.org/10.1007/978-3-319-40946-7_27
33. Wüstholz, V., Olivo, O., Heule, M.J.H., Dillig, I.: Static detection of DoS vulnerabilities in programs that use regular expressions. In: Legay, A., Margaria, T. (eds.) TACAS 2017. LNCS, vol. 10206, pp. 3–20. Springer, Heidelberg (2017). https://doi.org/10.1007/978-3-662-54580-5_1
34. Yu, X., Becchi, M.: GPU acceleration of regular expression matching for large datasets: exploring the implementation space. In: Computing Frontiers Conference, CF, pp. 18:1–18:10 (2013). https://doi.org/10.1145/2482767.2482791

On Verification of Smart Contracts via Model Checking

Yulong Bao[1,2], Xue-Yang Zhu[1,2(✉)], Wenhui Zhang[1,2], Wuwei Shen[3],
Pengfei Sun[1,2], and Yingqi Zhao[1,2]

[1] State Key Laboratory of Computer Science, Institute of Software, Chinese
Academy of Sciences, Beijing, China
{baoyl,zxy,zwh,sunpf,zhaoyq}@ios.ac.cn
[2] University of the Chinese Academy of Sciences, Beijing, China
[3] Department of Computer Science, Western Michigan University,
Kalamazoo, MI, USA
wuwei.shen@wmich.edu

Abstract. Combined with smart contracts, the application of blockchain techniques has grown faster and broader. However, it is very difficult to write secure and functionally correct smart contracts because of the openness of blockchain platforms. Formal verification, such as model checking, has been proven to be an effective way of guaranteeing security and correctness of systems. In this paper, we propose a novel model checking based framework, called mcVer, to support the verification of smart contracts written in Solidity. Built on model checking tool VERDS, the mcVer framework is able to verify not only safety properties but also liveness properties of smart contracts. For the properties that are not satisfied, mcVer produces a counter example by showing a sequence of statements in the original Solidity program as a hint for fault localization. We implemented the automatic transformation from a subset of the Solidity language to the modeling language of VERDS, that therefore provides automatic verification for smart contracts. Experiments are carried out on various cases, including checking contracts for finding typical security vulnerabilities and verifying properties of an access control smart contract. The experimental results demonstrate the flexibility and efficiency of mcVer.

1 Introduction

Since Bitcoin was first introduced in 2009 [32], the blockchain has been regarded as a promising but yet challenging technology. According to a recent study by Garther [16], the market value for the blockchain-based technology can exceed $3.1 trillion by 2030. Many cloud platform giants such as Microsoft, IBM, Amazon, Oracle have proposed Blockchain-as-a-Service (BaaS) solutions to support various enterprise scenarios such as financial services and supply chains. These

This work is partially supported by the National Natural Science Foundation of China
(No. 62072443).

Y. Aït-Ameur and F. Crăciun (Eds.): TASE 2022, LNCS 13299, pp. 92–112, 2022.
https://doi.org/10.1007/978-3-031-10363-6_7

solutions are based on programs called smart contracts [40]. However, due to the openness of blockchain platforms, people have suffered some devastating consequence caused by the errors in smart contracts. For instance, the infamous The DAO exploit [4] resulted in the loss of almost $60 million worth of Ether, and the Parity Wallet error caused $169 million worth of Ether to be locked forever [41]. Obviously, unsafe smart contracts not only result in huge financial loss but also seriously undermine the confidence about the development of blockchain-based technologies.

Realizing the importance of safe and secure smart contracts, researchers have conducted various types of studies [25, 27, 44] to reveal the nature of unsafe smart contracts as well as to detect such problems. As reported, many common vulnerabilities in the blockchain domain are related to nondeterminism [46], which is actually caused by concurrent calls. Model checking [17] has been successfully applied in the verification for many modern software systems with the concurrency feature. Generally, model checking techniques can be used to check various properties expressed by temporal logics [28], including safety properties and liveness properties. A *safety property* specifies that something bad never happens, while a *liveness property* specifies that something good will eventually happen, playing an important role in the correctness of smart contracts. Security requirements are usually a kind of safety properties.

While model checking techniques are promising for reducing the potential threats and errors of smart contracts, they currently require the skill of writing formal models and logic formulas, which is challenging for engineers who do not have solid mathematical background. Learning how to write formal models and specifications increases the learning curve and thus reduces the applicability of these techniques. We propose in this paper a novel framework **mcVer** to ease the difficulty of using model checking techniques and deal with the diversity of smart contract properties.

Our framework **mcVer** uses model checking tool VERDS [50] as the foundation to support the verification of smart contracts written in Solidity, which is a smart contract language of Ethereum [47]. The contributions of this paper are summarized as follows.

1. The **mcVer** framework is able to verify not only safety properties but also liveness properties of smart contracts. For the properties that are not satisfied, mcVer produces a counter example by showing a sequence of statements in the original Solidity program as a hint for fault localization.
2. We provide automatic verification for smart contracts by means of the automatic transformation from a subset of the Solidity language to the modeling language of VERDS.
3. We implement the framework and apply it to several case studies, including checking some typical security vulnerabilities and verifying properties, including liveness properties, of an access control smart contract [51].

The remainder of this paper is organized as follows. Related work is reviewed in Sect. 2. Solidity and VERDS are introduced in Sect. 3. We present the general idea of **mcVer** framework in Sect. 4 and illustrate the technical details in Sects. 5,

6 and 7. Case studies and experiments are shown in Sect. 8. Section 9 concludes and discusses limitations of **mcVer** and the future work.

2   Related Work

Luu Loi [27] and Atzei [9] summarized several types of common security vulnerabilities, such as Transaction-Ordering Dependency (TOD) and Reentrancy Vulnerability. Based on these types of common security vulnerabilities, a number of research efforts have been made to ensure the safety and security for smart contracts. The most explored are testing based techniques [21,48] and static analysis-based techniques, usually based on the symbolic execution, including Oyente [27], Securify [45], Slither [18], ETHBMC [20], Mythril [42], Sol-Met [22], SmartCheck [43], Ethainter [12], Manticore [30], VeriSmart [38] and FAIRCON [26]. However, these approaches heavily depend on known security patterns to detect errors and cannot guarantee the functional correctness in blockchain-based applications.

To overcome the limitation of above-mentioned approaches, formal verification techniques [15] have been proposed to verify the correctness of smart contracts. Research on formal verification of smart contracts starts with theorem proving based approaches. Hirai [24] uses theorem prover Isabelle [35] to verify smart contracts [23] and uses the Lem [31] to define a formal model for the Ethereum virtual machine (EVM). Bhargavan et al. [11] convert Solidity and EVM bytecode contracts into functional programming language F* [39]. Nehai et al. [34] translate smart contracts into models of Why3 [19]. The verification procedures in this kind of approaches generally require user's interaction and are difficult to deal with liveness properties. The verification procedure of **mcVer** is automatic and not only safety properties but also liveness properties can be verified in **mcVer**.

Model checking based techniques are also studied by many researchers. Albert et al. [7] use existing verification engines developed for C programs [10] to verify safety properties of low-level EVM code. Sukrit Kalra et al. [25] present ZEUS, which uses bounded model checking techniques to verify safety properties of smart contracts. Anton Permenev et al. [36] present VerX, which combines reduction of temporal safety verification to reachability checking, with symbolic execution and delayed abstraction. Mavridou [29], Nehai [33] and Abdellatif [8] present their work based on the model checking tool NuSMV [14]. A model-based framework VeriSolid is proposed in [29], which focuses more on the code generation procedure rather than verifying Solidity source code. Authors of [33] and [8] present work that verifies particular smart contracts. The former focuses on the contracts in the energy market field and the latter tries to verify a supply chain management smart contract. The NuSMV based methods are possible to deal with more properties, but existing work does not provide methodological techniques to support the verification of commonly developed contracts. Our framework **mcVer** is able not only to verify various properties but also implements the related tool to smooth the verification procedure that starts directly from the Solidity source code. The tool may return a counter example when a property is not satisfied, providing a further help for debugging. To the best of our knowledge, none of the formal method based work for the verification of smart contracts is able to provide such a functionality.

3   Solidity and VERDS

3.1   Solidity

Solidity is a programming language developed to write smart contracts that run on the EVM. A Solidity smart contract mainly consists of two parts, the variable declaration and the function definition. The former defines state variables used by the contract and the latter specifies the potential behavior of the contract. Figure 1, for example, shows partial code of our running example, aucSC, a simple auction contract modified from [1].

```
1  pragma solidity ^0.4.22;
2  contract Auction{
3      address public bene;
4      address public hBidder;
5      uint public hBid;
6      bool ended;
7      constructor(address _beneficiary)
           public {
8          bene = _beneficiary;
9      }
10     function bid() public payable{
11         require(!ended);
12         require(msg.value > hBid);
13         if (hBid!=0 ) {
14             require(hBidder.send(hBid)
                   );
15         }
16         hBidder = msg.sender;
17         hBid = msg.value;
18     }
19     function aucEnd() public{
20         require(!ended);
21         ended = true;
22         bene.send(hBid);
23     }
24 }
```

Fig. 1. aucSC, a smart contract for auction.

State variables of a smart contract are variables whose values are permanently stored in the blockchain and each has a type. For example, variables *bene* and *hBidder*, indicate addresses of the beneficiary and the current highest bidder of the auction, respectively. Variable *hBid* denotes the current highest bid and variable *ended* indicates whether an auction is ended or not.

Besides global state variables, there are implicit global variables that are defined by the EVM, including related accounts and balances. Once an account is created on the blockchain, it has an address as its identification and a variable to record the changes of its balance. When an account uses a smart contract, its address is the value of *msg.sender*, which is used but not defined in the contract. See aucSC for example. Accounts related to a smart contract include the account that deploys it (its owner), the accounts that use it (its users), and some accounts specified by the contract, e.g. the address of the beneficiary in sucSC. The balances related include its own balance and balances of the related accounts.

A function consists local variable declaration and statements. Functions can receive data via parameters, perform computation, manipulate state variables, and interact with other accounts. Functions are defined to operate on the states of the contract. The *constructor()* is a special function that is executed only once when the contract is deployed on the blockchain. The account who calls *constructor()* is the owner of the contract. Other functions can be called and executed many times during the lifecycle of the contract. For example, function *bid()*, which defines the bidding behavior, can be executed by arbitrary number of users before *aucEnd()*, which sets variable *ended* to be true. A function may also operate on the implicit global variables. An execution of a function may receive *msg.value* amount of money from its trigger *msg.sender*, and change the balances of related accounts.

We consider a subset of Solidity language that are sufficient to express most contracts. The supported subset is summarized in Fig. 2.

$$
\begin{aligned}
type ::=&\ address|bool|uint|mapping|enum|array|struct \\
operator ::=&\ +|-|*|/|++|--|+=|-=|*=|/= \\
logic\ op ::=&\ ||\ |\ \&\&\ |\ >\ |\ <\ |\ >=\ |\ <=\ |\ ! \\
statement ::=&\ assignment\ |\ condition\ statement \\
&\ |\ for\ statement\ |\ while\ statement \\
&\ |\ \textbf{continue}\ |\ \textbf{break}\ |\ \textbf{return}\ |\ \textbf{throw}\ |\ \textbf{require}
\end{aligned}
$$

Fig. 2. Subset of Solidity language **mcVer** supports

A call to a function of a contract activates an execution. The execution terminates after successfully updating the state of blockchain, or aborting and rolling back to the state before the call. While smart contracts allow the concurrent calls, the executions of concurrent calls are sequential due to the execution model of EVM [37]. We take this into account when formalize smart contracts.

3.2   Model Checking Tool VERDS

Model checking is considered one of the most practical applications of theoretical computer science in the verification of concurrent systems. The basic idea of model checking is to use the state transition system (S) to represent the behavior of the system, and the modal formula (F) to describe the properties of the system. In this way, the question of whether the system has the desired properties can be transformed into a question of whether S satisfies F. For finite state systems, this problem is algorithmically decidable. We use VERDS as the verification engine. VERDS is a model checking tool that has been applied in many aspects, such as the verification of SystemC design [49] and the verification of multi-agent systems [13]. The input to a model checking tool usually includes a system model and a specification. The modeling language of VERDS is called VERDS modeling language (VML). A verification model specified in VML is called a VERDS verification model (VVM), including a system model defined by the *guarded command transition systems* and specifications expressed by the *computation tree logic* (CTL).

Suppose p is any propositional atom, then CTL has the syntax given as follows.

$$
\begin{aligned}
\varPhi ::=&\ p|\neg\varPhi|\varPhi \wedge \varPhi|\varPhi \vee \varPhi|A\varPsi|E\varPsi \\
\varPsi ::=&\ X\varPhi|F\varPhi|G\varPhi|(\varPhi U\varPhi)
\end{aligned}
$$

Among them, Φ is the CTL formula and Ψ is the auxiliary path formula. The set of operators of CTL formula is divided into path operators and temporal operators. There are two kinds of path operators: $A\Psi$ indicates that on all paths Ψ should be true, and $E\Psi$ indicates that Ψ should be true on at least one path. The temporal operators are X, F, G, U. Two kinds of temporal operators are used in this paper: $F\Phi$ indicates that Φ will eventually be true on a certain state on a path; $G\Phi$ indicates that Φ should be satisfied for all the states on a path. Properties to be checked on guarded transition system can be of various kinds:

- safety: 'something bad never happens' is usually expressed in CTL as $AG(\neg p)$;
- liveness: 'something good will eventually happen' is usually expressed in CTL as $AF(p)$.

Each VVM consists of six parts: global alias definition, global variable declaration, initialization, module definition, process instantiation, and property specification. These six parts are distinguished by keywords DEFINE, VAR, INIT, MODULE, PROC and SPEC, respectively. Variables should be bounded.

A module in VVM is a template of a transition system, defined under keyword MODULE. Each module consists of four parts: module identifier and list of parameters, local variables declaration (VAR), local variables initialization (INIT), and collection of transitions (TRANS). A transition consists of two parts: logical expressions (guard) and assignments (command). When the logical expression is true, the assignment statement will be executed atomically. When logical expressions in different transitions are true at the same time, a random one of them will be executed. A process in PROC part is an instance of a module; a local variable x in a process $p0$ can be accessed using the form $p0.x$. Properties under verification are specified in SPEC part. If a property does not hold, a counterexample can be found in the CEX file returned by VERDS.

4   Overview of mcVer Framework

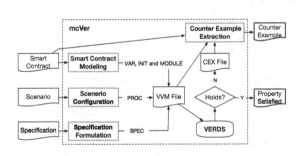

Fig. 3. Overall framework of **mcVer** .

The framework of **mcVer** is shown in Fig. 3, in which our main contributions are in boxes with purple border. The smart contract under verification are either entirely or partly translated into the VAR, INIT, and MODULE parts of a VVM; the scenario corresponds to the PROC part, and the specification is formulated as CTL formulas in the SPEC part. The model checker VERDS is then used to verify whether the smart contract satisfies required properties. If a property is not satisfied,

VERDS returns the trace indicating the problematic behavior in a CEX file. A counter example on the Solidity level is then extracted from it.

We present *Smart contract modeling* in the next section, *Scenario Configuration* and *Specification Formulation* in Sect. 6, and *Counter Example Extraction* in Sect. 7. Smart contract aucSC (Fig. 1) will be used as running example to help illustrating our ideas. Part of its corresponding VVM, aucVVM, is shown in Fig. 4. Details will be explained in the later sections.

```
1 DEFINE MAX=10                                          37    TRANS
2 VAR                                                    38      pc=0 & pCtrl=1 & order=1: pc=1 & pCtrl=0;
3     bene:{A,B,C,D,E,X,Z};  hBidder:{A,B,C,D,E,X,Z};    39      pc=1 & ended=0:          pc=2;
4     hBid:0..10; ended:0..1;                            40      pc=2 & msg_value>hBid:   pc=3;
5     balance[{A,B,C,D,E,Z}]:0..MAX; //global balance    41      pc=3 & hBid!=0:          pc=4;
6     pCtrl:0..1;      order:0..3;                        42      pc=4:    pc=5 & rcv=hBidder & amount==hBid & sta=1;
7     level0:0..1; level1:0..3; level2:0..1;             43      pc=5 & sta=0:            pc=6;
8     sta:0..1;   rtv:0..1;                              44      pc=6 & rtv=1:            pc=7;
9     rcv:{A,B,C,D,E,X}; amount:0..MAX;                  45      pc=3 & hBid=0:           pc=7;
10 INIT                                                   46      pc=7:              pc=8 & hBidder=msg_sender;
11     bene=X;  hBidder=X;   //X represents a Null address 47     pc=8:              pc=9 & hBid=msg_value ;
12     hBid=0; ended=0;                                   48      pc=1 & ended=1:          pc=9;
13     for{p:{A,B,C,D,E}}{balance[p]=5};  balance[Z]=0;   49      pc=2 & msg_value<=hBid:  pc=9;
14     pCtrl=0; order=0; // execution order control       50      pc=6 & rtv!=1:           pc=9;
15     level0=0; level1=0; level2=0;                      51      pc=9: pCtrl=1 & level1=level1+1 & balance[Z]=balance[Z]+msg_value
16     sta=0;  rtv=0; // send function                               & balance[msg_sender]=balance[msg_sender]-msg_value;
17     rcv=X;   amount=0;                                 52 MODULE send()
18 PROC                                                   53    VAR    pc:0..3;
19     o1: porderctrl();                                  54    INIT    pc=0;
20     p0: constructor(A,0,A);                            55    TRANS
21     p1: bid(B,2);       p2: bid(C,3);                  56      pc=0 & sta=1: pc=1;
22     p3: bid(D,4);       p4: aucEnd(A,0);               57      pc=1:          pc=2 & rtv=1;
23     s0: send();                                        58      pc=1:          pc=3 & rtv=0;
24 SPEC                                                   59      pc=2 :       pc=3 & balance[Z]=balance[Z]-amount
25     AF((order=3)&((hBidder=B)|(hBidder=C)|(hBidder=D)); //aucPr1          & balance[rcv]=balance[rcv]+amount;
26     AG(!(order=3)|(hBidder=D));               //aucPr2  60      pc=3:          pc=0 & sta=0;
27 MODULE porderctrl() // execution order control         61 MODULE constructor(msg_sender,msg_value, bene)
28    VAR                                                 62    VAR     pc:0..2;
29    INIT                                                63    INIT    pc =0;
30    TRANS                                               64    TRANS
31      level0=1&order=0:order=1;                         65      pc=0 & order=0: pc=1;
32      level1=3&order=1:order=2;                         66      pc=1: pc=2 & bene=_bene;
33      level2=1&order=2:order=3;                         67      pc=2: pCtrl=1 & level1=level1+1
34 MODULE bid(msg_sender,msg_value)                                  & balance[0]=balance[0]+msg_value
35    VAR   pc:0..9;                                                 & balance[msg_sender]=balance[msg_sender]-msg_value;
36    INIT pc=0;
```

Fig. 4. aucVVM, the corresponding VVM of aucSC.

5   Smart Contract Modeling

The behavior of smart contracts is defined by the *guarded command transition system*. To be intuitive, we describe the semantics of smart contracts directly with the VML. We discuss key points of mapping behavior of the EVM, variables, functions and function call in smart contracts to VVMs in this section.

Behavior of EVM. Due to the execution model of EVM, transactions are executed in a single-threaded manner. A boolean variable *pCtrl* is declared to control the execution of processes and is false by default. Only when *pCtrl* is true, a process except for that of *constructor* can move to the next step. When a process ends its execution, it releases the control by setting *pCtrl* to be true. Function *constructor* executes only once before all other functions. It needs not to check *pCtrl* to go. For example, a process instantiated from module *bid* in Fig. 4 is waiting until the control variable *pCtrl* becoming true (Line 38) to start its execution and change *pCtrl* to be false to block other process. It sets *pCtrl* to be true at the end of its execution (Line 51).

Related balances are explicitly defined as a global array *balance* in VVM. They are defined at Line 5 and initialized at Line 13 in Fig. 4, for example. The trigger address *msg.sender* and the amount of money *msg.value* are modeled as two parameters of each module in the VVM. See Line 34 in Fig. 4 for example. Changes of balances of related accounts are coded in the last transition of the module of each function.

State Variables. State variables of smart contracts are accordingly defined as bounded integer (in the VAR part) and initialized (in the INIT part) in the VVM. For readability, we use characters to represent the values of variables with address type. The address of contract under verification is set to be 'Z' by default. For example, Lines 3–4 and 11–12 in Fig. 4 are definition and initialization of state variables of aucSC in aucVVM. Constants is defined in the DEFINE part.

Functions. A function in a contract is modeled by a module in VVM, which is a guarded command transition system. By this we in fact define a transition system semantics for the behavior of contracts. Let S be the set of statements in a function and P_s be the label of statement s. Each statement in S is modeled as one or multiple transitions in VVM. Each module in VVM has an extra local variable pc to model the change of P_s. The mapping of statements in the subset of Solidity (Fig. 2) to VML is shown in Table. 1. The module in VVM of *bid()* in aucSC (Fig. 1) is shown in Fig. 4 (Lines 34–51). Line 34 declares the module identifier.

Table 1. Statements mapping

statement	solidity		VML
assignment	P_{s1}	$y = e;$	$pc = P_{s1} : y = e \ \& pc = P_{s2};$
	P_{s2}		
condition	P_{s1}	$if\,(cond)\,\{$	
	P_{s2}	$\ldots$	$pc = P_{s1} \ \& cond : pc = P_{s2};$
		$\}else\{$	$pc = P_{s1} \ \&!cond : pc = P_{s3};$
	P_{s3}	$\ldots\}$	
while	P_{s1}	$while\,(cond)\{$	$pc = P_{s1} \ \& cond : pc = P_{s2};$
	P_{s2}	$\ldots$	$pc = P_{s1} \ \&!cond : pc = P_{s4};$
	P_{s3}	$\}$	$pc = P_{s3} : pc = P_{s1};$
	P_{s4}	$\ldots$	
for	P_{s1}	$for(i = 0;\,cond;\,st)\{$	$pc = P_{s1} \ \& cond : pc = P_{s2};$
	P_{s2}	$\ldots$	$pc = P_{s1} \ \&!cond : pc = P_{s4};$
	P_{s3}	$\}$	$pc = P_{s3} : st \ \& pc = P_{s1};$
	P_{s4}	$\ldots$	
break		$while(cond_1)\{$	
		$\quad if(cond_2)\{$	
	P_{s1}	$\qquad break;\}$	$pc = P_{s1} : pc = P_{s2};$
		$\ldots\}$	
	P_{s2}	$\ldots$	
continue		$while(cond_1)\{$	
		$\quad if(cond_2)\{$	$pc = P_{s2} : pc = P_{s1};$
	P_{s2}	$\qquad continue;\}$	
		$\ldots\}$	
throw		$function\quad foo()\{$	
retrun		$\quad if(cond)\{$	
	P_{s1}	$\qquad throw;\}$	$pc = P_{s1} : pc = P_{s2};$
		$\ldots$	
	P_{s2}	$\}$	
require		$function\quad foo()\{$	
	P_{s1}	$\quad require(cond);$	$pc = P_{s1} \ \& cond : pc = P_{s2};$
	P_{s2}	$\ldots$	$pc = P_{s1} \ \&!cond : pc = P_{s3};$
	P_{s3}	$\}$	

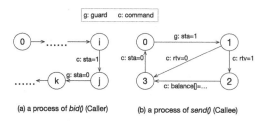

(a) a process of *bid()* (Caller)   (b) a process of *send()* (Callee)

Fig. 5. Illustration of function call.

Function Call. We use shared variables to handle calls between functions, which may be in the same contract or not. The caller and callee can execute in parallel, with the blocking feature. Once one function is active, the other one is blocked. Some callees may return uncertain values because they are defined outside and controlled by the environment, such as functions *transfer()* and *send()*. We model this uncertainty by using non-deterministic choice of transitions in a module.

A module to model function *send()* called in *bid()* in aucSC is shown in Lines 52–60 in Fig. 4, for example. Auxiliary variables *sta*, *rtv*, *rcv* and *amount* are defined as global variables (Lines 8–9) to model starting or ending the process, returned value, the address of the sender and the amount of money sent, respectively. A process of module *send()* starts when $sta = 1$ and sets *sta* to 0 and returns *rtv* when it finishes. At Lines 57 and 58, VERDS randomly chooses one transition to execute and so is the value of *rtv*. This makes the returned value non-deterministic. When *bid()* is trying to call *send()* (Line 42), it sets *sta* to 1 and then the execution does not resume until *sta* becomes 0. The interaction between the caller and the callee in a function call is depicted in Fig. 5.

6   Scenario Configuration and Specification Formulation

6.1   Scenario Configuration

A scenario defines how a contract is used. Since smart contracts are deployed on the blockchain, which is an open environment, the order of calls to its functions are not deterministic. This uncertainty is modeled as concurrency in **mcVer**. In some cases, e.g. sequential transactions submitted by the same account, the corresponding functions, i.e. callees, should be scheduled to execute sequentially.

We propose a scenario definition language (SDL), which is simple but capable of expressing both sequential and concurrent executions of function. Sequential execution of functions is separated by line shift and concurrent execution of functions is separated by symbol '|'. For example, in contract aucSC shown in Fig. 1, users can only call function *bid()* after the contract has been deployed. After its deployment (*constructor()*); there may be multiple users bidding at the same time; the owner may call function *aucEnd()* to end it. Suppose the owner is A and there are three bidders B, C and D bidding with amount 2, 3, 4, respectively. After the owner has deployed the contract on the blockchain, the three bidders can bid in any order. Then the owner ends the auction. The scenario, named aucSNR, is formulated in SDL as:

$$p0 : constructor(A, 0, A)$$
$$p1 : bid(B, 2) \mid p2 : bid(C, 3) \mid p3 : bid(D, 4)$$
$$p4 : aucEnd(A, 0)$$

This scenario is then translated into the PROC part of the VVM (Lines 18–23 in Fig. 4). The three biddings can be executed in any order, but can only be executed sequentially due to the execution model of the EVM. The execution order is controlled by variable *order*. The variable *leveli* indicates how many processes have been executed so far under *order* $= i$. Intuitively, variable *order* controls line execution, while *leveli* controls the execution of processes in the same line. For scenario aucSNR, for example, we have *level0* $\in [0, 1]$ and *level1* $\in [1, 3]$ because only one process $p0$ is executed under *order* $= 0$ but three concurrent processes $p1$, $p2$, $p3$ are executed under *order* $= 1$. A process control module *porderctrl()* is used to help execution order (Lines 27–33 in Fig. 4).

6.2   Specification

Specifications of smart contracts are defined under scenarios. For example there are some basic requirements for the aucSC contract:

1. Eventually there is a bidder win (liveness property);
2. The winner is always the bidder with the highest bid (safety property).

The requirements demand that after the auction is ended, 1) there is a winner and the winner must be one of the bidders, and 2) the winner must be the bidder with highest bid. Consider above mentioned scenario. There are three bidders. One of them will win. That is, *hBidder* $= B$, C or D. The bidder D pays the highest bid. When the value of the *order* reaches the maximum, 3 in this scenario, all processes are executed and the scenario finishes. We use a keyword *End* to indicate that the involved scenario is ended. Therefore, the requirements formulated under aucSNR are expressed by the following CTL formulas:

1. aucPr1: $AF((End)\&((hBidder = B)\mid(hBidder = C)\mid(hBidder = D)))$;
2. aucPr2: $AG(!(End)\mid(hBidder = D))$.

Where $!p\mid q$ is equivalent to $p\ implies\ q$. The specifications written in CTL formulas are used in the SPEC part of the VVM, shown in Fig. 4 (Lines 25–26).

7   Verification and Counter Example Extraction

The generated VVM is then verified by VERDS. If a property is satisfied, we can guarantee that the contract meets the corresponding requirement under the given scenario. Otherwise, VERDS may return a CEX file that records the trace of a counter example. A trace is a sequence of states generated by an execution of the contract. The procedure of counter example extraction starts from the trace. By the values of variables in states, we find the corresponding transitions in the VVM. Then according to Table 1, a reverted procedure of contract modeling is used to map the transitions to the Solidity contract. As such we have a counter example on the Solidity level. Below we illustrate the procedure by an example.

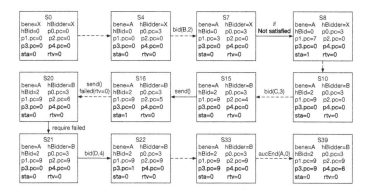

Fig. 6. A trace returned by VERDS.

By manually checking the aucSC contract (Fig. 1), it seems that it meets the second requirement (aucPr2). The result of the verification under scenario aucSNR, however, shows otherwise. That is, aucSC does not always choose the bidder with the highest bid as a winner. The trace returned by VERDS is shown in Fig. 6. The trace shows that when the three bidders bid sequentially in the order of bidder B, bidder C and then bidder D, the winner is bidder B. The corresponding order of calls on aucSC is shown in Fig. 7. Statements with process identifiers, i.e., p0, ..., p3 and p4, on the left are executed but the gray statements are not in a trace for a counter example.

```
p0   constructor(address _beneficiary)
     public {
p0      bene = _beneficiary;
p0   }
p1   call bid() public payable{
p1      require(!ended);
p1      require(msg.value > hBid);
p1      if (hBid!=0 ) {
            require(hBidder.send(hBid));
p1      }
p1      hBidder = msg.sender;
p1      hBid = msg.value;
p1   }
p2   call bid() public payable{
p2      require(!ended);
p2      require(msg.value > hBid);
p2      if (hBid!=0 ) {
p2         require(hBidder.send(hBid));
        }
        hBidder = msg.sender;
        hBid = msg.value;
p2   }
p3   call bid() public payable{
p3      require(!ended);
p3      require(msg.value > hBid);
p3      if (hBid!=0 ) {
p3         require(hBidder.send(hBid));
        }
        hBidder = msg.sender;
        hBid = msg.value;
p3   }
p4   call aucEnd() public{
p4      require(!ended);
p4      ended = true;
p4      bene.transfer(hBid);
p4   }
```

Fig. 7. A counter example of aucSC.

When bidder B bids, $p1$: $bid(B, 2)$ is called. At state S7, where $p1.pc = 3$ and $hBid = 0$, the condition of transition at Line 45 of aucVVM (Fig. 4) is satisfied, then $p1.pc$ is changed to 7, corresponding to the transition of Line 46 of aucVVM. By the information of the transitions in aucVVM, we then can find that after Line 13 of aucSC (Fig. 1), the execution go to Line 16, skipping Line 14, where is the gray line in Fig. 7.

The execution trace of $bid(C, 3)$ and $bid(D, 4)$ from the states shown in Fig. 6 to the execution path shown in Fig. 7 can be similarly explained.

In the counter example, after the first bidder, say, with bid 2, other higher biddings 3 and 4 may be aborted because the *send* operation fails. Recall that the return value of *send()* depends on what happens outside the contract and may return *true* or *false* nondeterministically. The subtle potential error is revealed by the counter example.

8 Case Studies and Experiments

We implemented **mcVer** and applied it to several case studies, including some reported contracts with typical security vulnerabilities [2,3,6] and an access control smart contract [51]. Our experiments are carried out on a machine with 3.10 GHz CPU, 512 GB RAM. The dataset is available on [5].

8.1 Security Vulnerabilities Checking

We show in this section some examples to illustrate how vulnerabilities such as Transaction-Ordering Dependency (TOD) and Reentrancy Vulnerability are revealed in **mcVer**.

Transaction-Ordering Dependency. Assume two transactions invoke a contract at the same time. If a final state depends on the order of these transactions, then a TOD vulnerability may exist. An attacker can enforce a specific execution order to make profit [27].

```
1   pragma solidity ^0.4.16;
2   contract EthTxOrderDependenceMinimal{
3       address public owner;
4       bool public claimed;
5       uint public reward;
6       constructor() public{
7           owner = msg.sender;
8       }
9       function setReward() public payable{
10          require(!claimed);
11          require(msg.sender == owner);
12          owner.transfer(reward);
13          reward = msg.value;
14      }
15      function claimReward(uint256
            submission) {
16          require(!claimed);
17          require(submission<10);
18          msg.sender.transfer(reward);
19          claimed = true;
20      }
21  }
```

Fig. 8. A contract with TOD [6], todSC

An example of a contract with TOD vulnerability [6] is shown in Fig. 8. Suppose the reward is first set to 3 by the owner A after the contract is deployed. Then user B sees the reward and tries to claim, and at the same time the owner resets the reward to 1. These two transactions may be executed in any order. The contract is first translated into a VVM with a module *setReward(msg_ sender, msg_ value)* to model function *setReward()*, a module *claimReward(msg_ sender, msg_ value, submission)* to model function *claimReward(uint submission)* and a module to model the constructor. The aforementioned scenario is configured as:

$$p0 : EthTxOrderDependenceMinimal(A, 0)$$
$$p1 : setReward(A, 3)$$
$$p2 : setReward(A, 1)|p3 : claimReward(B, 0, 3)$$

Suppose user B has a balance 5 before a transaction. After that, he should expect a balance to be 8, since the reward is 3 when he submits the transaction. Therefore, the property is denoted as follows.

$$AG(!(End)|(balance[B] = 8))$$

VERDS exhaustively explores the state space of the model and finds violation of the property. Therefore, a trace where the user's balance is only 6 at the end of the scenario is returned by VERDS as a counter-example. The trace shows that *setReward()* is executed before *claimReward()* and the reward is set to 1. Then, should B always have balance of 6 after the scenario? Verification of the following property shows otherwise, because *claimReward()* may also be executed first.

$$AG(!(End)|(balance[B] = 6))$$

The results show that a different execution order may lead to different balance of B. The TOD vulnerability is detected.

Reentrancy Vulnerability. If a function of a contract is called again before its previous invocations complete execution and the next call leads to inconsistency of balances of related accounts, a Reentrancy Vulnerability exists in the contract. The reason of TheDAO event is exactly that the Reentrancy Vulnerability in the DAO was exploited by attackers. A contract with Reentrancy Vulnerability is shown in Fig. 9. When function *withDraw*() is called, the statement *msg.sender.call.value(amount)*() in Line 8 will transfer some money to another contract and trigger its fallback function. When there is a callback to *withDraw*() in the fallback function, a reentrancy is formed and an attacker may withdraw more amount of money than his balance in the contract.

The contract is translated into a VVM with a set of modules. We set the number of callbacks to 1, because if there is a re-entry it will be found in one callback. An extra module *fallback*() is used to model *fallback* function in the external contract which is triggered automatically by *withDraw*(), and a module *withDraw_back*() is used to model the re-invoked *withDraw*() in *fallback* function. Suppose a user B first deposits 2 *wei* (a unit of Ether) into the contract by invoking

```
1  pragma solidity ^0.4.19;
2  contract Victim{
3    mapping(address => uint) public
         userBalance;
4    uint public amount=0;
5    function withDraw(){
6      uint amount = userBalance[msg.sender];
7      if(amount>0){
8        msg.sender.call.value(amount)();
9        userBalance[msg.sender] = 0;
10     }
11   }
12   function receiveEther() payable{
13     if(msg.value>0){
14       userBalance[msg.sender] += msg.
            value;
15     }
16   }
17 }
```

Fig. 9. Contract with Reentrancy [3], reSC

receiveEther() and then withdraws his money. The scenario is configured as follows.

$$p0 : receiveEther(B, 2)$$
$$p1 : withDraw(B, 0)$$

Suppose the initial balance of the user is 5, the required property is that his balance after the execution of the scenario is still 5. This property is formulated as follows.

$$AG(!(End)|(balance[B] = 5))$$

Checking this property with the above scenario, **mcVer** returns with *false*, meaning that the balance of the user is inconsistent before and after the scenario. The Re-entrancy Vulnerability is then detected.

Table 2. Checking time for security vulnerabilities.

Contract	Vul.	Bound		Execution Time (second)			
		MaxD	MaxI	Modeling	Veri	Counter Ex.	Total
todSC	TOD	2	8	0.071	3.41	0.003	3.484
reSC	Reentrancy	2	8	0.051	4.099	0.002	4.152

Experimental Results. Table 2 shows the time required for **mcVer** to detect the vulnerabilities contained in the above four cases. The bound of number of addresses, MaxD, and the bound of integer, MaxI, are shown in the third colomn. The procedures of model extraction and counter example generation are very fast, and the times required for verification of them are within several seconds.

8.2   Access Control Contract

The previously discussed properties related to security are all safety properties. In this section we study an access control contract [51] to show that **mcVer** can also deal with liveness properties.

Problem Description. The ubiquitous interconnection of physical objects has significantly accelerated data collection, aggregation, and sharing, making Internet of Things (IoT) one of the most basic architectures for applications in the smart health-care, smart transportation, and home automation domains. However, such interconnection may also bring serious security problems to IoT systems. If a system does not have secure access control, through intrusion into the system, unauthorized entities (attackers) can illegally access existing IoT devices by simply deploying their own resources. Therefore, the access control issue of the IoT has received extensive attention from academia and industry. The access control system should satisfy the following four requirements:

PR1. Regardless of whether a user has rights or not, the system should return a result;
PR2. Users who have no right to access can't get access rights;
PR3. Users with access rights can always obtain access rights;
PR4. Only specific users (such as administrators) can modify users' access rights.

```
1    contract AccessControlMethod{
2      address public owner;
3      address public subject;
4      address public object;
5      mapping(bytes32=>PolicyItem) policies;
6      mapping (bytes32 => BehaviorItem)
           behaviors;
7
8      constructor (address _subject) public{}
9      function policyAdd(bytes32 _action, bool
           _permission, uint minInterval, uint
           _threshold) public{}
10     function policyUpdate(bytes32 _action,
           bool _newPermission) public{}
11     function accessControl(bytes32 _action,
           uint _time) public{uint err;...}
12   }
```

Fig. 10. Access control contract [51].

We outline the contract and show it in Fig. 10. There are five global variables, among which *owner*, *subject* and *object* indicate the address who deployed the contract, the address of the accessing user and IoT device bound to the contract, respectively; the variables *policies* with mapping type are used to record the access policies. There are also three main functions in this contract. Function *AccessControlMethod*() is the constructor, initializing *owner*, *subject* and *object*. Function *policyAdd*() is used to add new access policy. Function *policyUpdate*() is used to update the access permissions in an access policy. Function *accessControl*() is used to get access rights. There is a local variable *err* in *accessControl*() representing whether a user can get access right. Different values of *err* represent different return results as shown in the following list.

1. $err = 0$ means right is granted;
2. $err = 1$ means punishment isn't ended and right is not granted;
3. $err = 2$ means user has no permission and right is not granted;
4. $err = 3$ means that although the user has the permission but he will be punished and right isn't granted, because he visits too frequently;
5. $err = 4$ means user has no permission and visit too frequently in the minimal interval, will be punished, right isn't granted;
6. $err = 5$ means the device that the user wants to visit is not current device and right isn't granted.

Modeling. For the verification of aforementioned four basic properties, we design three different scenarios. The first scenario, denoted by SNR1, is defined as:

$$p0 : constructor(A, 0, B)$$
$$p1 : policyAdd(A, 0, R, Y, 2, 2)$$
$$p2 : policyUpdate(A, 0, R, N) | p3 : accessControl(B, 0, R, 2)$$

In this scenario, administrator A deploys a contract for user B. He then sends a transaction calling *policyAdd* to add a new policy which allows B to read (R) the data on resource with identifier 3. This policy allows the user to visit the resource twice in interval 2 units of time. Then B tries to get access right and A tries to withdraw the permission for user B at the same time. Scenario SNR1 can be used to check properties PR1 and PR3, which are concretized and specified respectively by SNR1.pr1 and SNR1.pr2, shown as follows.

SNR1.pr1: $AF((End)\&(p3.err = 0|p3.err = 1|p3.err = 2|p3.err = 3|p3.err = 4|p3.err = 5))$
SNR1.pr2: $AG(!(End)|(p3.err = 0))$

The second scenario, SNR2, is defined as:

$$p0 : constructor(A, 0, B)$$
$$p1 : policyAdd(A, 0, R, Y, 2, 2)$$
$$p2 : policyUpdate(A, 0, R, N)$$
$$p3 : accessControl(B, 0, R, 2)$$

After *policyAdd* finishes, *policyUpdate* withdraws the permission of user B. The B tries to access the resource. Scenario SNR2 can be used to check properties PR1 and PR2, which are concretized and specified respectively by SNR2.pr1 and SNR2.pr2, shown as follows.

SNR2.pr1: $AF((End)\&(p3.err = 0|p3.err = 1|p3.err = 2|p3.err = 3|p3.err = 4|p3.err = 5))$
SNR2.pr2: $AG(!(End)|(p3.err = 2))$

The last scenario, SNR3, describes the situation that a user B with no permission tries to update his own permission and then tries to get access right:

$$p0 : constructor(A, 0, B)$$
$$p1 : policyAdd(A, 0, R, N, 2, 2)$$
$$p2 : policyUpdate(B, 0, R, Y)$$
$$p3 : accessControl(B, 0, R, 2)$$

Scenario SNR3 can be used to check properties PR1 and PR4, which are concretized and specified respectively by SNR3.pr1 and SNR3.pr2, shown as follows.

SNR3.pr1: $AF((End)\&(p3.err = 0|p3.err = 1|p3.err = 2|p3.err = 3|p3.err = 4|p3.err = 5))$
SNR3.pr2: $AG(!(End)|(p3.err = 2))$

The changes of permission can only be checked by the returned error code of *accessControl*(), so in this scenarios p3 is added and the formula SNR3.pr2 is the same as SNR2.pr2.

Table 3. Verification results for access control contract.

Requirements	Properties	Verification Results		Time (second)
PR1	SNR1.pr1	True	True	17.155
	SNR2.pr1	True		18.977
	SNR3.pr1	True		22.329
PR2	SNR2.pr2	True	True	17.367
PR3	SNR1.pr2	False	False	21.201
PR4	SNR3.pr2	False	False	19.019

Verification. After the contract, the scenarios and the property specification are translated into VVM, we verified the VVM using VERDS. The results are shown in Table 3. The first column list the names of requirements, the second column lists the related CTL formula, the third and forth columns are verification results, and the last column shows verification time for each property. The result for PR1 is true only when the verification results of SNR1.pr1, SNR2.pr1 and SNR3.pr1 are all true. From the results, we know that the contract doesn't meet PR3 and PR4. And the counter-example returned when verifying SNR3.pr2 shows that user B, who is not an administrator, successfully changes his own permission by calling function *policyUpdate*(), and gets the access right which violates PR4. All six properties are verified in about two minutes.

9 Conclusion and Future Work

In this paper, the model checking based framework, **mcVer**, has been proposed to support the verification of smart contracts written in Solidity. **mcVer** is able to verify a variety of properties of smart contracts. For the properties that are not satisfied, **mcVer** produces a counter example by showing a sequence of statements in the original Solidity program as a hint of where a faulty statement may be located. We have implemented **mcVer** and applied it to automatically checking various types of security vulnerabilities and properties of an access control smart contract. The results show that the proposed framework is flexible and efficient and can facilitate software development in the blockchain domain in terms of the diversity of detecting software breaches.

The limitations of **mcVer** framework come from two folds. The first is from the model checking technique itself, which can only deal with bounded systems and may suffer from state explosion issue when the model scales up. The second is that we have to configure the scenarios with particular values of parameters, which confines the space to be explored and limits the ability of **mcVer**. In the future, we will study the property-based contract modeling technique to reduce the size of the model to be verified and consider a better way to model the environment and user behaviors to broaden the scope of verification. Also, we will consider the impact of gas limitation to the behavior of contracts.

References

1. https://solidity-cn.readthedocs.io/zh/develop/solidity-by-example.html
2. https://bitcoinist.com/smart-contract-bug-disable-icon-icx-transfers/
3. https://blog.csdn.net/programmer_cjc/article/details/85987234
4. Analysis of the DAO exploit. https://hackingdistributed.com/2016/06/18/analysis-of-the-dao-exploit/

5. Dataset for mcver. https://gitee.com/fmpa/dataset-for-mcVer
6. Transaction order dependence. https://swcregistry.io/docs/swc-114
7. Albert, E., Correas, J., Gordillo, P., Román-Díez, G., Rubio, A.: SAFEVM: a safety verifier for Ethereum smart contracts. In: Proceedings of the 28th ACM SIGSOFT International Symposium on Software Testing and Analysis, pp. 386–389 (2019)
8. Alqahtani, S., He, X., Gamble, R., Mauricio, P.: Formal verification of functional requirements for smart contract compositions in supply chain management systems. In: Proceedings of the 53rd Hawaii International Conference on System Sciences (2020)
9. Atzei, N., Bartoletti, M., Cimoli, T.: A survey of attacks on ethereum smart contracts (SoK). In: Maffei, M., Ryan, M. (eds.) POST 2017. LNCS, vol. 10204, pp. 164–186. Springer, Heidelberg (2017). https://doi.org/10.1007/978-3-662-54455-6_8
10. Beyer, D., Keremoglu, M.E.: CPACHECKER: a tool for configurable software verification. In: Gopalakrishnan, G., Qadeer, S. (eds.) CAV 2011. LNCS, vol. 6806, pp. 184–190. Springer, Heidelberg (2011). https://doi.org/10.1007/978-3-642-22110-1_16
11. Bhargavan, K., et al.: Formal verification of smart contracts: short paper. In: Proceedings of the 2016 ACM Workshop on Programming Languages and Analysis for Security, pp. 91–96 (2016)
12. Brent, L., Grech, N., Lagouvardos, S., Scholz, B., Smaragdakis, Y.: Ethainter: a smart contract security analyzer for composite vulnerabilities. In: Proceedings of the 41st ACM SIGPLAN Conference on Programming Language Design and Implementation, pp. 454–469 (2020)
13. Chen, R., Zhang, W.: Checking multi-agent systems against temporal-epistemic specifications. In: the 24th International Conference on Engineering of Complex Computer Systems, pp. 21–30. IEEE (2019)
14. Cimatti, A., Clarke, E., Giunchiglia, F., Roveri, M.: NUSMV: a new symbolic model checker. Int. J. Softw. Tools Technol. Transf. 2(4), 410–425 (2000)
15. Clarke, E.M., Wing, J.M.: Formal methods: state of the art and future directions. ACM Comput. Surv. (CSUR) 28(4), 626–643 (1996)
16. Costello, K.: Gartner predicts 90% of current enterprise blockchain platform implementations will require replacement by 2021 (2019). https://www.gartner.com/en/newsroom/press-releases/2019-07-03-gartner-predicts-90-of-current-enterprise-blockchain
17. Clarke Jr., E.M., Grumberg, O., Kroening, D., Peled, D., Veith, H.: Model Checking, 2nd edn. MIT Press, Cambridge (2018)
18. Feist, J., Grieco, G., Groce, A.: Slither: a static analysis framework for smart contracts. In: 2019 IEEE/ACM 2nd International Workshop on Emerging Trends in Software Engineering for Blockchain (WETSEB), pp. 8–15. IEEE (2019)
19. Filliâtre, J.-C., Paskevich, A.: Why3—where programs meet provers. In: Felleisen, M., Gardner, P. (eds.) ESOP 2013. LNCS, vol. 7792, pp. 125–128. Springer, Heidelberg (2013). https://doi.org/10.1007/978-3-642-37036-6_8
20. Frank, J., Aschermann, C., Holz, T.: ETHBMC: a bounded model checker for smart contracts. In: 29th USENIX Security Symposium, pp. 2757–2774 (2020)
21. Grieco, G., Song, W., Cygan, A., Feist, J., Groce, A.: Echidna: effective, usable, and fast fuzzing for smart contracts. In: Proceedings of the 29th ACM SIGSOFT International Symposium on Software Testing and Analysis, pp. 557–560 (2020)
22. Hegedűs, P.: Towards analyzing the complexity landscape of solidity based ethereum smart contracts. Technologies 7(1), 6 (2019)

23. Hirai, Y.: Formal verification of deed contract in ethereum name service, November 2016. https://yoichihirai.com/deed.pdf
24. Hirai, Y.: Defining the ethereum virtual machine for interactive theorem provers. In: Brenner, M., et al. (eds.) FC 2017. LNCS, vol. 10323, pp. 520–535. Springer, Cham (2017). https://doi.org/10.1007/978-3-319-70278-0_33
25. Kalra, S., Goel, S., Dhawan, M., Sharma, S.: ZEUS: analyzing safety of smart contracts. In: Network and Distributed Systems Security (NDSS) Symposium, pp. 1–12 (2018)
26. Liu, Y., Li, Y., Lin, S.W., Zhao, R.: Towards automated verification of smart contract fairness. In: Proceedings of the 28th ACM Joint Meeting on European Software Engineering Conference and Symposium on the Foundations of Software Engineering, pp. 666–677 (2020)
27. Luu, L., Chu, D.H., Olickel, H., Saxena, P., Hobor, A.: Making smart contracts smarter. In: Proceedings of the 2016 ACM SIGSAC Conference on Computer and Communications Security, pp. 254–269 (2016)
28. Manna, Z., Pnueli, A.: The Temporal Logic of Reactive and Concurrent Systems: Specification. Springer, New York (2012). https://doi.org/10.1007/978-1-4612-0931-7
29. Mavridou, A., Laszka, A., Stachtiari, E., Dubey, A.: VeriSolid: correct-by-design smart contracts for ethereum. In: Goldberg, I., Moore, T. (eds.) FC 2019. LNCS, vol. 11598, pp. 446–465. Springer, Cham (2019). https://doi.org/10.1007/978-3-030-32101-7_27
30. Mossberg, M., et al.: Manticore: a user-friendly symbolic execution framework for binaries and smart contracts. In: 34th IEEE/ACM International Conference on Automated Software Engineering (ASE), pp. 1186–1189 (2019)
31. Mulligan, D.P., Owens, S., Gray, K.E., Ridge, T., Sewell, P.: Lem: reusable engineering of real-world semantics. In: the 19th ACM SIGPLAN international conference on Functional programming, pp. 175–188 (2014)
32. Nakamoto, S.: Bitcoin: a peer-to-peer electronic cash system. Technical report, Manubot (2019)
33. Nehaï, Z., Piriou, P., Daumas, F.: Model-checking of smart contracts. In: IEEE International Conference on Internet of Things (iThings) and IEEE Green Computing and Communications (GreenCom) and IEEE Cyber, Physical and Social Computing (CPSCom) and IEEE Smart Data (SmartData), pp. 980–987
34. Nehai, Z., Bobot, F.: Deductive proof of ethereum smart contracts using why3. arXiv preprint arXiv:1904.11281 (2019)
35. Nipkow, T., Wenzel, M., Paulson, L.C.: Isabelle/HOL – A Proof Assistant for Higher-Order Logic. LNCS, vol. 2283. Springer, Heidelberg (2002). https://doi.org/10.1007/3-540-45949-9
36. Permenev, A., Dimitrov, D., Tsankov, P., Drachsler-Cohen, D., Vechev, M.: VerX: safety verification of smart contracts. In: 2020 IEEE Symposium on Security and Privacy (SP), pp. 1661–1677 (2020)
37. Sergey, I., Hobor, A.: A concurrent perspective on smart contracts. In: Brenner, M., et al. (eds.) FC 2017. LNCS, vol. 10323, pp. 478–493. Springer, Cham (2017). https://doi.org/10.1007/978-3-319-70278-0_30
38. So, S., Lee, M., Park, J., Lee, H., Oh, H.: VeriSmart: a highly precise safety verifier for ethereum smart contracts. In: 2020 IEEE Symposium on Security and Privacy (SP), pp. 1678–1694 (2020)
39. Swamy, N., et al.: Dependent types and multi-monadic effects in F. In: Proceedings of the 43rd annual ACM SIGPLAN-SIGACT Symposium on Principles of Programming Languages, pp. 256–270 (2016)

40. Szabo, N.: Formalizing and securing relationships on public networks. First Monday **2**(9) (1997). https://firstmonday.org/ojs/index.php/fm/article/view/548

41. Thomson, I.: Parity: the bug that put $169m of ethereum on ice? Yeah, it was on the todo list for months (2017). https://www.theregister.com/2017/11/16/parity_flaw_not_fixed/

42. Thomson, I.: Mythril classic: security analysis tool for ethereum smart contracts (2018). https://github.com/ConsenSys/mythril

43. Tikhomirov, S., Voskresenskaya, E., Ivanitskiy, I., Takhaviev, R., Marchenko, E., Alexandrov, Y.: SmartCheck: static analysis of ethereum smart contracts. In: Proceedings of the 1st International Workshop on Emerging Trends in Software Engineering for Blockchain, pp. 9–16 (2018)

44. Tolmach, P., Li, Y., Lin, S.W., Liu, Y., Li, Z.: A survey of smart contract formal specification and verification. ACM Comput. Surv. **54**(7), 1–38 (2022)

45. Tsankov, P., Dan, A., Drachsler-Cohen, D., Gervais, A., Buenzli, F., Vechev, M.: Securify: Practical security analysis of smart contracts. In: Proceedings of the 2018 ACM SIGSAC Conference on Computer and Communications Security, pp. 67–82 (2018)

46. Wang, S., Zhang, C., Su, Z.: Detecting nondeterministic payment bugs in ethereum smart contracts. Proc. ACM Program. Lang. **3**, Article 189 (2019)

47. Wood, G., et al.: Ethereum: a secure decentralised generalised transaction ledger. Ethereum project yellow paper **151**, 1–32 (2014)

48. Wüstholz, V., Christakis, M.: Harvey: a greybox fuzzer for smart contracts. In: Proceedings of the 28th ACM Joint Meeting on European Software Engineering Conference and Symposium on the Foundations of Software Engineering, pp. 1398–1409 (2020)

49. Zeng, N., Zhang, W.: An executable semantics of SystemC transaction level models and its applications with VERDS. In: the 19th International Conference on Engineering of Complex Computer Systems, pp. 198–201 (2014)

50. Zhang, W.: VERDS: verification of hierarchical discrete systems by symbolic techniques. Manuscript (2013). http://lcs.ios.ac.cn/~zwh/verds

51. Zhang, Y., Kasahara, S., Shen, Y., Jiang, X., Wan, J.: Smart contract-based access control for the internet of things. IEEE Internet Things J. **6**(2), 1594–1605 (2018)

Equivalence of Denotational and Operational Semantics for Interaction Languages

Erwan Mahe[1]($\boxtimes$)(iD), Christophe Gaston[1](iD), and Pascale Le Gall[2](iD)

[1] Université Paris-Saclay, CEA, List, 91120 Palaiseau, France
erwan.mahe@cea.fr
[2] Université Paris-Saclay, CentraleSupélec, 91192 Gif-sur-Yvette, France

Abstract. Message Sequence Charts (MSC) and Sequence Diagrams (SD) are graphical models representing the behaviours of distributed and concurrent systems via the scheduling of discrete emission and reception events. So as to exploit them in formal methods, a mathematical semantics is required. In the literature, different kinds of semantics are proposed: denotational semantics, well suited to reason about algebraic properties and operational semantics, well suited to establish verification algorithms. We define an algebraic language to specify so-called interactions, similar to the MSC and SD models. It is equipped with a denotational semantics associating sets of traces (sequences of observed events) to interactions. We then define a structural operational semantics in the style of process algebras and prove the equivalence of the two semantics.

Keywords: Interactions · Sequence diagrams · Distributed & concurrent systems · Formal language · Denotational semantics · Operational semantics

1 Introduction

Modelling asynchronous communications between concurrent processes is possible under a variety of formalisms, such as process algebras [22], Petri Nets [4], series-parallel languages [11], distributed automata [1], or formalisms derived from Message Sequence Charts (MSC) [16]. MSCs are graphical models representing information exchanges between sub-systems. Various offshoots of MSCs, including UML Sequence Diagrams (UML-SD) [18], have been proposed and we call languages from that family "Interaction Languages" (IL). Interactions are interesting due to their graphical nature and ease of understanding. IL make it possible to describe scenarios using intuitions that are very easy to share: a) a vertical line per sub-system, called a lifeline, which from top to bottom describes the succession of events as perceived by the sub-system, b) exchanges of messages inducing causality relations between the lifelines, c) high-level operators such as parallel composition to structure simple scenarios.

© Springer Nature Switzerland AG 2022
Y. Aït-Ameur and F. Crăciun (Eds.): TASE 2022, LNCS 13299, pp. 113–130, 2022.
https://doi.org/10.1007/978-3-031-10363-6_8

So as to use interactions in formal methods, they have to be fitted with formal semantics. A major hurdle in defining those lies in the treatment of weak sequencing. Weak sequencing allows events taking place on different lifelines to occur in any order while strictly ordering those that take place on the same lifeline. The survey [17] provides an overview of solutions found in the literature. The most direct ones consist in defining semantics by translation: interactions are translated into models of other formalisms provided with formal semantics. Typical examples are Petri Nets [3], automata [10] or process algebra [8]. The main advantage of such approaches is that those formalisms are equipped with tools such as Model-Checker or Model-Based Testing tools. However, a notable drawback is that the target formalisms are defined on concepts (states, transitions, places...) that are quite different from the ones handled in ILs. Then it is difficult to know whether or not the objects resulting from the translation preserve the meaning associated to the original interaction. For example, in [8], the authors propose to translate UML-SD into Communicating Sequential Processes (CSP) [6]. UML-SD operators such as weak sequencing are encoded in a non-trivial manner, using sequence, parallel composition etc. as CSP does not introduce any similar operator, and as the translation is not presented exhaustively, it is not clear if the asynchronous nature of executions of UML-SD is fully reflected. Other approaches treat IL by equipping them with direct mathematical semantics, either denotational or operational. Denotational semantics either rely on partial order sets [15,23] or on algebraic operators [9]. Operational semantics [16] are given in the form of production rules similar to process algebra. Denotational semantics, based on sets of accepted execution traces, are close to intuition. They are well adapted to reason on and prove various properties about interactions. Operational semantics are closer to executable semantics and are well suited to prove the correctness of algorithms realizing formal analysis.

In this paper we set the basis of a framework to deal with interactions via two kinds of semantics (denotational and operational). While in [14,15] we formulated semantics for interactions by identifying the positions of communication actions using the Dewey notation, we now abstract away positions, to define a denotational semantics in an algebraic style as in [9] and an operational semantics in the style of Plotkin. Those new formulations enables us to prove the equivalence of the semantics (with an automated Coq proof available in [13]). To our knowledge, there are no similar equivalence results in the literature. In particular, in [15], there were only some tooled experiments hinting towards their equivalence. Our IL extends the one in [15] with additional loop mechanisms. Our denotational semantics can be seen as an extension of the one in [9] with repetition operators in the form of variants of the algebraic Kleene closure. We define a structural operational semantics in the fashion of process algebras [2]. It adopts some of the ideas introduced in [16,21] but is closer to usual structural operational semantics than the one in [16,21] which includes maps between sent and received messages or negative application rule conditions.

This paper is organized as follows: Sect. 2 introduces the concepts of interactions and traces. Section 3 presents the syntax of our IL and defines a trace semantics in denotational-style. In Sect. 4 a structural operational semantics is defined in the style of process calculi and we demonstrate its equivalence to the former in Sect. 5. Finally, in Sects. 6 and 7 we discuss some related works and we conclude. A formalisation using Coq of the main demonstrations is available in [13].

2   Basic Interactions and Intuition of Their Meaning

Interactions describe the behavior of distributed and concurrent systems based on their internal and external communications. They are defined over a signature $\Omega = (L, M)$ where L is a set of lifelines and M is a set of messages.

2.1   Preliminaries

The executions of systems are characterized by sequences of events called communication actions (actions for short) which are of two kinds: either the emission of a message $m \in M$ from a lifeline $l \in L$, denoted by $l!m$, or the reception of $m \in M$ by $l \in L$, denoted by $l?m$. $\mathbb{A}_\Omega$ denotes the set of actions over Ω. For any such action a, $\theta(a)$ denotes the lifeline on which a occurs.

Sequences of actions, called traces, are words in $\mathbb{A}_\Omega^*$, with "." denoting the concatenation operation and ϵ being the empty trace. We denote by $\mathbb{T}_\Omega = \mathbb{A}_\Omega^*$ the set of traces. Thus, for any two traces t_1 and t_2, $t_1.t_2$ is the trace composed of the sequence of actions of t_1 followed by the sequence of actions of t_2. We introduce operators to compose (sets of) traces, modeling different notions of scheduling: the strict sequencing (;), the interleaving ($||$) and the weak sequencing ($*$).

The set $t_1 ; t_2$ of strict sequencing of traces t_1 and t_2 is defined as $\{t_1.t_2\}$. By choosing ";" for denoting the extension of "." to sets of traces, we adopt the same notation as in [9] for the strict sequencing operator.

Interleaving allows elements of distinct traces to be reordered w.r.t. one another while preserving the order that is specific to each trace. The set $t_1 || t_2$ of interleavings of traces t_1 and t_2 is defined by:

$$\epsilon || t_2 = \{t_2\} \qquad\qquad t_1 || \epsilon = \{t_1\}$$
$$(a_1.t_1) || (a_2.t_2) = \{a_1.t \mid t \in t_1 || (a_2.t_2)\} \cup \{a_2.t \mid t \in (a_1.t_1) || t_2\}$$

By contrast, weak sequencing only allows such permutations when actions do not occur on the same lifeline. We define a predicate $t*l$ meaning that the trace t contains an action on the lifeline l (we say t has conflicts w.r.t. l):

$$\epsilon * l = \bot \qquad \text{and} \qquad (a.t) * l = (\theta(a) = l) \vee (t * l)$$

By overloading $*$, the set $t_1 * t_2$ of weak sequencing of t_1 and t_2 is defined by:

$$\epsilon * t_2 = \{t_2\} \qquad\qquad t_1 * \epsilon = \{t_1\}$$
$$(a_1.t_1) * (a_2.t_2) = \{a_1.t \mid t \in t_1 * (a_2.t_2)\} \cup \{a_2.t \mid t \in (a_1.t_1) * t_2, \ \neg(a_1.t_1 * \theta(a_2))\}$$

When defining $t'_1 \divideontimes t'_2$, the order of the actions in each trace is preserved and actions in t'_2 can only precede those in t'_1 that do not occur on the same lifeline. This explains the two subsets constituting $(a_1.t_1) \divideontimes (a_2.t_2)$: the first one contains all traces whose first action is a_1 and tail belongs to $t_1 \divideontimes (a_2.t_2)$ and the second one is empty if lifeline of a_2 occurs in $a_1.t_1$ (i.e. $\neg(a_1.t_1 \divideontimes \theta(a_2))$), and contains all traces whose first action is a_2 and tail belongs to $(a_1.t_1) \divideontimes t_2$ otherwise.

The previous binary operators ("$;$", "$\divideontimes$" and "$||$") defined on traces are canonically extended to sets of traces as follows: with $\diamond \in \{;, \divideontimes, ||\}$, $T_1 \diamond T_2$ is the union of all the sets $t_1 \diamond t_2$ with $t_1 \in T_1$ and $t_2 \in T_2$. The use of the strict sequencing ("$;$"), weak sequencing ("$\divideontimes$") and interleaving ("$||$") operators will be illustrated with Fig. 1 in Sect. 2.2.

2.2 Basic Interactions

An example of interaction is given in the left of Fig. 1. Lifelines l_1, l_2 and l_3 are drawn as vertical lines. Emission and reception actions are drawn as horizontal arrows carrying the transmitted messages m_1, m_2, m_3 and m_4 and which respectively exit the emitting lifeline or point towards the receiving lifeline. When a direct emission-reception causality occurs, we draw both actions as a single arrow from the emitter towards the receiver.

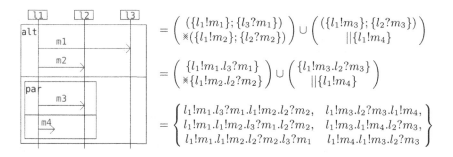

$$= \left(\begin{array}{c} (\{l_1!m_1\}; \{l_3?m_1\}) \\ \divideontimes(\{l_1!m_2\}; \{l_2?m_2\}) \end{array} \right) \cup \left(\begin{array}{c} (\{l_1!m_3\}; \{l_2?m_3\}) \\ ||\{l_1!m_4\} \end{array} \right)$$

$$= \left(\begin{array}{c} \{l_1!m_1.l_3?m_1\} \\ \divideontimes\{l_1!m_2.l_2?m_2\} \end{array} \right) \cup \left(\begin{array}{c} \{l_1!m_3.l_2?m_3\} \\ ||\{l_1!m_4\} \end{array} \right)$$

$$= \left\{ \begin{array}{ll} l_1!m_1.l_3?m_1.l_1!m_2.l_2?m_2, & l_1!m_3.l_2?m_3.l_1!m_4, \\ l_1!m_1.l_1!m_2.l_3?m_1.l_2?m_2, & l_1!m_3.l_1!m_4.l_2?m_3, \\ l_1!m_1.l_1!m_2.l_2?m_2.l_3?m_1 & l_1!m_4.l_1!m_3.l_2?m_3 \end{array} \right\}$$

Fig. 1. Example of a basic interaction & its trace semantics

The top to bottom direction relates to time passing. An action (arrow) drawn above another one generally occurs beforehand. This scheduling of actions corresponds to the weak sequencing operator. By contrast, strict sequencing may be used to enforce precedence relations between actions occurring on different lifelines. These two scheduling operators will be respectively denoted by the keywords seq and $strict$. Other keywords (alt, par, $loop$) will be also used for denoting other scheduling mechanisms. In Fig. 1, the arrow carrying m_1 and specifying its passing between l_1 and l_3 is modelled by the interaction $strict(l_1!m_1, l_3?m_1)$. Using the $strict$ operator here obliges $l_3?m_1$ to occur after $l_1!m_1$, which reflects the causality of the passing of message m_1 between l_1 and l_3. The fact that this arrow stands above that carrying m_2 can be modelled using the weak sequencing operator: $seq(strict(l_1!m_1, l_3?m_1), strict(l_1!m_2, l_2?m_2))$. Using seq here instead of $strict$ allows for instance $l_2?m_2$ to occur before $l_3?m_1$ even though the latter is drawn above. However $l_1!m_2$ cannot occur before $l_1!m_1$ because they both occur on l_1. Note that, in contrast to $strict$, the seq operator has no graphical representation in diagrams, as it corresponds to the default scheduling operator.

Parallel and alternative compositions can also be used. On Fig. 1, the passing of m_3 and the emission of m_4 are scheduled using parallel composition. In the diagram representation this corresponds to the box labelled with "par", modelled by the term $par(strict(l_1!m_3, l_2?m_3), l_1!m_4)$. Actions scheduled with par can occur in any order w.r.t. one another. Here, $l_1!m_4$ can occur before $l_1!m_3$, after $l_2?m_3$ or in between those two actions. Alternative composition is an exclusive non-deterministic choice between behaviors. Like par, alt is drawn as a box labelled with "alt". The global term describing the left of Fig. 1 is given by:

$$alt(seq(strict(l_1!m_1, l_3?m_1), strict(l_1!m_2, l_2?m_2)), par(strict(l_1!m_3, l_2?m_3), l_1!m_4))$$

2.3   Repetition Operators on Sets of Traces

Scheduling operators define compositions of traces obtained from enabling or forbidding the reordering of actions according to some scheduling policy. All three are associative (in addition, $\|$ is commutative) and admit $\{\epsilon\}$ as a neutral element. We define (Kleene) closures of those operators to specify repetitions[1]:

Definition 1 (Kleene closures). *For any* $\diamond \in \{;, \ast, \|\}$ *and any* $T \in \mathcal{P}(\mathbb{T}_\Omega)$, *the Kleene closure* $T^{\diamond *}$ *of* T *is defined by:* $T^{\diamond *} = \bigcup_{j \in \mathbb{N}} T^{\diamond j}$ *with* $T^{\diamond 0} = \{\epsilon\}$ *and* $T^{\diamond j} = T \diamond T^{\diamond (j-1)}$ *for* $j > 0$.

$$\left\{ \begin{array}{c} l_1!m_1.l_2!m_2, \\ l_2?m_1 \end{array} \right\}^{\ast *} = \left\{ \begin{array}{l} \epsilon, \\ l_1!m_1.l_2!m_2, \\ l_2?m_1, \end{array} \right. \left. \begin{array}{l} l_1!m_1.l_2!m_2.l_1!m_1.l_2!m_2, \\ l_1!m_1.l_1!m_1.l_2!m_2.l_2!m_2, \\ l_1!m_1.l_2!m_2.l_2?m_1, \\ l_2?m_1.l_2?m_1, \\ l_2?m_1.l_1!m_1.l_2!m_2, \\ l_1!m_1.l_2?m_1.l_2!m_2, \end{array} \quad \ldots \right\}$$

Fig. 2. Example illustrating the weak Kleene closure

The three Kleene closures $;*$, $\ast *$ and $\|*$ are respectively called, strict, weak and interleaving Kleene closures. Within the K-closure $T^{\diamond *}$ we can find traces obtained from the repetition (using $\diamond$ as a scheduler) of any number of traces of T. In the example from Fig. 2 we consider a set T containing two traces $l_1!m_1.l_2!m_2$ and $l_2?m_1$. The first 3 powersets of T (i.e. $T^{\ast 0} \cup T^{\ast 1} \cup T^{\ast 2}$) are

---

[1] For a set E, $\mathcal{P}(E)$ is the set of all subsets of E.

displayed, the rest of the weak K-closure of T (i.e. T^{**}) is represented by the
$\cdots$.

We have the property $T \diamond T^{\diamond *} = T^{\diamond *}$, analogous to the one defining replication
$!P$ (i.e. $!P = P|!P$) in the family of process calculi (e.g. see [19]), expressing
an unbounded number of copies of P along the parallel composition "|". For
$\diamond \in \{;, *, ||\}$ whenever $a.t \in T_1 \diamond T_2$ (with a and t any action and trace and T_1
and T_2 any sets of traces), it may be so that action a is taken from a trace $a.t'$
that belongs to either T_1 or T_2. Definition 2 introduces restricted versions of the
scheduling operators so as to impose action a to be taken from T_1.

Definition 2 (Restricted scheduling operators). *For any* $\diamond \in \{;, *, ||\}$,
we define the operator $\diamond^{\urcorner}$ *such that for any sets of traces* T_1 *and* T_2 *we have:*

$$T_1 \diamond^{\urcorner} T_2 = \{ t \in T_1 \diamond T_2 \mid (t = a.t') \Rightarrow (\exists t_1 \in \mathbb{T}_\Omega, \ s.t. \ (a.t_1 \in T_1) \ \wedge \ (t' \in \{t_1\} \diamond T_2)) \}$$

As an example, given $T_1 = \{l_1!m.l_1?m\}$ and $T_2 = \{l_2!m\}$, we have:

$$T_1 * T_2 = \left\{ \begin{array}{l} l_1!m.l_1?m.l_2!m, \\ l_1!m.l_2!m.l_1?m, \\ l_2!m.l_1!m.l_1?m \end{array} \right\} \quad \text{and} \quad T_1 *^{\urcorner} T_2 = \left\{ \begin{array}{l} l_1!m.l_1?m.l_2!m, \\ l_1!m.l_2!m.l_1?m \end{array} \right\}$$

We now define Head-First closures (abbr. HF-closure) of scheduling
operators.

Definition 3 (Head-first closures). *For any* $\diamond \in \{;, *, ||\}$, *we define the
Head-First closure of* $\diamond$ *as* $\diamond^{\urcorner *}$ *i.e. the Kleene closure of the restricted* $\diamond^{\urcorner}$ *operator.*

In the following we will show that HF-closure and K-closure are equivalent
for ; and || but that this is not the case for $*$.

Lemma 1. *For any* $\diamond \in \{;, ||\}$, $T \in \mathcal{P}(\mathbb{T}_\Omega)$, t *in* $\mathbb{T}_\Omega$ *and* $a \in \mathbb{A}_\Omega$ *we have:*

$$(a.t \in T^{\diamond *}) \Rightarrow (\exists t' \in \mathbb{T}_\Omega \ s.t. \ (a.t' \in T) \wedge \ (t \in \{t'\} \diamond T^{\diamond *}))$$

Proof. By induction on j given $a.t \in T^{\diamond j}$. For $||$, we use its commutativity. $\square$

Lemma 2 (Equivalence of HF & K closures for ; & ||). *For any set of
traces* T, *we have* $T^{;^{\urcorner}*} = T^{;*}$ *and* $T^{||^{\urcorner}*} = T^{||*}$.

Proof. By induction on a member trace t. $\square$

Let us detail a counter example showing that the weak K-closure ** and
the weak HF-closure $^{*^{\urcorner}*}$ are not equivalent. Given $T = \{l_1!m_1.l_2?m_1, \ l_2!m_2\}$,
let us consider the powerset T^{*2} of T. By definition, $\{l_2!m_2\} * \{l_1!m_1.l_2?m_1\} \subset$
T^{*2}. Here we can choose to take $l_1!m_1$ as a first action and therefore $t =$
$l_1!m_1.l_2!m_2.l_2?m_1 \in T^{*2}$. However, $t \notin T^{*^{\urcorner}}T = T^{*^{\urcorner}2}$ and more generally, for
any j smaller or greater that 2, $t \notin T^{*^{\urcorner}j}$. Hence, $T^{**} \not\subseteq T^{*^{\urcorner}*}$.

3   Syntax and Denotational Semantics

As noted earlier in Sect. 2.2, interactions terms are defined inductively. Basic building blocks include the empty interaction $\varnothing$ which specifies the empty behavior ϵ (observation of no action) and any atomic action a of $\mathbb{A}_\Omega$, which specifies the single-element trace a. More complex behavior can then be specified inductively using the binary constructors *strict*, *seq*, *par* and *alt* and the unary constructors $loop_S$ (strict loop), $loop_H$ (head loop up to $*$), $loop_W$ (weak loop) and $loop_P$ (parallel loop).

Definition 4 (Interaction Language). *We denote by $\mathbb{I}_\Omega$ the set of terms inductively defined by the set of operation symbols $\mathcal{F} = \mathcal{F}_0 \cup \mathcal{F}_1 \cup \mathcal{F}_2$ s.t.:*

- *symbols or arity 0 (constants) are $\mathcal{F}_0 = \{\varnothing\} \cup \mathbb{A}_\Omega$*
- *symbols of arity 1 are $\mathcal{F}_1 = \{loop_S,\ loop_H,\ loop_W,\ loop_P\}$*
- *symbols of arity 2 are $\mathcal{F}_2 = \{strict,\ seq,\ par,\ alt\}$*

In Definition 4 we define our Interaction Language (IL) as a set of terms $\mathbb{I}_\Omega$ inductively defined from the set of symbols $\mathcal{F}$ with arity in $\mathbb{N}$. The set $\mathcal{P}(\mathbb{T}_\Omega)$ of sets of traces admits the structure of a $\mathcal{F}$-algebra using operators introduced in Sect. 2. The denotational semantics of interactions is then defined in Definition 5 using the initial homomorphism associated to this $\mathcal{F}$-algebra.

Definition 5 (Denotational semantics). $\mathcal{A} = (\mathcal{P}(\mathbb{T}_\Omega), \{f^\mathcal{A} \mid f \in \mathcal{F}\})$ *is the $\mathcal{F}$-algebra defined by the following interpretations of the operation symbols in $\mathcal{F}$:*

$$
\begin{array}{llll}
& strict^\mathcal{A} = ; & loop_S^\mathcal{A} = ;^* \\
\varnothing^\mathcal{A} = \{\epsilon\} & seq^\mathcal{A} = * & loop_H^\mathcal{A} = *^{\neg}* \\
a^\mathcal{A} = \{a\} & par^\mathcal{A} = \| & loop_W^\mathcal{A} = ** \\
& alt^\mathcal{A} = \cup & loop_P^\mathcal{A} = \|^*
\end{array}
$$

The denotational semantics σ_d of $\mathbb{I}_\Omega$ is the unique $\mathcal{F}$-homomorphism $\sigma_d : \mathbb{I}_\Omega \to \mathcal{P}(\mathbb{T}_\Omega)$ between the free term $\mathcal{F}$-algebra[2] $\mathcal{T}_\mathcal{F}$ and $\mathcal{A}$.

The semantics of constants $\varnothing$ and $a \in \mathbb{A}_\Omega$ are sets containing a single element being respectively $\{\epsilon\}$ and $\{a\}$. The *strict*, *seq*, *par* and *alt* symbols are respectively associated to the ;, $*$, $\|$ and union $\cup$ operators on sets of traces. The use of the strict sequencing ("$;$"), weak sequencing ("$*$") and interleaving ("$\|$c) operators is illustrated on the right of Fig. 1 so as to compute the semantics of the interaction example given on the left of Fig. 1. For instance, from the second line to the third line, using distinct colours to better visualise the differences between scheduling operators, weak sequencing $\{l_1!m_1.l_3?m_1\} * \{l_1!m_2.l_2?m_2\}$ allows $l_1!m_2$ to be reordered before $l_3?m_1$ but not before $l_1!m_1$ while interleaving $\{l_1!m_3.l_2?m_3\} \| \{l_1!m_4\}$ allows $l_1!m_4$ to be placed anywhere w.r.t. $l_1!m_3$ and $l_2?m_3$. The resulting set of traces is given on the bottom right.

From a system designer perspective, using $loop_S$, $loop_H$, $loop_W$ or $loop_P$ is motivated by different goals:

---

[2] The free term $\mathcal{F}$-algebra is defined by interpreting symbols of $\mathcal{F}$ as constructors of new terms: for $f \in \mathcal{F}$ of arity j, for $t_1, \ldots t_j \in \mathbb{I}_\Omega$, $f(t_1, \ldots t_j)$ is interpreted as itself.

- With $loop_S(i)$, each instance of a repeatable behavior must be executed entirely before any other can start. We can use $loop_S$ to specify some critical repeatable behavior of which there can only exist one instance at a time.
- With $loop_P(i)$, all existing instances can be executed concurrently w.r.t. one another, and, at any given moment, new instances can be created. $loop_P$ can therefore be used to specify protocols in which any number of new sessions can be created and run in parallel.

4   A Structural Operational Semantics

Now we present our structural operational semantics. It relies on the definition (by structural induction) of two predicates: "$i \downarrow$" (the termination predicate) indicates that the interaction i accepts the empty trace and "$i \xrightarrow{a} i'$" (the execution relation) indicates that traces $a.t$ such that t is accepted by i' are accepted by i. The relation $\rightarrow$ allows the determination, for any interaction i, of which actions a can be immediately executed, and, of potential follow-up interactions i' which express continuations t of traces $a.t$ accepted by i. Defining an execution relation $\rightarrow$ is a staple of process calculus [2]. We will pay particular attention to the weak sequencing operator in Sect. 4.2 before defining $\rightarrow$ in Sect. 4.3.

4.1   Termination

By reasoning on the structure of an interaction term i, we can determine whether or not the empty trace ϵ belongs to its semantics. When this holds, we say that i terminates and use the notation $i \downarrow$ as in [2,16].

Definition 6 (Termination). *The predicate $\downarrow \subset \mathbb{I}_\Omega$ is such that for any i_1 and i_2 from $\mathbb{I}_\Omega$, any $f \in \{strict, seq, par\}$ and any $k \in \{S, H, W, P\}$ we have:*

$$\frac{}{\varnothing \downarrow} \qquad \frac{i_1 \downarrow}{alt(i_1, i_2) \downarrow} \qquad \frac{i_2 \downarrow}{alt(i_1, i_2) \downarrow} \qquad \frac{i_1 \downarrow \quad i_2 \downarrow}{f(i_1, i_2) \downarrow} \qquad \frac{}{loop_k(i_1) \downarrow}$$

All rules of Definition 6 are evident. The empty interaction $\varnothing$ only accepts ϵ, and thus terminates. An interaction with a loop at its root terminates because it is possible to repeat zero times its content. As $alt(i_1, i_2)$ specifies a choice, it terminates iff either i_1 or i_2 terminates. An interaction of the form $f(i_1, i_2)$, with f being a scheduling constructor, terminates iff both i_1 and i_2 terminate. The rules are consistent with the denotational semantics:

Lemma 3 (Termination w.r.t. σ_d). *For any $i \in \mathbb{I}_\Omega$, $(i \downarrow) \Leftrightarrow (\epsilon \in \sigma_d(i))$*

Proof. By induction on the term structure of interactions.   □

In summary, $i \downarrow$ means that i may terminate immediately, but because of non-determinism, depending on the nature of i, i may allow arbitrary long traces.

4.2 Dealing with Weak-Sequencing Using Evasion and Pruning

Weak sequencing only allows interleavings between actions that occur on different lifelines. As a result, within an interaction of the form $i = seq(i_1, i_2)$, some actions that can be executed in i_2 (i.e. such that $i_2 \xrightarrow{a} i'_2$) may also be executed in $seq(i_1, i_2)$, i.e. such that $seq(i_1, i_2) \xrightarrow{a} i'$. In other words, given a trace $a.t \in \sigma_d(i)$, action a might correspond to an action expressed by i_2. This is however conditioned by the ability of i_1 to express traces that have no conflict w.r.t. a so that a may be placed in front of what is expressed by i_1 when recomposing $a.t$.

We define the evasion predicate as a weaker notion than the termination predicate $\downarrow$. The evasion predicate "$\downarrow^*$" can be described as a form of local termination. For a lifeline l, we say that i evades l, denoted by $i \downarrow^* l$ if i accepts at least one trace that does not contain actions occurring on l.

Definition 7 (Evasion). *The predicate $\downarrow^* \subset \mathbb{I}_\Omega \times L$ is such that for i_1 and i_2 in $\mathbb{I}_\Omega$, $l \in L$, $a \in \mathbb{A}_\Omega$, $f \in \{strict, seq, par\}$ and $k \in \{S, H, W, P\}$ we have:*

$$\frac{}{\varnothing \downarrow^* l} \qquad \frac{\theta(a) \neq l}{a \downarrow^* l}$$

$$\frac{i_1 \downarrow^* l}{alt(i_1, i_2) \downarrow^* l} \qquad \frac{i_2 \downarrow^* l}{alt(i_1, i_2) \downarrow^* l} \qquad \frac{i_1 \downarrow^* l \qquad i_2 \downarrow^* l}{f(i_1, i_2) \downarrow^* l} \qquad \frac{}{loop_k(i_1) \downarrow^* l}$$

The empty interaction $\varnothing$ evades any lifeline as ϵ contains no action. An interaction reduced to a single action a evades l iff a does not occur on l. As for termination, an interaction with a loop at its root evades any lifeline because it accepts ϵ. Choice and scheduling operators are also handled in the same manner as for the termination predicate. Moreover, we consider the collision predicate $\cancel{\downarrow}^*$ by considering dual structural rules w.r.t. those defining the evasion predicate $\downarrow^*$ so that we have: $i \cancel{\downarrow}^* l$ iff $\neg(i \downarrow^* l)$.

Lemma 4 (Evasion w.r.t. σ_d).
For any $l \in L$ and $i \in \mathbb{I}_\Omega$, $(i \downarrow^* l) \Leftrightarrow (\exists\, t \in \sigma_d(i), \neg(t \cancel{\downarrow} l))$

Proof. By induction on the term structure of interaction.   □

Let us remark that, for any $i \in \mathbb{I}_\Omega$, if $i \downarrow$ then $\forall\, l \in L$, $i \downarrow^* l$. Indeed, ϵ has no conflict w.r.t. any l. The opposite does not hold: it suffices to consider $i = alt(l_1!m, l_2!m)$ and observe that $\forall\, l \in \{l_1, l_2\}$, $i \downarrow^* l$ holds while $i \downarrow$ does not.

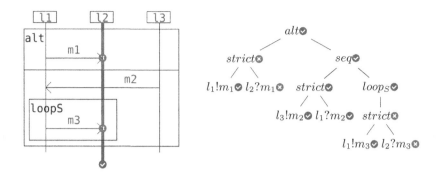

Fig. 3. Illustration of the evasion predicate (here w.r.t. lifeline l_2)

The application of the evasion predicate (w.r.t. lifeline l_2) is illustrated on Fig. 3. On the right is represented the syntactic structure of an interaction i, and, on the left, the corresponding drawing as a sequence diagram. On the syntax tree, the nodes are decorated with symbols ✓ (resp. ✗) to signify that the sub-interaction underneath that node evades (resp. collides with) l_2. Starting from the leaves we can decorate all nodes and conclude once the root is reached. By taking the right branch of the alternative and by choosing not to instantiate the loop, we can see that i accepts some traces that have no conflict w.r.t. lifeline l_2 (in our case, only the trace $l_3!m_2.l_1?m_2$). As a result the interaction i verifies $i \downarrow^* l_2$. On the diagram representation, evasion can be illustrated by drawing a line over l_2 the lifeline of interest. This line can be decomposed into several areas that are colored either in green or in red. The coloration depends on whether the sub-interaction corresponding to the operand evades or collides with l_2.

Provided that $i_1 \downarrow^* \theta(a)$, an action a that is executable in i_2 i.e. s.t. $i_2 \xrightarrow{a} i_2'$ is also executable in $i = seq(i_1, i_2)$. However, this is not enough to define a rule $seq(i_1, i_2) \xrightarrow{a} i'$ compatible with the semantics σ_d. i' must specify continuations t s.t. $a.t \in \sigma_d(i)$. Continuation traces t are built from traces $t_1 \in \sigma_d(i_1)$ and t_2 such that $\neg(t_1 \ast \theta(a))$ and $a.t_2 \in \sigma_d(i_2)$. By defining i_1' as the interaction which expresses exactly traces t_1 s.t. $\neg(t_1 \ast \theta(a))$ we may produce a rule $seq(i_1, i_2) \xrightarrow{a} seq(i_1', i_2')$. The computation of i_1' is called *pruning* and is defined as an inductive relation $\ast\!\!\longrightarrow$ s.t. $i \overset{l}{\ast\!\!\longrightarrow} i'$ indicates that the pruning of $i \in \mathbb{I}_\Omega$ w.r.t. $l \in L$ yields $i' \in \mathbb{I}_\Omega$. Pruning is defined so that $\sigma_d(i') \subseteq \sigma_d(i)$ is the maximum subset of $\sigma_d(i)$ that contains no trace conflicting with l (see Lemma 6).

Definition 8 (Pruning). *The pruning relation* $\ast\!\!\longrightarrow \subset \mathbb{I}_\Omega \times L \times \mathbb{I}_\Omega$ *is s.t. for any* $l \in L$, *any* $f \in \{strict, seq, par\}$ *and any* $k \in \{S, H, W, P\}$:

$$\frac{}{\varnothing \overset{l}{\nrightarrow} \varnothing} \qquad \frac{}{a \overset{l}{\nrightarrow} a} \, \theta(a) \neq l \qquad \frac{i_1 \overset{l}{\nrightarrow} i_1' \qquad i_2 \overset{l}{\nrightarrow} i_2'}{f(i_1, i_2) \overset{l}{\nrightarrow} f(i_1', i_2')}$$

$$\frac{i_1 \overset{l}{\nrightarrow} i_1' \qquad i_2 \overset{l}{\nrightarrow} i_2'}{alt(i_1, i_2) \overset{l}{\nrightarrow} alt(i_1', i_2')} \qquad \frac{i_1 \overset{l}{\nrightarrow} i_1'}{alt(i_1, i_2) \overset{l}{\nrightarrow} i_1'} \, i_2 \not\downarrow^* l \qquad \frac{i_2 \overset{l}{\nrightarrow} i_2'}{alt(i_1, i_2) \overset{l}{\nrightarrow} i_2'} \, i_1 \not\downarrow^* l$$

$$\frac{i_1 \overset{l}{\nrightarrow} i_1'}{loop_k(i_1) \overset{l}{\nrightarrow} loop_k(i_1')} \qquad \frac{}{loop_k(i_1) \overset{l}{\nrightarrow} \varnothing} \, i_1 \not\downarrow^* l$$

Evasion and pruning are intertwined notions. Indeed, as per Lemma 5 evasion is equivalent to the existence and unicity of a pruned interaction.

Lemma 5 (Conditional existence & unicity for pruning).
For any $i \in \mathbb{I}_\Omega$ and any $l \in L$, $(i \downarrow^* l) \Leftrightarrow (\exists! \; i' \in \mathbb{I}_\Omega \; s.t. \; i \overset{l}{\nrightarrow} i')$

Proof. By induction on the term structure of interactions. □

Let us comment on the rules defining the pruning relation. We have $\varnothing \overset{l}{\nrightarrow} \varnothing$ because the semantics of $\varnothing$ being $\{\epsilon\}$, there are no conflicts w.r.t. l. Any action $a \in \mathbb{A}_\Omega$ is prunable iff $\theta(a) \neq l$. In such a case, a needs not be eliminated and thus $a \overset{l}{\nrightarrow} a$. For $i = alt(i_1, i_2)$ to be prunable we must have either or both of $i_1 \downarrow^* l$ or $i_2 \downarrow^* l$. If both branches evade l they can be pruned and kept as alternatives in the new interaction term. If only a single one does, we only keep the pruned version of this single branch. For any scheduling constructor f, if $i = f(i_1, i_2)$, in order to have $i \downarrow^* l$ we must have both $i_1 \downarrow^* l$ and $i_2 \downarrow^* l$. In that case the unique interaction i' such that $i \overset{l}{\nrightarrow} i'$ is defined as the scheduling, using f, of the pruned versions of i_1 and i_2. For loops $i = loop_k(i_1)$ with $k \in \{S, H, W, P\}$, we distinguish two cases: (a) if $i_1 \not\downarrow^* l$ then any execution of i_1 will yield a trace conflicting l and repetitions should be forbidden; (b) if $i_1 \downarrow^* l$ repetitions are kept, given that i_1 can be pruned as $i_1 \overset{l}{\nrightarrow} i_1'$. This being the modification which preserves a maximum amount of traces, we have $loop_k(i_1) \overset{l}{\nrightarrow} loop_k(i_1')$.

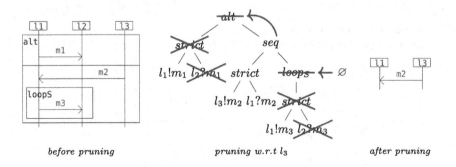

before pruning   pruning w.r.t l_3 after pruning

Fig. 4. Illustration of pruning

We have seen that the interaction i of Fig. 3 satisfies $i \downarrow^* l_2$. Therefore Lemma 5 implies the existence of a unique i' s.t. $i \xrightarrow{l_2}{*} i'$. Figure 4 illustrates the computation of i'. The blue lines represent the modifications in the syntax of i that occur during its pruning into i'. On Fig. 3 we decorated sub-interactions of i with ⊙ whenever they did not evade l_2. During pruning, those sub-interactions must be eliminated given that the resulting term must not express actions occurring on l_2. Hence, on Fig. 4, we have crossed in blue the problematic sub-interactions. The root node is an alt. Let us note $i = alt(i_1, i_2)$. On Fig. 3 we have seen that we have $i_1 \cancel{\downarrow}^* l_2$ and $i_2 \downarrow^* l_2$. Therefore we have $i \xrightarrow{l_2}{*} i'_2$ with i'_2 being such that $i_2 \xrightarrow{l_2}{*} i'_2$. This selection of the right branch of the alt is illustrated on Fig. 4 by the curved arrow which "replaces" the alt by the seq on its bottom right. There remains to determine i'_2 s.t. $i_2 \xrightarrow{l_2}{*} i'_2$. At the root of i_2 we have a seq. Let us note $i_2 = seq(i_A, i_B)$. As per Fig. 3 we have both $i_A \downarrow^* l_2$ and $i_B \downarrow^* l_2$ and therefore $i'_2 = seq(i'_A, i'_B)$ such that $i_A \xrightarrow{l_2}{*} i'_A$ and $i_B \xrightarrow{l_2}{*} i'_B$. Underneath i_A, no actions occur on l_2 and hence $i'_A = i_A$. At the root of i_B we have a $loops$. Let us note $i_B = loops(i_C)$. As per Fig. 3 we have $i_C \cancel{\downarrow}^* l_2$ and therefore $i'_B = \varnothing$ which is illustrated on Fig. 4 by the $\leftarrow \varnothing$ in blue, which "replaces" the $loops$ by $\varnothing$. Finally there remain $i' = seq(i_A, \varnothing)$, which is drawn on the right of Fig. 4.

Lemma 6 states that given $i \xrightarrow{l}{*} i'$, the pruned interaction i' exactly specifies all the executions of i that do not involve l.

Lemma 6 (Pruning w.r.t. σ_d). *For any $l \in L$ and any i and i' from $\mathbb{I}_\Omega$:*

$$(i \xrightarrow{l}{*} i') \Rightarrow (\sigma_d(i') = \{t \in \sigma_d(i) \mid \neg(t \divideontimes l)\})$$

Proof. By induction on the term structure of interactions.   □

4.3   Execution Relation and Operational Semantics

A structural operational semantic in the style of Plotkin [20] allows determining traces $t = a_1. \cdots .a_n$ through the assertion of a succession of predicates of the form $i_j \xrightarrow{a_j} i_{j+1}$ representing the evolution of the system. By expressing action a_j, the system goes from being modelled by i_j to being modelled by i_{j+1}.

Definition 9 (Execution relation).
The execution relation $\rightarrow \subset \mathbb{I}_\Omega \times \mathbb{A}_\Omega \times \mathbb{I}_\Omega$ is s.t.:

$$\frac{}{a \xrightarrow{a} \varnothing} \qquad \frac{i_1 \xrightarrow{a} i'_1}{alt(i_1, i_2) \xrightarrow{a} i'_1} \qquad \frac{i_2 \xrightarrow{a} i'_2}{alt(i_1, i_2) \xrightarrow{a} i'_2}$$

$$\frac{i_1 \xrightarrow{a} i'_1}{par(i_1, i_2) \xrightarrow{a} par(i'_1, i_2)} \qquad \frac{i_2 \xrightarrow{a} i'_2}{par(i_1, i_2) \xrightarrow{a} par(i_1, i'_2)}$$

$$\frac{i_1 \xrightarrow{a} i'_1}{strict(i_1, i_2) \xrightarrow{a} strict(i'_1, i_2)} \qquad \frac{i_2 \xrightarrow{a} i'_2}{strict(i_1, i_2) \xrightarrow{a} i'_2} i_1 \downarrow$$

$$\frac{i_1 \xrightarrow{a} i_1'}{seq(i_1, i_2) \xrightarrow{a} seq(i_1', i_2)} \qquad \frac{i_1 \ast\!\!\xrightarrow{\theta(a)} i_1' \quad i_2 \xrightarrow{a} i_2'}{seq(i_1, i_2) \xrightarrow{a} seq(i_1', i_2')}$$

$$\frac{i_1 \xrightarrow{a} i_1'}{loop_S(i_1) \xrightarrow{a} strict(i_1', loop_S(i_1))} \qquad \frac{i_1 \xrightarrow{a} i_1'}{loop_H(i_1) \xrightarrow{a} seq(i_1', loop_H(i_1))}$$

$$\frac{i_1 \xrightarrow{a} i_1' \quad loop_W(i_1) \ast\!\!\xrightarrow{\theta(a)} i'}{loop_W(i_1) \xrightarrow{a} seq(i', seq(i_1', loop_W(i_1)))} \qquad \frac{i_1 \xrightarrow{a} i_1'}{loop_P(i_1) \xrightarrow{a} par(i_1', loop_P(i_1))}$$

Many of the rules are directly similar to those in use for process algebras. In an interaction reduced to an action a, a may be executed with $\varnothing$ as remaining interaction. If within $i = alt(i_1, i_2)$, action a can be executed in either i_1 or i_2 with either $i_1 \xrightarrow{a} i_1'$ or $i_2 \xrightarrow{a} i_2'$ then it may be executed in i and the resulting interaction is either i_1' or i_2'. For $i = par(i_1, i_2)$, if we have either $i_1 \xrightarrow{a} i_1'$ or $i_2 \xrightarrow{a} i_2'$ then a may be executed in i and the resulting interaction naturally is either $par(i_1', i_2)$ or $par(i_1, i_2')$. Executing actions on the left of either a *strict* or a *seq* follows the same rule as in the case of a *par* because no precedence relations are enforced on the left-hand side. However, an action a may be executed on the right of $i = strict(i_1, i_2)$ only if i_1 terminates. Indeed, in that case i_1 may express the empty trace ϵ as per Lemma 3 and nothing prevents a to be the first action to be executed. The resulting interaction is then i_2' given that we force i_1 to express ϵ. Likewise, within $i = seq(i_1, i_2)$ there is a condition for executing an action a on the right. This condition is that $i_1 \downarrow^* \theta(a)$, which, as per Lemma 5 is implied by the condition $i_1 \ast\!\!\xrightarrow{\theta(a)} i_1'$. Finally, we obtain $i \xrightarrow{a} seq(i_1', i_2')$ given that $i_2 \xrightarrow{a} i_2'$ and that the pruning of i_1 up $\theta(a)$ yields i_1'.

Let us look at rules for loop operators $loop_S$, $loop_H$ and $loop_P$ which look the same, i.e. $loop_k(i) \xrightarrow{a} f(i', loop_k(i))$ under the condition $i \xrightarrow{a} i'$ and using the notation $(k, \diamond, f) \in \{(S, ;, strict), (H, \ast, seq), (P, ||, par)\}$.

Any $t \in \sigma_d(f(i', loop_k(i)))$ verifies $t \in \{t_1\} \diamond \sigma_d(loop_k(i))$ for a certain $t_1 \in \sigma_d(i')$. If action a comes from the first iteration of the loop i.e. $a.t \in \{a.t_1\} \diamond^\daleth \sigma_d(loop_k(i)) \subset \sigma_d(i) \diamond^\daleth \sigma_d(loop_k(i))$, it coincides with using the restricted operator $\diamond^\daleth$ as a scheduler. It turns out that $loop_H$ is explicitly associated to $^{\ast\daleth}\ast$ and thus the formulation of its rule is self-evident. In the case of $loop_S$ and $loop_P$ it is the fact that the HF and K-closures of ; and $||$ are equivalent (as per Lemma 2) which enables their respective rules to be formulated in this manner.

The rule for $loop_W$ allows for the first action to be taken from a later iteration of the loop. Let us consider $i = loop_W(i_1)$ and $a.t \in \sigma_d(i)$. The rule is formulated such that $t \in \sigma_d(seq(i', seq(i_1', i)))$ with $i\ast\!\!\xrightarrow{\theta(a)} i'$ and $i_1 \xrightarrow{a} i_1'$. Given that i is a loop, it is always prunable (Lemma 5) so there exists i' s.t. $i\ast\!\!\xrightarrow{\theta(a)} i'$. The fact that $t \in \sigma_d(seq(i', seq(i_1', i)))$ translates into having $t \in \sigma_d(i')\ast\sigma_d(i_1')\ast\sigma_d(i)$. Then, if a is taken from the first iteration of the loop, then, given that $\epsilon \in \sigma_d(i')$ (Lemma 6) we have $t \in \{\epsilon\}\ast\{t_1'\}\ast\sigma_d(i)$ with $t_1 = a.t_1' \in \sigma_d(i_1)$. If a is taken from the second iteration of the loop, let us consider $t_1 \in \sigma_d(i_1)$ the first iteration and $t_2 = a.t_2' \in \sigma_d(i_1)$ the second one (from which a is taken and hence $t_2' \in \sigma_d(i_1')$).

We have $t \in \{t_1\} \circledast \{t'_2\} \circledast \sigma_d(i)$ and the condition $\neg(t_1 \circledast \theta(a))$. This condition implies, as per Lemma 6 that $\{t_1\} \subset \sigma_d(i')$. The reasoning is the same when a is taken from later instances. Let us consider $a.t \in \{t_1\} \circledast \cdots \circledast \{t_{n-1}\} \circledast \{t'_n\} \circledast \sigma_d(i)$. We then have $\{t_1\} \circledast \cdots \circledast \{t_{n-1}\} \subset \sigma_d(i')$ because i' is either a loop (and therefore absorbing) or $\varnothing$ (all the t_j are then ϵ). Hence the rule indeed allows a to be taken from any iteration.

The predicates $\downarrow$ and $\rightarrow$ ground the operational semantics σ_o given below:

Definition 10 (Operational semantics). $\sigma_o : \mathbb{I}_\Omega \rightarrow \mathcal{P}(\mathbb{T}_\Omega)$ *is s.t.:*

$$\frac{i \downarrow}{\epsilon \in \sigma_o(i)} \qquad \qquad \frac{t \in \sigma_o(i') \qquad i \xrightarrow{a} i'}{a.t \in \sigma_o(i)}$$

4.4   Illustrative Example

On Fig. 5 we illustrate both the operational semantics and an example showcasing the difference between $loop_H$ and $loop_W$. Execution trees are drawn

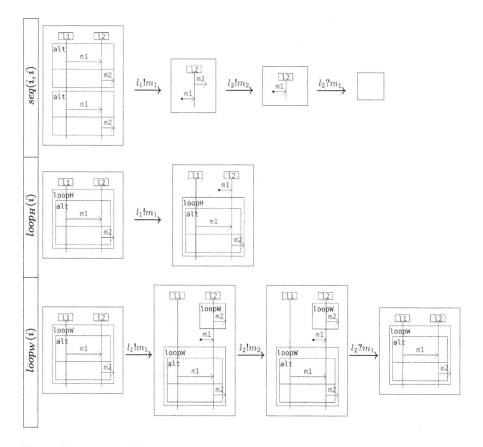

Fig. 5. Illustration of the operational semantics & of the counter-example from Sect. 2.3

with the help of the HIBOU tool described in [14]. We consider repetitions of $i = alt(strict(l_1!m_1, l_2?m_1), l_2!m_2)$. On the first row, we illustrate the construction of a trace accepted by $seq(i, i)$ where i is repeated twice using weak sequencing. Here, the second occurrence of action $l_1!m_1$ (at the bottom) is immediately executable because, with pruning, we can force the choice of the right branch of the first alternative which evades l_1. At the end, the trace $t = l_1!m_1.l_2!m_2.l_2?m_1$ is expressed by $seq(i, i)$. Now, if we consider $loop_H(i)$, we get what is illustrated on the second row of Fig. 5. We can manage to execute the first action $l_1!m_1$ but from that point, the second action of t which is $l_2!m_2$ is not executable. Indeed, the presence of $l_2?m_1$ at the top of the diagram prevents it to be executed. As $loop_H$ is associated to the weak HF-closure $^{*^\daleth}*$ and not to the K-closure **, it is therefore expected that t could not be accepted by $loop_H(i)$ in this example. However, on the third row of Fig. 5, $loop_W(i)$ can recognize t. The addition of the pruned version of the loop allows one to delay the determination of the instance as part of which the initial $l_1!m_1$ is executed.

5   Proving the Equivalence of both Semantics

In the following we prove the equivalence of σ_o and σ_d. A formalisation of the proofs using Coq is available in [13].

Let us at first prove that for any interaction i we have $\sigma_o(i) \subseteq \sigma_d(i)$. The first step to do so is to characterize the execution relation "$\rightarrow$" w.r.t. σ_d:

Lemma 7 (Property 1 of $\rightarrow$ w.r.t. σ_d). *For any $a \in \mathbb{A}_\Omega$, $t \in \mathbb{T}_\Omega$ and i and i' from $\mathbb{I}_\Omega$, $\left((i \xrightarrow{a} i') \wedge (t \in \sigma_d(i')) \right) \Rightarrow (a.t \in \sigma_d(i))$*

Proof. By induction on cases that make $i \xrightarrow{a} i'$ possible.   □

Lemma 7 and Lemma 3 state that the σ_d semantics accepts the same two construction rules (that for the empty trace ϵ and that for non empty traces of the form $a.t$) as those that define σ_o inductively. As a result any trace that is accepted according to σ_o is also be accepted according to σ_d:

Theorem 1 (Inclusion of σ_o in σ_d). *For any $i \in \mathbb{I}_\Omega$ we have $\sigma_o(i) \subseteq \sigma_d(i)$*

Proof. By induction on a member trace t.   □

Let us now prove the reciprocate, i.e. that for any interaction i, $\sigma_d(i) \subseteq \sigma_o(i)$. We provide, with Lemma 8, a second characterization of "$\rightarrow$" w.r.t. σ_d.

Lemma 8. (Property 2 of $\rightarrow$ w.r.t. σ_d). *For any $a \in \mathbb{A}_\Omega$, $t \in \mathbb{T}_\Omega$ and $i \in \mathbb{I}_\Omega$, $(a.t \in \sigma_d(i)) \Rightarrow \left(\exists~ i' \in \mathbb{I}_\Omega,~ (i \xrightarrow{a} i') \wedge (t \in \sigma_d(i')) \right)$*

Proof. By induction on the term structure of interactions.   □

Thanks to Lemma 8 and Lemma 3 we conclude with Theorem 2:

Theorem 2 (Inclusion of σ_d in σ_o). *For any $i \in \mathbb{I}_\Omega$ we have $\sigma_d(i) \subseteq \sigma_o(i)$*

Proof. By induction on a member trace t.   □

We have therefore proven both inclusion and can conclude that the operational semantics σ_o is indeed equivalent to the denotational-style semantics σ_d.

6   Related Works

Unlike some other works (e.g. [9]), we do not have a dedicated construction for the passing of a message from a lifeline to another. We formulate this in the form $strict(a!m, b?m)$, expressing that the emission of message m on lifeline a precedes its reception on b. In [17] a survey of formal semantics associated to UML-SDs is proposed. It is notable that UML-SDs are described semi-formally in the norm [18]. This allows for a rich language with operators such as *assert* or *negate* [5] which are not covered in our IL. However a full formalisation proves difficult, as explained in [5,17]. Most formal approaches rely on translations towards other formalisms [3] or consist in denotational semantics [23] that are most often based on partial order sets. The extent to which UML-SDs are formalised may vary [17]: some works formalize loops [12], others do not [9], and some only allow finitely many iterations [23]. In all cases where there are loops, only one loop operator is proposed and may correspond to either $loop_H$ or $loop_W$.

Our denotational semantics is inspired from [9]. We have completed their definitions dealing with loop operators. [16] introduces an operational semantics for MSC using a termination predicate and an execution relation. Similarities between [16] and our work include the use of pruning which, in [16], relates to a "permission relation". In [16], loops are not handled and there is no *strict* constructor: direct causal relations between actions occurring on different lifelines (e.g. emission-reception of a message) are handled by maps, updated during executions. Moreover, rules involve negative conditions such as $i \overset{g}{\nrightarrow}$ expressing that it is not possible to find an interaction i' verifying $i \overset{a}{\rightarrow} i'$. This way of doing reduces the set of rules to be considered, but does not give clear access to reasoning about the rule system itself, in particular reasoning about semantics equivalence. In [21], a loop construction for weak sequencing composition is considered in addition to the constructions discussed in [16]. Rules in [21] include two rules similar to our rules for $loop_H$ and $loop_W$ so that the semantics includes the two ways of dealing with composition according to the weak sequencing $⋇$.

Earlier works of ours [14,15] focused on the static analysis of traces against interactions. We have proposed an algorithmicised semantics allowing us, given an interaction i and an action a, to compute the follow-up interaction i' whose traces are licit extensions of a with respect to i. This previous semantics was defined in a functional style by identifying the actions likely to start a trace by means of their position in the interaction term. The use of positions makes the semantics less readable and understandable than a structural operational semantics *à la* process algebra, and hampers reasoning about the semantics. Novel contributions in this paper w.r.t. [14,15] consist in the distinction of $loop_W$ & $loop_H$, the formulation of a denotational semantics in an algebraic style rather than using precedence relations, the formulation of a structural operational semantics and primarily, a proof of equivalence between both semantics.

7 Conclusion and Further Work

In this paper we define an IL including weak and strict sequencing, parallel and alternative composition as well as four distinct loop operators to specify different kinds of repetition. We formulate the semantics of this IL: (1) in denotational-style, making use of composition & algebraic operators and (2) in operational-style by reconstructing accepted traces via the succession of atomic executions. The equivalence of both formulations is proven (Coq proof in [13]). We currently investigate how to enrich our language with some form of value passing i.e. instead of exchanging abstract messages we may interpret them concretely or symbolically with typed data. This last point is notably addressed in some process calculi frameworks [7].

References

1. Akshay, S., Bollig, B., Gastin, P., Mukund, M., Narayan Kumar, K.: Distributed timed automata with independently evolving clocks. In: van Breugel, F., Chechik, M. (eds.) CONCUR 2008. LNCS, vol. 5201, pp. 82–97. Springer, Heidelberg (2008). https://doi.org/10.1007/978-3-540-85361-9_10
2. Baeten, J.: Process algebra with explicit termination. Computing science reports, Technische Universiteit Eindhoven (2000)
3. Eichner, C., Fleischhack, H., Meyer, R., Schrimpf, U., Stehno, C.: Compositional semantics for UML 2.0 sequence diagrams using petri nets. In: Prinz, A., Reed, R., Reed, J. (eds.) SDL 2005. LNCS, vol. 3530, pp. 133–148. Springer, Heidelberg (2005). https://doi.org/10.1007/11506843_9
4. Haddad, S., Khmelnitsky, I.: Dynamic recursive petri nets. In: Janicki, R., Sidorova, N., Chatain, T. (eds.) PETRI NETS 2020. LNCS, vol. 12152, pp. 345–366. Springer, Cham (2020). https://doi.org/10.1007/978-3-030-51831-8_17
5. Harel, D., Maoz, S.: Assert and negate revisited: modal semantics for UML sequence diagrams. Softw. Syst. Model. **7**(2), 237–252 (2008)
6. Hoare, C.A.R.: Communicating Sequential Processes. Prentice-Hall, Hoboken (1985)
7. Ingólfsdóttir, A., Lin, H.: A symbolic approach to value-passing processes. In: Bergstra, J., Ponse, A., Smolka, S. (eds.) Handbook of Process Algebra, pp. 427–478. Elsevier Science, Amsterdam (2001). https://doi.org/10.1016/B978-044482830-9/50025-4
8. Jacobs, J., Simpson, A.: On a process algebraic representation of sequence diagrams. In: Canal, C., Idani, A. (eds.) SEFM 2014. LNCS, vol. 8938, pp. 71–85. Springer, Cham (2015). https://doi.org/10.1007/978-3-319-15201-1_5
9. Knapp, A., Mossakowski, T.: UML interactions meet state machines - an institutional approach. In: 7th Conference on Algebra and Coalgebra in Computer Science (CALCO). Leibniz International Proceedings in Informatics (LIPIcs), vol. 72 (2017)
10. Knapp, A., Wuttke, J.: Model checking of UML 2.0 interactions. In: Kühne, T. (ed.) MODELS 2006. LNCS, vol. 4364, pp. 42–51. Springer, Heidelberg (2007). https://doi.org/10.1007/978-3-540-69489-2_6
11. Lodaya, K., Weil, P.: Series-parallel languages and the bounded-width property. Theor. Comput. Sci. **237**(1–2), 347–380 (2000). https://doi.org/10.1016/S0304-3975(00)00031-1

12. Lu, L., Kim, D.K.: Required behavior of sequence diagrams: semantics and confor-mance. ACM Trans. Softw. Eng. Methodol. **23**(2), 1–28 (2014). https://doi.org/10.1145/2523108
13. Mahe, E.: Coq proof for the equivalence of the semantics. erwanm974.github.io/coq_hibou_label_semantics_equivalence/. Accessed 14 Oct 2021
14. Mahe, E., Bannour, B., Gaston, C., Lapitre, A., Le Gall, P.: A small-step approach to multi-trace checking against interactions. In: Proceedings of the 36th Annual ACM Symposium on Applied Computing, SAC 2021, pp. 1815–1822. Association for Computing Machinery, New York (2021). https://doi.org/10.1145/3412841.3442054
15. Mahe, E., Gaston, C., Gall, P.L.: Revisiting semantics of interactions for trace validity analysis. In: FASE 2020. LNCS, vol. 12076, pp. 482–501. Springer, Cham (2020). https://doi.org/10.1007/978-3-030-45234-6_24
16. Mauw, S., Reniers, M.A.: Operational semantics for MSC'96. Comput. Netw. **31**(17), 1785–1799 (1999). https://doi.org/10.1016/S1389-1286(99)00060-2
17. Micskei, Z., Waeselynck, H.: The many meanings of UML 2 sequence diagrams: a survey. Softw. Syst. Model. **10**(4), 489–514 (2011)
18. OMG: Unified Modeling Language v2.5.1, December 2017. omg.org/spec/UML/2.5.1/PDF
19. Parrow, J.: An introduction to the π-calculus. In: Bergstra, J.A., Ponse, A., Smolka, S.A. (eds.) Handbook of Process Algebra, pp. 479–543. Elsevier, North-Holland (2001)
20. Plotkin, G.: A structural approach to operational semantics. J. Log. Algebraic Program. **60–61**, 17–139 (2004). https://doi.org/10.1016/j.jlap.2004.05.001
21. Reniers, M.: Message sequence chart: syntax and semantics. Ph.D. thesis, Mathe-matics and Computer Science (1999). https://doi.org/10.6100/IR524323
22. Rensink, A., Wehrheim, H.: Weak sequential composition in process algebras. In: Jonsson, B., Parrow, J. (eds.) CONCUR 1994. LNCS, vol. 836, pp. 226–241. Springer, Heidelberg (1994). https://doi.org/10.1007/978-3-540-48654-1_20
23. Störrle, H.: Semantics of interactions in UML 2.0. In: 2003 Proceedings of IEEE Symposium on Human Centric Computing Languages and Environments, pp. 129–136, October 2003. https://doi.org/10.1109/HCC.2003.1260216

Automatic Classification of Bug Reports Based on Multiple Text Information and Reports' Intention

Fanqi Meng, Xuesong Wang[(✉)], Jingdong Wang[(✉)], and Peifang Wang

School of Computer, Northeast Electric Power University, Jilin City, Jilin, China
{mengfanqi,wangjingdong}@neepu.edu.cn, wxs970705@163.com

Abstract. With the rapid growth of software scale and complexity, a large number of bug reports are submitted to the bug tracking system. In order to speed up defect repair, these reports need to be accurately classified so that they can be sent to the appropriate developers. However, the existing classification methods only use the text information of the bug report, which leads to their low performance. To solve the above problems, this paper proposes a new automatic classification method of bug reports. The innovation is that when categorizing bug reports, in addition to using the text information of the report, the intention of the report (i.e. "suggestion" or "explanation") is also considered, thereby improving the performance of the classification. First, we collect bug reports from four ecosystems (Apache, Eclipse, Gentoo, Mozilla) and manually annotate them to construct an experimental data set. Then, we use Natural Language Processing technology to preprocess the data. On this basis, BERT and TF-IDF are used to extract the features of the intention and the multiple text information. Finally, the features are used to train the classifiers. The experimental result on five classifiers (including K-Nearest Neighbor, Naive Bayes, Logistic Regression, Support Vector Machine and Random Forest) show that our proposed method achieves better performance and its F-Measure achieves from 87.3% to 95.5% .

Keywords: Automatic classification · Bug report · Defect repair · Report intention

1 Introduction

Defect repair has an important impact on software quality assurance. It is the main activity in the later maintenance phase of software engineering. In recent years, with the vigorous development of the software engineering industry, the architecture complexity and code capacity of software systems have reached a new level that makes it difficult for developers to understand and manage [1]. This trend leads to a large number of bugs inevitably generated in the development process of software systems. To fix these bugs, developers must check the bug report [2]. The bug report describes the defects of the software system in the form of text, which contains multiple tags such as ID, Reporter, Summary, etc., as shown in Fig. 1. In the past, managers classified bug reports based on

© Springer Nature Switzerland AG 2022
Y. Aït-Ameur and F. Crăciun (Eds.): TASE 2022, LNCS 13299, pp. 131–147, 2022.
https://doi.org/10.1007/978-3-031-10363-6_9

tags so that they could assign the reports to appropriate developers to accomplish bug fixes. However, this is a very time-consuming task as there are too many bug reports to check manually. Moreover, due to the different experience and knowledge background of the reporter, the report submitted in the Bug Tracking System may have incorrect tags [3]. These wrong tags will cause the bug report to not be correctly assigned to the appropriate developers, thereby increasing the difficulty of defect repair [4, 5]. In order to reduce this impact and accelerate the speed of defect repair, the software engineering industry needs accurate and automated classification methods for bug reports.

ID	Product	Comp	Sev	Reporter	Summary	Assignee	Status
471699	Dirigibl	General	enh	nedelcho.delchev	Fine grained Roles	dirigible-inbox	NEW
473357	Dirigibl	General	enh	nedelcho.delchev	Entity objects discovery	dirigible-inbox	NEW
468971	Dirigibl	ide-work	enh	nedelcho.delchev	Provide list of available ExtensionPoints for Extension Wizard	dirigible-inbox	NEW
498003	CFT	General	blo	cforce	Spring STS 3.8.0 + CFT 1.0.1	cft-inbox	UNCO

Fig. 1. Several examples of bug report from Bugzilla

In recent years, many researchers have explored the automatic classification of bug reports. Among them, Antoniol et al. [6] classified bug reports via text mining technology. It proved that automatically classify reports into bug and other types through training models is effective and feasible. Zhou et al. [7] proposed a hybrid method combining text mining and data mining techniques to determine whether a new bug report is a real bug. This method also considers the structured information of the report on the basis of purely mining text description [5] (Such as severity and priority). Lamkanfj et al. [8] adopted machine learning technology to classify bug reports into severity and non-severity. Similarly, Tian et al. [9] proposed a nearest neighbor solution based on information retrieval to predict the severity of the bug report. They focused on predicting the five severity levels of the report, namely: Blocker, Critical, Major, Minor and Trivial. In addition, some scholars are concerned about the quality of bug reports [10] and the imbalance of data sets [11, 12] and other issues.

Reporters submit reports with clear intentions. After reading the summary of a large number of open source software bug reports, we found that the intention of the summary text content can be classified into two types: explanation or suggestion. However, there is no intention label in the Bug Tracking System. A large number of existing studies fail to consider the intention of the report when classifying bug reports, which lead to lower performance of their methods. Considering that these intentions will affect the classification of reports, the method in this paper incorporates the intentions of the report. Among them, the explanation refers to the description of the defect, such as a problem or the cause of the problem in a certain location, and the suggestion refers to a solution to the defect, such as how to deal with a certain problem. Table 1 shows real examples of software bug reports in four different ecosystems and their intention.

Table 1. Bug reports with intention tags

Ecosystem	Bug ID	Summary	Intention
Apache	63099	Regression in JMeter 5.0 due to fix of Bug 62478	Explanation
Eclipse	82281	logical structures table should sort on name	Suggestion
Gentoo	76636	Kernel module dvb-ttpci does not find its firmware	Explanation
Mozilla	277324	Copy XML doesn't work on #document nodes	Explanation

To sum up, the contributions of this paper are as follows:

(1) A new bug report classification method is proposed. Based on the text field classification, the intention of the report is additionally considered, and the report is classified as bug and no-bug.
(2) An automatic classification model was constructed based on the proposed method, and the classification performance of five classifiers (K-NN, NB, LR, SVM, RF) was observed. To measure the performance, the Accuracy, Precision, Recall, and F-measure are calculated.
(3) A dataset containing the intention and type of report that can be used by researchers to further explore the automatic classification of bug reports.

The rest of this paper is as follows: The Sect. 2 introduces the related work of bug report classification. The Sect. 3 introduces the proposed method. The Sect. 4 shows the experiment. The Sect. 5 discusses the experiment. Finally, the Sect. 6 summarizes the full text and puts forward insights on future work.

2 Related Work

Bug report classification helps developers understand and fix software defects. Due to the skyrocketing number of bug reports, manual classification has become time-consuming and laborious. For a long time, researchers have been exploring how to implement automatic classification of bug reports [18]. This section will summarize some existing research work.

The earliest bug classification method is Orthogonal Defect Classification (ODC) proposed by IBM's Chillarege et al. [19] in 1992. It is a method between qualitative analysis and quantitative analysis, including 13 categories (such as functions, interfaces, documents, etc.). In 2008, Antoniol et al. [6] proposed an automatic classification method for bug reports, using vector space technology to extract features, and training Decision Trees (DT), NB and LR classifiers to judge whether the report is a bug. The results show that the classification accuracy on Mozila, Eclipse and JBoss projects can reach 77% to 82%. In 2013, Pingclasai et al. [20] proposed a classification method to identify the authenticity of bugs. They adopted the topic model of Latent Dirichlet Allocation (LDA) combined with NB and Linear Logistic Regression (LLR) classifiers, and the accuracy of the three projects of HTTP-Client, Jackrabbit and Lucene reached 66%

to 76%, 65% to 77% and 71% to 82%. Similarly, kukkar et al. [13] applied a hybrid method to identify whether the report is a bug or non-bug in 2019, which integrates TM, NLP and ML technologies. They observed the performance of Term Frequency-Inverse Document Frequency (TF-IDF) and feature selection and K-NN classifiers on five different data sets (Mozilla, Eclipse, JBoss, Firefox, OpenFOAM). Experiments show that the performance of the K-NN classifier varies with different data sets, and its F-measure is 78% to 96%.

In addition, there are also researchers who classify the severity of bug reports. Menzies et al. [21] presented a new automated method called SERVERS in 2008. This method uses TF-IDF, InfoGain and Rule Learning technology to divide the severity of bug reports into 5 categories, from the most severe to the most insensitive. In 2011, Sari et al. [22] applied the InfoGain method to filter out 5 valid attributes from the 14 attributes reported in the bug report for severe and non-serious classification. These 5 attributes are component, qa_contact, summary, cc_list, and product. Their combination can achieve 99.83% accuracy on the SVM model. In 2016, Zhang et al. [23] improved the REP (i.e. REP theme) and K-NN algorithm to search for historical bug reports similar to new bugs, further extracted their features to predict the severity, and classified the bug reports into Blocker, Trivial, Critical, Minor, and Major. The results show that their proposed method can effectively improve the accuracy of the prediction of the severity of bug reports. In 2019, Kukkar et al. [24] believed that traditional Machine Learning classifiers could not capture some potentially important features of bug reports, so they proposed a classification method based on Deep Learning. The model uses the N-gram algorithm and Convolutional Neural Network (CNN) and Random Forest with Boosting to solve the multi-level severity prediction problem of bug reports. Their work has achieved good results, with an average accuracy rate of 96.34% in the five open source projects.

Not only limited to bug or severity, but also researchers have proposed different classification models from other perspectives. Du et al. [25] developed an automatic classification framework based on word2vec in 2017, which classified bug reports into different fault trigger categories from four granularities, including Bug/Non-Bug, BOH/MAN, ARB/NAM, and NAM/ARB. In 2014, Tan et al. [26] believed that semantic, security and concurrency problems are strongly related to software systems. Based on the above assumptions, they studied the distribution of these three types in projects such as Apache, Mozilla and Linux, and automatically classified bug reports into the above three types through machine learning technology. The average F-measure is about 70%. Recently, Catolino et al. [27] defined a new bug report classification pattern in 2019, including 9 defect types (Configuration issue, Network issue, Database-related issue, GUI-related issue, Performance issue, Permission/deprecation issue, Security issue, Program anomaly issue, Test code-related issue). Compared with Tan et al. [26], the method of Catolino et al. can provide a clearer and comprehensive overview of the types of bug reports. At the same time, the automatic model they built also achieved higher F-Measure and AUC-ROC (64% and 74%).

It can be seen from related work that many researchers have achieved good results in the automatic classification of bug reports. On the basis of existing research, the focus of this article is to add a new factor, that is, the intention of the report, when implementing the automatic classification of bug reports. We believe that increasing this factor will improve classification performance.

3   Methodology

This section details the proposed classification method for bug reports. The framework is shown in Fig. 2. First, we collect and manually mark bug reports in the open repository, and then perform preprocessing steps on them. Then, we use BERT and TF-IDF methods to extract features. And the text feature and frequency feature are merged and normalized. Next, we input the extracted features into five classifiers (including K-NN, NB, LR, SVM and RF). Finally, we categorize bug reports into bug and non-bug.

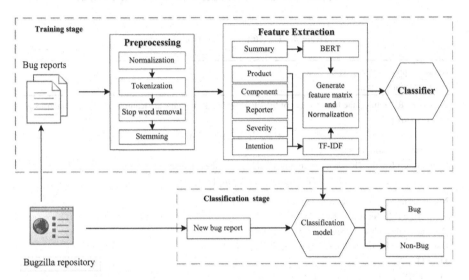

Fig. 2.   Framework of our approach

3.1   Preprocessing

This experiment uses manually marked bug reports as the experimental data set. The data is input in CSV file format, and text preprocessing steps are performed on the summary field, including normalization, tokenization, stop word removal, and stemming.

(1) Normalization: Its task is to unify all words and letters in the data into lowercase.
(2) Tokenization: Its task is to delete numbers, symbols, and punctuation. In this experiment, spaces are used to replace punctuation and numbers are deleted.
(3) Stop word removal: Its task is to delete common words that do not carry specific context-related information, thereby improving the classification performance of the model.
(4) Stemming: Its task is to remove the affixes of words and extract the main part to reduce the redundancy of text data.

3.2 Feature Extraction

After the preprocessing step, we use BERT to extract the text features of the summary field. The BERT model is a pre-training model proposed by Google [28], which can learn dynamic context word vectors and more comprehensively capture the features of word meaning, word position and sentence meaning. In this experiment, the output of the penultimate layer of the BERT model is used as the feature score. For fields other than the summary (i.e. product, component, reporter, severity, intention), the score is calculated using the TF-IDF algorithm. The TF-IDF algorithm can indicate the importance of the field in the document, which helps to increase the classification ability of the model. Finally, the text feature scores and frequency feature scores are spliced and fused to generate a feature matrix, and normalized. The steps are shown in Table 2.

Table 2. The steps of feature extraction

Input: preprocessed bug report data
Output: feature matrix

Step 1: BERT extracts the text features of the summary field and maps the features to a high- dimensional vector matrix (M1).

$$M1 = [V1, V2, \ldots \ldots Vn]$$

Vi = Feature vector, $i \in \{1,2,\ldots \ldots n\}$

Step 2: Calculate the TF-IDF scores of other fields except the summary to obtain the matrix (M2).

$$TF * IDF = Nw / N * log\left(D / \left(Dw + 1\right)\right)$$

Nw = The number of occurrences of the term w in the text

N = Total number of text entries

D = The total number of documents in the corpus

Dw = The number of documents containing the term w

$M2 = [Tp, Tc, Tr, Ts, Ta]$

Ti = TF-IDF score of i, $i \in \{p, c, r, s, a\}$

p = Product, c = Component, r = Reporter, s = Severity, a = Intention

Step 3: The feature matrix (M) is generated by fusing text features and frequency features, and normalized.

$$M = M1 + M2$$
$$M = [Tp, Tc, Tr, Ts, Ta, V1, V2, \ldots \ldots Vn]$$

Normalization method

$$X' = \left(X - X\_min\right) / \left(X\_max - X\_min\right)$$

X = Original data value, X_min = Minimum value of data, X_max = Maximum value of data

Step 4: Output feature matrix.

3.3 Classifier

In order to find the most suitable classifier for the proposed method, we input the extracted features into five classifiers for training respectively, and observe the performance of each classifier. These classifiers include K-NN, NB, LR, SVM and RF.

3.3.1 K-Nearest Neighbor

K-Nearest Neighbor is a supervised classification algorithm based on distance, which is often used in the field of data mining. The core idea is: if most of the k nearest neighbors of a sample in the feature space belongs to a certain category, the sample also belongs to this category and has the characteristics of the samples in this category. That is to say, for a given test sample and a way based on a certain distance measurement, the classification result of the current sample is predicted through the closest K training samples.

Suppose there is a training data set $T = \{(x_1, y_1), (x_2, y_2), ..., (x_N, y_N)\}$, where x_i is the feature vector of the sample, and $y = \{C_1, C_2, ..., C_k\}$ is sample category, $i = 1, 2, ..., N$. According to the selected distance metric, find the K nearest neighbors to x in the training set T, covering the x neighborhood $N_k(x)$ of these K points. According to the index that measures the similarity between samples, the nearest K known samples of each unknown category sample are searched out to form a cluster. The voting method is used in the neighborhood to vote on the searched known samples, that is, the label category with the most occurrences among the K samples is selected to determine the category y of x:

$$y = \arg\max \sum_{x_i \in N_i(x)} I(y_i = c_j) \tag{1}$$

In Eq. (1), $i = 1, 2, ..., N, j = 1, 2, ..., K$. Where I is an indicator function, and when $y_i = c_j$, I is 1, otherwise it is 0.

3.3.2 Naive Bayes

Naive Bayes classifier is a classification technique based on Bayes' theorem. It requires that each feature used for classification is independent and does not affect each other. The core idea is to calculate the category probability of each sample, and the category with the largest probability value is used as the final classification of the sample. Suppose there is a training data set, in order to calculate the probability that the sample y classified as x. According to Bayes' theorem:

$$p(x_i|y_1, y_2, \cdots, y_n) = \frac{p(x_i)}{p(y_1, y_2, \cdots y_n)} \prod_{k=1}^{n} p(y_k|x_i) \tag{2}$$

where $p(x_i)$ and $p(y)$ represent the a priori probabilities of category x_i and sample y, respectively. $p(y|x_i)$ represents the possibility that category x_i is sample y, and $p(x_i|y)$ represents the possibility that sample y is category x_i. Usually, when we deal with classification problems, the sample contains multiple features, which can be expressed $y = (y_1, y_2, ..., y_n)$. When each feature is independent of each other, it can be known from (2):

$$p(x_i|y_1, y_2, \cdots, y_n) = \frac{p(x_i)}{p(y_1, y_2, \cdots y_n)} \prod_{k=1}^{n} p(y_k|x_i) \tag{3}$$

Regarding $p(x_i)$ and $p(y_1, y_2, ..., y_n)$ as constants, after simplifying (3), we can get:

$$x_c = \arg\max \prod_{k=1}^{n} p(y_k|x_i) \tag{4}$$

where y_i is the feature of the data, and x_c is the classification result of the sample. In our experiment, y_i is the feature of the bug report represented by the vector, and the result of x_c has two types, including bug and non-bug.

3.3.3 Support Vector Machine

Support Vector Machine is a classifier based on statistical learning VC dimension and structural risk minimum theory. It finds a balance between classification ability (no error classification for any sample) and model complexity (classification accuracy of a specific sample) based on limited information, with the purpose of making the classifier get the best generalization ability. Suppose there is a linear sample set (x_i, y_i), $i = 1, 2, ..., n$, $x \in R^2$, y is the category label and $y \in \{-1, 1\}$. The linear discriminant function in d-dimensional space is:

$$g(x) = \omega \cdot x + b \tag{5}$$

If the linear classification line can accurately separate the two types of samples, the following conditions should be met:

$$y_i = 1 \Leftrightarrow g(x_i) = \omega \cdot x_i + b \geq 1 \tag{6}$$

$$y_i = -1 \Leftrightarrow g(x_i) = \omega \cdot x_i + b \leq -1 \tag{7}$$

Simplify (6) and (7) to get:

$$y_i(\omega \cdot x_i + b) \geq 1 \tag{8}$$

At this time, the classification interval is equal to $2/\|\omega\|$. When the condition $y_i(\omega \cdot x_i + b) \geq 1$ is satisfied, the minimum value of $\phi(\omega) = (\omega \cdot \omega)/2$ needs to be found. Apply Lagrange multiplier and satisfy Kuhn-Tucker conditions:

$$\alpha_i[y_i(\omega \cdot x_i + b) - 1] = 0 \tag{9}$$

Finally, the optimal classification function is obtained:

$$f(x) = \mathrm{sgn}([\omega^* \cdot x) + b^*] = \mathrm{sgn}\left[\sum_{i=1}^{k} a_i^* y_i(x_i \cdot x) + b^*\right] \tag{10}$$

where α_i^*, b^* is the parameter to determine the optimal hyperplane, and $(x_i \cdot x)$ is the inner product of the two vectors.

3.3.4 Logistic Regression

Logistic Regression, also known as logistic regression analysis, is a generalized linear regression classification model, which is often used in the field of data mining. Logistic regression is essentially a binary classification problem, and its dependent variable Y has two values {0, 1}. The formula of the multiple logistic regression classifier is as follows:

$$\pi(X_1, X_2, \ldots, X_n) = \frac{e^{Y_0 + Y_1 \cdot X_1 + \cdots + Y_n \cdot X_n}}{1 + e^{Y_0 + Y_1 \cdot X_1 + \cdots + Y_n \cdot X_n}} \tag{11}$$

where Xi is a vector describing the features of the data, and $1 \geq \pi \geq 0$ is the value on the logistic regression curve. In order to achieve classification, it is also necessary to set a threshold. For example, the threshold value in the model is 0.5, and x represents the text feature and frequency feature extracted from the bug report. When $\pi > 0.5$, the report is classified as bug; when $\pi < 0.5$,, the report is classified as non-bug.

3.3.5 Random Forest

Random Forest is a classification algorithm based on ensemble learning method, and its basic unit is decision tree. It includes "random" and "forest" parts. "Forest" means that the classifier consists of many trees, and it is based on ensemble learning theory. Random includes two aspects: one is for the training process. In order to ensure that all samples have a chance to be drawn once, the classifier randomly selects a training sample set, and the data used in each round of training is randomly selected from the original sample set with replacement. The other is for feature selection. Assuming that the original data has M features, S number of features are randomly selected from M features as candidate features of the training tree. After the training samples and features are determined, a decision tree is constructed on each training sample to get the prediction result. N samples can get N prediction models, and then use the model to predict the test samples, so that each sample can get N prediction results, and finally determine the final result through a simple majority voting principle. The formula of the model is as follows:

$$H(S) = \text{argMax} \sum_{i}^{n} I(h_i(S_i) = Y) \tag{12}$$

where $h_i(S_i)$ is a single decision tree, Y is the prediction result, and I is an indicator function.

4 Experiment

This experiment divides the training data and test data by 8:2, and extracts the features of the report summary field, other fields (product, component, reporter, severity), and intention, respectively. In order to find the most suitable classifier for the proposed method, we superimpose and fuse these three features in turn, and input them into five different machine learning classifiers (K-NN, NB, SVM, LR, RF) for experiments.

The experiments solved the following research questions:

RQ.1 Does adding the intention of the report improve the accuracy of the automatic classification for bug reports?

RQ.2 How about the performance of our proposed method on five different classifiers?

4.1 Dataset

In this study, we collected 2,230 bug reports from four ecosystems in the Bugzilla repository, respectively from Apache [14], Eclipse [15], Gentoo [16] and Mozilla [17]. Specifically, we select the reports whose status is "RESOLVED" or "VERIFIED" and the resolution is "FIXED". And extract their product, component, reporter, severity, and summary tags. On this basis, we manually marked the types and intention of these reports, and their type information statistics are shown in Table 3.

Table 3. Type statistics of our dataset

Ecosystem	Total	Bug	Non-Bug
Apache	446	296	150
Eclipse	658	419	239
Gentoo	511	294	217
Mozilla	615	425	190

4.2 Evaluation Metrics

To measure the performance of classification, we use Accuracy, Precision, Recall and F-Measure. Their definitions are as follows:

$$Accuracy = \frac{TP + TN}{TP + TN + FP + FN} \tag{13}$$

$$Precision = \frac{TP}{TP + FP} \tag{14}$$

$$Recall = \frac{TP}{TP + TN} \tag{15}$$

$$F - measure = 2 \times \frac{Precision \times Recall}{Precision + Recall} \tag{16}$$

where TP is the number of true positives, TN is the number of true negatives, FP is the number of false positives, and FN is the number of false negatives. In order to deal with the randomness caused by different data splits, ten-fold cross-validation is used to obtain the average value of evaluation metrics to measure the performance of classification.

4.3   Results

RQ1. Does Adding the Intention of the Report Improve the Accuracy of the Automatic Classification for Bug Reports?

We use three types of features that are sequentially fused and superimposed to train the classifier, and the average accuracy of the ten-fold cross-validation is shown in Table 4. Text represents the textual feature of the summary, Freq represents the word frequency feature of other fields (product, component, reporter, severity), and Intention represents the feature of the intention of the bug report. The unit of the values in the table is the percentage system. Text+Freq+Intention is the method we put forward.

Table 4. Average accuracy of all datasets

Ecosystem	Features	Classifier				
		K-NN	NB	LR	SVM	RF
Apache	Text	60.5	65.5	65.6	66.4	63.0
	Text+Freq	70.6	80.0	70.9	70.9	85.7
	Text+Freq+Intention	**90.4**	**89.2**	**90.8**	**91.0**	**91.7**
Eclipse	Text	61.5	63.7	65.0	64.6	61.0
	Text+Freq	66.4	66.1	65.2	64.4	73.1
	Text+Freq+Intention	**83.9**	**84.0**	**84.8**	**84.8**	**84.8**
Gentoo	Text	67.7	61.8	57.3	62.8	67.3
	Text+Freq	83.2	73.6	71.2	72.8	87.3
	Text+Freq+Intention	**91.8**	**85.1**	**86.1**	**87.7**	**94.5**
Mozilla	Text	65.2	66.8	65.0	69.4	67.5
	Text+Freq	75.3	70.4	72.0	72.3	78.2
	Text+Freq+Intention	**89.9**	**87.5**	**87.8**	**88.0**	**87.8**

RQ2. How About the Performance of Our Proposed Method on Five Different Classifiers?

The performance of our proposed method, which combines text, frequency and intention features (Text+Freq+Intention), on the five classifiers is shown in Figs. 3, 4, 5, 6 and 7. The x-axis represents the source of the data, and the y-axis represents the average value of the ten-fold cross-validation.

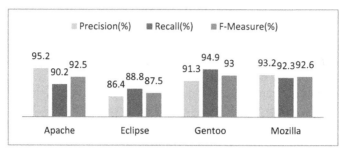

Fig. 3. The performance of all data on the K-NN classifier

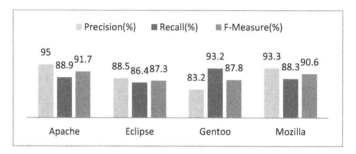

Fig. 4. The performance of all data on the NB classifier

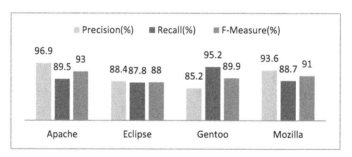

Fig. 5. The performance of all data on the SVM classifier

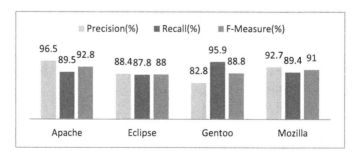

Fig. 6. The performance of all data on the LR classifier

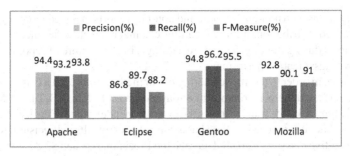

Fig. 7. The performance of all data on the RF classifier

5 Discussion

5.1 Experiment Analysis

Performance of our method: we combine the proposed approach with five different machine learning classifiers, and conduct experiments on the datasets of Apache, Eclipse, Gentoo, and Mozilla. Table 4 shows the average Accuracy of all data sets on different classifiers. Among them, the Apache data set has a maximum of 91.7%, the Eclipse data set has a maximum of 84.8%, the Gentoo data set has a maximum of 94.5%, and the Mozilla data set has a maximum of 89.9%. As can be seen from Table 4, compared with considering the text field of the report alone, after adding the intention factor of the report we proposed, the accuracy of the data sets of the four ecosystems on the five classifiers has been significantly improved. To explore why adding the binary feature of reporting intention can improve classification performance, we made statistics on the distribution of intention features and their correlation with labels (i.e. bug or non-bug) in the experimental dataset. The results are shown in Table 5.

Table 5. Distribution statistics of intention features for all data

Ecosystem	Type	Intention distribution	
		Explanation	Suggestion
Apache	Bug	265	31
	Non-bug	9	141
Eclipse	Bug	368	51
	Non-bug	49	190
Gentoo	Bug	284	10
	Non-bug	66	151
Mozilla	Bug	373	52
	Non-bug	23	167

From the above table, it can be concluded that there is an imbalance in the distribution of intention features in the dataset. Across the four ecosystems, bug reports included more explanations than non-bug reports, and non-bug reports included more suggestions. The imbalanced distribution of binary features can make the classifier more sensitive to different labels during training. Therefore, adding a binary feature of reported intention can improve classification performance.

In addition, in order to test the scalability of our method and select a classifier suitable for it, we also tested the performance of our approach on K-NN, NB, LF, SVM and RF classifiers. Figures 3, 4, 5, 6 and 7 shows the evaluation index value of each classifier. The results show that our proposed method has achieved good results in Precision, Recall and F-measure on five classifiers. In all data sets, the Precision reached 82.8% to 96.9%, the Recall reached 86.4% to 96.2%, and the F-measure reached 87.3% to 95.5%. Among the five classifiers, the comprehensive performance of Random Forest is better than other classifiers, and the performance of each classifier will change with the different data sets. Although the performance of our method changes with the classifier, the overall result is still a good level. This also means that when using our method to conduct a bug report classification, you can adjust the classifier according to different ecosystems and task requirements to achieve the best results. We believe our method is scalable.

Some of our thoughts:

(1) Bugs are harder to understand than non-bugs. Therefore, when faced with bug-type defects, only a few reporters can provide solutions, and most reporters can only describe the problem. This results in most reports where the intention is "explanations" are bugs, and those where the intention is "suggestions" are non-bugs.
(2) In the Bug Tracking System of open source software, the reporters are not only software developers and testers, but also a large number of users. The reporters who explain the defects are mostly users, and the reporters who can make suggestions for the defects are mostly software developers and testers. Because developers and testers have richer experience and knowledge than users, they have a better understanding of the code and architecture of the program, and can give advice on complex defects.
(3) The intention labels in this study are manually labeled, and this work seems to increase the training time of the automatic classification model, but we are to verify that the proposed method can improve the performance of automatic classification of bug reports. We think it is possible to add the label of reporting intention to the Bug Tracking System, so that reporters can explain their intentions when submitting reports, which can greatly reduce the time for manual labeling during model training. It is much easier for reporters to state their intentions than to judge whether a report is a bug.

5.2   Threats to Validity

In this part, we identified the following threats that may exist in this study.

Internal threat: The bug report tags of most open repositories contain errors. In order to avoid incorrect labeling to affect the performance of the model, the data set of this experiment is constructed by our manual labeling based on the data in the Bugzilla repository. Although we have flagged bugs or non-bugs in accordance with the rules proposed in the existing literature [29], due to differences in experience and knowledge background, there may be flagging errors that affect the performance of the model.

External threat: This research focuses on the 2,230 bug reports of the four ecosystems (Apache, Eclipse, Gentoo, Mozilla) to classify bugs or non-bugs. However, the performance of our method on other ecosystems is unknown, that is, the performance of our bug report classification model on data from other software systems may be higher or lower than the results of our experiments.

6   Conclusion and Future Work

In this study, we propose a new automatic classification approach for bug reports, that is, to increase the intention of the report based on the text information of the report. Our approach combines Text Mining, Natural Language Processing and Machine Learning technologies. We first collected 2,230 reports from the four ecosystems (Apache, Eclipse, Gentoo, Mozilla) in the bug repository, and manually marked their types and intention, with the goal of constructing the data set required for the research. Then, we perform preprocessing steps on the data, extract the text features of the report summary field and the word frequency features of other fields, and add the intention features of the report. Next, we superimpose these features and input them into five classifiers (K-NN, NB, SVM, LF, RF). Finally, we classify bug reports into bugs and non-bugs. The results show that, compared with simply extracting text information features for classification, adding the intention features of the report we proposed can significantly improve the performance of bug report classification. In the future, we will verify the proposed approach on more open source ecosystems, and combine Deep Learning technology to improve the performance of automatic classification of bug reports.

Acknowledgment. This work is supported by the Science and Technology Research Project of the Jilin Provincial Department of Education, "Research on Overtime Risk Assessment and Early Warning Technology of Industrial Control Code" (No. JJKH20210097KJ).

References

1. Meng, F., Cheng, W., Wang, J.: Semi-supervised software defect prediction model based on tri-training. KSII Trans. Internet Inf. Syst. **15**(11), 4028–4042 (2021)
2. Guo, S., Chen, R., Li, H.: Using knowledge transfer and rough set to predict the severity of android test reports via text mining. Symmetry **9**(8), 144–161 (2017)
3. Yang, G., Min, K., Lee, J.W.: Applying topic modeling and similarity for predicting bug severity in cross projects. KSII Trans. Internet Inf. Syst. **13**(3), 1583–1589 (2019)
4. Kim, S., Zhang, H., Wu, R., Gong, L.: Dealing with noise in defect prediction. In: 2011 33rd International Conference on Software Engineering (ICSE), pp. 481–490. ACM (2011)
5. Kochhar, P.S., Le, T.D.B., Lo, D.: Dealing with noise in defect prediction. In: 2014 11th Working Conference on Mining Software Repositories (MSR), pp. 296–299. IEEE (2014)
6. Antoniol, G., Ayari, K., Di, P.M., Khomh, F., Guéhéneuc, Y.G.: Is it a bug or an enhancement? A text-based approach to classify change requests. In: 2008 Conference of the Centre for Advanced Studies on Collaborative Research: Meeting of Minds, pp. 304–318 (2008)

7. Zhou, Y., Tong, Y., Gu, R., Gall, H.: Combining text mining and data mining for bug report classification. J. Softw.: Evol. Process **28**(3), 150–176 (2016)
8. Lamkanfi, A., Demeyer, S., Giger, E., Goethals, B.: Predicting the severity of a reported bug. In: 2010 7th IEEE/ACM Working Conference on Mining Software Repositories (MSR), pp. 1–10. IEEE (2010)
9. Tian, Y., Lo, D., Sun, C.: Information retrieval based nearest neighbor classification for fine-grained bug severity prediction. In: 2012 19th Working Conference on Reverse Engineering, pp. 215–224 (2012)
10. Feng, Y., Chen, Z., Jones, J., Fang, C., Xu, B.: Test report prioritization to assist crowdsourced testing. In: 2015 10th Joint Meeting on Foundations of Software Engineering, pp. 225–236 (2015)
11. Zhang, T., Chen, Y., Yang, X., Zhu, H.: Approach of bug reports classification based on cost extreme learning machine. J. Softw. **30**(5), 1386–1406 (2019)
12. Yang, X.L., Lo, D., Xia, X., Huang, Q., Sun, J.L.: High-impact bug report identification with imbalanced learning strategies. J. Comput. Sci. Technol. **32**(1), 181–198 (2017)
13. Kukkar, A., Mohana, R.: A supervised bug report classification with incorporate and textual field knowledge. Proc. Comput. Sci. **132**, 352–361 (2018)
14. http://bz.apache.org
15. http://bugs.eclipse.org
16. http://bugs.gentoo.org
17. http://bugzilla.mozilla.org
18. Zhang, T., Jiang, H., Luo, X., Chen, A.T.: A literature review of research in bug resolution: tasks, challenges and future directions. Comput. J. **59**(5), 741–773 (2016)
19. Chillarege, R., et al.: Orthogonal defect classification-a concept for in-process measurements. IEEE Trans. Softw. Eng. **18**(11), 943–956 (1992)
20. Pingclasai, N., Hata, H., Matsumoto, K.I.: Classifying bug reports to bugs and other requests using topic modelling. In: 2013 20th Asia-Pacific Software Engineering Conference (APSEC), vol. 2, pp. 13–18 (2011)
21. Menzies, T., Marcus, A.: Automated severity assessment of software defect reports. In: 2008 IEEE International Conference on Software Maintenance (ICSM), pp. 346–355. IEEE (2008)
22. Sari, G.I.P., Siahaan, D.O.: An attribute selection for severity level determination according to the support vector machine classification result. In: 1st International Conference on Information Systems for Business Competitiveness (ICISBC) (2012)
23. Zhang, T., Chen, J., Yang, G., Lee, B., Luo, X.: Towards more accurate severity prediction and fixer recommendation of software bugs. J. Syst. Softw. **177**(10), 166–184 (2016)
24. Kukkar, A., Mohana, R., Nayyar, A., Kim, J., Kang, B.G., Chilamkurti, N.: A novel deep-learning-based bug severity classification technique using convolutional neural networks and random forest with boosting. Sensors **19**(13), 2943–2964 (2019)
25. Du, X., Zheng, Z., Xiao, G., Yin, B.: The automatic classification of fault trigger based bug report. In: 2017 IEEE International Symposium on Software Reliability Engineering Workshops (ISSREW), pp. 259–265. IEEE (2017)
26. Tan, L., Liu, C., Li, Z., Wang, X., Zhou, Y., Zhai, C.: Bug characteristics in open source software. Empir. Softw. Eng. **19**(6), 1665–1705 (2013). https://doi.org/10.1007/s10664-013-9258-8
27. Catolino, G., Palomba, F., Zaidman, A., Ferrucci, F.: Not all bugs are the same: understanding, characterizing, and classifying bug types. J. Syst. Softw. **152**(10), 165–181 (2019)

28. Devlin, J., Chang, M.W., Lee, K., Toutanova, K.: BERT: pre-training of deep bidirectional transformers for language understanding. arXiv:1810.04805 (2018)

29. Herzig, K., Just, S., Zeller, A.: It's not a bug, it's a feature: how misclassification impacts bug prediction. In: 2013 35th International Conference on Software Engineering (ICSE), pp. 392–401. ACM (2013)

Collaborative Verification
of Uninterpreted Programs

Yide Du[1], Weijiang Hong[1,2], Zhenbang Chen[1(✉)], and Ji Wang[1,2]

[1] College of Computer, National University of Defense Technology, Changsha, China
{dyd1024,hongweijiang17,zbchen,wj}@nudt.edu.cn
[2] State Key Laboratory of High Performance Computing, National University of
Defense Technology, Changsha, China

Abstract. Given a set of uninterpreted programs to be verified, the
trace abstraction-based verification method can be used to solve them
once at a time. The verification of different programs is independent of
each other. However, the individual verification for each one is a waste
of resources if the programs behave similarly. In this work, we propose a
framework for the collaborative verification of a set of uninterpreted programs, which accumulates and reuses the abstract models of infeasible
traces to improve the verification's efficiency. We have implemented the
collaborative verification framework and the preliminary result demonstrate that our collaborative method is effective on the benchmark.

Keywords: Collaborative verification · Uninterpreted programs ·
CEGAR

1 Introduction

An uninterpreted program [11] is a program that works with arbitrary data
models and all of its functions have only a signature information and satisfy the
common property, *i.e.*, same inputs produce same outputs. Given a program $\mathcal{P}$
to be verified, we can over-approximate $\mathcal{P}$ by an uninterpreted version $\mathcal{P}_u$ and
do the verification. In most cases, the verification of $\mathcal{P}_u$ has a lower complexity.
However, even for uninterpreted programs, the verification problem is in general
undecidable [11]. Recently, a decidable class of uninterpreted programs called
coherent ones has been discovered [11]. Based on this result, a more effective trace
abstraction-based CEGAR-style [7] verification method for general uninterpreted
programs is proposed [8].

We notice that all this work are focus on the verification problem of a single
program, but there are many scenarios that a set of programs need to be verified. For example, the incremental verification plays an important role in the
area of regression verification as it can significantly improve the verification efficiency. During software development, only part of the software be changed and
due to the high complexity of program verification, there is no need to verify the

© Springer Nature Switzerland AG 2022
Y. Aït-Ameur and F. Crăciun (Eds.): TASE 2022, LNCS 13299, pp. 148–154, 2022.
https://doi.org/10.1007/978-3-031-10363-6_10

changed version from scratch. There are similar behaviors between different programs. Exploiting the similarity between softwares and reusing the verification results is an effective way to improve the efficiency of verification.

In this work, we propose a collaborative verification method to reuse the abstract models of infeasible traces during the CEGAR-style verification across different programs to improve the efficiency of verification.

The main contributions of this paper are as follows:

- We propose a framework for collaborative verification that can reuse the abstract models of infeasible traces to improve the efficiency of verification.
- We have implemented our framework in a prototype for uninterpreted programs and the preliminary result demonstrate that our collaborative method is effective on the benchmark.

Structure. The remainder of this paper is organized as follows. Section 2 gives a motivation example. The collaborative verification framework will be given in Sect. 3. Section 4 gives the preliminary evaluation results. Finally, Sect. 5 compares the related work, Sect. 6 introduces the next steps, and Sect. 7 concludes the paper.

2   Motivation

```
1  x := y;
2
3  if (z != n1){
4      x := g(x);
5      y := g(y);
6  } else {
7      x := f(x);
8      y := f(y);
9  }
10
11 assert(x = y);
```

(a) $\mathcal{P}_0$

```
1  x := y;
2
3  if (z != n1){
4      x := h(x);
5      y := h(y);
6  } else {
7      x := f(x);
8      y := f(y);
9  }
10
11 assert(x = y);
```

(b) $\mathcal{P}_1$

Fig. 1. The motivation example.

In Fig. 1 there are two uninterpreted programs in which $\mathcal{P}_1$ is obtained by modifying the program $\mathcal{P}_0$. Notice that all the traces of these two programs satisfy the equality of x and y at beginning, then apply the same functions on both x and y, so all of them satisfy the assertion in the end. If we use the CEGAR method with the congruence-based abstraction in [8] to verify them, we need 2 iterations, respectively.

We observe that $\mathcal{P}_1$ is the modified version of $\mathcal{P}_0$ and the false branch of them are the same. Therefore, we can conclude that the false branch of $\mathcal{P}_1$ is correct when $\mathcal{P}_0$ is verified to be correct, only the true branch of $\mathcal{P}_1$ need to be verified. In the scenario of software development and evolution, most of the traces are the same between two successive versions, it's no need to verify them from scratch. Based on these observations, we propose a collaborative verification method that reuses the abstract model of infeasible traces to improve the verification's efficiency. Next, we demonstrate the process of our collaborative verification method on this motivation example.

We use $\mathcal{A}_C$ to represent the accumulated model of infeasible traces, and $\mathcal{L}(\mathcal{A}_C)$ is empty at the beginning. First, $\mathcal{P}_0$ is verified to be correct by the CEGAR method, and the abstract models of the infeasible traces in $\mathcal{P}_0$ are merged with $\mathcal{A}_C$. When $\mathcal{P}_1$ is to be verified, its false branch can be removed by performing $\mathcal{A}_{\mathcal{P}_1} = \mathcal{A}_{\mathcal{P}_1} \backslash \mathcal{A}_C$ and the true branch can be verified by the CEGAR method. It takes only 2 and 1 iterations of refinement to successfully verify $\mathcal{P}_0$ and $\mathcal{P}_1$ respectively. Intuitively, the closer the programs to be verified, the more effective our collaborative verification method is.

3 Collaborative Verification Framework

We propose a collaborative verification framework based on the scheme of CEGAR for trace abstraction, which accumulates the abstract models of infeasible traces during the verification procedure, and the accumulated abstract models are later reused to facilitate other program's verification. The details can be found in Fig. 2.

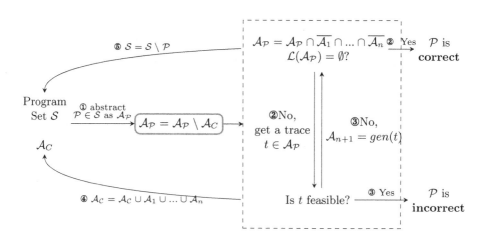

Fig. 2. Collaborative verification framework.

Our collaborative verification framework introduces an initial empty automata $\mathcal{A}_C$ to accumulates the abstract models during the verification progress. When verifying a set of programs $\mathcal{S}$, we pick one program $\mathcal{P}$ from them and abstract it to an FSA $\mathcal{A}_\mathcal{P}$ which include all the traces of $\mathcal{P}$. Then we wipe off those infeasible traces included in $\mathcal{A}_C$ by $\mathcal{A}_\mathcal{P} = \mathcal{A}_\mathcal{P} \backslash \mathcal{A}_C$. During the verification, we can conclude that $\mathcal{P}$ is correct if $\mathcal{L}(\mathcal{A}_\mathcal{P}) = \emptyset$ holds, otherwise, a trace t can be extracted from $\mathcal{L}(\mathcal{A}_\mathcal{P})$. If t is feasible, a real counter-example is found, and we can conclude that $\mathcal{P}$ is incorrect. Otherwise, we can abstract an FSA $\mathcal{A}_{n+1}$ from t which accept all the infeasible traces that with the same reason with t. Then, $\mathcal{A}_\mathcal{P}$ can be refined by $\mathcal{A}_{n+1}$. The CEGAR process continues until a feasible counter-example is found or $\mathcal{P}$ is concluded to be correct.

After the verification of each program is completed, the abstract models obtained during the verification process can be merged with $\mathcal{A}_C$ for reusing. When a new program is to be verified, $\mathcal{A}_C$ can be used to refine the program abstraction. The infeasible traces included in $\mathcal{A}_C$ can be removed directly without the CEGAR process. Thus, our framework shares the abstract models of infeasible traces within the programs in $\mathcal{S}$ to improve the verification's efficiency.

4   Preliminary Result

We have implemented a prototype for our collaborative verification framework in OCaml. We prepare to evaluate our collaborative verification framework on a set of similar programs. In the scenario of regression verification, during the software development and evolution, only part of the software be changed between two successive software versions and most of the program behavior is similar. Based on this scenario, we evaluate our collaborative method to answer the following question.

> Efficiency, *i.e.*, how efficient is our collaborative verification method compared to verifying each program individually when there are a set of uninterpreted programs to be verified?

Considering that there is no standard benchmark for similar programs, we convert some real-world programs from SV-COMP [15] to uninterpreted programs. These programs can be used as original programs in regression verification. To simulate the software evolution process, we randomly extract 10 correct programs as the initial programs and mutate them. Therefore we have 10 groups of similar programs that simulate software evolution.

All the experiments are carried out on a server with eight cores and 32G memory. The operating system is Ubuntu 18.04. We use the average value of three runs to eliminate the experimental errors.

The collaborative verification method is effective if the abstract models we collected reduces the number of refinements and further reduces the time cost of verification. We evaluate the collaborative verification method on the benchmark that simulates software evolution. Our preliminary results demonstrate that our collaborative verification method is effective, for the average speedups of 2.70x (1.11x–3.84x) on the benchmark.

5   Related Work

There are many existing works for collaborative verification. In some works [3–5], different verification tools are collaborated in different ways to improve verification efficiency and the ability to detect assertions. These methods have achieved good results, but all of them focus on a single program, while our work consider a set of similar programs. Such as the scenario of regression verification, the incremental verification is an efficient way to improve the verification's efficiency. There are different approachs to implement collaborative verification in different verification tools. For example, the function summaries [14], the abstraction precisions [2], the procedure summaries the state-space modeled by automata [1,10], and the loop summaries [6], the assertions in predicate analysis [16] and the counter-example traces [3] are reused to improves the efficiency of regression verification. Our approach reuses the abstract models of infeasible traces to improve the efficiency of verification.

Uninterpreted programs and their verification problems have been studied in many works. A decidable class of uninterpreted programs was found by Mathur *et al.* [11], based on this result, many decidable results [9,12,13] are proposed for different types of programs. For the verification problem of general uninterpreted program, CEGAR-based verification provide a general framework. A congruence-based trace abstraction method for infeasible traces was proposed by Hong *et al.* [8] and is more efficient than the interpolant-based trace abstraction method [7]. In this work, we implemented our collaborative verification framework based on Hong *et al.* [8]'s work.

6   Next Steps

The abstract models of infeasible traces are critical for the verification's efficiency, the better the generalization of the trace abstract models are, the less number of the program's refinement need. We studied the existing trace abstraction method [8] and found that the method does not distinguish the different reasons why a trace is infeasible. So we intend to propose a fine-grained generalization method to improve the generalization's ability.

Except for the scenario of regression validation, we are intend to consider more scenarios in which our approach is applicable, such as the component-based software development. In this scenario, programs are obtained by composing several designed components, and their behavior are similar. In the later evaluation, we are intend to explore the effect of different factors on the efficiency of our collaborative verification method, such as the verification order of programs and the different proportion of correct programs.

Furthermore, we plan to extend our collaborative verification framework to more types of programs and different verification tools.

7   Conclusion

This paper propose a collaborative verification framework for a set of uninterpreted programs. In some scenarios such as software development, there are similar traces between this set of uninterpreted programs. So we preserve the abstract models of infeasible traces during the verification process, when a new program is to be verified, the saved abstract models can be reused to do a refinement on it, thereby speeding up the overall verification speed. We have implemented our method and the preliminary results demonstrate that our method performs better on the benchmark.

Acknowledgments. This research was supported by the NSFC Programs (No. 62172429 and 62032024).

References

1. Beyer, D., Holzer, A., Tautschnig, M., Veith, H.: Information reuse for multi-goal reachability analyses. In: Felleisen, M., Gardner, P. (eds.) ESOP 2013. LNCS, vol. 7792, pp. 472–491. Springer, Heidelberg (2013). https://doi.org/10.1007/978-3-642-37036-6_26

2. Beyer, D., Löwe, S., Novikov, E., Stahlbauer, A., Wendler, P.: Precision reuse for efficient regression verification. In: Proceedings of the 2013 9th Joint Meeting on Foundations of Software Engineering, pp. 389–399 (2013)

3. Beyer, D., Wendler, P.: Reuse of verification results. In: Bartocci, E., Ramakrishnan, C.R. (eds.) SPIN 2013. LNCS, vol. 7976, pp. 1–17. Springer, Heidelberg (2013). https://doi.org/10.1007/978-3-642-39176-7_1

4. Christakis, M., Müller, P., Wüstholz, V.: Collaborative verification and testing with explicit assumptions. In: Giannakopoulou, D., Méry, D. (eds.) FM 2012. LNCS, vol. 7436, pp. 132–146. Springer, Heidelberg (2012). https://doi.org/10.1007/978-3-642-32759-9_13

5. Csallner, C., Smaragdakis, Y.: Check 'n'crash: combining static checking and testing. In: Proceedings of the 27th International Conference on Software Engineering, pp. 422–431 (2005)

6. He, F., Yu, Q., Cai, L.: Efficient summary reuse for software regression verification. IEEE Trans. Softw. Eng. (2020)

7. Heizmann, M., Hoenicke, J., Podelski, A.: Refinement of trace abstraction. In: Palsberg, J., Su, Z. (eds.) SAS 2009. LNCS, vol. 5673, pp. 69–85. Springer, Heidelberg (2009). https://doi.org/10.1007/978-3-642-03237-0_7

8. Hong, W., Chen, Z., Du, Y., Wang, J.: Trace abstraction-based verification for uninterpreted programs. In: Huisman, M., Păsăreanu, C., Zhan, N. (eds.) FM 2021. LNCS, vol. 13047, pp. 545–562. Springer, Cham (2021). https://doi.org/10.1007/978-3-030-90870-6_29

9. La Torre, S., Parthasarathy, M.: Reachability in concurrent uninterpreted programs. In: 39th IARCS Annual Conference on Foundations of Software Technology and Theoretical Computer Science (FSTTCS 2019). Schloss Dagstuhl-Leibniz-Zentrum fuer Informatik (2019)

10. Lauterburg, S., Sobeih, A., Marinov, D., Viswanathan, M.: Incremental state-space exploration for programs with dynamically allocated data. In: 2008 ACM/IEEE 30th International Conference on Software Engineering, pp. 291–300. IEEE (2008)

11. Mathur, U., Madhusudan, P., Viswanathan, M.: Decidable verification of uninterpreted programs. Proc. ACM Program. Lang. **3**(POPL), 1–29 (2019)
12. Mathur, U., Madhusudan, P., Viswanathan, M.: What's decidable about program verification modulo axioms? In: TACAS 2020. LNCS, vol. 12079, pp. 158–177. Springer, Cham (2020). https://doi.org/10.1007/978-3-030-45237-7_10
13. Mathur, U., Murali, A., Krogmeier, P., Madhusudan, P., Viswanathan, M.: Deciding memory safety for single-pass heap-manipulating programs. Proc. ACM Program. Lang. **4**(POPL), 1–29 (2019)
14. Sery, O., Fedyukovich, G., Sharygina, N.: Incremental upgrade checking by means of interpolation-based function summaries. In: 2012 Formal Methods in Computer-Aided Design (FMCAD), pp. 114–121. IEEE (2012)
15. SV-benchmarks. https://github.com/sosy-lab/sv-benchmarks
16. Yu, Q., He, F., Wang, B.Y.: Incremental predicate analysis for regression verification. Proc. ACM Program. Lang. **4**(OOPSLA), 1–25 (2020)

MSDetector: A Static PHP Webshell Detection System Based on Deep-Learning

Baijun Cheng[1], Yanhui Guo[1], Yan Ren[2], Gang Yang[3], and Guosheng Xu[1(✉)]

[1] School of Cyberspace Security, National Engineering Research Center of Mobile Network Security, Beijing University of Posts and Telecommunications, Beijing 100876, China
guoshengxu@bupt.edu.cn
[2] QI-ANXIN Technology Group Inc., Beijing, China
[3] School of Artificial Intelligence, Beijing University of Posts and Telecommunications, Beijing 100876, China

Abstract. Webshell is a web script containing malicious code fragment, which hackers could use to launch web attacks. Hence, it is of great signifiance to identify whether a web script contains malicious code fragments in the aspect of web security. However, the flexibility of scripting language such as PHP provides attackers the opportunities to obfuscate scripts, making it challenging for traditional rule-based webshell detectors to detect malicious code fragments. Deep learning brings new ideas for webshell detection and improves the effect of detectors. However, the effect of deep learning-based detectors depends on feature engineering and deep learning models. The feature representations and models adopted by existing methods fail to mine the syntactic and semantic features of webshell scripts. To tackle those problems, we design a new code representation called script sequence according to the characteristics of webshell and also we introduce new pretrain task to enhance understanding of deep learning model to syntax information of webshell code. This leads to the design and implementation of Malicious Script Detector (MSDetector). In order to evaluate MSDetector, we present a new PHP webshell dataset. Experimental results prove that MSDetector can achieve higher F1 score and accuracy than other approaches on the dataset.

Keywords: Webshell detection · Code representation · Deep learning

1 Introduction

In general, the web script which can be used to execute system commands, view databases, or combine some common operations to achieve some advanced spying behaviours is called Webshell, and it is a common web attack technology. Hacker could implant a malicious script into web applications through web vulnerabilities such as file upload or SQL injection. Webshell is often used for purposes

Supported by the National Natural Science Foundation of China (No.: 61873069).

Y. Aït-Ameur and F. Crăciun (Eds.): TASE 2022, LNCS 13299, pp. 155–172, 2022.
https://doi.org/10.1007/978-3-031-10363-6_11

such as permission maintenance and data theft. So it is of great significance to detect webshells.

Note that webshell can be written in all kinds of script languages. In this paper, we mainly focus on PHP scripts because it is the most widely used script language around the world.

In order to detect webshells, there have already been many rule-based detectors, such as NeoPI[1] and Shell-Detector[2]. Those approaches have two major drawbacks: they require experts to define rules and are prone to incur high false negative rates because they can only detect known webshell patterns. Hence, an ideal approach should effectively identify webshells with different kinds of patterns while trying not to rely on experts.

Deep Learning has been successful in the domains of computer vision and natural language processing. Recently, many researches [6,8,12,14,16,21,25,26] apply deep learning techniques to webshell detection, which mitigates manual labor to define rules and improves the performance of webshell detectors. However, there are still some problems to be solved. The effect of deep learning-based webshell detectors depends on feature engineering. The existing approaches mainly extract opcode sequence or text sequence from PHP code fragment as feature representation. The opcode sequence-based approaches abandon operands of PHP bytecodes, which could contain critical information of webshell. The text sequence-based approaches would lose syntactic information of PHP codes because they simply regard PHP code as natural language texts and some literals in PHP codes are hard to process by models. So those methods could not well mine syntactic and semantic information from PHP codes.

Our Solution. In this paper we present MSDetector, a new deep-learning based PHP webshell detector. We first present script sequence, a new sequence representation which is combined with lexical token sequence and string literal sequence of a PHP script file, then we leverage recent transformer-based [23] neural networks to embed script sequence into latent low-dimension vector space and classify it with a linear layer added to the top of transformer model.

We implement a customized script parser to transform a script file into script sequence, which is done by extracting lexical tokens and string literals when traversing the abstract synax tree(AST) of a script file. The tokens and string literals need symbolizing according to their types and contexts after being extracted. Also, there are some statements that are not related to webshell, we remove those statements when traversing AST. Token sequence and string literal sequence would be spliced together and separated by a special separator.

However, script sequence does not contain any syntactic information of code, directly using tree-structured neural network like TreeCNN [18] and TreeL-STM [20] to process ASTs is time-consuming. L. Buratti et al. [3] have proved that the structured information of code can be encoded by transformer-based model and is helpful in downstream tasks like vulnerability identification in source code, here we utilize CodeBert [7], which has already pre-trained on

---

[1] https://github.com/CiscoCXSecurity/NeoPI.
[2] http://www.shelldetector.com.

Masked Language Modeling (MLM) and Replaced Token Detection (RTD) for six programming languages including PHP, to learn structured information of PHP and detect webshell. We pre-train CodeBert on AST Node Tagging (ANT) task to make the model learn to map a lexical token to its corresponding node tag related to AST, here in pre-training stage, the script parser would not extract string literal sequence but to extract lexical tokens and their corresponding AST node types, and symbolize tokens. After pre-training, we fine-tune the model on webshell detection task. We evaluate our approach on a manually crafted dataset, experimental results prove that the fine-tunned model achieves better results than state-of-art approaches on accuracy, precision, recall and F1 scores.

The contributions of this work are summarized as follows:

- we present a new code representation: script sequence, to extract key features of webshell from PHP code.
- We pre-train transformer-based model on AST Node Tagging task to enhance the understanding of model to syntactic information of PHP code. The experimental results show that the enhanced transformer model is better than the previous model in webshell detection task.
- We implement MSDetector, and evaluate its effectiveness through our collected dataset. Experimental results show that MSDetector achieves higher accuracy and F1 score than baseline methods. Our tool is available at github[3].

2 Motivation

2.1 Framework Overview

Figure 1 shows the overall framework of MSDetector consisting of three phases: a pre-training phase, a training-phases and a detecting phase.

For the pre-training phase, in (a.1), MSDetector first parse a PHP script into its AST, and extract lexical tokens from terminal node, at the same time, the node tags of tokens would be generated according to the context of the terminal nodes. Also, lexicals tokens from AST terminal nodes would be symbolized after extraction. Next in (a.2), MSDetector start pre-training transformer model on a sequence tagging task called AST Node tagging with lexical token sequences as input and node tag sequences as labels, to make the model grasp the structured information of PHP code.

For the training phase, in (b.1), MSDetector extracts lexical token sequence in the same way as in pre-training phase. The difference is that MSDetector generates a string literal sequence instead of node tag sequence in this stage. Specifically, for every string literal in source code, MSDetector parse it first with a string parser and put the parsing result into string literal sequence. In (b.2), MSDetector concatenate lexical token sequence and string literal sequence into script sequence with a separator "[SEP]" separate them. The pre-trained transformer model will be fine-tuned to detect webshell in detecting phase.

---

[3] https://github.com/for-just-we/MSDetector.

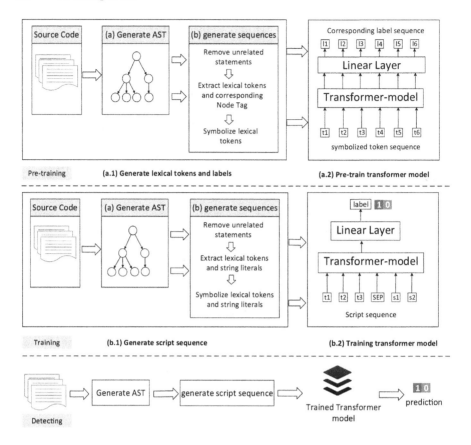

Fig. 1. Overview of MSDetector.

Note that in all three phases, statements in code that are not strongly related to webshell like "@set_time_limit(0);" will be ignored when MSDetector traverses AST, this would help reduce the length of token sequence and the noise in scripts.

2.2   Motivating Example

Figure 2 presents an example of generating lexical token sequence and node tag sequence in pre-training stage. Source code would be parsed into AST, the lexical tokens would appear in the terminal nodes of AST. MSDetector extracts every token in the terminal node except those nodes in ignored statements. Generally, MSDetector would set the parent node type of a given token as its node tag. Also, extracted tokens require symbolizing to construct a canonical form of the textual representation, this would help reduce noise imposed by irregular user-defined names. Here, we only consider symbolizing user-defined class names, function names and variable names. In this example, function name "foo" is symbolized to "func1", variable name "$var". is symbolized to "$var1".

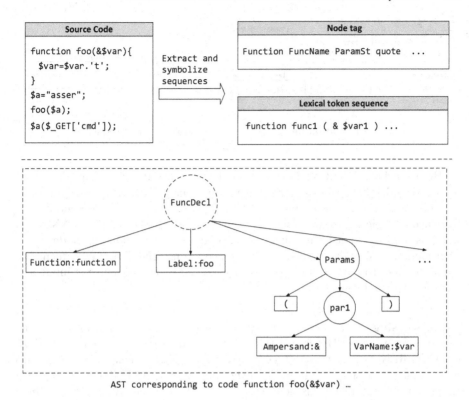

Fig. 2. Illustration for the process of extracting node tag sequence and token sequence from AST.

Figure 3 illustrates how MSDetector extract script sequence given the same sample in Fig. 2. The code concatenate string literals "asser" and "t" into "assert" and assign it to variable "$a", then the script call function "assert" through variable "$a", with its parameter passed via get requests. Here, MSDetector puts "t", "asser" and "cmd" into string literal sequences.

3   MSDetector

3.1   Pre-training Transformer Model

Abstract syntax tree (AST) is an important structure produced by compiler. Previous works [15,27] proved that it could be used to improve the performance of code analysis tasks. But utilizing tree-structured neural networks to process AST is often time-consuming. Nevertheless, learning AST features by transformer-based language model has been proved to be feasible. Hence we utilize AST node tagging (ANT) pre-training task proposed by L.Buratti [3], which is a sequence labelling task for transformer model to capture the grammatical roles of each component of the linearized AST.

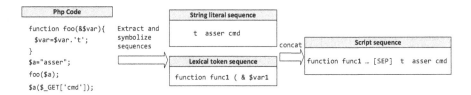

Fig. 3. Illustration for the process of generating script sequence.

Here we choose the CodeBert [7] model which has already been pre-trained on MLM and RTD tasks as our main transformer model. Our work is mainly to fine-tuning the language model. For the source code, we represent it as a sequence of lexical tokens. We implement a script parser based on ANTLR[4], which is used to extract the token sequence and the corresponding node tag as corresponding label by traversing AST. Then we use the node tag sequence as sequence label to train CodeBert model with the token sequence as input and cross entropy as loss function.

Preprocessing. In this stage, we extract lexical token sequence and node tag sequence for a given PHP script. Here we first parse PHP source code into AST by ANTLR. Note that the AST generated by ANTLR is usually too large thus hard to parse, we simplify the AST in the same way as ASTMiner[5]. Formally, a simplified AST of a script is denoted as $A = (N, T)$ where $N = \{nn1, ..., nn_k\}$ is the non-terminal node set and $T = \{tn_1, ..., tn_l\}$ is the terminal node set. Let $P(n)$ represent the parent node of node n and $Type(n)$ represent the node type of n. The script parser intializes a symbolic table ST first to store the identifiers need mapping and their symbolic names. Then traversing A and generate token sequence and tag sequence from terminal nodes in following rules:

– (a) For a terminal node tn whose node type $Type(tn)$ is "Label", script parser will check the node type of its parent node $Type(P(tn))$ and generate corresponding tag according to $Type(P(tn))$. At the same time, if the node token is function name or class name, token generator will check whether the token is in ST and add the token to ST if not, then replace original token with its symbolic name in the lexical token sequence. The symbolic name is usually a common identifier together with a separate index (i.e. func1, func2, class1, class2).
– (b) For terminal node tn whose node type $Type(tn)$ is "VarName", script parser will check whether its parent node type $Type(P(tn))$ is "FuncCall" because calling a method by a variable name is allowed in PHP, and the node tag would be "FuncCall" if so, otherwise "VarName". Also, variable name will be symbolized in the same way as in rule (a).

---

[4] https://www.antlr.org/.
[5] https://github.com/JetBrains-Research/astminer.

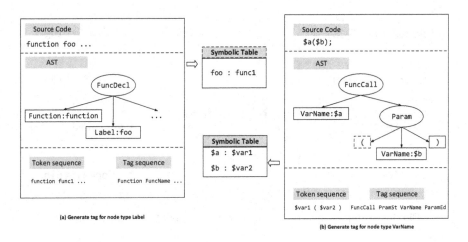

Fig. 4. Examples illustrating our key ideas in generating tag sequences and lexical token sequences.

- (c) For terminal node whose node type $Type(tn)$ represent numerical value such as "Decimal", script parser will directly use the node type as tag and the token will be replaced by symbolic name "number".
- (d) For terminal node whose node type $Type(tn)$ is "StringConstant", script parser will directly use "StringConstant" as tag and compute the symbolic name of the string literal with a string parser.
- (e) For other type of terminal node, script parser will directly use node type as tag and lexical token without any symbolization.

Figure 4 illustrates our key ideas in generating lexical token sequences and corresponding node tag sequences. In (a), when visting the terminal node "Label:foo", script parser checks the parent node type of the terminal node is "FuncDecl", then it set the node tag to "FuncName" and add it to tag sequence, meanwhile, it symbolizes "foo" into "func1", and add "foo:func1" to the symbolic table as a key value pair. In (b), the parent node type of "VarName:$a" is FuncCall, hence the tag for $a is FuncCall while the tag is still "VarName" for $b, those variable names are symbolized too after extracting tags.

Note that there are some statements not related to webshell in some scripts. For example, "error_reporting(0)", "set_time_limit(0);". We simply ignore those statements when traversing ASTs to reduce noise imposed by unrelated statements.

The string parser in above rule.(d) computes symbolic name of a string literal in following steps:

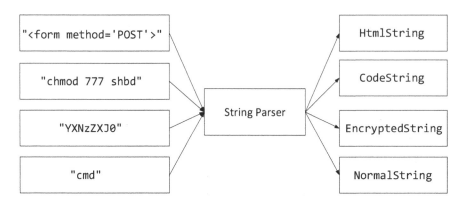

Fig. 5. Examples illustrating the parsing results of some string literals.

- (1) Check whether the string is HTML code by detecting whether there are html keywords. If there are, set the symbolic name to "HtmlString" or go to next step.
- (2) Check whether the string constant contains PHP code or symtem command by the matching of some keywords (function name, such as "system". If there are, set the symbolic name to "CodeString" or go to next step.
- (3) We calculate the information entropy of the string. If it exceeds a preset threshold, we believe it is an encrypted string and set the corresponding symbolic name to "EncryptedString", or go to next step.
- (4) Otherwise, it is an ordinary string, the symbolic name is set to "NormalString".

Figure 5 illustrates the parsing results of some string literals from scripts we have so far collected, we define four kinds of string constant which commonly show up in webshells.

Pre-train Transformer Model. After preprocessing, wo get lexical token sequence C as input to CodeBert and corresponding node tag sequence L as the label of C. Codebert tokenizer would add two special tokens $[CLS]$ and $[EOS]$ to C at the start and end. Therefore, we need to add start and end special tokens at the beginning and end of L.

CodeBert utilizes Bert architecture which is complicated transformer-based model and views the source code as flattened text sequence. Like other transformer-based models, CodeBert takes sequence of tokens as input and return sequence of fine-tuned embedding vectors for each token respectively. Formally, it can be denoted as:

$$H = [h_{cls}, h_{c_1}, h_{c_2}, ..., h_{c_m}, h_{eos}] = f(X = [[CLS], c_1, ..., c_m, [EOS]]) \quad (1)$$

where f is the CodeBert model, X is the input token sequence, $H \in R^{M \times 768}$ is the output of CodeBert model, $h_i \in R^{768}$ and M is length of input/output sequence. When tokenizing the token in the sequence, following Feng Z [7], we split each token into WordPieces [24], for example, token "$var1" will be split into three subtokens "$", "var", "1", hence we should align the length of the tags to 3. Here we simply use BIO mode, for example, the tag "VarName" for "$var1" will be transformed into tags "B-VarName", "I-VarName" and "I-VarName".

In this sequence labelling task, we add a linear layer $W_{ast} \in R^{768 \times |V_{ast}|}$ followed by softmax. V_{ast} stands for AST token_kind set. The cross entropy loss is used as the loss function.

The forward propagation process of a single sample is as follows:

$$pred = softmax(H.W_{ast})   \tag{2}$$

where $pred \in R^{M \times |V_{ast}|}$ is the pred sequence of the model output, $pred_i \in R^{|V_{ast}|}$ is the probability distribution of the i-th token in the output sequence.

The loss of a single sample is calculated as follows

$$loss = -\frac{1}{M} \sum_{i=1}^{M} \sum_{j=1}^{|V_{ast}|} l_{ij} log(pred_{ij})   \tag{3}$$

$pred_{ij}$ is the probability of i-th token belonging to j-th label of the V_{ast}. $l_i \in R^{|V_{ast}|}$ is the label of the i-th token, which is a one-hot vector.

3.2   Training Transformer Model and Detecting Webshell

Our goal is to statically identify whether a PHP script contains malicious fragments without prior knowledge. We regard webshell detection as a binary classification problem.

As shown in Fig. 1. In training phase, for given PHP scripts, MSDetector generates their corresponding script sequences after parsing it into ASTs, and then feeds those script sequences to pre-trained CodeBert model to fine-tune it on webshell detection task, then fine-tuned model can be used to detect whether a script sequence corresponding to a PHP script contains malicious code fragments in detecting phase.

Preprocessing. In this stage, MSDetector aim at generating script sequence for a given PHP script. The process is similar to preprocessing stage in pre-training stage (Sect. 3.1). The lexical token sequence of a PHP script is extracted in the same among all the pre-training phase, training phase and detecting phase. The difference between the two processes is that in training and detecting phase, the script parser extracts string literal sequences rather than node tag sequences for scripts when traversing ASTs. The string literal sequence of a script is initialized with an empty list and the extraction of it is done by string parser used in preprocessing stage of pre-training phase (Sect. 3.1). Here, a string literal would be added to string literal sequence only if it is identified as "CodeString" or "NormalString" by string parser.

Fine-Tuning Transformer Model and Detecting Webshell. In the last stage, the script parser extracts script sequence X composed of lexical token sequence C and string literal sequence W with a special separator between them.

- Where $X^{'}$ is the input to CodeBert, we denote it as:
  $X^{'} = [[CLS], c_1^{'}, c_2^{'}, ..., c_m^{'}, [SEP], w_1^{'}, w_2^{'}, ..., w_n^{'}, [EOS]]$
- The output $H^{'}$ of CodeBert can be denoted as:
  $H^{'} = [h_{cls}^{'}, h_{c_1}^{'}, h_{c_2}^{'}, ..., h_{c_m}^{'}, h_{sep}^{'}, h_{w_1}^{'}, h_{w_2}^{'}, ..., h_{w_n}^{'}, h_{eos}^{'}]$

Webshell detection is a binary classification task. Input the sample PHP code and output whether the sample belongs to Webshell. The final classification result only depends on the $h_{cls}^{'}$ vector output by CodeBert. We add a linear layer W. We use cross entropy as loss function.

The forward propagation process of a single sample is as follows

$$p = sigmoid(h_{cls}^{'}.W) \tag{4}$$

where p represents the probability that the sample belongs Webshell.

The loss of a single sample is calculated as follows

$$loss = -(y.log(p) + (1 - y).log(1 - p)) \tag{5}$$

where y is the label of the sample.

In detecting phase, if $p > 0.5$, then MSDetector will take input as webshell otherwise normal script.

4   Experiment and Evaluation

We seek to evaluate the benefits of MSDetector by answering the following questions:

- RQ1: Can representing PHP codes with script sequences achieve higher webshell detecting capability than text-based representation?
- RQ2: Can ANT pre-training task improve the webshell detecting capability of MSDetector?
- RQ3: How does MSDetector perform compare to the other webshell detection methods?

4.1   Experimental Configuration and Evaluation Criteria

The experimental platform includes Inter (R) Xeon (R) CPU e5-2603v4@1.70 GHz, 64 GB memory, NVIDIA geforce GTX Titan X. The operating system used in the experiment is Ubuntu 20.04. The development environment includes Java for source code analysis and python for vectorization. The development tools include anaconda3.

The CodeBert model we use is the same as RoBERTa-base, The total number of model parameters is 125M and already pre-trained by Feng Z [7]. We set maximum length of model input sequence to 512. We use SGD optimizer with learning rate 0.01 and weight decay 0.0001, batch size is set to 64 and dropout is used with rate 0.1 to avoid overfit. We randomly shuffle each dataset.

We evaluate MSDetector on four commonly used metrics: accuracy, precision, recall and F1 score which are defined as follows.

- accuracy: $ACC = \frac{TP+TN}{TP+TN+FN+FP}$
- precision: $P = \frac{TP}{TP+FP}$
- recall rate: $R = \frac{TP}{TP+FN}$
- F1 score: $F1 = \frac{2 \times recall \times prec}{recall+prec}$.

Where TP is the number of true positive samples, FP is the number of false positive samples, TN is the number of true negative samples and FN is the number of false negative samples.

4.2 Datasets

In the pre-training phase, we utilizes CodeSearchNet corpus [10]. The dataset covers six programming languages including Java, Python, PHP. We select the PHP part as our pre-training corpus. Before pre-training, we restore each PHP code in the corpus to a script file. Since all functions in the dataset are intercepted from the internal functions of the user-defined class, with private, public, static and other modifiers, ANTLR is likely to throw exceptions when parsing these functions. Therefore these modifiers must be removed, then a PHP tag will be added to the script file. However, code parsing errors still exist, we filter out those codes with parsing errors. At last, there are about 524682 functions left in the training set and 24523 functions left in the test set.

As for webshell datasets. We mainly download webshell and normal samples from data sources listed in Table 1. Those data samples contain large amounts of PHP files with more than 2000 lines of code, which is beyond the scope of CodeBert model. Therefore we manually perform data clean operation to refine our datasets, by manually splitting large PHP files into several small PHP files while retaining the semantic information of webshell. Data clean took us about 480 h.

After that, we split the dataset into test set and training set. The training set includes 3280 malicious scripts and 3226 normal scripts. The test set includes 930 malicious scripts and 987 normal scripts (dubbed "Testset-1").

Also, in order to verify the effectiveness of MSdetector against some unknown webshells, we manually inject some malicious code fragments into normal scripts to get a new dataset (dubbed "Testset-2"), which includes 180 malicious scripts and 184 normal scripts.

4.3 Experiments for Answering RQ1

In order to evaluate the advantages of script sequence representation over PHP codes, we conduct experiments with the following two source code representations.

Table 1. Data sources

	Url
Webshell samples	https://github.com/tanjiti/WebshellSample
	https://github.com/JohnTroony/PHP-Webshells
	https://github.com/learnstartup/4tweb
Normal samples	https://github.com/johnshen/PHPcms
	https://github.com/WordPress
	https://github.com/phpmyadmin/phpmyadmin
	https://github.com/smarty-php/smarty
	https://github.com/yiisoft/yii

- text-based representation: PHP scripts are simply treated as texts and tokenized into text sequences in the same way in natural language processing (NLP).
- script sequence representation: PHP scripts are parsed into ASTs and the ASTs would be simplified, and a sequence generator will traverse over ASTs to extract lexical tokens and string literals for every script. Then, extracted token sequence and string literal sequence will be spliced into script sequence.

Both text sequence and script sequence will be input to CodeBert model. We fine-tune one CodeBert model for text-based representation and one for script sequence. And test them on both Testset-1 and Testset-2. The comparison are summarized in Table 2. We observe that script sequences lead to better result than text sequences in both testsets, including a 4.3% improvement in accuracy, a 4.4% improvement in precision, a 4.5% improvement in recall rate and a 4.5% improvement in F1 score on Testset-1. The performance difference on Testset-2 is similar to that on Testset-1.

This can be attributed to the advantage of script sequence that it reduces noise imposed by irregular literals and highlight the semantic features in webshells by analysing AST. This can be justified by the following example.

Figure 6 describes an webshell example. Consider those tokens marked yellow or green are string literals or irregularly named variables or classes which are hard to be vectorized because those tokens are usually out of the vocabulary of embedding tools, meaning they could impose noise. Here the string literals marked yellow are parsed by string parser into token "EncryptedString" indicating those are encrypted string literals that are not commonly shown in normal PHP scripts, the user-defined variable and class names are symbolized to corresponding symbolic names to lower distraction caused by personalized naming. Also, some tokens marked red are not related to webshell, we simply ignore them. Other string literals marked blue are extracted to string literal sequence to preserve the features in string constants.

ANSWER: MSDetector utilizing script sequence representation is substantially more effective than MSDetector using text-based representation, owing to the aforementioned advantage of script sequence.

Table 2. Compare two different kinds of code representations.

Code representation	Testset	ACC (%)	P (%)	R (%)	F1 (%)
text sequence	Testset-1	94.6	94.7	94.1	94.4
	Testset-2	91.3	92.3	90.0	91.1
script sequence	Testset-1	98.9	99.1	98.6	98.9
	Testset-2	95.1	95.5	94.4	95.0

```
class PNLK{
    function __destruct(){
        $FQHZ='xk%uoq'^"\x1b\x19\x40\x14\x1b\x14";
        @$FQHZ=$FQHZ('',$this->PZAF);
        return @$FQHZ();
    }
}
$pnlk=new PNLK();
@$pnlk->PZAF=&$_POST['test'];
```

```
text sequence
class PNLK { function __destruct ( ) { $FQHZ =
xk%uoq \x1b\x19\x40\x14\x1b\x14 @ $FQHZ =  $FQHZ
( , $this ->  PZAF return @ $FQHZ ( ) ; } }
$pnlk = new PNLK ( ) ; @ $pnlk -> PZAF = &
$_POST [ test ] ;
```

```
script sequence
class class1 { function __destruct ( ) { $var1
= EncryptedString EncryptedString a $var1 =
$var1 ( , $this -> var2 return $var1 ) ; } }
$var3 = new class1 ( ) ; $var3 -> var2 =
$_POST [ ] ; [SEP] test
```

Fig. 6. The comparison between text sequence and script sequence. (Color figure online)

4.4 Experiments for Answering RQ2

In order to measure the contribution of AST Node Tagging task to MSDetector, we conduct experiments to compare identification capability of CodeBert before and after pre-training.

Table 3 presents the result. It indicates that, AST Node Tagging task does some help with webshell detection task. Although the score is not much improved, Only about 1% improvement in accuracy and F1 score on Testset-1 and 1.6% improvement in accuracy and F1 score on Testset-2, we can still learn that the transformer-based model has the ability to learn the syntax information of AST and perform better on downstream tasks like webshell detection.

ANSWER: MSDetector could learn syntax information of PHP through ANT pre-training task and perform better on downstream tasks like detection.

4.5 Experiments for Answering RQ3

In order to evaluate the effectiveness and preciseness of MSdetector in identifying webshells with known ground truth, we compare MSdetector and some state-of-the-art webshell detectors in terms of their capabilities in identifying webshells in target programs with known ground truth.

Table 3. Compare CodeBert before pre-training and that after pre-training.

CodeBert	Testset	ACC (%)	P (%)	R (%)	F1 (%)
Before pre-training	Testset-1	97.9	99.2	96.3	97.8
	Testset-2	93.4	92.9	93.9	93.4
After pre-training	Testset-1	98.9	99.1	98.6	98.9
	Testset-2	95.1	95.5	94.4	95.0

For rule-based detectors, we consider Shell-Detector. For deep-learning based detectors we consider the opcode-based methods including RF-opcode [6] which vectorize opcode sequence with fasttext [1] then utilize random forest model [2] to achieve a binary classifier and CNN-opcode [16] utilizing CNN to classify opcode sequences of PHP scripts and text-based methods such as CNN-text [21] and GRU-text [12] utilizing CNN [4] and GRU [5] with attention mechanism [17] to classify text sequence of PHP scripts respectively. We choose these detectors for comparison since they are the state-of-the-art.

Table 4 summarizes the comparison. We observe that:

– Rule-based detector Shell-detector achieves low scores on four metrics, this is due to the inefficiency of manually writing rules.
– MSDetector outperforms other deep-learning based approaches on both of the two datasets. This is because MSDetector makes full use of the syntactic and semantic features of webshells by utilizing pre-trained transformer model and script sequence.

ANSWER: MSDetector is more effective than the state-of-the-art rule-based and deep-learning based webshell detectors in the field of webshell detection.

5   Limitations

This paper has several limitations. **First,** MSDetector focuses on detecting webshells in PHP program because many dynamic features of PHP facilitate obfuscation of malicious code. Extending MSDetector to accommodate other script languages is an interesting future work. **Second,** MSDetector requires scripts that can be parsed into ASTs by tools like ANTLR, so it does not work well when a script cannot be parsed into AST. **Third,** the string parser used to parse string literals is base on human-defined rules and could incur false parsing results sometimes, it is interesting to parse string literals with machine learning techniques in future work. **Fourth,** the transformer model learn syntax information of PHP code by AST Node Tagging task, it is worth exploring other kinds of pre-training task to make the model learn higher-level semantic information of the code and apply pre-trained model to other kinds of downstream tasks.

Table 4. Compare MSDetector with state-of-the-art webshell detectors.

Detector	Testset	ACC (%)	P (%)	R (%)	F1 (%)
MSDetector	Testset-1	**98.9**	**99.1**	**98.6**	**98.9**
	Testset-2	**95.1**	**95.5**	**94.4**	**95.0**
PHP-Shell-Detector	Testset-1	73.4	80.6	59.5	68.5
	Testset-2	65.9	100	31.1	47.4
CNN-text	Testset-1	86.2	82	91.6	86.5
	Testset-2	83.8	87.1	78.9	82.8
GRU-text	Testset-1	93.8	97.3	89.7	93.3
	Testset-2	90.3	91.9	88.3	90.1
RF-opcode	Testset-1	92.8	93.7	91.2	92.4
	Testset-2	85.2	85	85	85
CNN-opcode	Testset-1	89.6	91.2	86.9	89.0
	Testset-2	78.5	92.5	61.7	74

6   Related Work

6.1   Static Webshell Detection

The identification of webshell can be divided into dynamic detection, log analysis and static detection. Static detection aims directly to script files while dynamic detection relies on runtime behaviour, log analysis is mainly used to check the system errors after it is intruded. Hence static detection is faster than dynamic analysis and log analysis, and it can detect problems before attackers execute malicious code. Reference [22] proposed a method based on optimal threshold to identify malicious code files in web applications. It uses statistical method to count the frequency of malicious functions and command execution functions in malicious script files, but they are easily bypassed by malicious scripts after encryption. Y. Fang [6] uses fasttext and random forest algorithm classifier to construct the webshell detecting system for PHP scripts. In [8,14,16,25,26], PHP opcode sequence are used as code representation, combined with TF-IDF, word2vec and multi-layer perceptron (MLP) neural network respectively to detect Webshell. F. Tao [21] regarded PHP scripts as text sequences and classified it with deep learning model. T Li [12] regard PHP as two-dimensional text, and use word2vec to pre-train a word embedding tool on PHP text sequences first, and then use gated recurrent network and attention mechanism to generate vector representation for a given PHP script and classify it with a dense layer.

6.2   Code Representation

In addition to the researches of webshell detection, the representation of source code is also an important research. In [9,11,19], source codes are parsed into programming token sequences as the input features to neural networks. TBCNN [15] parses the source code into AST and transforms AST into binary tree, and then calculates the vector representation of the whole binary AST with tree convolutional neural network. ASTNN [27] splits each large AST into many statement subtree sequence, encodes each single subtree with TreeLSTM [18], and utilizes the bidirectional RNN model to calculate the vector representation of whole sequence. Devign [28] uses code analysis tool Joern[6] to extract the token sequence, AST, CFG of C language source code, and creates DFG of source code based on CFG, then creates joint graph representation of program based on these four structures, and vectorizes joint graph with gated graph neural network [13].

6.3   Pre-trained Models for Programming Languages

With the successes of pre-training model in NLP, the pre-training model for source code also gets rapid development, which promotes the development of code intelligence. Microsoft research team released CodeBert [7] model, which is a bi-modal pre-training language model for natural language and programming language. The research team utilizes masked language modeling (MLM) and replaced token detection (RTD) to pre-train CodeBert, and achieved good results in downstream tasks such as code search and code document generation. L. Buratti [3] proposed C-Bert, which uses AST Node Tagging task to pre-train the model on C language corpus, and achieves good results on vulnerability identification. Experiments show that this method is not inferior to the code detection method based on graph representation.

7   Conclusions

We introduce a novel webshell detecting system MSDetector, which first parses a PHP script into a joint sequence called script sequence composed of lexical token sequence and string literal sequence of that script to preserve key features of webshells, then utilizes a transformer model to determine whether this script contains malicious code. For the purpose of letting the model learn the syntactic information of PHP source codes and semantic information of webshells, we pre-train transformer model on AST Node Tagging task on a large PHP corpus, then we fine-tune the transformer model on a small-scaled webshell datasets. We have applied MSDetector to a webshell dataset and demonstrate that MSDetector outperforms other state-of-the-art methods.

References

1. Bojanowski, P., Grave, E., Joulin, A., Mikolov, T.: Enriching word vectors with subword information. Trans. Assoc. Comput. Linguistics **5**, 135–146 (2017). https://transacl.org/ojs/index.php/tacl/article/view/999
2. Breiman, L.: Random forests. Mach. Learn. **45**(1), 5–32 (2001)

---

[6] https://joern.readthedocs.io/en/latest/.

3. Buratti, L., et al.: Exploring software naturalness through neural language models. CoRR abs/2006.12641 (2020). https://arxiv.org/abs/2006.12641
4. Chen, Y.: Convolutional neural network for sentence classification. Master's thesis, University of Waterloo (2015)
5. Cho, K., et al.: Learning phrase representations using RNN encoder-decoder for statistical machine translation, pp. 1724–1734 (2014). https://doi.org/10.3115/v1/d14-1179
6. Fang, Y., Qiu, Y., Liu, L., Huang, C.: Detecting webshell based on random forest with fasttext. In: Proceedings of the 2018 International Conference on Computing and Artificial Intelligence, ICCAI 2018, Chengdu, China, 12–14 March 2018, pp. 52–56. ACM (2018). https://doi.org/10.1145/3194452.3194470
7. Feng, Z., et al.: CodeBERT: a pre-trained model for programming and natural languages. In: EMNLP 2020, pp. 1536–1547 (2020). https://doi.org/10.18653/v1/2020.findings-emnlp.139
8. Guo, Y., Marco-Gisbert, H., Keir, P.: Mitigating webshell attacks through machine learning techniques. Future Internet **12**(1), 12 (2020). https://doi.org/10.3390/fi12010012
9. Harer, J.A., et al.: Automated software vulnerability detection with machine learning. arXiv preprint arXiv:1803.04497 (2018)
10. Husain, H., Wu, H.H., Gazit, T., Allamanis, M., Brockschmidt, M.: CodeSearchNet challenge: evaluating the state of semantic code search. arXiv preprint arXiv:1909.09436 (2019)
11. Iyer, S., Konstas, I., Cheung, A., Zettlemoyer, L.: Summarizing source code using a neural attention model. In: Proceedings of the 54th Annual Meeting of the Association for Computational Linguistics, ACL 2016, 7–12 August 2016, Berlin, Germany, Volume 1: Long Papers. The Association for Computer Linguistics (2016). https://doi.org/10.18653/v1/p16-1195
12. Li, T., Ren, C., Fu, Y., Xu, J., Guo, J., Chen, X.: Webshell detection based on the word attention mechanism. IEEE Access **7**, 185140–185147 (2019). https://doi.org/10.1109/ACCESS.2019.2959950
13. Li, Y., Tarlow, D., Brockschmidt, M., Zemel, R.S.: Gated graph sequence neural networks (2016). http://arxiv.org/abs/1511.05493
14. Lu, J., Tang, Z., Mao, J., Gu, Z., Zhang, J.: Mixed-models method based on machine learning in detecting webshell attack. In: CIPAE 2020: 2020 International Conference on Computers, Information Processing and Advanced Education, Ottawa, ON, Canada, 16–18 October 2020, pp. 251–259. ACM (2020). https://doi.org/10.1145/3419635.3419716
15. Mou, L., Li, G., Zhang, L., Wang, T., Jin, Z.: Convolutional neural networks over tree structures for programming language processing. In: Schuurmans, D., Wellman, M.P. (eds.) Proceedings of the Thirtieth AAAI Conference on Artificial Intelligence, 12–17 February 2016, Phoenix, Arizona, USA, pp. 1287–1293. AAAI Press (2016). http://www.aaai.org/ocs/index.php/AAAI/AAAI16/paper/view/11775
16. Nguyen, N., Le, V., Phung, V., Du, P.: Toward a deep learning approach for detecting PHP webshell. In: Proceedings of the Tenth International Symposium on Information and Communication Technology, Ha Noi, Ha Long Bay, Vietnam, 4–6 December 2019, pp. 514–521. ACM (2019). https://doi.org/10.1145/3368926.3369733
17. Pappas, N., Popescu-Belis, A.: Multilingual hierarchical attention networks for document classification, pp. 1015–1025 (2017). https://aclanthology.org/I17-1102/

18. Roy, D., Panda, P., Roy, K.: Tree-CNN: a hierarchical deep convolutional neural network for incremental learning. Neural Netw. **121**, 148–160 (2020). https://doi.org/10.1016/j.neunet.2019.09.010

19. Sajnani, H., Saini, V., Svajlenko, J., Roy, C.K., Lopes, C.V.: SourcererCC: scaling code clone detection to big-code. In: Dillon, L.K., Visser, W., Williams, L.A. (eds.) Proceedings of the 38th International Conference on Software Engineering, ICSE 2016, Austin, TX, USA, 14–22 May 2016, pp. 1157–1168. ACM (2016). https://doi.org/10.1145/2884781.2884877

20. Tai, K.S., Socher, R., Manning, C.D.: Improved semantic representations from tree-structured long short-term memory networks, pp. 1556–1566 (2015). https://doi.org/10.3115/v1/p15-1150

21. Tao, F., Cao, C., Liu, Z.: Webshell detection model based on deep learning. In: Sun, X., Pan, Z., Bertino, E. (eds.) ICAIS 2019. LNCS, vol. 11635, pp. 408–420. Springer, Cham (2019). https://doi.org/10.1007/978-3-030-24268-8_38

22. Tu, T.D., Guang, C., Xiaojun, G., Wubin, P.: Webshell detection techniques in web applications. In: Fifth International Conference on Computing, Communications and Networking Technologies (ICCCNT), pp. 1–7. IEEE (2014)

23. Vaswani, A., et al.: Attention is all you need, pp. 5998–6008 (2017). https://proceedings.neurips.cc/paper/2017/hash/3f5ee243547dee91fbd053c1c4a845aa-Abstract.html

24. Wu, Y., et al.: Google's neural machine translation system: Bridging the gap between human and machine translation. CoRR abs/1609.08144 (2016). http://arxiv.org/abs/1609.08144

25. Xiao-Bo, X.U., Nie, X.M.: A method of detecting webshell based on multi-layer perception. Commun. Technol. **51**, 895–900 (2018)

26. Zhang, H., Xue, Z., Shi, Y.: Improved method of detecting webshell based on multi-layer perception. Commun. Technol. **52**, 179–183 (2019)

27. Zhang, J., Wang, X., Zhang, H., Sun, H., Wang, K., Liu, X.: A novel neural source code representation based on abstract syntax tree. In: Atlee, J.M., Bultan, T., Whittle, J. (eds.) Proceedings of the 41st International Conference on Software Engineering, ICSE 2019, Montreal, QC, Canada, 25–31 May 2019, pp. 783–794. IEEE/ACM (2019). https://doi.org/10.1109/ICSE.2019.00086

28. Zhou, Y., Liu, S., Siow, J.K., Du, X., Liu, Y.: Devign: effective vulnerability identification by learning comprehensive program semantics via graph neural networks, pp. 10197–10207 (2019). https://proceedings.neurips.cc/paper/2019/hash/49265d2447bc3bbfe9e76306ce40a31f-Abstract.html

Extending Process Algebra with an Undefined Action

S. Arun-Kumar[(✉)]

Department of Computer Science and Engineering, Indian Institute of Technology Delhi,
Hauz Khas, New Delhi 110 016, India
sak@cse.iitd.ac.in

Abstract. Extensional equivalences in process algebra have sometimes led
authors to conflate divergence with deadlock [8], divergence with livelock
[4,5,12] and deadlock with livelock [9] (e.g. $\mathbf{T} = \tau.\mathbf{T} \approx \mathbf{0}$ in CCS).

Following Scott [10,11] we take divergence to mean undefinedness and define
a basic extended process algebra (BXPA) to include "partially" defined processes and their behaviours. We define a behavioural preorder, called lifted strong
bisimilarity and show that it is a precongruence on BXPA. Divergent processes
are the least elements in the preorder and lie below both deadlocks and livelocks
which are mutually incomparable.

We extend the notion of logical characterisations of behavioural equivalences
to that of behavioural preorders using a parameterised Hennessy-Milner Logic
(PHML) and prove the characterisation of the pre-bisimilarity using techniques
developed in [6,9] and [3].

Keywords: Concurrency · Process algebra · Hennessy-Milner logic ·
Bisimulation · Prebisimulations · Lifted strong bisimilarity

1 Motivation and Related Work

Divergence, Deadlock and Livelock in Process Algebra. In denotational semantics
[10,11], divergence is identified with undefinedness, i.e. the least solution of the equation $X \Leftarrow X$ is the function that is undefined everywhere.

A blocked or deadlocked process is one that is incapable of engaging in any
action, while a livelocked process is one that may engage in infinite "internal chatter"
($\mathbf{T} = \tau.\mathbf{T}$) but is incapable of engaging with the environment[1]. A livelocked process
consumes computational cycles and energy. In the testing framework [4,5] and the pre-
bsimulation framework of Walker [12], both the equations $X \Leftarrow X$ and $X \Leftarrow \tau.X$ have
the same least solution.

We take the view that both deadlock and livelock are well-defined and incomparable
with each other and from divergence. Further divergent processes are less defined than
any well-defined process.

Taking a line through denotational semantics we adjoin a special undefined action $\perp$
to the set of actions and use it to define partially defined processes. A divergent process

---

[1] The CCS process $R = (P|Q)\backslash a \sim \tau.R$, where $P = a.P$ and $Q = \bar{a}.Q$ is one such since $R \sim \mathbf{T}$.

© Springer Nature Switzerland AG 2022
Y. Aït-Ameur and F. Crăciun (Eds.): TASE 2022, LNCS 13299, pp. 173–179, 2022.
https://doi.org/10.1007/978-3-031-10363-6_12

is one that cannot perform any other action. A partially defined process is one that may evolve into a divergent one.

In this paper we attempt to formulate an expanded view of processes to include partially defined processes in the above sense, and try to distinguish divergence, deadlock and livelock from each other.

Organisation and Contribution. We start with some basic notions and notations of labelled transition systems (LTS) in Sect. 2. In Sect. 3, we define a basic process algebra (BXPA) to include partially defined processes, by expanding the action set to include an undefined action. In Sect. 4 we define a strong pre-bisimulation relation on processes which yields a preorder $\sqsubseteq$ that we call lifted strong bisimilarity and is a precongruence on BXPA. BXPA/$\sqsubseteq$ yields a partial order on processes with a least element viz. the totally undefined process Ω which is distinct from both deadlock and livelock. We also define a parameterised Hennessy-Milner Logic [3] and prove a characterisation of lifted strong bisimilarity. Section 5 is the conclusion.

In addition to the usual notions of theorem, proposition, lemma and corollary we also have "fact(s)" which typically are either well-known or follow directly from definitions or some previous remarks.

2   Labelled Transition Systems: Basics

Definition 1. *A* **labelled transition system (LTS)** $\mathbb{L}[L]$ *over a set of* **labels** L *is a tuple* $\mathbb{L}[L] = \langle S, L, \longrightarrow \rangle$, *where* S *is a (possibly infinite) set of* **states** *and* $\longrightarrow \subseteq S \times L \times S$ *is the* **transition relation**. (s, ℓ, t) *is written* $s \xrightarrow{\ell} t$; s *is the* source, ℓ *is the* label *and* t *is the* target *of the transition. A* **rooted LTS** *is a LTS* $\mathbb{L}[L]$ *with a distinguished* **start state** $s_0 \in S$ *and denoted* $\langle S, L, \longrightarrow, s_0 \rangle$. _ *denotes a place-holder in the following.*

- $s \xrightarrow{\ell} \_ = \{t \in S \mid s \xrightarrow{\ell} t\}$ *is the set of* ℓ*-successors of* s.
- $L(s) = \{\ell \in L \mid \exists t[s \xrightarrow{\ell} t]\}$ *is the set of labels from* s.
- $Succ(s) = \bigcup_{\ell \in L} s \xrightarrow{\ell} \_ = \{t \mid \exists \ell \in L[s \xrightarrow{\ell} t]\}$ *is the set of successors of* s
- $Targets(\longrightarrow) = \{t \in S \mid \exists s \in S[t \in Succ(s)]\}$.
- $Der(s) = \{s\} \cup \bigcup_{t \in Succ(s)} Der(t)$ *is the set of derivatives of* s.

A **sub-LTS** *of* $\mathbb{L}[L]$ *at a state* $s_0 \in S$ *is the rooted LTS* $\langle Der(s_0), L, \longrightarrow, s_0 \rangle$. *By convention* $s \xrightarrow{\epsilon} s$ *and for any* $x = ay \in L^+$, $s \xrightarrow{x} s'$ *if* $s \xrightarrow{a} s'' \xrightarrow{y} s'$ *for some* $s'' \in S$.

Definition 2. *A binary relation* $\mathcal{R} \subseteq S \times T$ *between (sub-)LTSs* $\mathbb{L}[L] = \langle S, L, \longrightarrow \rangle$ *and* $\mathbb{M}[L] = \langle T, L, \longrightarrow \rangle$ *is a* **natural bisimulation** *if* $s\mathcal{R}t$ *implies for all labels* $\ell \in L$, $s \xrightarrow{\ell} s' \Rightarrow \exists t' \in T[t \xrightarrow{\ell} t' \wedge s'\mathcal{R}t']$ *and* $t \xrightarrow{\ell} t'' \Rightarrow \exists s'' \in S[s \xrightarrow{\ell} s'' \wedge s''\mathcal{R}t'']$. s *is said to be* **naturally bisimilar** *to* t *(denoted* $s \sim t$*) if* $s\mathcal{R}t$ *for some natural bisimulation* $\mathcal{R}$ *(notation:* $\mathcal{R} \vdash s \sim t$*).*

Fact 1. *Unions, relational converses and (relational) compositions of natural bisimulations are also natural bisimulations. Natural bisimilarity* ($\sim$) *is the largest natural bisimulation and is an equivalence relation.*

3 Basic Extended Process Algebra (BXPA)

Definition 3. *Let $A_\perp = A \cup \{\perp\}$ be the set of all **actions** where A is a countable set of (uninterpreted but) well-defined actions and $\perp \notin A$ is a special undefined action with $\perp < a$ for each $a \in A$.*

Our notion of a process is a (sub-)LTS of $\mathbb{L}[A_\perp] = \langle S, A_\perp, \longrightarrow \rangle$. It is convenient for us to introduce an undefined action $\perp$ which is the only action that can be performed by the totally undefined process Ω (to be defined below). This action is less defined than any other action from the action set A. Once a process descends to a state that performs $\perp$, it remains in that state and can perform only $\perp$ then on and can never recover to a well-defined state. The traces that we need to consider are therefore from $A^* \perp^*$. Since a process may only perform sequences of actions of the form $x\perp^*$ for any $x \in A^*$ we find it convenient to quotient out the set $A^* \perp^*$ by the equation $\boxed{x\perp\perp = x\perp}$ to yield the set of normal forms $A^{*?}_\perp = A^* \cup A^*\perp$ of finite sequences of actions.

Notational Convention. x, y, z denote words from A^* and u, v, w denote words from $A^{*?}_\perp$. In general any $u \in A^*_\perp$ is of the form $u = x\perp$ where $x \in A^*$.

Definition 4. *Let $\leq \subseteq A^{*?}_\perp \times A^{*?}_\perp$ be the smallest relation such that for all $x, y \in A^*$, $x \leq x$ and $x\perp \leq xy\perp \leq xy$. $u < v$ if $u \leq v \not\leq u$ for all $u, v \in A^{*?}_\perp$.*

Fact 2

1. *For all $x, y \in A^*$, $x \leq y$ iff $x = y$.*
2. *$\perp < \epsilon$, where ϵ is the empty trace. and $\perp < a$ for every $a \in A^2$.*
3. *$a\perp < a = a\epsilon$.*
4. *$\langle A^{*?}_\perp, \leq \rangle$ is a partial order.*
5. *$\langle A_\perp, \leq \rangle$ and $\langle A_{\perp,\epsilon} \leq \rangle$ are both flat complete partial orders (cpo), where $A_{\perp,\epsilon} = A_\perp \cup \{\epsilon\}$.*

Definition 5 (Process). *A **(partial) process** is a sub-LTS $\langle Der(s_0), A_\perp, \longrightarrow, s_0 \rangle$ satisfying the **irrecoverability** constraint $\boxed{\forall s \in Der(s_0)[s \xrightarrow{\perp} s' \Rightarrow A_\perp(s') = \{\perp\}]}$. The process is **total** if $s \not\xrightarrow{\perp} s'$ for all $s, s' \in Der(s_0)$. If $s_0 \xrightarrow{u} t$ for $t \in Der(s_0)$ and $u \in A^{*?}_\perp$, then $s_0 \xrightarrow{u} t$ is a **behaviour** of the process.*

Fact 3. *If $\langle S, A_\perp, \longrightarrow, s_0 \rangle$ is a process then so is $\langle Der(s), A_\perp, \longrightarrow, s \rangle$ for any $s \in S$.*

Notational Conventions and Terminology

1. Processes are identified with their start states (Fact 3) and all relations between processes are also relations between their start states.
2. Upper-case latin letters P, Q, R etc. (possibly decorated) denote processes.
3. Lower-case initial latin letters a, b, c etc. (possibly decorated) denote individual actions (including $\perp$ and the empty trace ϵ).

---

[2] In particular $\perp < \tau$ if $\tau \in A$.

In the sequel, we restrict ourselves to the set of (partial) processes $\mathbb{P}[A_\perp]$ defined below.

Definition 6. *The structure* $\mathbf{P}[A_\perp] = \langle \mathbb{P}[A_\perp], \Omega, \mathbf{0}, \{a._- \mid a \in A\}, \Sigma \rangle$ *where*

- **Omega.** $\Omega \stackrel{df}{=} \langle \{s_0\}, A_\perp, \{s_0 \stackrel{\perp}{\longrightarrow} s_0\}, s_0 \rangle$ *is the totally undefined process,*
- **Nil.** $\mathbf{0} \stackrel{df}{=} \langle \{s_0\}, A_\perp, \emptyset, s_0 \rangle$ *is the "terminated", "blocked", "deadlocked" or "stop" process,*
- **Prefixing.** $a.P \stackrel{df}{=} \langle S \cup \{s_0'\}, A_\perp, \longrightarrow \cup \{s_0' \stackrel{a}{\longrightarrow} s_0\}, s_0' \rangle$, *for any* $P = \langle S, A_\perp, \longrightarrow, s_0 \rangle$, $a \in A$, *and* $s_0' \notin S$,
- **Summation.** *For any sequence* $[P_i \mid i \in I, P_i = \langle S^i, A_\perp, \longrightarrow_i, s_0^i \rangle]$ *of processes indexed by a set I, their sum is* $\sum_{i \in I} P_i \stackrel{df}{=} \langle S, A_\perp, \longrightarrow, s_0 \rangle$ *where* $s_0 \notin \bigcup_{i \in I} S^i$ *and*
  - $S = Der(s_0) = \{s_0\} \cup \biguplus_{i \in I} Targets(\longrightarrow_i)$,
  - $s_0 \stackrel{a}{\longrightarrow} t$ *if for some* P_i, $i \in I$, $s_0^i \stackrel{a}{\longrightarrow}_i t \in S^i$,
  - $s \stackrel{a}{\longrightarrow} t$ *if* $s \stackrel{a}{\longrightarrow}_i t$ *for some* $i \in I$, $s, t \in Der(s_0)$.

is called **Basic Extended Process Algebra (BXPA).**

$\mathbb{P}[A_\perp]$ contains processes with infinite behaviours too. We do not allow prefixing with the undefined action. In the case of summation, the root s_0 is a new state representing the effect of coalescing all the start states s_0^i, $i \in I$. However, whether an s_0^i belongs to S depends on whether it is a proper derivative of itself. For example, given $P = \langle \{s_0^P\}, A_\perp, \{s_0^P \stackrel{a}{\longrightarrow} s_0^P\}, s_0^P \rangle$ and $Q = \langle \{s_0^Q, t^Q\}, A_\perp, \{s_0^Q \stackrel{b}{\longrightarrow} t^Q\}, s_0^Q \rangle$ the set of states in their sum ($S = \{s_0, s_0^P, t^Q\}$) would include s_0^P and t^Q but would exclude s_0^Q.

By convention $\sum_{i \in \emptyset} P_i \equiv \mathbf{0}$ and (by abuse of notation) $\Omega \equiv \perp.\Omega$. When $|I| = 2$ we use the binary infix symbol "+", (e.g. $P_1 + P_2$) to denote their sum. Let $[P_i \mid 1 \leq i \leq n]$ be any finite sequence of processes. We write $P_1 + \cdots + P_n$ to denote $\sum_{1 \leq i \leq n} P_i$.

Proposition 1. $\mathbb{P}[A_\perp]$ *is an idempotent abelian monoid under + with* $\mathbf{0}$ *as identity. Further*

1. $P \stackrel{a}{\longrightarrow} P', a \in A$ *implies* $P \sim a.P' + P$.
2. $P \stackrel{\perp}{\longrightarrow} P'$ *implies* $P' \sim \Omega$ *and hence* $P \sim \Omega + P$.
3. **(Canonical form upto $\sim$).** $P \sim [\Omega+] \sum_{a \in A, P \stackrel{a}{\longrightarrow} P_a} a.P_a$[3].

Parallel Composition. To ensure that the composition of two processes yields a process (that satisfies the irrecoverability constraint of Definition 5) we impose a **strict-ness** condition $\boxed{(P \stackrel{\perp}{\longrightarrow} \_ \lor Q \stackrel{\perp}{\longrightarrow} \_) \implies ((P \otimes Q \stackrel{\perp}{\longrightarrow} \Omega) \land (Q \otimes P \stackrel{\perp}{\longrightarrow} \Omega))}$ that guarantees that $\mathbb{P}[A_\perp]$ is closed under $\otimes$. The expansion laws follow for the various composition operators akin to those defined in CSP, CCS and SCCS. We refer the reader to the extended report for the details.

---

[3] where "$[\Omega+]$" indicates that Ω occurs only if $P \stackrel{\perp}{\longrightarrow}$.

4 Lifted Strong Bisimulations and PHML

In [1] bisimulation was generalised to (ρ, σ)-bisimulation for binary relations ρ and σ on the set of actions. Further in [2] many bisimilarities defined in the literature were shown to inherit their nice algebraic and relational properties from the properties of the underlying relations on actions.

Definition 7. *A binary relation $\mathcal{R}$ on processes is a* **lifted strong bisimulation (LSB)** *if for all states s, t, sRt implies for all $a, b \in A_{\perp, \epsilon}$, (1) $s \xrightarrow{a} s' \Rightarrow \exists b, t'[a \leq b \wedge t \xrightarrow{b} t' \wedge s'Rt']$ and (2) $t \xrightarrow{b} t' \Rightarrow \exists a, s'[a \leq b \wedge s \xrightarrow{a} s' \wedge s'Rt']$. $s \sqsubseteq t$ (equivalently $t \sqsupseteq s$) if there exists a LSB $\mathcal{R}$ such that sRt (we write $\mathcal{R} \vdash s \sqsubseteq t$ to denote this fact). $s \sqsupseteq t$ if $s \sqsubseteq t$ and $s \sqsupseteq t$.*

LSB is an instance of the more general (ρ, σ)-bisimulation [1] with $\rho = \sigma = \leq$. By theorem 4.1 part 1 in [1], $\sqsubseteq$ is a preorder.

Example 1. Let $P \stackrel{df}{=} a.b.0$ and $Q \stackrel{df}{=} a.b.\Omega$. Then $Q \sqsubseteq P$. However $P_1 \stackrel{df}{=} \Omega + P \not\sqsubseteq Q \not\sqsubseteq P_1$. Let $P_2 \stackrel{df}{=} \Omega + Q$. Then we have $P_2 \sqsubseteq Q \not\sqsubseteq P_2$.

Theorem 4 (Precongruence). *The operators of $\mathbf{P}[A_\perp]$ are monotonic under $\sqsubseteq$ and the relation $\sqsubseteq$ is a precongruence on $\mathbf{P}[A_\perp]$.*

In [9] Milner has defined what it means for a logic to characterise a behavioural equivalence relation viz. that two processes are behaviourally equivalent if and only if they satisfy the same set of logical properties. In [6] the definition was generalised to the logical characterisation of behavioural *preorders*, in terms of containment of sets of properties. We give a definition below that subsumes both Milner's definition for behavioural equivalences and the one in [6].

Definition 8. *Let $(\mathcal{L}, \models^X)$ be a logic consisting of a language $\mathcal{L}$ and a relation $\models^X \subseteq \mathbb{P} \times \mathcal{L}$. $(\mathcal{L}, \models^X)$* **characterises** *a behavioural preorder $\leq$ over $\mathbb{P}$ if for any $P, Q \in \mathbb{P}$, $P \leq Q$ iff $\mathcal{L}_X(P) \subseteq \mathcal{L}_X(Q)$, where $\mathcal{L}_X(P) = \{\phi \in \mathcal{L} \mid P \models^X \phi\}$. $P \subseteq_X Q$ iff $\mathcal{L}_X(P) \subseteq \mathcal{L}_X(Q)$.*

In [3] the authors have generalised Hennessy-Milner Logic (HML) to a parameterised form called PHML corresponding to the parameterisation of bisimulations and bisimilarities in [1]. In general however, PHML defined over a set of "observables" (which may or may not be the set of "actions") is not a modal logic unless certain conditions are met. Rather, it is a negation-free logic which reduces to a modal logic whenever the parameters ρ and σ are preorders satisfying the conditions (see theorem 4.1 in [1])

- ρ and σ are both equivalences and so $\sqsupseteq_{(\rho,\sigma)}$ is an equivalence, or else
- the preorders ρ and σ are not equivalences and
  - either $\rho = \sigma$ in which case $\sqsupseteq_{(\rho,\rho)}$ is a preorder,
  - or $\rho = \sigma^{-1}$ in which case $\sqsupseteq_{(\rho,\sigma)}$ is an equivalence.

We have $\sqsubseteq = \quad\square_{(\leq,\leq)}$ since it is induced by the preorder (actually partial order) $\leq \subseteq A_{\perp,\epsilon} \times A_{\perp,\epsilon}$. Hence PHML [3] applied to our present context ($\rho = \leq = \sigma$) directly yields a modal logic.

Definition 9. $\phi :: = \mathbf{tt} \mid \mathbf{ff} \mid \langle a\rangle\phi \mid [a]\phi \mid \bigwedge_{i\in I}\phi_i \mid \bigvee_{i\in I}\phi_i$, where $a \in A_{\perp,\epsilon}$ and I is an indexing set, is the BNF of the language $\mathcal{L}_{(\leq,\leq)}$[4]. $\bigwedge_{i\in\emptyset}\phi_i \equiv \mathbf{tt}$ and $\bigvee_{i\in\emptyset}\phi_i \equiv \mathbf{ff}$ by convention.

Definition 10 (Satisfaction). $\models^S \subseteq \mathbb{P} \times \mathcal{L}$ is the smallest (infix) relation defined by induction on the structure of formulae for any process P and any action $a \in A_{\perp,\epsilon}$.

$$P \models^S \mathbf{tt} \text{ for each } P \in \mathbb{P} \qquad P \models^S \mathbf{ff} \text{ for no } P \in \mathbb{P}$$
$$P \models^S \langle a\rangle\phi \text{ iff} \qquad\qquad P \models^S [a]\phi \text{ iff}$$
$$\exists b \in A_{\perp,\epsilon} : b \geq a, P' : \qquad \forall b \in A_{\perp,\epsilon} : b \leq a, P' :$$
$$[P \xrightarrow{b} P' \wedge P' \models^S \phi] \qquad [P \xrightarrow{b} P' \Rightarrow P' \models^S \phi]$$
$$P \models^S \bigwedge_{i\in I}\phi_i \text{ iff } \forall i \in I[P \models^S \phi_i] \quad P \models^S \bigvee_{i\in I}\phi_i \text{ iff } \exists i \in I[P \models^S \phi_i]$$

P **satisfies** ϕ if $P \models^S \phi$ and $\mathcal{L}_S(P) = \{\phi \mid P \models^S \phi\}$. $P \subseteq_S Q$ if $\mathcal{L}_S(P) \subseteq \mathcal{L}_S(Q)$ for processes P, Q,

Theorem 5 then directly follows from definition 5 and theorem 3 of [3].

Theorem 5 (Logical characterisation of $\sqsubseteq$). $P \sqsubseteq Q$ if and only if $\mathcal{L}_S(P) \subseteq \mathcal{L}_S(Q)$.

By defining an affirmation relation (analogous to that in [7]) which omits the observability of $\perp$ (i.e. omitting the modalities $\langle\perp\rangle$ and $[\perp]$) we may show that the discrimination power of the modal logic remains unchanged. Hence they may be dispensed with altogether. We refer the reader to the extended report for the details.

5   Conclusion

We have expanded the notion of process to include agents which are capable of performing an undefined action. By stipulating that it lies below all other actions, we have been able to define a totally undefined process Ω which lies below all other processes. In particular, $\Omega \sqsubseteq \mathbf{0} \not\sqsubseteq \Omega$. We may also include a distinguished silent action τ in the action set A. Since all actions in A are mutually incomparable, deadlock ($\mathbf{0}$) and livelock ($\mathbf{T}$) will not be equated by the relation $\sqsubseteq$.

We have not explicitly addressed the question of recursion. However, it is easy to see that guarded recursion equations made up of only well-defined actions, will yield unique fixpoints as solutions. It is also clear that if $\tau \in A$, then the two equations $X \Leftarrow X$ and $X \Leftarrow \tau.X$ would yield different (least) solutions Ω and $\mathbf{T}$ respectively (upto $\sqsubseteq$), with $\Omega \sqsubseteq \mathbf{T} \not\sqsubseteq \Omega$.

Future Work. The relation $\sqsubseteq$ could be used as a refinement relation which allows a progression from a totally undefined process to one which satisfies a certain specification (expressed in terms of the properties or the behaviours that need to be satisfied).

---

[4] For the present, we are assuming that every action in $A_{\perp,\epsilon}$ including the undefined action $\perp$ is observable; this may be relaxed.

The fact that the algebra is closed (upto ~) under the various parallel composition operators opens up the possibility that a formal specification language could potentially use more than one parallel composition operator. The challenge in designing such a language would then rest on defining a suitable syntax and a structural operational semantics that is faithful to our model. We conjecture that it may be useful in hardware-software codesign.

References

1. Arun-Kumar, S.: On bisimilarities induced by relations on actions. In: Proceedings 4th IEEE International Conference on Software Engineering and Formal Methods, Pune, India. IEEE Computer Society Press (2006)
2. Arun-Kumar, S., Bagga, D.: Parameterised bisimulations: some applications. In: Höfner, P., Jipsen, P., Kahl, W., Müller, M.E. (eds.) RAMICS 2014. LNCS, vol. 8428, pp. 208–225. Springer, Cham (2014). https://doi.org/10.1007/978-3-319-06251-8_13
3. Bagga, D., Arun-Kumar, S.: Logical characterization of parameterised bisimulations. In: Hung, D., Kapur, D. (eds.) ICTAC 2017. LNCS, vol. 10580, pp. 51–69. Springer, Cham (2017). https://doi.org/10.1007/978-3-319-67729-3_4
4. De Nicola, R., Hennessy, M.C.B.: Testing equivalences for processes. Theoret. Comput. Sci. **34**, 83–133 (1983)
5. Hennessy, M.C.B.: Algebraic Theory of Processes. MIT Press, Boston (1988)
6. Korade, N., Arun-Kumar, S.: A logical characterization of efficiency preorders. In: Liu, Z., Araki, K. (eds.) ICTAC 2004. LNCS, vol. 3407, pp. 99–112. Springer, Heidelberg (2005). https://doi.org/10.1007/978-3-540-31862-0_9
7. Milner, R.: A modal characterisation of observable machine-behaviour. In: Astesiano, E., Böhm, C. (eds.) CAAP 1981. LNCS, vol. 112, pp. 25–34. Springer, Heidelberg (1981). https://doi.org/10.1007/3-540-10828-9_52
8. Milner, R.: Calculi for synchrony and asynchrony. Theoret. Comput. Sci. **25**, 267–310 (1983)
9. Milner, R.: Communication and Concurrency. Prentice-Hall International (1989)
10. Scott, D.S.: Data types as lattices. SIAM J. Comput. **5**(3), 522–587 (1976)
11. Scott, D.S.: Domains for denotational semantics. In: Nielsen, M., Schmidt, E.M. (eds.) ICALP 1982. LNCS, vol. 140, pp. 577–610. Springer, Heidelberg (1982). https://doi.org/10.1007/BFb0012801
12. Walker, D.J.: Bisimulation and divergence in CCS. In: Third Annual Symposium on Logic in Computer Science, pp. 186–192. IEEE Computer Society Press, Edinburgh, July 1988

Machine-Assisted Proofs for Institutions in Coq

Conor Reynolds$^{(\boxtimes)}$ⓘ and Rosemary Monahanⓘ

Maynooth University, Maynooth, Ireland
{conor.reynolds,rosemary.monahan}@mu.ie

Abstract. The theory of institutions provides an abstract mathematical framework for specifying logical systems and their semantic relationships. Institutions are based on category theory and have deep roots in a well-developed branch of algebraic specification. However, there are no machine-assisted proofs of correctness for institution-theoretic constructions—chiefly satisfaction conditions for institutions and their (co)morphisms—making them difficult to incorporate into mainstream formal methods. This paper therefore provides the details of our approach to formalizing a fragment of the theory of institutions in the Coq proof assistant. We instantiate this framework with the institutions *FOPEQ* for first-order predicate logic and *EVT* for the Event-B specification language, both of which will serve as an illustration and evaluation of the overall approach.

1 Introduction

The theory of institutions dates to Joseph Goguen and Rod M. Burstall's 1984 paper [7] and the subsequent more detailed analysis in 1992 [8]. An institution is a mathematical realisation of the notion of "logical system" which does not commit to any single concrete system. The key insight is that many general results about logical systems do not depend in any interesting way on the details of that system.

In her PhD thesis [6], Marie Farrell uses the theory of institutions to provide a semantics for the Event-B formal modelling method with an eye to addressing some drawbacks of the Event-B language—namely the lack of standardised modularisation constructs. *EVT* was shown by Farrell [6], on paper, to support such constructs.

Indeed, the theory of institutions has been applied to a wide variety of languages and formal methods; CLEAR [2], CSP [15], and UML [10] have been given an institution-theoretic semantics, to name but a few. The HETS tool for heterogeneous specification [12] has the largest single repository of such institutions and their logical relationships, represented mainly by institution morphisms and comorphisms; but as far as we know there are no machine-checked

Funded by the Irish Research Council (GOIPG/2019/4529).

Y. Aït-Ameur and F. Crăciun (Eds.): TASE 2022, LNCS 13299, pp. 180–196, 2022.
https://doi.org/10.1007/978-3-031-10363-6_13

proofs that these constructions are correct. Many of the requirements—checking that categories are really categories, that functors are really functors, as well as satisfaction conditions for institutions and for the (co)morphisms that relate them—amount in some parts to simple bookkeeping, and in other parts to more novel and interesting results.

We hence provide here a framework in the Coq proof assistant [5] for interactive machine-assisted proofs for institutions and an instantiation of this framework to two institutions: the institution *FOPEQ* for first-order predicate logic and the institution *EVT* for Event-B. Coq has two properties desirable for this work. First, it is based on a dependent type theory called the calculus of inductive constructions (CIC) which makes the representation of mathematical objects and the subtle constraints that they impose on one another easier than in a system without dependent types. Second, it is an interactive proof assistant rather than an automated proof assistant. The user can design automated tactics that can discharge many simple goals, but crucially Coq allows the user to step in and spell out the proofs in detail if necessary. Our framework is available on GitHub at https://github.com/ConorReynolds/coq-institutions.

We build directly on the work done by Emmanuel Gunther, Alejandro Gadea, and Miguel Pagano [9] formalizing multi-sorted universal algebra in Agda. We also note some other work in this direction in Coq by Venanzio Capretta [3], and by Gianluca Amato, Marco Maggesi and Maurizio Parton and Cosimo Perini Brogi [1] which makes use of homotopy type theory—but none go quite as far as defining institutions or instantiating first-order logic at the time of this writing. This is the first such formalization of which we are aware.

We will begin by laying the basic mathematical groundwork for institution theory, multi-sorted universal algebra, and first-order predicate logic, before explaining how these concepts are defined in our Coq developments. First-order logic is an extremely central institution, on which many others build (including *EVT*) and provides an appropriate first example. We then provide the same treatment for *EVT* as a further case study, and to provide a concrete example of one institution building on another.

2 Mathematical Background

Institutions are based on category theory. A *category* consists of a collection of objects, and a collection of arrows or morphisms between those objects, subject to some straightforward laws. A *functor* is a map between categories which preserves the categorical structure—more precisely, it preserves identity morphisms and composition of morphisms. Definitions for these concepts can be found in Emily Riehl's freely available *Category Theory in Context* [14]. We only require very light familiarity with categories and functors for this paper.

Definition 1. *An* institution [7] *consists of*

- *a category* Sig *of signatures;*
- *a sentence functor* Sen : Sig → Set*;*

- a *model functor* $\mathsf{Mod} : \mathsf{Sig}^{\mathsf{op}} \to \mathsf{Cat}$*; and*
- a *semantic entailment relation* $\models_\Sigma \subseteq |\mathsf{Mod}(\Sigma)| \times \mathsf{Sen}(\Sigma)$ *for each* $\Sigma \in \mathsf{Sig}$,

such that for any signature morphism $\sigma : \Sigma \to \Sigma'$, *any sentence* $\phi \in \mathsf{Sen}(\Sigma)$, *and any model* $M' \in \mathsf{Mod}(\Sigma')$, *the satisfaction condition holds:*

$$M' \models_{\Sigma'} \mathsf{Sen}(\sigma)(\phi) \quad \textit{iff} \quad \mathsf{Mod}(\sigma)(M') \models_\Sigma \phi$$

ensuring that a change in signature induces a consistent change in the satisfaction of sentences by models.

The signatures contain non-logical symbols: data types, constants, functions, and so on. The sentence functor explains how to build sentences over the non-logical symbols. The model functor explains how to interpret the symbols in any given signature. The semantic entailment relation explains how to decide if a given sentence is true or false in a given model. The requirement that the signatures form a category, and that the sentence and model constructors are functors, is due to the central concept of a *signature morphism*, a mapping between signatures—a "change in notation". If the sentence construction is a functor then we can be sure that signature translations preserve the sentence structure.

The satisfaction condition explains how the components should interact with one another, and in particular how they behave under a change in signature. Without such a condition, the semantic entailment relation $\models$ could behave just as expected on one signature, but behave utterly erratically on another. But we expect the entailment relation $\models$ to change only so much with a change in signature. The satisfaction condition ensures that satisfaction of sentences by models is consistent under a change in signature.

2.1   First-Order Predicate Logic

We provide a brief account of multi-sorted universal algebra and first-order predicate logic, in preparation for a formal encoding in Coq (Sect. 4); see Sannella and Tarlecki's *Foundations of Algebraic Specification* [17] for details.

Definition 2. *An* S*-indexed set is a family of sets* $X = (X_s)_{s \in S}$.

Definition 3. *A* signature *is a 3-tuple* $\langle S, \mathscr{F}, \mathscr{P} \rangle$ *where* S *is a set of sorts,* $\mathscr{F}$ *is a* $(\mathsf{List}(S) \times S)$*-indexed set of function symbols, and* $\mathscr{P}$ *is a* $\mathsf{List}(S)$*-indexed set of predicate symbols.*

Here $\mathsf{List}(A)$ is just as expected: the set of all finite sequences of elements from A. The idea is that a symbol $F \in \mathscr{F}_{w,s}$ has arity w and result sort s, and a predicate symbol $P \in \mathscr{P}_w$ has arity w and no result sort (since it represents a predicate). If the signature is clear from context, we instead write $F : \prod_i w_i \to s$ for function symbols, and $P : \prod_i w_i \to \mathsf{Prop}$ for predicate symbols. If a function symbol C has arity nil and result sort s, then it is called a constant symbol and we denote it $C : s$.

As a running example, let stackSig be a signature consisting of the symbols required to describe a stack. It has two sorts elem and stack; some function symbols empty : stack, push : elem × stack → stack, and pop : stack → stack; and a predicate symbol isEmpty : stack → Prop.

Definition 4. *Let* $\Sigma = \langle S, \mathscr{F}, \mathscr{P} \rangle$ *and* $\Sigma' = \langle S', \mathscr{F}', \mathscr{P}' \rangle$ *be two signatures. A signature morphism* $\sigma : \Sigma \to \Sigma'$ *consists of a function* $\sigma_{sorts} : S \to S'$, *which will usually be written* σ, *as well as a pair of functions*

$$\sigma_{funcs} : \prod_{w,s} \mathscr{F}_{w,s} \to \mathscr{F}'_{\sigma(w),\sigma(s)}$$

$$\sigma_{preds} : \prod_{w} \mathscr{P}_w \to \mathscr{P}'_{\sigma(w)}$$

respectively mapping sorts, function symbols, and predicate symbols, in such a way that the sorts are translated consistently with σ_{sorts}. *We define* $\sigma(w)$ *as the action of* σ_{sorts} *on each of the sorts in* w.

Definition 5. *An* algebra A *for a signature* $\Sigma = \langle S, \mathscr{F}, \mathscr{P} \rangle$ *consists of three functions* $\langle A_{sorts}, A_{funcs}, A_{preds} \rangle$, *all of which we denote by* A, *each respectively interpreting the sorts, function symbols, and predicate symbols as sets, functions, and predicates:*

- *for any sort* $s \in S$, $A(s)$ *is a set, which we typically denote* A_s;
- *for any* $F \in \mathscr{F}_{w,s}$, *we have* $A(F) : A_{w_1} \times \cdots \times A_{w_n} \to A_s$; *and*
- *for any* $P \in \mathscr{P}_w$, *we have* $A(P) \subseteq A_{w_1} \times \cdots \times A_{w_n}$.

Algebras give meaning to the symbols in a signature. Consider again our running example stackSig; we could interpret the sort elem as the set $\mathbb{N}$ of natural numbers, and the sort stack as the set $\mathsf{List}(\mathbb{N})$ of lists of natural numbers; the function symbols empty, push, and pop as nil $\in \mathsf{List}(\mathbb{N})$, cons : $\mathbb{N} \times \mathsf{List}(\mathbb{N}) \to \mathbb{N}$, and tail : $\mathsf{List}(\mathbb{N}) \to \mathbb{N}$, respectively; and the predicate symbol isEmpty as the predicate $\{s \mid s = \mathsf{nil}\} \subseteq \mathsf{List}(\mathbb{N})$. We are by no means bound to this interpretation, of course.

Definition 6. *Let* Σ *and* Σ' *be signatures, let* $\sigma : \Sigma \to \Sigma'$ *be a signature morphism, and let* A' *be a* Σ'-algebra. *The* reduct algebra $A'|_{\sigma}$ *is a* Σ-algebra *defined at each component of the algebra to be* $A' \circ \sigma$.

Algebras are best thought of (loosely) as functions providing a concrete denotation for the symbols in a signature—functions from symbols to "real" mathematical objects. In the presence of a change in signature $\sigma : \Sigma \to \Sigma'$, a Σ'-algebra can interpret symbols in Σ by first applying σ and interpreting the resulting Σ'-symbol; hence we "precompose" A' by σ to obtain a Σ-algebra. Note that the direction is reversed; we are taking Σ'-algebras to Σ-algebras using $\sigma : \Sigma \to \Sigma'$. Now is a good time to note the contravariance of the model functor in the definition of an institution: if $\sigma : \Sigma \to \Sigma'$ then $\mathsf{Mod}(\sigma) : \mathsf{Mod}(\Sigma') \to \mathsf{Mod}(\Sigma)$.

The following pair of definitions explain how we may build more complex expressions, which we will call *terms*, out of the basic symbols of a signature.

Definition 7. *A set of* variables *for a signature* $\Sigma = \langle S, \mathscr{F}, \mathscr{P} \rangle$ *is an S-indexed set.*

Definition 8. *A* term *over a signature* $\Sigma = \langle S, \mathscr{F}, \mathscr{P} \rangle$ *with variables in X is defined inductively as follows.*

- *A variable $x \in X_s$ is a term of sort s.*
- *A constant symbol $C \in \mathscr{F}_{\text{nil},s}$ is a term of sort s.*
- *If $|w| = n > 0$, then given terms $t_1 : w_1, \ldots, t_n : w_n$ and a function symbol $F \in \mathscr{F}_{w,s}$, the expression $F(t_1, \ldots, t_n)$ is a term of sort s.*

Terms explain how sorted variables and symbols may be put together. For example, let x : elem and s : stack be two variables; then $\mathsf{push}(x, s)$: stack is a valid term; as is $\mathsf{push}(x, \mathsf{push}(x, s))$. But, for example, $\mathsf{pop}(x)$ is not since x has the wrong sort.

With terms and algebras defined, all that is left is to define first-order sentences.

Definition 9. *Let $\Sigma = \langle S, \mathscr{F}, \mathscr{P} \rangle$ be a signature. The* sentences *of first-order logic are built from the logical symbols $=, \rightarrow, \neg, \wedge, \vee, \forall, \exists$. The atomic sentences are*

- *$u = v$ for terms u and v with the same sort; and*
- *$P(t_1, \ldots, t_n)$ for any predicate symbol $P \in \mathscr{P}_w$ and terms t_i.*

The sentences in general are defined inductively as follows:

- *Any atomic sentence ϕ is a sentence.*
- *The expressions $\neg \phi$, $\phi \rightarrow \psi$, $\phi \wedge \psi$, $\phi \vee \psi$, $\forall x.\ \phi$ and $\exists x.\ \phi$, for any sentences ϕ, ψ and variable x, are all sentences.*

We can now write sentences like $\forall x.\ \forall s.\ \mathsf{pop}(\mathsf{push}(x, s)) = s$. The interpretation of first-order sentences is defined by induction on the sentence structure. We will give a more precise account in Sect. 4.

3   Institutions in Coq

Coq is an interactive proof assistant for higher-order logic based on a dependent type theory called the *calculus of inductive constructions* (CIC). Dependent type theories allow for extremely elegant representation of complex mathematical objects such as those found in category theory, institution theory, universal algebra, etc. All of the work presented here is formalised fully in Coq.

We depend on a formalization of category theory by John Wiegley [20]. Morphisms between objects a and b are denoted a ~> b, and functors between categories C and D are denoted C --> D. The generic form of an institution can be defined directly as a dependent record.

```
Class Institution :=
{ Sig : Category ;
  Sen : Sig --> SetCat ;
  Mod : Sig^op --> SetCat ;
  interp : ∀ (Σ : Sig), Mod Σ -> Sen Σ -> Prop ;
  sat : ∀ (Σ Σ' : Sig) (σ : Σ ~> Σ') (φ : Sen Σ) (M' : Mod Σ'),
    interp M' (fmap[Sen] σ φ) <-> interp (fmap[Mod] σ M') φ }.
```

Here **interp** refers to the semantic entailment relation $\models$ for an institution and **SetCat** refers to the category of sets, which here just means the category of Coq types and functions. The term **fmap** is short for "functor map" and describes the action of a functor on morphisms. For the purposes of this paper, we implement so-called *set/set institutions* [11], in which the target of Mod is Set, the category of sets, and not Cat, the category of all small categories.

Our focus for this paper is on an instantiation of this object to *FOPEQ*, the institution for first-order predicate logic, and *EVT*, the institution for Event-B defined in [6]. Since *EVT* builds on *FOPEQ*, we will begin with *FOPEQ* and work up.

4   First-Order Logic in Coq

We partially build upon a formalization of multi-sorted universal algebra in Agda [9], though we deviate in many of the details. As we define objects in Coq, we will make reference back to their mathematical definitions from Sect. 2.1. We do not show everything, only what we deem crucial to follow the basic idea of the formalization.

4.1   Representing FOL

Signatures (cf. Definition 3) are represented by a dependent record, mirroring the mathematical definition exactly.

```
Record Signature :=
{ Sorts : Type ;
  Funcs : list Sorts -> Sorts -> Type ;
  Preds : list Sorts -> Type }.
```

An algebra (cf. Definition 5) for a signature needs to interpret sorts as Coq types and the function and predicate symbols as Coq functions with the right type.

For this we use *heterogeneous lists*—henceforth *h-lists*—following Gunther *et al.* [9]. A heterogeneous list can contain elements of different types, as distinguished from a homogeneous list which contains only elements of a single type. Our definition of h-lists comes from Chlipala's CPDT [4], where the reader can find a more detailed description of the implementation details.

Let $\mathcal{U}$ be a universe of types. Given an index type $I : \mathcal{U}$, a list $w : \text{List}(I)$ and a type family $A : I \to \mathcal{U}$ which selects for each $i : I$ a type $A_i : \mathcal{U}$, we can build a h-list $v : \mathsf{HList}(A, w)$ which contains $|w|$ elements and where the ith element of v, denoted v_i, has the type A_{w_i}. For example, if $w = [\mathbb{N}, \mathsf{bool}, \mathsf{string}]$ and if A is the identity, then $\langle 3, \mathsf{true}, \text{'hello'}\rangle$ would be a valid h-list of type $\mathsf{HList}(A, w)$. Another example, more pertinent to our discussion: Consider again our running example stackSig. Let $I = \{\mathsf{elem}, \mathsf{stack}\}$, let $w = [\mathsf{elem}, \mathsf{stack}]$, and let $A : I \to \mathcal{U}$ be defined by $\mathsf{elem} \mapsto \mathbb{N}$ and $\mathsf{stack} \mapsto \mathsf{List}(\mathbb{N})$. Then $\langle 2, [3, 4]\rangle$ would be a valid term of type $\mathsf{HList}(A, w)$.

A h-list is a concrete implementation of a kind of dependent n-tuple; that is to say, $\mathsf{HList}(A, w)$ is a concrete Coq encoding of the dependent sum $\sum_i A(w_i)$. Now, let $\Sigma = \langle S, \mathcal{F}, \mathcal{P}\rangle$ be a signature, let $F \in \mathcal{F}_{w,s}$ and let A be a Σ-algebra. Since $\mathsf{HList}(A, w) \to A(s) \cong \sum_i A(w_i) \to A(s)$, we should interpret $A(F)$ as a function $\mathsf{HList}(A, w) \to A(s)$.

```
Record Algebra Σ :=
{ interp_sorts : Sorts Σ -> Type ;
  interp_funcs w s : Funcs Σ w s -> HList interp_sorts w -> interp_sorts s ;
  interp_preds w : Preds Σ w -> HList interp_sorts w -> Prop }.
```

We are so far no different from Gunther *et al.* [9]. Our first deviation is in the definition of variables and terms (cf. Definition 8).

```
Inductive Term : Sorts Σ -> Type :=
| var s : member s Γ -> Term s
| term w s : Funcs Σ w s -> HList Term w -> Term s.
```

Variables (cf. Definition 7) are not represented here by members of an indexed set; instead they are dependent de Bruijn indices—see CPDT chapter nine [4]. The member type is exactly as it appears there; a term $i : \mathsf{member}(s, \Gamma)$ can be thought of as a constructive proof that s appears at index i in the list Γ. By defining variables this way, we can quite easily define quantifiers which correctly track the locations of free variables, as we will see.

Signature morphisms (cf. Definition 4) are the cornerstone of institution theory; much of the implementation depends on this definition.

```
Record SigMorphism Σ Σ' :=
{ on_sorts : Sorts Σ -> Sorts Σ' ;
  on_funcs w s : Funcs Σ w s -> Funcs Σ' (map on_sorts w) (on_sorts s) ;
  on_preds w : Preds Σ w -> Preds Σ' (map on_sorts w) }.
```

No surprises here, but note that we must translate the sorts in **on_funcs** and **on_preds** using **on_sorts**. With this we can now define reduct algebras (cf. Definition 6).

```
Definition ReductAlgebra (σ : SigMorphism Σ Σ') (A' : Algebra Σ') : Algebra Σ :=
{| interp_sorts := interp_sorts A' ∘ σ ;
   interp_funcs := λ w s F, interp_funcs A' (on_funcs σ F) ∘ reindex σ ;
   interp_preds := λ w P, interp_preds A' (on_preds σ P) ∘ reindex σ |}.
```

Note that the function reindex is computationally the identity but converts between the equivalent types $\mathsf{HList}(A \circ f, w)$ and $\mathsf{HList}(A, \mathsf{map}\ f\ w)$.

We can now start to build the syntactic and semantic structure of first-order sentences. The syntax is as follows.

```
Inductive FOL : list (Sorts Σ) -> Type :=
| Forall Γ s : FOL (s :: Γ) -> FOL Γ
| Exists Γ s : FOL (s :: Γ) -> FOL Γ
| Equal Γ s : Term Σ Γ s -> Term Σ Γ s -> FOL Γ
| Pred Γ w : Preds Σ w -> HList (Term Σ Γ) w -> FOL Γ
| ...
```

We omit the other connectives since their definitions are straightforward. Syntactically, a quantifier accepts as argument a sentence in which at least one variable appears free and binds it. If ψ is a sentence with context $s :: \Gamma$, then the sentence $Q_s.\ \psi$ is a sentence with context Γ, where Q is either quantifier. Formally, we have the following syntactic formation rule:

$$\frac{s :: \Gamma \vdash \phi}{\Gamma \vdash Q_s.\ \phi}$$

To interpret a first-order sentence, we must decide what the logical symbols mean and what values the free variables will get. If θ is an environment providing values for the variables in Γ, then we denote the semantic interpretation of a sentence ϕ with free variables from Γ by an algebra A with environment θ by $A \vDash^\theta \phi$. Precisely, in the case of the quantifiers, we have

$$A \vDash^\theta \mathsf{Forall}_s(\psi) \quad \text{iff} \quad \text{for all } x \in A_s \text{ we have } A \vDash^{x,\theta} \psi$$
$$A \vDash^\theta \mathsf{Exists}_s(\psi) \quad \text{iff} \quad \text{there exists } x \in A_s \text{ such that } A \vDash^{x,\theta} \psi$$

This setup makes the definition of the semantic entailment relation relatively painless. (The triple-colon operator denotes the cons function for h-lists.)

```
Fixpoint interp_fol (A : Algebra Σ) (φ : FOL Σ Γ) (θ : HList A Γ) : Prop :=
  match φ with
  | Forall s ψ => ∀ x : A s, interp_fol A ψ (x ::: θ)
  | Exists s ψ => ∃ x : A s, interp_fol A ψ (x ::: θ)
  | Equal u v  => eval_term A u θ = eval_term A v θ
  | Pred P ts  => interp_preds A P (map_eval_term A ts θ)
  | ...
```

The institution $FOPEQ$ requires closed first-order sentences, i.e. sentences of the form $\psi : \mathsf{FOL}(\Sigma, \mathsf{nil})$; hence $A \vDash \psi$ will really mean $\mathsf{interp\_fol}(A, \psi, \mathsf{hnil})$.

The relation above relies on two mutually-defined term evaluation functions, for which we use the **coq-equations** library [18].

```
Equations eval_term (A : Algebra Σ) (t : Term Σ Γ s)
   : HList A Γ -> A s := {
  eval_term _ (var i) θ := HList.nth θ i ;
  eval_term A (term F args) θ := interp_funcs A F (map_eval_term A args θ)
} where map_eval_term (A : Algebra Σ) (args : HList (Term Σ Γ) w)
   : HList A Γ -> HList A w := {
  map_eval_term _ () _ := () ;
  map_eval_term A (t ::: ts) θ :=
    eval_term A t θ ::: map_eval_term A ts θ }.
```

On variables, it looks up the right value in the environment. On terms, it inter-
prets the function symbol with the given algebra and calls itself on the function
symbol's arguments. It is possible to write this function (and others) without
coq-equations, but this gives the best computational behaviour and plays relatively nicely with the proofs.

4.2   Proofs and Proof Strategy

There are some more definitions that are crucial for proving the satisfaction
condition for first-order predicate logic. The following mutually-defined functions
promote signature morphisms to term translations:

```
Equations on_terms (σ : SigMorphism Σ Σ') (t : Term Σ Γ s)
   : Term Σ' (map σ Γ) (σ s) := {
  on_terms σ (var i) := var (reindex_member σ i) ;
  on_terms σ (term F args) := term (on_funcs σ F) (map_on_terms σ args)
} where map_on_terms (σ : SigMorphism Σ Σ') (args : HList (Term Σ Γ) w)
   : HList (Term Σ' (map σ Γ)) (map σ w) := {
  map_on_terms σ () := () ;
  map_on_terms σ (t ::: ts) := on_terms σ t ::: map_on_terms σ ts }.
```

Applying a signature translation to a variable amounts only to a reindexing; all
the work is happening at the type level, but the underlying "number" i doesn't
change. To apply a signature translation to a term, we just apply it to the
function symbol and then apply it to all its arguments. Promoting this a level
higher to first-order sentences is a simple matter, since the sentence structure
will be ignored by signature morphisms.

We will also need to define a custom induction principle for terms; the induction principle automatically generated by Coq is too weak because it is missing
a hypothesis in the case where the term has the form $F(t_1, \ldots, t_n)$; namely that
the predicate $P : \prod_i A_i \to \mathsf{Prop}$ holds for all $t_1, \ldots, t_n$. In Coq this is represented
by HForall $P \langle t_1, \ldots, t_n \rangle$.

```
Context (Σ : Signature) (Γ : list (Sorts Σ)).
Context (P : ∀ s, Term Σ Γ s -> Prop).

Hypothesis var_case : ∀ s (m : member s Γ), P s (var m).
Hypothesis term_case :
  ∀ w s (F : Funcs Σ w s) (args : HList (Term Σ Γ) w),
  HForall P args -> P s (term F args).

Equations term_ind' s (t : Term Σ Γ s) : P s t := {
  term_ind' s (var i) := var_case _ i ;
  term_ind' s (term F args) := term_case _ _ F args (map_term_ind' _ args)
} where map_term_ind' w (args : HList (Term Σ Γ) w) : HForall P args := {
  map_term_ind' s () := I ;
  map_term_ind' s (t ::: ts) := conj (term_ind' _ t) (map_term_ind' _ ts) }.
```

Proofs Involving Indexed Types. Consider how to define the composition of two signature morphisms σ and τ. Doing so directly will result in a type-level mismatch between map τ (map σ w) and map $(\tau \circ \sigma)$ w. Of course, these terms are propositionally equal via the proof $p = $ map_map σ τ w; so we need to mention this to Coq at the point of definition. As an example, here is the definition of the composition of two first-order signature morphisms, simplified for readability.

```
Definition comp_FOSig
  (τ : SigMorphism B C) (σ : SigMorphism A B) : SigMorphism A C :=
{| on_sorts := τ ∘ σ ;
  on_funcs w s F :=
    rew (map_map σ τ w) in (on_funcs τ (on_funcs σ F)) ;
  on_preds w P :=
    rew (map_map σ τ w) in (on_preds τ (on_preds σ P)) |}.
```

Many definitions in our developments take a similar form. Proofs of most propositions involving such terms should follow by computation and induction on the involved identity proofs—an *identity proof* being a proof of the form $p : x = y$. We call upon a range of tactics and rewriting strategies for identity proofs, many of which are defined in `Coq.Init.Logic` and some of which come from the homotopy type theory [19] Coq developments, specifically `Basics/PathGroupoids.v`.

Proofs about terms caused the most consternation. Using the following lemma,

```
Lemma map_on_terms_hmap (σ : SigMorphism Σ Σ') (ts : HList (Term Σ Γ) w) :
  map_on_terms σ ts = reindex σ (HList.map (on_terms σ) ts).
```

we can write map_on_terms in terms of hmap and on_terms; this exposes reindex, which we may convert into rew using some combination of the following two lemmas.

```
Lemma reindex_id (v : HList A is) :
  reindex idmap v = rew (map_id is)^ in v.
```

```
Lemma reindex_comp (f : I -> J) (g : J -> K) (v : HList (A ∘ (g ∘ f)) is) :
  rew (map_map f g is) in reindex g (reindex f v) = reindex (g ∘ f) v.
```

This process pulls out the hidden identity proof such that it may be combined with others. We then required the lemma

```
Lemma map_ext_HForall (f g : ∀ i, A i -> B i) (v : HList A w) :
  HForall (λ i x, f i x = g i x) v <-> hmap f v = hmap g v.
```

for converting the hypothesis generated by our custom induction principle for terms into a useful rewrite rule.

There is one more trick we employ, and for which we must assume proof irrelevance. Often the subject of an identity proof is of the form $x :: xs$, as in, for example, p' : map id $(x :: xs) = x :: xs$. If one has a proof p : map id $xs = xs$, then in fact f_equal (cons x) p is also a proof that map id $(x :: xs) = x :: xs$. By proof irrelevance, p' and f_equal (cons x) p are themselves equal, but the point is that the latter form has useful structure that we can exploit. This is not always necessary—often the simplify_eqs tactic is enough—but we found it indispensable in proofs which required more careful rewriting of identity proofs.

The Proof of Satisfaction. Throughout the process, we identified at least one non-obvious lemma required for the proof of satisfaction for first-order logic.

Lemma 1. *Let* $\sigma : \Sigma_1 \to \Sigma_2$ *be a signature morphism, let* t_1 *be a* Σ_1-*term with* Σ_1-*context* Γ_1, *and let* A_2 *be a* Σ_2-*algebra. Let* θ : $\mathsf{HList}(A_2|_\sigma, \Gamma_1)$ *be a valuation of the variables in* Γ_1. *Then*

$$A_2^{\sigma(\theta)}(\sigma(t_1)) = (A_2|_\sigma)^\theta(t_1)$$

Since θ is a h-list, the action of σ on θ is just a reindexing; hence we obtain $\sigma(\theta)$: $\mathsf{HList}(A_2, \mathsf{map}\ \sigma\ \Gamma_1)$. The specific requirement generated by the proof of satisfaction, for one of the atomic sentences, $t_1 = t_2$, is

$$A' \models^{\sigma(\theta)} (\sigma(t_1 = t_2)) \quad \text{iff} \quad (A'|_\sigma) \models^\theta (t_1 = t_2)$$

Lemma 1 is a strict strengthening of this requirement, since it shows in fact that the terms under analysis are equal. This lemma handles the atomic sentences; the other cases follow without much trouble.

5   Formalizing *EVT*

Readers should consult the backmatter of [16] for a summary of the Event-B language by Thai Son Hoang. Not much, if any, familiarity with the system will be required beyond what we describe here. Event-B machines consist, at the most basic level, of discrete state-transitions called *events*. Our approach is to use first-order sentences to represent updates to the machine state; for example, the variable-update statement x := x + 1 is written as a first-order sentence $x' = x + 1$. The unprimed variables represent the state of the machine before an event, the primed variables represent the state of the machine after an event.

We will formally describe a more generic institution for Event-B than is presented in Farrell [6], dropping event names from the representation. We will call this institution *EVT* where there is no room for confusion. We found that defining *EVT* without event names results in simplified constructions and gives us more room for defining potential extensions to *EVT*—but, crucially, without changing the details of the proof of satisfaction. For a short account of a formalization that matches Farrell's more closely, see [13].

First, we'll define signatures and signature morphisms for *EVT*.

Definition 10. *An EVT-signature $\hat{\Sigma}$ is a 3-tuple $\langle \Sigma, X, X' \rangle$ where Σ is a first-order signature and X and X' are $\mathsf{Sorts}(\Sigma)$-indexed sets, such that $(-)' : X \to X'$ is an equivalence.*

Definition 11. *An EVT-signature morphism $\hat{\sigma} : \hat{\Sigma}_1 \to \hat{\Sigma}_2$ consists of a first-order signature morphism $\sigma : \Sigma_1 \to \Sigma_2$ and two variable morphisms $\mathsf{on\_vars} : X_1 \to X_2$ and $\mathsf{on\_vars}' : X'_1 \to X'_2$ such that the following diagram commutes.*

$$
\begin{array}{ccc}
X_1 & \xrightarrow{\ \mathsf{on\_vars}\ } & X_2 \\[2pt]
{\scriptstyle (-)'}\Big\uparrow\Big\downarrow & & \Big\uparrow\Big\downarrow{\scriptstyle (-)'} \\[2pt]
X'_1 & \xrightarrow[\ \mathsf{on\_vars}'\ ]{} & X'_2
\end{array}
$$

In all cases where not otherwise specified, the *EVT*-signature $\hat{\Sigma}$ is given by $\langle \Sigma, X, X' \rangle$.

A standard construction in institution theory is the *signature extension*. We add variables by adding them directly into the signature as constant function symbols.

Definition 12. *Let $\Sigma = \langle S, \mathscr{F}, \mathscr{P} \rangle$ be a first-order signature and let X be an S-indexed set. The expansion of Σ by X is a first-order signature $\Sigma + X$ which is equal to Σ everywhere except on the constant function symbols; $\Sigma + X$ has constant symbols $\mathscr{F}_{\mathsf{nil},s} + X_s$, for each $s \in S$.*

To model signatures of the form $\Sigma + X$, we need only expand a given Σ-algebra by a valuation $X \to A$.

Definition 13. *Let $\Sigma = \langle S, \mathscr{F}, \mathscr{P} \rangle$ be a first-order signature and let A be a Σ-algebra. Let X be an S-indexed set of variables and let $\theta : X \to A$ be a valuation of variables. The expansion of A by θ is a $(\Sigma + X)$-algebra A^θ, which behaves like A on symbols from Σ and takes variables $x \in X_s$ to $\theta(x) \in A_s$.*

Definition 14. *A $\hat{\Sigma}$-model M is a 3-tuple $\langle A, \theta, \theta' \rangle$, where A is a Σ-algebra and $\theta : X \to A$ and $\theta' : X \to A$ are valuations of variables.*

To illustrate what we have so far, consider the following example. A model for a $(\Sigma + X + X')$-sentence consists of a Σ-algebra A and two valuations of the variables $\theta : X \to A$ and $\theta' : X' \to A$, usually referred to as a Σ-states—θ is the pre-state and θ' is the post-state. One possible model for the sentence $x' = x + 1$ consists of the usual algebra for natural numbers, a pre-state $x \mapsto 2$, and a post-state $x' \mapsto 3$. One possible model for the sentence $s' = \mathsf{push}(x, s)$ consists of an algebra for a stack of characters, a pre-state $x \mapsto \mathrm{e}$, $s \mapsto [\mathrm{v}, \mathrm{t}]$, and a post-state $s' \mapsto [\mathrm{e}, \mathrm{v}, \mathrm{t}]$. Here, x' can consistently be assigned anything. If we wish to avoid this, we can assume that sentences ψ which don't mention a given primed variable x' are really shorthand for $\psi \wedge (x' = x)$.

Let us formally define the sentences for EVT. Note that $\mathsf{FOSen}(\Sigma)$ denotes the set of all first-order Σ-sentences.

Definition 15. *Let $\hat{\Sigma}$ be an EVT-signature. A $\hat{\Sigma}$-sentence is either an* initialization *sentence* $\mathsf{Init}(\phi)$ *where* $\phi \in \mathsf{FOSen}(\Sigma + X')$, *or an* event *sentence* $\mathsf{Event}(\phi)$ *where* $\phi \in \mathsf{FOSen}(\Sigma + X + X')$.

Initialization sentences constrain the range of possible initial states for a machine; often only one such state is possible. There is no previous state yet, so any initialization sentence is built over $\Sigma + X'$. Event sentences explain how an event updates the state, and therefore can access both pre- and post-variables; thus event sentences are built over $\Sigma + X + X'$.

Finally, let's define the semantic entailment relation for EVT.

Definition 16. *Let $\hat{\Sigma}$ be an EVT-signature, $M = \langle A, \theta, \theta' \rangle$ a $\hat{\Sigma}$-model, and ψ an EVT-sentence. We define $M \models \psi$ by induction on ψ: $M \models \mathsf{Init}(\phi)$ if $A^{\theta'} \models \phi$; and $M \models \mathsf{Event}(\phi)$ if $A^{\theta + \theta'} \models \phi$.*

5.1 Representing EVT

We have a much easier job here than we did for first-order predicate logic since EVT builds directly on $FOPEQ$. We rely on a couple of major first-order constructions. First, we will define signature extensions by a set of variables (cf. Definition 12). Note that **Indexed I** is the category of indexed types $I \to \mathcal{U}$.

```
Definition SigExpand (Σ : FOSig) (X : Indexed (Sorts Σ)) : FOSig :=
{| Sorts := Sorts Σ ;
   Funcs := λ w s, match w with
                   | [] => Funcs Σ [] s + X s
                   | _  => Funcs Σ w s
                   end ;
   Preds := Preds Σ |}.
```

The main part of an algebra expansion (cf. Definition 13) is given by the following function; no other part of the algebra is changed.

```
Equations alg_exp_funcs
    (A : Algebra Σ) (θ : X ~> A) w s (F : Funcs (SigExpand Σ X) w s)
    : HList A w -> A s :=
  alg_exp_funcs [] s (inr C) := λ _, θ s C ;
  alg_exp_funcs [] _ (inl F) := interp_funcs A F ;
  alg_exp_funcs (_ :: _) _ F := interp_funcs A F .
```

EVT-signatures (cf. Definition 10) are represented exactly as they are given mathematically.

```
Record EvtSignature :=
{ base :> Signature ;
  Vars  : Sorts base -> Type ;
  Vars' : Sorts base -> Type ;
  prime_rel : Primed Vars Vars' }.
```

Here **prime_rel** is the proof that $(-)' : X \to X'$ is an equivalence.

For *EVT* signature morphisms (cf. Definition 11), we simply define on_vars' in terms of on_vars to simplify matters.

```
Record EvtSigMorphism Σ Σ' : Type :=
{ on_base :> SignatureMorphism Σ Σ' ;
  on_vars : Vars Σ ~> Vars Σ' ∘ on_base }.

Definition on_vars' (σ : EvtSigMorphism Σ Σ') : Vars' Σ ~> Vars' Σ' ∘ σ :=
  λ s x, prime (σ s) (on_vars σ (unprime s x)).
```

EVT-models (cf. Definition 14) and *EVT*-sentences (cf. Definition 15) also offer no surprises.

```
Record EvtModel Σ :=
{ base_alg :> Algebra Σ ;
  env  : Vars Σ ~> base_alg ;
  env' : Vars' Σ ~> base_alg }.

Inductive EVT Σ : Type :=
| Init  : Sen[FOL] (SigExpand Σ (Vars' Σ)) -> EVT Σ
| Event : Sen[FOL] (SigExpand Σ (Vars Σ ⊕ Vars' Σ)) -> EVT Σ.
```

Finally, the semantic entailment relation for *EVT* (cf. Definition 16) defers directly to entailment for *FOPEQ*.

```
Definition interp_evt (M : EvtModel Σ) (φ : EVT Σ) : Prop :=
  match φ with
  | Init  ψ => AlgExpansion (base_alg M) (env' M) ⊨ ψ
  | Event ψ => AlgExpansion (base_alg M) (join_vmaps (env M) (env' M)) ⊨ ψ
  end.
```

Here, **join_vmaps** stitches two valuations $\theta : X \to M$ and $\theta' : X' \to M$ (with the same target) into $\Theta : X + X' \to M$.

5.2   Proofs and Proof Strategy

Most of the tricks we needed for first-order logic apply just as well here. The main additional proof strategy emerged while proving equality for dependent records.

As an example, let's consider EVT signature morphisms. To prove that two EVT signature morphisms are equal, we need to prove that they are equal componentwise—the first-order signature morphisms have to agree everywhere, as do the two variable morphisms. The proofs that the variable morphisms are equal *appear* at first to depend on the proof that the base first-order signature morphisms are equal. But actually, that's not strictly the case; we only need to know that the first-order signature morphisms agree on sorts to prove that the two variable morphisms are equal.

We can write custom equality lemmas which state the dependencies between proofs more precisely. Here is one such lemma for EVT signature morphisms.

```
Lemma eq_evtsigmorphism (σ σ' : EvtSigMorphism Σ Σ')
  (p' : on_sorts σ = on_sorts σ')
  (p : on_base σ = on_base σ')
  (q : rew [λ σs, Vars Σ ~> Vars Σ' ∘ σs] p' in
        on_vars σ = on_vars σ')
  : σ = σ'.
```

Here we build a proof that two signature morphisms are equal from proofs that they are equal at each of their components. Note that q depends on p' only, and not p. Normally the dependency is on p—but p' is typically much simpler than p and is all that is necessary. Often p' is refl, meaning rew computes away, simplifying the proofs considerably.

Most other constructions and proofs revolved around signature and model extensions. The following was the main non-trivial lemma which we identified while proving the satisfaction condition for EVT. Note that the following holds for *any* indexed sets X_1 and X_2 and *any* function $f : X_1 \to X_2 \circ \sigma$.

Lemma 2. *Let* $\sigma : \Sigma_1 \to \Sigma_2$ *be a first-order signature morphism, let* $f : X_1 \to X_2 \circ \sigma$ *be a variable morphism, let* A_2 *be a* Σ_2-*algebra, and let* $\theta_2 : X_2 \to A_2$ *be a valuation of variables. Then*

$$(A_2|_\sigma)^{\theta_2 \circ f} = (A_2^{\theta_2})|_{\sigma + f}$$

We're taking some liberties with the notation. Note that $\theta_2 \circ f$ is a shorthand for $\lambda s, x.\ \theta_2(\sigma(s), f(s, x))$ and $\sigma + f : \Sigma_1 + X_1 \to \Sigma_2 + X_2$ is a shorthand for the extension of σ by f.

The proof of satisfaction itself proceeds by two cases, both of which are essentially the same, and both of which rely on the satisfaction condition for $FOPEQ$ and Lemma 2, with f instantiated to different maps in each.

6   Conclusion

We have detailed the most important points of our formalisation of two institutions in Coq: the institution $FOPEQ$ for first-order predicate logic, and the institution *EVT* for Event-B. According to the `cloc` tool[1] we have over 3,000 significant lines of Coq developments, not including the many experimental or variant implementation attempts. Initial progress was slow, but the overall approach was successful; the satisfaction condition is fully formalized for both—with some difficulty for *FOPEQ*, but with far greater ease for *EVT*. Furthermore, both institutions have many reusable components which will aid in the construction of other concrete institutions and with proving their satisfaction conditions. Proofs involving indexed types in Coq are notoriously difficult, but we suspect for the purposes of our formalism that they are all difficult in the same way, so that the lessons we learn here can be applied more generally.

Having a formal framework for defining institutions continues to be useful in our own work. Indeed, we have already begun applying it to the problem of integrating linear-time temporal logic with Event-B specifications. We have also defined some institution-independent constructions not covered here, specifically modal and linear-time temporal logics over an arbitrary institution.

We intend in the future to add more concrete institutions to this framework; to show that both *FOPEQ* and *EVT* have the amalgamation property; to build more institution-independent constructions; to improve proof automation for institutions; and to define and verify some institution (co)morphisms. This work could also, in time, become a fully formal basis for the work already done for the HETS tool for heterogeneous specification.

References

1. Amato, G., Maggesi, M., Parton, M., Brogi, C.P.: Universal Algebra in UniMath (2020). https://arxiv.org/abs/2007.04840
2. Burstall, R.M., Goguen, J.A.: The semantics of clear, a specification language. In: Bjørner, D. (ed.) Abstract Software Specifications. LNCS, vol. 86, pp. 292–332. Springer, Heidelberg (1980). https://doi.org/10.1007/3-540-10007-5_41
3. Capretta, V.: Universal algebra in type theory. In: Bertot, Y., Dowek, G., Théry, L., Hirschowitz, A., Paulin, C. (eds.) TPHOLs 1999. LNCS, vol. 1690, pp. 131–148. Springer, Heidelberg (1999). https://doi.org/10.1007/3-540-48256-3_10
4. Chlipala, A.: Certified Programming with Dependent Types: A Pragmatic Introduction to the Coq Proof Assistant. MIT Press (2013). http://adam.chlipala.net/cpdt/
5. Coq Development Team: The Coq Proof Assistant. https://coq.inria.fr/
6. Farrell, M.: Event-B in the Institutional Framework: Defining a Semantics, Modularisation Constructs and Interoperability for a Specification Language. Ph.D. thesis, National University of Ireland Maynooth (2017). http://mural.maynoothuniversity.ie/9911/
7. Goguen, J.A., Burstall, R.M.: Introducing institutions. In: Clarke, E., Kozen, D. (eds.) Logic of Programs 1983. LNCS, vol. 164, pp. 221–256. Springer, Heidelberg (1984). https://doi.org/10.1007/3-540-12896-4_366
8. Goguen, J.A., Burstall, R.M.: Institutions: abstract model theory for specification and programming. J. ACM **39**(1), 95–146 (1992). https://doi.org/10.1145/147508.147524

---

[1] https://github.com/AlDanial/cloc.

9. Gunther, E., Gadea, A., Pagano, M.: Formalization of universal algebra in Agda. Electron. Notes Theor. Comput. Sci. **338**, 147–166 (2018). https://doi.org/10.1016/j.entcs.2018.10.010

10. Knapp, A., Mossakowski, T., Roggenbach, M., Glauer, M.: An institution for simple UML state machines. In: Egyed, A., Schaefer, I. (eds.) FASE 2015. LNCS, vol. 9033, pp. 3–18. Springer, Heidelberg (2015). https://doi.org/10.1007/978-3-662-46675-9_1

11. Mossakowski, T., Goguen, J., Diaconescu, R., Tarlecki, A.: What is a logic? In: Logica Universalis, pp. 111–133. Birkhäuser Basel (2007)

12. Mossakowski, T., Maeder, C., Lüttich, K.: The heterogeneous tool set, HETS. In: Grumberg, O., Huth, M. (eds.) TACAS 2007. LNCS, vol. 4424, pp. 519–522. Springer, Heidelberg (2007). https://doi.org/10.1007/978-3-540-71209-1_40

13. Reynolds, C.: Formalizing the institution for Event-B in the coq proof assistant. In: Raschke, A., Méry, D. (eds.) ABZ 2021. LNCS, vol. 12709, pp. 162–166. Springer, Cham (2021). https://doi.org/10.1007/978-3-030-77543-8_17

14. Riehl, E.: Category Theory in Context. Dover Modern Math Originals, Dover Publications, Aurora (2017)

15. Roggenbach, M.: CSP-CASL—a new integration of process algebra and algebraic specification. Theor. Comput. Sci. **354**(1), 42–71 (2006). https://doi.org/10.1016/j.tcs.2005.11.007

16. Romanovsky, A., Thomas, M. (eds.): Industrial Deployment of System Engineering Methods. Springer, Heidelberg (2013). https://doi.org/10.1007/978-3-642-33170-1

17. Sannella, D., Tarlecki, A.: Foundations of Algebraic Specification and Formal Software Development. Monographs in Theoretical Computer Science. An EATCS Series, Springer, Heidelberg (2012). https://doi.org/10.1007/978-3-642-17336-3

18. Sozeau, M.: Equations: a dependent pattern-matching compiler. In: Kaufmann, M., Paulson, L.C. (eds.) ITP 2010. LNCS, vol. 6172, pp. 419–434. Springer, Heidelberg (2010). https://doi.org/10.1007/978-3-642-14052-5_29

19. Univalent Foundations Program: Homotopy Type Theory: Univalent Foundations of Mathematics (2013). https://homotopytypetheory.org/book. Institute for Advanced Study

20. Wiegley, J.: Category Theory in Coq. https://github.com/jwiegley/category-theory

Optimizing Trans-Compilers in Runtime Verification Makes Sense – Sometimes

Hannes Kallwies[✉], Martin Leucker, Meiko Prilop, and Malte Schmitz

Institute for Software Engineering and Programming Languages, Universtity of Lübeck,
Lübeck, Germany
{kallwies,leucker,prilop,schmitz}@isp.uni-luebeck.de

Abstract. This paper considers two kinds of optimizations for a specification language compiler for stream-based runtime verification: (i) the manual addition of core functions with dedicated translation schemas and (ii) an improved initialization that simplifies subsequent constant propagation. We employ both optimizations within the open source runtime verification framework TeSSLa, which comes with a trans-compiler as synthesis tool which translates TeSSLa specifications to Scala code eventually running on the JVM. Our evaluation shows that the first optimization improves the efficiency of the resulting monitor significantly while the second gets lost within the variety of optimizations present for the back end systems.

1 Introduction

Runtime verification is the discipline that checks whether a run of a system meets its specification [1]. To this end, a specification is typically transformed into a monitor that checks the run of the system and assigns a verdict assessing to which extend the observation meets the specification. Central research questions in the field of runtime verification are the development of specification languages and the synthesis of monitors from such specifications especially for obtaining efficient monitors in terms of time and memory.

While traditionally specifications are often formulated in temporal logics such as LTL [2], a large number of extensions of specification languages have been proposed, especially to cope with computations on data [3–5]. One branch of this line of research emerged into the field of stream runtime verification (SRV) where observations of the system are considered as *streams* and the specification as a stream transformation. Prominent examples are Lola [6], RTLola [7], Striver [8], or TeSSLa [9]. Such languages have similarities with functional programming languages and can be considered as data flow languages, in which the transformation of data is the primary goal [10]. However, the development of compilers synthesizing efficient monitors is still an active research question. In this paper we study two aspects of building compilers for data flow languages. As object of study, we take the language and tool set TeSSLa, which is available as open source and can be used as a testing target for corresponding research questions. When designing a language, it is desirable to restrict to few (core) operators to limit the burden of analyzing the language from a formal perspective. Moreover providing support for a few core operators in a compiler seems to reduce the development

© Springer Nature Switzerland AG 2022
Y. Aït-Ameur and F. Crăciun (Eds.): TASE 2022, LNCS 13299, pp. 197–204, 2022.
https://doi.org/10.1007/978-3-031-10363-6_14

effort. Though from a user's perspective, it is desirable to have a large number of operators supporting the rapid development of specifications. A common approach to address these two conflicting design goals is to provide a small number of core operators and a large amount of syntactic sugar on top of the core language to define new functionality within the language and provide standard libraries. Following this approach TeSSLa comes with six operators but is enriched with a standard library providing a large number of extensions which are formulated in TeSSLa's macro language. TeSSLa comes with a reference implementation of a compiler, which supports TeSSLa's core operators as well as the definition of functions and macro expansion. A TeSSLa specification is translated into a Scala program which is then compiled using the Scala compiler and eventually executed on the JVM [11].

However, many specifications result in long Scala programs and an important question arises as our first question studied in this paper: *Would it make sense to support further, commonly used macros, directly by the TeSSLa compiler rather than unfolding/compiling them during compilation time?* In this paper we answer this question positively. Note that the answer to this question is not obvious as one might hope that optimizations during compilation of the resulting Scala program as well as the optimizations typically performed by the Just-in-Time compiler on the JVM yield efficient monitors already. We show that this is not the case.

Compiler optimization is an active research area since decades. A large number of optimizations have been proposed in the literature. The area of runtime verification asks for further, dedicated optimizations. In [12], several optimizations have been shown to be useful for obtaining efficient monitors; leading us to our second research question: *Do standard optimizations for functional languages during the TeSSLa compilation process yield more efficient monitors?* As an example, we consider an optimization which chooses a smart order for variable declarations to avoid dummy initialization and mark variables as constants if possible. This optimization primarily reduces the length of the generated code and improves readability, which in turn simplifies debugging of the compiler a lot. Furthermore, one may also expect this optimization to support the backend compiler by showing opportunities for constant propagation. However, our experiment shows that this kind of optimization does *not* improve the overall efficiency. In fact, especially the Just-in-Time compiler of the JVM already performs similar optimizations.

From a broader perspective, the first optimization can be considered a *high-level* optimization while the second optimization is more a *low level* optimization. Very vaguely and of course arguably, our findings support the rule of thumb that high-level optimization are difficult to achieve automatically while low-level optimizations are handled effectively by today's compilers.

2   TeSSLa and Its Reference Compiler

TeSSLa is a stream tranformation language, i.e., a TeSSLa specification defines how so-called input streams are tranferred into so-called output streams, potentially making use of so-called intermediate streams. In our setting a stream is a function mapping timestamps from a time domain (e.g. $\mathbb{N}$ or $\mathbb{R}$) to values from the stream's data domain $\mathbb{D}$ or $\bot$ if the stream has no event at the timestamp. Syntactically, a TeSSLa specification is an equation system where each left hand side is a variable and each right-hand side is a TeSSLa term. A TeSSLa term is built up from variables of the equation system and the core operators described below. The semantics of a TeSSLa specification is then the minimal fixpoint solution of the equation system, which is shown to exist [9]. The core operators are: (i) **nil** is the empty stream, containing no events, (ii) **unit** is a stream containing a single event at timestamp 0, (iii) **time**(s) is the stream that contains events exactly at the same positions as s but with the timestamps of these events as values, (iv) **lift**$(f)(s_1, \ldots, s_n)$ is the stream that contains events with the values $f(v_1, \ldots, v_n)$ where $v_1, \ldots, v_n$ are the current values of $s_1, \ldots, s_n$ (or $\bot$ in case they have no value at the current timestamp). However **lift** only produces events if any of its input streams has one. Hence one cannot generate an event with **lift**, if there is no other event at this exact timestamp. (v) **last**(v, t) is the stream that contains the previous event of stream v always when the so-called trigger stream t has an event. (vi) **delay**(d, r) is the stream with events always t time units after the last reset (event of r or the stream itself), where t is the value of d at the last reset. With **delay** events can be generated at timestamps where no other stream has an event.

Every monotonous, continuous and future-independent stream transformation can be expressed by these six operators [9]. However for a comfortable usage of such a language it is crucial to have the possibility to define macros for common combinations of such operators. This also sets the basis for the creation of a standard library as known from other languages. Furthermore it is important to include a possibility to define functions which can be lifted in the specification language. As such, TeSSLa comes with the possibility to define functions on values (not streams). Both features are supported by the open-source reference implementation of TeSSLa[1] which we investigate in this paper. The concrete usage can be seen in the example specification in Fig. 1.

```
1    def one = 1
2    def addOne(i: Option[Int]): Option[Int] = Some(getSome(i) + one)
3    def count[T](x: Events[T]): Events[Int] = o where {
4        def o : Events[Int] = default(lift1(last(o, x), addOne), 0) }
5    in x: Events[Int]
6    def o = count(x)
7    out o
```

Fig. 1. TeSSLa example specification

For the sake of the example, the specification defines a constant *one* and a function *addOne*. The function takes an integer, wrapped into an option container, adds one, and returns the result after wrapping it into a Some container again. Note that this function operates on a plain value, not on streams, however the function is lifted to a stream in line 4. As described above a function which is lifted has to be able to deal with the $\bot$ value, this is why the function returns and receives values of type Option[...].

In lines 3 and 4 the specification contains the definition of the macro **count**. The macro receives a stream x of generic type T whose events shall be counted and returns an integer stream o. The stream o is defined in line 4 and results from lifting the function

---

[1] https://www.tessla.io/.

addOne from line 2 to *last(o, x)*, which reproduces the last value of *o* whenever *x* has an event. The default around the **lift** initializes stream *o* with value 0.

Finally in lines 5 to 7 an input stream *x* of type integer is declared and an output stream *o* is defined. Stream *o* results from applying the **count** macro on *x*.

3   The TeSSLa Compiler and Optimizations

In order to make a TeSSLa specification executable, a trans-compiler to the programming language Scala has been developed. This way a monitor can be generated from a TeSSLa specification and be run on the Java Virtual Machine (JVM). The compilation procedure from TeSSLa to Scala consists of three steps (see Fig. 2): In the first step all macros (like **count** in Fig. 1) are resolved. As result one gets an equivalent TeSSLa specification with no macros but only stream definitions using the six core stream operators presented in Sect. 2 and definitions of constants (e.g. *one* from Fig. 1) and non-stream functions (e.g. the functions *addOne*). This TeSSLa fragment is called *TeSSLa Core*.

Fig. 2. Phases of the TeSSLa to Scala compilation

In the second step *TeSSLa Core* is translated to a generic imperative language used inside of the compiler, the *Intermediate Code*. Therefore the compiler follows the standard synchronous evaluation scheme which is also used for trans-compilation of similar languages [13–16]: Every stream defined in the Core specification is represented by a bunch of variables, indicating the stream's current value, error state, if it has an event at the current timestamp etc. Furthermore for every core operator in the Core specification there is an if block created in which the mentioned variables get actualized values assigned if an event on the corresponding stream is triggered. These if blocks are ordered to guarantee a correct evaluation of the specification and put into a while loop which is iterated for every timestamp where any stream has an event in a strictly ascending order. At the end of the while loop new input values are consumed and output values are printed. The constants and non-stream functions from the TeSSLa Core are straightforwardly translated to constants and imperative functions which are bound to names and referenced from inside the if blocks.

Finally, the *Intermediate Code* is translated to a specific imperative language, in our case Scala code, which can then be further compiled to an executable monitor.

3.1   Expansion of the Language Core and the DSL

The first optimization targets the translation of macros. As mentioned before, when reducing a TeSSLa specification to the *TeSSLa Core*, all macros are replaced by an equivalent nesting of the six core operators. The example of the *count* macro suggests that such a nesting can be quite extensive, as several if blocks have to be included (one for **last**, **lift**, ...). Also note that the *default* is not one of the core functions but also a macro defined in the standard library and also consists of a nesting of **unit** and **lift**. This shows how the use of macros quickly increases the number of involved core operators.

Now the first optimization is to extend the set of core functions and to provide an optimized translation schema for those, which is achieved by adding further macros manually by means of an imperative-language-like domain specific language (DSL) which describes the statements of the generated code. For example, via the DSL it is possible to add a procedure for the direct translation of the *count* macro without unrolling the macro to core functions: one if block is generated for each usage of *count* in the specification and added to the while-loop. The guard evaluates this generated if block to true if there is an event on the stream to be counted. The value variable of the corresponding stream is then incremented by 1 within the body of the if.

For this kind of optimization it is necessary that the macro translation has been built into the compiler manually, the advanced translation can hardly be directly inferred from the macro definition. However, the TeSSLa implementation from this paper comes with a rich standard library of macros which are vastly used in specifications and independent from the concrete specification. We implemented a direct translation of ten of these macros.

3.2   Usage of Smart Initializations Within the Monitors

The second optimization carried out relates to the translation of constants and functions from TeSSLa specifications. The example from Fig. 1 requires a translation of the constant *one* and the function *addOne*. Note that functions can principally be recursive and also mutual recursive and thus must be declared before they are defined. A straight-forward solution to this is first defining all constants and functions in the generated code and afterwards assigning their final values. However, in some imperative languages, like Scala, a declaration without value assignment is not possible for non-class variables. Hence this method requires dummy initializations:

```
1    var one  : Int = 0
2    var addOne : Function1[Option[Int], Option[Int]] = null
3    one = 1
4    addOne = (i : Option[Int]) => {Some(i.get + one)}
```

However, one can easily see that in this example the reassignments of *zero* and *addOne* are not necessary, they could be initialized directly with their final value, as long as *one* is defined before its usage inside of *addOne*. Note that if variables are recursively dependent on each other this is not possible, then some must be a dummy-initialized to break the chain of dependencies. We implemented a greedy algorithm to optimize the initialization order of variables in the generated code and avoid dummy initializations. Foremost this optimization reduces the generated code and makes it better readable. Furthermore it is also possible to mark the variables which are not reassigned as constants (keyword *val* in Scala). This could aid the backend compiler during optimizations like constant propagation. The resulting code would then only consist of line 3 and 4 with the *val* keyword prepended.

In fact the optimization also has impact on the generated Java byte-code. The unoptimized implementation first initializes the variable *one* with 0 and then overwrites it with 1. The Java bytecode at the top right results from this implementation, while the direct initialization of *one* ultimately results in the bytecode at the bottom right. The val keyword has no effect.

```
0:  iconst_0
1:  istore_3
2:  iconst_1
3:  istore_3
```

```
0:  iconst_1
1:  istore_3
```

4 Evaluation

For the evaluation of the performance gain of the optimizations, the execution times of six monitors with and without optimizations were measured and compared. Three of these specifications consist of a single macro call (*average*, *boolFilter*, *count*) for which a direct translation was implemented and three are complex specifications (*accSum*, *election*, *filterByTime*) from practical scenarios. The generated monitors were tested without any optimizations, with one of the two new optimizations and finally using both optimizations. The generated Scala monitors are inevitably compiled to Java bytecode by means of the Scala compiler and finally executed on a JVM. The Scala compiler supports optional optimizations for the entered Scala code. In order to discuss the impact of the Scala optimizations, especially in correlation with our optimizations, we ran all monitors with and without Scala optimizations enabled. To receive stable results the measurements were repeated ten times and preceeded by a JIT warm-up.

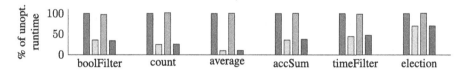

Fig. 3. Measurement results: ■ Without optimizations, □ extended Core optimization, ▨ no TeSSLa but Scala optimizations, ■ Both TeSSLa and Scala optimizations.

The JVM uses a so-called Just-in-Time (JiT) compiler to execute Java bytecode. The code entered is first interpreted while individual program sections are compiled at the same time [17]. Due to thread scheduling, garbage collection and side effects of the underlying system, the process of JiT compilation is non-deterministic [18,19]. An advantage of compilation at runtime is that the entire context of the program to be executed is also available to a JiT compiler. On the basis of this information, extensive optimizations can be done on the bytecode to be executed [20].

Our measurement results are depicted in Fig. 3. The optimization around the extension of the language kernel is reflected in runtime improvements of up to 90% for the simple examples and from 30% to about 65% for the complex ones (compare blue and yellow bars). These optimizations are also not adopted by the Scala compiler or the JiT compiler, as can be seen from the green bars in comparison to the yellow ones.

Improved initializations, on the other hand, did not lead to any improvement in the runtime of the monitors (not shown). In fact, we recognized that it is possible for the Scala compiler to remove unused variable assignments from the Java bytecode when its optimizations are enabled. Even without our optimization the Scala compiler with enabled optimization flag produces the same bytecode as presented for the optimized case in Sect. 3.2. Furthermore, also the JiT Compiler is able to perform these optimizations and a subsequent constant propagation [21]. Hence the second optimization did not show any speedups.

These results give a good idea of which optimizations make sense within a trans-compiler. The ability of both, the Scala and JiT compilers, to distinguish between constants and variables and to remove unused variable assignments [22] shows that especially small optimization possibilities are often already adopted at other points in the compilation process. Optimizations that change the structure of the programs, on the other hand, are quite useful and more often result in significant runtime improvements than peephole optimizations.

5 Summary

In this paper we studied the effect of compiler optimization in the setting that a (specification) language is trans-compiled into a language for which powerful, optimizing compilers and runtime environments exist. We studied two optimizations in the setting of stream-runtime verification, more specifically for the language TeSSLa. Arguably oversimplifying our experiments suggest that optimizations affecting significantly the structure of the code are not well supported by the back-end compilers (and hence improve the resulting code), while "simple" optimizations are already taken care of by the backend compilers.

References

1. Leucker, M., Schallhart, C.: A brief account of runtime verification. J. Log. Algebraic Program. **78**(5), 293–303 (2009)
2. Pnueli, A.: The temporal logic of programs. In: Proceedings of the 18th IEEE Symposium on the Foundations of Computer Science (FOCS-77), IEEE Computer Society Press, Providence, Rhode Island, pp. 46–57 (1977)
3. Barringer, H., Goldberg, A., Havelund, K., Sen, K.: Rule-based runtime verification. In: Steffen, B., Levi, G. (eds.) VMCAI 2004. LNCS, vol. 2937, pp. 44–57. Springer, Heidelberg (2004). https://doi.org/10.1007/978-3-540-24622-0_5
4. Barringer, H., Rydeheard, D.E., Havelund, K.: Rule systems for run-time monitoring: from eagle to ruler. J. Log. Comput. **20**(3), 675–706 (2010)
5. Barringer, H., Falcone, Y., Havelund, K., Reger, G., Rydeheard, D.: Quantified event automata: towards expressive and efficient runtime monitors. In: Giannakopoulou, D., Méry, D. (eds.) FM 2012. LNCS, vol. 7436, pp. 68–84. Springer, Heidelberg (2012). https://doi.org/10.1007/978-3-642-32759-9_9
6. D'Angelo, B., et al.: LOLA: runtime monitoring of synchronous systems. In: TIME, IEEE Computer Society, pp. 166–174 (2005)

7. Faymonville, P., Finkbeiner, B., Schwenger, M., Torfah, H.: Real-time stream-based monitoring. CoRR abs/1711.03829 (2017)
8. Gorostiaga, F., Sánchez, C.: Striver: stream runtime verification for real-time event-streams. In: Colombo, C., Leucker, M. (eds.) RV 2018. LNCS, vol. 11237, pp. 282–298. Springer, Cham (2018). https://doi.org/10.1007/978-3-030-03769-7_16
9. Convent, L., Hungerecker, S., Leucker, M., Scheffel, T., Schmitz, M., Thoma, D.: TeSSLa: temporal stream-based specification language. In: Massoni, T., Mousavi, M.R. (eds.) SBMF 2018. LNCS, vol. 11254, pp. 144–162. Springer, Cham (2018). https://doi.org/10.1007/978-3-030-03044-5_10
10. Johnston, W.M., Hanna, J.R.P., Millar, R.J.: Advances in dataflow programming languages. ACM Comput. Surv. 36(1), 1–34 (2004)
11. Lindholm, T., Yellin, F.: The Java Virtual Machine Specification. 2nd edn. Addison Wesley (1999)
12. Baumeister, J., Finkbeiner, B., Kruse, M., Schwenger, M.: Automatic optimizations for stream-based monitoring languages. In: Deshmukh, J., Ničković, D. (eds.) RV 2020. LNCS, vol. 12399, pp. 451–461. Springer, Cham (2020). https://doi.org/10.1007/978-3-030-60508-7_25
13. Halbwachs, N., Raymond, P., Ratel, C.: Generating efficient code from data-flow programs. In: Maluszyński, J., Wirsing, M. (eds.) PLILP 1991. LNCS, vol. 528, pp. 207–218. Springer, Heidelberg (1991). https://doi.org/10.1007/3-540-54444-5_100
14. Amagbégnon, P., Besnard, L., Le Guernic, P.: Implementation of the data-flow synchronous language SIGNAL. In: PLDI, ACM, pp. 163–173 (1995)
15. Finkbeiner, B., Oswald, S., Passing, N., Schwenger, M.: Verified rust monitors for Lola specifications. In: Deshmukh, J., Ničković, D. (eds.) RV 2020. LNCS, vol. 12399, pp. 431–450. Springer, Cham (2020). https://doi.org/10.1007/978-3-030-60508-7_24
16. Kallwies, H., Leucker, M., Scheffel, T., Schmitz, M., Thoma, D.: Aggregate update problem for multi-clocked dataflow languages. In: CGO, IEEE, pp. 79–91 (2022)
17. Aycock, J.: A brief history of just-in-time. ACM Comput. Surv. 35(2), 97–113 (2003)
18. Barrett, E., Bolz, C.F., Killick, R., Mount, S., Tratt, L.: Virtual machine warmup blows hot and cold. CoRR abs/1602.00602 (2016)
19. Georges, A., Buytaert, D., Eeckhout, L.: Statistically rigorous java performance evaluation. In: Proceedings of the 22nd Annual ACM SIGPLAN Conference on Object-Oriented Programming Systems, Languages and Applications. OOPSLA 2007, New York, NY, USA, Association for Computing Machinery, pp. 57–76 (2007)
20. Adl-Tabatabai, A.R., Cierniak, M., Lueh, G.Y., Parikh, V., Stichnoth, J.: Fast, effective code generation in a just-in-time Java compiler. 33, 280–290 (1998)
21. Dragos, I.: Compiling Scala for Performance. PhD thesis, École Polytechnique Fédérale de Lausanne (2010)
22. Ivanov, V.: JVM JIT-compiler overview. http://cr.openjdk.java.net/~vlivanov/talks/2015_JIT_Overview.pdf at Oracle. Accessed 31 May 2021

Testing Vehicle-Mounted Systems: A Stepwise Symbolic Execution Approach for OSEK/VDX Programs

Haitao Zhang$^{(\boxtimes)}$ and Bowen Pu

School of Information Science and Engineering, Lanzhou University,
Lanzhou 730000, China
{htzhang,pubw20}@lzu.edu.cn

Abstract. OSEK/VDX is a standard for automotive embedded systems, and it has been widely adopted by many automotive companies to develop a vehicle-mounted system. However, the ever increasing complexity of developed OSEK/VDX multi-tasking programs has created a challenge to ensure reliability. This paper presents an efficient approach that applies a new variety of symbolic execution called stepwise symbolic execution to explore paths included in an OSEK/VDX multi-tasking program for checking its reliability. A series of experiments have been carried out to investigate the performance of the approach based on an implemented prototype tool. The experimental results indicate that the proposed approach is capable of performing a much more wider and deeper exploration on the OSEK/VDX programs compared with the existing testing techniques.

Keywords: Symbolic execution · OSEK/VDX · Sequentialization

1 Introduction

With the development of automotive industry and electronic technology, vehicles become more intelligent benefiting from the widespread usage of vehicle-mounted software systems. Even so, the automotive intelligence is still in a primary level, because manufacturers use different platforms and specifications in the development. To reunify the development standard of vehicle-mounted software systems, European automobile manufacturer association issues a standard called OSEK/VDX [1] since 1994. The OSEK/VDX is a set of standards for real-time architecture of automotive embedded systems, as a fusion of the German Open Systems and their Interfaces for the Electronics in Motor Vehicles (OSEK) standard and the French Vehicle Distributed eXecutive (VDX) standard. Currently, it has gained widespread usage in automotive manufacturers such as BMW, Audi, and Volkswagen, and research groups such as the Institut de Recherche en Communications et Cybernetique de Nantes (IRCCyN) and Toyohashi Open Platform for Embedded Real-time Systems (TOPPERS).

© Springer Nature Switzerland AG 2022
Y. Aït-Ameur and F. Crăciun (Eds.): TASE 2022, LNCS 13299, pp. 205–219, 2022.
https://doi.org/10.1007/978-3-031-10363-6_15

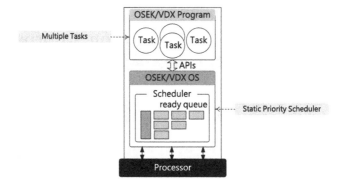

Fig. 1. Architecture of OSEK/VDX vehicle-mounted system.

In general, a developed OSEK/VDX vehicle-mounted system includes two important components, one is operating system (OS), and the other one is program. As illustrated in Fig. 1, a developed OSEK/VDX program contains multiple tasks. When the program is loaded to run, the OSEK/VDX OS manipulates tasks to execute on a processor in concurrent mode, in which a *deterministic* scheduling policy [2] called static priority policy is responsible for scheduling tasks—a ready queue with different priorities is in charge of determining the scheduling order of tasks with the different or the same priorities. In addition, tasks can invoke application interfaces (APIs) for requesting OSEK/VDX OS to support various services, such as activate a suspended task dynamically. As a result of the concurrency and dynamic scheduling of tasks, developers face a challenge to evaluate the reliability of a developed OSEK/VDX program because of the complex executions.

Random testing [3] is currently considered as an automatic and practical solution in the automotive industry to check a developed OSEK/VDX program. The random testing runs a given program with a random input in practical way and is usually scalable to perform a deep exploration in the examination process [4]. However, it is hard to complete the exploration of all paths included in an OSEK/VDX program with low cost, i.e., the probability of selecting particular inputs that cause buggy behavior may be astronomically small since the range of behaviors covered by random testing is often vanishingly small in comparison to all the possible behaviors of the program [5]. In order to obtain a high-coverage, this paper presents an approach that can perform a wide exploration for the *deterministic* scheduler based OSEK/VDX concurrent programs based on symbolic execution technique [6].

As a matter of fact, symbolic execution technique has got great development and already been applied to detect different types of programs with the increasing computation power of computers as well as the advances in theorem proving and constraint solving technologies. For example, R. Majumdar and K. Sen show a hybrid concolic testing method [4] that interleaves random testing with concolic execution [7] to obtain both a deep and a wide exploration for sequential programs. In addition, for concurrent programs with *non-deterministic* scheduling behaviors, many existing symbolic execution methods have also been proposed such as [8]. Unfortunately, these existing works are not suitable to deal with a given OSEK/VDX program because it is a *deterministic* scheduler based concurrent program.

In order to make symbolic execution suitable in dealing with the deterministic scheduler based OSEK/VDX concurrent programs, the approach presented in this paper first translates a given OSEK/VDX program into a sequential model by means of the work presented in [2]. After that, a new exploring technique named stepwise symbolic execution is proposed to desire a high-coverage by inheriting advantages of the existing symbolic execution methods. The stepwise symbolic execution is a new variety of hybrid concolic testing, that takes the breadth-first search concolic testing [7] to achieve a wide coverage, and then a constraint solver based random testing is started from a state to achieve a precise deep coverage when the concolic testing generates a test input over a time budget from the state. According to the proposed approach, a prototype tool has been built on top of CUTE [7]. Based on the prototype tool, a series of experiments are conducted to investigate the performance of the stepwise symbolic execution approach. In the conducted experiments, benchmarks are selected from papers [2,9,10] and the advanced hybrid concolic testing technique [4] is considered as a comparison object. The experimental results indicate that the proposed approach is capable of performing a much more wider and deeper exploration on the OSEK/VDX programs in comparison to the existing testing techniques.

There are four primary contributions in this paper: (*i*) the approach shown in this paper expands the application scope of symbolic execution in the *deterministic* scheduler based concurrent programs; (*ii*) a new variety of symbolic execution called stepwise symbolic execution is proposed in this paper, which can make symbolic execution more powerful in performing a high-coverage exploration on the *deterministic* scheduler based concurrent programs; and (*iii*) the approach can be considered as a guideline to evaluate other *deterministic* scheduler based concurrent programs by using symbolic execution, such as the round robin concurrent programs and AUTOSAR concurrent programs.

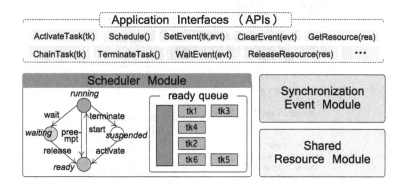

Fig. 2. Structure of the OSEK/VDX OS and corresponding APIs.

2   OSEK/VDX Background and Motivating Example

2.1   Scheduler of OSEK/VDX OS

A program developed on OSEK/VDX OS consists of multiple tasks, especially OSEK/VDX OS supports two types of tasks in the development, i.e., extended tasks and basic tasks. Extended tasks are able to synchronously execute via events while the basic tasks are unable. As shown in Fig. 2, the states of an extended task are switched on *running*, *suspended*, *ready* and *waiting*. A basic task absent the *waiting* state in comparison to the extended tasks. In the scheduling process, a *deterministic* scheduler called static priority scheduling policy is in charge of scheduling tasks to execute on one processor, which supports Mix-preemptive strategy (Full- and Non-preemptive strategies) and a ready queue is used to organize the execution order of tasks. In addition, four APIs (e.g., *TerminateTask*, *ActivateTask*, *Schedule* and *ChainTask*) are provided by the OSEK/VDX scheduler module for dynamically switching the states of tasks.

2.2   Running Example

The OSEK/VDX standard does not allow developers to create tasks dynamically in the development of a program, i.e., all tasks are static and must be declared in advance. As shown in Fig. 3, an OSEK/VDX program includes two files: a source file and a configuration file. The source file can be coded in C programming language, used to present the concrete behaviors of a program. The configuration file contains all configuration data of a program. In the configuration file, the type of a

```
Source file                              Configuration file
int speed;                               Task contask
bool despeed;                            {
int Getspeed() {···}                       Type=Basic;
bool Identify(int _speed) {···}            Priority=2;
                                           Schedule=Full;
Task contask() {                           Autostart=True;
L1   speed=Getspeed();                    }
     despeed=Identify(speed);
     if(despeed == false)
        ActivateTask(plustask);          Task plustask
     else                                {
        ActivateTask(minustask);           Type=Basic;
     //goto L1 if program is not broken     Priority=3;
     TerminateTask();                       Schedule=Non;
}                                           Autostart=False;
                                          }
Task plustask() {
L2   speed++;
     TerminateTask();                     Task minustask
}                                         {
                                            Type=Basic;
Task minustask() {                          Priority=3;
L3   while(speed>30)                        Schedule=Non;
        speed=speed-10;                     Autostart=False;
     TerminateTask();                     }
}
```

Fig. 3. Running example.

task is set by the attribute Type with the value Basic or Extended. The priority of a task is assigned by the attribute Priority with a signless integer, and a higher priority task holds a higher value. Schedule is in charge of determine whether a lower priority task can be preempted by a higher priority task, where Full and Non stand for such preemption is allowed and forbidden, respectively. Autostart is used to configure the initial states of tasks and holds two values True and False. If a task within an OSEK/VDX program is configured as True, the task locates at *ready* state when the program is loaded to run; otherwise, it locates at *suspended* state.

Figure 3 illustrates an OSEK/VDX program to reveal the execution characteristics of OSEK/VDX programs. The program consists of three tasks: *contask*, *plustask* and *minustask*. Two functions Getspeed() and Identify(_speed) are called by *contask* in the program, where the function Getspeed() is to get the current speed of vehicle, and the function Identify(_speed) is to identify whether the speed of vehicle should be decreased according to the condition of road and the current speed, i.e., the identification of road condition is based on the machine learning algorithms [11]. When the program is loaded to run on the OSEK/VDX OS, *contask* will be first dispatched to execute since the attribute Autostart of *contask* is configured as True in contrast with the tasks *plustask* and *minustask*. After the executions of functions Getspeed() and Identify(_speed), the API *ActivateTask(plustask)* or *ActivateTask(minustask)* is invoked by *contask* in if-else branches. For example, assume that the API *ActivateTask(minustask)* is invoked by *contask*. After that, the OSEK/VDX scheduler responses to this API invocation and then activates *minustask* (i.e., the state of *minustask* will be transferred from *suspended* state to *ready* state). When the program runs here, *minustask* will preempt the execution of currently running *contask* because the attribute Schedule of *contask* is set to Full and *minustask* holds a higher priority. In the next step, *minustask* gets processor to run until the API *Terminate-Task()* is invoked (*TerminateTask()* is used to terminate the execution of a running task and the state of the running task will be switched to *suspended* state). Once *minustask* is terminated, the OSEK/VDX scheduler will assign processor resource to *contask* again from its preempted point. Similarly, in the another branch, when *contask* invokes API *ActivateTask(plustask)*, *plustask* will preempt the execution of *contask* and terminate itself by invoking *TerminateTask()*.

Execution Characteristics. Based on the running example, the execution characteristics of the OSEK/VDX programs are summarized below.

1. Tasks within an OSEK/VDX program are concurrently executed under the scheduling of OSEK/VDX OS, and the running task can be explicitly determined by the OSEK/VDX scheduler.
2. Tasks can invoke APIs to change their states, and the invoked APIs can dynamically update the scheduling order of tasks.

Owing to the concurrency and dynamic scheduling of tasks, ensuring the reliability of the developed OSEK/VDX programs has become a challenge in the automotive industry. Next section will present an approach called stepwise symbolic execution to alleviate this challenge.

3   Symbolic Execution for OSEK/VDX Programs

3.1   Overview

The approach proposed in this paper allows the existing symbolic execution methods to successfully test the OSEK/VDX programs. To realize this target, the approach first translate a given OSEK/VDX program into a sequential model by means of a sequentialization technique presented in [2]. After that, a new variety of hybrid concolic testing approach named stepwise symbolic execution is proposed for desiring both a wide and a deep exploration by inheriting advantages of the existing symbolic execution methods. Compared with the existing hybrid concolic testing, the proposed approach takes the breadth-first search concolic testing to achieve a wide coverage, and then a constraint solver based random testing is started from a state to achieve a precise deep coverage when the concolic testing generates a test input over a time budget from the state.

3.2   Sequentialization of OSEK/VDX Programs

In order to successfully use symbolic execution techniques to generate a rich testing inputs for a developed OSEK/VDX program, the program is translated into an equivalent sequential model in the preliminary stage. In this paper, the sequentialization technique [2] is adopted to perform a sequential process. After that, as shown in Fig. 4, the running example can be translated into a sequential model which contains all execution traces of the running program. Based on

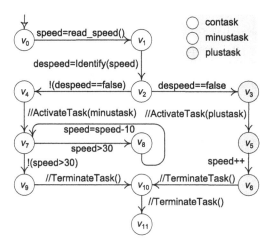

Fig. 4. Sequential model for the running example.

the sequential model, the existing symbolic execution techniques can directly explore the OSEK/VDX program and then generate a wide input for testing the OSEK/VDX program. Note that the mapped APIs in the sequential model are only for sequentialization process, which are omitted in the test generation by using symbolic execution.

3.3   Background of Symbolic Execution Techniques

If an OSEK/VDX program is translated into a sequential model, it can obtain both a deep and a wide exploration of the state space with the help of the existing symbolic execution techniques such as classic symbolic execution [12], concolic testing technique [7] and hybrid testing technique [4]. In the classic symbolic execution, a program is formally represented as a tree Λ, where a node n in the program tree Λ consists of an assignment statement block of the program, and condition statements in the program correspond to the branches of the program tree Λ, especially each branch signifies a constraint that determines a path p of the program tree Λ. The definition of a path p is shown in Definition 1. In the exploration process, symbolic variables are employed to execute the program instead of concrete values of inputs. The goal of the classic symbolic execution is to systematically solve symbolic constraints along paths for generating different concrete values for inputs so that as many different paths as possible would be taken. The classic symbolic execution can effectively handle a simple program with high-coverage. Unfortunately, for large or complex programs, it is computationally intractable to precisely maintain and solve the constraints required for test generation caused by the complex data structures and undecidable constraints.

Recently, a technique named concolic testing technique has been proposed as a variant of symbolic execution. In contrast with the classic symbolic execution, this technique is to simultaneously search a program with both concrete values and symbolic variables in order to simplify the symbolic constraints generated along a path by using the corresponding concrete execution. Even though the technique can deal with the complex data structures as well as the constraints that go beyond the solving ability of constraint solver, it is commonly limited to small units of code and path lengths of at most about fifty thousand basic blocks as a result of the capacity limitation of constraint solver [13].

Definition 1. A path p in a program tree Λ is an execution sequence $p: n_0 \xrightarrow{c_1} n_1 \xrightarrow{c_2} \cdots, n_{i-1} \xrightarrow{c_i} n_i, \cdots \xrightarrow{c_p} n_p$, where $n_i \in \Lambda$ is a state of path p consisting of an assignment statement block, c_i is a branch statement, n_0 is the initial state, n_p is the terminal or halt state, and p is the length of p.

Hybrid concolic testing technique is developed based on an interleaving exploration between the traditional random testing and the concolic testing in order to make symbolic execution more powerful. Compared with the concolic testing technique, it starts exploration by performing the traditional random testing and then the concolic testing is switched to carry out an exhaustive bounded depth search when the random testing is not capable of covering a new state of a program. The hybrid testing technique substantially wants to take both deep capability of the random testing and wide capability of the concolic testing to achieve a high-coverage. However, the technique may miss the wide capability when the random testing is hard to achieve a high-coverage and meanwhile the concolic testing is invalid for solving the constraints along an uncovered path.

3.4   Stepwise Symbolic Execution

In this paper, a new symbolic execution technique named stepwise symbolic execution is developed for exploring large-scale OSEK/VDX programs by inheriting the advantages of the existing symbolic execution techniques.

3.4.1   Exploration Mode

The stepwise symbolic execution explores a program by using both the concolic testing and a special random testing in an interactive way. In the exploration process, the breadth first search (BFS) based concolic testing is first started to achieve a wide coverage, where the amount of constraints to be solved by constraint solver is increased in a gradual manner along the states of paths. If the concolic testing generates a test input from a state n_i over a time budget ξ, a restricted random testing is then started from the state n_i to desire a deep coverage by using a number of random inputs——the constraint solver is called to generate λ random inputs under the constraints from the initial state n_0 to the state n_i. Note that the time budget ξ is a threshold for limiting the running time of constraint solver in each exploration, that should be smaller than the disabled time of constraint solver.

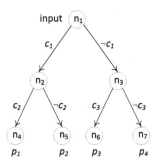

Fig. 5. A simple program tree.

3.4.2   Detail Explanation with an Example

Figure 5 shows a simple program tree that consists of four paths: p_1, p_2, p_3 and p_4. Since the BFS based concolic testing is first used to perform exploration in the stepwise symbolic execution technique, one of concrete input values is first employed to execute the program tree. Here, assume that the path p_2 is taken under the concrete input values. Then, the negative branch $\neg c_1$ is considered as a constraint to generate new concrete values for input by means of constraint solver, where suppose that the new concrete values trigger the path p_4. In the next round, the branch c_2 is taken and used to construct a constraint formula $(c_1 \wedge c_2)$ for generating concrete input values for trigging the path p_1 according to the concrete execution of path p_2. After that, the constraint formula $(\neg c_1 \wedge c_3)$ is constructed and used to feed constraint solver for making the path p_3 being tested.

Unfortunately, in contrast with the simple example shown in Fig. 5, a practical program is usually complex and large which would result in constraint solver expensive in dealing with a constraint formula corresponding to a long path under a short time. For example, assume that the used constraint solver is fast to deal with one constraint but is expensive to handle more constraints, obvious that the BFS based concolic testing is impossible to perform a full-coverage for the example shown in Fig. 5 within a short time. To overcome this problem, the restricted random testing is then launched to continue exploration.

The quintessence of restricted random testing is to generate some explicit concrete values for input so that as many different paths as possible would be saturated. For achieving this target, the constraint solver as a random generator is repeatedly called to produce a number of concrete input values with a constraint formula until an uncovered path is taken or the number of produced inputs is over a set random times λ, where the constraint formula is a conjunctive form consisting of a sub-path and a negative constraints with regard to each generated concrete values.

Compared with the traditional random testing, the restricted random testing may need more time to complete random process, but it is more precise in coverage process because its random process is under constraint restrictions. For instance, assume that the shown example holds one input variable x and the paths p_2 and p_4 are taken with the concrete input values $\{x = 3\}$ and $\{x = 6\}$ respectively after first round of the BFS based concolic testing, i.e., the constraints corresponding to branches c_1 and $\neg c_1$ were solved to generate concrete input values for variable x. If the restricted random testing is considered to cover path p_1 in the next step, the constraint formula $(c_1 \wedge (x \neq 3))$ is then passed to constraint solver.

Here, suppose that the constraint solver specifies $\{x = 2\}$ but the concrete input value of variable x is still not able to trigger the path p_1. For this situation, the constraint solver will be called again to generate a new input value for variable x with the constraint formula $(c_1 \wedge (x \neq 3) \wedge (x \neq 2))$. Obviously, the restricted random testing is possible to trigger the path p_1 by repeatedly calling constraint solver to generate a different concrete input for variable x.

3.4.3 Algorithm of Stepwise Symbolic Execution

Once a given OSEK/VDX program is translated into a sequential model, it is possible to convert the sequential model into a program tree by unfolding loops as κ branches. After that, the stepwise symbolic execution is started to generate enough test suite for the given OSEK/VDX program. The key process of the stepwise symbolic execution has been abstracted as a formal algorithm which is shown in Algorithm 1. The algorithm holds four parameters $\Lambda, \xi, \lambda, \Psi$ as input and returns an output Γ, where Λ is program tree of a given OSEK/VDX program, ξ and λ are the limitations for the running time of concolic testing and the times of restricted random testing in each exploration respectively, Ψ is the given limitation used to terminate the algorithm such as the amount of running time and coverage rate, $\Gamma = \{(\tau_1, p_1), (\tau_2, p_2), \cdots, (\tau_i, p_i)\}$ is a set used to record the generated test input τ_i and its covered path p_i. In the algorithm, the function $Execute(\Lambda, \tau_i)$ executes a program tree Λ with the input τ_i and

---

Algorithm 1. Key processes of stepwise symbolic execution

Require: $\Lambda \ \xi \ \lambda \ \Psi$
Ensure: Γ

 1: declare a variable $c := 0$, a variable $i = 0$ and a set $P := \{\}$, where c is used to count running time, P is in charge of recording execution path p, i is index;
 2: generate a concrete values for input τ_i by using random testing
 3: $p_i := Execute(\Lambda, \tau_i)$;
 4: $P := P \cup \{p_i\}$, $\Gamma := \Gamma + \{(\tau_i, p_i)\}$;
 5: $\Delta := Explore(\Lambda, n_0)$, where n_0 is the root node of program tree Λ;
 6: initialize a queue Q, $Q.Enqueue(\Delta)$, $n := Q.Dequeue()$;
 7: **while** $Q.isEmpty() \neq false$ and Ψ is true **do**
 8:     **if** $c < \xi$ **then**
 9:         $i++$;
10:         $\psi := Formula(P, n)$;
11:         $\tau_i := Solver(\psi)$;
12:         $c := SolveTime(\psi)$;
13:         $p_i := Execute(\Lambda, \tau_i)$;
14:         **if** $P \cap \{p_i\} = \oslash$ **then**
15:             $P := P \cup \{p_i\}$, $\Gamma := \Gamma + \{(\tau_i, p_i)\}$;
16:         **end if**
17:         $\Delta := Explore(\Lambda, n)$, $Q.Enqueue(\Delta)$;
18:         $n := Q.Dequeue()$, $\Delta := Explore(\Lambda, n)$
19:         $Q.Enqueue(\Delta)$;
20:         $n := Q.Dequeue()$;
21:     **else**
            $c := 0$, $j := 0$;
22:         **while** $j < \lambda$ **do**
23:             $\tau_i := Solver(\psi)$, $p_i := Execute(\Lambda, \tau_i)$;
24:             **if** $P \cap \{p_i\} = \oslash$ **then**
25:                 $P := P \cup \{p_i\}$, $\Gamma := \Gamma + \{(\tau_i, p_i)\}$, $i++$;
26:             **end if**
27:             $\psi := Restrict(\psi, \tau_i)$;
28:             $j++$
29:         **end while**
30:     **end if**
31: **end while**
32: **return** Γ;

---

returns an executed path p_i from program tree Λ. Δ is a set with order used to record nodes of Λ that is returned by function $Explore(\Lambda, n)$, where the executed node is in front of the unexecuted node, and returned nodes by function $Explore(\Lambda, n)$ are the children nodes of node n. The function $Formula(P, n)$ is used to extract the sub-path $(n_0, \cdots, n)$ from the executed path set P and to translate the extracted sub-path into constraint formula ψ. The function $Solver(\psi)$ is in charge of negating the last condition of ψ and calling constraint solver to return a concrete values for input τ_i. The function $SolveTime(\psi)$ is used to count the solving time of constraint solver in order to realize the switch from concolic testing to restricted random testing. The function $Restrict(\psi, \tau_i)$ is to construct the conjunction constraint formula ψ with τ_i for supporting the restricted random testing.

4   Experiment and Evaluation

4.1   Experiments and Benchmarks

According to the presented approach, a prototype toolkit is implemented based on the Visual Studio 2015 with about 7600 lines of C++ code. A series of experiments are conducted to evaluate the efficiency and capability of the proposed approach by using the implemented toolkit. The used ten benchmarks are randomly selected from the sixty OSEK/VDX programs that are shown the papers [2,9,10] in order to desire a relatively fair evaluation. In addition, the pure random testing technique and hybrid concolic testing technique is considered as a comparison object.

Based on the selected benchmarks, two types of experiments are carried out to investigate the proposed approach on ability of path coverage and consumption of time. In the first type of experiments, the path coverage percentage is fixed to 80% and then the consumption on time is set as an investigated point. Compared with the first experiments, the time budget is fixed to 2000 seconds in the second type of experiments, but the path coverage rate is investigated. All of the experiments are conducted on the Intel i7-3770 CPU with 4G RAM. The experimental results for the first experiments and the second experiments are listed in Table 1 and Table 2, respectively. In the tables, #v is the number of symbolic variables, #b is the number of branches, and #l is the number of loops. "memory" and "time" are the memory consumption and time consumption measured in MByte and seconds (s), respectively. "coverage" is a percentage of the number of covered paths to the amount of paths included in a program. "PRT", "HCT" and "SSE" stand for the pure random testing (PRT), hybrid concolic testing (HTC) and stepwise symbolic execution (SSE). Furthermore, in the conducted experiments, the loop bound κ is set to 10, the time budget ξ and random times λ in the stepwise symbolic execution approach are set to $2s$ and 20, respectively.

4.2 Experimental Results

The experimental results shown in Table 1 indicate that the pure random testing is almost impossible to achieve the fixed path coverage (80%) within 3000 s. In comparison to the pure random testing, the hybrid concolic testing technique and the stepwise symbolic execution approach are both capable of achieving a high-coverage (80%) within a short time (< 300 s) when the explored benchmarks hold a few of symbolic variables and branches such as the benchmarks 1 and 2 shown in Table 1. The high-coverage benefits from the concolic testing, i.e., the explored benchmarks are not complex that allows constraint solver to quickly generate a precise value for input. However, alongside the increasing number of symbolic variables, branches as well as loops, the compared hybrid concolic testing technique takes a long time (> 2000 s or > 3000 s) to complete the fixed path coverage rate such as the benchmarks 4 and 5 shown in Table 1. Compared with this technique, the stepwise symbolic execution is a cost-effective technique, that can successfully active the goal within a short time (< 2000 s) except the benchmark 5 shown in Table 1. This is because, the compared hybrid testing technique uses the traditional random testing to explore the benchmarks, which is expensive to achieve a wide exploration since the random inputs usually result in the same paths being taken. In contrast, the stepwise symbolic execution takes the constraint solver based random testing to produce a number of concrete input values when the concolic testing runs out of the time budget, that is more cost-efficient owning to the precise search.

As shown in Table 2, the pure random testing is almost impracticable to complete the exploration of all paths within 2000 s. In contrast with the pure random

Table 1. Comparison: PRT, SSE and HCT under the fixed coverage (**80%**)

| No. | #v | #b | #l | Sequentialization | | PRT | HCT | SSE |
				Time (s)	Memory (Mb)	Time (s)	Time (s)	Time (s)
1	14	28	0	0.2	3.9	>3000	570	500
2	16	49	0	0.7	5.1	>3000	980	843
3	24	10	4	1.1	6.2	>3000	1897	1732
4	13	32	7	1.4	7.7	>3000	>2000	1984
15	12	12	9	2.1	8.2	>3000	>3000	>2000

Table 2. Comparison: PRT, SSE and HCT under the fixed time (**2000 s**)

| No. | #v | #b | #l | Sequentialization | | PRT | HCT | SSE |
				Time (s)	Memory (Mb)	Cov. (%)[a]	Cov. (%)	Cov. (%)
1	8	21	0	0.8	3.1	16.4	100	100
2	24	17	1	1.3	3.8	14.3	72.4	86.4
3	13	19	4	1.4	4.4	10.2	64.1	74.1
4	18	20	5	1.7	4.7	9.1	56.6	63.9
5	19	18	7	2.4	4.9	7.4	47.8	58.4

[a]cov. stands for coverage

testing, the hybrid concolic testing technique as well as the stepwise symbolic execution have the ability to obtain a full-coverage (100%) under 2000 s if the explored benchmarks are not large such as the benchmark 1. The outstanding ability is performed by the concolic testing, since the explored benchmarks just contain a few of symbolic variables, branches and loops which are not beyond the capability of the concolic testing. However, the compared hybrid concolic testing technique will perform a low-coverage when the benchmarks hold more symbolic variables, branches and loops, especially the coverage rate drops quickly. Compared with this technique, the coverage rate of the stepwise symbolic execution approach is also dropped with the growth of complexity of benchmarks, but the coverage rate is greater than the hybrid concolic testing, which benefits from the constraint solver based random testing.

Overall, it is easy to find that the stepwise symbolic execution is an efficient technique that is capable of performing both a wide and a deep exploration for large-scale OSEK/VDX programs compared with the pure random testing and the hybrid concolic testing technique.

5   Related Work

With the development of constraint solver [14,15], symbolic execution has won much attention as an effective technique benefiting from its high-coverage in test suite generation. Currently, many advanced methods have already been proposed for making symbolic execution more practical in the software testing. For example, in the scope of solving constraints, the automatic tools CUTE [7] and KLEE [16] use an optimization strategy to avoid the similar constraints to be repeatedly solved by constraint solver. The optimization strategy is based on the characteristic that many paths usually hold the same constraints which will lead to the similar inputs to be generated by constraint solver. Therefore, by using this characteristic, the input results generated by the previous same constraints can be reused to improve the speed of constraint solving in the next solving process. Compared with these existing works, this paper presents a new testing approach which is a new variety of symbolic execution techniques.

Systematically explore a complex program that hold a large number of branches and loops is a challenge in symbolic execution, since these branches and loops will make the path space in exponential growth. To overcome this challenge, some advanced techniques have been proposed based on the heuristic techniques and sound program analysis techniques. For example, the paper [17] shows a heuristic technique that takes the static CFG of a given program to guide the exploration toward the path closest from an uncovered instruction. In the technique, exploration process favors the visited statements that were run the fewest times in previous. In contrast with the heuristic techniques, a technique [18] for reducing the number of paths is proposed based on the sound program analysis techniques. In the technique, the select expression is used to combine branches. Furthermore, a counter-example guided refinement [19] based lazy test generation technique is presented in paper [20]. The technique employs the concolic symbolic execution to explore a program, but a trustworthy function called in the program such as a STL function is abstracted as an unconstrained formula in order to reduce the paths from the function to be explored. Currently, these advanced techniques are not taken into account in this paper. In the future, these advanced techniques will be applied in the stepwise symbolic execution for implementing a more efficient tool. Besides the shown existing works, there have been many methods that apply formal method such as model checking to verify the developed OSEK/VDX OS and programs such as [21,22]. These existing works are different from this paper, because this paper focuses on the generation of testing inputs rather than model checking.

6   Conclusion and Future Work

This paper presents a new stepwise symbolic execution approach that is in a position to perform both a wide and a deep exploration for the deterministic scheduler based OSEK/VDX multi-tasking programs. In the future, a more complete tool will be developed based on current prototype tool.

References

1. Lemieux, J.: Programming in the OSEK/VDX Environment. CMP, Suite 200 Lawrence, KS 66046, USA (2001)
2. Zhang, H., Cheng, Z., Li, G., Liu, S.: autoC: an efficient translator for model checking deterministic scheduler based OSEK/VDX applications. Sci. China Inf. Sci. **61**(5), 1–15 (2017). https://doi.org/10.1007/s11432-016-9039-4
3. Zamli, K.Z., Din, F., Kendall, G., Ahmed, B.S.: An experimental study of hyper-heuristic selection and acceptance mechanism for combinatorial t-way test suite generation. Inf. Sci. **399**, 121–153 (2017)
4. Majumdar, R., Sen, K.: Hybrid concolic testing. In: International Conference on Software Engineering (ICSE), pp. 416–426 (2007)
5. Offutt, A.J., Hayes, J.H.: A semantic model of program faults. ACM SIGSOFT Softw. Eng. Notes **21**(3), 195–200 (1996)
6. Cadar, C., et al.: Symbolic execution for software testing in practice-preliminary assessment. In: International Conference on Software Engineering (ICSE), pp. 1066–1071 (2011)
7. Sen, K., Marinov, D., Agha, G.: CUTE: a concolic unit testing engine for C. In: The Joint 10th European Software Engineering Conference (ESEC) and 13th ACM SIGSOFT Symposium on the Foundations of Software Engineering (FSE-13), pp. 263–272 (2005)
8. Bucur, S., Ureche, V., Zamfir, C., Candea, G.: Parallel symbolic execution for automated real-world software testing. In: European Conference on European Conference on Computer Systems, pp. 183–198 (2011)
9. Zhang, H., Li, G., Sun, D., Lu, Y., Hsu, C.: Verifying cooperative software: a SMT-based bounded model checking approach for deterministic scheduler. J. Syst. Architect. **81**, 7–16 (2017)
10. Zhang, H., Li, G., Cheng, Z., Xue, J.: Verifying OSEK/VDX automotive applications: a Spin-based model checking approach. Softw. Test. Verification Reliab. **28**(3), 1662 (2018)

11. Gass, S.I., Fu, M.C.: Machine learning. Encyclopedia of Operations Research and Management Science, Springer, Boston, MA (2013)
12. Khurshid, S., PĂsĂreanu, C.S., Visser, W.: Generalized symbolic execution for model checking and testing. In: Garavel, H., Hatcliff, J. (eds.) TACAS 2003. LNCS, vol. 2619, pp. 553–568. Springer, Heidelberg (2003). https://doi.org/10.1007/3-540-36577-X_40
13. Jhala, R., Majumdar, R.: Path slicing. In: Programming Language Design and Implementation, pp. 38–47 (2003)
14. De Moura, L., Bjorner, N.: Satisfiability Modulo theories: introduction and applications. Commun. ACM **54**(9), 69–77 (2011)
15. Ábrahám, E., Kremer, G.: Satisfiability checking: theory and applications. In: De Nicola, R., Kühn, E. (eds.) SEFM 2016. LNCS, vol. 9763, pp. 9–23. Springer, Cham (2016). https://doi.org/10.1007/978-3-319-41591-8_2
16. Cadar, C., Dunbar, D., Engler, D.: KLEE: unassisted and automatic generation of high-coverage tests for complex systems programs. In: USENIX Conference on Operating Systems Design & Implementation, pp. 209–224 (2009)
17. Burnim, J., Sen, K.: Heuristics for scalable dynamic test generation. In: IEEE/ACM International Conference on Automated Software Engineering, pp. 443–446 (2008)
18. Collingbourne, P., Cadar, C., Kelly, P.H.J.: Symbolic crosschecking of floating-point and SIMD code. In: Conference on Computer Systems, pp. 315–328 (2011)
19. Segelken, M.: Abstraction and Counterexample-Guided Construction of ω-Automata for Model Checking of Step-Discrete Linear Hybrid Models. In: Damm, W., Hermanns, H. (eds.) CAV 2007. LNCS, vol. 4590, pp. 433–448. Springer, Heidelberg (2007). https://doi.org/10.1007/978-3-540-73368-3_46
20. Majumdar, R., Sen, K.: LATEST: lazy dynamic test input generation. In: Technical Report UCB/EECS-2007-36, EECS Department, University of California (2007)
21. Deifel, H., Göttlinger, M., Milius, S., Schröder, L., Dietrich, C., Löhmann, D.: Automatic verification of application-tailored OSEK kernels. In: Formal Methods in Computer Aided Design, pp. 196–203 (2017)
22. Waszniowski, L., Jan, K., Zdenek, H.: Case study on distributed and fault tolerant system modeling based on timed automata. J. Syst. Softw. **82**(10), 1678–1694 (2009)

Dynamic Specification Mining Based on Transformer

Ying Gao[1], Meng Wang[1(✉)], and Bin Yu[2]

[1] Cyberspace Security and Computer College, Hebei University,
Baoding 071000, China
`wangmnxd@163.com`
[2] Institute of Computing Theory and Technology,
Xidian University, Xi'an 710071, China

Abstract. Software specifications play an important role in improving the quality of software. In order to mine software specifications, many automated technologies have been proposed based on finite-state automaton (FSA). Among these technologies, the representative one is the Deep Specification Miner (DSM) using deep learning to conduct specification mining. However, the quality of the mining specifications is not very accurate due to the long-term dependence and other inherent defects of the Recurrent Neural Networks (RNNs) used in DSM.

In this paper, we propose a dynamic specification mining approach based on the Transformer framework to improve accuracy. With this approach, we improve DSM by using the Transformer framework instead of RNNs to capture global dependencies between input and output. Specifically, taking execution traces of software systems as input, a Transformer model can be constructed. Meanwhile, a heuristic algorithm is used to find a subset of traces that can represent all traces. Further, feature values of trace prefixes of each trace in the trace subset are calculated by the Transformer model, and then they are input into clustering algorithms. Finally, some finite-state automata (FSAs) can be obtained by the clustering algorithms, and according to the F_1-measure of each FSA, an FSA with the best index can be regarded as the final model. The proposed approach has been implemented in a tool named DSM-T and experiments include 11 target classes that have been conducted to evaluate the effectiveness of the approach. Experiments show that the average F_1-measure of our method reaches 93.13%, which is 21.16% higher than DSM.

Keywords: Transformer · Specification mining · Finite-state machine · Attention mechanism · Formal method

1 Introduction

Software specifications are of great importance in the software development life cycle (SDLC). They can help to improve the efficiency of software development,

© Springer Nature Switzerland AG 2022
Y. Aït-Ameur and F. Crăciun (Eds.): TASE 2022, LNCS 13299, pp. 220–237, 2022.
https://doi.org/10.1007/978-3-031-10363-6_16

ensure software quality, and guide the use of a software system. Especially, for large-scale software systems, the role of complete specifications is more obvious.

However, software specifications are usually ignored by designers due to hard deadlines and 'short-time-to-market' requirements. This results in the lack of software specifications. Moreover, software specifications are usually not updated by developers as software evolution, which leads to the inconsistency between a software system and its software specifications. In these cases, the quality of requirement specifications is generally poor.

In order to verify software systems using formal methods such as model checking and theorem proving, software specifications should be specified in a formal way. Furthermore, it is very time-consuming and difficult to manually write formal specifications since this work requires developers to have the requisite skills and experience. Thus, it is necessary to mine formal specifications automatically.

Nowadays many techniques have been proposed for automatically mining interesting specifications in software systems. These techniques can be roughly classified into two categories: static specification mining [21,22] and dynamic specification mining [2,6]. The former mines software specifications directly from the source code of software systems without executing these systems, but it cannot deal with large-scale systems well. Whereas the latter mines software specifications from execution traces of systems, where the mined specifications are usually expressed in temporal logic formulas [9], or finite-state automaton (FSA) [1,8]. However, the quality of mined specifications is not perfect yet.

In 2018, Tien-Duy et al. [17,18] proposed Deep Specification Miner (DSM) based on deep learning in order to mine high-quality FSA-based specifications. In DSM, a rich set of execution traces is used to train a language model based on Recurrent Neural Networks (RNNLM). However, the RNNLM has its inherent defects. On the one hand, it cannot be calculated in parallel because the calculation of the hidden layer state at time t depends not only on the sentence input word X_t at time t, but also on the hidden layer state $S_{(t-1)}$ at time $t-1$. However, the latter can only be sequentially transmitted through the information transmission channel. On the other hand, it cannot solve the long-term dependence problem. After many stages of propagation, the gradient disappears or explodes.

In this paper, we improve the DSM and propose a dynamic specification mining approach using Transformer technology [23]. Here we apply Transformer to the field of specification mining and use it to capture temporal relationships among methods in execution traces of a program. First, we need to input the target software into the test case generation tool to generate test cases that cover as many paths as possible in the software. Then, we execute test cases and get rich execution traces. The Transformer model is trained by execution traces. At the same time, in order to improve mining efficiency, we extract a subset of traces that can cover all adjacent method pairs of execution traces. Next, we input the trace subset into the Transformer model, obtaining the feature values of trace prefixes of each trace in the trace subset, and then the feature values are input into the k-means, hierarchical, and dbscan clustering algorithms to obtain multiple FSAs. We choose one FSA that best expresses software behavior as the final model.

The main contributions of our work are four-fold.

(1) An approach for applying Transformer technology in the field of Natural Language Processing (NLP) to dynamic specification mining is proposed.
(2) We extend clustering algorithms used in DSM with the dbscan clustering algorithm which does not need to enter the number of clusters in advance.
(3) We have implemented our approach in a tool DSM-T[1].
(4) We evaluate our approach on 11 target library classes presented in [17]. The experimental results show the effectiveness of our approach. The average F_1-measure of the results reaches 93.13%, which is superior to the most related tools: k-tail [1], SEKT [15], CONTRACTOR++ [15], TEMI [15], and DSM [17].

The remainder of the paper is organized as follows. Section 2 introduces the preliminary knowledge of this work. Section 3 presents our dynamic specification mining approach. We evaluate our approach in Sect. 4. Section 5 presents the related work and Sect. 6 concludes the paper.

2   Preliminary

2.1   Seq2seq Model

Seq2seq is a model that transforms one sequence into another, and it is widely used in the NLP field. Figure 1 is the most abstract representation of a common seq2seq model using two RNNs.

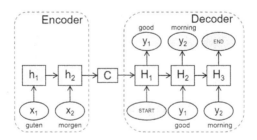

Fig. 1. Seq2seq model with RNNs

It can be seen the seq2seq model is composed of the encoder-decoder architecture. The encoder converts the input sequence $X = \langle x_1, x_2 \rangle$ into an intermediate semantic vector C through the hidden layer state h_i at each moment, that is,

---

[1] https://github.com/gaoying11/Dynamic-Specification-Mining-based-on-Transformer.

$C = q(h_1, h_2)$, where q represents some kind of nonlinear neural network. The decoder generates the output of the current moment according to the semantic vector C, the state and the output of the hidden layer at the previous moment, that is, $y_j = g(y_{j-1}, H_{j-1}, C)$, where g is a nonlinear multi-layer neural network.

Since the encoder stores all the input sequence information into a fixed semantic vector C, the information which is previously entered will be covered by the information entered later. Thus, C may not completely represent the information of the whole sequence. Besides, the encoder-decoder framework considers each word in the input sequence with the same weight, and the importance of different inputs is not reflected. Take the machine translation task as an example. If we want to translate German "guten morgen" to English "good morning". When translating the target sequence word "good", the word "guten" has the greatest impact and the impact of other words should be very small.

2.2 Attention Mechanism

Because of the limitation of the encoder-decoder, an attention mechanism is proposed [4]. The core of the attention mechanism is the ability to selectively focus on useful parts of the input sequence.

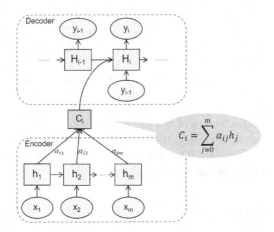

Fig. 2. Seq2Seq model with attention mechanism

The encoder-decoder model with an attention mechanism can learn the importance of each element from the sequence, and then combine the elements according to their importance. This indicates that the encoder will obtain multiple semantic vectors, and different semantic vectors are composed of different sequence elements combined with different weight parameters. As shown in Fig. 2, α_{ij} can be regarded as a probability, reflecting the importance of h_j. The higher the value of α_{ij}, the greater the impact of the hidden layer h_j on the output results. In this way, the semantic vector C is obtained by the weighted summation of each element according to its importance.

2.3 Transformer Model

The Transformer was proposed by Google in [23] for machine translation tasks in 2017. Since then, the remarkable effect of the Transformer in many specific tasks has caused considerable repercussions. The Transformer is also composed of an encoder and a decoder. However, it abandons the commonly used RNNs in the traditional encoder-decoder framework and adopts a full attention structure. In this way, it not only solves the long-term dependency problem caused by the traditional encoder-decoder framework during encoding, but also avoids the sequential structure of RNNs to achieve parallel computing.

3   Dynamic Specification Mining Based on Transformer

In this section, we present an approach based on Transformer to dynamically mining specifications expressed in FSA.

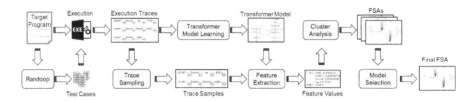

Fig. 3. Overview of our approach

As shown in Fig. 3, the core of our approach includes six steps: trace generating, Transformer model learning, trace sampling, feature extraction, clustering analysis and model selection. The details of the specification mining approach are explained in the following subsections.

3.1   Trace Generating

As in [17], we use the test cases generated by Randoop, a test case generation tool. Randoop is a unit test generator for Java. The tool generates test cases through random tests. We collect rich execution traces by executing test cases, that is, obtaining the calling sequence between methods. A trace tr can be expressed as $tr = \langle f_1, f_2, ..., f_n \rangle$, where f_i $(1 \leq i \leq n)$ is a method call.

Fig. 4. Top-level view of the Transformer

3.2 Transformer Model Learning

In general, we want to use the Transformer to achieve the purpose of using the current method prefix to predict the next method in the trace.

As shown in Fig. 4, taking an execution trace $\langle\langle START\rangle, StackAr, makeE mpty, push, top, \langle END\rangle\rangle$ as an example, where $\langle START\rangle$ and $\langle END\rangle$ represent the start and end marks of the trace respectively. If the current is the start flag, then the next method we want to predict is $StackAr$. If the current method prefix is $\langle StackAr\rangle$, then the next predicted method should be $makeEmpty$. By analogy, it can be found that the output sequence is the result of shifting the input sequence to the left by one bit. Until $\langle END\rangle$ is predicted.

Trace Preprocessing. In order to train the Transformer model, it is necessary to preprocess all execution traces. First, a method dictionary MI is built to map each method m_h appearing in the input trace set to a method index i where $i \in N$. That is, $MI[m_h] = i$. Accordingly, each trace can be converted into a sequence of method indexes. The Transformer model we want to train only considers execution traces of a fixed length. It is assumed that the fixed length is N. Then, for a trace longer than N, we only take the first N method indexes in the trace index sequence as training data. For a trace shorter than N, we use 0 to fill the trace index sequence to the specified length N. As shown in Fig. 5, we suppose the trace set we deal with is $TR = \{tr_1, tr_2, tr_3\}$, where $tr_1 = \langle\langle START\rangle, StackAr, top, mE, tAP, top, mE, \langle END\rangle\rangle$, $tr_2 = \langle\langle START\rangle$, $StackAr, mE, push, tAP, top, push, top, \langle END\rangle\rangle$ and $tr_3 = \langle\langle START\rangle$, $StackAr, mE, push, top, \langle END\rangle\rangle$. Among them, mE means method $makeEmpty$, tAP means method $topAndPop$. A method dictionary MI is created which maps methods $\langle START\rangle$, $StackAr$, top, mE, tAP, $\langle END\rangle$ and $push$ to method indexes from 1 to 7, respectively. Thus, tr_1, tr_2 and tr_3 can be converted into method index sequence $tri_1 = \langle 1, 2, 3, 4, 5, 3, 4, 6\rangle$, $tri_2 = \langle 1, 2, 4, 7, 5, 3, 7, 3, 6\rangle$ and $tri_3 = \langle 1, 2, 4, 7, 3, 6\rangle$. We assume the fixed length N of a trace we are processing is 8. Then tri_2 is truncated into sequence $\langle 1, 2, 4, 7, 5, 3, 7, 3\rangle$ and tri_3 becomes $\langle 1, 2, 4, 7, 3, 6, 0, 0\rangle$ by filling 0 in the rest of positions.

Training the Transformer Model. The framework of the Transformer model is shown in Fig. 6. It contains Embedding Layer, Positional Embedding, Encoder component, Decoder component and Softmax Layer. By taking a preprocessed trace $tri = \langle f_1, f_2, ..., f_n\rangle$ in the trace set and a predicted trace prefix $tr_o^i =$

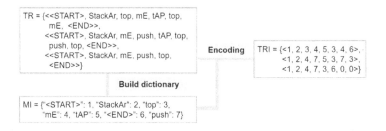

Fig. 5. Data processing.

$\langle f'_1, f'_2, ..., f'_i \rangle$ as input, the Transformer model predicts the next called method after tr^i_o. In practice, the model calculates a vector $P_{tr^i} = \langle P_{m_1}, P_{m_2}, ..., P_{m_k} \rangle$, where m_1, m_2, ..., m_k are all methods appearing in the trace set, and P_{m_j} ($1 \leq j \leq k$) represents the probability of occurrence of method m_j after tr^i_o. Then the index of method m_h i.e., $MI[m_h]$ with the highest probability P_{m_h} is chosen and added to the predicted trace prefix, i.e. $tr^{i+1}_o = \langle f'_1, f'_2, ..., f'_i, MI[m_h] \rangle$. The framework is explained in the following.

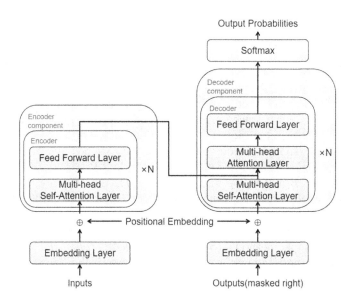

Fig. 6. The framework of the Transformer model

Embedding Layer. For a method index sequence generated by trace preprocessing, a word vector with dimension d is generated for each method in the sequence using the word embedding algorithm. Thus, all word vectors for methods in the trace form a matrix $Words$ with dimension $N \times d$, where N is the fixed length of a trace in the Transformer model process.

Positional Embedding. Since the Transformer relies solely on the attention mechanism, no positional information is included in the model. We adopt the formula proposed in [23] that can calculate the position information in the sequence. And the word order information is combined with the word vector to achieve the purpose of enhancing the input, so that the model has the position information. Moreover, the formula can be applied to sequences of arbitrary length.

For a method at position *pos* $(0 \leq pos < N)$ in the trace, a positional embedding vector PE with dimension d which is the same as the dimension of the word vector can be calculated using the following formula:

$$
\begin{aligned}
PE_{(pos,2i)} &= \sin \frac{pos}{1000^{\frac{2i}{d}}}, \\
PE_{(pos,2i+1)} &= \cos \frac{pos}{1000^{\frac{2i}{d}}}.
\end{aligned}
\tag{1}
$$

where i $(0 \leq i < d/2)$ is an integer, $PE_{(pos,2i)}$ and $PE_{(pos,2i+1)}$ calculate the value at $2i$ (even-numbered dimension) and $2i + 1$ (odd-numbered dimension) when the vector PE is at position *pos*. Positions of all methods in a trace also form a matrix PES with dimension $N \times d$. Then we obtain the true matrix representation of a trace by adding matrix $Words$ and PES.

Encoder Component. It is composed of multiple encoders, and each encoder contains a multi-head self-attention layer and feed forward layer. The multi-head self-attention layer contains multiple self-attention heads. When encoding a specific method in the input trace, a single self-attention head can help to view and calculate the degree of correlation with other methods in the trace. Multiple self-attention heads allow the model to focus on different aspects of information. By integrating all aspects of information obtained from all self-attention heads, more abundant information can be captured. The feed forward layer is mainly used for non-linear transformation.

Decoder Component. It is composed of multiple decoders. In addition to the multi-head self-attention layer and feed forward layer, there is a multi-head attention layer in each decoder. The attention layer associates a source trace with a target trace and calculates the correlation of each method in the target trace to each method in the source trace, where a source trace is an input sequence after being processed by the Encoder component, and a target trace is an output sequence composed of methods with the highest probability of occurrence in each prediction before.

Softmax Layer. The final output of the decoder component will be projected into a logits vector. Here, our model has learned N different methods from the trace set, so the logits vector is a vector of length N. Each cell corresponds to the score of a method. The softmax function turns the score into a probability. The cell with the highest probability is selected, and its corresponding method is used as the output of the round.

3.3   Trace Sampling

In order to improve the efficiency and reduce the cost of specification mining, we select a subset of traces that can represent the set of all traces. Intuitively, we look for the smallest trace subset which can cover all adjacent method pairs appearing in the set of all traces. For a trace $tr = \langle f_1, f_2, ..., f_n \rangle$, we call (f_i, f_{i+1}) $(1 \leq i < n)$ as the pair of methods appearing in trace tr.

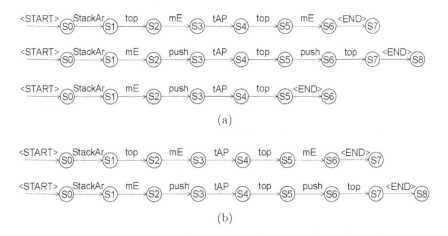

Fig. 7. (a) Set TR of three traces (b) Set TR' of two traces

Example 1. As shown in Fig. 7(a), there are 12 method pairs in set TR of three traces, namely $\{(\langle START \rangle, StackAr), (StackAr, mE), (mE, push), (push, tA$ $P), (tAP, top), (top, \langle END \rangle), (StackAr, top), (top, mE), (mE, tAP), (mE, \langle E$ $ND \rangle), (top, push), (push, top)\}$. Actually, set TR' of two traces in Fig. 7(b) contains the same method pairs as in Fig. 7(a). Therefore, we can reduce the three traces in Fig. 7(a) to the two traces in Fig. 7(b).

We use the same sampling strategy as DSM. To obtain a subset from all traces, we record the method pairs that appear in the set of all traces and the number of traces in which the method pair appears. From them, we select the method pair with the least number of traces and select the shortest one of the traces in which the method pair appears to be added to the subset of traces. Next, the method pair that does not exist in the trace subset and has the least number of traces appearing in the trace set is selected for a new round of sampling. Until the trace subset contains all method pairs in the execution trace.

Through the experiment, we found that the quality of the final model obtained by using all traces to extract feature values compared to using a subset of traces is very close, so a subset of traces can be extracted by considering the adjacency pairs.

3.4   Feature Extraction

In order to provide more information to the clustering algorithms, we take a combination of values of two types as the feature value. In this step, we take the trace subset obtained in Subsect. 3.3 and the Transformer model obtained in Subsect. 3.2 as input. First, each trace in the trace subset is preprocessed to an index sequence with a fixed length N. Then taking the index sequence and a predicted trace prefix $tr_o^i = \langle f_1', f_2', ..., f_i' \rangle$ as input of the Transformer model, a vector $P_{tr_o^i} = \langle P_{m_1}, P_{m_2}, ..., P_{m_k} \rangle$ containing the probability of each method m_r $(1 \leq r \leq k)$ appearing in the trace set being called after tr_o^i can be calculated. Further, logarithm processing is performed on each probability value in the vector to obtain the value of the first type $log(P_{tr_o^i})$ as shown in Table 1. The value of the second type $F_{tr_o^i} = \langle F_{m_1}, F_{m_2}, ..., F_{m_k} \rangle$ is determined by the position where each method m_r $(1 \leq r \leq k)$ appears in tr_o^i. If method m_r appears just one time at position j in tr_o^i, the value is j $(F_{m_r} = j)$; and if method m_r appears multiple times in tr_o^i, the average value of the multiple positions is chosen; otherwise, if method m_r does not appear in tr_o^i, the value is 0 $(F_{m_r} = 0)$.

Table 1. Feature values

Feature	Value
$log(P_{tr_o^i})$	$\langle log(P_{m_1}), log(P_{m_2}), ..., log(P_{m_k}) \rangle$, where $m_1, m_2, ..., m_k$ are all methods appearing in the trace set and P_{m_r} $(1 \leq r \leq k)$ is the probability that m_r is called after tr_o^i.
$F_{tr_o^i}$	$\langle F_{m_1}, F_{m_2}, ..., F_{m_k} \rangle$, where F_{m_r} $(1 \leq r \leq k)$ is the position at which method f_i' appears in tr_o^i.

Example 2. We perform feature extraction on the first trace shown in Fig. 7(b). If the predicted trace prefix is $tr_o^5 = \langle \langle START \rangle, StackAr, top, mE, tAP \rangle$, the probability of each method being called after tr_o^5 can be calculated using the trained Transformer model. Then by performing a logarithmic operation on the resulting probability, we can obtain the feature value of the first type. That is, $log(P_{\langle START \rangle}) = -2.0458$, $log(P_{StackAr}) = -1.0236$, $log(P_{top}) = -0.5237$, $log(P_{mE}) = -0.5557$, $log(P_{tAP}) = -1.8996$, $log(P_{push}) = -1.1884$, $log(P_{\langle END \rangle}) = -1.0809$.

Further, we calculate the feature value of the second type. According to the position of each method, and then obtain $F_{\langle START \rangle} = 1, F_{StackAr} = 2, F_{top} = 3, F_{mE} = 4, F_{tAP} = 5, F_{push} = F_{\langle END \rangle} = 0$. Therefore, the feature value of the current predicted trace prefix tr_o^5 is $\langle -2.0458, -1.0236, -0.5237, -0.5557, -1.8996, -1.1884, -1.0809, 1, 2, 3, 4, 5, 0, 0 \rangle$.

3.5   Cluster Analysis

In DSM, the authors use k-means and hierarchical clustering algorithms, but they need to determine a reasonable number of clusters k in advance. In addition, the random selection of k initial cluster center points in k-means also has a great impact on the clustering results. Therefore, in our work, we incorporate the dbscan clustering algorithm, which does not need to know the number of clusters. Moreover, dbscan can handle clusters of different sizes or shapes and is less susceptible to noise and outliers.

We cluster feature values obtained in Subsect. 3.4 by k-means, hierarchical and dbscan clustering algorithms and obtain $2 * (max\_clusters - 1) + 1$ FSAs, where $max\_clusters$ represents the maximum number of clusters that we set in advance. Both the k-means and hierarchical clustering algorithms generate $max\_clusters - 1$ FSAs, while the dbscan clustering algorithm generates 1 FSA. Figure 8 shows one FSA we obtained through a hierarchical clustering algorithm.

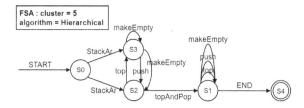

Fig. 8. An FSA obtained by hierarchical clustering algorithm

3.6   Model Selection

Precision and Recall are usually used to evaluate FSA and they can be defined as follows:

$$Precision(F) \overset{\text{def}}{=} \frac{|\ \mathbb{MP}_{TR}\ |}{|\ \mathbb{MP}_{TR} \cup fsa\_pairs(F)\ |} \tag{2}$$

where F is the evaluated FSA, $\mathbb{MP}_{TR}$ represents all method pairs appearing in the input trace set TR, and $fsa\_pairs(F)$ represents method pairs appearing in F. Note that we call a method pair (x, y) appears in F if x and y are labeled at two adjacent edges in F, respectively.

$$Recall \overset{\text{def}}{=} \frac{|\ accepted\_traces\ |}{|\ TR\ |} \tag{3}$$

where $|\ accepted\_traces\ |$ represents the number of traces that the generated FSA can accept, and $|\ TR\ |$ represents the number of all execution traces. Using just one of Precision or Recall to evaluate FSA cannot comprehensively evaluate the advantages and disadvantages of FSA. Higher Precision means an FSA can accept fewer traces that should not be accepted, while higher Recall means an

FSA can accept more traces that should be accepted. Thus, we combine Precision and Recall to obtain F_1-measure as the actual scoring criteria of FSA.

$$F_1 \stackrel{\text{def}}{=} 2 \times \frac{Precision \times Recall}{Precision + Recall} \tag{4}$$

4 Experiment

We have implemented the proposed approach in a tool named DSM-T and evaluated our approach to answer the following questions.

(1) How effective is DSM-T?
(2) How does DSM-T compare to existing specification mining algorithms?

4.1 DataSet

We use 11 target library classes to evaluate the effectiveness of DSM-T. These target classes have been studied in previous work [15–17].

Table 2. Target library classes

Target library class	M	Recorded method calls
ArrayList	18	22,996
LinkedList	7	4,847
HashSet	8	257,428
HashMap	11	67,942
Hashtable	8	89,811
Signature	5	205,386
Socket	21	130,876
ZipOutputStream	5	43,626
StringTokenizer	5	336,924
StackAr	7	132,826
NFST	5	95,149

Table 2 shows the information of all target library classes. Column "Target Library Class" lists the names of all target library classes. Column "M" represents the number of methods defined in the target class. Column "Recorded Method Calls" presents the number of recorded method calls in all execution traces of the target class.

In this benchmark, *ArrayList* is the implementation of a variable-size array of list interfaces. *LinkedList* is mainly used to create the data structure of the

linked list. *HashSet* implements the set interface, which does not allow dupli-
cate elements and does not guarantee the order of elements. *HashMap* is a hash
table, which stores key-value mapping, and has fast access speed. *Hashtable* is a
part of the original *java.util*, which is a concrete implementation of a dictionary.
The *Signature* class is used in Java to provide a digital signature algorithm for
applications. *Socket* class provides a rich set of network communication methods and properties. *Zipoutputstream* can write the content directly to the zip
package. *Stringtokenizer* class implements iterator and enumeration interface.
The above nine target class libraries are all from the Java development kit. In
addition, there are two other class libraries, *StackAr* from the Daikon project
and *NFST* which is short for *NumberFormatStringTokenizer* from Apache
Xalan.

4.2   Experience Setting

Table 3. F_1-measure (%): "CON++" is CONTRACTOR++, "SEKT 1" is State-
Enhanced 1-tail, "SEKT 2" is State-Enhanced 2-tail, "NFST" is NumberFormatString-
Tokenizer, "–" means that the result is not available.

Class	Tools							
	1-tail	2-tail	SEKT 1	SEKT 2	CON++	TEMI	DSM	DSM-T
ArrayList	13.96	13.13	36.03	13.86	13.07	16.87	22.21	78.63
LinkedList	27.15	25.72	86.02	26.67	24.52	7.51	30.98	88.66
HashSet	20.88	21.27	52.22	20.88	21.27	23.34	76.84	94.66
HashMap	25.41	8.71	68.94	–	–	–	86.71	98.49
Hashtable	42.39	33.58	92.78	–	–	–	79.92	96.11
Signature	61.54	64.25	66.88	62.05	63.98	39.06	100.00	100.00
Socket	35.89	31.52	55.15	34.73	28.37	–	54.24	93.01
ZipOutputStream	46.36	47.42	62.80	47.91	–	–	88.82	95.07
StringTokenizer	52.88	52.97	21.30	52.15	–	–	100.00	96.55
StackAr	16.54	16.54	34.91	16.54	16.54	–	74.38	94.19
NFST	24.57	25.52	30.40	24.56	25.78	11.80	77.52	89.09
Average	33.42	30.97	55.22	33.26	27.65	19.72	71.97	93.13

The experiments have been carried out on a 64-bit Ubuntu 18.04 LTS with a
3.20 GHz Intel(R) Core(TM) i7-8700 processor and 8 GB memory.

Transformer Model Constructs. We build the Transformer model in Ten-
sorFlow 1.15. For each target library class, we repeat the training 5 times, and
take the average of the 5 results as the final result. The encoder component and
the decoder component are composed of 8 encoders and 8 decoders, respectively.
The multi-head self-attention layer has 8 self-attention heads, and the multi-
head attention layer also has 8 attention heads. In the process of training the

model, we use dropout [13] to alleviate the occurrence of over-fitting, which has a regularization effect to a certain extent.

Clustering. In our tool DSM-T, we use clustering methods *KMeans*, *AgglomerativeClustering* and *DBSCAN* in the *sklearn.cluster* module of python to perform the clustering of feature values. In the experiments, we set the maximum number *max_clusters* of clusters to 20, and generate $2 * (max\_clusters - 1) + 1 = 39$ FSAs. In other words, for hierarchical clustering and k-means clustering algorithms, 19 FSAs are generated respectively, and the number of clusters ranges from 2 to 20.

4.3 Experiment Results and Analyses

We compare our tool DSM-T with DSM in [17] and four dynamic FSA inference techniques including k-tail [1], CONTRACTOR++ [15], SEKT [15] and TEMI [15]. K-tail $(k = 1, 2)$ represents traces-only strategy, which means that the model is only inferred from execution traces; CONTRACTOR++ stands for invariants-only strategy, indicating that it only infers the model from invariants; SEKT $(k = 1, 2)$ infers the model from execution traces and then uses invariants to enhance it; TEMI infers the model from invariants and then enhances it by execution traces.

Table 3 gives the experimental results on the benchmark. Column "Class" lists the names of all target library classes. Columns "1-tail", "2-tail", "SEKT 1", "SEKT 2", "CON++", "TEMI", "DSM" and "DSM-T" show the F_1-measure of the final FSA generated by each tool. The results show that for all library classes, 1-tail, 2-tail, SEKT 1, DSM and DSM-T can output the final FSAs, and SEKT 2, CON++ and TEMI fail on 2, 4 and 6 classes. On an average, our F_1-measure of the final FSAs can reach 93.13%, which improved by 21.16 % compared with the best performing tool DSM in the other 7 tools.

5   Related Work

In recent years, specification mining has received extensive attention. Some temporal specification mining techniques have been proposed, which can roughly be classified into two categories. One takes execution traces and predefined property templates [10–12, 19, 24–26] expressed in the temporal logic formula as input, and outputs properties that meet all execution traces. The other is to generate FSA-like models [5, 14, 15, 17], which can describe dynamic behaviors of entire systems.

5.1   Mining Properties Expressed in Temporal Logic Formulas

In the work of this category, every event type appearing in the property template is replaced by an event instance in execution traces to obtain a property instance, then it is checked whether all traces satisfy this property. If so, this property instance is output as the final property. Property templates are usually expressed in regular expressions, Linear Temporal Logic (LTL) [19], Propositional Projection Temporal Logic (PPTL) [26,27], and other custom formats.

Texada [19] can be used to extract specifications of arbitrary length and complexity in LTL. Texada takes the user-defined LTL property template and execution traces as input, and outputs a set of property instances. At the same time, Texada also supports properties with imperfect confidence. To do that, Texada provides two controls: confidence threshold and support threshold. Between them, the confidence threshold refers to the minimum proportion of the number of traces that satisfy the property instance to the total number of traces, and the support threshold refers to the minimum number of traces that satisfy the property instance.

Most of the existing research focuses on the specification of event sequences. Few technologies consider the actual duration between events, which is crucial in real-time systems. Eugene Asarin et al. [3] proposed a technique to mine property instances of execution traces that satisfy the given timed regular expressions (TRE) template, where TRE extends regular expressions by providing additional operators to specify timing constraints between events. At the same time, a timing automaton is synthesized for a given TRE. The timed automaton is then used as a checker to verify whether the traces meet the corresponding TRE.

5.2 Mining Properties Expressed in FSA-Like Model

The specification mining work of this category generates a model similar to FSA. Usually, an initial model is generated from execution traces. The initial model is then refined according to various methods to obtain the final model. Existing approaches often refine the initial model by the k-tail algorithm [20], the Contractor [7], or adding various restrictions to it [5,15].

The k-tail algorithm [1] was proposed in 1972 by A.W. Biermann and J.A. Feldman for automatic mining of software specifications from execution traces, and it is the basis for many techniques for mining FSA-based specifications. The existing k-tail algorithm merges each pair of states with the sequence of the next k identical calls (hence the term "k-tail").

Contractor [7] is an FSA-based model for describing software behavior based on program invariants, but it requires manually specified invariants. In order to be able to handle dynamically inferred invariants, Krka et al. improved it and built a new tool Contractor++ [15] which can process invariants inferred by Daikon and filter out invariants that are not meaningful.

Krka et al. [15] measured the impact of different types of input data on the quality of inferred FSA-based specification models and proposed four strategies for dynamically inferring FSA models. For the proposed strategy, new reasoning techniques SEKT and TEMI are implemented, so that different techniques correspond to different reasoning strategies and the experimental results of each technique are analyzed. Their experimental results show that although the precision of the generative model is higher, the recall is still at a lower level.

6   Conclusion

In this work, we improve Deep Specification Miner (DSM) and employ Transformer technology which is widely used in the NLP field to mine FSA-based specifications. We have evaluated our approach by conducting experiments on 11 target library classes and proven the effectiveness of our approach.

The biggest difference between our work and DSM is the use of the Transformer as a feature extractor for execution traces. The Transformer not only avoids the long-term dependency problem of the original work, but also enables to obtain the target region that needs to be focused on, and invest more resources in this region to obtain more details about the target that needs to be focused on. In addition, we use the location of the current method as a class of feature values in the feature extraction step, which not only distinguishes whether the current method has appeared in the method prefix, but also provides information about the location of the method. More information is provided for the subsequent steps. Then, in the clustering analysis stage, the clustering algorithms taken in the original paper need to determine the number of clusters in advance, and the optimal number of clusters is not the same for different data sets, so we added the dbscan clustering algorithm to use density as a criterion for clustering as well.

In the future, we plan to add likely invariant information to the specification model to further improve the accuracy of the model.

Acknowledgments. This research is supported by Hebei Natural Science Foundation under grant No. F2020201018, Science and Technology Research Project of Higher Education in Hebei Province under grant No. QN2021020 and Advanced Talents Incubation Program of the Hebei University under grant No. 521000981346.

References

1. Biermann, A.W., Feldman, J.A.: On the synthesis of finite-state machines from samples of their behavior. IEEE Trans. Comput. **100**(6), 592–597 (1972). https://doi.org/10.1109/TC.1972.5009015
2. Ammons, G., Bodík, R., Larus, J.R.: Mining specifications. ACM SIGPLAN Not. **37**(1), 4–16 (2002). https://doi.org/10.1145/565816.503275
3. Asarin, E., Caspi, P., Maler, O.: Timed regular expressions. J. ACM **49**(2), 172–206 (2002). https://doi.org/10.1145/506147.506151
4. Bahdanau, D., Cho, K., Bengio, Y.: Neural machine translation by jointly learning to align and translate. Comput. Sci. (2014)
5. Beschastnikh, I., Brun, Y., Schneider, S., Sloan, M., Ernst, M.: Leveraging existing instrumentation to automatically infer invariant-constrained models. In: SIGSOFT/FSE 2011; ACM SIGSOFT Symposium on Foundations of Software Engineering (2012). https://doi.org/10.1145/2025113.2025151
6. Bonato, M., Guglielmo, G.D., Fujita, M., Fummi, F., Pravadelli, G.: Dynamic property mining for embedded software. In: Jerraya, A., Carloni, L.P., Chang, N., Fummi, F. (eds.) Proceedings of the 10th International Conference on Hardware/Software Codesign and System Synthesis, CODES+ISSS 2012, Part of

ESWeek 2012 Eighth Embedded Systems Week, Tampere, Finland, 7–12 October 2012, pp. 187–196. ACM (2012). https://doi.org/10.1145/2380445.2380479

7. Caso, G.D., Braberman, V., Garbervetsky, D., Uchitel, S.: Automated abstractions for contract validation. IEEE Trans. Softw. Eng. **38**(1), 141–162 (2012)

8. Cicchello, O., Kremer, S.C.: Inducing grammars from sparse data sets: a survey of algorithms and results. J. Mach. Learn. Res. **4**(4), 603–632 (2003). https://doi.org/10.1162/153244304773936063

9. Ernst, M., Cockrell, J., Griswold, W.G., Member, IEEE: Dynamically discovering likely program invariants to support program evolution. IEEE Trans. Softw. Eng. **27**(2), 99–123 (2002). https://doi.org/10.1109/32.908957

10. Gabel, M.: Fully automatic mining of general temporal properties from dynamic traces. Proc. Fse (2008)

11. Gabel, M., Su, Z.: Online inference and enforcement of temporal properties. In: Proceedings of the 32nd ACM/IEEE International Conference on Software Engineering - vol. 1, ICSE 2010, Cape Town, South Africa, 1–8 May 2010 (2010). https://doi.org/10.1145/1806799.1806806

12. Gabel, M., Su, Z.: Symbolic mining of temporal specifications. In: ACM/IEEE International Conference on Software Engineering (2008). https://doi.org/10.1145/1368088.1368096

13. Hinton, G.E., Srivastava, N., Krizhevsky, A., Sutskever, I., Salakhutdinov, R.R.: Improving neural networks by preventing co-adaptation of feature detectors. Comput. Sci. **3**(4), 212–223 (2012). https://doi.org/10.9774/GLEAF.978-1-909493-38-4_2

14. Jian-Guang, F.U., Shengqi, L.I.: Mining program workflow from interleaved logs. research.microsoft.com (2010). https://doi.org/10.1145/1835804.1835883

15. Krka, I., Brun, Y., Medvidovic, N.: Automatically mining specifications from invocation traces and method invariants. ACM (2013). https://doi.org/10.1145/2635868.2635890

16. Le, T., Le, X., Lo, D., Beschastnikh, I.: Synergizing specification miners through model fissions and fusions (T). In: IEEE/ACM International Conference on Automated Software Engineering (2015). https://doi.org/10.1109/ASE.2015.83

17. Le, T., Lo, D.: Deep specification mining. ACM, pp. 106–117 (2018). https://doi.org/10.1145/3213846.3213876

18. Le, T.B., Bao, L., Lo, D.: DSM: a specification mining tool using recurrent neural network based language model. In: Leavens, G.T., Garcia, A., Pasareanu, C.S. (eds.) Proceedings of the 2018 ACM Joint Meeting on European Software Engineering Conference and Symposium on the Foundations of Software Engineering, ESEC/SIGSOFT FSE 2018, Lake Buena Vista, FL, USA, 04–09 November 2018, pp. 896–899. ACM (2018). https://doi.org/10.1145/3236024.3264597

19. Lemieux, C., Park, D., Beschastnikh, I.: General LTL specification mining (T). In: IEEE/ACM International Conference on Automated Software Engineering (2016). https://doi.org/10.1109/ASE.2015.71

20. Lorenzoli, D., Mariani, L., Pezzè, M.: Automatic generation of software behavioral models. In: ACM/IEEE International Conference on Software Engineering (2008). https://doi.org/10.1145/1368088.1368157

21. Peleg, H., Shoham, S., Yahav, E., Yang, H.: Symbolic automata for static specification mining. In: Logozzo, F., Fähndrich, M. (eds.) SAS 2013. LNCS, vol. 7935, pp. 63–83. Springer, Heidelberg (2013). https://doi.org/10.1007/978-3-642-38856-9_6

22. Shoham, S., Yahav, E., Fink, S.J., Pistoia, M.: Static specification mining using automata-based abstractions. IEEE Trans. Softw. Eng. **34**(5), 651–666 (2008). https://doi.org/10.1109/TSE.2008.63

23. Vaswani, A., et al.: Attention is all you need (2017). https://doi.org/10.5555/3295222.3295349

24. Weimer, W., Necula, G.C.: Mining temporal specifications for error detection. In: Halbwachs, N., Zuck, L.D. (eds.) TACAS 2005. LNCS, vol. 3440, pp. 461–476. Springer, Heidelberg (2005). https://doi.org/10.1007/978-3-540-31980-1_30

25. Yang, J., Evans, D., Bhardwaj, D., Bhat, T., Das, M.: Perracotta: mining temporal API rules from imperfect traces. In: ICSE (2006). https://doi.org/10.1145/1134285.1134325

26. Zhang, N., Yuan, X., Duan, Z.: Propositional projection temporal logic specification mining. In: Wu, W., Zhang, Z. (eds.) COCOA 2020. LNCS, vol. 12577, pp. 289–303. Springer, Cham (2020). https://doi.org/10.1007/978-3-030-64843-5_20

27. Zhang, N., Yu, B., Tian, C., Duan, Z., Yuan, X.: Temporal logic specification mining of programs. Theor. Comput. Sci. **857**, 29–42 (2021). https://doi.org/10.1016/j.tcs.2020.12.032

Dynamic Environment Simulation
for Database Performance Evaluation

Chunxi Zhang[1(✉)], Rong Zhang[2], and Kai Liu[1]

[1] Shanghai Stock Exchange, Shanghai 200000, China
{chxzhang,kliu}@sse.com.cn
[2] East China Normal University, Shanghai 200000, China
rzhang@dase.ecnu.edu.cn

Abstract. The wide popularity and the maturity of cloud platform promote the development of Cloud Native database systems. On-demand resource configuration or application is an attractive feature of cloud platforms, but its complexity in resource management challenges the benchmarking of database performance, which is no longer in a standalone test environment. Sharing or contending of resources aggravates the dynamics of environment, which can influence database performance much. In order to expose the real performance in production environment, environment simulation is prerequisite for benchmarking databases. Although Docker Containers have been promoted to isolate resources, we still cannot achieve the true resource isolation. In this paper, we first define four kinds of workload generators corresponding to the key environmental dimensions, then builds a multi-factor linear regression model to calculate the correlation among workloads, and finally designs an algorithm to simulate the dynamical changes of environment. It is the first work to provide a complete and dynamic simulation to environment. We conduct comprehensive experiments on the open source DBMSs by running the standard benchmarks to verify the effectiveness of our work.

Keywords: Simulation · Environment · Evaluation

1 Introduction

The wide popularity and the maturity of cloud platforms promote the development of Cloud Native software systems, since cloud has the advantages of manageability, scalability and elasticity. In the latest work [4,9], it has been mentioned that there are more and more businesses migrating from the private environment to the public cloud. Execution or processing of businesses/workloads can be deployed on the same cloud for parallel executions. Cloud providers charge users based on the on-demand resources. Though it is an attractive feature to service providers, it brings new challenges for software evaluations, because of its sharing or contending of resources among different softwares. Addtionally, in order to make full use of the cloud resources, resource providers usually sell more

© Springer Nature Switzerland AG 2022
Y. Aït-Ameur and F. Crăciun (Eds.): TASE 2022, LNCS 13299, pp. 238–255, 2022.
https://doi.org/10.1007/978-3-031-10363-6_17

quotients for larger profits, with the assumption that the intensity of workloads is usually lighter than the expectation. It then aggravates resource snatch and generates performance vibration.

In such a case, resource isolation is prerequisite to guarantee stable service quality, which is usually achieved by Virtual Machines (abbr. VMs) and Docker Containers (abbr. DCs) [3]. For each VM, resources are assigned in advance, while DCs compete for shared resources at runtime. VMs have higher startup overhead with all VMs launched at the beginning but DCs are lightweight without guest OS, which are launched when needed. Compared to VMs, DCs are more portable and efficient. But DCs can only provide the ability to package and run an application in a loose isolated environment, which is not a through solution due to the following reasons:

- Public resources, e.g., memory, processing unit or page cache, are shared among all DCs. Contention for resources and interference of actions become severer when using DCs by different applications.
- DCs are usually deployed on distributed nodes. Besides the resource consumed by each DC itself, distributed communication costs much more sharing bandwidth.

We run the standard YCSB workloads [6] on TiDB[1] on a four-node UCloud cluster[2], each of which is configured with 32 GB CPU cores, 128 GB Memory and 1 TB Disk. We set concurrency 100. When CPU is occupied more by TiDB, the throughputs increase obviously, shown in Fig. 1(a); when we set up more TiDB dockers, either the performance of the whole cluster All_TPS or the performance of each TiDB instance has become lower, shown in Fig. 1(b). So along with the development of cloud native softwares, traditional evaluation methods are challenged for its static or exclusive test environment requirement and the provided performance may deviate obviously from the results under in-production environment.

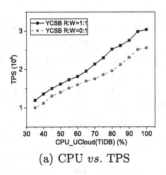

(a) CPU *vs.* TPS

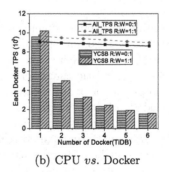

(b) CPU *vs.* Docker

Fig. 1. Database performance *vs.* Resources

[1] TiDB: https://pingcap.com/en/.
[2] UCloud: https://www.ucloud.cn/.

In production environment, resource consumption status (or environment status) is generated mainly by the following elements:

- Coexistence of different applications causes varied resource occupations, which can change dynamically.
- Complete isolation between applications is impossible. Snatch of Resource is violent, especially for intensive read or write workloads.
- Complex influence among different workloads makes it tough to simply count the resource requirement of an application.

How to model and simulate the open and dynamic production environment is useful for both cloud service providers and software developers, e.g. DB suppliers. For cloud service providers, they can optimize cloud resource configuration more reasonable considering both profit and service quality; for software developers, they can evaluate their products authenticity and support their resource application on the cloud platform. In this paper, we propose a workload generator for dynamic environment simulation. Firstly, we analyze and define four kinds of workload generators for four dimensions of resources, i.e., CPU, Memory, Disk IO and Network. Secondly, considering the resource consumption by each workload generator itself, we define a multi-order polynomial linear regression model to quantify the input of each workload. Then, we model the bi-impact between workloads. Finally, a dynamic environment status generation algorithm is proposed based on a multi-factor regression model. Comprehensive experiments are launched to demonstrate the effectiveness of our model.

The paper is organized as followings. In Sect. 2, we summarize the related work. In Sect. 3, we define four workload generators for environment. In Sect. 4, we design the workload association model and the dynamic environment simulation algorithm. In Sect. 5, we demonstrate the validity of our design through experiments and conclusions are made in Sect. 6.

2   Related Work

Migrating production environments from corporate-owned data centers to cloud-based services is becoming popular [4]. Traditional performance engineering methods of the development and delivery of software systems are challenged by the non-deterministic characteristics of cloud platform. In such an environment, the form and/or parameters of the target deployment environment cannot be controlled in advance. It brings the difficulty to diagnose the causes of performance issues during testing. It may be severe when highly variable workloads run on the target platform competing with each other for resources. Addtionally, to explore the cost-benefits of cloud services adequately, the execution performance of their applications should be reliably exploited. So it is mentioned that the credible peformance tuning should be launched in production environment. However, the black box nature of public clouds and the cloud usage costs has become a barricade along the way of performance evaluation for cloud application [7,9], which also leads to expensive parameter optimization [1]. And it is usually not a possible way to do performance testing on production platform. Specifically, in the domain of database performance debugging, slow queries are sensitive to the fluctuation of production environment [15]. It is obvious that simulation of production environment is critical to promote software systems to the cloud platform.

Environment simulation is to run a set of generated workloads to replicate the environment status, which is necessary for performance evaluation [13,14,16,17]. There are two ways to generate workloads [2]. One is defining an analytic approach, such as mathematical models, which can be parameterized to simulate the behaviors of users or the characteristics of specific workloads. The other one is to collecting the running traces and generate workloads according the running status. Currently, most of the simulation is based on the first way, i.e., to define an analytic task. In work [2], it proposes a workload generator which helps to benchmark database systems in an environment similar to the real world in terms of resource status. It creates Memory-bound, CPU-bound, and I/O-bound workloads seperately, which will be used to create a composite workload similar to real jobs running in practice. In ProWGen [5], it defines a workload generator by using mathematical models to simulate the feature of web page references for evaluating web proxy caches. Gismo [11] creates scalable request streams for benchmarking web streaming media delivery techniques. Considering the real workload characteristics, file access behaviours are modeled based on a user-oriented synthetic workload generator [12]. In [10], though it proposes to evaluate a DBMS by simulating its running environment, it does not consider the network resource or the bi-impact between resources. All these work simplifies the simulation to a single dimension, e.g., CPU, or a particular application. The simulation method cannot simulate the dynamicity of environment. Previous work usually define one kind of workload to control the consumption of system resources, which can not fully simulate the dynamicity and capture the complex intercorrelation of real application environment, i.e., resource status, by mathematical models. And the dynamic changes of resource status have not been captured yet. So in this paper, we provide an effective workload generator for dynamic resource status simulation, which can improve performance evaluation, help performance optimization and configure resource requirement.

3   Workload Generator Definition

First of all, we define four types of fundamenal workload generators corresponding to CPU, Memory, Disk IO and Bandwidth, shown in Table 1. These defined generators have the property of parameter sensitivity, and we can easily construct adpative workload composition model for simulating environment status. We define and implement the resource consumption workloads in different ways shown in Table 1.

There are two ways to generate the simulation workloads. One is to call the kernel operations in Operation System (OS), and the other one is to consume resources by means of software coding. We have found that both methods are

242   C. Zhang et al.

almost equally effective as shown in Fig. 2. We generate workloads to occupy 8% CPU, Memory and Disk resources respectively in different ways, i.e., Linux kernel function and software program. We demonstrate the performance discrepancy of MySQL by running the standard YCSB benchmark with R:W=1:1 and concurrency 60. Since there is no Linux kernel functions to control the usage of Network, so we do not compare the generation effect of Network here. We can see there are only slender performance difference in TPS (*transactions per second*) by taking two different ways to generate resource consumption. So in our design, considering the implementation simplicity, we define and implement the resource consumption workloads in different ways shown in Table 1.

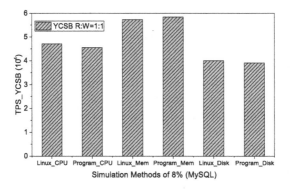

Fig. 2. Resource consumption with different simulation methods

Table 1. Simulation workloads

Category	Workload type	Method	Sensitive resource
CPU-bound	Java program	Multi-thread Π Calculation	**CPU**, Memory
Memory-bound	C++ program	Multi-thread string srray creation	**Memory**, CPU
IO-bound	Shell Script	Multi-thread file write	**Disk IO**, CPU
Network-bound	Java program	Netty	**Bandwidth**, CPU, Memory

In order to control the resource status in fine granularity, simulation workloads are defined from two dimensions. The first is the semantic dimension corresponding to the four categories shown in Table 1, i.e., CPU, Memory, Disk IO and Bandwidth. The second is the quantification dimension for subtle status simulation, which is realized by adjusting the parameters in workload generation functions.

3.1   Workload Generator Definition

CPU-Bound Workload: We define a computation intensive workload for CPU, i.e., Π *calculation* in Eq. 1. The intensity is controled by Gregory-Leibniz series based on n and the number of threads tn in calculation. The larger n or the bigger tn consumes more CPU resource. It is implemented by *Java*, which will consume memory to launch *Java* program.

$$\frac{\Pi}{4} = \sum_{n=0}^{\infty} \frac{(-1)^n}{2 \cdot n + 1} \tag{1}$$

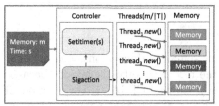

Memory-bound Workload

Fig. 3. Memory workload generation

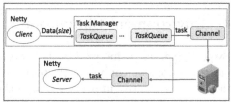

Network-bound Workload

Fig. 4. Network workload generation

Memory-Bound Workload: We define a multi-thread array space applying function by *new()* in *C++* program to control memory consumption as shown in Fig. 3. There is no contention for memory applying among threads T so as to avoid additional CPU resource consumption for space lock management. Considering the expect memory consumption m for a time period s, threads communicate with Linux signal function *Sigaction* to coordinate the execution time period set by *Setitimer*. Since this kind of software-based resource occupation also consumes CPU resource, each thread applies $m/\|T\|$ memory initially, which will be adjusted according to the global resource status considering the interaction among workloads.

IO-Bound Workload: We take Linux disk operation command *dd* for multi-thread disk IO operation, and the amount of IO, i.e., $io = \|T\| \cdot bs \cdot k$, is controlled by the number of threads $\|T\|$, the quantity $bs = size$ of each write and the total round of writing $count = k$ of each thread. We write default '0' to a file, e.g., $file_i$, by */dev/zero*. At the end of test, we erase the file $file_i$ by writing */dev/urandom*. Even though we call the kernel function for IO consumption, it has a positive impact to CPU for the involved calculation operation.

$$Write \ file : \# \ dd \ if = /dev/zero$$
$$of = file_i \ \ bs = size \ count = k;$$
$$Erase \ file : \# \ dd \ if = /dev/urandom \ \ of = file_i$$

Network-Bound Workload: Netty software[3] is programmed to generate network-bound workload as shown in Fig. 4. We first set the percentage of bandwidth usage, i.e., *size*; then we pack a string for each *TaskQueue* in Task Manager considering about the capacity (*iops=Input/Output Operations Per Second*) of each queue, and stream it to *Channel* continuously. Netty connects to the target server(s) in an non-blocking way to simulate data *dispatch/receive* actions. Java code is implemented to call Netty and calculate the size of data for transferring, so network-bound workload has impact on both CPU and Memory.

These workload generators do not exist isolatedly, and they may have impacts on each other as we have explained. For each generator, we list the affected resources in Table 1. These impaction will be catched and used to adjust the inputs (requirements) to our generators, which will be modeled in next section.

4　Environment Simulation

Even though we define workloads Ψ on four semantic dimensions, i.e., environment space E, we cannot easily produce the resource status isolatedly because they have interactive impacts on each other as shown in Table 1. For example, if we execute $\Pi calculation$ to consume CPU, it can not guarantee no consumption for other resources, e.g., memory, for even java program itself takes up memory. So directly assigning expect values, e.g. CPU usage, to generators can not generate the ideal environment status in a high probability. It may produce an environment deviation defined in **Definition 1** between the expected value and the generated value considering the mutual influence among simulation functions. Our purpose is to minimize the *devs* along all dimensions.

Definition 1 For an environment variable $e_i \in E$, given the expected value x_i and the generated value y_i by the generation function $\Psi_i \in \Psi$, **Environment Deviation** dev_i is defined as the deviation between x_i and y_i, i.e. $dev_i = \frac{\|x_i - y_i\|}{x_i}$ with $y_i = \Psi_i(x_i)$.

4.1　Workload Modeling on Each Individual Dimension

For a single dimension $e_i \in E$, considering its generation function Ψ_i, we formalize the environment status simulation as a multi-order polynomial linear regression problem defined by Eq. 2, with x_i, y_i as the observed and generated value for e_i, and α_j as the model parameter.

$$\begin{cases} \hat{y}_i & = \Psi_i(x_i) = \alpha_0 + \sum_{j=1}^{n} \alpha_j x_i^j \\ y_i & = \hat{y}_i + \epsilon_i \end{cases} \quad (2)$$

The generation problem can be achieved by minimizing ϵ_i, that is

$$\arg\min_{\alpha} dev_i(x_i) = \arg\min_{\alpha} \|y_i - \hat{y}_i\|$$

---

[3] Netty: https://netty.io/.

Supposing $x^0 = 1$, we then have $X^T \cdot X \cdot \alpha = X^T \cdot Y$ where $x[k]$ and $y[k]$ are the kth pair of training data on e_i.

$$X = \begin{pmatrix} 1 & x[1] & ... & x^n[1] \\ 1 & x[2] & ... & x^n[2] \\ ... & ... & ... & ... \\ 1 & x[m] & ... & x^n[m] \end{pmatrix}, \quad \alpha = \begin{pmatrix} \alpha_0 \\ \alpha_1 \\ ... \\ \alpha_m \end{pmatrix}, \quad Y = \begin{pmatrix} y[1] \\ y[2] \\ ... \\ y[m] \end{pmatrix}$$

Then for each environment dimension, we have its own multi-order regression function formulated by α, which does not care about the mutual influence among generators.

4.2 Modeling Environment by Learning Workload Interaction Among Dimensions

Bi-Impact Modeling Between Dimensions. In Eq. 2, it aims to simulate the resource consumption on an individual dimension. As we have explained that the four dimensions of environment status may have impacts on each other, represented by z. We then formulate this kind of impact from dimension e_i to the other one e_j by $\hbar_j(y_i)$ and the total impact for e_j is z_j defined in Eq. 3 with n as the order which is usually small and set by experiment.

$$\hat{z}_j(i) = \hbar_j(y_i) = \beta_0 + \sum_{k=1}^{n} \beta_k \cdot y_i^k; \quad \hat{z}_j = \sum_{i=1 \wedge i \neq j}^{4} (z_j(i)); \tag{3}$$

Considering the impact between the simulation workloads, we can learn all β parameter by solving $\underset{\beta}{\arg\min} \, dev_i(x) = \underset{\beta}{\arg\min} \| \hat{z}_j(i) - z_j(i) \|$.

Environment Status Generation Model. For simulating resource consumption status x_i on dimension e_i by our generator, considering the mutual influence of generators, i.e. Ψ, we get the expect input, i.e., y_i', usually $y_i' < x_i$. We can formalize the impact from dimensions other than e_i by:

$$\tilde{\Psi}_i(x_i) = \Psi_i(x_i - z_i) = y_i', \tag{4}$$

where z_i is the impact function from other dimensions. Given the resource status x_i on dimension e_i, we can calculate the corresponding input requirement y_i' by Eq. 4. But the formulation here is still based on the impacts from any two signle dimensions, which is not general enough to catch the complex interaction among dimensions.

Based the bi-impact mode in Eq. 4, we define the final environment simulation model catching the mutual impacts among different dimensions by defining a multi-factor linear regression model in Eq. 5. It guarantees to generate a consistent status on any dimension e_i considering the existence of all other three dimensions.

$$\Gamma_{i,\theta}(y') = \theta_0 + \sum_{i=1}^{4} \theta_i \cdot y_i' \tag{5}$$

For dimension e_i, we have the observed value x_i corresponding to input y_i'. In order to have a good fitting function, we optimize and minimize the cost function $J(\theta)$ as shown in Eq. 6.

$$\arg\min_{\theta} J(\theta) = \arg\min_{\theta} \frac{1}{2p} \sum_{k=1}^{p} (\Gamma_{i,\theta}(y'[k]) - x_i[k])^2, \tag{6}$$

p is the training data size, and $y'[k] \in Y'$ and $x_i[k] \in X_i$ are the kth pair of training data instances in Y' and X_i.

We take the stochastic gradient descent algorithm to resolve the parameters θ for each dimension as shown in Eq. 7.

$$\theta_i := \theta_i - \omega \cdot \frac{\partial J(\theta)}{\partial \theta_i}, \quad with \ i = 0...k.$$

$$:= \theta_i - \omega \cdot \frac{\partial \frac{1}{2p} \sum_{k=1}^{p} (\Gamma_{i,\theta}(y'[k]) - x_i[k])^2}{\partial \theta_i}$$

$$:= \theta_i - \omega \frac{1}{p} \sum_{k=1}^{p} \cdot (\Gamma_{i,\theta}(y'[k]) - x_i[k]) \cdot y_i'[k] \tag{7}$$

The iterative parameter generation algorithm is shown in Algorithm 1, which is controlled by θ and can stop early if the cost J_{old} is less than predefined value τ (line 21–24). θ is initialized to 1 on each dimension in line 3, which is calculated and updated by stochastic gradient descent algorithm in line 14–20. For each round of θ assignment, we can get the cost J_{old}. The algorithm will stop if it reaches the maximum number of iteration $iterNum$ or the cost is small enough compared to τ in line 22. In this algorithm, the time complexity is determined by the number of samples and the rounds of iterations, i.e. $O(p * iterNum)$.

Algorithm 1: MutiDimension Model

Input:

X_i, Y_i, Z_i:a set of training data set for dimension e_i, with X_i as the target environment status, Y_i as the input values for the workload generator and Z_i as bi-impacts from other dimension to e_i;

α: fitting parameters for environment simulation on the single dimension e_i in Equation 2;

β: fitting parameters for the bi-impact simulation from other dimensions to dimension e_i in Equation 3;

$iterNum$: the iterative number; ω: the step size for adjustment.

Output: θ: fitting parameter set for multiDimension model on e_i in Equation 5.

1 **multiDimensionModel**$(X_i, Y_i, Z_i, \alpha, \beta, iterNum, \omega)$
2 {
3   Initialize:
4     $\theta[\,] \leftarrow 1$; $J_{old} \leftarrow 0$;
5     $\Psi_i(X_i) = \alpha_0 + \sum_{j=1}^{n} \alpha_j \cdot X_i^j$;
6     $Z_j(i) = \hbar_j(Y_i) = \beta_0 + \sum_{j=1}^{n} \beta_j \cdot Y_i^j$;
7     $Y_i' = \Psi_i(X_i - Z_i)$;
8     $\theta = $ **gradientDescentMulti**$(X_i, Y_i', \theta, \omega, iterNum)$;
9 }
10 **gradientDescentMulti**$(X_i, Y_i', \theta, \omega, iterNum)$
11 {
12   $p \leftarrow size(X_i)$;
13   **for** $iter = 1 : iterNum$ **do**
14     $temp[\,] = zeros(size(\theta))$;
15   **for** $j = 1 : size(\theta)$ **do**
16       $temp[j] == \theta_j - \omega \frac{1}{p} \sum_{k=1}^{p} \cdot (\Gamma_{i,\theta}(Y'[k]) - X_i[k]) \cdot Y_i'[k]$;
17   **end**
18   **for** $j = 1 : size(\theta)$ **do**
19       $\theta[j] = temp[j]$;
20   **end**
21   calculate cost J_{old};
22   **if** $J_{old} <= \tau$ **then**
23   break;
24   **end**
25   **end**
26 }

4.3 Dynamic Environment Simulation

Environment may keep changing along the time. In Algorithm 2, we show the simulation of dynamic environment changing. Inputs X, Y and Z are four dimensional arrays with each dimension corresponding to one type of resource, e.g., e_d. A, B and Θ are metrices sized $4 \times (n+1)$ with n as the parameter size and each row, e.g., A_d, corresponds to the model paramters for environment dimension e_d, i.e., $\alpha_d, \beta_d,$ and θ_d in $learnParameter$ ($line\ 14$–18) with $\|\alpha_d\| = n$, $\|\beta_d\| = n$ and $\|\theta_d\| = n$. Supposing we have a list of environment changing time points in $\hat{T}$, between which are the stable time periods for the environment status, we have the simulation targets O. For each time period $\hat{t} \in \hat{T}$, according to the target resource comsumption $o_d \in O$, i.e., x in Eq. 4, it simulates the input y_d, i.e., y' in Eq. 4, for our generator, which is put into $\hat{Y}_d$ ($line\ 4$–9). Our final generator inputs are stored in $\hat{Y}$.

Algorithm 2: Dynamic Environment Status Simulation

Input:
X, Y, Z: a set of training data, with X as the target environment status,
Y as the input values for workload generators and Z as bi-impacts
between any two dimensions;
$\hat{T}$: the set of inflexion points of environment status;
O: the target environment status;
$iterNum$: the iterative number; ω: the step size for adjustment.
Output: $\hat{Y}$: the generated environment status.

1 **DynamicEnvironmentGeneration**$(X, Y, Z, O, \hat{T}, iterNum, \omega)$
2 {
3   θ=**learnParameter**$(X, Y, Z, iterNum, \omega)$;
4 **for** each dimension e_d **do**
5   **for** each time period $\hat{t}$ in $\hat{T}$ **do**
6        $y_d = \theta_{(d,0)} + \sum_{i=1}^{4} \theta_{(d,i)} \cdot o_d$;
7        $\hat{Y}_d \leftarrow y_d$;
8   **end**
9     $\hat{Y} \leftarrow \hat{Y}_d$;
10 **end**
11 Return $\hat{Y}$;
12 }
13
14 **learnParameter**$(X, Y, Z, iterNum, \omega)$ {
15    $A \leftarrow$ **individualDimensionModel**(X, Y);
16    $B \leftarrow$ **bi-impactModel**(Y, Z);
17    $\Theta \leftarrow$ **multiDimensionModel**$(X, Y, Z, A, B, iterNum, \omega)$;
18 }

---

5   Experiment Results

Experimental Setting: Our experiments are conducted on 4 nodes configured in RAID-5 on CentOS v.6.5. Each node is equipped with 2 Intel Xeon E5-2620 @ 2.13 GHz CPUs, 130GB memory and 3 TB HDD disk. Nodes are connected using 1 Gigabit Ethernet. We deploy a centralized DB, i.e., MySQL ($v.5.6.28$) and a distributed DB, TiDB ($v.4.0.0$) on different environment status which are simulated by different workloads to verify the effectiveness of our work.

Baseline: We take *Jeong* [10] as the comparison baseline. It simulates CPU, Memory, and Disk I/O consumptions without Network. *Jeong* defines a computation intensive task to simulate CPU usage define as *the number of CPU × CPU Clock Speed (MHz) × System Clock Speed (MHz) × Correction Factor. Correction Factor* is used to adjust CPU consumption considering the possible interaction from other computer actions, if any. It occupies memory by using a multithread data reading from disk into memory with the number of threads set to 5. For Disk IO simulation, it assigns a branch of threads to write the queued small files to disk parallelly.

Workloads: In different environment, we run two representative workloads shown in Table 2 on MySQL and collect the real performance. By simulating the running environment, we also collect the simulated performance data from MySQL, which is compared with the real performance. According to TPC-C requirement, we set the number of warehouses is equal to the execution thread numbers. The threshold for cost is $\tau = 1e - 6$.

Table 2. Benchmark workloads

Database	Workload	Transaction ratio	Concurrecy
MySQL	TPC-C	New-Order: Payment: Order-Status: Delivery: Stock-Level = 45:43:4:4:4	20
			60
	YCSB	Write:Read=1:1	30
			60
			120

5.1 Environment Workload Demonstration

We first demonstrate the effectiveness of workload generators for environment simulation on each dimension. When we simulate one dimension, we clear all operations on other dimensions. For each dimension e_i, we randomly generated $1K$ groups of workloads, i.e. y_i, and executed to get the real workload , i.e. x_i, and the impact on other dimension z_i, which are used to learn the parameters α, β and θ.

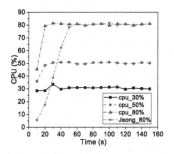

Fig. 5. CPU consumption generation

CPU-Bound Workload. Supposing we have the target CPU consumption set to 30%, 50% and 80%, by controling the complexity, i.e., n, Π calculation can reach to our targets by 20s shown in Fig. 5. The deviations between the simulations and the targets are small, among which the biggest is less than 1%. In our experiment, we find that Π calculation has no requirement to *Disk* or *Network Bandwidth* but has a little requirement to *Memory*, less than 1%. Though *Jeong* can have almost the result as we do by taking almost 2× more time, its generation is adjusted by *Correction Factor* which has lower adjustion efficiency than our model.

Memory-Bound Workload. We keep applying space for an array to consume Memory. The array can be filled by a multi-thead mode. Supposing we have the target memory consumption set to 30%, 50% and 80%. For 80% memory consumption, we take both the two-thread generation mode, i.e., $Memory\_2\_80\%$ and the single-thread generation mode, i.e., $Memory\_1\_80\%$. It is easy to see that the small memory required, the faster to reach the target Fig. 6(a). For 30% and 50% memory consumption requirements, it needs only less than 5s to reach the targets in a single-thread mode. For 80% memory consumption, though $Memory\_2\_80\%$ is 2× faster than $Memory\_1\_80\%$ to occupy memory, its CPU consumption is 2× higher as shown in Fig. 6(b). By running our workload to generate memory environment, CPU is also comsumed, usually less than 6% in total by the single thread mode as shown in Fig. 6(b). *Jeong* reads data from disk is slower than our method to generate the same size of memory consumption and also costs much more CPU resources shown in Fig. 6.

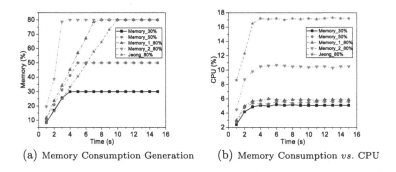

(a) Memory Consumption Generation   (b) Memory Consumption *vs.* CPU

Fig. 6. Memory consumption

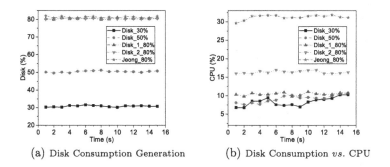

(a) Disk Consumption Generation   (b) Disk Consumption *vs.* CPU

Fig. 7. Disk IO consumption

IO-Bound Workload. We keep writing data to Disk by using a Linux disk operation command *dd* in a multi-thread mode, and CPU is used to calculate for adusting writing speed. Supposing IO consumptions are set to 30%, 50% and 80%. As shown in Fig. 7(a), we can see that both our method and *Jeong* can reach the target setting very soon, around 1s, but the CPU consumption by our generator is much smaller than that by *Jeong*. *Jeong* takes the software program method to simuate disk consumption in a multi-thread mode and each thread shall maintain a queue for managing the writing files, which costs additional more CPU resources. Our method can write the required size of data directly without managing any files in advance. *Jeong* then has 2× higher CPU usages than our multi-thread generation mode, i.e., $Disk\_2\_80\%$. Our additional CPU consumption is bound by 10% in a single-thread mode as shown in Fig. 7(b). Since we do not keep any data in memory, the additional memory consumption is only about 0.1%, which is insignificant in simulation.

Network-Bound Workload. Bandwidth consumption is simulated by Netty. We control the bandwidth consumption by adjusting the number of transmission per second, i.e., *iops* and the data size for transmission. Supposing we have the bandwidth occupation set to 30%, 50% and 80% as shown in Fig. 8, it is easy to reach our target environment by around 1s as shown in Fig. 8(a). Since it has high uncertainty on cluster network, the adjustion calculation costs more CPU than the other workloads, which is between 7% − 15% as shown in Fig. 8(b).

Summarization. According to these experiments, we can see that 1) worload generator usually has an interaction with each other; 2) our simulation method is more efficient than *Jeong* which does not provide simulation to Network.

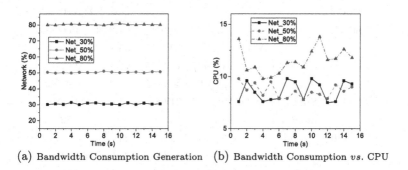

(a) Bandwidth Consumption Generation (b) Bandwidth Consumption *vs.* CPU

Fig. 8. Bandwidth consumption

5.2 Environment Simulation

Based on the bi-impact between workloads, we bulid the final simulation model in Eq. 5. We compare the simulated environment, i.e., *GeneValue* with the real environment, i.e., *RealValue*, by *deviation* defined in Eq. 8 on the four dimensions with 100 groups of test data. The deviations for CPU, Memory, Disk IO and Network are 3.78%, 1.46%, 3.73% and 2.96%, respectively. It means that our model is effective in environment simulation.

$$deviation = \frac{|RealValue - GeneValue|}{RealValue} \tag{8}$$

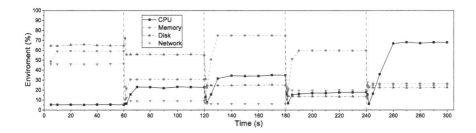

Fig. 9. Fitting lines for dynamic environment simulation

Dynamic Simulation of Environment. We generate 5 groups of resource consumption requirements randomly, and each group of resouce status will last for 60s. So we have 300s running environment status in total as shown in Table 3. Our model can simulate each group of resource consumption very well bound by 5% deviation. In Fig. 9, it shows the effectiveness of our workload generation model considering the dynamic changes at the time points of 60s, 120s, 180s and 240s segmented by the dashed red lines. We can see that our model can reach the simulation targets, i.e. corresponding to the changes, in 10s.

Table 3. Deviation for dynamic environment simulation

Period(s)		CPU	Memory	Disk IO	Network
0–60	Target	5.35%	58.91%	64.34%	45.69%
	SimulatedValue	5.41%	59.56%	65.17%	46.64%
	deviation	1.1%	1.1%	1.3%	2.1%
60–120	Target	22.74%	30.69%	55.07%	8.94%
	SimulatedValue	23.02%	31.08%	55.63%	9.18%
	deviation	1.24%	1.27%	1.1%	2.72%
120–180	Target	34.44%	74.68%	24.15%	6.15%
	SimulatedValue	34.87%	75.6%	24.95%	6.31%
	deviation	1.27%	1.22%	3.3%	2.5%
180–240	Target	17.85%	59.7%	13.65%	19.55%
	SimulatedValue	17.37%	60.32%	13.81%	19.93%
	deviation	−2.6%	1.03%	1.18%	1.98%
240–300	Target	67.62%	26.3%	22.21%	24.64%
	SimulatedValue	68.41%	26.62%	22.69%	25.13%
	deviation	1.16%	1.22%	2.17%	2.01%

Environment Simulation Based on Real Applications. We launch YCSB and TPC-C workloads generated by OLTP-Bench [8] on MySQL by varying access thread sizes (60 and 120 for YCSB, 20 and 60 for TPC-C) and collect four groups of resource consumption status by nmon[4]. Since environment is not stable along with the running of benchmark workloads, for each benchark, we monitor and collect its resource consumption every 2s, and calculate the average resouce status for simulation. The simulation *deviation* is shown in Table 4, among which the *deviation* between *GeneValue* and *RealValue* is bound by 5%.

Table 4. Environment simulation on real applications

No.	Workload		CPU	Memory	Disk IO	Network
G1	$YCSB^{60}$	Target	62.51%	4.16%	19.68%	5.4%
		SimulatedValue	63.92%	4.21%	20.35%	5.51%
		deviation	2.25%	1.2%	3.4%	5.51%
G2	$YCSB^{120}$	Target	71.65%	4.34%	18.98%	9.6%
		SimulatedValue	72.92%	4.38%	19.53%	9.15%
		deviation	1.7%	1%	2.89%	−4.6%
G3	$TPC\text{-}C^{20}$	Target	23.95%	5.34%	31.28%	3.1%
		SimulatedValue	24.52%	5.40%	32.85%	3.21%
		deviation	2.37%	1.12%	5.0%	3.5%
G4	$TPC\text{-}C^{60}$	Target	27.83%	9.61%	32.54%	3.56%
		SimulatedValue	29.03%	9.87%	31.03%	3.61%
		deviation	4.31%	2.7%	−4.6%	1.4%

5.3   Evaluation on Database

In order to demonstrate the effectiveness of our simulation model, we run two database services on YCSB and TPC-C benchmarks concurrently shown in Table 5. We have four groups of experiments, i.e., $G1 - G4$. In each group, the two sets of experiments are launched on $YCSB$ and $TPC\text{-}C$ acting as an environment generator and a service provider mutually. And the *IdeaValue* is generated by running workloads exclusively on our cluster. For example, in $G1$, when we launch 30 threads to run $YCSB$, i.e., $YCSB^{30}$, it consumes resources on our cluster; when we run $TPC\text{-}C$ by 20 threads simultaneously, i.e., $TPC\text{-}C^{20}$, the impact from $YCSB^{30}$ makes $TPC\text{-}C^{20}$ low down its performance from its ideal TPS=1342 to 881. If we take our simulation model to simulate the resource consumed by $YCSB^{30}$, the TPS for $TPC\text{-}C^{20}$ is 816 with the *deviation*=7.37% compared to the target 881. Similarly, if $TPC\text{-}C^{20}$ acts as an environment generator, $YCSB^{30}$ lowers down its performance from ideal TPS=39428 to 28778; and if we simulate the environment from $TPC\text{-}C^{20}$, the performance of $YCSB^{30}$ lows down by 7.03% to 26754. In Table 6, we run TPC-C^{30} on distibuted TiDB deployed on four nodes. On each node we run the YCSB workloads with different concurrency, i.e., 10-40 to generate the running environment for TiDB.

---

[4] nmon: http://nmon.sourceforge.net/pmwiki.php?n=Main.HomePage.

We take the environment simulation model to simulate the resource consumption by YCSB on MySQL and then run TPC-C^{30} on TiDB again. We can find the the performance deviation for TiDB is only 5.34%. So our simulation model can simulate the environment well for the applications which may coexist with others.

Table 5. Performance deviation for benchmark workloads on MySQL

No.	Workload	IdeaValue		TPS	Workload	IdeaValue		TPS
G1	$YCSB^{30}$	39482	Target	28778	$TPC\text{-}C^{20}$	1342	Target	881
			GeneValue	26754			GeneValue	816
			deviation	7.03%			*deviation*	7.37%
G2	$YCSB^{30}$	39482	Target	24856	$TPC\text{-}C^{60}$	1546	Target	965
			GeneValue	23595			GeneValue	917
			deviation	5.07%			*deviation*	4.97%
G3	$YCSB^{60}$	52254	Target	37788	$TPC\text{-}C^{20}$	1342	Target	652
			GeneValue	36094			GeneValue	616
			deviation	4.48%			*deviation*	5.52%
G4	$YCSB^{60}$	52254	Target	32546	$TPC\text{-}C^{60}$	1546	Target	765
			GeneValue	30557			GeneValue	716
			deviation	6.11%			*deviation*	6.41%

Table 6. Performance deviation for benchmark workloads on TiDB

Environment generator	Workload	Test DB	Workload	Performance (TPS)
$MySQL_{N1}$	$YCSB^{10}$	TiDB	TPC-C^{30}	target = 712
$MySQL_{N2}$	$YCSB^{20}$			GeneValue = 674
$MySQL_{N3}$	$YCSB^{30}$			deviation = 5.34%
$MySQL_{N4}$	$YCSB^{40}$			

6   Conclusion

In our work, we present a workload generator for environment simulation. We define a multi-order polynomial linear regression model for each resource, and consider the influence of workload of each resource on resources. Then, we design a multi-factor linear regression model to reflect the impaction among workload generators. We launch a comprehensive set of experiments to verify the effectiveness of the model based on micro and macro evaluations.

References

1. Bao, L., Liu, X., Wang, F., Fang, B.: ACTGAN: automatic configuration tuning for software systems with generative adversarial networks. In: Proceedings of the ASE, pp. 465–476. IEEE (2019)

2. Barford, P., Crovella, M.: Generating representative web workloads for network and server performance evaluation. In: Proceedings of the ACM SIGMETRICS, pp. 151–160 (1998)
3. Bhimani, J., et al.: Docker container scheduler for I/O intensive applications running on NVMe SSDs. IEEE Trans. Multi-Scale Comput. Syst. **4**(3), 313–326 (2018)
4. Bondi, A.B.: Challenges with applying performance testing methods for systems deployed on shared environments with indeterminate competing workloads: position paper. In: Proceedings of the ACM/SPEC, pp. 41–44 (2016)
5. Busari, M., Williamson, C.: ProWGen: a synthetic workload generation tool for simulation evaluation of web proxy caches. Comput. Netw. **38**(6), 779–794 (2002)
6. Cooper, B.F., Silberstein, A., Tam, E., Ramakrishnan, R., Sears, R.: Benchmarking cloud serving systems with YCSB. In: Proceedings of the ACM SoCC, pp. 143–154 (2010)
7. Diamantopoulos, D., Hagleitner, C.: HelmGemm: managing GPUs and FPGAs for transprecision GEMM workloads in containerized environments. In: Proceedings of the ASAP, vol. 2160, pp. 71–74. IEEE (2019)
8. Difallah, D.E., Pavlo, A., Curino, C.: OLTP-Bench: an extensible testbed for benchmarking relational databases. Proc. VLDB Endow. **7**(4), 277–288 (2013)
9. He, S., Manns, G., Saunders, J., Wang, W., Pollock, L., Soffa, M.L.: A statistics-based performance testing methodology for cloud applications. In: Proceedings of the ESEC and SFSE, pp. 188–199 (2019)
10. Jeong, H.J., Lee, S.H.: A workload generator for database system benchmarks. In: Proceedings of the iiWAS, pp. 813–822. Citeseer (2005)
11. Jin, S., Bestavros, A.: GISMO: a generator of internet streaming media objects and workloads. ACM SIGMETRICS Perform. Eval. Rev. **29**(3), 2–10 (2001)
12. Kao, W.-I., Iyer, R.K.: A user-oriented synthetic workload generator. In: Proceedings of the ICDCS, pp. 270–271. IEEE Computer Society (1992)
13. Kerr, J., Reddy, P., Kosti, S., Izzetoglu, K.: UAS operator workload assessment during search and surveillance tasks through simulated fluctuations in environmental visibility. In: Schmorrow, D.D., Fidopiastis, C.M. (eds.) HCII 2019. LNCS (LNAI), vol. 11580, pp. 394–406. Springer, Cham (2019). https://doi.org/10.1007/978-3-030-22419-6_28
14. Li, Y., Zhang, R., Yang, X., Zhang, Z., Zhou, A.: Touchstone: generating enormous query-aware test databases. In: Proceedings of the USENIX ATC, pp. 575–586 (2018)
15. Ma, M., et al.: Diagnosing root causes of intermittent slow queries in cloud databases. Proc. VLDB Endow. **13**(8), 1176–1189 (2020)
16. Schäfer, D., Edinger, J., Breitbach, M., Becker, C.: Workload partitioning and task migration to reduce response times in heterogeneous computing environments. In: Proceedings of the ICCCN, pp. 1–11. IEEE (2018)
17. Tabebordbar, A., Beheshti, A., Benatallah, B., Barukh, M.C.: Feature-based and adaptive rule adaptation in dynamic environments. Data Science and Engineering **5**(3), 207–223 (2020). https://doi.org/10.1007/s41019-020-00130-4

Extending SysML with Refinement and Decomposition Mechanisms to Generate Event-B Specifications

Racem Bougacha[1], Régine Laleau[2](✉) ⓘ, Simon Collart-Dutilleul[3], and Rahma Ben Ayed[1]

[1] Institut de Recherche Technologique Railenium, 59300 Famars, France
{racem.bougacha,rahma.ben-ayed}@railenium.eu
[2] Univ Paris Est Creteil, LACL, 94010 Creteil, France
laleau@u-pec.fr
[3] COSYS-ESTAS, Univ Gustave Eiffel, 59650 Villeneuve d'Ascq, France
simon.collart-dutilleul@univ-eiffel.fr

Abstract. SysML, dedicated to system design, provides graphical models. One of the strengths of these graphical models is that they can be validated by domain experts. However, the semantics of SysML is given in natural language, which does not allow formal and rigorous reasoning necessary for critical systems for which safety and security are major concerns. Our project aims at modeling and verifying high-level architectures of critical complex systems, in particular railways systems, that must be validated by domain experts. For that, we propose to combine SysML and the Event-B formal method. To master the complexity of such systems, Event-B provides refinement and decomposition mechanisms that allow a step-by-step design and make proofs easier to discharge. This paper proposes to extend SysML with safety relevant Event-B mechanisms that enable an automatic translation from SysML diagrams to Event-B specifications. We focus on diagrams that facilitate high-level architecture design, namely package, block-definition, state-transition and sequence diagrams.

Keywords: SysML · Formal specification · Event-B method · High-level architecture · Model transformation

1 Introduction

Complex systems such as information technology systems, railways systems, air traffic control, and other cyber-physical systems, are composed of a set of subsystems. They generally are heterogeneous in that they integrate various kinds of components as mechanical, electronic, or software components. Therefore their design requires the collaboration of domain experts and the use of a common language to communicate with each other to build a consistent model. Moreover

© Springer Nature Switzerland AG 2022
Y. Aït-Ameur and F. Crăciun (Eds.): TASE 2022, LNCS 13299, pp. 256–273, 2022.
https://doi.org/10.1007/978-3-031-10363-6_18

their design depends on solutions that can address interplay between their subsystems. Then complex systems should be represented as a layered hierarchy of sub-systems and a model of high-level architectures supporting a layered hierarchy is needed. Such a high-level architecture must enable the specification of the main functional elements of a system, together with its interfaces and interactions. It constitutes a framework common to all the domain experts involved in the design of the system.

Our work is part of the the Autonomous Freight Train (AFT) project under the Autonomous Train program [2]. A recent study of technological efforts concerning the use of formal methods in railways performed in 2017 [3] concludes by claiming: "This analysis has shown a dominance of the UML modeling language for high-level representation of system models ...". However, the semantics of UML is given in natural language, which does not allow formal and rigorous reasoning necessary for critical systems for which safety and security are major concerns. The use of formal methods is thus recommended and the study also claims that "this analysis has shown a large variety of formal tools used, with a dominance of the tools associated to the B family". This is reaffirmed in [11].

Our work aims at modeling and verifying High-Level Architectures (HLA) of critical complex systems, in particular railways systems, that must be validated by domain experts. For that, we propose to combine SysML [22] and the Event-B [5] formal method. We prefer using SysML rather than UML since SysML offers a set of concepts more relevant to model systems and is recommended by the AFT project partners. Indeed, the AFT project reuses the RailTopoModel[1] that contains a SysML-based functional ontology of a railway infrastructure. Moreover, the European initiative EULYNX[2] has defined a standard SysML-based model of railways signalling system components.

To master the complexity of such systems, Event-B provides refinement and decomposition mechanisms that allow a step-by-step design and make proofs easier to discharge. This paper proposes to extend SysML with safety relevant Event-B mechanisms that enable an automatic translation from SysML diagrams to Event-B specifications. We focus on diagrams that facilitate high-level architecture design, namely package, block-definition, state-transition and sequence diagrams.

The remainder of the paper is organized as follows. Section 2 briefly describes SysML and Event-B. This is followed by a presentation of the proposed SysML extensions in Sect. 3. Section 4 presents an illustration of the SysML extensions on a case study. Section 5 describes a set of rules that allows to automatically generate Event-B specifications from the SysML extensions. Section 6 discusses the related work. Finally, Sect. 7 reports our conclusions and presents future work.

---

[1] http://www.railtopomodel.org/en/. It is a standard for the representation of railway infrastructure-related data.

[2] https://www.eulynx.eu/.

2   Background

2.1   SYSML

Systems Modeling Language (SYSML) [15, 22] is a modeling language for systems engineering applications. SYSML, a UML profile, is used in system engineering whereas UML is more appropriated to software engineering. SYSML is composed of nine types of diagrams. Over these diagrams, in HLA graphical modeling, we are interested in package, block definition, state machine and sequence diagrams. In the following we give the SYSML concepts of these diagrams that we need to model HLAs.

Package diagram is a static structural diagram that shows the relationships among packages and their contents. It allows to group the structures of a model and defines high level relationships between these groupings. This diagram encompasses two main elements: "Package" representing a graphical node and "Dependency" representing a graphical path that links different packages and how they depend on each other. Note that the semantics of "Dependency" is very informal and can be adapted for particular needs. A "Package" element is made up of a number of "Packageable elements". In SYSML, almost any element can be enclosed within a package. In HLA modeling, we are interested in "Block", "State-machine", "Sequence diagram" packageable elements and in "Package" itself which is also a packageable element and thus can contain other packages.

A Block Definition Diagram (BDD) is a structural diagram. As HLA is represented as a set of system/sub-systems layered hierarchy we are only interested in basic modeling elements of this diagram. These two basic elements are "Block" and "Relationship". A "Block" defines a collection of features used to describe a system, sub-system, component or other system elements. A "Relationship" relates together one or more blocks. It participates in describing the structure of a system, sub-system or component. In SYSML block relationships encompass many types of links. To model HLAs, we are interested in two types of relationships: "Association" and "Composition". These concepts come from UML class diagrams, with the same semantics. The extract of BDD meta-model, used for HLA modeling, is presented in Fig. 1.

To model the behavior of a block, a state machine diagram is used. Such a diagram is composed of two basic elements: states and transitions. It describes the state changes of a block instance during its life cycle. These changes are triggered by events associated to the transitions of the diagram. We have extracted all the concepts of SYSML state-machine diagrams that we need to model HLAs. They are presented in the meta-model of Fig. 2.

To display the interactions between users, objects, systems and entities within the system, a sequence diagram is used. We will detail this diagram in Sect. 3.2.

2.2   Event-B

EVENT-B [5] is a formal method to specify discrete systems based on mathematical notations, predicate logic and set theory. An EVENT-B specification is com-

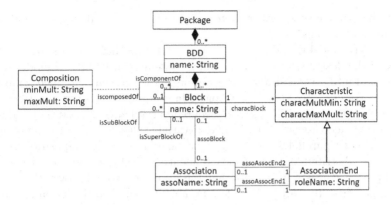

Fig. 1. SYSML BDD meta-model

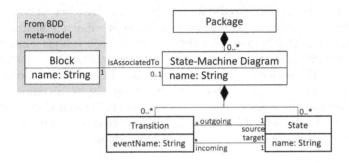

Fig. 2. SYSML state-machine diagram meta-model

posed of two main elements which are "Machines" and "Contexts". A "Machine" represents the dynamic part of the model and it specifies the behavioral properties of the system by variables and a set of events composed of guards and actions. The possible values that the variables hold are restricted using an invariant . The guard of an event is a condition that must be satisfied for the event to be triggered and the action describes the update of state variables. Proof obligations are generated to verify that the execution of each event maintains the invariant. A "Context" contains the static part of the model and it can be seen by machines. EVENT-B is based on two main mechanisms to master the complexity of a system which are refinement and model decomposition.

Refinement is a process that allows to gradually introduce the different parts that constitute the system starting from an abstract model to a more concrete one. It is applied to enrich or modify a model in order to augment its functionalities. A machine refinement consists in adding new variables and/or replacing existing variables by new ones. Events can be refined and new ones can be introduced. The refinement of an event has to verify that the guard of the refined event should be stronger than the guard of the abstract one and the effect of the refined action should be stronger than the effect of the abstract one. A context can also be extended with other contexts by adding new modeling elements (sets, constants and axioms).

EVENT-B model decomposition is a powerful mechanism to scale the complexity of the design of large and complex systems. An EVENT-B model can be decomposed into several simple sub-components which can be refined separately and more comfortably than the whole. Many approaches allow to decompose an EVENT-B model, particularly, the shared-variable decomposition [4] and the shared-event decomposition [13]. Shared-variable decomposition is suitable for shared memory parallel systems, whereas shared-event decomposition is more suitable for distributed system development. The shared-variable decomposition approach consists in distributing the events of a model over the selected sub-components. It allows the introduction of shared variables and external events. These ensure that the behavior of shared variables is preserved in all sub-components. After that, further refinements then concentrate on how each sub-component processes shared state variables. The shared-event decomposition is a set of events that are synchronized and shared by sub-components. This approach defines a partial version of a global event in each sub-machine, when the variables of a global event are distributed between separate sub-machines. This is to simulate the action of the global event on the considered variables. The recomposition of the refined sub-components gives rise to a component which should refine the initial abstract component. This is the shared-event decomposition that we have adopted for HLA modeling as we can consider that a system composed of sub-systems acts as a distributed system.

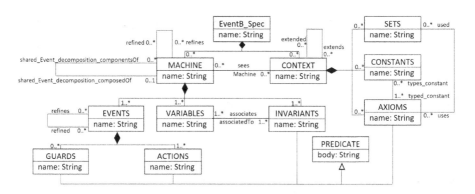

Fig. 3. EVENT-B meta-model

Figure 3 shows a proposed meta-model of the EVENT-B restricted to the presented concepts that are relevant to our use.

EVENT-B method is supported by several industrial tools, such as AtelierB [7], Rodin [6] and ProB [23]. These tools allow to generate proof obligations and to automatically and/or interactively discharge them. Animation, model-checking are also possible. In our project we use AtelierB. Its formal language is BSYSTEM, an EVENT-B syntactic variant.

3   SysML Extensions with Refinement and Decomposition Mechanisms

The aim of our approach is to provide an automatic translation from SysML diagrams to Event-B specifications. Two interesting characteristics of Event-B are the refinement and decomposition mechanisms that facilitate a step-by-step design and make proofs easier to discharge. This allows to master the complexity of complex systems. Therefore, we propose to extend SysML with these Event-B mechanisms to enable an automatic translation. These extensions are applied on two SysML diagrams, the package and sequence diagrams.

3.1   SysML Package Diagram Extensions

To model a system HLA in a layered hierarchy of sub-systems, we have chosen to create a package diagram, each package corresponding to a system of these hierarchy. Such a package contains a BDD, the associated state machines and a sequence diagram that defines the interactions between the blocks. To represent the links between these packages, two kinds of relationships have been introduced. The first one is inspired from the refinement link of Event-B and is called "HLA_refines". It is defined between two packages and is used to detail the behavior of the parent package. For this, new blocks and a new sequence diagram are introduced in the child package. This new sequence diagram describes the interactions between blocks to satisfy the parent behavior.

The second relationship, called "HLA_decompose", comes from the fact that some blocks of a package can be considered as sub-systems because they have their own life and can exist independently of the other blocks. In this case, they become new packages and the link with the parent package is "HLA_decompose" link. This concept corresponds to the decomposition mechanism of Event-B, more precisely the shared-event decomposition since the systems/sub-systems we consider behave as distributed systems.

To represent these system/sub-systems relationships, the SysML package diagram meta-model is extended by introducing new meta-classes, as described by the grey boxes in Fig. 4 "HLA_refines" and "HLA_decompose", as sub-classes of the meta-class "Dependency".

3.2   SysML Sequence Diagram Extension

To display the interactions between users, objects, systems and entities within a system, a sequence diagram is used. This diagram represents the sending and receiving of messages between the interacting entities called lifelines. The intersection of a message arrow and a lifeline is represented by the element "Message Occurrence". We have adapted the sequence diagram meta-model of SysML to our approach. Figure 5 shows our meta-model. First, we impose that each message corresponds to a transition in the state machine of the block associated to the target lifeline. Second, as we have introduced a refinement link between packages, we need to specify that a message of the refining package is a refinement

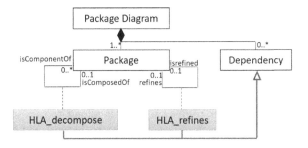

Fig. 4. SYSML extended package diagram meta-model

of a message of the refined package. This is achieved by adding a new meta-class in the meta-model, called "Refines_Message", sub-class of the meta-class "Message".

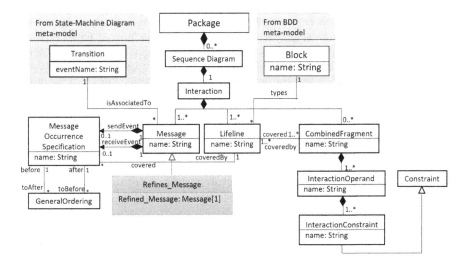

Fig. 5. Extract of SYSML extended sequence diagram meta-model

4   Illustration of the SYSML Extensions

Our work is part of the the Autonomous Freight Train (AFT) project under the Autonomous Train program [2]. As AFT data and case studies are of high level of confidentiality, to describe the SYSML extensions, we use in this paper an extract of the Landing Gear System case study [10].

We start our modeling by creating a new package diagram. It contains the package "LandingGearSystemL0" that describes the main system. There is a unique block called "Landing Gear System", its state-machine diagram and a sequence diagram that show the main functionalities and the behavior of a landing gear system, that is to extend and retract a landing gear (Fig. 6).

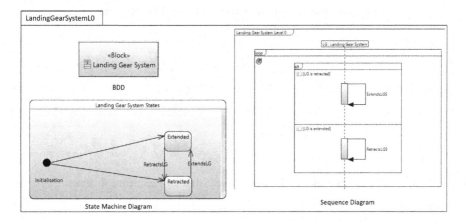

Fig. 6. Main system package

The Landing Gear System is composed of three sub-systems ("Pilote Sub-System", "Digital SubSystem" and "Mechanical SubSystem") and a "Pilot" to command the extension and retraction of the gear. Therefore, the behavior of the main system is satisfied by the result of the behavior describing these entities interplay. Following the description presented in Subsect. 3.1, we create a second package "LandingGearSystemL1" which encompasses the different entities and the composition relationship with their parent system.

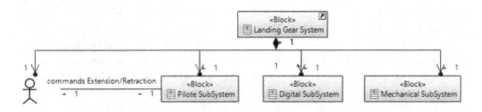

Fig. 7. Sub-systems package "LandingGearSystemL1" block diagram

The package "LandingGearSystemL1" contains the BDD describing the sub-systems (see Fig. 7), the state-machine diagrams for all the sub-systems (Fig. 8 shows this of the "Mechanical SubSystem") and the sequence diagram, an extract

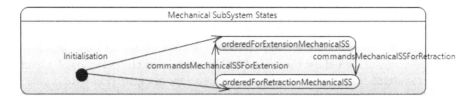

Fig. 8. State diagram of the mechanical SubSystem

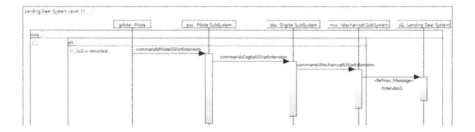

Fig. 9. Extract of the "LandingGearSystemL1" sequence diagram

Fig. 10. Packages refinement   **Fig. 11.** Packages decomposition

of it is shown in Fig. 9, defining the Pilot/sub-systems process which refines the main system process.

We use the "HLA_refines" link between "LandingGearSystemL0" and "LandingGearSystemL1" to express that "LandingGearSystemL1" refines "LandingGearSystemL0" (see Fig. 10). More precisely, in the "LandingGearSystemL1" sequence diagram, the message "ExtendsLG" allows the extension of the "Landing Gear System" by the sub-systems processes interplay. It is a refinement of the message "ExtendsLGS" of the sequence diagram of the "LandingGearSystemL0", which is specified by the "Refines_Message" stereotype (see Fig. 9).

Now, we want to describe more precisely the behavior and the structure of the three sub-systems "Pilote SubSystem", "Digital SubSystem" and "Mechanical SubSystem". This is achieved by creating a new package for each of them. Therefore the package "LandingGearSystemL1" is decomposed into the three newly created packages using the "HLA_decompose" link (see Fig. 11). Each of the packages can then be described by a BDD, representing its structure and in particular its possible sub-systems, the state machines associated to some blocks and a sequence diagram.

The process of refinement/decomposition can be applied again. The full specification of the HLA modeling of the case study can be found in [12].

5   SysML to Event-B Translation

In this section, we first present the rules that allow to obtain an Event-B specification from a SysML model. Then the implementation of the translation rules is described and a discussion ends the section.

5.1   Translation Rules

Three sets of rules have been defined. The first one considers elements related to a package. The second one deals with the SysML refinement extensions and the last one with SysML decomposition extension. These rules take meta-models as input and output. The source meta-models are the SysML meta-models described in Figs. 1, 2, 4, 5 and the target meta-model is the Event-B meta-model of Fig. 3.

Translation of Package Elements. The rules of Table 1 allow to translate a package diagram, that gives an Event-B project, and a package, that must not be a decomposed package, inside a package diagram. Each package gives an Event-B machine and an Event-B context.

It should be noted that in Tables 1 and 2, E_X designates the result of the translation of X.

Table 1. Translation rules for a package diagram

		SysML concepts		Event-B concepts	
Rule	Translation of	Element	Constraint	Element	Constraint
1	Package diagram	PD	PD is a Package diagram	E_PD	E_PD ∈ EventB_Spec
2	Package that is not a decomposed package	P	P ∈ SysML_Package P ∉ ran(HLA_decompose)	E_P_M E_P_CONT	E_P_M ∈ MACHINE E_P_CONT ∈ CONTEXT E_P_M SEES E_P_CONT

The rules of Table 2 are applied for the elements of a given package. Note that we have deliberately omitted to present the translation rules of some elements of the BDD meta-model of Fig. 1, in particular "Composition", "Association", "AssociationEnd" and "Characteristic" since these rules are the same as those used for translating the equivalent concepts in class diagrams [16]. Furthermore they are not used in this paper.

The first three rules in Table 2 are rather straightforward. Rule 6 expresses that a lifeline L of a block B is translated by a constant E_LC, instance of the abstract set E_B_S associated to B, and a variable E_LV that represents the current state of E_LC in the state machine associated to B.

Figure 12 shows the EVENT-B specification obtained from the block "MechanicalSubSystem" and its linked lifeline "mss" of the sequence diagram (see Figs. 7, 8, 9).

Table 2. Translation rules for elements of a package

		SYSML concepts		Event-B concepts	
Rule	Translation of	Element	Constraint	Element	Constraint
3	Block	B	B ∈ SYSML _Block	E_B_S	E_B_S ∈ SETS
4	State-machine of a block	SM, B	SM ∈ SYSML _State-machine SM is associated to B	E_SM	E_SM ∈ SETS
5	State-machine states	$S_1, S_2, \ldots S_n$ SM	S_i ∈ SYSML _States SM ∈ SYSML _State-machine S_i is a state of SM	E_S_1,E_S_2, …E_S_n	E_S_i ∈ CONSTANTS E_SM={E_S_1,E_S_2,…E_S_n}
6	Lifeline of a sequence diagram associated to a block	L,B, SM	L ∈ SYSML _Lifeline L is an instance of block B, SM is the state diagram associated to B B and SM have already been translated	E_LC, E_LV	E_LC ∈ CONSTANTS E_LC ∈ E_B_S E_LV ∈ VARIABLES (E_LV ∈ {E_LC} → E_SM) ∈ INVARIANTS (E_LV :∈ {E_LC} → E_SM) ∈ INITIALISATION
7	Sequence diagram message that is not a refined message	M	M ∈ SYSML _Message	E_M	E_M ∈ EVENTS

Rule 7 needs to be more precisely defined. An EVENT-B event E_M obtained from the translation of a message M is of the form **SELECT** G_M **THEN** A_M **END** where G_M are the guards and A_M are the actions. G_M and A_M are obtained as follows.

Let SQ be a sequence diagram. A message M is defined between two lifelines L_1, its origin, and L_2, its destination (L_1 and L_2 are not necessary different). L_1 (L_2, resp.) is associated to block B_1 (B_2, resp.). Let SM_1 (SM_2, resp.) be the state machine associated to B_1 (B_2, resp.). M is associated to a transition T of SM_2. Let SS_2 be the source state of T and TS_2 be the target state of T.

Note that Rule 5 gives E_SS_i (E_TS_i, resp.) as the EVENT-B elements associated to SS_i (TS_i, resp.). Rule 6 gives E_L_iC and E_L_iV as the EVENT-B elements associated to L_i.

– Calculation of A_M

$A\_M \triangleq E\_L_2V(E\_L_2C) := E\_TS_2$

The current state of E_L_2C corresponding to the lifeline L_2 is the target state of the transition T.

– Calculation of G_M

```
SYSTEM
LandingGearSystemL1_CONT
SETS
MechanicalSubSystem; MechanicalSubSystemStates; ...
CONSTANTS
mss, orderedForExtensionMechanicalSS, orderedForRetractionMechanicalSS
PROPERTIES
mss ∈ MechanicalSubSystem ∧ MechanicalSubSystem ={mss} ∧
orderedForExtensionMechanicalSS ∈ MechanicalSubSystemStates ∧
orderedForRetractionMechanicalSS ∈ MechanicalSubSystemStates ∧
orderedForRetractionMechanicalSS ≠ orderedForExtensionMechanicalSS ∧
MechanicalSubSystemStates ={orderedForExtensionMechanicalSS, orderedForRetractionMechan-
icalSS} ∧
...
END
```

```
REFINEMENT
LandingGearSystemL1
REFINES
LandingGearSystemL0
SEES
LandingGearSystemL1_CONT, LandingGearSystemL0_CONT
VARIABLES
mssState, ...
INVARIANTS
mssState ∈ {mss} → MechanicalSubSystemStates ∧ ...
INITIALISATION
mssState :∈ {mss} → MechanicalSubSystemStates ∥ ...
...
END
```

Fig. 12. Application of rules 3, 4, 5, 6 on block *MechanicalSubSystem*

- If M is the first message of SQ and SQ has a guard called G_SQ (defined as an Interaction Constraint in the sequence diagram meta-model) then
  $G\_M \triangleq G\_SQ \wedge E\_L_2V(E\_L_2C) = E\_SS_2$
- Else, let $Prev\_M$ be the message of SQ that precedes M. Its lifeline destination is necessary L_1 and $Prev\_M$ corresponds to a transition T' of SM_1 whose source state is SS_1 and target state TS_1.
  $G\_M \triangleq E\_L_1V(E\_L_1C) = E\_TS_1 \wedge E\_L_2V(E\_L_2C) = E\_SS_2$
  This means that M is triggered after $Prev\_M$ (i.e. the current state of E_L_1C is the target state of the transition T' and the current state of E_L_2C is the source state of T).

Let us take the example of the message "commandsMechanicalSSForExtension". The previous message in the sequence diagram of Fig. 9 is "commandsDigitalSSForExtension".

$commandsMechanicalSSForExtension \triangleq$
  SELECT $dssState(dss) = orderForExtensionDigitalSS \wedge$
  $mssState(mss) = orderedForRetractionMechanicalSS$
  THEN $mssState(mss) := orderedForExtensionMechanicalSS$
  END

Translating. SYSML **refinement extension to** EVENT-B. Two rules are defined to translate the two SYSML package and sequence diagram refinement extensions.

- **Machine Refinement Rule** is defined as follows:
  Let P_1 and P_2 two SYSML packages such that P_2 "HLA_refines" P_1. P_1 and P_2 are translated into EVENT-B according to Rule 2 and give E_P_1_M and E_P_2_M machines.
  In E_P_2_M, two clauses are added to express the SYSML package refinement:
  - E_P_2_M **REFINES** E_P_1_M
  - E_P_2_M **SEES** E_P_1_CONT
- **Event Refinement Rule** is defined as follows:
  Let P_1 and P_2 two SYSML packages such that P_2 "HLA_refines" P_1. P_1 and P_2 are translated into EVENT-B according to Rule 2 and Machine Refinement Rule. This gives E_P_1_M and E_P_2_M machines such that E_P_2_M refines E_P_1_M.
  Let M_1 (M_2, resp.) a SYSML message of the sequence diagram of P_1 (2, resp.) such that M_2 "Refines_Message" M_1. M_1 is translated according to Rule 7:
  $$E\_M_1 \triangleq \textbf{SELECT } G\_M_1 \textbf{ THEN } A\_M_1 \textbf{ END}$$

  Then M_2 is translated by:
  $$E\_M2 \text{ ref } E\_M1 \triangleq \textbf{SELECT } G\_M_1 \wedge E\_LVM_2(E\_LCM_2) = E\_SSM_2$$
  $$\textbf{THEN } A\_M_1 \parallel E\_LVM_2(E\_LCM_2) := E\_TSM_2 \textbf{ END}$$

Translating. SYSML **decomposition extension to** EVENT-B. As already stated, we use the shared-event decomposition approach [13] of EVENT-B to translate the SYSML package decomposition extension. First all the variables of the machine to be decomposed are assigned to one of the decomposed machines called "Interface". Then the elements linked to a variable are assigned in the relevant decomposed machine.

The Machine Decomposition Rule is defined as follows.

Let P, P_1 and P_2 three SYSML packages such that P is "HLA_decompose" into P_1 and P_2. Recall that it means that P_1 and P_2 are sub-systems of P and then corresponds to the blocks B_1 and B_2 in P. P is translated into EVENT-B according to Rule 2 and give E_P_M machine.

- E_P_M machine is shared-event decomposed into two machines called E_P_1_Interface and E_P_2_Interface that correspond to P_1 and P_2. Each E_P_i_Interface contains the elements of E_P_M linked to the B_i block: SEES clause, variables, invariant and the events that read or modify these variables.
- E_P_i_Interface is refined by a machine called E_P_i_M that contains the translation of the elements of P_i (blocks, sequence diagram, state machines).

Figure 13 shows the "MechanicalSubSystem_Interface" machine obtained after decomposing the "LandingGearSystem1" machine (see Fig. 11).

```
SYSTEM
MechanicalSubSystem_Interface
SEES
LandingGearSystemL1_CONT, LandingGearSystemL0_CONT
VARIABLES
mssState
INVARIANTS
mssState ∈ {mss} → MechanicalSubSystemStates
INITIALISATION
mssState :∈ {mss} → MechanicalSubSystemStates
EVENTS
commandsMechanicalSSForRetraction ≜
SELECT
mssState(mss)=orderedForExtensionMechanicalSS
THEN
mssState(mss):=orderedForRetractionMechanicalSS END;
commandsMechanicalSSForExtension ≜
SELECT
mssState(mss)=orderedForRetractionMechanicalSS
THEN
mssState(mss):=orderedForExtensionMechanicalSS END;
ExtendsLG ≜
SELECT
mssState(mss)=orderedForExtensionMechanicalSS
THEN
skip END;
RetractsLG ≜
SELECT
mssState(mss)=orderedForRetractionMechanicalSS
THEN
skip END;
END
```

Fig. 13. MechanicalSubSystem_Interface

5.2 Implementation

SysML to Event-B translation is performed in two phases. The first phase is a model-to-model transformation which implements the above rules. The second phase is a model-to-text transformation which allows to generate textual formal specifications in order to be integrated in AtelierB for formal verification purposes.

Model-to-Model Translation. The rules have been implemented using Query View Transformation (QVT) language. QVT is a defacto standard specification for model transformation standard published by the Object Management Group (OMG) [8]. Particularly, we focus on QVT-Operational (QVTo), introduced as part of the MOF (Meta Object Facility) standard (OMG, 2011). Although other known transformation languages could be used to implement this transformation such as ATL [18], they are not standards of the OMG. A set of 35 rules have been implemented with around 700 lines of code spread over four modules which concern contexts, machines, decomposition and a main module to synchronize the first three modules.

Model-to-Text Translation. This step generates automatically an Event-B textual specification from the resulting Event-B models of the previous step using Acceleo [21]. Acceleo is a template based technology allowing to automatically produce any kind of source code from any data source available in EMF format. This textual specification could be introduced into provers such as AtelierB [7], model-checkers and animators such as ProB [23] to verify the consistency of the modeled system.

5.3 Discussion

As a consistent way to validate the application of the proposed translation rules in order to verify the correctness of the generated results, we have applied these rules on a set of case studies, i.e. railways system case studies and the landing gear system case study [10] used in Sect. 4. The full EVENT-B specification resulted from applying the proposed transformation on the HLA models of the landing gear system case study is presented in [12].

After that, the generated specification is introduced in AtelierB to be formally verified and in ProB to animate the execution scenarios. This verification generates automatically a set of proof obligations corresponding to the modeled functional properties without any non-functional properties integration, and proof obligations from the application of model decomposition. These proofs are of type invariant preservation, non-deterministic action feasibility and well-definedness. For the landing gear system case study, the verification of the generated EVENT-B specification required to discharge 136 proof obligations, all automatically discharged using AtelierB. The table summarizing the proof activity of the landing gear system can be found in [12].

6   Related Work

Automatic transformation of SysML/UML models into formal specifications was the subject of several research work e.g. [16,19,24] and [25]. However, the aim of our work is the modeling of HLA for complex systems, particularly railways systems, and their system/subsystems hierarchy. That is why we focus the section on works dealing with HLA modeling and verification, or system/subsystems refinement and decomposition relationships.

Papers [14] and [18] present the CHESS Toolset, a tooled MDE approach for cross-domain modeling of industrial complex systems. These works are based on an extension of UML, SysML and MARTE modeling languages and separation of concerns achieved through the specification of well-defined design views, each of which addresses a particular aspect of the problem. The CHESS toolset allows code generation toward multiple language targets and property description, verification, preservation and dependability through a dedicated UML profile. FUML [1] is a subset of the standard Unified Modeling Language (UML). This subset is limited to the structural modeling of UML, such as classes, associations and behavior modeling using UML activities. A model constructed in FUML is therefore executable in exactly the same sense as a program in a traditional programming language, but it is written with the level of abstraction and richness of expression of a modeling language. Despite these approaches support HLA models based on SysML or UML and allow formal verification and property preserving, however, they do not allow to model decomposition and refinement mechanisms which are particularly well suited to HLA modeling.

SysML extensions and its alignment with formal method concepts have been the subject of numerous works. Papers [17] and [20] propose SysML extensions based on SysML diagrams refinement to enable reasoning. They define a semantics for refinement and for a representative collection of elements from the UML4SysML profile (blocks, state machines, activities, and interactions) used in combination. The semantics is defined in CML (COMPASS Modelling Language), a formal language based on VDM (Vienna Development Method) and CSP (Communicating Sequential Processes). However they do not support model decomposition which is an important mechanism to design complex systems.

Paper [9] provides the reasoning and the rationale for designing the formal methods demonstrator in Railway Environment. The design concerns the usefulness of formal methods from the point of view of the infrastructure managers and the adoption of a semi-formal SysML notation within formal methods, such as Event-B demonstrator process.

7 Conclusion

This paper proposes SysML extensions to be aligned with Event-B refinement and decomposition mechanisms in order to automatically translate SysML models of HLA to Event-B specifications. These extensions are applied on two SysML parts. The first part is about package diagrams which are customized to represent the decomposition of system/sub-systems hierarchies and the refinement of a system by its sub-systems interplay. The second part consists in extending sequence diagrams with stereotypes applied on messages to refine the parent system task by the collaboration of its sub-systems processes. A set of rules are defined to translate SysML models into Event-B specifications in order to formally verify them using AtelierB.

Work in progress aims at enriching SysML models with non-functional properties such as security and safety. Bidirectional transformation for traceability of Event-B specifications to identify errors on the original SysML models is also required. Furthermore, we are aware that the correctness of the proposed translation rules should be addressed.

Acknowledgements. This research work contributes to the french collaborative project AFT (Autonomous Freight Train), with SNCF, Alstom Transport, Hitachi Rail STS, Capgemini Engineering and Apsys. It was carried out in the framework of IRT Railenium, Valenciennes, France, and therefore was granted public funds within the scope of the French Program "Investissements d'Avenir".

References

1. Object Management Group, Semantics of a Foundational Subset for Executable UML Models (FUML). https://www.omg.org/spec/FUML/1.5/About-FUML/
2. The autonomous train program. https://railenium.eu/train-autonome/
3. ASTRAIL European project D4.1 - report on analysis and on ranking of formal methods (2017). http://www.astrail.eu/download.aspx?id=bb46b81b-a5bf-4036-9018-cc6e7d91e2c2
4. Abrial, J.R.: Event model decomposition. Technical report/[ETH, Department of Computer Science 626 (2009)
5. Abrial, J.R.: Modeling in Event-B: System and Software Engineering. Cambridge University Press, Cambridge (2010)
6. Abrial, J., Butler, M.J., Hallerstede, S., Hoang, T.S., Mehta, F., Voisin, L.: Rodin: an open toolset for modelling and reasoning in Event-B. Int. J. Softw. Tools Technol. Transf. **12**(6), 447–466 (2010). https://doi.org/10.1007/s10009-010-0145-y
7. Atelier, B.: Atelier B tool. https://www.atelierb.eu/en/atelier-b-tools/
8. Barendrecht, P.J.: Modeling transformations using QVT operational mappings. Eindhoven University of Technology Department of Mechanical Engineering Systems Engineering Group, Research project report, Eindhoven (2010)
9. Basile, D., et al.: Designing a demonstrator of formal methods for railways infrastructure managers. In: Margaria, T., Steffen, B. (eds.) ISoLA 2020. LNCS, vol. 12478, pp. 467–485. Springer, Cham (2020). https://doi.org/10.1007/978-3-030-61467-6_30
10. Boniol, F., Wiels, V.: The landing gear system case study. In: Boniol, F., Wiels, V., Ait Ameur, Y., Schewe, K.-D. (eds.) ABZ 2014. CCIS, vol. 433, pp. 1–18. Springer, Cham (2014). https://doi.org/10.1007/978-3-319-07512-9_1
11. Bonvoisin, D.: 25 years of formal methods at RATP. In: International Railway Safety Council (IRSC2016) (2016). https://international-railway-safety-council.com/wp-content/uploads/2017/09/bonvoisin-25-years-of-formal-methods-at-ratp.pdf
12. Bougacha, R.: The landing gear system case study. https://github.com/RacemBougacha/Landing-Gear-System.git
13. Butler, M.: Decomposition structures for Event-B. In: Leuschel, M., Wehrheim, H. (eds.) IFM 2009. LNCS, vol. 5423, pp. 20–38. Springer, Heidelberg (2009). https://doi.org/10.1007/978-3-642-00255-7_2
14. Cicchetti, A., et al.: CHESS: a model-driven engineering tool environment for aiding the development of complex industrial systems. In: Goedicke, M., Menzies, T., Saeki, M. (eds.) IEEE/ACM International Conference on Automated Software Engineering, ASE 2012, Essen, Germany, 3–7 Sep 2012, pp. 362–365. ACM (2012). https://doi.org/10.1145/2351676.2351748
15. Holt, J., Perry, S.: SysML for Systems Engineering, vol. 7. IET, Stevenage (2008)
16. Laleau, R., Mammar, A.: An overview of a method and its support tool for generating B specifications from UML notations. In: The Fifteenth IEEE International Conference on Automated Software Engineering, ASE 2000, Grenoble, France, 11–15 Sep 2000, pp. 269–272. IEEE Computer Society (2000). https://doi.org/10.1109/ASE.2000.873675
17. Lima, L., et al.: An integrated semantics for reasoning about SysML design models using refinement. Softw. Syst. Model. **16**(3), 875–902 (2015). https://doi.org/10.1007/s10270-015-0492-y

18. Mazzini, S., Favaro, J.M., Puri, S., Baracchi, L.: CHESS: an open source methodology and toolset for the development of critical systems. In: Bordeleau, F., Bruel, J., Dingel, J., Gérard, S., Muccini, H., Mussbacher, G., Voss, S. (eds.) Joint Proceedings of the 12th Educators Symposium (EduSymp 2016) and 3rd International Workshop on Open Source Software for Model Driven Engineering (OSS4MDE 2016) co-located with the ACM/IEEE 19th International Conference on Model Driven Engineering Languages and Systems (MODELS 2016), Saint Malo, France, 3 Oct 2016. CEUR Workshop Proceedings, vol. 1835, pp. 59–66. CEUR-WS.org (2016). http://ceur-ws.org/Vol-1835/paper09.pdf

19. Mentré, D.: SysML2B: automatic tool for B project graphical architecture design using SysML. In: Butler, M., Schewe, K.-D., Mashkoor, A., Biro, M. (eds.) ABZ 2016. LNCS, vol. 9675, pp. 308–311. Springer, Cham (2016). https://doi.org/10.1007/978-3-319-33600-8_26

20. Miyazawa, A., Cavalcanti, A.: Formal refinement in SysML. In: Albert, E., Sekerinski, E. (eds.) IFM 2014. LNCS, vol. 8739, pp. 155–170. Springer, Cham (2014). https://doi.org/10.1007/978-3-319-10181-1_10

21. Musset, J., et al.: Acceleo user guide, vol. 2 (2006). http://acceleo.org/doc/obeo/en/acceleo-2.6-user-guide

22. OMG: OMG systems modeling language, version 1.3. http://www.omgsysml.org/ (2012)

23. ProB: The ProB animator and model checker. https://prob.hhu.de/

24. Salunkhe, S., Berglehner, R., Rasheeq, A.: Automatic transformation of SysML model to Event-B model for railway CCS application. In: Raschke, A., Méry, D. (eds.) ABZ 2021. LNCS, vol. 12709, pp. 143–149. Springer, Cham (2021). https://doi.org/10.1007/978-3-030-77543-8_14

25. Snook, C., Butler, M.: UML-b: formal modeling and design aided by UML. ACM Trans. Softw. Eng. Methodol. **15**(1), 92–122 (2006)

Development of Monitoring Systems for Anomaly Detection Using ASTD Specifications

El Jabri Chaymae[1]([✉]), Frappier Marc[1], Ecarot Thibaud[1],
and Tardif Pierre-Martin[2]

[1] Computer Science Department at Université de Sherbrooke,
GRIF, Québec, Canada
{chaymae.el.jabri,marc.frappier,thibaud.ecarot}@usherbooke.ca
[2] Management School at Université de Sherbrooke, Québec, Canada
pierre-martin.tardif@usherbrooke.ca

Abstract. Anomaly-based intrusion detection systems are essential defenses against cybersecurity threats because they can identify anomalies in current activities. However, these systems have difficulties providing entity processing independence through a programming language. In addition, a degradation of the detection process is caused by the complexity of scheduling the training and detection processes, which are required to keep the anomaly detection system continuously updated. This paper shows how to use the algebraic state-transition diagram (ASTD) language to develop flexible anomaly detection systems. This paper provides a model for detecting point anomalies using the unsupervised nonparametric technique Kernel Density Estimation to estimate the probability density of event occurrence. The proposed model caters for both the training and the detection phase continuously. The ASTD language streamlines the modeling of detection systems thanks to its process algebraic operators that provide a solution to overcome these challenges. By delegating the combination of anomaly-based detection processes to the ASTD language, the effort and complexity are reduced during detection models development. Finally, using a qualitative evaluation, this study demonstrates that the algebraic operators in the ASTD specification language overcome these challenges.

Keywords: Intrusion detection system · Anomaly detection · Specification language · Formalization · Algebra operators

1 Introduction

Critical systems and sensitive infrastructure are increasingly subject to an intensification of cyberattacks, the complexity of which increases throughout multiple offensives. To adequately counter the risks that are not always identified and known, these systems must have a defense with the main characteristic of

© Springer Nature Switzerland AG 2022
Y. Aït-Ameur and F. Crăciun (Eds.): TASE 2022, LNCS 13299, pp. 274–289, 2022.
https://doi.org/10.1007/978-3-031-10363-6_19

quickly and effectively detecting a threat or abnormal behavior. These threats, which are often composed of a variety of combined tactics and techniques that adversaries may employ to achieve their objectives, are increasingly challenging to detect due to their inherent heterogeneity and complexity [26].

Detecting these threats is challenging because of detecting heterogeneous attacks with various variants, the need to quickly obtain a representative and up-to-date dataset for the training phase, and the management of internal processes and alarm handling of an intrusion detection system (IDS). Indeed, IDSs must detect a wide range of attacks whose nature can vary within a given system substrate [8,19]. In addition, the management of the processes running within the detection systems is of great complexity, mainly due to the number of entities present in the ever-growing infrastructures, whose topology is constantly changing and which are deployed on a large scale [22]. It is also about getting representative datasets of these changes faster and processing a massive amount of generated alerts to reduce the number of false positives, or irrelevant alerts [10,25]. These various challenges have highlighted the difficulty of adapting IDSs to changes. These difficulties impact IDS based on dynamic signatures and anomaly detection.

To answer these difficulties of adaptation, particular works of [2,30] have examined several approaches, such as the combination of different learning techniques or the use of a better classification using labeling before the training phase. However, specific challenges persist with these works, particularly the lack of flexibility due to the process scheduling during the training and detection phases executed in parallel [12] and the entity profiles independence to be monitored [13]. More specifically, process scheduling is a persistent issue during IDS' development. Indeed, programming languages do not have predefined formal operations ensuring the interaction between the multiple processes, complicating continuous improvement and reducing reusability. The next challenge is the unique treatment of the entities of a system to be monitored. Indeed, the processing is unique for all the characteristics of the entities. It is impossible to differentiate the entities because the training and detection model parameters are specified a priori. A final issue is the interruption of detection when renewing training data because the feedback loop is not continuous or automated.

In order to answer appropriately to these functional issues, it was hypothesized that the use of the algebraic state transition diagrams (ASTDs) formalization language [4] would make it possible to meet effectively to these challenges. ASTD is an executable, modular and graphical notation that allows for the composition of hierarchical state machines using process algebra operators such as flow, sequence, quantified interleaving, and parallel synchronization [27]. Indeed, using algebra operators specific to the IDS' development coming from this language should improve the reliability and flexibility of these systems. The research work presented in this article aims to formalize the development of intrusion detection systems and to achieve three objectives:

– Separate the coordination of the processes from the actions constituting the model;
– Provide independent processing of each entity that constitutes the system to be monitored;
– Ensure continuous processing of events between the training and detection phase.

This paper is structured as follows. Section 2 first explores the existing anomaly detection tools by selecting those that allow continuous event flow management and those that offer heterogeneous processing of the system substrate profiles. Then, in Sect. 3 a new methodology for detecting point anomalies is presented based on the graphical specification of the detection model. The methodology is illustrated through a case study in the Microsoft365 environment. The different actions that make up the model and the execution steps of this new specification will be described. Finally, in Sect. 4 a qualitative evaluation is proposed to show that using ASTD meets formalization, reusability, and modularity objectives that next-generation IDSs need to counter increasingly complex attacks and motley.

2   Related Work

In the literature, some tools offer the possibility of detecting anomalies in a data set, each using a different methodology. There are those specific to anomaly detection, others more related to the processing and analysis of event logs, and others that present advanced functionalities in the statistical processing of data.

Several industrial approaches exist to perform anomaly detection by signature or behavior. The first approach is carried out with the Snort tool. Snort [20] provides a low-level signature language to express and detect multi-stage Advanced Persistent Threats (APT) attacks. However, Snort is a stateless language that offers minimal event correlation capabilities. This limitation has the effect of triggering more redundant true positives and false positives. Suricata [1] is based on the same inference mechanism as Snort, so it is very complex to make combinations to detect complex attacks. Zeek [18] was proposed to overcome some limitations of Snort by providing an event-driven scripting language to precisely specify and identify APT. The writing of Zeek scripts is essentially programming using functions and global variables. However, Zeek being a scripting language, is less abstract than approaches based on process algebra composition operators. Zeek functions are monolithic; that is, there is a single function for each event, and this function must address all cases of occurrence of this event, making it complex to deal with state-dependent reactions for this event.

BeepBeep 3 [5] is mainly a data stream query engine. It provides processors and functions that define recurrent operations on event logs. BeepBeep 3 aims to present reusable, tested, and general toolkits that reduce the development effort of continuous event processing and express this processing in a more readable way and with a higher level of abstraction. BeepBeep 3 does not present predefined processors for anomaly detection, although such extensions exist [21]. BeepBeep forms more complex computations on the data by composing (or piping) processors between them, which is achieved by letting the output of one processor be the input of another. It does not present a large selection of relationships that can be established between different processors. The specification of anomaly detection is more representative and simpler by ASTDs than with BeepBeep 3. This argument means that modularity is not present with BeepBeep compared to methods based on process algebra.

Palisade [9] is an anomaly detection framework. It is motivated by the need to remotely detect anomalies and combine a set of detectors with improving the detection system's accuracy. Palisade ensures that the different detectors can operate in parallel on the same data set thanks to its architecture composed of nodes that communicate via Redis, a distributed data streaming architecture. Palisade does not handle anomaly detection in interleaved events as it is intended for embedded systems. The detection is performed on the entity's data to which the framework is connected. Palisade does not present a graphical representation or an additional level of abstraction to develop an intrusion detection system. However, it is necessary to browse its source code to extend or reuse systems based on Palisade, making it less flexible than ASTD.

Project-R is one of the oldest tools for statistical data processing and statistical calculations. It is a GNU project developed by the R programming language [7]. It has advanced features like time series analysis, clustering, classification, etc. Thus it can be used in anomaly detection according to machine learning techniques [3,24], especially at the stage of establishing the model describing the system's normal behavior. R does not offer the possibility of combining statistical processing, which causes a considerable loss of time during execution. PqR [15] improves R, whose main objective is the acceleration of calculations. PqR structure calculations as tasks by adding the possibility of parallelizing, pipelining, and merging tasks when certain conditions are met. The modularity and reusability of an IDS made with R depends on the developer.

The management of Interleaved Event Inputs in [17] raises the need to separate interleaved events produced by different users or for other purposes during intrusion detection. It allows distinguishing between data elements representing different behaviors and locating where the intrusion is. Research works in [14,23] indicate that the detection of anomalies in data streams and environments that dynamically change properties requires the updating of training data to preserve the accuracy of the detection system.

The ASTD specification language, through its compiler cASTD [16], allows continuous data stream processing and combines the processes constituting the detection system through algebraic operators. In the following, a case study will be presented that demonstrates how to process coordination, entity processing independence, and automation of training data update can be provided by the ASTD specification of the detection system.

3   Case Study

The case study detects unexpected events in end-user activity data streams from various Microsoft online services such as Exchange, Azure AD, and SharePoint. They are collected in real-time using a Microsoft365 API. Unexpected events occur at times of the day when the user is not usually active. Data streams are made up of events representing activities performed by various users. Among the attributes associated with an activity are:

- ID : uniquely identifies each event
- CreationTime: determines the date and time in Coordinated Universal Time (UTC) that the user performed the activity. It has the following format YYYY-mm-ddTHH:MM:ssZ.
- UserId : the user who performed the action

The events are interleaved: they contain events from different users not recognized (identified) a priori (i.e., the IDS does not have access to a database of existing/registered users; it discovers them on the fly). Events are not always received in the chronological order of their realization, and some events are received very late.

Anomaly detection proceeds according to the following steps:

- We establish a model describing a user's activity during the day. This model estimates the probability density of a user's activity during the 1440 min of the day using the non-parametric technique kernel density estimation (KDE).
- A minimum threshold is set that defines the lowest probability density to classify an event as expected.
- The new events are compared with the learned reference model. If the event has occurred for a minute for which the probability density is below the threshold, the event is considered to be an anomaly.

KDE has been used in unexpected event detection in an application established in collaboration with the company Sherweb [11]. The experiments performed demonstrated that the model meets its statistical function by modeling the active hours of a user even when ignoring the exact values of the model parameters. In addition, it turns out that the reported events are abnormal in terms of user behavior and not necessarily performed by an attacker. The model's threshold is chosen considering that a significant threshold value will classify more events as abnormal, which requires more investigation by the company security analyst.

The update of the training data is done by implementing a sliding window.The events are grouped by week by assigning them a week number calculated from the DateCreation attribute, which we call henceforth a *period*. A *period* is defined as YYYYWW, where YYYY denotes the year and WW denotes the week's number. Two types of periods are needed: *UsedPeriods* and *AccumulatedPeriods*. *UsedPeriods* are used to calculate the current KDE model, and *AccumulatedPeriods* are the periods received after the computation of the current KDE, and that will be used to compute the next KDE. To update the training data two conditions must be satisfied:

- The accumulation of at least n period
- Obtaining at least k events in the accumulated periods

These conditions were put in place to ensure that the sample of data used for training was representative and that the profile learned by KDE was reliable.

Figure 1 represents the data renewal process.

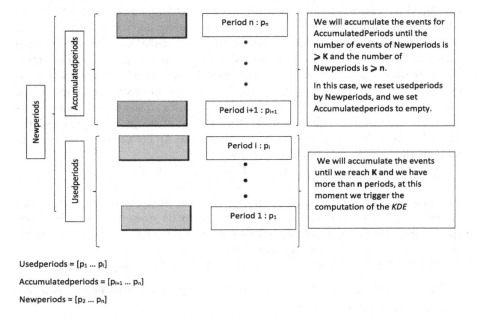

Usedperiods = [p_1 ... p_i]

Accumulatedperiods = [p_{i+1} ... p_n]

Newperiods = [p_2 ... p_n]

Fig. 1. Methodology for updating training data.

Having accumulated at least n periods in *UsedPeriods* and obtained k events associated with these periods, we launch the computation of the KDE, then we remove the first period from *UsedPeriods* and we add the periods of *AccumulatedPeriods* to *UsedPeriods*. Finally, we empty the list *AccumulatedPeriods*, and we continuously repeat this process.

In what follows, we present the graphical specification of the detection system by highlighting the process algebra operators used and their functionalities. Then we define the different actions governing the specification of the detection system and the methodology for updating the training data.

3.1   Graphical Specification of the IDS

ASTD specifications are created using the **eASTD** editor. The specification is built using state-transition machines, which are combined using process algebra operators, called *ASTD types*. Thus, an ASTD of a given type contains an operator, attributes (i.e., state variables), and an executable code (action) which is executed every time the ASTD is executed. Each ASTD type has a specific graphical representation.

Figure 2 provides the graphical representation of the ASTD specification of our model. Its top-level operator is a quantified interleave, denoted by ||| in the top-left tab; it is a unary operator, thus it applies to its sub-ASTD *Detect_Anomalous_Event_Times*. It declares a quantified variable userid of type int. ASTD was initially intended for information system (IS) modeling. The quantified interleave operator, taken from the CSP [6] language, gave ASTD an advantageous property not present in other modeling languages such as UML, which consists in the possibility of representing multiple instances of the same entity in an explicit and concise way [4]. In our context, the quantified interleave operator allows one to treat each user independently by associating an instance of its sub-ASTD *Detect_Anomalous_Event_Times* to each user. Thus, each user has its own copy of this sub-ASTD, and it can store the specific information related to a user. It is important to note that the quantification variable userid has an unbounded domain which allows the ASTD to treat all the users without the need to recognize them before.

ASTD *Detect_Anomalous_Event_Times* is of type flow, denoted by Ψ; it is a binary operator similar to AND-state in Statecharts. The flow operator was added to the ASTD language in [29], because often the same event is part of several attacks, and flow allows this event to be executed on each attack specification that can execute it. It allows for executing the same input event on both the training and detection processes.

ASTD *Detect_Anomalous_Event_Times* has the following attributes:

- *EventsByWeek* : $map\langle int, vector\langle double\rangle\rangle$; it contains the period as a key, and a list of event minutes.
- $n : int$; the minimum number of periods to accumulate to launch the calculation of the KDE
- $k : int$; defines the number of events that a user should have in n periods, in order to compute the KDE and build his profile.
- *threshold* : *double*; defines the lowest probability to classify an event as expected
- *UsedPeriods* : $vector\langle int\rangle$; it contains the indices of the periods in EventsBy-Week which will provide the calculation of the KDE after having accumulated a minimum of K events for these periods.
- *AccumulatedPeriods* : $vector\langle int\rangle$; it is used to renew the data used for the calculation KDE.
- *startKDE* : *bool* ; is used to launch the KDE calculation when it is true.
- *UserKDE* : $vector\langle double\rangle$; it contains the current KDE calculated.
- *Alerts* : $vector\langle string\rangle$; it contains the ID of the suspicious events.

Detect_Anomalous_Event_Times contains two sub-ASTDs: *Computation* and *Alerting*, which in turn have access to the previous attributes. The event e is executed by each sub-ASTD which can execute it.

The ASTD *Computation* is of type Automaton. It has as an action *KDE_Computation* which takes as parameters the following variables and

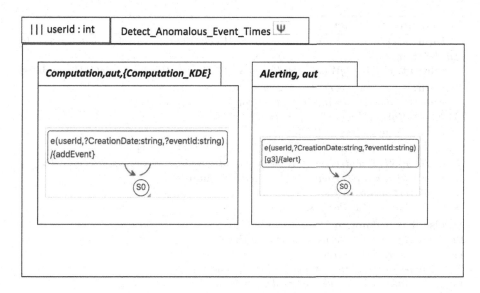

Fig. 2. ASTD graphical specification.

attributes: *userId, EventsByWeek, userkde, UsedPeriods, AccumulatedPeriods, startkde*; it is responsible for the KDE computation after checking the value of *startKDE*. ASTD *Computation* is a state machine that contains a single state with a loop transition labeled with event *e* and it has an action *addEvent(userId, CreationTime, EventsByWeek, UsedPeriods, AccumulatedPeriods, startkde, k, n)*, which adds the events received to the map *EventsByWeek* and manages the periods. The execution of actions occurs in a bottom-up way, which means that transition actions are executed first, followed by ASTD actions. Thus, action *addEvent* is executed before action *KDE_Computation*. ASTD *Computation* manages the attribute *EventsByWeek* and the computation of the KDE profile when it is possible.

The ASTD *Alerting* is also a state machine. It contains only one state with a loop transition also labeled with *e*, and it has an action *alert(userkde, userId, CreationDate, ID, alerts, threshold)*, which is in charge of checking if the probability of occurrence of the received event is lower than the threshold. In that case, the event is reported by adding its *ID* to the vector of alerts. The transition is guarded with condition *g3 = userkde. size()!=0*, which ensures that the *userkde* is not empty.

3.2 Action Definitions

First of all we define the three main actions (*addEvent, Computation_KDE, alert*), then we introduce some methods responsible for partial calculations.

Action *addEvent* (see Algorithm 1) updates the training data structure (*EventsByWeek*) and triggers the KDE computation. For each event received,

---

Algorithm 1. addEvent

Input: $userId, CreationDate, EventsByWeek, UsedPeriods, AccumulatedPeriods,$ $startKDE, n, k$

Output: $EventsByWeek, UsedPeriods, AccumulatedPeriods, startKDE$ updated

1: $period \leftarrow Compute\_period(CreationDate)$
2: $value \leftarrow Compute\_minute(CreationDate)$
3: $EventsByWeek[period].append(value)$
4: **if** $UsedPeriods.size()! = 0$ **then**
5:     $last\_used\_period \leftarrow UsedPeriods[\ UsedPeriods.size() - 1]$
6: **if** $calculNbrEvents(EventsByWeek, UsedPeriods) \leq k$ **or** $UsedPeriods.size() \leq$ n **or** $diffnext(last\_used\_period, period) > 0$ **then**
7:     **if** $period$ **not in** $UsedPeriods$ **then**
8:         $insert(UsedPeriods, period)$
9: **else if** $period$ **not in** $UsedPeriods$ **then**
10:     **if** $AccumulatedPeriods.size() == 0$ **then**
11:         $startKDE \leftarrow true$
12:     **if** $period$ **not in** $AccumulatedPeriods$ **then**
13:         $insert(AccumulatedPeriods, period)$
14: $NewPeriods \leftarrow UsedPeriods[2:] + AccumulatedPeriods$
15: **if** $calculNbrEvents(EventsByWeek, NewPeriods)$ $\geq$
    k **and** $calculNbrEvents(EventsByWeek, AccumulatedPeriods)$ $\geq$
    2 **and** $UsedPeriods.size() \geq n$ **then**
16:     $EventsByWeek.erase(UsedPeriods[1])$
17:     $UsedPeriods \leftarrow NewPeriods$
18:     $AccumulatedPeriods \leftarrow [\ ]$
19:     $NewPeriods \leftarrow [\ ]$

---

we calculate the minute of the day and the period in which it occurred from the *CreationDate* by the *Compute_minute* and *Compute_period* methods, respectively. The minute obtained is then added to the *EventsByWeek* map according to its period. The condition of line 6 allows to build the list *UsedPeriods* and to ensure the continuity of the order between *UsedPeriods* and *AccumulatedPeriods* by verifying that the inserted period is less than the last period of *UsedPeriods*. If this condition (in line 6) is not satisfied, it means that the computation of the KDE from the data associated with *UsedPeriods* is possible. To ensure that we have received enough or all events from the last *UsedPeriods* period, we check-in line 10 that we have not yet received an event from a brand new period that does not exist in *UsedPeriods*. The condition in line 12 ensures that the *AccumulatedPeriods* list is built until the conditions for updating the training data are satisfied.

Then we create the *NewPeriods* list by taking the *UsedPeriods* list deprived of its first period and the periods of *AccumulatedPeriods*. The condition in line 15 checks if *NewPeriods* can be the new *UsedPeriods* that will be used for the computation of the new profile and that there are at least two events associated with the *AccumulatedPeriods*; this is to ensure that the first period of *Used-*

Periods is not deleted before being included in the KDE calculation because the first event of the *AccumulatedPeriods* is responsible for starting the KDE computation.

Algorithm 2. Computation_KDE

> **Input:** *EventsByWeek, UsedPeriods, AccumulatedPeriods, startKDE, userKDE*
> **Output:** *userKDE* updated

1: **if** *startKDE* **then**
2:    *userKDE*.clear()   ▷ **reset** *userKDE*
3:    **for** key in *EventsByWeek*.keys() **do**
4:       **if** key not in *UsedPeriods* **and** key not in *AccumulatedPeriods* **then**
5:          *EventsByWeek*.erase(key)
6:    *fusion(EventsByWeek, UsedPeriods, fusiondata)*
7:    *userKDE ← computationoftheKDE*
8:    *startKDE ← false*

Action *Computation_KDE* (See algorithm 2) computes the KDE after verifying the value of *startKDE*. In this case, it resets the *userKDE*, cleans up the map *EventsByWeek* by deleting the periods not existing in *UsedPeriods* and *AccumulatedPeriods*, merges the data in *EventByWeek* from the *UsedPeriods* into a single list and starts the KDE computation.

Algorithm 3. alert

> **Input:** *userKDE, ID, CreationDate, alerts, threshold*
> **Output:** *alerts* updated

1: *value ← Compute_minute(CreationDate)*
2: **if** *userKDE[value] ≤ threshold* **then**
3:    add *ID* to *alerts*

Action *Alert* (see Algorithm 3) compares the probability of occurrence of the event and the threshold. It computes the minute of occurrence of the received event. It retrieves the probability of occurrence of events at this minute using *userKDE*, compares the probability to a threshold. If the probability is less than the threshold, *ID* is added to the alerts list.

The *numweek* method receives as input the day, month and year. It returns the number of the week associated with this date. The *calculNbrEvents* method receives as input a map of event data and a list of periods. It returns the number of values (events) for those periods in the map. The *diffnext⟨period1, period2⟩* method calculates the difference between two periods, assuming that period2 > period1.

The *insert* method (See Algorithm 4) inserts the periods in the lists *UsedPeriods* and *AccumulatedPeriods*. The insertion of the periods in the two lists is done while keeping an ascending order. This order in the lists is created to ensure the order of the events and identify the events received late: It sometimes happens that there are events that are received after one month of their occurrence. Therefore, it would be relevant to delete them when calculating the current KDE profile. These events can be determined because they belong to a period very far from the first period of the current period list (a difference of more than three periods between the old period and the first period of the list). If we receive an event corresponding to an old period, this period will not be inserted into the list.

Algorithm 4. insert

    Input: *vec, period*
    Output: *vec* updated

1: $it \leftarrow upper\_bound(vec.begin(), vec.end(), period)$ ▷
   `upper_bound return an iterator pointing to the first period in the`
   `range [vec.begin(),vec.end()) which compares greater than period`
2: **if** $it ==vec.begin()$ **and** $it! = vec.end()$ **then** ▷ `if vec is not empty and period`
   `should be inserted at the beginning of vec`
3:     $diff \leftarrow diffnext(value\ at\ it, period)$
4:     **if** $diff \le 3$ **then**
5:         insert *period* at the position pointed by *it*
6: **else**
7:     insert *period* at the position pointed by *it*

3.3   IDS Code Generation

The generation of the IDS source code is done by compiling the ASTD specification by the cASTD compiler [28]. The latter produces code in C++ programming language from an ASTD specification in JSON. The compilation takes place in the following four steps :

– Parsing the ASTD specification in JSON and producing an ASTD object model by the ASTD Parser.
– Translation from ASTD to an intermediate model (IM) using the ASTD Compiler.
– Translation from IM to a programming language like C++ using the IM Translator.
– Code optimization by removing redundant calculations

The specification is first modeled using the eASTD editor, which generates the specification in JSON. This specification and the code defining the set of operations required for the training and detection processes are passed as input to the cASTD. It generates as output the source code in the C++ programming language and the associated program (monitor) that will be executed on the data streams (see Fig. 3). The source code is composed of the helper file, which calls the constructors associated with given string types; the logger file, which allows debugging of the generated program; the IDS source code file, which contains the translated code of the ASTD specifications; and the makefile for linking and compilation. This makefile calls the native compiler corresponding to the C++ language and is automatically executed by cASTD to produce the IDS executable.

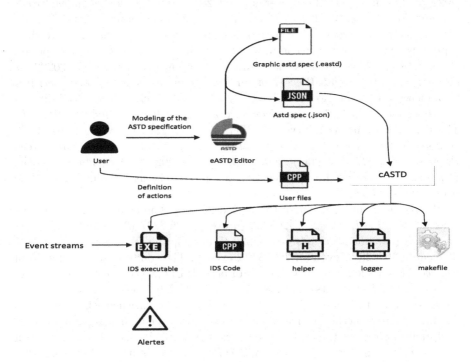

Fig. 3. IDS code generation.

3.4   Example of Specification Execution

To clarify the period management methodology, we proceed with an explicit example. It is assumed that a user's events are received with the following sequence of periods: [202225, 202225, 202225, 202221, 202227, 202227, 202227, 202228, 202228, 202228,202228 , 202229, 202229, 202226]. We take $k = 10$, $n = 3$ and $threshold = 0.001$.

When the first three events are received, the lists of periods are as follows: $UsedPeriods = [202225$ (3 $events$)$]$, $AccumulatedPeriods = [\,]$ and $NewPeriods = [\,]$, according to the condition in line 6 of the $addEvent$ method

We receive the event of period 202221, which is supposed to be inserted in the first position in $UsedPeriods$, in order to keep the list in ascending order. However when we compute the difference between the first period of $UsedPeriods$ 202224 and 202221, we obtain 4 which is greater than 3 so the period 202221 will not be inserted in *UsedPeriods* according to the method insert (Algorithm 4). The lists of periods remains unchanged: *UsedPeriods* = [202225(3*events*)], *AccumulatedPeriods* = [] and *NewPeriods* = [].

The following seven events [202227, 202227, 202227, 202228, 202228, 202228, 202228] will be inserted in *UsedPeriods* according to the method *addEvent* (Algorithm 1). The lists of periods will have the following content: *UsedPeriods* = [202225 (3 events), 202227 (3 events), 202228 (4 events)], *AccumulatedPeriods* = [] and *NewPeriods* = [202227 (3 events), 202228 (3 events)].

We receive the event of the period 202229, *UsedPeriods* contains more than n periods, the number of events associated to it is equal to k, the last period of *UsedPeriods* 202228 is less than 202229, which means that period 202228 is finished, and *AccumulatedPeriods* is empty. So all the conditions are satisfied to launch the computation of the KDE : *startKDE* receives true. According to the condition in line 11 of *addEvent*, we add 202229 to *AccumulatedPeriods*. The period lists are as follows: *UsedPeriods* = [202225 (3 events), 202227 (3 events), 202228 (4 events)], *AccumulatedPeriods* = [202229(1*event*)] and *NewPeriods* = [202227 (3 events), 202228 (3 events), 202229 (1 event)]. Then the *Computation_KDE* method is executed to compute the user profile that will be stored in *UserKDE*.

We receive another event of the period 202229. The content of the periods is as follows: *UsedPeriods* = [202225 (3 events), 202227 (3 events), 202228 (4 events)], *AccumulatedPeriods* = [202229 (2 event)] and *NewPeriods* = [202227 (3 events), 202228 (3 events), 202229 (2 event)]. The condition in the line 15 of *addEvent* is satisfied, we renew the list of periods to have the following: *UsedPeriods* = [202227 (3 events), 202228 (3 events), 202229 (2 event)], *AccumulatedPeriods* = [] and *NewPeriods* = []. The condition *g3* is satisfied which allows to execute the *Alert* method which classifies the event as being normal or abnormal.

Finally we receive the event of the period 202226, which, as the condition of the line 6 of *addEvent*, is inserted in *UsedPeriods*, to obtain the following lists: *UsedPeriods* = [202226 (1 event), 202227 (3 events), 202228 (3 events), 202229 (2 events), 202229 (2 events)], *AccumulatedPeriods* = [] and *NewPeriods* = [202227 (3 events), 202228 (3 events), 202229 (2 events), 202229 (2 events)]. This event also passes through the detection process as *g3* is satisfied.

4   Evaluation and Discussion

The flow operator coordinated the two sub-ASTDs of the training and detection processes. A received event is added to the training data structure and evaluated against the learned model if already computed. This means that the training data is fed simultaneously as the detection is maintained. The fact that the two sub-ASTDs share the attributes inherited from the parent ASTD reinforces this coordination, as the model computed by the first sub-ASTD is used to perform the detection at the second sub-ASTD.

The quantified interleave operator creates the sub-ASTD for each entity processed, which means that there are as many independent IDS as there are entities.

The advantage of the processing independence of the different users in the developed case study is that the update of the training data is done depending on the user's activity, not blindly at the same time for all entities. Each entity has its own attributes, and in the ASTD language, an attribute can be initialized by the value returned by a method. The initialization can also be dependent on the properties of the entity.

The automation of the training data update has been implemented according to if-else instructions; this is possible thanks to continuous data processing. The reference profile is renewed when a new training data set meets defined conditions. This was achieved in the case study by the executable code *Computation_KDE*, responsible for recalculating the KDE profile according to the value of the boolean *startKDE*, which is executed directly after the execution of the action *addEvent* that checks the value of *startKDE*.

The ASTD language formalized the scheduling and coordination of the various IDS processes, which reduces the mental load and the effort required for the development. The modeling of the specification in a graphical representation facilitates modifying or extending the specification. The cASTD tool with its IDS source code generation methodology ensures the modularity and reusability of the IDS specification. Modularity results from the separation of the reading of the data flows, the operations composing the system, and the coordination of the different processes. Reusability is due to the fact that the IDS code generated by cASTD can be compiled and executed in any environment.

The IDS specification was executed on a dataset containing 3,827,551 events of 10 distinct users collected over 10 weeks from one of our industrial collaborators operating a Microsoft365 SAS, using an Intel Core i7 processor machine with frequency 3 GHz × 8 and 32 GB of RAM. The execution took 1 h:34 min:13 s (wall clock time) and 138 MB of RAM, which represents an average execution time of 1.476 ms by event. This Microsoft365 site collects around 40 million events per week, so our generated code can clearly cope with this workload. In [28] a comparison was made between cASTD and other event processing tools (BeepBeep v3, MonPoly, iASTD); it turned out that cASTD is the fastest among them.

5 Conclusion

A study on the use of ASTDs in the context of intrusion detection systems is presented in this paper. This study demonstrates the simplicity of allowing data updates without interrupting the detection process and the creation of modularity at the level of each user that can be treated independently. The ASTD language made it possible to coordinate the anomaly detection model's different processes by using the algebra operators. Evaluation conducted in this paper shows that ASTD specification language can be used to develop anomaly-based detection systems. The cASTD tool that has been used to compile the specifications has shown to be efficient in terms of execution time.

The anomaly detection application presented in the case study is of point type detection. Future works will be carried out to develop other types of anomaly detection that are contextual or collective. A new evaluation will present the advantages of the ASTD specification language in terms of flexibility to apply other estimation calculation methods. The hope founded by this formalization work can allow greater resilience of detection systems in the face of new modern threats. Moreover, the work carried out in this study shows that this could be a probable solution to the current detection problems.

References

1. Home (2022). http://suricata-ids.org/
2. Ahmad, I., Basheri, M., Iqbal, M.J., Rahim, A.: Performance comparison of support vector machine, random forest, and extreme learning machine for intrusion detection. IEEE Access **6**, 33789–33795 (2018). https://doi.org/10.1109/ACCESS.2018.2841987
3. Bauder, R., Khoshgoftaar, T.: Multivariate anomaly detection in medicare using model residuals and probabilistic programming (2017). https://aaai.org/ocs/index.php/FLAIRS/FLAIRS17/paper/view/15429
4. Frappier, M., Gervais, F., Laleau, R., Fraikin, B., St-Denis, R.: Extending statecharts with process algebra operators. Innovations Syst. Softw. Eng. **4**, 285–292 (2008). https://doi.org/10.1007/s11334-008-0064-1
5. Hallé, S.: Event Stream Processing with BeepBeep 3: Log Crunching and Analysis Made Easy (2018)
6. Hoare, C.A.R.: Communicating sequential processes. Commun. ACM **21**(8), 666–677 (1978)
7. Ihaka, R., Gentleman, R.: R: a language for data analysis and graphics. J. Comput. Graph. Stat. **5**(3), 299–314 (1996). http://www.jstor.org/stable/1390807
8. Kasinathan, P., Pastrone, C., Spirito, M.A., Vinkovits, M.: Denial-of-service detection in 6lowpan based internet of things. In: 2013 IEEE 9th International Conference on Wireless and Mobile Computing, Networking and Communications (WiMob), pp. 600–607 (2013)
9. Kauffman, S., Dunne, M., Gracioli, G., Khan, W., Benann, N., Fischmeister, S.: Palisade: a framework for anomaly detection in embedded systems. J. Syst. Architect. **113**, 101876 (2021)
10. Khakurel, N., Bhagat, N.: Advanced engineering and ICT-convergence 2019 (ICAEIC-2019), p. 22 (2019)
11. Létourneau, L.S., El Jabri, C., Frappier, M., Tardif, P.M., Lépine, G., Boisvert, G.: Statistical approach for cloud security: Microsoft office 365 audit logs case study. In: 2021 51st Annual IEEE/IFIP International Conference on Dependable Systems and Networks Workshops (DSN-W), pp. 15–18. IEEE (2021)
12. Lifandali, O., Abghour, N.: Deep learning methods applied to intrusion detection: survey, taxonomy and challenges. In: 2021 International Conference on Decision Aid Sciences and Application (DASA), pp. 1035–1044 (2021). https://doi.org/10.1109/DASA53625.2021.9682357
13. Liu, G., Yi, Z., Yang, S.: Letters: a hierarchical intrusion detection model based on the pca neural networks. Neurocomput. **70**(7–9), 1561–1568 (2007). https://doi.org/10.1016/j.neucom.2006.10.146
14. Nakayama, H., Kurosawa, S., Jamalipour, A., Nemoto, Y., Kato, N.: A dynamic anomaly detection scheme for aodv-based mobile ad hoc networks. IEEE Trans. Veh. Technol. **58**(5), 2471–2481 (2008)

15. Neal, R.M.: Speed improvements in pqr: current status and future plans
16. Nganyewou Tidjon, L.: Modélisation formelle des systèmes de détection d'intrusions. Ph.D. thesis, Institut polytechnique de Paris (2020)
17. Pao, H.K., Lee, F.R., Lee, Y.J.: Dealing with interleaved event inputs for intrusion detection. J. Inf. Sci. Eng. **35**(1), 223–242 (2019)
18. Paxson, V.: Bro: a system for detecting network intruders in real-time. In: Proceedings of the 7th Conference on USENIX Security Symposium - volume 7, p. 3. SSYM 1998, USENIX Association, USA (1998)
19. Raza, S., Wallgren, L., Voigt, T.: Svelte: real-time intrusion detection in the internet of things. Ad Hoc Netw. **11**(8), 2661–2674 (2013). https://doi.org/10.1016/j.adhoc.2013.04.014. https://www.sciencedirect.com/science/article/pii/S1570870513001005
20. Roesch, M.: Snort: lightweight intrusion detection for networks. In: LISA (1999)
21. Roudjane, M., Rebaïne, D., Khoury, R., Hallé, S.: Real-time data mining for event streams. In: 2018 IEEE 22nd International Enterprise Distributed Object Computing Conference (EDOC), pp. 123–134. IEEE (2018)
22. Sanchez, L. et al.: Smartsantander: the meeting point between future internet research and experimentation and the smart cities. In: 2011 Future Network & Mobile Summit, pp. 1–8. IEEE (2011)
23. Sun, R., Zhang, S., Yin, C., Wang, J., Min, S.: Strategies for data stream mining method applied in anomaly detection. Cluster Comput. **22**(2), 399–408 (2018). https://doi.org/10.1007/s10586-018-2835-2
24. Szmit, M., Adamus, S., Szmit, A., Bugała, S.: Implementation of Brutlag's algorithm in Anomaly detection 3.0. In: 2012 Federated Conference on Computer Science and Information Systems (FedCSIS), pp. 685–691 (2012)
25. Thakkar, A., Lohiya, R.: A review of the advancement in intrusion detection datasets. Procedia Comput. Sci. **167**, 636–645 (2020)
26. Thakkar, A., Lohiya, R.: A review on machine learning and deep learning perspectives of ids for iot: recent updates, security issues, and challenges. Arch. Comput. Meth. Eng. **28**(4), 3211–3243 (2021). https://doi.org/10.1007/s11831-020-09496-0
27. Tidjon, L.N., Frappier, M., Mammar, A.: Intrusion detection using ASTDs. In: Barolli, L., Amato, F., Moscato, F., Enokido, T., Takizawa, M. (eds.) AINA 2020. AISC, vol. 1151, pp. 1397–1411. Springer, Cham (2020). https://doi.org/10.1007/978-3-030-44041-1_118
28. Tidjon, L.N.: Formal modeling of intrusion detection systems. Ph.D. thesis, Institut Polytechnique de Paris; Université de Sherbrooke (Québec, Canada) (2020)
29. Tidjon, L.N., Frappier, M., Leuschel, M., Mammar, A.: Extended algebraic state-transition diagrams. In: 2018 23rd International Conference on Engineering of Complex Computer Systems (ICECCS), pp. 146–155. IEEE (2018)
30. Zhang, F., Kodituwakku, H.A.D.E., Hines, J.W., Coble, J.B.: Multilayer data-driven cyber-attack detection system for industrial control systems based on network, system, and process data. IEEE Trans. Ind. Inf. **15**, 4362–4369 (2019)

A Language-Based Causal Model for Safety

Marcello Bonsangue[1], Georgiana Caltais[2(✉)], Hui Feng[1],
and Hünkar Can Tunç[3]

[1] Leiden University, Leiden, Netherlands
{m.m.bonsangue,h.feng}@liacs.leidenuniv.nl
[2] University of Twente, Enschede, Twente, Netherlands
g.g.c.caltais@utwente.nl
[3] Aarhus University, Aarhus, Denmark
tunc@cs.au.dk

Abstract. Inspired by the seminal works on causal analysis by Halpern and Pearl, in this paper we introduce a causal model based on counterfactuals, adapted to finite automata models and with safety properties defined by regular expressions. The latter encode undesired execution traces. We devise a framework that computes actual causes, or minimal traces that lead to states enabling hazardous behaviours. Furthermore, our framework exploits counterfactual information and identifies modalites to steer causal executions towards alternative safe ones. This can provide systems engineers with valuable data for actual debugging and fixing erroneous behaviours. Our framework employs standard algorithms from automata theory, thus paving the way to further generalizations from finite automata to richer structures like probabilistic or KAT automata.

Keywords: Causal models · Counterfactuals · Regular languages · Automata · Safety

1 Introduction

Causal models and associated causal inference machineries are precious tools for the interpretation and explanation of systems failures. Current testing and verification frameworks such as equivalence checking, for instance, assess whether or not systems comply to their specifications, and at most will produce a counterexample in case the system fails. Causal analysis, instead, plays an important role in explaining complex phenomena that are actual sources of hazards by adding, for example, additional information to counterexamples on how to avoid the hazard.

A notion of causality often embraced and adopted by computer scientists was introduced by Halpern and Pearl in their seminal works [9,10]. Their causal model encodes complex logical structures of multiple events that contribute to undesired effects, or hazards. In essence, the model is based on the the so-called alternative worlds, originally proposed by Lewis [17]. In short, Lewis assumes

© Springer Nature Switzerland AG 2022
Y. Aït-Ameur and F. Crăciun (Eds.): TASE 2022, LNCS 13299, pp. 290–307, 2022.
https://doi.org/10.1007/978-3-031-10363-6_20

the existence of worlds satisfying a sufficiency condition, where both the cause and the effect occur, and other worlds satisfying a necessity condition, in which neither the cause nor the effect occur. This enables formulating the counterfactual argument, which defines a first condition to be satisfied by a cause, namely: when the presumed cause does not occur, the effect will not occur either. More complex aspects such as redundancy and preemption are also captured by the causal model in [9,10]. For an intuition, redundancy refers to simultaneous events that play the same role in enabling an undesired effect. Orthogonally, preemption refers to subsequent events that have the same power to enable the effect. In both cases, the counterfactual test alone cannot determine the actual cause. Last, but not least, causes in the spirit of [9] comply to a minimality requirement which guarantees that only the relevant set of causal events is identified.

Related Work. Along time, several notions of causality have been proposed, each of which tailored to the type of the system under analysis, and associated correctness specifications. Of particular interest for this paper are the works in [4, 5,15]. The aforementioned results propose trace-based adoptions of causality á la Halpern and Pearl, applicable to automata models. These, in combination with model checking-based methodologies, enabled computing causes for the violation of safety and liveness properties in Kripke structures and labelled transition systems, for instance.

Our work is closely related to the contribution in [5]. Given an automaton model, the naive goal is to identify the shortest sequence of actions that enable the effect, i.e., that can bring the system into a hazardous state. These are called "causal traces". Note that, in contrast with the often tedious counterexamples identified by model-checkers, the minimality of causal traces implies concise descriptions of systems faults. Thus, causal traces encode essential information for systems engineers, for instance, and they can serve as a debugging aid. As previously stated, in the spirit of Halpern and Pearl, our definition of causality imposes a sufficiency condition: namely, whenever a causal trace is executed, the effect is reached as well. However, important information on how to actually avoid/fix hazardous behaivours can be extracted based on the aforementioned set of alternative worlds (or traces in our model), that do not lead to an undesired effect. Hence, we designed our causal model in the spirit of the counterfactual criterion of Lewis and identified modalities to avoid hazardous scenarios. Similarly to [4,5,15], we call these escape options – "events causal by their non-occurrence". This information can be exploited in order to steer an execution towards an alternative safe one, with immediate applicability in synthesizing schedulers, for instance.

A rich body of work successfully exploited the counterfactual argument for fault analysis and debugging techniques. Examples related to counterexample explanation in model checking are the works in [7,8,21], for instance. In [7] the authors propose a framework for understanding errors in ANSI C programs, based on distance metrics for program executions. In [8] the cause describing the error includes the identification of source code fragments crucial to distinguishing success from failure, and differences in invariants between failing and non-failing runs. Distance criteria have also been exploited in [21], in combination with the so-called nearest neighbor queries to perform fault localization. The why-because-analysis in [14] was used to reason about aviation accidents, in a framework where Lamport's Temporal Logic of Actions (TLA) described both the behavior of a system, the (history of) hazards and the sequence of the states leading to an accident. The work in [23] provides a comprehensive approach to systematic debugging including, among others, delta debugging – a technique for isolating minimal input to reproduce an error.

For finer notions of causal dependencies that distinguish between interleaving and true concurrency, for instance, we refer to event structures [2,20]. Nevertheless, in our work, we adhere to the approaches in [4,5,15], and do not take into consideration the order of events along execution traces.

Our Contributions. We propose a shifting bisimulation setting presented in [5] to a trace based setting in the context of regular languages and automata theory. The benefits are multifold. For instance, the paradigm change facilitates the application of more standard algorithms from automata theory, in contrast with the rather ad-hoc procedures in [4,5,15]. Furthermore, the current framework enables using an expressive logic for defining safety properties in terms of regular expressions (or automata), instead of the ordinary Hennessy-Milner logic. The language based approach to causality enables representing both hazards and causal explanations in terms of automata – a format better accepted by engineers. In addition, in this paper, we use regular languages (or full regular expressions including Kleene-star) to encode non-occurrence of events. Previous related works such as [4,5,15] can only provide finite sets of runs steering an execution towards an alternative safe one. Orthogonal to the aforementioned results, the current approach entails a "may" semantics of causality, instead of "must"; nevertheless, we believe that the approach can be easily modified to cater for the "must" version. Besides, in contrast with the results in [5], steering executions are guaranteed not to jump over hazardous states by simply concatenating sequences causal by their non-occurrence and the causal trace. The ultimate goal of the current work is to generalize from finite automata to richer structures like probabilistic automata and NetKAT automata [1,6].

Structure of Paper. In Sect. 2 we provide an overview of regular languages and associated automata theory aspects. A running example is introduced in Sect. 3. Section 4 defines the language-based model of causality, whereas in Sect. 5 we show how to compute actual causes and safe computations. In Sect. 6 we provide an experimental evaluation of our method and in Sect. 7 we discuss how our model can be extended with tests and assignments. Section 8 concludes our work.

2 Preliminaries

In this section we recall few basic facts about regular languages, finite automata, and regular expressions [18].

Let A be a finite set of actions that we refer to as an *alphabet*. A *word* or *string* over A is a finite sequence $a_1 \ldots a_n$ of elements from A. We denote by ε

the empty word, i.e. the sequence of length 0, and write A^* to denote the set of (possibly empty) words over A. A *language* L is just a subset of words, that is $L \subseteq A^*$. We call a word w' to be a *prefix* of a word w whenever $w = w'w''$. A word w' is said to be a *sub-word* of a word w, if w' is obtained by deleting one or more elements of A at some not necessarily adjacent positions in w. We denote by $sub(w)$ the set of all sub-words of w. Note that $sub(\varepsilon) = \emptyset$. Also, $\varepsilon \in sub(w)$ but $w \notin sub(w)$ for every non empty word w.

A *finite automaton* (FA) is a 5-tuple $M = (S, A, i, \longrightarrow, F)$, where S is a finite set of states, $i \in S$ is the initial state, $F \subseteq S$ is the set of accepting states and $\longrightarrow \subseteq S \times A \times S$ is the transition relation. For simplicity, we write $s \xrightarrow{a} t$ whenever $(s, a, t) \in \longrightarrow$. A transition relation is called deterministic if for all $s \in S$ and $a \in A$ if $s \xrightarrow{a} t_1$ and $s \xrightarrow{a} t_2$ then $t_1 = t_2$.

A string $w \in A^*$ is accepted by an automaton M from a state s if either (1) $w = \varepsilon$ and $s \in F$, or (2) $w = aw'$ and there exists $s \xrightarrow{a} t$ such that w' is accepted by M from the state t. The *language accepted* by a FA M is the set $L(M) = \{w \in A^* \mid M \text{ accepts } w \text{ from } i\}$. Since for every FA M we can build a FA N with a deterministic transition relation such that $L(M) = L(N)$, without loss of generality we will consider only finite automata with a deterministic transition relation.

A language L over the alphabet A is said to be *regular* if there exists a finite automaton M accepting it, that is $L(M) = L$. The class of all regular languages is closed under union, intersection, concatenation, complement and Kleene star. Here language union and intersections are the usual set theoretic operations, whereas concatenation of two languages L_1 and L_2 is given by the set $L_1 \cdot L_2 = \{w_1 w_2 \mid w_1 \in L_1 \wedge w_2 \in L_2\}$. Finally, for a language L, its Kleene star closure is defined by $L^* = \bigcup_{n \in \mathbb{N}} L^n$ where $L^0 = \{\varepsilon\}$ and $L^{n+1} = L \cdot L^n$ for all $n \in \mathbb{N}$, thus denoting the concatenation of a language with itself a finite number of time.

In this paper, we are interested in system communicating by message passing, and thus we will always assume that the alphabet A is partitioned in three disjoint subsets A_I, A_O, and A_P of input, output and private actions, respectively. Notationally, for $a \in A$ we write $a?$ if a is an input action in A_I and $a!$ if a is an output action in A_O, and use no markings for private actions in A_P. We use σ to denote an action that can be either input, output or private.

Let A and B be two alphabets with disjoint private actions, and assume the set P is disjoint from Q. Given two finite automata $M = (P, A, i, \longrightarrow_M, E)$ and $N = (Q, B, j, \longrightarrow_N, F)$ their *parallel composition* is defined by the finite automaton $M \parallel N = (P \times Q, \Sigma, < i, j >, \longrightarrow, E \times F)$ where $\Sigma_I = (A_I \backslash B_O) \cup (B_I \backslash A_O)$, $\Sigma_O = (A_O \backslash B_I) \cup (B_O \backslash A_I)$, $\Sigma_P = (A_P \cup B_P) \cup (A_I \cap B_O) \cup (A_O \cap B_I)$, and $\longrightarrow$ is the least transition relation such that

$$\frac{p \xrightarrow{\sigma}_M p' \quad \sigma \notin B}{\langle p, q \rangle \xrightarrow{\sigma} \langle p', q \rangle} \qquad \frac{q \xrightarrow{\sigma}_N q' \quad \sigma \notin A}{\langle p, q \rangle \xrightarrow{\sigma} \langle p, q' \rangle}$$

$$\frac{p \xrightarrow{a?}_M p' \quad q \xrightarrow{a!}_N q'}{\langle p, q \rangle \xrightarrow{a} \langle p', q' \rangle} \qquad \frac{p \xrightarrow{a!}_M p' \quad q \xrightarrow{a?}_N q'}{\langle p, q \rangle \xrightarrow{a} \langle p', q' \rangle}$$

The topmost rules are about either private actions that are not affected by the other automaton or communication actions that do not involve the other automaton. The two rules at the bottom are about complementary communication actions $a!$ and $a?$ that are synchronized resulting in the private action a. Note that when $A = B$ with $A_I = B_O$, $A_O = B_I$ and $A_P = B_P = \emptyset$ then parallel composition reduces to the product automata where all actions synchronize. In the case A is completely disjoint from B then parallel composition results in the so-called shuffle product. Other variation of synchronization product could be defined in a similar way, including multi-process synchronization, hiding of successful communication, value passing synchronization (for a finite value domain) and synchronization parameterized by a finite subset of actions.

For the characterization of the parallel composition of two languages we need first to introduce the *projection* function. Given two alphabets A_1 and A_2 we define the projection $\pi_i : (A_1 \cup A_2)^* \rightarrow A_i^*$ by $\pi_i(\varepsilon) = \varepsilon$, and $\pi_i(\sigma \cdot w) = \sigma \cdot \pi_i(x)$ if $\sigma \in A_i$, and $\pi_i(w)$ otherwise. Because projections are surjective functions they have inverse π_i^{-1} returning the set of strings that are projected into a given one. More precisely, we define the *inverse projection* by $\pi_i^{-1}(w) = \{x \in (A_1 \cup A_2)^* \mid \pi_i(x) = w\}$ for every $w \in A_i^*$. Projections and their inverses can extended to languages by applying them to all the strings in the language. In general we have that $\pi_i(\pi_i^{-1}(L)) = L$ but for the converse it only holds that $L \subseteq \pi_i^{-1}(\pi_i(L))$. Note that if two alphabets A_1 and A_2 have disjoint private actions and we partition $A_1 \cup A_2$ as in the alphabet of the parallel composition of two automata, then projections will assign private actions of $A_1 \cup A_2$ to either private, input or output actions in A_i unambiguously. Similarly, inverse projections assign private actions to private actions, but may assign input and output actions to private ones.

The *parallel composition* of two languages $L_1 \subseteq A_1^*$ and $L_2 \subseteq A_2^*$ is the language $L_1 \parallel L_2$ on the alphabet $A_1 \cup A_2$ defined as $\pi_1^{-1}(L_1) \cap \pi_2^{-1}(L_2)$. Basically, the intersection takes care that dual communication actions will be synchronized, and that disjoint private events will be shuffled with the others. As expected, we have that $L(M_1 \parallel M_2) = L(M_1) \parallel L(M_2)$, implying that regular languages are closed under parallel composition [22].

We conclude this section by introducing extended regular expressions, that we may use as alternative syntax to FAs in order to reason about causality in complex systems composed of several components potentially communicating with each other.

Given an alphabet A including communication actions, *extended regular expressions* are given by the following grammar:

$$e ::= 0 \mid 1 \mid a \mid a? \mid a! \mid e \,;\, e \mid e + e \mid e \parallel e \mid e^*, \tag{1}$$

where $a \in A_P$, $a?$ implies $a \in A_I$, and $a!$ implies $a \in A_O$. In process theoretic terms, 0 denotes no behavior, 1 denotes a terminating process. The further building blocks of processes are (communication) actions. Processes can be composed sequentially, non-deterministically, in parallel, or can loop a finite number of times. Communication between process terms is performed based on synchronizations between opposite communication actions, that play thus a sender, respectively, receiver role. In the sequel we often use A as shorthand for the regular expression obtained by the finite set of every action in A, and $\neg a$ as a shorthand for the set of every action in A except a. Note that in general we could extend negation to all regular expression, as regular languages are closed under complement.

Ordinary regular expressions are expressions without any parallel composition. Except for the parallel composition we assume that an action cannot be used as input and output in the same 'sequential' expression, i.e., regular expression with no occurrence of the $\parallel$ operator. With this mild restriction we can associate to each regular expressions e a language $L(e)$ inductively as follows:

$$
\begin{array}{lll}
L(0) = \emptyset & L(e_1\,;\,e_2) = L(e_1) \cdot L(e_2) & \\
L(1) = \{\varepsilon\} & L(e_1 + e_2) = L(e_1) \cup L(e_2) & L(e^*) = L(e)^* \\
L(a) = \{a\} & L(e_1 \parallel e_2) = L(e_1) \parallel L(e_2) &
\end{array}
$$

It is well known [11] that the language of an ordinary regular expression is regular. The same holds for our extended regular expressions, as we have seen that regular languages are closed under parallel composition. This implies that for every (extended) regular expression e there exists an automaton M such that $L(e) = L(M)$. We will not describe the construction here as it is outside the scope of this paper.

3 A Railway Crossing Example

In this section we recall the railway crossing example from [5], and adapt it to our present setting. The example consists of a car, a train, and a gate of a crossing that communicates with the train. The gate can communicate its the status of being closed ($Gc!$) or open ($Go!$). The status changes to closed only after the gate receives a message from the train that is approaching the crossing ($Ta?$), and it can change to open only after it receives the message that the train leaves the crossing ($Tl?$). The behavior of the gate is described by the following regular expression:

$$
G = (Go!^* \,; (1 + Ta?\,; Gc!^* \,; Tl?))^*.
$$

When a train is approaching the crossing, it sends a message ($Ta!$). After that, it will actually enter the crossing (Tc) and then send a message informing its departure from the crossing ($Tl!$). This behavior is described by the following regular expression:

$$
T = Ta!\,; Tc\,; Tl!.
$$

Finally, a car can approach the crossing (Ca), wait as long as the gate is closed ($Gc?$), eventually observe the gate being open ($Go?$), and only then it may enter the crossing (Cc) and leave the crossing afterwards (Cl). The regular expression encoding this is given by:

$$
C = Ca\,; Gc?^* \,; Go?\,; Cc;\, Cl.
$$

The FAs corresponding to the above three regular expression are illustrated in Fig. 1. Note that the car can enter the crossing only after the gate is open, whereas the gate enters the state of being open only after a train signals its departure.

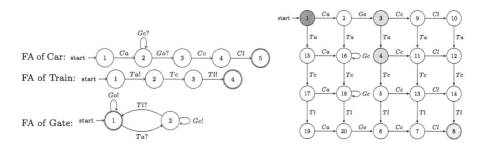

Fig. 1. The car, train and gate as FAs   **Fig. 2.** The railway system as a FA

In Fig. 2 we see the automaton describing the railway system that results by the parallel composition of the three regular expressions: $C \parallel T \parallel G$ where, for simplicity, we renamed the states. For example, the initial state ① corresponds to the state $\langle 1, 1, 1 \rangle$ and the only accepting state is ⑧ corresponding to $\langle 5, 4, 1 \rangle$. The red states ③ and ④ will be used in the next section as examples of states leading to a hazard situation: a car entering the crossing and not leaving it before the train enters the crossing too.

4   A Language-Based Causal Model

In this section we introduce a notion of causality with respect to a so-called *hazard*, or *effect* expressed in terms of regular expressions. The current causal framework is inspired from the model introduced in [5] and massaged into the setting of FAs with the goal to use trace semantics instead of bisimulation, and define different system properties in terms of regular expressions (such as reachability) instead of the ordinary Hennessy-Milner logic.

In short, a hazard is a regular language specified by a regular expression e (or the corresponding automaton). It is said to occur in a FA M representing our model whenever there is a finite (and possibly empty) string $c = a_0 \ldots a_n$ in M such that after c we may observe the hazard, that is, $L(c\,;\,e) \cap L(M) \neq \emptyset$. In this case, we say that c may enable the hazard e in M. Additional conditions that have to be satisfied by c, such as minimality and non-occurrence of events, are formalized in Definition 1.

For an intuition, consider the railway crossing example of the previous section. A hazardous situation can happen whenever both the train and the car enter the crossing, and none of them leaves the crossing before the other one enters it. The regular expression encoding this hazard is:

$$e = (Cc\,;\,(\neg Cl)^*\,;\,Tc + Tc\,;\,(\neg Tl)^*\,;\,Cc)\,;\,A^* \tag{2}$$

Note that the hazard situation can terminate with any string in A^*. This is to guarantee that after a trace c enables e, their concatenation will contain behaviors accepted by the automaton, and thus the hazard is observed. It is straightforward to see that in the FA in Fig. 1 it is possible to reach the above hazard with the string $c_1 = Ca\,Go$ leading to the state ③, but also with the string $c_2 = Ca\,Go\,Ta$ leading to the state ④. In fact, the intersection of the language of the hazard e with that of the automaton M starting from either state ③ or ④ instead of ① is non-empty. Furthermore, state ③ and ④ are both reachable from the initial state ①.

We may say that c_1 does a better job at describing the relevant sequence of actions that, if triggered, lead to a hazard because it is a *minimal* sequence enabling it. Moreover, we see that it is possible to avoid the hazard by "decorating" the string c_1 with the strings Ta, $TcTl$ and, respectively, $CcCl$. This can result, for instance, in the string $w = Ta\,\underline{Ca}\,TcTl\,\underline{Go}\,CcCl$ which does not lead to a hazard. Sequences such as Ta, $TcTl$ and $CcCl$ are called *causal by non-occurrence* in works such as [4,5]. Non-occurrence is essential for describing how certain dangerous situations, if controllable, can be avoided within a system. This concept plays an important role in our definition of causality.

As formalized in Definition 1, non-occurrence of events is captured in terms of the so-called *computations* [5]. The latter are strings in a regular language, typically denoted by π, built on top of a string $c = a_0 \ldots a_n$, and "decorated" with strings $d_0^i, \ldots, d_{n+1}^i$, with $i \in I$, where I is a finite set of integers, such that:

$$w \in \pi \;\;\Rightarrow\;\; w = d_0^i a_0 d_1^i \cdots a_n d_{n+1}^i.$$

Intuitively, given a trace c that enables a hazard, strings in π describe all the alternative runs (such as w above) that execute all actions in c and avoid the hazard. The only requirement is that all strings specified by π are observable executions of M; i.e., for a given FA M, $\pi \subseteq L(M)$. Notice that π being a regular language means that it can be expressed as a regular expression r, and because all strings in π contain c as subword, we have $r = \Sigma_{j,k} r_k^j$ with $r_k^j = r_0^j; a_0; r_1^j; \ldots a_k; r_{k+1}^j$ for some finite indexes j and k and regular expressions r_{k+1}^j. For simplicity, we sometimes write r in lieu of π.

The next definition formally introduces *decorated causes* for a FA M with respect to a hazard e.

Definition 1 (Causality for FAs). *Let $M = (S, A, s_0, \rightarrow, F)$ be a FA, e be a regular expression over A, denoting a hazard, and $c \in A^*$. We say that the computation π built on top of c, with $\pi \subseteq L(M)$, is a decorated cause of the hazard e if*

AAC1: *The string c may enable e – $L(c\,;\,e) \cap L(M) \neq \emptyset$*
AAC2.1: *If the effect e is not observed then it has not been caused by c –*
$\forall w \in L(M) \backslash L(A^*\,;\,e) : (L(w\,;\,e) \cap L(M) = \emptyset) \Rightarrow (c \notin sub(w) \vee w \in \pi)$.
AAC2.2: *Strings of π are safe, i.e., they do not cause the effect e –*
$\forall w \in \pi : w \notin L(A^*\,;\,e) \wedge (L(w\,;\,e) \cap L(M) = \emptyset)$

AAC3: *Minimality –*

*for all $c' \in sub(c)$ there is no computation π' built on top of c' with $\pi' \subseteq L(M)$, that satisfies **AAC1–AAC2.2** with respect to the string c' and the hazard e.*

We call c as above a causal trace, *and sometimes write $Cause_c(e, M)$ to denote the corresponding decorated cause π. We let $Causes(e, M)$ be the union of all $Cause_c(e, M)$.*

Intuitively, **AAC1** identifies a scenario where the string c enables the hazard e in M. Note that **AAC1** entails a "may" semantics of causality, instead of "must", as c does not always have to lead to e. Catering for the "must" version requires modifying **AAC1** to $L(c\,;\,e) \subseteq L(M)$. **AAC2.1** is a necessity condition according to which, if a word w cannot enable e, then either w does not contain the causal trace c (meaning it is an execution bringing not to the hazard), or it has been decorated with events that eliminate the possibility of executing the hazard. Note that **AAC2.1** can be equivalently expressed (by modus tollens) as a sufficiency condition stating that a string w enables the hazard e whenever the causal trace is contained in w but it is not decorated with elements causal by their non-occurrence that would avoid the execution of the hazard:

$$\forall w \in L(M)\backslash L(A^*\,;\,e) \,:\, (c \in sub(w) \wedge w \notin \pi) \Rightarrow (L(w\,;\,e) \cap L(M) \neq \emptyset)$$

AAC2.2 requires causal traces decorated with events causal by their non-occurrence to avoid the hazard. Furthermore, note that c itself cannot be a safe computation in π, because otherwise **AAC2.2** would contradict **AAC1**. Observe that **AAC2.2** is reminiscent of the traditional counterfactual criterion of Lewis, as it allows to test the dependence of e on c under certain contingencies encoded, in our case, in terms of non-occurrence of events. We refer to [10] for more insight on the so-called *structural contingencies*. **AAC3** is the minimality condition that requires to consider decorated causes entailed by the shortest causal traces c satisfying **AAC1–AAC2.2**.

We conclude the section with a few examples intended to clarify certain aspects of the above definition and the differences with the work [5]. To begin with, we illustrate the role played by loops in the decorations of computations.

Example 1. Consider the automaton M_1 in Fig. 3 and let the hazard be expressed by the regular expression $e = c\,;\,A^*$, meaning that we have to avoid executing action c.

Clearly, the string $a\,b$ is a possible cause for the hazard. Hence, $Cause_{ab}(e, M_1)$ for this example can be encoded via the regular expression: $a\,;\,f\,;\,h^*\,;\,b\,;\,g$. Note that as a result of considering the decorations as regular expressions, all finite repetitions of the loop are conveniently represented with the Kleene star operator. The work in [5] handles loops in the decorations by unfolding the loop only a finite number of times specified a-priori, hence, only the string afh^nbg would be describing hazard avoidance, for all $n \leq k$ and some fixed k.

In the second example, we consider the case when there are no possible decorations to steer a causal trace away from its hazard.

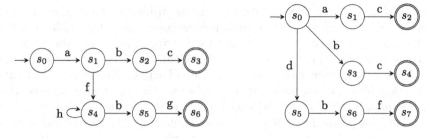

Fig. 3. Automaton M_1 **Fig. 4.** Automaton M_2

Example 2. Consider the automaton M_2 in Fig. 4 and let the hazard be as before expressed by the regular expression $e = c$; A^*.

In this example, there are two possible causal traces, namely, a and b. There are no possible decorations for the causal trace a to make it avoid the hazard, whereas, there exists a decoration for the causal trace b with $Cause_b(e, M_2) = d$; b; f. Whenever there are no computations π satisfying Definition 1 for e in M w.r.t. a trace c, we say that the hazard e, if enabled by c, is *unavoidable* in M.

In the above two examples there was no actual difference if we would have used c as hazard instead of the regular expression c; A^*. In the next example we show a FA where the two expressions entail different decorated causes.

Example 3. Consider the automaton M_3 in Fig. 5 and the hazards $e = c$; A^* and $e' = c$.

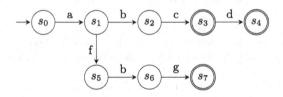

Fig. 5. Example 3

For both hazards, ab is the causal trace, but

$$Cause_{ab}(e, M_3) = a\,;\, f\,;\, b\,;\, g$$
$$Cause_{ab}(e', M_3) = a\,;\, f\,;\, b\,;\, g \;+\; a\,;\, b\,;\, c\,;\, d$$

Observe that the string $abcd$ is considered safe (i.e., avoids the hazard) according to $Cause_{ab}(e', M_3)$ but is not considered safe in $Causes_{ab}(e, M_3)$, wheres the string $afbg$ is considered safe in both cases. This is different than the usual notion of safety (modeled as in e and thus forbidding any possible continuation after the hazard) as e' allow to overpass the hazard if the system does not stop there. In fact, the expression e' asserts that the trace cannot halt with the action c. Accordingly, both $abcd$ and $afbg$ are valid strings that satisfy this condition and thus avoid the hazard e'. On the other hand, the expression e asserts that the action c followed by any possible sequence of actions (i.e., in A^*) constitutes a violation, hence, the action c cannot be observed at any point in an execution. Therefore, only $afbg$ is a valid execution that will avoid the hazard e. It is essentially not possible to define properties similar to e with the approach in [5], as they allow jumping over a hazardous state while executing strings in π.

5   Computing Causes

Given a FA $M = (S, A, i, \longrightarrow, F)$ and an effect specified by a regular expression e on A, we show an algorithm for computing the set $Causes(e, M)$ using standard operations on automata and graphs. The algorithm first computes the set of loop-free traces that lead to the hazard e. Then, for each one of them, it determines the associated computation satisfying conditions **AAC2.1–AAC2.2** in Definition 1. The union of all such computations will give a first approximation of the set $Causes(e, M)$. We will then show below how to obtain precisely the set $Causes(e, M)$ by requiring the minimality condition **AAC3** in Definition 1.

Algorithm 1: Computing Causes

Input: A FA $M = (S, A, i, \longrightarrow, F)$, an effect e.
Output: The set of decorated causes $Causes(e, M)$.

(1) Compute the set of traces that lead to e by following the steps:
  (1.1) For all $s \in S$, construct the FA $P_s = (S, A, s, \longrightarrow, F)$ and compute the following intersection:
  $L(P_s') = L(P_s) \cap L(e)$.
  (1.2) Construct the automaton $P = (S, A, i, \longrightarrow, F')$ where $F' = \{s \mid L(P_s') \neq \emptyset\}$.
  (1.3) Compute all simple paths from the intial states i and a final state $f \in F$ in P.
  (1.4) Let $CausalTraces$ be the set of all strings in $L(P)$ labeling the paths computed in (1.3).
(2) For all $c = a_0 \ldots a_n \in CausalTraces$, compute $Cause_c(e, M)$ by :

$$(L(A^*; a_0; A^*; \ldots; A^*; a_n; A^*) \setminus \{c\}) \cap (L(M) \setminus (L(A^*; e) \cup L(P)))$$

(3) Return the union of all the languages computed in step (2) as Causes(e, M).

Next, we discuss the underlying ideas behind the certain steps of Algorithm 1 and then provide a proof of correctness for the algorithm. We first compute all traces that enable e by constructing in steps (1.1) and (1.2) the automaton P that accepts exactly all traces in M possibly causing the effect e. The only difference between the automata P and M is their set of final states. The procedure for constructing P first involves constructing a set of automata P_s, for all the states s of the automaton M, such that s is the initial state in P_s and accepts strings of the language of the hazard e. If the intersection of $L(P_s)$ with $L(e)$ is non-empty, then the corresponding state is considered as a final state in the automaton P (step (1.2)). As a result, the strings in $L(P)$ are exactly those strings bringing M to a state of where the hazard is activated. For our railway crossing example in Sect. 3 with the hazard given by the regular expression in (2), the automaton P would be the one in Fig. 2 with states ③ and ④ as the only final states.

In step (1.3) we compute $CausalTraces$ as the subset of strings accepted by P via a simple path starting from the initial state and ending in a final state. These paths correspond to the set of loop-free traces that lead to the hazard e. While this condition does not guarantee minimality (see discussion below) it already reduces the set of possibly causal traces to a finite set. In general, $L(P)$ will be infinite, if it involves a loop in the automaton.

For each of the above finitely many causal traces, in step (2), we compute the set of associated computations. For a given possibly causal trace c, this is done by subtracting all the traces which enable the effect (i.e., $L(P)$) and all the traces which observe the effect (i.e., $L(A^*; e)$) from $L(M)$ and then take the intersection of the resulting language with the language resulted from c decorated with non-occurrence in all possible ways. Note that the intersection computed in step (2) may be empty, meaning that the hazard e is unavoidable when executing the actions of c. For our running example in Sect. 3, the possibly causal traces computed by the algorithm are $CaGo$ and $CaGoTa$. Examples of strings in the associated computations are $CaGoTaCcClTcTl$ and $CaGoCcClTaTcTl$. Note that the first string avoids the hazard for both possibly causal traces, while the latter is a string that avoids the hazard for $CaGo$.

Finally, the union of the resulting languages in the step (2) of Algorithm 1 is returned as a first approximation of the set of all decorated causes of M for the hazard e. For this set, the following theorem guarantees that conditions **AAC1–AAC2.2** hold. However, condition **AAC3** may fail to hold.

Theorem 1. *The computations in $Causes(e, M)$ returned by Algorithm 1 satisfy conditions* **AAC1–AAC2.2** *by construction.*

Proof. The set $Causes(e, M)$ returned by Algorithm 1 is obtained as the union of all $Causes_c(e, M)$ for all $c \in CausalTraces$. Elements in this sets are obtained in step (1.4). These strings are computed based on the language that the automaton P (constructed in step (1.2)) recognizes. By construction, $x \in L(P)$ implies there is $y \in L(e)$ such that $xy \in L(M)$. Hence $L(x; e) \cap L(M) \neq \emptyset$. Since $CausalTraces \subseteq L(P)$, condition **AAC1** holds.

In order to show that **AAC2.1** holds for some $c \in CausalTraces$, take a string x accepted by M that is not in $L(A^*; e)$. Assume that $L(x; e) \cap L(M) = \emptyset$. Then $x \notin L(P)$ because otherwise, as we have just seen above, there would exist $y \in L(e)$ such that $xy \in L(M)$. Therefore, $x \in L(M) \backslash (L(A^*; e) \cup L(P))$. Because $CausalTraces \subseteq L(P)$, it follows that $x \neq c$ for any possibly causal trace c. We have now two cases: for every $c \in CausalTraces$ either $c \in sub(x)$ or not. In the latter case **AAC2.1** holds. In the other case $c \in sub(x)$ and thus $x \in L(A^*; a_0; A^*; \ldots; A^*; a_n; A^*)$, from which it follows based on step (2) that $x \in Causes_c(e, M)$, and thus **AAC2.1** holds.

It remains to show that **AAC2.2**. For some possibly causal trace $c \in CausalTrace$ let $x \in Cause_c(e, M)$. We must show that $x \notin A^*e$ and that $L(x; e) \cap L(M) = \emptyset$. The first part of the conjunction in **AAC2.2** holds because by the construction in step (2) $Cause_c(e, M)$ cannot contain strings from $L(A^*; e)$. Similarly, the second part of the conjunction holds because $L(P)$ is subtracted from $L(M)$ in the same step.

Condition **AAC3** does not necessarily hold for $Cause_c(e, M)$ used by the Algorithm 1. In fact, for possibly causal traces $x, y \in CausalTraces$, if $x \in sub(y)$ then any sub-string of x is also a sub-string of y. In other words, for $a_0 \cdots a_n = x \neq y = b_0 \cdots b_m$ we have

$$L(A^*; a_0; A^*; \ldots; A^*; a_n; A^*) \subseteq L(A^*; b_0; A^*; \ldots; A^*; b_m; A^*) \qquad (3)$$

By step (2) of Algorithm 1 we thus have that $Causes_x(e, M) \subseteq Causes_y(e, M)$. Note that it must be the case that $m > n$ for $x \in sub(y)$. We can therefore easily compute the smallest sets of safe computations by removing from the set $CausalTraces$ all strings y that have another possibly causal trace $x \in CausalTraces$ of smaller length as sub-word. In our running example, the trace $CaGo$ is clearly a sub-word of the other one $CaGoTa$, and indeed, the computation for $CaGoTa$ is included in the computation for $CaGo$ as well. Hence, only the causal trace $CaGo$ satisfies the minimality condition **AAC3** .

6   Experimental Evaluation

In this section, we provide an experimental evaluation and assess the applicability of our method. We developed a tool prototype implementing our approach and evaluated the time performance by computing the decorated causes on randomly generated FAs with growing size. The implementation is based on Python and closely follows Algorithm 1. The inputs to our tool are a FA and a regular expression which describes the effect on the given FA. The output of our tool is an automaton which characterizes the set of all decorated causes with respect to the given inputs. In our implementation we utilized the BRICS automaton library [19] for performing standard automaton operations.

We evaluated our tool in the following experimental setting: we generated random FAs by using the libalf [3] framework. In the process of generating FAs we fixed the size of the alphabet to 5. We then generated over 1000 FAs with increasing number of states and achieved a maximum of 300 states. Figure 6 shows an example of a FA with 5 states that was generated randomly by libalf. For each generated FA we also randomly computed an effect for which the decorated causes are determined. We fixed the size of the effect length to 3. All the experiments were conducted on a computer running Ubuntu 20.04.3 with 8 core 1.8GHz Intel i7-10510U processor and 16 GB RAM.

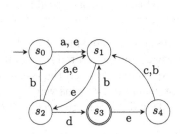

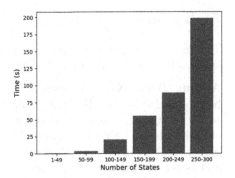

Fig. 6. Randomly generated FA with 5 states.

Fig. 7. Experimental results

The results of our experiments are displayed in Fig. 7. We group the randomly generated FAs by their number of states and report the average running times in each group. We only report the times of the experiments in which the decorated causes were not empty. The results indicate that for relatively small FAs with less than 100 states, a result is obtained within 10 s. For larger FAs with 250 to 300 states, a result is obtained in 3 min on average and within 15 min at maximum. We remark that these results are obtained without any attempts to tailor the standard automaton operations to our setting.

Table 1. Average size of obtained decorated causes.

	Number of states in the input FA					
	1–49	50–99	100–149	150–199	200–249	250–300
# States	71	185	266	422	484	560
# Transitions	236	654	997	1565	1862	2177
# Potential Causes	81	328	10476	21932	44750	73318
# (Minimal) Causes	3	8	10	18	10	22

In Table 1 we summarize some information on the automata that recognize the decorated causes returned by the algorithm. Depending on the number of states of the automata given as input, we report the average number of states and transitions of the returned automata, the average number of causes and the average number of minimal causes obtained. As to be expected, the size of the automata of the output increased linearly with that of the input. However, the number of potential causal traces computed increases exponentially. That is not the case for the number of minimal causal traces, as it increases only marginally when the size of the input increases. In fact, in the majority of the cases, the number of minimal causes is less than 5, regardless of the size of the given input automaton.

7   Extensions

To illustrate the generality of our causal model we briefly discuss possible extensions so to consider addition of tests and assignments.

Adding Tests: KAT. The set of regular expressions we considered in (1) can be extended with a set B of Boolean tests that we assume generated from a finite set At of atoms, meaning that every $b \in B$ is equivalent modulo the equations of the Boolean algebra to a finite disjunction of atoms in At. This way one can model basic programming constructs, like conditionals, loops, guarded actions, and assertions using tests in B and actions in A.

Kozen [12] showed that the above extensions of regular expressions, called KAT (Kleene algebra with tests) expressions, plays the same role with regular sets of guarded strings as ordinary regular languages play for regular expressions. Here a *guarded string* is an ordinary string over the alphabet $A \cup At$, such that the symbols in A alternate with the atoms At. Formally, a guarded language is a subset of $(At \times A)^* \times At$.

A *deterministic KAT automaton* recognizing guarded strings [13] is just a deterministic finite automaton $(S, \Sigma, i, \longrightarrow, F)$ with $\Sigma = At \times A$ and $F \subseteq S \times At$. The only differences are thus the transition relations that is now labeled by guarded actions (α, a), and the accepting states, that are now labeled with atoms marking the end of an accepted string. The idea is that an action a is executed only when its guard α (pre-condition) is true, and a string is accepted only in states where the post-condition holds. We say that a guarded string $w \in (At \times A)^* \times At$ is accepted by a KAT automaton M from a state s if either (1) $w = \alpha$ and $(s, \alpha) \in F$, or (2) $w = (\alpha, a)w'$ and there exists $s \xrightarrow{\alpha,a} t$ such that w' is accepted by M from the state t. The *language accepted* by a KAT automaton M is the set $L(M) = \{ w \in (At \times A)^* \times At \mid M \text{ accepts } w \text{ from } i \}$.

Our causal model for automata extends naturally to KAT automata by considering hazards e as KAT-expressions and causes c as strings in $(At \times A)^*$. Safe computations in M for the hazard e with respect to c are non-empty strings of $L(M)$ satisfying **AAC1** as in Definition 1 but with respect to the alphabet $(At \times A)$ instead of A only. Also the algorithm for computing causes needs basically no adjustment, but for the way how operations on automata are computed.

Adding Assignments: NetKAT. NetKAT [1] is a network programming model, which is used for specifying and verifying the packet-processing behavior of software-defined networks. In a nutshell, it is a variation on KAT that considers actions not as abstract elements of an alphabet A but rather as state transformers, like assignments, that are executed when a precondition α is satisfied and modify it into a post-condition β.

For a given set of atoms At of a Boolean algebra B, a *deterministic NetKAT automaton* [6] is a deterministic FA $M = (S, \Sigma, i, \longrightarrow, F)$ such that $\sigma = At \times At$ and $F \subseteq S \times (At \times At)$. The transition relation $\longrightarrow$ is thus labeled by pairs of atoms (α, β) and so are the accepting states. The interpretation of these pair of atoms is that they represent pre-conditions and post-conditions of one-step executions.

A string $w \in At \times At \times At^*$ is accepted by M from a state s only when post-conditions match the subsequent pre-condition, meaning that either (1) $w = \alpha\beta$ and $(s, \alpha, \beta) \in F$, or (2) $w = (\alpha\beta)w'$ and there exists $s \xrightarrow{\alpha,\beta} t$ such that $\beta w'$ is accepted by M from the state t. Note that in the last condition is crucial that w' is not the empty string. The *language accepted* by a NetKAT automaton M is the set $L(M) = \{w \in At \times A \times At^* \mid M \text{ accepts } w \text{ from } i\}$.

As for KAT automata, our causal model for automata extends naturally to NetKAT automata too, with hazard represented by NetKat expressions [6], causes as strings in At^*, and safe computations as strings in $L(M)$ that can be projected into a cause by deleting some atoms and satisfying the rest of the conditions of Definition 1.

8   Conclusions

In this paper we moved the causal model proposed in [5] from labeled transition systems to finite automata in order to obtain a language-based causal model for safety. The model is in-line with the notion of causality described in a logical context in [9] in the sense that a hazard may be observed if and only if it has been caused. Analogously to the alternative worlds of Lewis [16], we also considered decorated causes as alternative to causes in the sense that they allow executing all actions of a cause interleaved with other actions that guarantee hazard avoidance.

We treated only the case when causes *may* enable a hazard while strings of the decorated causes must avoid it. While it can be interesting to consider a stronger notion of causes as strings c that bring the automaton M to states where the hazard e is inevitable for any of its possible extensions (i.e., by changing **AAC1** to $L(c\,;e) \subseteq L(M)$), such a change would imply that there would be no causes in our railway system example.

We have also presented an algorithm to compute decorated causes, relying only on basic automata theoretic operations. The algorithms could be improved, using model checking techniques for marking those states in which a hazard is enabled, and search techniques to find the decorated causes avoiding marked states. Also, it would be interesting to move from automata back to labeled transition systems but remaining into a trace setting, with hazard specified as LTL-properties.

Finally, we briefly discussed extensions of our work to KAT and NetKAT automata. Clearly, more work needs to be done here, both to precisely set the definitions and to show the applicability of the method to, for example, find causes of a hazard in a software defined network.

Acknowledgments. The work of Georgiana Caltais and Hünkar Can Tunç was supported by the DFG project "CRENKAT", no. 398056821.

References

1. Anderson, C.J., et al.: NetKAT: semantic foundations for networks. In: The 41st Annual ACM SIGPLAN-SIGACT Symposium on Principles of Programming Languages, POPL 2014, San Diego, CA, USA, 20–21 January 2014, pp. 113–126 (2014). https://doi.org/10.1145/2535838.2535862
2. Arbach, Y., Karcher, D.S., Peters, K., Nestmann, U.: Dynamic causality in event structures. Logical Methods Comput. Sci. **14**(1) (2018). https://doi.org/10.23638/LMCS-14(1:17)2018
3. Bollig, B., Katoen, J.-P., Kern, C., Leucker, M., Neider, D., Piegdon, D.R.: libalf: the automata learning framework. In: Touili, T., Cook, B., Jackson, P. (eds.) CAV 2010. LNCS, vol. 6174, pp. 360–364. Springer, Heidelberg (2010). https://doi.org/10.1007/978-3-642-14295-6_32
4. Caltais, G., Guetlein, S.L., Leue, S.: Causality for general LTL-definable Properties. In: Finkbeiner, B., Kleinberg, S. (eds.) Proceedings 3rd Workshop on formal reasoning about Causation, Responsibility, and Explanations in Science and Technology, CREST@ETAPS 018, Thessaloniki, Greece, 21 April 2018. EPTCS, vol. 286, pp. 1–15 (2018). https://doi.org/10.4204/EPTCS.286.1
5. Caltais, G., Mousavi, M.R., Singh, H.: Causal reasoning for safety in Hennessy Milner logic. Fund. Inform. **173**, 217–251 (2020). https://doi.org/10.3233/FI-2020-1922
6. Foster, N., Kozen, D., Milano, M., Silva, A., Thompson, L.: A coalgebraic decision procedure for NetKAT. In: Proceedings of the 42nd Annual ACM SIGPLAN-SIGACT Symposium on Principles of Programming Languages, POPL 2015, Mumbai, India, 15–17 January 2015, pp. 343–355 (2015). https://doi.org/10.1145/2676726.2677011
7. Groce, A., Chaki, S., Kroening, D., Strichman, O.: Error explanation with distance metrics. Int. J. Softw. Tools Technol. Transf. (STTT) **8**(3), 229–247 (2006)
8. Groce, A., Visser, W.: What went wrong: explaining counterexamples. In: Ball, T., Rajamani, S.K. (eds.) SPIN 2003. LNCS, vol. 2648, pp. 121–136. Springer, Heidelberg (2003). https://doi.org/10.1007/3-540-44829-2_8
9. Halpern, J.Y.: A modification of the Halpern-Pearl definition of causality. In: Yang, Q., Wooldridge, M.J. (eds.) Proceedings of the Twenty-Fourth International Joint Conference on Artificial Intelligence, IJCAI 2015, Buenos Aires, Argentina, 25–31 July 2015, pp. 3022–3033. AAAI Press (2015). http://ijcai.org/Abstract/15/427
10. Halpern, J.Y., Pearl, J.: Causes and explanations: a structural-model approach: part 1: causes. In: Breese, J.S., Koller, D. (eds.) UAI 2001: Proceedings of the 17th Conference in Uncertainty in Artificial Intelligence, University of Washington, Seattle, Washington, USA, 2–5 August 2001, pp. 194–202. Morgan Kaufmann (2001). https://dslpitt.org/uai/displayArticleDetails.jsp?mmnu=1&smnu=2&article_id=100&proceeding_id=17
11. Kleene, S.C.: Representation of events in nerve nets and finite automata. Autom. Stud. **34**, 3–42 (1956)
12. Kozen, D.: Kleene algebra with tests. ACM Trans. Program. Lang. Syst. **19**(3), 427–443 (1997)
13. Kozen, D.: Automata on guarded strings and applications. Mat. Contemp. **24**, 117–139 (2003)
14. Ladkin, P., Loer, K.: Analysing aviation accidents using WB-analysis - an application of multimodal reasoning. In: AAAI Spring Symposium. AAAI (1998). https://www.aaai.org/Papers/Symposia/Spring/1998/SS-98-04/SS98-04-031.pdf

15. Leitner-Fischer, F., Leue, S.: Causality checking for complex system models. In: Giacobazzi, R., Berdine, J., Mastroeni, I. (eds.) VMCAI 2013. LNCS, vol. 7737, pp. 248–267. Springer, Heidelberg (2013). https://doi.org/10.1007/978-3-642-35873-9_16

16. Lewis, D.: Causation. J. Philos. **70**, 556–567 (1973)

17. Lewis, D.: Counterfactuals. Blackwell Publishers, Hoboken (1973)

18. Martin, J.C.: Introduction to Languages and the Theory of Computation, vol. 4. McGraw-Hill, New York (1991)

19. Møller, A.: dk.brics.automaton – finite-state automata and regular expressions for Java (2021). http://www.brics.dk/automaton/

20. Nielsen, M., Plotkin, G.D., Winskel, G.: Petri nets, event structures and domains, part I. Theor. Comput. Sci. **13**, 85–108 (1981). https://doi.org/10.1016/0304-3975(81)90112-2

21. Renieris, M., Reiss, S.: Fault localization with nearest neighbor queries. In: 18th International Conference on Automated Software Engineering (2003)

22. Shabana, H., Volkov, M.V.: Optimal synchronization of partial deterministic finite automata. CoRR abs/2002.01045 (2020). https://arxiv.org/abs/2002.01045

23. Zeller, A.: Why Programs Fail: A Guide to Systematic Debugging. Elsevier, Amsterdam (2009)

Consistency of Heterogeneously Typed Behavioural Models: A Coalgebraic Approach

Harald König[1,2] and Uwe Wolter[3]([✉])

[1] University of Applied Sciences, FHDW, Hanover, Germany
harald.koenig@fhdw.de
[2] Høgskulen på Vestlandet, Bergen, Norway
[3] University of Bergen, Bergen, Norway
uwe.wolter@uib.no

Abstract. Systematic and formally underpinned consistency checking of heterogeneously typed interdependent behavioural models requires a common metamodel, into which the involved models can be translated. And, if additional system properties are imposed on the behavioural models by modal logic formulae, the question arises, whether these formulae are faithfully translated, as well.

In this paper, we propose a formal methodology based on natural transformations between coalgebraic specifications, which enables state-space preserving translations into a category of homogeneously typed systems, and we determine mild assumptions for the transformations to guarantee preservation and reflection of truth of translated formulae.

Keywords: Heterogeneous behavioural models · Coalgebra · Reactive system · Modal logic · Category Theory

1 Introduction and Motivation

In model-based software projects, heterogenous (ly structured) but interdependent behavioural models can occur. These models may, however, prescribe the same (or overlapping parts of the same) real-world behaviour: A class diagram may prescribe domain services, a BPMN[1] diagram may model a process, in which these services are invoked (in a certain sequence). Although the behaviour of these systems is based on states and state changes, the concrete stimuli and effects of state changes are different. Beside the above example, there are labelled transition systems with or without output (per state or per transition), deterministic or non-deterministic, possibly timed or probabilistic.

Model checking is an automated technique that, given a finite-state model of a system and a formal property, systematically checks whether this property

---

[1] https://www.omg.org/spec/BPMN/2.0/PDF.

© Springer Nature Switzerland AG 2022
Y. Aït-Ameur and F. Crăciun (Eds.): TASE 2022, LNCS 13299, pp. 308–325, 2022.
https://doi.org/10.1007/978-3-031-10363-6_21

holds for (a given state or computation path in) that model. Usually, the property is given in terms of a formula in modal logic. Automatic verification of this formula is carried out on a homogeneously structured transition structure, which is derived from the behavioural structure of a system, usually a Kripke Frame. To consequently model check a complete ensemble of interacting, but *heterogeneously structured* artefacts, formulas of modal logic can only formally be imposed on them, if the different involved types of transition structures are translated into a homogeneous transition structure. We call a formula, which spreads over different systems an *inter-model constraint*. In the sequel, we will consider such an ensemble of heterogeneously typed transition structures. Formulas can be imposed on single *local* components or they are *global* inter-model constraints.

In this paper, we propose a formalism for the translation of components' shapes into a common transition structure, enabling uniform formal reasoning about their interaction. The translation will not alter the state space, but only the transition structure. When translating local components' behaviour into a common formalism, formulas imposed on the local component, e.g. liveness or termination properties, must also be translated. Moreover, these local constraints interact with the global inter-model constraints: They might contradict each other or the former is a logical consequnce of the latter, etc. Thus, the following *research questions* arise:

1. How can we formally define the translation into a common type of transition structure?
2. Can we expect preservation (and reflection) of formula validity during a translation? If not, which requirements must the translation fulfill for formula validity invariance?

We will use *coalgebras* for the all-embracing metamodel of reactive systems. We think that this is the consequent continuation of the theory of *institutions* [19], where algebraic specifications (understood as endofunctors $\mathcal{F}$), specification morphisms (natural transformations between functors), and logical formulas enable a comprehensive view on heterogeneous data structures. It is an old insight [18] that dualisation of the structure maps of algebras enables an elegant description of behavioural systems instead of data structures and that logical formulas in the algebraic settings are replaced by formulas of a modal logic. Finally, coalgebras enable a comprehensive view on heterogeneous behavioural structures.

In this paper, we present the following novelties:

- We show how to synchronize reactive systems of different behavioural specifications in general. For this, we use coalgebras and corresponding specification morphisms.
- We provide a criterion characterizing preservation and reflection of validity of modal logic formulas during translation along specification morphisms.

The investigated temporal operators are based on predicates imposed on state spaces, i.e. we emphasize more the branching-time perspective of CTL

(Computation Tree Logic) than the linear-time perspective of LTL (Linear Temporal Logic). For a comparison of these two logics, see [1].

Section 2 presents a practical problem, which has already been elaborated in a similar form in [11] and which is picked up in the paper each time a theoretical result must be illustrated. Section 3 reports on the necessary background and Sect. 4 presents the main results (Proposition 1 and 2) and applies them to the running example. Sections 5 and 6 conclude the paper.

2   Running Example

The process of fixing bugs, which have been reported as tickets by users of a software application, may be captured in a BPMN diagram, which models the ticket handling workflow. Automatic activities in this workflow rely on the existence of services provided by a backend system, seeing Activity "Analyse Ticket Database" in Fig. 1.

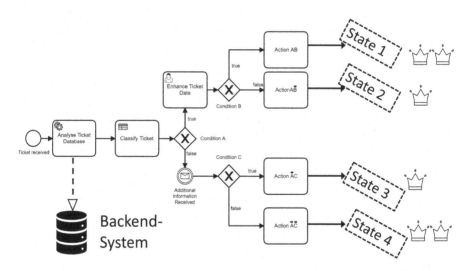

Fig. 1. BPMN model with different decision points

Abstraction in BPMN Models: For the sake of simplicity we assume that each service task requests exactly one method of the backend system and that the output of the method call does not directly influence the process instance's state, e.g. the (business rule) task "Classify Ticket" is always the successor of "Analyse Ticket Database" independent of the output of the invoked method in the latter task.

The further activities in Fig. 1 are as follows:

– The automatic activity "Analyse Ticket Database" invokes a method in the backend system, which exploits a knowledge database, in order to provide (semi-)automatically a solution for the current ticket. Depending on this data and the ticket classification, evaluation of *Condition A* decides, which of the following two branches is chosen.

- In the upper branch, a user activity enhances possibly missing information in the ticket. In the lower branch, more information is received by an intermediate catching event.
- Evaluation of *Condition B* and *Condition C* depend on this additional data and trigger one of the four activities $\{AB, A\overline{B}, \overline{A}C, \overline{A}\,\overline{C}\}$, which may or may not be automatic tasks and which may update the backend system with new information.

Consequently, the state of the data in the backend system influences state changes of the process instance and vice versa, thus:

The behaviours of the backend system and the workflow management system mutually depend on each other.

The software application may be run by customers of a software company, who sells this software, or it may as well be a ready-to-use solution built by a company on its own. In either case, service-level agreements (SLA) are offered in order to ensure the quality of bug fixing for the users. A typical agreement prescribes solutions to be provided as a software patch, which automatically updates the current software version and removes the reported bug (high-quality solution). In contrast, a low-quality solution is a temporary workaround being carried out by the user, for example, a change in the configuration of the application.

Often these promises are subject to certain preconditions: A software patch will be provided, only if the user's software runs in a certain mature version (and not in a recently offered "Alpha"-version). This information may or may not be present prior to process start: If the information is not already stored in the backend system, it has to be retrieved by further inquiries, e.g. "Enhance Ticket Data", in Fig. 1.

Let us assume that a high-quality solution like the patch provisioning is present, if one of the actions AB or $\overline{A}\,\overline{C}$ has terminated, two crowns at state 1 and 4 in Fig. 1 (a single crown indicates low-quality solutions). It is then a goal for the software provider to guarantee his promise by using a formal model checking procedure. For this, a predicate V is defined which holds in a certain state, if the given software **V**ersion of the ticket reporter is some mature version. Furthermore, one can define a predicate H, which can be imposed on states of BPMN processes indicating the possibility to provide a **H**igh-Quality Solution. Since the process is not yet finished in states 1 to 4, predicate H could be invalidated due to other activities or events, hence we formulate the SLA by

"Inter-Model Constraint" φ: If the system is in a state with property V, then for each computation path, we eventually reach a state, from which henceforth property H holds.

Of course, this formula interacts with already given formulas on the local systems for example termination or liveness requirements of the BPMN-workflow. If ψ is such a formula, one has to ensure for instance, that φ and ψ are not contradictory.

Moreover, if ψ is a logical consequence of φ, it is not required to be checked, but can be considered to be fulfilled, if φ holds.

The goal is now to use established model checkers to prove validity of the involved temporal formulas. In order to check validity of inter-model-constraints, one has to define a comprehensive state space of Backend System and BPMN process models especially taking into account their interactions (see above). We face two problems:

1. How can we formally define this comprehensive state space?
2. Shall validity of a local constraint ψ be checked on the local state space or on the comprehensive state space? Can we expect to obtain the same result?

A challenge is to cope with *private* and *common* features of these two transition structures: A feature is private, if it is known only to one of the structures and not known to the other, e.g. the backend system knows nothing about incoming events and roles (not shown in Fig. 1) of the BPMN process, the BPMN process does not consider outputs of the backend system's methods. An exception is the output of a condition's evaluation, which we can, however, interpret as an event, which lets an event-based gateway decide the alternative. Finally, common behaviour of both systems are states and method-call-triggered state changes (requests in the BPMN tasks and invocations of methods in the backend system).

In the next sections, we show how to translate different types of transition structures into an appropriate common transition structure. We illustrate our general approach by encoding (1) stateful backend systems and (2) BPMN process models as coalgebras.

3 Background

3.1 Notation

We use the following notations: $\mathcal{SET}$ is the category of sets and total mappings. For two sets X and Y we write Y^X for the set of all total maps from X to Y. Special sets are $1 = \{*\}$ (any singleton set) and $2 = \{\texttt{true}, \texttt{false}\}$. Instead of the set of all partial maps $A \xrightarrow{f} B$ between two sets A, B we consider the set of all total maps $A \xrightarrow{f} 1 + B$, i.e. $f(x)$ is undefined if and only if $f(x) = *$. Both sets are isomorphic in $\mathcal{SET}$.

For functors between different categories we will use calligraphic letters like $\mathcal{F}$, $\mathcal{G}$, or $\mathcal{H}$. $\mathcal{ID}$ is the identity functor on $\mathcal{SET}$. Application of a functor $\mathcal{F} : \mathbb{C} \to \mathbb{D}$ will always be written without parentheses, e.g. $\mathcal{F}X$ (for objects) and $\mathcal{F}f$ (for morphisms). The power set functor is $\wp : \mathcal{SET} \to \mathcal{SET}$. $\wp_{fin} : \mathcal{SET} \to \mathcal{SET}$ will denote the functor assigning to a set the set of its *finite* subsets. For $X \xrightarrow{f} Y$ and a subset $A \subseteq X$, defined by a condition ϕ, we write

$$f(A) := \{f(x) \in Y \mid \phi(x)\} \text{ if } A = \{x \in X \mid \phi(x)\},$$

$$X \xrightarrow{\;\;f\;\;} Y$$

$$\begin{array}{ccc} \mathcal{F}X & \xrightarrow{\;\mathcal{F}f\;} & \mathcal{F}Y \\ {\scriptstyle \eta_X} \downarrow & & \downarrow {\scriptstyle \eta_Y} \\ \mathcal{G}X & \xrightarrow{\;\mathcal{G}f\;} & \mathcal{G}Y \end{array}$$

Fig. 2. Naturality square

which is the application of $\wp f$ to A. To distinguish f from this counterpart, we often write $f(\_)$ for $\wp f$ and likewise for $\wp_{fin} f$.

Diagrams always depict commutative diagrams, e.g. the square in Fig. 2 is automatically assumed to be commutative, specifying the condition for a natural transformation $\eta : \mathcal{F} \Rightarrow \mathcal{G}$, i.e. a family $(\eta_X)_{X \in |\mathbb{C}|} : \mathcal{F}X \to \mathcal{G}X$ of $\mathbb{D}$ morphisms indexed by $\mathbb{C}$'s object collection (which we denote by $|\mathbb{C}|$) if $\mathcal{F}, \mathcal{G} : \mathbb{C} \to \mathbb{D}$.

3.2 Coalgebras

The investigation of *heterogenous* (ly typed) reactive systems requires a meta-model, which captures as many behavioural specifications as possible. A behavioural "specification" describes the way a system interacts with the environment. For deterministic labeled transition systems (DLTS) over an alphabet A, this specification is the set $(1 + X)^A$, because for each system state a partial map assigns to an event $a \in A$ (from the environment) at most one follow-up state. In contrast to that, non-deterministic finitely-branching systems (NLTS) are based on an assignment $x \mapsto c(x) \in \wp_{fin}(A \times X)$ for all states x, i.e. $(a, y) \in c(x)$ means that in state x the event a may cause a state change from x to y. [2]

We obtain a common template for encoding different types of transition structures: They can formally be described by an assignment $\mathcal{F} : |\mathcal{SET}| \to |\mathcal{SET}|$, e.g. $X \mapsto (1 + X)^A$ for DLTS or $X \mapsto \wp_{fin}(A \times X)$ for NLTS. Analogously, one can find similar assignments for all other types of transition structures. Moreover, in all cases, cf. [18], these assignments extend to functors $\mathcal{F} : \mathcal{SET} \to \mathcal{SET}$.

Example 1 (LTS). *The functor*

$$\mathcal{G} : \left\{ \begin{array}{l} \mathcal{SET} \longrightarrow \mathcal{SET} \\ X \xrightarrow{\ f\ } Y \ \mapsto\ (1 + X)^A \xrightarrow{\ (id_1 + f) \circ \_\ } (1 + Y)^A \end{array} \right.$$

encodes DLTS and NLTS are specified by the functor

$$\wp_{fin}(A \times \_) : \left\{ \begin{array}{l} \mathcal{SET} \longrightarrow \mathcal{SET} \\ X \xrightarrow{\ f\ } Y \ \mapsto\ \wp_{fin}(A \times X) \xrightarrow{\ (id_A \times f)(\_)\ } \wp_{fin}(A \times Y) \end{array} \right.$$

Example 2 (Modules of Object-Oriented Programs, [9,17]). *A package or a module of classes in an object-oriented environment with n visible methods $(m_j(x : I_j) : O_j)_{j=1..n}$ in its facade can be encoded as a coalgebra for the functor $\mathcal{F}_1$, which maps a set X to the Cartesian product of the family $((O_j \times X)^{I_j})_{j=1..n}$ of sets of maps*

$$\mathcal{F}_1 X = \prod_{j=1}^{n} (O_j \times X)^{I_j}.$$

---

[2] Other examples of reactive systems are finite or infinite streams, automata with output (i.e. UML state charts), activity diagrams or BPMN diagrams (with or without guard conditions) and probablistic or timed automata [18].

An $\mathcal{F}_1$-*system* $c : X \rightarrow \mathcal{F}_1 X$ *represents a tuple* $(m_1, ..., m_n)$ *of maps, in which* $m_j(x)$ *is the application of method* m_j *for input* $i \in I_j$. *Depending on state* x, *it produces an output* $o \in O_j$ *and a new state* $x' \in X$.

Generalizing Example 1 and 2, we define

Definition 1 ($\mathcal{F}$-Coalgebra). *Let* $\mathcal{F} : \mathcal{SET} \rightarrow \mathcal{SET}$ *be a functor. An* $\mathcal{F}$-*coalgebra* (X, c) *or* $\mathcal{F}$-*system is a map* $X \xrightarrow{c} \mathcal{F}X$.

In the context of coalgebras, $\mathcal{F}$ *is called a (specification of a)* transition struc- *ture and* c *is the (transition) structure map.*

Furthermore, $\mathcal{F}$-coalgebras constitute themselves a category: A *homomor- phism* between $\mathcal{F}$-coalgebras (X, c) and (Y, d) is a map $h : X \rightarrow Y$, for which

$$d \circ h = \mathcal{F}h \circ c.$$

Note that homomorphisms not only preserve, but also reflect the transition struc- ture: The graph $\{(x, h(x)) \mid x \in X\}$ of h yields a bisimilarity on $X \times Y$ [18].

It is then easy to see that we can give the following definition, see also [18].

Definition 2 (Category of $\mathcal{F}$-Coalgebras). *The category* $\mathcal{F}$-*Coalg has objects* $\mathcal{F}$-*coalgebras, see Definition 1, and morphisms the* $\mathcal{F}$-*coalgebra homo- morphisms. Identities are identical maps* id_X *and composition is composition of set maps.*

The existence of initial objects in categories of algebras yields many impor- tant insights such as the principle of induction, initial semantics and term gener- ation [22]. Dually, it is important that categories of $\mathcal{F}$-coalgebras possess a *final* object.[3] Corresponding resulting aspects are the principles of final semantics: The unique arrow from a coalgebra into the final object usually assigns to each state its behavioural semantics w.r.t. bisimilarity [10], for coalgebras with no proper quotient one obtains the principle of coinduction, which is a template for recursive implementations of algorithms e.g. on streams [18] etc.

Not every functor $\mathcal{F}$ yields reasonable coalgebras, especially for practical purposes in computer science, because there may not be a final object in $\mathcal{F}$-Coalg. A prominent example is the power set functor $X \mapsto \wp(X)$. Using Lambek's Theorem ("If $\mathcal{F}$-Coalg possesses a final object (Z, ζ), then ζ is a bijection.", see [10], Lemma 2.3.3.) and Cantor's diagonal argument ($X \ncong \wp(X)$ for all sets X), it is clear that there is no final object in $\wp$-Coalg. It is, however, possible to show that this deficit vanishes, if one restricts to the functor $\wp_{fin}(\_)$, see Sect. 3.1.

Because of these natural restrictions, we will consider the following restricted collection of $\mathcal{SET}$-endofunctors, whose respective category of coalgebras can be shown to possess a final object [18], and which are sufficient to deal with all important types of transition structures in computer science:

---

[3] An initial/a final object in a category $\mathbb{C}$ is an object $0/1$, for which there is exactly one morphism $0 \rightarrow X$/exactly one morphism $X \rightarrow 1$ for all $X \in |\mathbb{C}|$.

Definition 3 (Kripke Polynomial Functors - $\mathcal{KPF}$, [10]). *The collection $\mathcal{KPF}$ of $\mathcal{SET}$-endofunctors is defined inductively as follows:*

(1) $\mathcal{ID}$ is in $\mathcal{KPF}$

(2) The functor $Const_A$ defined by $Const_A(X \xrightarrow{f} Y) = A \xrightarrow{id_A} A$ is in $\mathcal{KPF}$ for each set A.

(3) If $\mathcal{F}_1, \mathcal{F}_2 \in \mathcal{KPF}$, so is the functor $\mathcal{F}_1 \times \mathcal{F}_2$ defined by

$$(\mathcal{F}_1 \times \mathcal{F}_2)(X \xrightarrow{f} Y) = \mathcal{F}_1 X \times \mathcal{F}_2 X \xrightarrow{\mathcal{F}_1 f \times \mathcal{F}_2 f} \mathcal{F}_1 Y \times \mathcal{F}_2 Y .$$

(4) If I is an index set and in an I-indexed collection $(\mathcal{F}_i)_{i \in I}$, all $\mathcal{F}_i$ are in $\mathcal{KPF}$, then so is the functor $\coprod_{i \in I} \mathcal{F}_i$ defined by [4]

$$(\coprod_{i \in I} \mathcal{F}_i)(X \xrightarrow{f} Y) = \coprod_i \mathcal{F}_i X \xrightarrow{\coprod_i \mathcal{F}_i f} \coprod_i \mathcal{F}_i Y .$$

(5) If A is a set and $\mathcal{F} \in \mathcal{KPF}$, then so is the functor $\mathcal{F}^A$ defined by

$$\mathcal{F}^A(X \xrightarrow{f} Y) = (\mathcal{F}X)^A \xrightarrow{\mathcal{F}f \circ -} (\mathcal{F}Y)^A .$$

(6) If $\mathcal{F} \in \mathcal{KPF}$, then so is the functor $\wp_{fin}(\mathcal{F})$ defined by

$$(\wp_{fin}(\mathcal{F}))(X \xrightarrow{f} Y) = \wp_{fin}(\mathcal{F}X) \xrightarrow{(\mathcal{F}f)(\_)} \wp_{fin}(\mathcal{F}Y) .$$

It can be shown that automata with output (Moore and Mealy Machines) as well as automata with final states can be encoded using $\mathcal{KPF}$'s, the latter by $Const_2 \times \mathcal{F}$ for an arbitrary $\mathcal{F}$ in $\mathcal{KPF}$.

From now on, we always assume the involved functors to be contained in $\mathcal{KPF}$. Moreover, we use the following shorthand notation for an $\mathcal{F}$-coalgebra: For any $x \in X$ and $y \in c(x)$, we write $x \rightsquigarrow y$ to indicate the possibility for x to transition to y due to structure map c. If an alphabet A is involved, this can be extended to

$$x \xrightsquigarrow{a} y ,$$

for $a \in A$, for instance for $\mathcal{F} = \wp_{fin}(A \times \_)$ and an $\mathcal{F}$-coalgebra (X, c) with $(a, y) \in c(x)$.

3.3   Signature Morphisms

The example in Sect. 2 deals with two different behavioural systems: BPMN diagrams and class diagrams (for which behaviour is described by specifying, how a method application changes the object structure at runtime). In the literature the two different metamodels are also called *signatures*. In universal algebra,

---

[4] For a family $(A_i)_{i \in I}$ of sets the coproduct (sum) $\coprod_{i \in I} A_i$ denotes the disjoint union of all the sets A_i, $i \in I$.

signature morphisms are the tool of choice to relate algebras of different signatures. It is an old observation, that (unsorted) signatures can also be encoded with $\mathcal{SET}$-endofunctors $\mathcal{T}$, where algebras are maps $\alpha : \mathcal{T}X \to X$, and if categories of algebras are defined in such a way, then it is easy to see that signature morphisms can be encoded as natural transformations between the respective specifying functors [3]. Moreover, these transformations yield - by precomposition - a "forgetful" functor in the opposite direction between the respective categories of algebras.

For coalgebras, we use the dual approach: Given a natural transformation $\eta : \mathcal{F} \Rightarrow \mathcal{G}$, an $\mathcal{F}$-system (X, c) can be translated by postcomposition

$$X \xrightarrow{\;c\;} \mathcal{F}X \xrightarrow{\;\eta_X\;} \mathcal{G}X$$
$$\underbrace{}_{\eta_X \circ c}$$

into a $\mathcal{G}$-system $(X, \eta_X \circ c)$. For $\mathcal{F}$-Coalg-homomorphism $h : (X, c) \to (Y, d)$, we obtain $\mathcal{G}h \circ (\eta_X \circ c) = (\eta_Y \circ d) \circ h$ by naturality, thus:

Lemma 1 (Co-Forgetful Functor). *Let $\eta : \mathcal{F} \Rightarrow \mathcal{G}$ be a natural transformation between two set-endofunctors. The assignment $c \mapsto \eta_X \circ c$ extends to a functor*

$$\mathcal{U}_\eta : \begin{cases} \mathcal{F}\text{-}Coalg \longrightarrow \mathcal{G}\text{-}Coalg \\ (X, c) \xrightarrow{\;h\;} (Y, d) \;\; \mapsto \;\; (X, \eta_X \circ c) \xrightarrow{\quad h \quad} (Y, \eta_Y \circ d) \end{cases}$$

Example 3 (Translation of Backend Behaviour to DLTS). *In our running example of Sect. 2, we can now translate transition structures of the backend system to DLTS. For this we use functor $\mathcal{F}_1$ from Example 2 to encode the available services $m_1, ..., m_n$ (methods) of the backend as an $\mathcal{F}_1$-system. Note that all methods decompose into two projections: $m_j = (m_{j,1}, m_{j,2}) : I_j \to O_j \times X$. Since we want the DLTS to be prepared for additional events, we choose for the functor $\mathcal{G}$ of Example 1*

$$A := I + \coprod_{j=1}^{n} I_j$$

as its input alphabet, where I is an arbitrary set of additional input stimuli. The translation is given by the following family of mappings indexed over $X \in |\mathcal{SET}|$:

$$\eta_X : \begin{cases} \prod_{j=1}^{n} (O_j \times X)^{I_j} \to (1 + X)^A \\ (m_1, ..., m_n) \;\; \mapsto \lambda i. \begin{cases} m_{j,2}(i) \,, & \textit{if } i \in I_j \textit{ for some } j \\ * \,, & \textit{if } i \in I \end{cases} \end{cases}$$

where we denoted the result of η_X by a λ-expression. We omit the easy proof of naturality of $\eta : \mathcal{F}_1 \Rightarrow \mathcal{G}$ but emphasize that the translation along η forgets outputs and enables the behaviour embedding of the backend system in a transition structure with extended input options.

3.4 Predicate Lifting

The heart in the description of temporal operators in the next Sect. 3.5 is the transformation of truth of a property from one state to its sucessor state(s) by a structure map c in an $\mathcal{F}$-coalgebra (X, c). Truth, however, is based on predicates. If a predicate P like "Eventually a state is reached, which guarantees a high-quality solution." is true on a state x, we write $P(x)$, and we can equivalently describe P as a subset of the state set, namely those states where P holds. That is, the notations

$$P(x), x \in P \text{ and } x \models P$$

for $P \subseteq X$ (or equivalently $P \hookrightarrow X$) will synonymously be used. If x satisfies a predicate, we want to reason whether $c(x)$ satisfies this predicate, too. However, $c(x) \in \mathcal{F}X$ is not a single state, but - according to $\mathcal{F}$ - a more complex entity depending on the type of transition structure $\mathcal{F}$.

Hence it is necessary to transform (lift) predicates that are imposed on elements of a fixed set X to predicates on $\mathcal{F}X$. We recall inductively defined predicate lifting from Chapter 6 of [10] for $\mathcal{KPF}$'s: The operator

$$\mathrm{Pred}(\mathcal{F}) : \wp(X) \to \wp(\mathcal{F}X)$$

is defined on $\mathcal{KPF}$'s as follows: For $P \subseteq X$

(1) $\mathrm{Pred}(\mathcal{ID})(P) = P$
(2) $\mathrm{Pred}(Const_A)(P) = A$
(3) $\mathrm{Pred}(\mathcal{F}_1 \times \mathcal{F}_2)(P) = \mathrm{Pred}(\mathcal{F}_1)(P) \times \mathrm{Pred}(\mathcal{F}_2)(P)$
(4) $\mathrm{Pred}(\coprod_{i \in I} \mathcal{F}_i)(P) = \coprod_{i \in I} \mathrm{Pred}(\mathcal{F}_i)(P)$
(5) $\mathrm{Pred}(\mathcal{F}^A)(P) = \{f : A \to \mathcal{F}X \mid \forall a \in A : f(a) \in \mathrm{Pred}(\mathcal{F})(P)\}$
(6) $\mathrm{Pred}(\wp_{fin}(\mathcal{F}))(P) = \{U \subseteq \mathcal{F}X \mid U \subseteq \mathrm{Pred}(\mathcal{F})(P)\}$

We illustrate this definition for DLTS: Let $\mathcal{F}X = (1+X)^A$, then we calculate the lift of predicate $P \subseteq X$ along the syntactical structure of $\mathcal{F}$: $\mathrm{Pred}(1 + \_)(P) = \mathrm{Pred}(Const_1)(P) + \mathrm{Pred}(\mathcal{ID})(P) = 1 + P$ and with that

$$\mathrm{Pred}(\mathcal{F})(P) = \{f : A \to 1 + X \mid \forall a \in A : f(a) \in 1 + P\}$$

i.e. the lifted predicate is true for $f \in (1 + X)^A$, if *all* $f(a) \in P$ or $f(a) = *$, i.e. for each $a \in A$ all successor states, if any, must fulfill the predicate. This can also be expressed by saying that $\mathrm{Pred}(\mathcal{F})(P)$ contains exactly those f, for which $f(A) \subseteq 1 + P = \mathrm{Pred}(1 + \_)(P)$, thus, in this example, $\mathrm{Pred}(\mathcal{F})(P) = (1 + P)^A = \mathcal{F}P$. Indeed, this observation is always true, cf. [10], Lemma 6.1.6.:

Lemma 2 (Predicate Lifting). *Let $\mathcal{F}$ be a $\mathcal{KPF}$, $X \in |\mathcal{SET}|$, then for each predicate $P \xrightarrow{m} X$*

$$\mathrm{Pred}(\mathcal{F})(P) \xrightarrow{\mathcal{F}m} \mathcal{F}X$$

is the inclusion arrow of the lift, i.e., especially, $\mathrm{Pred}(\mathcal{F})(P) = \mathcal{F}P$.   □

By structural induction along the definition of $\mathrm{Pred}(\mathcal{F})$ one can also prove:

Lemma 3 (Predicate Lifting is monotone). *In the above setting*

$$P_1 \subseteq P_2 \Rightarrow \mathrm{Pred}(\mathcal{F})(P_1) \subseteq \mathrm{Pred}(\mathcal{F})(P_2)$$

3.5   Temporal Operators

The basic temporal operator is the "next time"-Operator $\bigcirc$. All other operators can be derived from it (of course by using the basic logical operators $\neg$ (negation) and $\wedge$ (conjunction)). A temporal operator depends on a given $\mathcal{F}$-system (X, c) and is usually determined by an operation on subsets P (predicates) of X: If $P \subseteq X$, we denote with $\bigcirc P$ the subset of $\mathcal{F}X$, which contains those states, which reach states in P after a single application of structure map c.

Note that $\bigcirc$ usually depicts a path operator, i.e. $\bigcirc P$ holds for a computation path, if P holds on the second state. Our approach is more general in that it defines this operator for arbitrary transition structures. We will work with the following formal definition:

Definition 4 (Next Time Operator). *Let $\mathcal{F}$ be a $\mathcal{KPF}$ and (X, c) be an $\mathcal{F}$-system. We call*

$$\bigcirc_{\mathcal{F}, c} : \begin{cases} \wp(X) \to \wp(X) \\ \quad P \mapsto c^{-1}(\mathrm{Pred}(\mathcal{F})(P)) \end{cases}$$

the Next Time-Operator. *For $x \in X$ we write $x \models_{\mathcal{F}, c} \bigcirc P$, if $x \in \bigcirc_{\mathcal{F}, c} P$, equivalently, if $c(x) \in \mathrm{Pred}(\mathcal{F})(P)$, or short*

$$x \models \bigcirc P$$

if $\mathcal{F}$ and c are clear from the context.

E.g., for DLTS: $x \models \bigcirc P \iff \forall a \in A, x' \in X : (x \overset{a}{\rightsquigarrow} x' \Rightarrow x' \models P)$.

In the sequel, fixed points of operators on power sets are important. Clearly, a fixed point of an operator $op : \wp(X) \to \wp(X)$ is a subset Q of X, for which $op(Q) = Q$. They are of major importance, if one considers monotone operators (i.e. $P \subseteq Q \Rightarrow op(P) \subseteq op(Q)$) on the boolean algebra $(\wp(X), \subseteq)$, because a consequence of the Theorem of Knaster and Tarski [20] yields

Lemma 4 (Fixed Points). *A monotone operator $op : \wp(X) \to \wp(X)$ possesses a least and a greatest fixed point written $\mu S.op(S)$, $\nu S.op(S)$, resp. Furthermore, if X is a finite set, there is $n_0 \in \mathbb{N}$, such that*

$$\mu S.op(S) = \bigcup_{k=0}^{n_0} op^k(\emptyset) \ \text{and} \ \nu S.op(S) = \bigcap_{k=0}^{n_0} op^k(X).$$

Remark 1 (Finiteness). *We do not formulate the Knaster-Tarski Theorem in its full generality for arbitrary (infinite) sets, because we do not want to deal with the intricacies of approximants in the modal μ-calculus [4].*

$\bigcirc_{\mathcal{F}, c}$ is a monotone operator by Lemma 3, and so is the operator $\neg \bigcirc_{\mathcal{F}, c} \neg S$ where $\neg S$ denotes set complementation. Hence - from Lemma 4 - we can introduce the following existential path operators: For a fixed $\mathcal{F}$-system (X, c) and subsets P and Q of X

- $\exists\Box P := \nu S.(P \cap \neg \bigcirc \neg S)$ (henceforth)
- $\exists P\,\mathcal{U}\,Q := \mu S.(Q \cup (P \cap \neg \bigcirc \neg S))$ (until)

In words: $x \models \exists\Box P$, if there is a computation path starting at state x, on which P holds forever, $x \models \exists P\,\mathcal{U}\,Q$, if on a path from x, P holds for a while (maybe never) *until* Q holds once.

It is well-known [1] that all important temporal operators (e.g. of CTL) can be derived from these two operators, e.g. the constant `true` (intersection of an empty collection of sets) and further operators like $\exists\Diamond P = \exists\mathsf{true}\,\mathcal{U}\,P$ and with that

$$\forall\Box P := \neg\exists\Diamond\neg P$$

denoting that henceforth on all paths property P holds. Similarly

$$\forall\Diamond P := \neg\exists\Box\neg P$$

means, that for all computation paths, P holds eventually. We write $\Omega_{\mathcal{F},c}$ for any such temporal operator Ω, if the dependency from $\mathcal{F}$ and c is important.

The goal of the next section is to give an answer to both research questions on page 2: We define an appropriate common type of transition structure in order to formally define the *inter-model constraint*

$$\varphi := (\,V \Rightarrow \forall\Diamond(\forall\Box P)\,)$$

on page 4 in Sect. 2 and show that checking local formulas is independent of the underlying transition structure.

4   Formula Translation

4.1   Truth Preservation

In this section, we investigate how truth can be translated from $\mathcal{F}$-Coalg to $\mathcal{G}$-Coalg with the co-forgetful functor $\mathcal{U}_\eta : \mathcal{F}$-Coalg $\to \mathcal{G}$-Coalg from Lemma 1 based on a natural transformation $\eta : \mathcal{F} \Rightarrow \mathcal{G}$ for two $\mathcal{KPF}$'s $\mathcal{F}$ and $\mathcal{G}$. The results are important fundaments for the question, how formulas of temporal logic in different reactive systems interact with each other in a heterogeneous modeling environment. In this context, the following definition is important:

$$P \overset{m}{\hookrightarrow} X$$

$$\begin{array}{ccc} \mathrm{Pred}(\mathcal{F})(P) & \overset{\mathcal{F}m}{\hookrightarrow} & \mathcal{F}X \\ {\scriptstyle\eta_P}\big\downarrow & & \big\downarrow{\scriptstyle\eta_X} \\ \mathrm{Pred}(\mathcal{G})(P) & \overset{\mathcal{G}m}{\hookrightarrow} & \mathcal{G}X \end{array}$$

Fig. 3. Naturality square for predicate inclusion

Definition 5 (Cartesian along Inclusions).
A natural transformation $\eta : \mathcal{F} \Rightarrow \mathcal{G}$ between functors $\mathcal{F}, \mathcal{G} : \mathcal{SET} \to \mathcal{SET}$ is said to be Cartesian along inclusions, *if we have in the naturality square in Fig. 3 that*[5]

$$\eta_X^{-1}(\mathrm{Pred}(\mathcal{G})(P)) \subseteq \mathrm{Pred}(\mathcal{F})(P).$$

---

[5] Equivalently: The square in Fig. 3 is a pullback square.

Our first result is

Proposition 1 (Compatibility of Next Time Operator). *Let $\eta : \mathcal{F} \Rightarrow \mathcal{G}$ for two $\mathcal{KPF}$'s $\mathcal{F}$ and $\mathcal{G}$ and $\mathcal{U}_\eta : \mathcal{F}$-Coalg $\rightarrow \mathcal{G}$-Coalg the emerging co-forgetful functor from Lemma 1. Let (X, c) be an $\mathcal{F}$-system and P a predicate, then the next time operator is compatible with transformations:*

$$\forall x \in X : x \models_{\mathcal{F},c} \bigcirc P \Rightarrow x \models_{\mathcal{G},\mathcal{U}_\eta c} \bigcirc P \tag{1}$$

If furthermore η is Cartesian along inclusions, implication (1) is an equivalence.

Proof. Note that (by the definition of Pred(_)) for any structure map d:

$$x \models_{\_,d} \bigcirc P \iff d(x) \in \text{Pred}(\_)(P).$$

Fix a set X. The assumption of (1) is $c(x) \in \text{Pred}(\mathcal{F})(P)$. From Lemma 2, we know that the square in Fig. 3 commutes. Thus by the Def. of $\mathcal{U}_\eta$

$$(\mathcal{U}_\eta c)(x) = \eta_X(c(x)) = \mathcal{G}m(\eta_P(x)) = \eta_P(x) \in \text{Pred}(\mathcal{G})(P),$$

i.e. $x \models_{\mathcal{G},\mathcal{U}_\eta c} \bigcirc P$. Cartesian along inclusions yields $c(x) \in \text{Pred}(\mathcal{F})(P)$, if $\eta_X(c(x)) = (\mathcal{U}_\eta c)(x) \in \text{Pred}(\mathcal{G})(P)$. □

The following example shows that we cannot expect translation to always reflect truth, i.e. the precondition in the second part of Proposition 1 is necessary. For $\mathcal{F} = (\_)^A$ and $\mathcal{G} = 1 + \_$. We consider the natural transformation

$$\eta_X : \begin{cases} X^A \rightarrow 1 + X \\ f \mapsto * \end{cases}$$

which intuitively removes all transitions from an $\mathcal{F}$-system. Now consider the property $P = \texttt{false}$, i.e. $P = \emptyset$. Obviously for an $\mathcal{F}$-system (X, c), $x \models_{\mathcal{G},\mathcal{U}_\eta c} \bigcirc \emptyset$ for all $x \in X$, because for $d := \mathcal{U}_\eta c$ we obtain

$$\bigcirc_{\mathcal{G},d} P = d^{-1}(\text{Pred}(\mathcal{G})(\emptyset)) = d^{-1}(1 + \emptyset) = d^{-1}(1) = X$$

since $d(x) = *$ for all $x \in X$. This is also intuitively clear, because a property holds in all successor states, if there are no such states. However, $x \not\models_{\mathcal{F},c} \bigcirc \emptyset$ for all $x \in X$, because all x possess transitions in an $\mathcal{F}$-system. And η is not Cartesian along inclusions: $\eta_X^{-1}(1 + P) = X^A \not\subseteq \emptyset = \emptyset^A$.

The following result delineates conditions for preservation and reflection of truth w.r.t. all temporal operators. We formulate it for finite state sets X, see Remark 1, which is sufficient for practical applications in software engineering.

Proposition 2 (Truth Preservation and Reflection). *Let $\eta : \mathcal{F} \Rightarrow \mathcal{G}$ for two $\mathcal{KPF}$'s $\mathcal{F}$ and $\mathcal{G}$, which is Cartesian along inclusions, and $\mathcal{U}_\eta : \mathcal{F}$-Coalg $\rightarrow \mathcal{G}$-Coalg the emerging co-forgetful functor from Lemma 1. Let (X, c) be an $\mathcal{F}$-system with finite state set X and Ω any of the above mentioned temporal operators, then:*

$$\forall x \in X : x \models_{\mathcal{F},c} \Omega P \iff x \models_{\mathcal{G},\mathcal{U}_\eta c} \Omega P \tag{2}$$

Proof. For the two elementary operators $\exists\Box$ and $\exists_{-}\mathcal{U}_{-}$, this follows from Lemma 4 and Proposition 1 by simple induction, because X is a finite set. The result then easily propagates to all derived operators, like $\forall\Box$ and $\forall\Diamond$, and furthermore to all nested formulas. $\qquad\Box$

This result causes truth preservation and reflection along specification morphisms $\eta : \mathcal{F} \Rightarrow \mathcal{G}$ of all temporal formulas, thus enabling validity checks being independent of whether they are carried out in the category of $\mathcal{F}$-systems or in the category of $\mathcal{G}$-systems, respectively.

4.2   The Case Study Revisited

Examples 1, 2, and 3 showed how to encode the backend system and the common platform and provided the translation of the former to the latter. Our goal is now to provide a corresponding translation of a BPMN process model to the common platform. We assume the state space of a BPMN diagram to be a set of possible token distributions in the diagram, cf. [21], equivalently it can be seen as the set of enabled tasks and events, cf. [8]. Hence, we can encode BPMN models as coalgebras for the functor

$$\mathcal{F}_2 = (1 + {}_{-})^n \times (1 + {}_{-})^E \times ((1 + {}_{-}) \times R)^T.$$

Here E is the set of catch events in the process model, e.g. "Additional Information Received" in Fig. 1, T is the set of non-automatic tasks, e.g. "Enhance Ticket Data" or (the business rule task) "Classify Ticket" and R is set of roles in the process model assigned to user tasks, e.g. "IT-Staff" for the above user task. For the sake of simplicity, we assume that each automatic task calls exactly one method in the backend system.

   Then the transition structure is given by assigning to a state $x \in X$ a triple $c(x) = (h_1, h_2, h_3)$ of maps. The function application $h_1(j)$ specifies, whether in state x an automatic task is ready to request method m_j with successor state x' (if $h_1(j) = x' \neq *$) or whether this is not the case $(h_1(j) = *)$, i.e., the successor state is independent of input and output of the called method, cf. remark on abstraction in BPMN models in Sect. 2. Similarly, $h_2(e)$ specifies, whether in state x, the process is ready to receive event $e \in E$ or not, and $h_3(t) = (h_{3,1}(t), h_{3,2}(t))$ indicates whether a user task $t \in T$ with role assignment $h_{3,2}(t) \in R$ produces successor state $h_{3,1}(t)$ (or is disabled, if $h_{3,1}(t) = *$). The next goal is to find a natural transformation η' in

$$\mathcal{F}_1 \overset{\eta}{\Longrightarrow} \mathcal{G} \overset{\eta'}{\Longleftarrow} \mathcal{F}_2$$

In order to translate input-independent part h_1 to LTS where the alphabet distinguishes between all elements $i \in I_j$, the map $h_1(j) : I_j \to X$ is a constant map. Furthermore, we have to bear in mind that process instances evolve due to events and user activities. Hence we allow these ingredients in the common platform and choose for the functor $\mathcal{G} : \mathcal{SET} \to \mathcal{SET}$ in Example 1 and 3:

$$A := I + \coprod_{j=1}^{n} I_j \quad \text{with} \quad I := E + T.$$

Then the transformation

$$\eta_Y' : \begin{cases} (1+Y)^n \times (1+Y)^E \times ((1+Y) \times R)^T \to (1+Y)^A \\ \\ \quad (h_1, h_2, h_3) \qquad\qquad \mapsto \lambda z. \begin{cases} h_1(j) \ , \ \text{if } z = i \in I_j \\ h_2(e) \ , \ \text{if } z = e \in E \\ h_{3,1}(t) \ , \ \text{if } z = t \in T \end{cases} \end{cases}$$

additionally forgets role assignments and thus faithfully translates the BPMN model into a DLTS.

4.3 Handshaking

Let (X, c) be a backend system ($\mathcal{F}_1$-system) and (Y, d) be a BPMN model ($\mathcal{F}_2$-system), then the two translated systems $\mathcal{U}_\eta c$ and $\mathcal{U}_{\eta'} d$ can be synchronized over a set of common communication channels, in our case the touch points are the methods $\{m_1, \ldots, m_n\}$ together with their inputs, i.e. it is the set

$$H := \coprod_{j=1}^{n} I_j.$$

The resulting system $s := \mathcal{U}_\eta c \,\|_H\, \mathcal{U}_{\eta'} d$, is the parallel composition whose components communicate synchronously (handshake) over channels H and all actions outside H are independent and therefore can be executed autonomously in an interleaved manner [1].

Furthermore formula φ can now be formulated based on the specification $\mathcal{G}$ of the common transition structures. Model checking means then to ask whether in a certain state $(x, y) \in X \times Y$ of the composed $\mathcal{G}$-system formula φ holds:

$$(x, y) \overset{?}{\models}_{\mathcal{G}, s} \varphi$$

Assume now, an additional formula ψ has been imposed on (X, c) or (Y, d), then the question is, how φ and ψ interact: Are they contradictory? Does one of them logically imply the other? Is a syntactical combination, e.g. $\psi \Rightarrow \varphi$, valid? etc. ... Because φ only lives on our LTS-platform ($\mathcal{G}$-systems) and ψ lives either in $\mathcal{F}_1$- or in $\mathcal{F}_2$-systems, it is desirable, to know whether $x \models \psi$ is true independent of whether we check in $\mathcal{G}$ or in $\mathcal{F}_{1/2}$.

It follows now immediately from the definition of η (Example 1) and η' (see above in the present section), that both natural transformations are Cartesian along inclusion: Whenever $P \subseteq X$, then for any map m (or h) in the domain of η_X (or η_X'), such that its η_X-image maps into P, whenever the values shall be in X, we immediately see, that this is also the case for m, i.e. $\eta_X^{-1}((1+P)^A) \subseteq \mathcal{F}_{1/2} P$.

Hence Proposition 2 guarantees this independence and all model checks can be carried out on the common platform.

5   Related Work

Practical Approaches: The general idea of transforming different behavioural formalisms to a single semantic domain to reason about crosscutting concerns is nothing new [7]. [14] developed consistency checking for sequence diagrams and statecharts based on CSP, while Petri nets were used for the same scenario in [24]. Nevertheless, all approaches utilize fixed types of transition systems and no common framework, which can capture all possible types of transition structures. [6] tackles the problem of dealing with relationships between heterogeneous behavioural models. They coordinate the different models using a dedicated coordination language, which we formalize using morphisms between behavioural specifications.

Theoretical Approaches: Reasoning about heterogenously typed transition structures leads to the general theory of *(co-)institutions*, in which the same functor $\mathcal{U}_\eta$ as above is used to build the covariant model functor. In addition to our approach, a concrete (contravariant) functor for formula translation (of modal logics) is used: [5] defines (many-sorted) specification morphisms $\mathcal{F} \to \mathcal{G}$ as natural transformations from $\mathcal{G}$ to $\mathcal{F}$ and shows that formulae are preserved and reflected, if the negation operator is omitted (positive logic), see also [2]. [16] proves three different types of logics for coalgebras to be institutions. Another approach are parametrized endofunctors as comprehensive behavioural specifications, where the overall structure can be studied in terms of cofibrations [13]. [23] investigates co-institutions purely dual to classical institutions [19]. Finally, a good overview over the connection between coalgebars and modal logic is [12].

6   Future Work

More General Translations: We plan to use more general natural transformations to relate specifications $\mathcal{F}$ and $\mathcal{G}$. An established possibility [18] is to investigate translation properties, when using

$$\eta : \mathcal{H}\mathcal{F} \Rightarrow \mathcal{G}\mathcal{H}$$

for some reasonably chosen functor $\mathcal{H} : \mathcal{SET} \to \mathcal{SET}$. This yields the translation of an $\mathcal{F}$-system (X, c) to the $\mathcal{G}$-system $(\mathcal{H}X, \eta_X \circ \mathcal{H}c)$ and thus enables transformation of the state space, too. The question is, whether we can expect similar results as above for this kind of translations.

Refined Formulas: Formulas of modal logic can be refined w.r.t. to input symbols, e.g. you want to express that property P holds after a transition with structure map c only *if there was a certain input/event*. A formalisation of this is described in [10], Chapter 6.5., which enables defining formulas as in Hennessy-Milner-Logic [15].

Evaluation and Implementation: Finally, we want to investigate, how application (framework)s for checking behavioural consistency in heterogeneous modeling scenarios can be implemented based on the insights of the present paper. It is a goal to formally underpin already existing work [11].

References

1. Baier, C., Katoen, J.P.: Principles of Model Checking. The MIT Press, Cambridge (2008)
2. Balan, A., Kurz, A., Velebil, J.: An institutional approach to positive coalgebraic logic. J. Log. Comput. **27**(6), 1799–1824 (2017)
3. Barr, M., Wells, C.: Category Theory for Computing Sciences. Prentice Hall, Hoboken (1990)
4. Bradfield, J.C., Stirling, C.: Modal logics and mu-calculi: an introduction. In: Bergstra, J.A., Ponse, A., Smolka, S.A. (eds.) Handbook of Process Algebra, pp. 293–330. North-Holland/Elsevier (2001). https://doi.org/10.1016/b978-044482830-9/50022-9
5. Cîrstea, C.: An institution of modal logics for coalgebras. J. Log. Algebraic Program. **67**(1–2), 87–113 (2006)
6. Deantoni, J.: Modeling the behavioral semantics of heterogeneous languages and their coordination. In: 2016 Architecture-Centric Virtual Integration (ACVI), pp. 12–18. IEEE (2016)
7. Engels, G., Küster, J.M., Heckel, R., Groenewegen, L.: A methodology for specifying and analyzing consistency of object-oriented behavioral models. In: Tjoa, A.M., Gruhn, V. (eds.) Proceedings of the 8th European Software Engineering Conference Held Jointly with 9th ACM SIGSOFT International Symposium on Foundations of Software Engineering 2001, Vienna, Austria, 10–14 September 2001, pp. 186–195. ACM (2001). https://doi.org/10.1145/503209.503235
8. Fiadeiro, J.L.: Categories for Software Engineering. Springer, Heidelberg (2005). https://doi.org/10.1007/b138249
9. Jacobs, B.: Objects and classes, co-algebraically. In: Freitag, B., Jones, C.B., Lengauer, C., Schek, H. (eds.) Object Orientation with Parallelism and Persistence (The Book Grow Out of a Dagstuhl Seminar in April 1995), pp. 83–103. Kluwer Academic Publishers (1995)
10. Jacobs, B.: Introduction to Coalgebra: Towards Mathematics of States and Observation. Cambridge Tracts in Theoretical Computer Science, vol. 59. Cambridge University Press, Cambridge (2016). https://doi.org/10.1017/CBO9781316823187
11. Kräuter, T.: Towards behavioral consistency in heterogeneous modeling scenarios. In: ACM/IEEE International Conference on Model Driven Engineering Languages and Systems Companion, MODELS 2021 Companion, Fukuoka, Japan, 10–15 October 2021, pp. 666–671. IEEE (2021). https://doi.org/10.1109/MODELS-C53483.2021.00107
12. Kurz, A.: Coalgebras and modal logic. Course Notes for ESSLLI 2001 (2001)
13. Kurz, A., Pattinson, D.: Coalgebras and Modal Logic for Parameterised Endofunctors. Centrum voor Wiskunde en Informatica (2000)
14. Küster, J.M.: Towards inconsistency handling of object-oriented behavioral models. Electron. Notes Theor. Comput. Sci. **109**, 57–69 (2004). https://doi.org/10.1016/j.entcs.2004.02.056
15. Milner, R.: Communication and Concurrency, vol. 84. Prentice Hall, Englewood Cliffs (1989)
16. Pattinson, D.: Translating logics for coalgebras. In: Wirsing, M., Pattinson, D., Hennicker, R. (eds.) WADT 2002. LNCS, vol. 2755, pp. 393–408. Springer, Heidelberg (2003). https://doi.org/10.1007/978-3-540-40020-2_23
17. Reichel, H.: An approach to object semantics based on terminal co-algebras. Math. Struct. Comput. Sci. **5**(2), 129–152 (1995). https://doi.org/10.1017/S0960129500000694

18. Rutten, J.J.M.M.: Universal coalgebra: a theory of systems. Theor. Comput. Sci. **249**(1), 3–80 (2000). https://doi.org/10.1016/S0304-3975(00)00056-6
19. Sannella, D., Tarlecki, A.: Foundations of Algebraic Specification and Formal Software Development. Springer, Heidelberg (2012). https://doi.org/10.1007/978-3-642-17336-3
20. Tarski, A.: A lattice-theoretical fixpoint theorem and its applications. Pac. J. Math. **5**, 285–309 (1955)
21. Van Gorp, P., Dijkman, R.: A visual token-based formalization of BPMN 2.0 based on in-place transformations. Inf. Softw. Technol. **55**(2), 365–394 (2013). https://doi.org/10.1016/j.infsof.2012.08.014. Special Section: Component-Based Software Engineering (CBSE), 2011
22. Wechler, W.: Universal Algebra for Computer Scientists. Springer, Heidelberg (1992). https://doi.org/10.1007/978-3-642-76771-5
23. Wolter, U.: (Co)institutions for coalgebras. Reports in informatics 415 (2016)
24. Yao, S., Shatz, S.M.: Consistency checking of UML dynamic models based on Petri net techniques. In: 2006 15th International Conference on Computing, pp. 289–297. IEEE (2006)

Improving Adversarial Robustness of Deep Neural Networks via Linear Programming

Xiaochao Tang[1], Zhengfeng Yang[1]([✉]), Xuanming Fu[1], Jianlin Wang[2], and Zhenbing Zeng[3]

[1] Shanghai Key Lab of Trustworthy Computing, East China Normal University, Shanghai, China
{xctang,xmfu}@stu.ecnu.edu.cn, zfyang@sei.ecnu.edu.cn
[2] School of Computer and Information Engineering, Henan University, Kaifeng, China
jlwang@henu.edu.cn
[3] Department of Mathematics, Shanghai University, Shanghai, China
zbzeng@shu.edu.cn

Abstract. Adversarial training provides an effective means to improve the robustness of neural networks against adversarial attacks. The nonlinear feature of neural networks makes it difficult to find good adversarial examples where project gradient descent (PGD) based training is reported to perform best. In this paper, we build an iterative training framework to implement effective robust training. It introduces the Least-Squares based linearization to build a set of affine functions to approximate the nonlinear functions calculating the difference of discriminant values between a specific class and the correct class and solves it using LP solvers by simplex methods. The solutions found by LP solvers turn out to be very close to the real optimum so that our method outperforms PGD based adversarial training, as is shown by extensive experiments on the MNIST and CIFAR-10 datasets. Especially, our methods can provide considerable robust networks on CIFAR-10 against the strong strength attacks, where the other methods get stuck and do not converge.

Keywords: Linear programming · PGD · Robust training · Adversarial training

1 Introduction

Deep neural networks have shown remarkable performance in various applications, ranging from speech recognition [17], natural language processing [2] and games playing [18,35] to medical diagnosis [1] and vehicle control [5] where they achieve human-level intelligence.

However, it has been discovered by researchers [4,38] that neural networks suffer from heavy robustness issues, that is modern neural network classifiers are able to achieve very high accuracy on image classification tasks but are sensitive to small, adversarially chosen perturbations to the inputs.

Given an image x that is correctly classified by a neural network, a malicious attacker may find a small adversarial perturbation δ such that the perturbed image $x + \delta$,

Y. Aït-Ameur and F. Crăciun (Eds.): TASE 2022, LNCS 13299, pp. 326–343, 2022.
https://doi.org/10.1007/978-3-031-10363-6_22

though visually indistinguishable from the original image, is assigned to a wrong class with high confidence by the network. As their integration into the safety-critical systems continues to grow, there is a great need in training robust neural networks against such perturbations.

Researchers have proposed a variety of defense methods to improve the robustness of neural networks, which are not only accurate on the data, but also immune to attacks using adversarial examples. Most of the existing defenses are based on adversarial training [3, 12, 15, 19, 27]. The rationale of these approaches is to find worst-case examples and feed them to the model during training or constraining the output not to change significantly under small perturbations. Adversarial training can be formulated as a robust optimization problem which takes the form of a non-convex min-max problem. It treats the adversarial training as a procedure, that is, maximizes the loss function caused by the adversarial example crafted from the input x within the $\epsilon-$ball and then tries to minimize the maximal value of the loss by regulating model parameters. Due to the non-convex activation functions in DNNs, the problem for pursuiting the optimal adversarial examples is NP-hard [21]. Thus adversarial training can only rely on approximate methods to solve the inner maximization problem.

Multiple attempts have been made the inner maximization problem tractable. They have focused on effective first-order attack methods to generate adversarial examples. For instance, Fast Gradient Sign Method (FGSM) was introduced in [15] to generate adversarial examples based on computing the gradient of the loss function for the current value of the model parameters. The recent study [28] has shown that first-order methods can reliably solve the problem where the Projected Gradient Descent (PGD) method could find a better solution than any other first-order methods as it is the strongest attack that utilizes the local first-order information about the network. It is now widely believed that models adversarially trained via the PGD attack are robust since small adversarially trained networks can be formally verified [8, 39, 43], and larger models could not be broken on public challenges [28, 47].

The first-order adversarial attack methods are directly based on gradient information, i.e., by calculating the partial derivatives of the target loss function to the element of adjacency matrix [6, 10]. In this manner, the generated adversarial network may easily drop into poor local maxima and thus overfit the model, leading to lower transferability across models. In this paper, we introduce *EMRobust*, an adversarial training method to improve the robustness of DNNs via Easily-Misclassified examples. Unlike many existing and contemporaneous methods which rely on gradient computation to find a solution, we build a linear programming (LP) by approximating the inner maximization problem and efficiently solve it by calling LP solvers. The solution to the linear program is supposed to be very close to the optimal solution of the inner maximization problem. In other words, the solution to the associated LP problem may bring big losses, and thus is called an easily-misclassified example. To build the linear programming problem, Least-Squares-based linearization helps to obtain a set of affine functions approximate the nonlinear classifier functions which calculates the difference of discriminant values between a specific label and the correct label. Compared to the popular PGD-based method for the success attack rate against the model, our LP-based method can find stronger adversarial examples than PGD attacks (see

Table 1 and Table 2). Furthermore, through a lot of experiments we show empirically that our method, based on easily-misclassified examples pursuit, is numerically stable and accounts for both classification accuracy and robustness.

To summarize, the contributions of this paper are:

- We construct a relaxed linear programming problem for approximating the non-convex inner maximization problem, and then call LP solver to obtain an easily-misclassified example.
- An adversarial training method based on easily-misclassified examples generation is proposed to improve the robustness of DNNs.
- We empirically evaluate our method on six different networks trained on the MNIST and CIFAR-10 datasets, demonstrating the advantage of our method in the form of high robustness to PGD attacks. Our *EMRobust* can surpass the results of the other adversarial training methods [24,27].

The rest of this paper is organized as follows. In Sect. 2, we provide a brief background on deep neural networks and adversarial robustness. In Sect. 3, we describe our adversarial training method. Then, in Sect. 4 we show the experiments on benchmarks, illustrating the effectiveness of our algorithm. In Sect. 5 we discuss related work, and conclude in Sect. 6.

2   Preliminaries

In this section, we provide the background on deep neural networks (DNNs) and describe the adversarial robustness of DNNs.

2.1   Deep Neural Networks

A deep neural network $\mathcal{N}$ is a tuple $\langle \mathcal{X}, \mathcal{T}, \Phi \rangle$, where $\mathcal{X} = \{x^{[0]}, \ldots, x^{[k]}\}$ is a set of layers, $\mathcal{T} = \{T_1, \ldots, T_k\}$ consists of affine functions between layers, and $\Phi = \{\phi_1, \ldots, \phi_k\}$ is a set of activation functions. More specifically, $x^{[0]}$ is the input layer, $x^{[k]}$ is the output layer, and $x^{[1]}, \ldots, x^{[k-1]}$ are called hidden layers. Each layer $x^{[i]}, 0 \leq i \leq k$ is associated to an s_ℓ-dimensional vector space, in which each dimension corresponds to a neuron. For each $1 \leq i \leq k$, the affine function is written as $T_i(x^{[i-1]}) = W^{[i]} x^{[i-1]} + \mathbf{b}^{[i]}$, where $W^{[i]}$ and $\mathbf{b}^{[i]}$ are called the weight matrix and the bias vector, respectively. Furthermore, for each layer $x^{[i]}$, the value of each neuron in the hidden layer is assigned by the affine function T_i using the values of neurons in the previous layer, and then applying the activation function ϕ_i, i.e., $x^{[i]} = \phi_i(W^{[i]} x^{[i-1]} + \mathbf{b}^{[i]})$, with the activation function ϕ_i being applied element-wise.

There are some typical activation functions, such as the rectified linear unit (ReLU), sigmoid, softmax and tanh function [14]. And the commonly used ReLU is defined as $\text{ReLU}(x) = \max(0, x)$. Given a vector $\mathbf{x} \in \mathbb{R}^n$, the definition of $\phi(\mathbf{x})$ is extended to apply component-wise to $\mathbf{x}$, i.e.,

$$\phi(\mathbf{x}) = [\phi(x_1), \ldots, \phi(x_n)]^T.$$

From the mapping point of view, the i-th layer can be seen as the mapping image of the $(i-1)$-th layer. For each non-input layer $x^{[i]}$, $1 \leq i \leq k$, we can define a function $f^{[i]} : \mathbb{R}^{s_{i-1}} \rightarrow \mathbb{R}^{s_i}$, with

$$f^{[i]}(x) = \phi^{[i]}(W^{[i]}x + \mathbf{b}^{[i]}), 1 \leq i \leq k. \tag{1}$$

Therefore, a DNN $\mathcal{N}$ is expressed as the composition function $f : \mathbb{R}^{s_0} \rightarrow \mathbb{R}^{s_k}$, such that

$$f(x) = f^{[k]}(f^{[k-1]}(\cdots (f^{[1]}(x)))). \tag{2}$$

Given an input $x^{[0]}$, the DNN $\mathcal{N}$ assigns the label selected with the largest logit of the output layer $x^{[k]}$:

$$\ell = \arg\max(f(x^{[0]})) = \arg\max_{1 \leq j \leq s_k}(x_j^{[k]}). \tag{3}$$

In this paper, we focus on one of the most common architectures feed-forward DNN classifiers with ReLU activation functions.

2.2 Adversarial Robustness

We begin with formally defining the notion of robustness, and introducing the adversarial training of DNNs.

Given a DNN $\mathcal{N}$ with its associated function f and an input point x_0, we now define ϵ-robustness for a DNN $\mathcal{N}$ on x_0. Let $B_\epsilon(x_0)$ be the ℓ_∞-ball of radius $\epsilon \in \mathbb{R}_{>0}$ around the point x, i.e.,

$$B_\epsilon(x_0) = \{x \mid \|x - x_0\|_\infty \leq \epsilon\}.$$

We say that an input region $B_\epsilon(x_0)$ has the same label if any input x chosen from $B_\epsilon(x_0)$ has the same label as x_0 has. This property that the ϵ-ball around the point having the same label is called as $\epsilon-robustness$. Formally, we have the following definition. mon definition for *robustness*.

Definition 1 ($\epsilon-$**Robustness**). *Given a DNN with its associated function f, and an input point x_0. The ϵ-robustness of f at point x_0 holds if and only if $\mathcal{N}$ assigns the same label to all inputs within $B_\epsilon(x_0)$, i.e.,*

$$\arg\max(f(x)) = \arg\max(f(x_0)), \ \forall x \in B_\epsilon(x_0). \tag{4}$$

We say that $\mathcal{N}$ on x_0 is ϵ-robust.

Given a DNN $\mathcal{N}$ and its associated function $f : \mathbb{R}^{s_0} \rightarrow \mathbb{R}^{s_k}$, f_i denotes the function of the $i-$th element of f. Suppose $\mathcal{N}$ assigns the label ℓ to x_0, that is, $\ell = \arg\max f(x_0)$. Accordingly, the target of $\epsilon-$robustness verification with respect to x_0 is to determine whether any input selected randomly from $B_\epsilon(x_0)$, satisfies

$$\forall x \in B_\epsilon(x_0) \ \forall \tilde{\ell} \neq \ell : \ f_\ell(x) > f_{\tilde{\ell}}(x). \tag{5}$$

On the contrary, for an input x_0 with the correct label ℓ, we say that $\mathcal{N}$ w.r.t. x_0 is ϵ-unrobust if there exists an input $x \in B_\epsilon(x_0)$ such that $\arg\max(f(x)) \neq \ell$ is satisfied. In other words, x is misclassified if the logit of some incorrect label $\tilde{\ell}$ is larger than the logit of ℓ on x. Therefore, the existence of a misclassification $x \in B_\epsilon(x_0)$ is equivalent to x_0 ϵ-unrobust. Moreover, the problem of finding a misclassified example within $B_\epsilon(x_0)$ can be written as the following optimization problem:

$$p = \max_{x \in B_\epsilon(x_0)} \{ \max\{ f_{\tilde{\ell}}(x) - f_\ell(x), \ \tilde{\ell} \neq \ell \} \}. \tag{6}$$

It is seen that the network $\mathcal{N}$ on x_0 is ϵ-roubst if and only if the objective of the optimization problem (6) is negative, i.e., $p < 0$. Alternatively, once the optimum $p > 0$, the corresponding optimizer, denoted by x^*, is a misclassified example. Moreover, the optimization problem is to find an example x^* within $B_\epsilon(x_0)$ such that the logit of some incorrect label subtracting the logit of the correct label is maximized.

The following concept of robust accuracy, adapted from [44], is used to measure the robustness of the given DNN.

Robust Accuracy. Given a DNN $\mathcal{N}$ with a test set of labeled inputs $\{(x_i, y_i)\}_{i=1}^n$, the robust accuracy is the percentage of test samples for which the model $\mathcal{N}$ is ϵ-robust.

The optimization problem (6) for proving the ϵ-robustness on the given input can be written as the corresponding mixed integer linear programming. Due to the high computational complexity, the relaxed certification methods, such as abstraction-refinement and convex optimization, are able to yield *lower* bounds for robust accuracy. On the other hand, the first-order adversarial attacks, such as projected gradient descent (PGD) [24] or Deepfool [30], provide *upper* bounds for robust accuracy. In this paper, we will employ the popular adversarial attack PGD method, to measure the robust accuracy of the given DNN $\mathcal{N}$.

3   Training for Adversarial Robustness

A common method for adversarial training usually focuses on searching adversarial examples into the training set, and then training the DNN model with the updated training set to improve its robustness. Given a training dataset $\mathcal{D}$, the regular training is to obtain network weights θ by minimizing the following loss function, i.e.,

$$\min \mathbb{E}_{(x,y)\sim\mathcal{D}}(L(\theta, x, y)). \tag{7}$$

For a given ϵ-ball, the robust training is to obtain the network weights by minimizing the following loss function, i.e.,

$$\min \mathbb{E}_{(x,y)\sim\mathcal{D}} \max_{\tilde{x} \in B_\epsilon(x)} (L(\theta, \tilde{x}, y)). \tag{8}$$

As stated in prior work [21], the above min-max problem (8) is NP-hard. Therefore, generating adversarial examples approaches, based on adversarial attack techniques such as projected gradient descent(PGD), are applied to yield the approximate solutions of the inner maximization problem in (8). Instead of injecting adversarial examples, in this work we adopt linear programming to generate easily-misclassified examples. Specifically, we build an iterative training framework, wherein each iteration proceeds in two stages:

Compute Easily-Misclassified Examples. Given some inputs chosen randomly from the training set, for each input we apply a linear approximation and linear programming solving method for computing the associated easily-misclassified example with respect to the current DNN model. Precisely, given a DNN $\mathcal{N}$ and an input x_0, the task of inspecting an adversarial example with $B_\epsilon(x_0)$ can be equivalently expressed as a nonlinear optimization problem. To speedup the solving process, a surrogate is to relax the derived non-linear optimization as a linear programming problem to generate an *easily-misclassified* example (See Sect. 3.1).

Train the Model by Using Easily-Classified Examples. We construct the new loss function composing of normal examples and easily-misclassified ones obtained from the above step, and then run the training step to update the network (See Sect. 3.2).

3.1 Generating Easily-Misclassified Examples

Given a DNN $\mathcal{N} : \langle \mathcal{X}, \mathcal{T}, \Phi \rangle$, and an input point x_0 with its label ℓ, recall that $\epsilon-$robustness of x_0 is to verify whether any input $x \in B_\epsilon(x_0)$ satisfies the condition (5). In other words, $\mathcal{N}$ on x_0 is $\epsilon-$unrobust if and only if

$$\max_{x \in B_\epsilon(x_0)} \left\{ \max\{ f_{\tilde{\ell}}(x) - f_\ell(x), \ \tilde{\ell} \neq \ell \} \right\} > 0. \tag{9}$$

Accordingly, to inject an adversarial example in $B_\epsilon(x_0)$, one can construct the following nonlinear optimization problem:

$$\left. \begin{array}{l} p = \max\{ \ \max\{ \ f_{\tilde{\ell}}(x) - f_\ell(x), \ \tilde{\ell} \neq \ell \ \}\} \\ \text{s.t. } \|x - x_0\|_\infty \leq \epsilon, \end{array} \right\} \tag{10}$$

whose objective function is piece-wise. By introducing an auxiliary variable t, it can be transformed to an equivalent optimization problem by forming the epigraph problem,

$$\left. \begin{array}{l} p = \ \min \ t \\ \text{s.t. } \max_{\tilde{\ell} \neq \ell} f_{\tilde{\ell}}(x) - f_\ell(x) \leq t, \\ \|x - x_0\|_\infty \leq \epsilon. \end{array} \right\} \tag{11}$$

The constraint $\max_{\tilde{\ell} \neq \ell} f_{\tilde{\ell}}(x) - f_\ell(x) \leq t$ in (11) can then be expressed as a set of separate ones, i.e.,

$$f_{\tilde{\ell}}(x) - f_\ell(x) \leq t, \ \tilde{\ell} \neq \ell.$$

By doing so, the optimization problem (10) is equivalently written as the following one,

$$\left. \begin{array}{l} p = \ \min \ t \\ \text{s.t. } f_{\tilde{\ell}}(x) - f_\ell(x) \leq t, \ \tilde{\ell} \neq \ell, \\ \|x - x_0\|_\infty \leq \epsilon, \end{array} \right\} \tag{12}$$

with variables t and x.

Remark 1. Depending the equivalence between (10) and (12), consequently, capturing an adversarial example in the ϵ-ball of x_0 is equivalent to solve the nonlinear optimization problem (12). Precisely, the positivity of the optimum p for (12) is equivalent to the ϵ-unrobustness of x_0. Furthermore, the corresponding optimizer x^* of (12) is an adversarial example in $B_\epsilon(x_0)$.

Linear Approximation. Observing (12), we can find that the third constraints are linear, whereas the second ones are nonlinear, which are arising from the activation functions in the given DNN. As we know, the optimization problem (12) may be intractable. To make it tractable, one may compute the linear approximations for the nonlinear constraints in (12), thus can derive a linear programming problem. Instead of attacking the nonlinear optimization problem, the above linear encoding is able to seize a relaxed solution of (12), which can be regarded as an *easily-misclassified* example within $B_\epsilon(x_0)$.

Now let us explain how to apply the Least-Squares based linearization procedure to approximate the nonlinear constraints in (12). Specifically, given a DNN $\mathcal{N} : \langle \mathcal{X}, \mathcal{T}, \Phi \rangle$, with the associated function $f : \mathbb{R}^{s_0} \to \mathbb{R}^{s_k}$ and the input point x_0. We first construct a rectangular mesh M in $B_\epsilon(x_0)$ with a mesh spacing $s \in \mathbb{R}_+$ and the corresponding mesh point set $\{x_1, \ldots, x_t\}$. For each nonlinear function $f_{\tilde{\ell}}(x) - f_\ell(x), \tilde{\ell} \neq \ell$, we construct a point set $\mathcal{S}_{\tilde{\ell}} = \{(x_1, y_{\tilde{\ell},1}), \ldots, (x_t, y_{\tilde{\ell},t})\}$, where $y_{\tilde{\ell},j}, 1 \leq j \leq t$ are the evaluations of the function $f_{\tilde{\ell}} - f_\ell$ at the points x_j,

$$y_{\tilde{\ell},j} = f_{\tilde{\ell}}(x_j) - f_\ell(x_j).$$

For each point set $\mathcal{S}_{\tilde{\ell}}$, one can easily use the Least-Squares method to obtain an affine function, denoted by $h_\ell(x)$, to approximate the nonlinear function $f_{\tilde{\ell}} - f_\ell$, i.e.,

$$h_{\tilde{\ell}}(x) \approx f_{\tilde{\ell}}(x) - f_\ell(x), \ \tilde{\ell} \neq \ell. \tag{13}$$

Figure 1 illustrates the Least-Squares based on linearlization procedure to deal with a binary case. Figure 1(a) depicts a nonlinear binary classifier $[f_1(x), f_2(x)]$ within an interval $[-0.3, 0.3]$, where $f_1(x)$ and $f_2(x)$ respectively represent the probability of each category. As shown in Fig. 1(b), we construct the point set including the evaluations of $f_2(x) - f_1(x)$, and apply the Least-Squares method to obtain the linear approximate function $h_2(x)$ plotted with the red dashed line. Meanwhile, for the classifiers $f_1(x)$ and $f_2(x)$, one can also use the first-order linearization around $x_0 = 0$ to get the approximate linear classifiers, denoted by $g_1(x)$ and $g_2(x)$:

$$g_j(x) = f_j(0) + \nabla f_j(0)^T(x), \ j = 1, 2. \tag{14}$$

The associated first-order linearization approximation is $g_2(x) - g_1(x)$, plotted with the green dashed line in Fig. 1(b). In comparison with the method based on the first-order linearization approximation, our Least-Squares based method is able to yield the tight linear approximation. The reason is that the least-squares based method can minimize the mean square error, but first-order linearization approximation method may not.

Based on the above linearization procedure, the optimization problem (12) for generating easily-misclassified example within $B_\epsilon(x_0)$ can be relaxed into the following optimization problem:

$$p^* = \begin{aligned} &\min \ t \\ &\text{s.t. } h_{\tilde{\ell}}(x) \leq t, \quad \tilde{\ell} \neq \ell, \\ &\quad \|x - x_0\|_\infty \leq \epsilon, \end{aligned} \tag{15}$$

where $h_{\tilde{\ell}}(x)$ are the corresponding affine approximations of $f_{\tilde{\ell}} - f_\ell$ as in (14). To summarize, the LP solver can be applied to solve the above optimization problem (15), whose optimizer is an easily-misclassified example within $B_\epsilon(x_0)$.

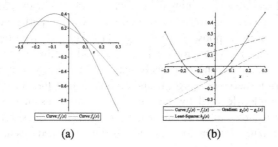

(a)   (b)

Fig. 1. Illustration of the linearization for nonlinear constraints.

3.2 Improving Adversarial Robustness with Easily-Misclassified Examples

Recall that our aim is to solve the min-max optimization problem (8) for improving adversarial robustness. Given a data set $X = \{(x_i, y_i), i = 1, \ldots, N\}$, the min-max optimization problem in (8) can be formulated as follow:

$$\frac{1}{N} \min \sum_{i=1}^{N} \max_{\tilde{x}_i \in B_\epsilon(x_i)} (L(\theta, \tilde{x}_i, y)). \tag{16}$$

As proposed in [24], a hyperparameter in a loss function is introduced to control the relative weight of adversarial examples. In this manner, training this new loss function can increase both the test accuracy and the robustness. On the other hand, following the idea shown in [24,33], batch normalization can also be deployed during the training. Therefore, suppose the current minibatch is $B = \{x_1, \ldots, x_m\}$, we can formulate the training loss function as following:

$$(1 - \alpha)\frac{1}{m} \sum_{i=1}^{m} L(\theta, x_i, y_i) + \alpha\frac{1}{m} \sum_{i=1}^{m} \max_{\tilde{x}_i \in B_\epsilon(x_i)} L(\theta, \tilde{x}_i, y_i), \tag{17}$$

where α is a hyperparameter that governs the relative weight of the regular loss and the robust loss. Notes that $\alpha \in [0, 1]$. And if $\alpha = 0$, (17) is equivalent to a standard training loss.

As stated in Sect. 3.1, here we use the linear relaxation technique to seek an easily-misclassified example. Concretely, during the training process, it trains the model to obtain the current network $\mathcal{N}$ with its associated function $f_{\hat{\theta}}(x)$ parameterized by $\hat{\theta}$. In this stage, for each sample $x_i, 1 \leq i \leq m$ in the minibatch B, we solve the corresponding linear programming problem (15) with $f_{\hat{\theta}}(x)$ and obtain its optimizer, denoted by $\hat{x}_i$. Having such easily-misclassified examples $\hat{x}_1, \ldots, \hat{x}_m$, we can build the new loss function:

$$Loss = (1 - \alpha)\frac{1}{m} \sum_{i=1}^{m} L(\theta, x_i, y_i) + \alpha\frac{1}{m} \sum_{i=1}^{m} L(\theta, \hat{x}_i, y_i). \tag{18}$$

Training Procedure. Given a training data set X and a network structure, we provide a method to train the adversarial robust network model, which is performed by an iterative scheme. More precisely, suppose $f_{\theta^{(t)}}(x)$ is a DNN parameterized by $\theta^{(t)}$, which are obtained from iteration t. At iteration $t+1$, we first read minibatch $B = \{x_1, \ldots, x_m\}$. For each sample x_i in B, one can easily establish the linear programing problem based on the current network $f_{\theta^{(t)}}(x)$, and further obtain the corresponding easily-misclassified example, denoted by $\hat{x}_i$. The loss function as in (18) is constructed by using the normal examples x_i and easily-misclassified ones $\hat{x}_i$. Afterwards we update θ by minimizing the new loss function. Detailed procedures are summarized in Algorithm 1.

Algorithm 1: *RobustTrain* (Robust Training of network via Easily-misclassified Examples)

    Input: Network $f_\theta(x)$ parameterized by θ;
           Training set X; minibatch size m;
           Perturbation radius ϵ;
           Hyperparameter $\alpha \in [0, 1]$.
    Output: Robust network $f_\theta(x)$ with θ.
1   Initialize parameter θ selected randomly;
2 **while** *stopping criterion not met* **do**
3   Sample a minibatch $B = \{(x_1, y_1), \ldots, (x_m, y_m)\}$ from the training set X.
4   **for** $j = 1, 2, \cdots, m$ **do**
5   Establish the optimization problem (15) from θ and x_j;
6   Call an LP solver to obtain its optimizer $\hat{x}_j$;
7   Make a new minibatch $B_{adv} = \{(\hat{x}_1, y_1) \ldots, (\hat{x}_m, y_m)\}$;
8   Construct $Loss$ as in (18) from B and B_{adv}.
9   Minimize $Loss$ to obtain its optimizer θ^*;
10   Apply update: $\theta \leftarrow \theta^*$;
11 **return** θ *and the robust network* $f_\theta(x)$.

---

4   Experiments

In this section, we evaluate the performance of our tool: EMRobust against two state-of-the-art methods proposed by Madry et al. [27] and Kurakin et al. [24] respectively, based on two benchmark datasets in the literate: MNIST [25] and CIFAR-10 [22] are used. Here, how does the configuration of parameters: the number of epochs and the hyperparameter α affect the performance of training is studied at first, and performance comparison on adversarial example generation and adversarial robustness training are made using the good parameter configuration. All the experiments are run on an Ubuntu 18.04.3 LTS server with a 2.7 GHz Intel Core i7 CPU with 64 GB RAM, and a NVIDIA GTX 2080Ti GPU.

MNIST. The networks *MNIST Small*, *MNIST Large* [42] and *MNIST Chall* [27] used in experiments, are all ConvNet architectures. These models are trained by the Adam optimizer with a fixed learning rate of 10^{-4}, a batch size of 32 on MNIST dataset. For adversarial training, we perform a 40 steps PGD attack with the step size of 0.01 and use a uniform random initialization within the L_∞-ball of radius ϵ_{train} for all adversarial training methods.

CIFAR-10. Two ConvNet architectures *CIFAR Small* and *CIFAR Large* [42] and one ResNet network *CIFAR Chall* [27] are chosen for generating models. Models are trained on CIFAR-10 dataset with a batch size of 32, using the Adam optimizer with a fixed learning rate of 10^{-4}. All adversarial training is based on PGD attacks with 40 iterations with the step size $2/255$ and random start points.

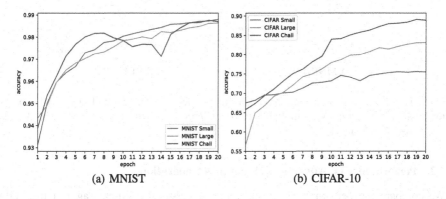

(a) MNIST   (b) CIFAR-10

Fig. 2. Test accuracies of EMRobust with different epochs on MNIST (a) and CIFAR-10 (b).

4.1 Effect of Parameters

We first investigate how does the number of epochs affect the training results. To identify the number of epochs adequate for EMRobust training method, we train several models with different epochs over a range of maximum epochs K, and then plot the final test accuracy of each trained model in Fig. 2. The overall trend of accuracy keeps increasing with the increase of training epochs, but its increasement slows down as the epoch becomes larger. For example, as shown in Fig. 2(a) and Fig. 2(b), the test accuracies of all networks becomes almost stable when the epoch goes from 16 to 20, and after that we could not achieve notable improvement on performance by increasing the epoch. Based on this result, we fix the training epoch to 20 in the following experiments.

The hyperparameter α in (17) is used to tune the balance between the regular loss and the robust loss. To evaluate its impact on *MNIST Small* model and *CIFAR Small*, we start EMRobust with different fixed values of α in the range $\{0.1, 0.2, \ldots, 0.9, 1\}$. The results on *MNIST Small* model and *CIFAR Small* model are reported in Fig. 3. It is shown that the test accuracy of *MNIST Small* remains steady at around 1.0, whereas that of *CIFAR Small* network is about 0.8. As for the robust accuracies, they rise gradually within $\alpha = 0.9$ and the optimum values are within $[0.9, 1.0]$. In Fig. 3(a), the robust accuracy reaches the optimal at the point $\alpha = 0.9$. In Fig. 3(b), the optimal α for the robust accuracy is in the range $[0.9, 1]$. To find the optimal α, we tune α from 0.9 to 1.0 with a step-size of 0.05. The procedure turns out that the robust accuracy reaches to the optimal at the point $\alpha = 0.95$.

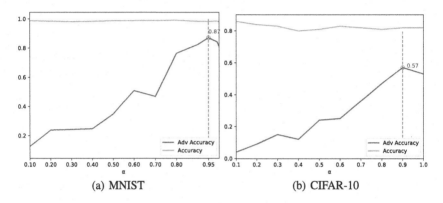

(a) MNIST   (b) CIFAR-10

Fig. 3. The effects of hyper-parameter α on the training accuracy on clean and adversarial samples for (a) *MNIST Small* model with $\epsilon = 0.3$ and (b) *CIFAR Small* model with $\epsilon = 8/255$, under the L_∞-norm PGD-40 attack.

4.2 Performance on Adversarial Examples Generation

We compare the performance on generating adversarial examples against the PGD attacks with different steps on the L_∞-norm. In Table 1 and Table 2 show the results, where PGD-N denotes PGD with N steps. The performance is compared using adversarial success rate, that is, the attack success rate of adversarial examples generated by PGD-5, 10, 20, 40 and our LP strategy at different ϵ. Table 1 shows the results on three standard networks trained on MNIST. The performance of PGD attacks increases significantly with the number of iterations. It is observed that the LP based approach achieves the same level of success in standard PGD-40 attack, but consistently superior to other attacks. It is also seen that in the PGD attack algorithm where the number of iterations gets larger than 10 and our LP method, the perturbation radius matters a lot. For example, when the attack radius increases from 0.1 to 0.3, the strength of LP based adversarial examples are improved by 46.75%. As Table 2, similar results are obtained when experiments are implemented on the CIFAR-10 dataset.

4.3   Performance on Robust Training

To demonstrate the effectiveness of EMRobust, we conduct experiments on different networks and datasets. We compare the performance against two existing state-of-the-art robust training schemes: [27] and [24]. In [27], the adversarial robustness of neural networks is studied through the lens of robust optimization, while in [24], adversarial training is scaled to large models and datasets. We train robust networks of three different architectures under the L_∞-norm PGD-40 attacks of various perturbations ϵ. The performance on robustness is measured by clean accuracy and adversarial accuracy.

Table 1. Adversarial examples on MNIST

Model	ϵ	PGD-5	PGD-10	PGD-20	PGD-40	LP
MNIST Small	0.1	15.54	59.98	63.43	64.18	**67.91**
	0.2	15.54	59.98	97.81	98.51	**98.75**
	0.3	15.54	59.98	97.81	**99.99**	99.95
MNIST Large	0.1	16.18	51.91	52.83	52.91	**53.14**
	0.2	16.23	53.97	94.62	**96.73**	96.10
	0.3	16.21	52.95	98.73	99.83	**99.89**
MNIST Chall	0.1	7.70	30.90	32.80	33.60	**34.13**
	0.2	7.70	30.90	93.20	94.40	**95.60**
	0.3	7.70	30.90	93.20	**99.80**	99.31

Table 2. Adversarial examples on CIFAR-10

Model	ϵ	PGD-5	PGD-10	PGD-20	PGD-40	LP
CIFAR Small	2/255	90.23	90.41	90.46	90.47	**91.13**
	4/255	98.07	98.21	98.24	**98.24**	93.11
	8/255	99.96	99.98	99.98	**99.98**	99.81
	16/255	100	100	100	100	100
CIFAR Large	2/255	82.12	82.50	81.69	**83.71**	73.91
	4/255	95.12	94.51	94.87	**95.64**	91.9
	8/255	98.92	99.01	99.13	99.14	**99.32**
	16/255	99.12	99.13	99.25	99.45	**99.80**

Results on MNIST. Table 3 presents the evaluation results of the three techniques under the attack of $\epsilon = 0.1$ and 0.3 on MNIST models, where the best result are put in bold fonts.

For the three MNIST networks, each of which is attacked by adversarial examples yielded from the two perturbations: 0.1 and 0.3, there should be twelve best results on the two index: ACCURACY and ADVERSARIAL ACCURACY. Clearly, our *EMRobust* produces ten of them.

As for the average values, for the three models that against the adversarial examples with the perturbation 0.1, the ACCURACY of the model towards clean examples, produced by Madry's method, Goodfellow's method and our *EMRobust*, are 99.16%, 99.21% and 99.72%, respectively. The ADVERSARIAL ACCURACY towards adversarial examples, produced by the three methods, are 96.02%, 95.81% and 97.74%, respectively. Meanwhile, for the three models against the perturbation 0.3, the ACCURACY of the model, trained by the three methods, are 97.99%, 98.66% and 99.06%, respectively. The ADVERSARIAL ACCURACY of the three models are 90.47%, 85.09% and 91.54%, respectively. Our *EMRobust* produces the best average results of all the indexes.

When the perturbation is strengthened from 0.1 to 0.3, both the ACCURACY and ADVERSARIAL ACCURACY of the models drops. However, our *EMRobust* stably provides the best results.

Table 3. Performance on adversarial robustness training

Network	ϵ	Madry et al.		Goodfellow et al.		EMRobust	
		ACCURACY	ADV. ACCURACY	ACCURACY	ADV. ACCURACY	ACCURACY	ADV. ACCURACY
MNIST Small	0.1	98.95	94.84	98.98	93.99	**99.71**	**98.21**
	0.3	96.31	85.23	97.90	84.96	**99.61**	**87.34**
MNIST Large	0.1	99.23	97.56	99.24	97.31	**99.83**	**98.51**
	0.3	**99.26**	95.16	99.24	95.80	99.22	**96.13**
MNIST Chall	0.1	99.40	95.67	99.41	96.12	**99.63**	**96.51**
	0.3	98.42	91.04	**98.83**	74.52	98.35	**91.15**
CIFAR Small	4/255	67.23	62.74	78.23	60.23	**83.48**	**63.54**
	8/255	-	-	-	-	**75.61**	**57.34**
CIFAR Large	4/255	81.23	65.12	74.23	67.23	**82.65**	**68.23**
	8/255	-	-	-	-	**83.32**	**65.17**
CIFAR Chall	4/255	87.67	61.27	90.21	63.12	**91.23**	**64.37**
	8/255	82.34	48.49	86.13	42.77	**89.12**	**49.21**

Results on CIFAR-10. In Table 3, we compare the performance of *EMRobust* to the other two methods on CIFAR-10 for ϵ of $4/255$ and $8/255$. Furthermore, show the result accompanied with the increase of the perturbation, Fig. 4 plots the performance on *CIFAR Small* networks trained by three adversarial training methods under the perturbations with $\epsilon = 2/255, 4/255, 6/255$ and $8/255$.

There should be six best results for the three networks with two perturbations each. Our *EMRobust* gives all the six best results. Consider the average values, for the models against the perturbation 0.1, their ACCURACY and ADVERSARIAL ACCURACY are 78.71%, 80.89%, 85.79% and 63.04%, 63.53%, 65.38%, respectively. Again, for the successful models against to the perturbation 0.3, their ACCURACY and ADVERSARIAL ACCURACY are 82.34%, 86.13%, 89.12% and 48.49%, 42.77%, 49.21%, respectively. Our *EMRobust* improves the models on all the two aspects.

Figure 4 shows that our *EMRobust* reliably outperforms the other two methods when the perturbations gets larger and larger. When ϵ is set to $2/255$, that is, a relatively small strength of attack, the performance of *EMRobust* trained model is comparable with the other types of models. As the perturbation bound gets larger, *EMRobust*'s clean and adversarial accuracy degrades gracefully, while when ϵ is set to $6/255$ or lager, both of Madry's and Goodfellow's methods get stuck after many iterations and thus fail to converge to a usable model. The same similar situation happens in *CIFAR Large* network. For all the cases, our *EMRobust* does not get stuck and successfully return models with acceptable accuracy.

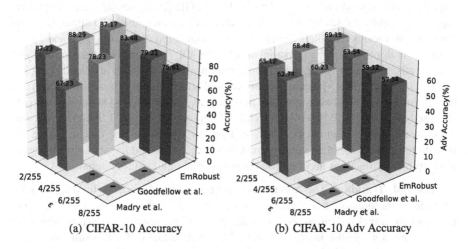

(a) CIFAR-10 Accuracy   (b) CIFAR-10 Adv Accuracy

Fig. 4. Accuracy and robustness of *CIFAR Small* network trained with three methods against attacks of different strengths. The attack strengths are $\epsilon \in \{2/255, 4/255, 6/255, 8/255\}$. The same color denotes the models are trained by the same method while the shade of square columns denotes the level of robustness of the networks under different perturbation bounds. The notation "$-$" indicates the training method does not converge under a given attack.

Table 3 shows that *EMRobust* can yield models achieving both high robustness and high clean accuracy in all cases, which demonstrates the most important advantage of *EMRobust*. On the one hand, it is well-known that robustness training usually sacrifices the accuracy of the model on clean samples. Our *EMRobust* training can provide better robustness against adversarial examples than the state-of-the-art adversarial training methods on adversarial examples while retaining the highest accuracy on the original examples. On the other hand, our *EMRobust* shows its potential to producing robust models against strong adversarial attacks, where stats-of-the-art training methods fail to converge.

5   Related Work

Adversarial Attacks. The existence of adversarial examples was firstly reported by Szegedy et al. [38] where adversarial perturbations were found by box-constrained L-BFGS optimization. After that, Goodfellow et al. presented the Fast Gradient Sign Method (FGSM) to generate adversarial examples in one iteration [15] in which the sign of gradient gives the direction of perturbations. Later, many variants of FGSM were developed. R+FGSM proposed by Tramèr et al. [41] enhanced the classical FGSM with a randomization step. Kurakin et al. [23] extended the FGSM by applying it multiple times with a small step size to find better adversarial examples, called the Basic Iterative Method. The iterative FGSM attack was further improved by adding multiple random restarts or introducing random initialization points [43]. The projected gradient descent (PGD) attack is a kind of iterative attack which integrates multiple iterations with the projection on the ϵ−ball. The study on PGD [28] gives strong evidences on supporting it to be the strongest first-order attack. Since then, the PGD attack has been enhanced by various techniques, such as using momentum to boosting [13] and generalizing to multiple types of adversarial attacks [29,40]. [16] improves transferability of adversarial examples by linear backpropagating using off-the-shelf attacks that exploit gradients. Carlini et al. [9] formulated adversarial attacks as optimization instances and solved them using stochastic gradient descent. Like us, Moosavi-Dezfooli et al. [31] proposed an iterative LP based attack called Deepfool. However, it linearized the network as a hyperplane and seeked the smallest perturbation as the distance from the input to the hyperplane in an iterative manner while our method linearize the difference of discriminant functions and can find the adversarial input without iteration.

Adversarial Training. The robustness gained from adversarial training heavily depends on the quality of the adversarial examples used. Training on examples from non-iterative attacks such as FGSM only improve robustness against non-iterative attacks, and not against iterative attacks like PGD attacks. As a result, to defend strong adversarial attacks, many research has built defenses on PGD adversarial training or embedded PGD attacks into the training. Representative works include Supervised Sparse Coding [37], matrix estimation [46], logit pairing [32], Feature Denoising [45], Defensive Quantization [26], Thermometer Encoding [7], PixelDefend [36], L2-nonexpansive nets [34], Jacobian Regularization [20] and Stochastic Activation Pruning [11]. All these works utilize the classic PGD attacks different from EMRobust proposed in the paper.

6   Conclusion

In this paper, we have presented a new adversarial training method called EMRobust, which raises the robustness of neural networks using easily misclassified examples. A linear program is constructed to approximate the optimal problem that finds the adversarial examples inducing the maximum loss within the allowed perturbation. LP solvers turn out to find solutions very near to the optimum which enable EMRobust to produce robust neural networks readily. The evaluation on MNIST and CIFAR-10 datasets demonstrates that EMRobust brings more robustness improvement for those networks than the PGD based method does even under strong strength attacks.

Acknowledgment. This research is supported by the National Natural Science Foundation of China under Grant 12171159 and Shanghai Trusted Industry Internet Software Collaborative Innovation Center.

References

1. Amato, F., Lopez, A., Pena-Mendez, E.M., Vanhara, P., Hampl, A., Havel, J.: Artificial neural networks in medical diagnosis. J. Appl. Biomed. **11**(2), 47–58 (2013)
2. Andor, D., et al.: Globally normalized transition-based neural networks. In: Proceedings of the 54th Annual Meeting of the Association for Computational Linguistics, ACL 2016, Berlin, Germany, 7–12 August 2016, Volume 1: Long Papers (2016)
3. Athalye, A., Carlini, N., Wagner, D.A.: Obfuscated gradients give a false sense of security: circumventing defenses to adversarial examples. In: Proceedings of the 35th International Conference on Machine Learning, ICML 2018, Stockholmsmässan, Stockholm, Sweden, 10–15 July 2018, pp. 274–283 (2018)
4. Biggio, B., et al.: Evasion attacks against machine learning at test time. In: Blockeel, H., Kersting, K., Nijssen, S., Železný, F. (eds.) ECML PKDD 2013. LNCS (LNAI), vol. 8190, pp. 387–402. Springer, Heidelberg (2013). https://doi.org/10.1007/978-3-642-40994-3_25
5. Bojarski, M., et al: Efficient visualization of CNNs for autonomous driving. In: 2018 IEEE International Conference on Robotics and Automation, ICRA 2018, pp. 1–8 (2018)
6. Bojchevski, A., Günnemann, S.: Adversarial attacks on node embeddings (2018)
7. Buckman, J., Roy, A., Raffel, C., Goodfellow, I.J.: Thermometer encoding: one hot way to resist adversarial examples. In: 6th International Conference on Learning Representations, ICLR 2018, Vancouver, BC, Canada, 30 April–3 May 2018, Conference Track Proceedings (2018)
8. Carlini, N., Katz, G., Barrett, C., Dill, D.L.: Provably minimally-distorted adversarial examples. arXiv preprint arXiv:1709.10207 (2017)
9. Carlini, N., Wagner, D.A.: Adversarial examples are not easily detected: bypassing ten detection methods. In: Proceedings of the 10th ACM Workshop on Artificial Intelligence and Security, pp. 3–14 (2017)
10. Chen, J., Wu, Y., Xu, X., Chen, Y., Zheng, H., Xuan, Q.: Fast gradient attack on network embedding. arXiv preprint arXiv:1809.02797 (2018)
11. Dhillon, G.S., et al.: Stochastic activation pruning for robust adversarial defense. In: 6th International Conference on Learning Representations, ICLR 2018, Vancouver, BC, Canada, 30 April–3 May 2018, Conference Track Proceedings (2018)
12. Ding, G.W., Sharma, Y., Lui, K.Y.C., Huang, R.: Max-margin adversarial (MMA) training: direct input space margin maximization through adversarial training. arXiv preprint arXiv:1812.02637 (2018)
13. Dong, Y., et al.: Boosting adversarial attacks with momentum. In: 2018 IEEE Conference on Computer Vision and Pattern Recognition, CVPR 2018, Salt Lake City, UT, USA, 18–22 June 2018, pp. 9185–9193 (2018)
14. Goodfellow, I., Bengio, Y., Courville, A.: Deep Learning. MIT Press, Cambridge (2016)
15. Goodfellow, I.J., Shlens, J., Szegedy, C.: Explaining and harnessing adversarial examples. In: 3rd International Conference on Learning Representations, ICLR 2015, San Diego, CA, USA, 7–9 May 2015, Conference Track Proceedings (2015)
16. Guo, Y., Li, Q., Chen, H.: Backpropagating linearly improves transferability of adversarial examples. In: Larochelle, H., Ranzato, M., Hadsell, R., Balcan, M.F., Lin, H. (eds.) Advances in Neural Information Processing Systems, vol. 33, pp. 85–95. Curran Associates Inc., New York (2020)
17. Hinton, G., et al.: Deep neural networks for acoustic modeling in speech recognition: the shared views of four research groups. IEEE Signal Process. Mag. **29**(6), 82–97 (2012)
18. Hosu, I., Rebedea, T.: Playing atari games with deep reinforcement learning and human checkpoint replay. CoRR abs/1607.05077 (2016)

19. Huang, R., Xu, B., Schuurmans, D., Szepesvári, C.: Learning with a strong adversary. arXiv preprint arXiv:1511.03034 (2015)
20. Jakubovitz, D., Giryes, R.: Improving DNN robustness to adversarial attacks using jacobian regularization. In: Computer Vision - ECCV 2018–15th European Conference, Munich, Germany, 8–14 September 2018, Proceedings, Part XII, pp. 525–541 (2018)
21. Katz, G., Barrett, C., Dill, D.L., Julian, K., Kochenderfer, M.J.: Reluplex: an efficient SMT solver for verifying deep neural networks. In: Majumdar, R., Kunčak, V. (eds.) CAV 2017. LNCS, vol. 10426, pp. 97–117. Springer, Cham (2017). https://doi.org/10.1007/978-3-319-63387-9_5
22. Krizhevsky, A., Nair, V., Hinton, G.: The CIFAR-10 dataset home page (2009). https://www.cs.toronto.edu/~kriz/cifar.html
23. Kurakin, A., Goodfellow, I.J., Bengio, S.: Adversarial examples in the physical world. In: 5th International Conference on Learning Representations, ICLR 2017, Toulon, France, 24–26 April 2017, Workshop Track Proceedings (2017)
24. Kurakin, A., Goodfellow, I.J., Bengio, S.: Adversarial machine learning at scale. In: Proceedings International Conference on Learning Representations (ICLR), pp. 1–17 (2017)
25. LeCun, Y., Cortes, C., Burges, C.J.: The MNIST database of handwritten digits home page (1998). http://yann.lecun.com/exdb/mnist/
26. Lin, J., Gan, C., Han, S.: Defensive quantization: when efficiency meets robustness. In: 7th International Conference on Learning Representations, ICLR 2019, New Orleans, LA, USA, 6–9 May 2019 (2019)
27. Madry, A., Makelov, A., Schmidt, L., Tsipras, D., Vladu, A.: Towards deep learning models resistant to adversarial attacks. arXiv preprint arXiv:1706.06083 (2017)
28. Madry, A., Makelov, A., Schmidt, L., Tsipras, D., Vladu, A.: Towards deep learning models resistant to adversarial attacks. In: 6th International Conference on Learning Representations, ICLR 2018, Vancouver, BC, Canada, 30 April–3 May 2018, Conference Track Proceedings (2018)
29. Maini, P., Wong, E., Kolter, J.Z.: Adversarial robustness against the union of multiple perturbation models. CoRR abs/1909.04068 (2019)
30. Moosavi-Dezfooli, S., Fawzi, A., Frossard, P.: DeepFool: a simple and accurate method to fool deep neural networks. In: IEEE Conference on Computer Vision and Pattern Recognition(CVPR), pp. 2574–2582 (2016)
31. Moosavi-Dezfooli, S., Fawzi, A., Frossard, P.: DeepFool: a simple and accurate method to fool deep neural networks. In: 2016 IEEE Conference on Computer Vision and Pattern Recognition, CVPR 2016, Las Vegas, NV, USA, 27–30 June 2016, pp. 2574–2582 (2016)
32. Mosbach, M., Andriushchenko, M., Trost, T.A., Hein, M., Klakow, D.: Logit pairing methods can fool gradient-based attacks. CoRR abs/1810.12042 (2018)
33. Na, T., Ko, J.H., Mukhopadhyay, S.: Cascade adversarial machine learning regularized with a unified embedding. In: Proceedings International Conference on Learning Representations (ICLR) (2018)
34. Qian, H., Wegman, M.N.: L2-nonexpansive neural networks. In: 7th International Conference on Learning Representations, ICLR 2019, New Orleans, LA, USA, 6–9 May 2019 (2019)
35. Silver, D., et al.: Mastering the game of go with deep neural networks and tree search. Nature **529**(7587), 484–489 (2016)
36. Song, Y., Kim, T., Nowozin, S., Ermon, S., Kushman, N.: PixelDefend: leveraging generative models to understand and defend against adversarial examples. In: 6th International Conference on Learning Representations, ICLR 2018, Vancouver, BC, Canada, 30 April–3 May 2018, Conference Track Proceedings (2018)

37. Sulam, J., Muthukumar, R., Arora, R.: Adversarial robustness of supervised sparse coding. In: Larochelle, H., Ranzato, M., Hadsell, R., Balcan, M.F., Lin, H. (eds.) Advances in Neural Information Processing Systems, vol. 33, pp. 2110–2121. Curran Associates, Inc., New York (2020)
38. Szegedy, C., et al.: Intriguing properties of neural networks. In: Proceedings of the International Conference on Learning Representations (ICLR 2014) (2014)
39. Tjeng, V., Tedrake, R.: Verifying neural networks with mixed integer programming. CoRR abs/1711.07356 (2017)
40. Tramèr, F., Boneh, D.: Adversarial training and robustness for multiple perturbations. In: Advances in Neural Information Processing Systems 32: Annual Conference on Neural Information Processing Systems 2019, NeurIPS 2019, Vancouver, BC, Canada, 8–14 December 2019, pp. 5858–5868 (2019)
41. Tramèr, F., Kurakin, A., Papernot, N., Goodfellow, I.J., Boneh, D., McDaniel, P.D.: Ensemble adversarial training: attacks and defenses. In: 6th International Conference on Learning Representations, ICLR 2018, Vancouver, BC, Canada, 30 April–3 May, 2018, Conference Track Proceedings (2018)
42. Wong, E., Kolter, J.Z.: Provable defenses against adversarial examples via the convex outer adversarial polytope, vol. 12, Stockholm, Sweden, pp. 8405–8423 (2018)
43. Wong, E., Rice, L., Kolter, J.Z.: Fast is better than free: Revisiting adversarial training. In: 8th International Conference on Learning Representations, ICLR 2020, Addis Ababa, Ethiopia, 26–30 April 2020 (2020)
44. Xiao, K.Y., Tjeng, V., Shafiullah, N.M.M., Madry, A.: Training for faster adversarial robustness verification via inducing reLU stability. In: International Conference on Learning Representations (2019)
45. Xie, C., Wu, Y., van der Maaten, L., Yuille, A.L., He, K.: Feature denoising for improving adversarial robustness. In: IEEE Conference on Computer Vision and Pattern Recognition, CVPR 2019, Long Beach, CA, USA, 16–20 June 2019, pp. 501–509 (2019)
46. Yang, Y., Zhang, G., Xu, Z., Katabi, D.: ME-Net: towards effective adversarial robustness with matrix estimation. In: Proceedings of the 36th International Conference on Machine Learning, ICML 2019, Long Beach, California, USA, 9–15 June 2019, pp. 7025–7034 (2019)
47. Zhang, H., Yu, Y., Jiao, J., Xing, E.P., Ghaoui, L.E., Jordan, M.I.: Theoretically principled trade-off between robustness and accuracy. arXiv preprint arXiv:1901.08573 (2019)

AllSynth: Transiently Correct Network Update Synthesis Accounting for Operator Preferences

Kim Guldstrand Larsen[1], Anders Mariegaard[1], Stefan Schmid[2,3], and Jiří Srba[1(✉)]

[1] Aalborg University, Aalborg, Denmark
{kgl,am,srba}@cs.aau.dk
[2] TU Berlin, Berlin, Germany
[3] University of Vienna, Vienna, Austria
stefan_schmid@univie.ac.at

Abstract. The increasingly stringent dependability requirements on communication networks as well as the need to render these networks more adaptive to improve performance, demand for more automated approaches to operate networks. We present AllSynth, a symbolic synthesis tool for updating communication networks in a provably correct and efficient manner. AllSynth automatically synthesizes network update schedules which transiently ensure a wide range of policy properties (expressed in the LTL logic), also during the reconfiguration process. In particular, in contrast to existing approaches, AllSynth symbolically computes and compactly represents *all* feasible solutions. At its heart, AllSynth relies on a novel, two-level and parameterized use of BDDs which greatly improves performance. Indeed, AllSynth not only provides formal correctness guarantees and outperforms existing state-of-the-art tools in terms of generality, but often also in terms of runtime as documented by experiments on a benchmark of real-world network topologies.

1 Introduction

A more automated operation of communication networks is considered one of the most important research problems in networking today, for two main reasons. *First*, communication networks and their configurations are highly complex, forcing operators to become "masters of complexity" [24]; many major Internet outages over the last years were caused by human errors [5,12,15]. Today's manual approach hence stands in stark contrast to the increasingly stringent dependability requirements on communication networks, which are a critical infrastructure of our digital society. *Second*, network traffic is not only growing explosively but also features much temporal and spatial structure [4,6,48]; this introduces a significant potential to improve operational efficiency by rendering networks more adaptive towards the actual traffic patterns they serve.

Motivated by the vision of more automated networks [17], over the last years, great efforts were made in laying the foundations for automated network verification, and in designing synthesis tools [3,16,27,42,45]. Furthermore, motivated

© Springer Nature Switzerland AG 2022
Y. Aït-Ameur and F. Crăciun (Eds.): TASE 2022, LNCS 13299, pp. 344–362, 2022.
https://doi.org/10.1007/978-3-031-10363-6_23

by the benefits of more adaptive network operations, e.g., to improve availability and performance [28], automated tools for consistently updating network configurations have been developed [11,23,38,43,46] which overcome the limitations of existing hand-crafted algorithms [2,34,37]. However, the computation of provably consistent network update schedules remains challenging, due to the required performance and expressiveness. The performance requirements are multidimensional: network update schedules should not only be quickly computable but also account for operator preferences, like requiring that certain switches or routers are updated first. However, existing approaches only provide one update sequence that may not be preferred by the network operator.

Our Contributions. We present an automated network update synthesis tool, *AllSynth*, that computes and represents in a compact BDD form *all* correct update sequences that respect various logical properties expressible in linear temporal logic (LTL) [41] like reachability, waypointing and service chaining. *AllSynth* comes with formal correctness guarantees and for situations in which *provably* no simple update schedule exists, it can make suggestions for alternative solutions (where the same switch is updated multiple times).

Despite being more general, *AllSynth* significantly outperforms state-of-the-art tools in terms of runtime on all non-trivial real-world networks from the standard Topology Zoo benchmark [29]. The update synthesis problem solved by *AllSynth* is NP-hard, even if restricted to preserving the basic loop-freedom and waypointing properties [34]. To combat the complexity of the problem, *All-Synth* exploits a novel two-level use of binary decision diagrams (BDDs) [32] to compactly encode not only the network topology and policy invariant, but also the set of *all* correct update sequences.

The fact that *AllSynth* computes all feasible update sequences enables future use cases for the tool, such as finding an optimal schedule, providing multiple alternative solutions and filtering based on operator requirements (e.g. some switches must be updated before the rest or in a certain order). The source code of *AllSynth* and all our experimental artefacts are available at [31].

Related Work. Motivated by the benefits of adaptive and software-defined (i.e., programmable) communication networks [30], as well as the increasingly stringent dependability requirements, the question of how to correctly update network configurations has received much attention over the last years. A recent survey summarizes over one hundred approaches [19].

In their seminal work, Reitblatt et al. [43] showed that a strong per-packet consistency can be achieved using packet versioning during reconfigurations. Their approach, which was subsequently studied intensively in the literature [8,10,20,25,26,33,40], has the drawback that it requires packet header modifications and additional memory at the nodes: switches and routers need to store forwarding rules for each version.

A clever alternative approach, introduced by Mahajan and Wattenhofer [37], schedules batches of updates over time, where the set of updates within a batch can take effect in any order without harming consistency. This approach has also been explored extensively already [2,14,21,34–36,47], however, it can only be used to provide a subset of the consistency properties of [43]. This in turn motivated hybrid approaches such as FLIP [46]. Interestingly, similar to *All-Synth*, FLIP also supports alternative solutions in case a simple update cannot be found. However, in contrast to FLIP which relies on a heuristic algorithm, *AllSynth* only presents alternative solutions in case a simple solution *provably* does not exist. Furthermore, while FLIP resorts to a packet tagging alternative (which consumes header space and switch memory), *AllSynth* is light-weight and fully symbolic approach aiming at updating nodes multiple times.

The need for supporting more general or even customizable consistency properties [49] as well as more automated synthesis approaches [18,23,39] has already received attention in the literature as well. However, our approach is the first one that is using the BDD-based technology for the synthesis and representation of *all* correct network updates. The competing tool NetSynth [38] for update synthesis is relying on an incremental enumeration of candidates of update sequences that are then verified by external model checkers, like NuSMV [13], and the tool terminates as soon as the first correct update sequence is found.

2   A Model for Update Synthesis

Before we formally define our problem, we shall provide an intuitive motivation for the update synthesis problem. In Fig. 1 we see a simple network with four nodes (routers). Packets from the source node s are forwarded to the destination node d along the solid edges (links) that represent the initial routing configuration. The network operator aims to change this routing to an alternative one represented by the dashed edges. The task is to schedule the order of node updates (changing the forwarding function at the updated node from the solid edge to the dashed one) so that in every intermediate routing configuration we preserve the reachability between s and d and at the same time always visit the waypoint node v_1 (representing for example a firewall).

If the node s is updated first, the new routing will follow the path s, v_2, d which preserves the reachability property but not the waypointing. On the other hand, if we first update the node v_2, we create an undesirable forwarding loop $s, v_2, v_1, v_2, v_1, \ldots$ which

Fig. 1. Update synthesis problem

breaks the reachability property. Hence the only option is to update first the node v_1, after which we have a correct forwarding path s, v_1, d satisfying both reachability and waypointing. After this we can update the node v_2 because this update does not change the forwarding path and lastly, we update the node s that completes the update sequence from the initial to the final routing. We are now ready to provide the formalization of the update synthesis problem.

We model the network as a multigraph, allowing us to describe multiple connections between nodes (i.e., switches or routers, which are treated as synonyms in the following); these connections can have different quantitative attributes (e.g. latency). Henceforth, we adopt graph-theory terminology and refer to such connections or links as edges.

Definition 1 (Network Topology). *A network topology is a directed multi-graph $G = (V, E, \mathsf{src}, \mathsf{tgt})$ where V is the set of nodes, E is the set of edges and $\mathsf{src}, \mathsf{tgt} \colon E \to V$ are respectively the* source *and* target *functions.*

In order to route traffic from a node v_0 to a node v', each node v has a forwarding rule that specifies an appropriate outgoing edge e such that $\mathsf{src}(e) = v$. This rule can be per-flow or apply to multiple flows; in the following, we do not explicitly distinguish between the two scenarios. Not all nodes need to have defined their forwarding edge (e.g. the target node v' or the nodes that are not involved in packet forwarding from v_0 to v'). We capture this formally by the notion of a routing configuration.

Definition 2 (Routing Configuration). *A routing configuration, or routing for short, in a network topology $G = (V, E, \mathsf{src}, \mathsf{tgt})$ is a partial function $\rho \colon V \rightharpoonup E$ such that $\mathsf{src}(\rho(v)) = v$ for all $v \in V$ where $\rho(v)$ is defined.*

For a given network topology $G = (V, E, \mathsf{src}, \mathsf{tgt})$ with the source node $v_0 \in V$, a routing configuration ρ defines a unique sequence of edges (a path) that is finite if the routing is loop free; otherwise it is infinite. In the finite case, the *path* is given by $\pi = e_0 e_1 \cdots e_n$ such that $\rho(\mathsf{tgt}(e_{i-1})) = e_i$ for all i, $0 \leq i \leq n$, where by convention $\mathsf{tgt}(e_{-1}) = v_0$ and where $\rho(\mathsf{tgt}(e_n))$ is undefined. The corresponding sequence of *traversed nodes* is then $\overline{\pi} = \mathsf{src}(e_0)\mathsf{src}(e_1) \cdots \mathsf{src}(e_n)\mathsf{tgt}(e_n)$. In the infinite case, the *path* is given by $\pi = e_0 e_1 \cdots$ such that $\rho(\mathsf{tgt}(e_{i-1})) = e_i$ for all $i \geq 0$ where as before $\mathsf{tgt}(e_{-1}) = v_0$. The sequence of *traversed nodes* is given by the infinite sequence $\overline{\pi} = \mathsf{src}(e_0)\mathsf{src}(e_1) \cdots$. If $\overline{\pi} = v_0 v_1 \ldots$ is a (finite or infinite) sequence of nodes then we refer to its suffix $v_i v_{i+1} \ldots$ by $\overline{\pi}_i$ and to the initial node v_0 by $\overline{\pi}[0]$. For a node $v_0 \in V$ and routing ρ, we let $\pi_\rho(v_0)$ denote the unique (finite or infinite) path induced by ρ from the source node v_0 and let $\overline{\pi}_\rho(v_0)$ be the corresponding sequence of traversed nodes.

2.1 Routing Policies

We shall now define an LTL-based logic [41] that allows us to describe the policy of acceptable routings (both statically and transiently).

Definition 3 (Policy Syntax). *For a network topology $G = (V, E, \mathsf{src}, \mathsf{tgt})$, a policy φ is constructed according to the following LTL-based abstract syntax, where $v \in V$:*

$$\varphi ::= \mathsf{true} \mid v \mid \neg\varphi \mid \varphi \wedge \varphi \mid \mathsf{NoLoop} \mid X\,\varphi \mid \varphi\,U\,\varphi .$$

In addition to the classical LTL operators, our logic includes a loop freedom predicate. We now give the formal semantics of our logic, interpreted both on infinite and finite paths [22].

$$\mathsf{Reach}(d) \equiv \mathsf{true}\,U\,d$$

$$\mathsf{Waypoint}(v,d) \equiv \neg\mathsf{Reach}(d) \vee (\neg d\,U\,v \wedge \mathsf{Reach}(d))$$

$$\mathsf{MultiWaypoint}(W,d) \equiv \bigvee_{v \in W} \mathsf{Waypoint}(v,d)$$

$$\mathsf{Service}(\omega,d) \equiv \begin{cases} \mathsf{true} & \text{if } |\omega| = 0 \\ \neg\mathsf{Reach}(d)\,\vee & \text{if } \omega = v \circ \omega' \\ \left(\bigwedge_{v' \in \omega'} \neg v' \wedge \neg d\right)\,U\,(v \wedge \mathsf{Service}(\omega',d)) & \text{where } v \in V \end{cases}$$

Fig. 2. Encoding of standard policies where $v,d \in V$, $\emptyset \neq W \subseteq V$ and $\omega \in V^*$

Definition 4 (Policy Semantics). *For a network topology* $G = (V,E,\mathsf{src},\mathsf{tgt})$, *satisfaction of a policy* φ *by a path* $\pi \in E^* \cup E^\omega$, *written* $\pi \models \varphi$, *holds iff the corresponding sequence of traversed nodes* $\overline{\pi}$ *satisfies* $\overline{\pi} \models \varphi$, *defined inductively on the structure of* φ *as follows:*

$\overline{\pi} \models \mathsf{true}$	*always*	$\overline{\pi} \models v$	*iff* $\overline{\pi}[0] = v$
$\overline{\pi} \models \neg\varphi$	*iff* $\overline{\pi} \not\models \varphi$	$\overline{\pi} \models \varphi_1 \wedge \varphi_2$	*iff* $\overline{\pi} \models \varphi_1$ *and* $\overline{\pi} \models \varphi_2$
$\overline{\pi} \models \mathsf{NoLoop}$	*iff* $\overline{\pi}$ *is finite*	$\overline{\pi} \models X\,\varphi$	*iff* $\overline{\pi}_1 \models \varphi$
$\overline{\pi} \models \varphi_1\,U\,\varphi_2$	*iff* $\exists j \forall i < j.\overline{\pi}_j \models \varphi_2$	*and* $\overline{\pi}_i \models \varphi_1$.	

We now formulate some standard routing policies as presented in Fig. 2. The simplest policy, $\mathsf{Reach}(d)$, specifies that the destination node d must eventually be reached while $\mathsf{Waypoint}(v,d)$ asks that any path reaching the destination d must necessarily pass through waypoint node v. For multiple alternative waypoints, $\mathsf{MultiWaypoint}(W,d)$ specifies that any path reaching destination d must necessarily pass through *either* of the waypoints in W. Finally, $\mathsf{Service}(\omega,d)$ ensures that the sequence of waypoints in ω is visited in this fixed order.

2.2 Update Synthesis

In the following we assume a fixed network topology $G = (V,E,\mathsf{src},\mathsf{tgt})$. An *update* $u \in E \cup V$ on G under a current routing configuration ρ specifies that the source node of edge u (if $u \in E$) must now forward its traffic along u or that the routing for the node u (if $u \in V$) is set to undefined. We write ρ^u for the new routing configuration, defined for any $v \in V$ as

$$\rho^u(v) = \begin{cases} u & \text{if } u \in E \text{ and } v = \mathsf{src}(u) \\ undefined & \text{if } u = v \\ \rho(v) & \text{otherwise.} \end{cases}$$

We inductively extend this notation to sequences of updates by letting $\rho^\varepsilon = \rho$ and $\rho^{wu} = (\rho^w)^u$ for any $w \in (E \cup V)^*$ and $u \in E \cup V$. An update sequence may in general contain an arbitrary number of updates that change multiple times the routing of the same node, however an important set of update sequences is the class of *simple* update sequences, meaning that each update changes the routing for a given node v from its initial routing $\rho_i(v)$ directly to its final routing $\rho_f(v)$.

Definition 5 (Simple Updates). *Let ρ_f be the final routing. An update u is simple if $\rho_f(\mathsf{src}(u)) = u$ whenever $u \in E$ and $\rho_f(\mathsf{src}(u))$ is undefined whenever $u \in V$. A simple update sequence is then a sequence of simple updates, where each update appears at most once.*

A basic property of simple update sequences is that any reordering results in the same final routing configuration i.e., if w is a simple update sequence and w' is any permutation of w, then $\rho^w = \rho^{w'}$ for any routing ρ.

Although any reordering of a simple update sequence yields the same final routing configuration, the intermediate routing configurations induced by each update may not respect a given policy invariant. This is also the case for general update sequences. We therefore say that an update sequence is *correct* with respect to a policy φ and a node v, if the unique path from v induced by any intermediate routing configuration satisfies φ.

Definition 6 (Update Correctness). *An update sequence $w \in (E \cup V)^*$ on network topology G with initial routing configuration ρ is* correct *with respect to source node v_0 and a policy φ, if $\pi_{\rho^{w'}}(v_0) \models \varphi$ for any prefix w' of w.*

The network update synthesis problem is thus the problem of constructing a correct update sequence that updates an initial routing to a desired final routing.

Definition 7 ((Simple) Update Synthesis Problem). *Given a topology G, an initial routing configuration ρ_i, a final routing configuration ρ_f, source node $v_0 \in V$ and a policy φ, the* simple update synthesis problem *asks to construct a simple update sequence w that is correct with respect to v_0 and φ such that $\rho_i^w = \rho_f$. The* update synthesis problem *omits the requirement that the constructed update sequence is simple.*

In the following, we let $P = (G, \rho_i, \rho_f, v_0, \varphi)$ denote a (simple) update synthesis problem and say that a constructed update sequence w that satisfies the conditions above is a *solution*. For any simple update synthesis problem P, the set of solutions is always finite. This is not the case for the *general* problem as there may be infinitely many (longer and longer) solutions.

While much prior work focused on simple update problems, there are examples which are only solvable with a general solution (as supported by our approach). To see this, consider the network topology in Fig. 3a with initial and final routings visualised respectively as solid and dashed lines in Fig. 3b. We fix the source node s and the policy $\varphi = \mathsf{Waypoint}(v_2, d) \wedge \mathsf{Reach}(d)$ requiring that waypoint v_2 must be visited before reaching d. An update of any node v from the initial to the final routing violates φ—either by introducing a loop or it bypasses the waypoint. Hence there is no correct simple update sequence. However, the update sequence that first updates s to route to v_2, followed by the update of

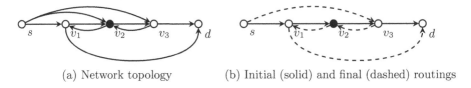

(a) Network topology   (b) Initial (solid) and final (dashed) routings

Fig. 3. Update synthesis problem with only a general solution

the nodes v_1, v_2 and v_3 and finally updating s again to route to v_3 is a correct update sequence.

2.3 Simple Update Sequence Reordering

In case of simple update sequences, we shall now argue that for routing policies that (i) include the preservation of reachability between the source and a target, and (ii) for which it holds that once a packet is delivered, no further routing is defined from the target node, we can reorder certain updates in the sequence without invalidating the correctness of the sequence. More specifically, we shall show that if a node routing is to be changed from undefined to some concrete edge, we can safely schedule such updates (in any order) to the very beginning of the update sequence. Similarly, all nodes that change their current routing into undefined can be scheduled (again in arbitrary order) at the end of the update sequence.

Lemma 1. *Let w be a solution to a simple update synthesis problem $P = (G, \rho_i, \rho_f, v_0, \varphi)$ where $\varphi = \mathsf{Reach}(d) \wedge \varphi'$ for any policy φ' and where $\rho_i(d)$ and $\rho_f(d)$ are undefined.*

1. *If $w = w_1 \circ u \circ w_2$ where $u \in E$ is an update s.t. $\rho_i(\mathsf{src}(u))$ is undefined then $u \circ w_1 \circ w_2$ is a solution to P.*
2. *If $w = w_1 \circ u \circ w_2$ where $u \in V$ updates the routing in u to undefined then $w_1 \circ w_2 \circ u$ is a solution to P.*

Lemma 1 can be used to identify all nodes that have an undefined forwarding function in ρ_i and schedule them to the beginning of the update sequence. Symmetrically, all updates that change a node forwarding to an undefined value (in the routing ρ_f), can be placed at the end of

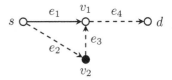

Fig. 4. Counter example for $\mathsf{Waypoint}(v_2, d)$; initial/final routing is in solid/dashed lines

the update sequence. This may simplify the synthesis of the update sequence by analysing only the nodes that have a defined forwarding function both in the initial and final routing.

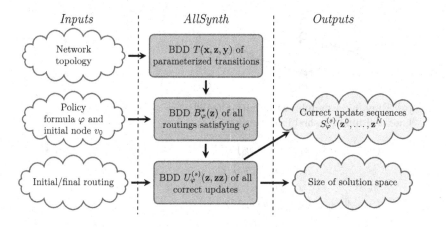

Fig. 5. *AllSynth* workflow

The requirement in Lemma 1 that the policy must enforce at least the reachability of d is essential, as illustrated in Fig. 4 where $e_2 \circ e_3 \circ e_4$ is a correct update sequence preserving $\mathsf{Waypoint}(v_2, d)$. This is because until the last update, the destination d is not reachable and hence the waypointing policy trivially holds. However, even though the routing of v_1 is undefined in the initial routing, moving the update e_4 to the beginning of the update sequence creates a transient forwarding following the path $e_1 e_4$ and violates $\mathsf{Waypoint}(v_2, d)$.

3   The AllSynth Tool and the Synthesis Algorithm

The diagram in Fig. 5 illustrates the main components of *AllSynth*. The inputs to *AllSynth* are the network topology G, a policy of interest φ, as well as the initial routing ρ_i and final routing ρ_f from the node v_0.

From the input network topology G, a BDD representation of the edges in G is combined with the input policy φ and a source node v_0 to produce a BDD representing all routing configurations ρ where the unique path $\pi_\rho(v_0)$ satisfies φ. This BDD is then in turn combined with the initial and final routing configurations ρ_i and ρ_f, to construct a BDD representation of all correct update sequences.

We shall now present our algorithmic solution to the update synthesis problem, based on a symbolic encoding of routing configurations using BDDs. This encoding allows for an efficient fixed-point computation of those routing configurations that satisfy a given routing policy, and subsequently to find a correct update sequence solving the synthesis problem.

Boolean decision diagrams [32] are data structures for the compact representation of a Boolean function. A BDD is a rooted directed acyclic graph (DAG), with nonleaf nodes labeled by Boolean variables, and leaf nodes labeled with 0 (false) or 1 (true). Each node that is labelled by a variable has two outgoing edges, a solid one representing the true assignment to the variable and a dotted

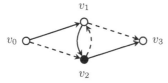

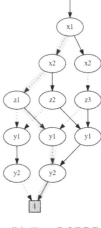

(a) Running example with initial (solid line) and final (dashed line) routings

$$(\neg x_1 \wedge \neg x_2 \wedge z_1 \wedge \neg y_1 \wedge y_2) \vee$$
$$(\neg x_1 \wedge \neg x_2 \wedge \neg z_1 \wedge y_1 \wedge \neg y_2) \vee$$
$$(\neg x_1 \wedge x_2 \wedge z_2 \wedge y_1 \wedge y_2) \vee$$
$$(\neg x_1 \wedge x_2 \wedge \neg z_2 \wedge y_1 \wedge \neg y_2) \vee$$
$$(x_1 \wedge \neg x_2 \wedge z_3 \wedge y_1 \wedge y_2) \vee$$
$$(x_1 \wedge \neg x_2 \wedge \neg z_3 \wedge \neg y_1 \wedge y_2)$$

(c) Expression T

(b) T as ROBDD

Fig. 6. Running example and encoding of the transition function

one for the false assignment. By following the paths from the root to the leaf labelled with 1, we obtain all satisfying Boolean assignments. BDDs were introduced by Lee [32] and later Bryant [9] presented their reduced ordered version (ROBDD), where the ordering between the Boolean variables are fixed along each path from the root to a leaf, and isomorphic parts are combined. We show how to exploit ROBDDs for solving the update synthesis problem.

First, let us recall how to encode subsets of a finite set S using Boolean expressions—hence ROBDDs. The encoding is relative to a given enumeration $s_0, s_1, s_2, \ldots s_{|S|-1}$ of S and it is based on $n = \lceil \log(|S|) \rceil$ Boolean variables $\mathbf{x} = x_1, x_2, \ldots, x_n$. Now, any truth assignment μ to $\mathbf{x}$ may be seen as a binary encoding of a natural number $n(\mu) \in \mathbb{N}$ and hence an encoding of the $n(\mu)$'th element $s_{n(\mu)} \in S$. We shall use the short notation $s(\mu)$ for the element $s_{n(\mu)}$ as well as the notation $\mathbf{x}(s)$ to denote a Boolean expression over $\mathbf{x}$ encoding the singleton-set $\{s\}$. Now any Boolean expression $t(\mathbf{x})$ over $\mathbf{x}$ may be seen as encoding the subset $[\![t(\mathbf{x})]\!] = \{ s_{n(\mu)} \mid \mu \text{ satisfies } t(\mathbf{x}) \} \subseteq S$.

Example 1. Consider the network topology in Fig. 6a with the nodes $V = \{v_0, v_1, v_2, v_3\}$ enumerated by the given indices. We encode any subset of V by a Boolean expression over two Boolean variables x_1, x_2—note that the encoding of e.g. $\{v_1\}$ is $\mathbf{x}(v_1) = \neg x_1 \wedge x_2$ as the binary encoding of v_1 is 01. Conversely, the subset identified by the Boolean expression $t \equiv \neg x_1 \vee \neg x_2$ is $[\![t]\!] = \{v_0, v_1, v_2\}$ as the binary encoding of v_0, v_1, v_2 are 00, 01, 10, respectively.

BDD Encoding of Routing Configurations. Let $G = (V, E, \mathsf{src}, \mathsf{tgt})$ be a network topology and let $v \in V$. We denote by E_v the set of edges having v as a source-node, i.e. $E_v = \{e \in E \mid \mathsf{src}(e) = v\}$. Now, a routing configuration $\rho \colon V \rightharpoonup E$

is isomorphic to indicating for each node v whether $\rho(v)$ is defined and if so to identify an element from E_v. For the Boolean encoding of (sets of) elements from E_v we use, as described above, $\lceil \log(|E_v|) \rceil$ Boolean variables $\mathbf{z}_v$. To indicate the definedness of $\rho(v)$, we use an additional Boolean variable z_v^d. To encode the possible transitions between nodes v and v' enabled by a given routing configuration ρ, we use Boolean variables $\mathbf{x}$ for encoding the source node v and equally many Boolean variables $\mathbf{y}$ for encoding the target node v'. The following Boolean expression T encodes the possible transitions:

$$T(\mathbf{x}, \mathbf{z}_{v_0}, \ldots, \mathbf{z}_{v_k}, z_{v_0}^d, \ldots, z_{v_k}^d, \mathbf{y}) = \bigvee_{v \in V} \bigvee_{e \in E_v} \big(\mathbf{x}(v) \wedge \mathbf{z}_v(e) \wedge z_v^d \wedge \mathbf{y}(\mathsf{tgt}(e)) \big)$$

where $V = \{v_0, \ldots, v_k\}$.

Example 2. Reconsidering the network topology from Fig. 6a, we shall use three Boolean variables z_1, z_2, z_3 for encoding routing configurations in terms of their choice of successor-node from v_0, v_1 and v_2[1]. Using the encoding of nodes from Example 1, the possible transitions between nodes are given by the Boolean expression T in Fig. 6c. The resulting unique ROBDD in Fig. 6b with only 11 non-leaf nodes illustrates the compactness of the ROBDD data structure (the missing edges lead to 0). The highlighted path encodes the transition (routing) from v_0 to v_1 under the initial routing. Here the chosen ordering of the Boolean variables is crucial. Alternative orderings, e.g. with the $\mathbf{z}$ variables being tested first respectively last results in ROBDDs with 25 respectively 17 non-leaf nodes.

BDD Encoding of Routing Policies. Now let $G = (V, E, \mathsf{src}, \mathsf{tgt})$ be a network topology and let φ be a routing policy expressed in the LTL logic of Definition 3. Using Boolean variables $\mathbf{x}$ for encoding nodes and Boolean variables $\mathbf{z}$ for encoding routing configurations[2], we shall construct an ROBDD $B_\varphi(\mathbf{x}, \mathbf{z})$ such that: $(v, \rho) \in [\![B_\varphi(\mathbf{x}, \mathbf{z})]\!]$ if and only if $\pi_\rho(v) \models \varphi$ where $\pi_\rho(v)$ is the unique path starting in the node v following the the routing configuration ρ.

Definition 8. *Let $G = (V, E, \mathsf{src}, \mathsf{tgt})$ be a network topology and φ a routing policy. We define the ROBDD $B_\varphi(\mathbf{x}, \mathbf{z})$ inductively on φ as follows:*

$$B_{\mathsf{true}}(\mathbf{x}, \mathbf{z}) = 1$$
$$B_v(\mathbf{x}, \mathbf{z}) = \mathbf{x}(v)$$
$$B_{\neg\varphi}(\mathbf{x}, \mathbf{z}) = \neg B_\varphi(\mathbf{x}, \mathbf{z})$$
$$B_{\varphi_1 \wedge \varphi_1}(\mathbf{x}, \mathbf{z}) = B_{\varphi_1}(\mathbf{x}, \mathbf{z}) \wedge B_{\varphi_2}(\mathbf{x}, \mathbf{z})$$
$$B_{\mathsf{NoLoop}}(\mathbf{x}, \mathbf{z}) \stackrel{\mathsf{min}}{=} \forall \mathbf{y}.(T(\mathbf{x}, \mathbf{z}, \mathbf{y}) \rightarrow B_{\mathsf{NoLoop}}(\mathbf{y}, \mathbf{z}))$$
$$B_{X\varphi}(\mathbf{x}, \mathbf{z}) = \exists \mathbf{y}.\big(T(\mathbf{x}, \mathbf{z}, \mathbf{y}) \wedge B_\varphi(\mathbf{y}, \mathbf{z}) \big)$$
$$B_{\varphi_1 U \varphi_2}(\mathbf{x}, \mathbf{z}) \stackrel{\mathsf{min}}{=} B_{\varphi_2}(\mathbf{x}, \mathbf{z}) \vee \big(B_{\varphi_1}(\mathbf{x}, \mathbf{z}) \wedge \exists \mathbf{y}.\big(T(\mathbf{x}, \mathbf{z}, \mathbf{y}) \wedge B_{\varphi_1 U \varphi_2}(\mathbf{y}, \mathbf{z}) \big) \big)$$

---

[1] In this running example, we shall for simplicity assume that routing configurations are total functions, e.g. that the variables z_v^d are true.

[2] Recall that $\mathbf{z}$ consists of variables $\mathbf{z}_{v_1}, \ldots, \mathbf{z}_{v_k}$ and $z_{v_1}^d, \ldots, z_{v_k}^d$.

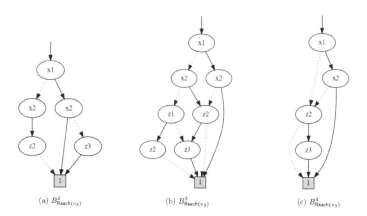

(a) $B^2_{\mathsf{Reach}(v_3)}$ (b) $B^3_{\mathsf{Reach}(v_3)}$ (c) $B^4_{\mathsf{Reach}(v_3)}$

Fig. 7. Increasing approximants $B^n_{\mathsf{Reach}(v_3)}$

In the above definition we exploit that ROBDDs are closed under Boolean operations as well as Boolean quantification. In the cases NoLoop and $\varphi_1\,U\,\varphi_2$, the changes of Boolean variables used in the parameter lists in the right-hand sides are obtained by simple substitution of variables, an operation that may efficiently be performed on ROBDDs. Finally, note that the definitions of B_{NoLoop} and $B_{\varphi_1\,U\,\varphi_2}$ are given as minimal fixed points. These fixed points, e.g. B_{NoLoop}, are obtained after a finite number of applications of the corresponding right-hand sides on increasing approximations B^n_{NoLoop}, starting with $B^0_{\mathsf{NoLoop}} = 0$, and terminating when $B^{n+1}_{\mathsf{NoLoop}} = B^n_{\mathsf{NoLoop}}$.

Lemma 2. *We have* $(v, \rho) \in [\![B_\varphi(\mathbf{x}, \mathbf{z})]\!]$ *if and only if* $\pi_\rho(v) \models \varphi$.

Example 3. Consider the network topology from Fig. 6a with the routing policy $\mathsf{Reach}(v_3)$. Given the LTL-definition of $\mathsf{Reach}(v_3)$, the ROBDD $B_{\mathsf{Reach}(v_3)}$ is given by the limit of the following inductively defined sequence: $B^{n+1}_{\mathsf{Reach}(v_3)}(\mathbf{x}, \mathbf{z}) = \mathbf{x}(v_3) \vee \exists.\mathbf{y}.\big(T(\mathbf{x}, \mathbf{z}, \mathbf{y}) \wedge B^n_{\mathsf{Reach}(v_3)}(\mathbf{y}, \mathbf{z})\big)$ with $B^0_{\mathsf{Reach}(v_3)} = 0$. Figure 7 provides some of the approximants with $B^4_{\mathsf{Reach}(v_3)}$ found to be the least fixed point.

We shall denote by $B^*_\varphi(\mathbf{z})$ the ROBDD $\exists\mathbf{x}.B_\varphi(\mathbf{x}, \mathbf{z}) \wedge \mathbf{x}(v_0)$, where $v_0 \in V$ is the source node. Rather than using BDDs for model-checking that individual routing configurations satisfy a given policy φ one by one, $B^*_\varphi(\mathbf{z})$ characterizes exactly in one single ROBDD the full set of routing configurations satisfying φ.

Example 4. Recall the network topology from Fig. 6a and the Boolean encoding of routing configurations and nodes from Example 2. Now consider the routing policies $W = \mathsf{Waypoint}(v_2, v_3)$ and $R = \mathsf{Reach}(v_3)$. The resulting ROBDDs for B^*_R, B^*_W and $B^*_{W \wedge R}$ are given in Fig. 8. It can be concluded that there are 6, 6 respectively 4 routing configurations satisfying the policies R, W respectively $R \wedge W$. Moreover, both ρ_i and ρ_f satisfy all three policies.

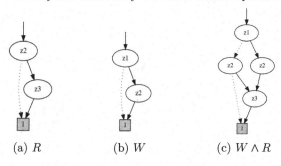

(a) R (b) W (c) $W \wedge R$

Fig. 8. Encoding of different routing policies

BDD Encoding of Update Sequences. Again let $G = (V, E, \text{src}, \text{tgt})$ be a network topology and let φ be a routing policy, with ρ_i respectively ρ_f being initial respectively final routing configuration. We shall show how to symbolically synthesize correct (simple) update sequences using BDD encodings. The basis of the synthesis is the ROBDD $B_\varphi^*(\mathbf{z})$ encoding all routing configurations that are correct with respect to φ using Boolean variables $\mathbf{z} = \mathbf{z}_{v_0} \dots \mathbf{z}_{v_k}, z_{v_0}^d, \dots, z_{v_k}^d$. For simple updates it suffices to use single Boolean variables z_{v_j}, with z_{v_j} encoding $\rho_i(v_j)$ and $\neg z_{v_j}$ encoding $\rho_f(v_j)$, i.e. in case $\rho_f(v_j) \neq \rho_i(v_j)$. To encode a simple update between configurations ρ and ρ' we shall use Boolean variables $\mathbf{z}$ for encoding ρ and a corresponding (distinct) sequence of Boolean variables $\mathbf{zz}$ for encoding ρ'. The following Boolean expression U_φ^s encodes the set of possible simple updates that preserve correctness with respect to φ.

$$U_\varphi^s(\mathbf{z}, \mathbf{zz}) = B_\varphi^*(\mathbf{z}) \wedge B_\varphi^*(\mathbf{zz}) \wedge \exists i. \left[z_{v_i} \wedge \neg zz_{v_i} \wedge \bigwedge_{j \neq i} z_{v_j} = zz_{v_j} \right]$$

Note that in this simple update the routing configuration changes for exactly one node v_i from the setting in the initial configuration ρ_i, encoded as z_{v_i}, to the setting in final configuration ρ_f, encoded as $\neg zz_{v_i}$. In the general case, the update can change the setting of any node arbitrarily, as given by the following Boolean expression U_φ.

$$U_\varphi(\mathbf{z}, \mathbf{zz}) = B_\varphi^*(\mathbf{z}) \wedge B_\varphi^*(\mathbf{zz}) \wedge \exists i. \left[\mathbf{z}_{v_i} \neq \mathbf{zz}_{v_i} \wedge \bigwedge_{j \neq i} \mathbf{z}_{v_j} = \mathbf{zz}_{v_j} \right]$$

Lemma 3. *We have* $(\rho, \rho') \in \llbracket U_\varphi(\mathbf{z}, \mathbf{zz}) \rrbracket$ *(resp.* $\llbracket U_\varphi^s(\mathbf{z}, \mathbf{zz}) \rrbracket$*) iff* $\rho \neq \rho'$ *and there exists an update (resp. simple update) u such that $\rho^u = \rho'$, $\pi_\rho(v_0) \models \varphi$ and $\pi_{\rho'}(v_0) \models \varphi$, where v_0 is the given source node.*

To enable synthesis of correct (simple) update sequences, the following recursively defined ROBDD is key.

$$R_\varphi^s(\mathbf{z}, \mathbf{zz}) \stackrel{\min}{=} \mathbf{z}(\rho_f) \vee \exists \mathbf{zzz}. \big(U_\varphi^s(\mathbf{z}, \mathbf{zz}) \wedge R_\varphi^s(\mathbf{zz}, \mathbf{zzz}) \big) \qquad (1)$$

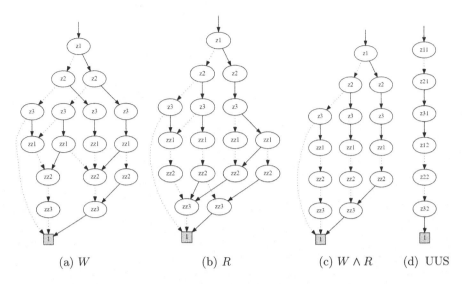

Fig. 9. Encoding of all correct simple update-steps (a–c); unique update sequence (UUS) for $W \wedge R$ (d)

The expression encodes the set of simple updates that preserve correctness with respect to φ while ensuring reachability of the final routing configuration.

Lemma 4. *We have* $(\rho, \rho') \in [\![R_\varphi^s(\mathbf{z}, \mathbf{zz})]\!]$ *iff there exists a correct simple update sequence* $w = u_0 u_1 \cdots u_k$ *with respect to* ρ *and* φ *such that* $\rho' = \rho^{u_0}$ *and* $\rho^w = \rho_f$.

All correct, simple update sequences of length N may now be characterized by the following Boolean expression, where $\mathbf{z}^i$ are (distinct) Boolean variables encoding the routing configuration after i updates:

$$S_\varphi^s(\mathbf{z}^0, \ldots, \mathbf{z}^N) = \mathbf{z}^0(\rho_i) \wedge \mathbf{z}^N(\rho_f) \wedge \bigwedge_{i=0}^{N-1} R_\varphi^s(\mathbf{z}^i, \mathbf{z}^{i+1}) \qquad (2)$$

Theorem 1. *We have* $(\rho_0, \rho_1, \ldots, \rho_N) \in [\![S_\varphi^s(\mathbf{z}^0, \ldots, \mathbf{z}^N)]\!]$ *iff there exists a simple correct update sequence* $w = u_0 u_1 \cdots u_{N-1}$ *with respect to* φ *and* ρ_0 *such that* $\rho_{k+1} = \rho_k^{u_k}$ *for all* k *with* $0 \leq k < N$, $\rho_0 = \rho_i$ *and* $\rho_N = \rho_f$.

For the synthesis in the general case: simply replace U_φ^s in (1) with U_φ to get a ROBDD R_φ characterizing (general) update sequences leading to ρ_f. Now, replace R_φ^s with R_φ in (2) to get a characterization of all correct (general) update sequences of length N.

Example 5. Consider again the network topology from Fig. 6a and the routing policies $W = \mathsf{Waypoint}(v_2, v_3)$ and $R = \mathsf{Reach}(v_3)$. The full sets of correct simple update-steps with respect to W, R and $W \wedge R$ are given by the ROBDDs R_W^s, R_R^s and $R_{W \wedge R}^s$ given in Fig. 9(a–c). Instantiating Eq. (2) with these ROBDDs reveals that there are 3, 3 respectively 1 correct simple update sequences of length 3 with respect to the routing policies W, R respectively $W \wedge R$.

The unique simple update sequence for $W \wedge R$ (ignoring the initial and final routing configurations) is given by the ROBDD in Fig. 9(d)[3]. Here the values suggested for the first three Boolean variables z_1^1, z_2^1, z_3^1 indicate that the routing configuration after the first update is given by the edges $(v_0, v_2), (v_1, v_2), (v_2, v_3)$. Similarly, the values of the last three Boolean variables z_1^2, z_2^2, z_3^2 indicate the edges $(v_0, v_2), (v_1, v_3), (v_2, v_3)$ as the configuration after the second update. Note, that in case there is no correct (simple) update sequence the resulting ROBDD becomes empty (just consisting of the node false).

4   Implementation and Evaluation

Our tool *AllSynth* is implemented in Python and relies on a Cython wrapper [1] of the CUDD [44] package for manipulation of ROBDD. From a given network topology with the initial and final routing, the tool produces either a simple or general update sequence satisfying a given policy, as well as the information about the number of possible solutions. As all such correct solutions are symbolically represented in a compact way as an ROBDD, it is possible to generate alternative solutions without any additional computational effort.

We evaluate *AllSynth* against two state-of-the-art update synthesis tools, NetSynth [38] and FLIP [46]. NetSynth can compute only a simple update sequence or inform the user that there is no solution; the synthesis of general update sequences is not supported. FLIP can synthesise sequences of steps (groups of switches or routers) in which order the network can be updated, however, if such a sequence does not exist, the tool may introduce additional forwarding rules and use tagging of packets. As NetSynth and FLIP do not support general update sequences, compare the running times only for simple updates.

All experiments are executed on Ubuntu 14.04 cluster with 2.3 GHz AMD Opteron 6376 processors with 2 h timeout and 14 GB memory limit. A reproducibility package is available in [31].

We consider a scalable synthetic topology and the standard benchmark of 261 real-world network topologies from the Topology Zoo dataset [29]. The class of synthetic topologies, referred to as *diamond* topologies, are overtaken from the NetSynth evaluation benchmark [38] and are formed by disjoint initial and final routing paths that only share the initial and final node. The size of the problem is defined to be the sum of the lengths of the two paths—we include instances of sizes up to 2000. The Topology Zoo instances are five times sequentially concatenated in order to obtain larger topologies where the size of the update problems ranges from 20 to 679. We display the 50 most difficult instances of the problem.

We consider three classes of update policies: Reach(d), MultiWaypoint(W, d) and Service(ω, d). For MultiWaypoint(W, d), we let every $5th$ node on both the

---

[3] Note that zij in the figure is to be read as the variable z_i^j.

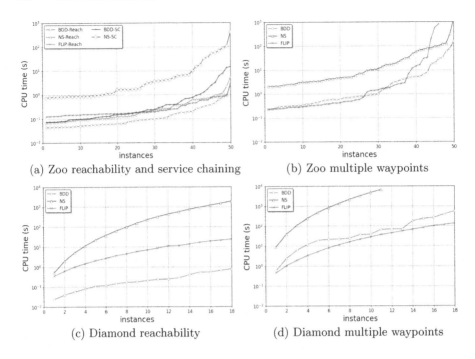

Fig. 10. Experimental results

initial and final path be included in W. For $\mathsf{Service}(\omega, d)$, the sequence ω is generated by including every $5th$ node that is traversed by both the initial and final path. Because the diamond update problem consists of two disjoint paths, the service chaining policy is not considered here. The policy language of NetSynth is identical to our LTL-based specifications and hence it is able to directly express all these properties. On the other hand, the policy input to FLIP enumerates all admissible subpaths that are considered, in logical disjunction. The encoding of the service chaining policy then entails an exhaustive enumeration of all paths that satisfy the service chaining policy and we therefore do not include FLIP in our service chaining experiments.

Results. The experiments are summarized in a number of so-called *cactus plots* [7] in Fig. 10, where for each method all instances of the problem are independently sorted from the fastest to the slowest one and plotted on the x-axis, and the y-axis (note the logarithmic scale) shows the increasing running time. If some curve does not reach to the right end of the plot, this means that the corresponding tool is not able to solve the remaining instances within the given timeout and memory limit. While cactus plots do not provide instance-to-instance runtime comparison, they provide an overall performance evaluation of the different tools.

For the experiments on the collection of real networks from the Topology Zoo presented in Figs. 10a and 10b, we notice that none of the tools has difficulty solving the synthesis of the plain reachability policy and it takes less than 10 s for all instances—here our approach has a slight margin. For waypointing, while FLIP is performing well on small instances, it shows a noticeable penalty once it reaches the most difficult problems where its running time quickly deteriorates and it is as the only tool not able to solve some of the largest instances. We maintain about one order of magnitude advantage over NetSynth (NS), which is the case also for service chaining.

Results for diamond topologies are given in Figs. 10c and 10d. We observe that for reachability our computation of all solutions is almost one order of magnitude faster than FLIP and several orders of magnitude faster than NetSynth (both tools terminate as soon as they find the first correct update sequence). For waypointing, we still significantly outperform NetSynth and we are almost comparable with FLIP which shows better performance at the largest instances.

In conclusion, our experiments demonstrate that *AllSynth*, based on the symbolic BDD technology, not only significantly outperforms state-of-the-art tools on all non-trivial real-world networks, but also provides higher generality. Indeed, *AllSynth* computes *all* solutions, compared to only one solution returned by Net-Synth or a more general sequence of update steps generated by FLIP. This aspect is important for the practical usage by network operators as it allows them to iteratively choose the most suitable update sequence.

5   Conclusion

We presented an efficient approach for synthesizing correct update sequences for software-defined networks. In contrast to existing tools, our approach is fully symbolic and relies on BDD technology. As a result, we are able to represent *all* solutions to the update synthesis problem in a succinct binary tree, preserving generic routing policies (e.g., service chaining) that can be described in the LTL logic. Our prototype implementation of *AllSynth* outperforms the state-of-the-art tools NetSynth and FLIP in many scenarios (e.g., on the real-world Internet topologies), while at the same time extending the generality.

Our experiments focused on the generation of simple update sequences (at most one update per flow per switch), similar to the methodology used in Net-Synth and FLIP. *AllSynth* however also supports a novel generalization where a switch can be updated several times. This is particularly useful for the instances of the update synthesis problem that do not have any simple solution. In this case, NetSynth does not provide any alternative (and in fact does not terminate even on relatively small negative instances); FLIP may degrade to a two-phase commit strategy that is less preferable as it requires the duplication of forwarding rules as well as additional packet header space. *AllSynth* instead tries to suggest a general update sequence that does not require packet tagging.

Acknowledgements. The research is partly funded by the Vienna Science and Technology Fund (WWTF), project WHATIF (ICT19-045), the ERC Advanced Grant LASSO, the Villum Investigator Grant S4OS, DFF project QASNET as well as DIREC: Digital Research Centre Denmark.

References

1. dd python package (2021). https://github.com/tulip-control/dd
2. Akhoondian Amiri, S., Dudycz, S., Schmid, S., Wiederrecht, S.: Congestion-free rerouting of flows on DAGs. In: 45th International Colloquium on Automata, Languages, and Programming (ICALP), vol. 107, pp. 143:1–143:13. Schloss Dagstuhl-Leibniz-Zentrum fuer Informatik (2018)
3. Anderson, C.J., et al.: NetKAT: semantic foundations for networks. ACM SIGPLAN Notices **49**(1), 113–126 (2014)
4. Avin, C., Ghobadi, M., Griner, C., Schmid, S.: On the complexity of traffic traces and implications. In: Proceedings of the ACM SIGMETRICS (2020)
5. Beckett, R., Mahajan, R., Millstein, T., Padhye, J., Walker, D.: Don't mind the gap: bridging network-wide objectives and device-level configurations. In: Proceedings of the 2016 ACM SIGCOMM Conference, pp. 328–341 (2016)
6. Benson, T., Akella, A., Maltz, D.A.: Network traffic characteristics of data centers in the wild. In: Proceedings of the 10th ACM SIGCOMM Conference on Internet Measurement, pp. 267–280 (2010)
7. Brain, M.N., Davenport, J.H., Griggio, A.: Benchmarking solvers, SAT-style. In: Proceedings of the 2nd International Workshop on Satisfiability Checking and Symbolic Computation co-located with the 42nd International Symposium on Symbolic and Algebraic Computation (ISSAC 2017). CEUR, vol. 1974, pp. 1–15. CEUR-WS.org (2017)
8. Brandt, S., Förster, K.T., Wattenhofer, R.: On consistent migration of flows in SDNs. In: IEEE INFOCOM 2016-The 35th Annual IEEE International Conference on Computer Communications, pp. 1–9. IEEE (2016)
9. Bryant: Graph-based algorithms for boolean function manipulation. IEEE Trans. Comput. **C3-5**(8), 677–691 (1986). https://doi.org/10.1109/TC.1986.1676819
10. Canini, M., Kuznetsov, P., Levin, D., Schmid, S.: A distributed and robust SDN control plane for transactional network updates. In: 2015 IEEE Conference on Computer Communications (INFOCOM), pp. 190–198. IEEE (2015)
11. Černý, P., Foster, N., Jagnik, N., McClurg, J.: Optimal consistent network updates in polynomial time. In: Gavoille, C., Ilcinkas, D. (eds.) DISC 2016. LNCS, vol. 9888, pp. 114–128. Springer, Heidelberg (2016). https://doi.org/10.1007/978-3-662-53426-7_9
12. Chirgwin, R.: Google routing blunder sent Japan's internet dark on friday (2017). https://www.theregister.co.uk/2017/08/27/google_routing_blunder_sent_japans_internet_dark/
13. Cimatti, A., Clarke, E.M., Giunchiglia, F., Roveri, M.: NUSMV: a new symbolic model checker. Int. J. Softw. Tools Technol. Transf. **2**(4), 410–425 (2000). https://doi.org/10.1007/s100090050046
14. Dudycz, S., Ludwig, A., Schmid, S.: Can't touch this: consistent network updates for multiple policies. In: 2016 46th Annual IEEE/IFIP International Conference on Dependable Systems and Networks (DSN), pp. 133–143. IEEE (2016)
15. Duluth News Tribune: Human error to blame in minnesota 911 outage (2018). https://www.ems1.com/911/articles/389343048-Officials-Human-error-to-blame-in-Minn-911-outage/
16. El-Hassany, A., Tsankov, P., Vanbever, L., Vechev, M.: Netcomplete: practical network-wide configuration synthesis with autocompletion. In: 15th {USENIX} Symposium on Networked Systems Design and Implementation ({NSDI} 2018), pp. 579–594 (2018)

17. Feamster, N., Rexford, J.: Why (and how) networks should run themselves. arXiv report (2017)
18. Finkbeiner, B., Gieseking, M., Hecking-Harbusch, J., Olderog, E.R.: Model checking data flows in concurrent network updates (full version). arXiv preprint arXiv:1907.11061 (2019)
19. Foerster, K., Schmid, S., Vissicchio, S.: Survey of consistent software-defined network updates. IEEE Commun. Surv. Tutor. **21**(2), 1435–1461 (2019)
20. Foerster, K.T.: On the consistent migration of unsplittable flows: upper and lower complexity bounds. In: 2017 IEEE 16th International Symposium on Network Computing and Applications (NCA), pp. 1–4. IEEE (2017)
21. Foerster, K.T., Luedi, T., Seidel, J., Wattenhofer, R.: Local checkability, no strings attached:(a) cyclicity, reachability, loop free updates in SDNs. Theoret. Comput. Sci. **709**, 48–63 (2018)
22. Giacomo, G.D., Vardi, M.Y.: Linear temporal logic and linear dynamic logic on finite traces. In: Proceedings of the 23rd International Joint Conference on Artificial Intelligence (IJCAI 2013), pp. 854–860. AAAI Press (2013)
23. Glavind, M., Christensen, N., Srba, J., Schmid, S.: Latte: improving the latency of transiently consistent network update schedules. In: Proceedings of 38th International Symposium on Computer Performance, Modeling, Measurements and Evaluation (PERFORMANCE) (2020)
24. Heller, B., et al.: Leveraging SDN layering to systematically troubleshoot networks. In: Proceedings of the Second ACM SIGCOMM Workshop on Hot Topics in Software Defined Networking, pp. 37–42 (2013)
25. Jin, X., et al.: Dynamic scheduling of network updates. In: ACM SIGCOMM Computer Communication Review, vol. 44, no. 4, pp. 539–550. ACM (2014)
26. Kazemian, P., Chang, M., Zeng, H., Varghese, G., McKeown, N., Whyte, S.: Real time network policy checking using header space analysis. In: Presented as part of the 10th USENIX Symposium on Networked Systems Design and Implementation (NSDI 2013), pp. 99–111 (2013)
27. Kazemian, P., Varghese, G., McKeown, N.: Header space analysis: static checking for networks. In: Presented as part of the 9th {USENIX} Symposium on Networked Systems Design and Implementation ({NSDI} 2012), pp. 113–126 (2012)
28. Kellerer, W., Kalmbach, P., Blenk, A., Basta, A., Reisslein, M., Schmid, S.: Adaptable and data-driven softwarized networks: review, opportunities, and challenges. In: Proceedings of the IEEE (PIEEE) (2019)
29. Knight, S., Nguyen, H.X., Falkner, N., Bowden, R.A., Roughan, M.: The internet topology zoo. IEEE J. Sel. Areas Commun. **29**(9), 1765–1775 (2011). https://doi.org/10.1109/JSAC.2011.111002
30. Kreutz, D., Ramos, F.M., Verissimo, P.E., Rothenberg, C.E., Azodolmolky, S., Uhlig, S.: Software-defined networking: a comprehensive survey. Proc. IEEE **103**(1), 14–76 (2014)
31. Larsen, K., Mariegaard, A., Schmid, S., Srba, J.: Reproducibility package for: the hazard value: a quantitative network connectivy measure accounting for failures, March 2022. https://doi.org/10.5281/zenodo.6534948
32. Lee, C.Y.: Representation of switching circuits by binary-decision programs. The Bell Syst. Tech. J. **38**(4), 985–999 (1959). https://doi.org/10.1002/j.1538-7305.1959.tb01585.x
33. Liu, H.H., Wu, X., Zhang, M., Yuan, L., Wattenhofer, R., Maltz, D.: zUpdate: updating data center networks with zero loss. In: ACM SIGCOMM Computer Communication Review, vol. 43, no. 4, pp. 411–422. ACM (2013)

34. Ludwig, A., Dudycz, S., Rost, M., Schmid, S.: Transiently secure network updates. ACM SIGMETRICS Perform. Eval. Rev. **44**(1), 273–284 (2016)
35. Ludwig, A., Marcinkowski, J., Schmid, S.: Scheduling loop-free network updates: it's good to relax! In: Proceedings of the 2015 ACM Symposium on Principles of Distributed Computing, pp. 13–22. ACM (2015)
36. Ludwig, A., Rost, M., Foucard, D., Schmid, S.: Good network updates for bad packets: waypoint enforcement beyond destination-based routing policies. In: Proceedings of 13th ACM Workshop on Hot Topics in Networks (HotNets), p. 15. ACM (2014)
37. Mahajan, R., Wattenhofer, R.: On consistent updates in software defined networks. In: Proceedings of 12th ACM Workshop on Hot Topics in Networks (HotNets), p. 20. ACM (2013)
38. McClurg, J., Hojjat, H., Cerný, P., Foster, N.: Efficient synthesis of network updates. In: Proceedings of the 36th ACM SIGPLAN Conference on Programming Language Design and Implementation, Portland, OR, USA, 15–17 June 2015, pp. 196–207 (2015). https://doi.org/10.1145/2737924.2737980
39. McClurg, J., Hojjat, H., Černý, P., Foster, N.: Efficient synthesis of network updates. In: ACM SIGPLAN Notices, vol. 50, no. 6, pp. 196–207. ACM (2015)
40. Monsanto, C., Reich, J., Foster, N., Rexford, J., Walker, D.: Composing software defined networks. In: 10th USENIX Symposium on Networked Systems Design and Implementation (NSDI 2013), pp. 1–13 (2013)
41. Pnueli, A.: The temporal logic of programs. In: 18th Annual Symposium on Foundations of Computer Science, Providence, Rhode Island, USA, 31 October–1 November 1977, pp. 46–57. IEEE Computer Society (1977). https://doi.org/10.1109/SFCS.1977.32
42. Prabhu, S., Chou, K.Y., Kheradmand, A., Godfrey, B., Caesar, M.: Plankton: scalable network configuration verification through model checking. In: 17th USENIX Symposium on Networked Systems Design and Implementation ({NSDI} 2020), pp. 953–967 (2020)
43. Reitblatt, M., Foster, N., Rexford, J., Schlesinger, C., Walker, D.: Abstractions for network update. ACM SIGCOMM Comput. Commun. Rev. **42**(4), 323–334 (2012)
44. Somenzi, F.: CUDD: CU decision diagram package release 3.0.0. University of Colorado at Boulder (2015). http://vlsi.colorado.edu/~fabio/CUDD/
45. Steffen, S., Gehr, T., Tsankov, P., Vanbever, L., Vechev, M.: Probabilistic verification of network configurations. In: Proceedings of the Annual Conference of the ACM Special Interest Group on Data Communication on the Applications, Technologies, Architectures, and Protocols for Computer Communication, pp. 750–764 (2020)
46. Vissicchio, S., Cittadini, L.: FLIP the (flow) table: fast lightweight policy-preserving SDN updates. In: 35th Annual IEEE International Conference on Computer Communications, INFOCOM 2016, San Francisco, CA, USA, 10–14 April 2016, pp. 1–9 (2016). https://doi.org/10.1109/INFOCOM.2016.7524419
47. Zerwas, J., et al.: AHAB: data-driven virtual cluster hunting. In: Proceedings of IFIP Networking (2018)
48. Zhang, Q., Liu, V., Zeng, H., Krishnamurthy, A.: High-resolution measurement of data center microbursts. In: Proceedings of the 2017 Internet Measurement Conference, pp. 78–85 (2017)
49. Zhou, W., Jin, D., Croft, J., Caesar, M., Godfrey, P.B.: Enforcing customizable consistency properties in software-defined networks. In: Proceedings of 12th USENIX Symposium on Networked Systems Design and Implementation (NSDI 2015), pp. 73–85 (2015)

End-to-End Heat-Pump Control Using Continuous Time Stochastic Modelling and UPPAAL STRATEGO

Imran Riaz Hasrat, Peter Gjøl Jensen[✉], Kim Guldstrand Larsen, and Jiří Srba

Department of Computer Science, Aalborg University, Aalborg, Denmark
{imranh,pgj,kgl,srba}@cs.aau.dk

Abstract. Heatpump-based floor-heating systems for domestic heating offer flexibility in energy-consumption patterns, which can be utilized for reducing heating costs—in particular when considering hour-based electricity prices. Such flexibility is hard to exploit via classical Model Predictive Control (MPC), and in addition, MPC requires a priori calibration (i.e. model identification) which is often costly and becomes outdated as the dynamics and use of a building change. We solve these shortcomings by combining recent advancements in stochastic model identification and automatic (near-)optimal controller synthesis. Our method suggests an adaptive model-identification using the tool CTSM-R, and an efficient control synthesis based on Q-learning for Euclidean Markov Decision Processes via UPPAAL STRATEGO. On a virtual Danish family-house from the OpSys project, we demonstrate up to 33% reduction in heating cost while retaining comparable comfort to a standard bang-bang controller. Furthermore, we show the flexibility of our method by computing the Pareto-frontier that visualizes the cost/comfort tradeoff.

Keywords: Model identification · Strategy syntheses · Heat-pump control · Floor heating

1 Introduction

Space heating is the primary source of energy consumption in residential and commercial buildings, consuming more than 40% of the energy delivered to such facilities [8]. Intelligent control of heating systems promises to reduce this energy use, thereby countering global warming effects and CO2 emissions.

Model Predictive Controllers (MPCs) have been demonstrated as an efficient method for control of domestic heating systems with the potential for both energy and cost reductions [1,18,26]. In the classical setting of MPC, an approximate system model under control is constructed before application and paired with a control objective. In the setting of a domestic heating system, such a model describes heat dynamics of the house and external effects that may impact the temperature of the house, for instance, residential behaviour,

© Springer Nature Switzerland AG 2022
Y. Aït-Ameur and F. Crăciun (Eds.): TASE 2022, LNCS 13299, pp. 363–380, 2022.
https://doi.org/10.1007/978-3-031-10363-6_24

outdoor temperature or solar radiation contributing to the temperature of the rooms. This model also defines the possible actions of the controller along with the impact of these control-actions on the behaviour of the system. When the given model is paired with a control objective (e.g. minimize cost and maximize comfort), (model, objective)-pairing induces an *optimization*-problem. Depending on the formalism used to describe the model and control objective, different *solvers* can be used to obtain the next optimal control action to use. As a result, one can apply the MPC-controller in a tight and periodic loop of "observe, solve, act" to control the system.

This paper targets a floor-heating heat-pump control problem for a standard family house. In the case of domestic heating systems, three significant challenges appear in the classical MPC application:

– the heating dynamics of a house is not known a priori,
– the behaviour and dynamics of a house change over the lifetime of the house,
– the design, tuning and deployment of MPC for learning near-optimal control strategies to minimize a desired objective function is not straightforward.

To address these issues, we propose a framework for model-identification for use with the tool UPPAAL STRATEGO extending on the concept presented by Larsen et al. [18]. In particular, we introduce the model estimation into the loop of the regular MPC-control. We employ the tool CTSM-R (continues time stochastic modelling in R) [17] to identify the house model by utilizing the *historical data* of the house. We further propose an online strategy synthesis approach where the controller periodically predicts the control decisions with the current room temperatures and weather forecast knowledge. The controller explores partial state space and learns near-optimal strategies within the given price budget based on the selected learning method. Under the learned strategies, the controller optimizes and computes every decision ahead of time to make it ready to be applied for the next time interval. The main contributions of the method are as follows.

1. Developing data-driven thermal dynamics and constant coefficient estimations using CTSM-R.
2. Modelling a case-house in STRATEGO using the estimated heat transfer coefficients and thermal dynamics.
3. Employing STRATEGO MPC to learn near-optimal control strategies for operating the heat-pump.
4. Analysing the efficiency of the STRATEGO controller to handle the trade-off between heating cost and user comfort.

Related Work: Several domestic heating systems have been discussed in the literature. Vogler-Finck et al. [26] study the house dynamics where the control objective is given in the restricted form of linear equations. They apply *grey-box* modelling facility from MATLAB System Identification toolbox [20] to identify a model for predictive control. They examine three family houses of different ages and the results witness reduced carbon footprint of heating by MPC optimization based on energy and CO2. However, they use a simple deterministic model for MPC whereas we apply a stochastic model for MPC with an online strategy synthesis approach. An alternative approach is adopted by Larsen et al. [18] who utilize the tool STRATEGO [6,7] to obtain *near-optimal* control-optimization for switch-controlled hybrid stochastic systems. The authors suggest an online and compositional synthesis approach for a family-house floor heating system, focusing purely on maximizing comfort and disregarding energy consumption. In our work, we instead optimize for multiple objectives (comfort and cost) and introduce a model identification approach into the loop of an MPC control.

For large and complex systems, model identification becomes an important aspect of MPC control to identify a relatively simple and reduced-order model to make it practically controllable in real-time. However, Prívara et al. [22] describe that model identification is one of the main practical obstacles for large scale use of MPC. The *grey-box* modelling is one of the commonly used approaches that require a small data-set for model identification. Ferracuti et al. [9] and Fonti et al. [10] utilise low-order *grey-box* models to detect short-term (15 min, 1 h and 3 h horizons) thermal behaviour of a real building while Reynders et al. [23] used *grey-box* approach to identify reduced-order energy building models. However, these works do not offer a controller synthesis for the identified models. We create a specialised model for a fully automatic heat-pump case where we first identify the model and then use it for strategy synthesis and evaluation.

Vinther et al. [25] propose *black-box* approach to estimate MPC models from multiple Artificial Neural Network (ANN) techniques with a Genetic Algorithm (GA) to predict the future set-points (for room temperatures) in an existing floor heating system. Furthermore, Nassif et al. [21] also use ANN with GA for optimisation of a HVAC system. Harasty et al. [11] apply a differential evolution (DE) algorithm with ANN for MPC control and optimisation of room temperature for the conservation of cultural heritage. These approaches are based on offline learning, but we offer an online learning approach where the control decisions are predicted periodically for the near future by considering the real-time, making them applicable in practice even for long-lasting horizons.

2   Usecase and Method

We demonstrate our approach on a $150m^2$ experimental family house sketched in Fig. 1. The house consists of four rooms of different sizes and material properties: *Room 1* is the designated living room with a build-in kitchen, *Room 2* and *Room 4* are bedrooms, and *Room 3* serves as the bathroom with a light concrete floor as opposed to the light wooden floors of the other rooms. The system uses hot water as a means of heat distribution. The house in question has a high-fidelity DYMOLA model, which has been constructed and compared to a physical model through the OpSys project [15]. As it is standard for existing houses, the heating system has two layers of control: room thermostats (with a fixed mechanical bang/bang controller), and a heat-pump (for which we derive a controller). The model reflects a realistic scenario where an existing building is

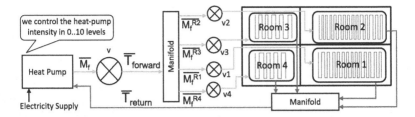

Fig. 1. An Overview of the four-rooms family house equipped with floor-heating.

retrofitted with an intelligent heat-pump. Notice here that each room thermostat acts independently of the heat-pump and the other thermostats; it is simply concerned with opening the flow of hot water when the room temperature drops below a certain set point (fixed to 22° in our experiments). This implies that the only control-point of concern is the intensity of the heat-pump.

The system is designed as a closed-loop system with a fixed distribution-key. This means that the ingoing massflow of water $(\overline{M_f})$ must be distributed to the rooms via the manifold. Conventionally the manifold is calibrated s.t. a fixed proportion of water is designated to each room. This distribution-key we denote $\overline{M_f}^{R_x}$ for a room x. The individual room thermostats regulate the binary valves v_x. This implies that the massflow is re-distributed (proportionally) to the remaining open valves if certain valves are shut. Furthermore, we denote by $\overline{T}_{forward}$ and $\overline{T}_{return}$ the forward and return water temperature.

The main purpose of the heat-pump is to balance the difference between the room temperatures $\tilde{T}_r^x$ and a given set point T_g with the cost of heating $cost(\tau) = price_\tau \cdot w_\tau$, which is a time-dependent function of the energy consumption of the heat-pump w_τ (determined directly by the controller) and the market electricity price $(price_\tau)$ which varies on an hourly basis and is known 24 h in advance.

Naturally, a consumer wishes to weight comfort against cost, and we can thus state the optimization criteria and introduce the $0 \leq W_{comf} \leq 1$ weighting factor that allows for such tuning. This allows us to derive the following (W_{comf}-parameterized) fitness function for our controllers for a period τ_0 to τ_n given that the heat-pump settings, energy prices and room temperatures (denoted $\tilde{T}_r^i(\tau)$) are known for the duration for k rooms as:

$$F(\tau_0, \tau_n) = \int_{\tau_0}^{\tau_n} \left(((1 - W_{comf}) \cdot cost(x)) + W_{comf} \cdot \sqrt{\sum_i^k (T_g - \tilde{T}_r^i(x))^2} \right) dx \tag{1}$$

Notice that this function penalizes more significant deviations of temperatures in a squared fashion while the cost increase has a linear impact on fitness.

2.1   Methodological Overview

While a high-fidelity model for DYMOLA is provided, this model is infeasible for practical experiments both due to its high computational effort caused by

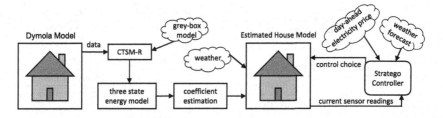

Fig. 2. Estimation and control process using observed data

the high fidelity and due to licensing issues making massive parallel experiments unfeasible. The overview of our suggested approach can be seen in Fig. 2. We initially derive a low-fidelity model of the thermal dynamics of the building via a data-driven *grey-box* model estimation using the CTSM-R software [16]. The CTSM-R library allows finding best-fit parameters for a stochastic model based on samples of a (virtual) house. The specific grey-box formulation is given in Sect. 3 along with an evaluation of its performance. Notice that the model-identification problem is constructed s.t. the estimation can be computed in a decomposed manner, i.e. a model is computed individually for each room, and the set of models is later recomposed. We do so to avoid an explosion in computational effort from a large set of variables to estimate. While this *grey-box* model yields us the internal heat coefficients (how the energy dissipates between rooms or a heater), it does not capture the heat transfer from the hot water flowing through the pipes. Therefore, we derive a model capturing the relationship between internal temperature changes and the drop in the heat-carrying water, yielding us the return water temperature ($\overline{T}_{return}$).

Given these two thermal models, we can instantiate a Euclidean Markov Decision Process (EMDP) [13] from which Stratego MDP model can learn near-optimal control strategies. This model simulates both the behaviour of the house but also contains models of the expected weather and the future energy price prediction. We use this model for both evaluation and predictive control in our experimental setup, including an experiment with varying degrees of noise in the model used for predictive control. For instance, we replay a historical weather scenario during the evaluation while the predictive controller only has access to an approximate weather forecast.

3   Thermal Model Identification

The CTSM-R software[17] allows for continuous-time *grey-box* model identification. The general method of CTSM-R is based around maximum likelihood estimation and a gradient-decent approach for convergence. It identifies Continuous Time Stochastic Model and estimates the embedded parameters. CTSM-R has been successfully applied for the identification and estimation of physical system models, e.g., heat thermodynamics of buildings and walls, thermostats and radiators, and more [5,24,27].

Data	Description
$\tilde{T}_r^i$	room i air temp.[°C]
$\overline{M^i}$	room i water mass flow [kg/s]
$\overline{T_f}$	water temp. exiting heat-pump [°C]
$\dot{T}_a$	outside temp. [°C]
$T^i{}_{return}$	water temp. exiting room i [°C]
$\dot{S}^i$	solar heat to room i [Watt]

(a) Measured data

Constant	Description
α_h^i	floor to room air
α_e^i	envelope to room
α_s^i	solar radiation to room
α_w^i	pipes to floor
α_a^i	envelope to outdoors
α_n^i	room i to room n
β_h^i	floor heat capacity
β_h^e	envelope heat capacity

(b) Heat exchange coefficients

$$\frac{d\tilde{T}_r^i}{dt} = \alpha_h^i(\tilde{T}_h^i - \tilde{T}_r^i) + \alpha_e^i(\tilde{T}_e^i - \tilde{T}_r^i) + \alpha_s^i \cdot \dot{S}^i \tag{2}$$

$$\frac{d\tilde{T}_h^i}{dt} = \frac{\alpha_h^i}{\beta_h^i}(\tilde{T}_r^i - \tilde{T}_h^i) + \alpha_w^i \cdot \overline{M^i}(\overline{T_f} - \tilde{T}_h^i) \tag{3}$$

$$\frac{d\tilde{T}_e^i}{dt} = \frac{\alpha_e^i}{\beta_e^i}(\tilde{T}_r^i - \tilde{T}_e^i) + \alpha_a^i(\dot{T}_a - \tilde{T}_e^i) + \sum_{\substack{n=1 \\ n \neq i}}^{N} \alpha_n^i(\hat{T}_r^n - \tilde{T}_e^i) \tag{4}$$

(c) Proposed three state energy model

Fig. 3. The thermodynamics system with the input data and the heat transfer coefficients where $i \in \{1, 2, 3, 4\}$ and, (α), (β) are "resistance" and "capacity"

We model the thermal dynamics of the house as presented in Eqs. (2)–(4) from Fig. 3. For readability, we annotate the system in the following way: predicted state-variables by a tilde, e.g. $\tilde{T}_r^i$, inputs directly affected by the two levels of controls (i.e. the *heat-pump* or the *room thermostat*) with an overline, e.g. $\overline{M^i}$, impact of nature with a dot, e.g. $\dot{T}_a$, and constants (to be estimated) are left without decoration.

The thermal dynamics model follows a classical three-state framework consisting of room temperature $(\tilde{T}_r^i)$, heater temperature $(\tilde{T}_h^i)$ and envelope temperature $(\tilde{T}_e^i)$. This approach is similar to what was presented in [16]; however, we here consider the rooms as individual model identification problems to overcome instability in the model identification when the number of coefficients to be estimated grows. Here the room temperature $(\tilde{T}_r^i)$ is directly affected by the heater (relative to the coefficient α_h^i), the envelope (relative to the coefficient α_e^i) and the direct solar radiation of the room ($\dot{S}^i$ relative to the coefficient α_s^i). The room temperature directly impacts the heater temperature $(\tilde{T}_h^i)$, but also receives energy from the in-flowing hot water which is proportional to the flow-rate $\overline{M^i}$ and the relative difference to the forward temperature of the water $(\overline{T_f})$. The envelope $(\tilde{T}_h^i)$ models the energy transfer through the walls surrounding the room. The envelope thus exchanges energy with the room itself $(\tilde{T}_r^i)$, the outside world $\dot{T}_a$ (proportional to the coefficient α_a^i) and with the other rooms of the house (the last sum term of Eq. (4)).

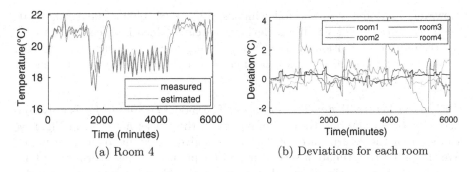

(a) Room 4   (b) Deviations for each room

Fig. 4. Predicted and measured indoor temperatures

A legend of the variables used can be seen in Fig. 3a for data-variables and Fig. 3b for the transfer coefficients. Given a time-series of historical data of the variables presented in Fig. 3a (excluding $\tilde{T}_h^i$ and $\tilde{T}_e^i$), the CTSM-R software can estimate the heat transfer coefficients presented in Fig. 3b. The model is estimated s.t. the suggested coefficients allow us to predict $\tilde{T}_r^i$ with a high accuracy given known values for the massflow and temperature of the feed-in water and the environmental influences such as sun and outdoor temperature.

Decomposed Grey-Box Modelling. Notice here that the presented model only considers a single room. This implies that the identification can be done on a room-to-room basis without the explosion in the coefficients to be estimated. In general, this allows us for faster model identification. This implies repeating the same model-identification scheme four times but with different indexing. As we shall see later, four such identified models can be recomposed to form a complete model with high predictive power.

Evaluation of the Estimations. We shall now assess the quality of our proposed model-identification. The model is identified on a time-series consisting of data generated by the high-fidelity DYMOLA model using historical weather input from February 05, 2009, from Aalborg, Denmark and five days forward at a sample rate of 60 s. We note that the model estimation for the values is completed in less than 7 min for each room. Remark here that the data used for the estimation contains some effects not captured by Eqs. (2)–(4); notably occupants and cooking activities, contributing to significant noise in the system.

To estimate the quality of the model, we compute a 6000 min time-series in DYMOLA and compare the predicted room temperatures of each of the identified room-models to the reference computed by DYMOLA. In Fig. 4a we see a head-to-head comparison for Room 4 where we can observe that the identified model demonstrates good predictive power. In particular, we note that no divergent behaviour is observed. The deviation of each room from measured data can be seen in Fig. 4b. Excluding Room 1, the largest average deviation observed for all rooms is less than 1 C°, and in general, kept below 0.5 C° of difference.

However, in Room 1 in the following intervals 1000–1400, 2400–2900, 3800–4300, 4700–5400 min, significant deviation occurs, which is traced back to the unaccounted contribution of heat from cooking activities which are expected to be unobservable in a real application—and not captured during the model identification.

Estimating Return-Water Temperatures. The model created so far is only concerned with the internal transfer of energy in the house; however, in Fig. 1 we can see that the return-water of the rooms is given as input to the heat-pump. We thus need to estimate a second model for predicting the return-water temperature. We here again adopt a data-driven approach and derive a model of this temperature-drop directly from data. We here assume a simple linear model; the increase in temperature of a room is assumed to be primarily due to energy dissipation from the heater. While this assumption is true in a closed system (due to the principle of conservation of energy), we here know that the assumption is incorrect: external influences occur, such as loss and gain of energy from neighboring rooms. This assumption allows us to establish the relationship described in Eqs. (5)–(6), and using historical data for $\overline{T}_{forward}$, $\tilde{T}_h^i$ and $\tilde{T}_r^i$ we can estimate the coefficients α, β and intercept γ. Again, these coefficients allow us to later predict the value of $\overline{T}_{return^i}$ for use in our full predictive model. Notice that prior to model-identification, we filter out data points where the water is not flowing (i.e. the local thermostat has shut off the supply). It is observed that while the return temperatures are all above 32 C°, the absolute mean error in estimating them is for all the rooms between 0.74 C° and 0.95 C°.

$$Energy_{loss}^i = \overline{T}_{forward} - \tilde{T}_h^i \tag{5}$$

$$Energy_{gain}^i = \tilde{T}_h^i - \tilde{T}_r^i \tag{6}$$

$$\overline{T}_{forward} - \overline{T}_{return^i} \approx \alpha \cdot Energy_{loss}^i + \beta \cdot Energy_{gain}^i + \gamma \tag{7}$$

4 Modelling in UPPAAL STRATEGO

We can create a complete predictive model given the two identified thermal models. For doing so, we use the UPPAAL tool suit [2–4,19] which has been successfully applied in many industrial projects for verification, performance analysis, and strategy synthesis. UPPAAL STRATEGO [7] is a branch of the tool that provides machine learning-based techniques for strategy synthesis and cost optimization of different controllers from Priced Timed MDPs. It has a rich modelling formalism for stochastic and hybrid games and control synthesis exploiting efficient reinforcement learning facilities. In UPPAAL systems are modelled as networks of finite-state automata processes. The processes communicate with each other through channels or shared variables, and real-valued clocks facility is available in the tool to capture critical timing aspects of a system. In addition, STRATEGO provides C-library support [14] which offers a convenient way to construct complex interactions with other libraries and historical data, for instance, STRATEGO itself.

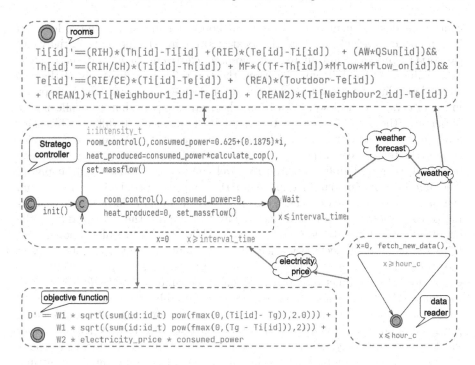

Fig. 5. Overall system composition

The overall composition of the system as a model in STRATEGO can be seen in Fig. 5. We design sub-parts of the system as separate templates (parameterizable automata). The dashed-line areas in Fig. 5 represent that the model has four templates: *Room*, *HeatPumpController*, *DataReader* and *ObjectiveFunction*. In the *Room* template, we express the continuous variables $\tilde{T}_r^i$, $\tilde{T}_h^i$ and $\tilde{T}_e^i$ (developed in Eqs. 2–4) as real-time clocks which evolve with time, but with rate-expressions matching the identified models. The *DataReader* template reads the *weather* and *day-ahead electricity price* information from the data file into the model. The *ObjectiveFunction* template implements the *fitness/optimization* function (see Eq. 1). The *HeatPumpController* template implements the control mechanism of the controller where choices for using different energy levels for heat-pump are made.

STRATEGO handles this heating problem as a *stochastic hybrid game*. In this model, solid edges indicate controllable actions, and dashed lines indicate uncontrollable (controlled by the environment) actions. Circles are denoted locations, and the double-circle indicate the initial location of automata and arrows are called *edges*. An (instantiated) set of templates constitute a Network of (Hybrid Stochastic) Timed Game Automata (which semantically gives us an EMDP) where a state is given by a location vector (one for each template instance) and an assignment of concrete values to any variable. The system may then evolve by respecting guards and invariants – in particular, those that restrict the continuous development of clocks wrt our house dynamics. The initial location is committed (marked by a C in the locations) forcing the model to initially call the **init**() function, initializing the *weather, electricity price* and *solar radiations* values. At the following location, the controller may take any of the two edges depending on the amount of energy it decides to operate the heat-pump in an interval; in the lower transition, the heat-pump is shut off while in the upper uses the *select* statement to compactly implement 10 different intensity levels of the controller (encoded in the type intensity_t). I.e. the controller assigns the temporary variable i a discrete value from *intensity* (range between 0 and 10) to reflect different intensity level choices to operate the heat-pump. The function roomControl() implements the bang/bang controllers of the room thermostats, which decides whether to periodically open or close the valves leading to each room, this directly gives a way to compute the distribution of the ongoing flow by the setMassFlow() function. The variable consumed_power contains the amount of electricity selected by the controller for each intermediate interval during strategy synthesis while heat_produced is the produced heat for every interval. The function calculate_cop() calculates the *Coefficient of Performance* (COP) value used to measure the produced heat. Notice that the COP value, for a given return-water temperature and outdoor temperature, provides a gearing of input to output energy; i.e. at a COP value of 2, a single kWh of power yields 2kWh of energy. Such gearing is normally found in the technical specifications of a heat-pump. This gearing, along with the pump intensity-setting, massflow and the return-water temperature, allows for the computation of the *forward* temperature and using the equations for return-water temperature. The return-water temperature is computed based on the previous time-step, and the relative changes in the indoor temperatures allow us to predict this value using the developed equations from Sect. 3. At the wait location, the invariant x<= interval bounds the system to stay there until the value of clock x (local clock) reaches interval i.e. 15-min. The constant interval is the control frequency of the heat-pump. The guard x>=interval prevents the system from making this transition before spending 15 min at the wait location, after which the clock x is reset to zero, allowing for timing a new interval.

Evaluation Using STRATEGO: We use the provided model for both learning and evaluation in our experiments. However, in the evaluation phase, the control choices of the STRATEGO controller template are restricted to follow those suggested by a call to an external library, implying that the controller is invoked for every simulated 15 min. When we evaluate the system under the control of a bang-bang controller, this call returns either full intensity or the 0 intensity value. When the STRATEGO itself is used as a controller instead, the call instantiates the above templates—but instead of evaluating, it will synthesize a controller by repeated sampling.

4.1   Learning by STRATEGO

To attain a predictive controller, STRATEGO trains on the instantiated model, using the initial state estimate by exploiting repeated sampling and Q-learning.

This allows the tool to factor in temporal changes such as weather and price changes of the near future. However, four problems arise:

1. not all variables are observable, specifically only the room-temperatures ($\tilde{T}_r^i$), the weather forecast and the price projection can be observed,
2. controllers take time to compute, leading to a delay from observation to reaction,
3. the development of the real world (or evaluation model) can deviate over time, and
4. both weather forecasts and prices have a limited horizon.

The latter points we shall discuss in Sect. 4.2, and let us instead here address the first issue.

Initial State Estimation: In our three-state thermodynamics model, the changes in room temperature ($\tilde{T}_r^i$) are directly dependent on two hidden states, i.e., floor temperature ($\tilde{T}_h^i$) and envelope temperature ($\tilde{T}_e^i$). The states are unobservable and they intuitively track the abstract value of "energy stored in the heater" and "energy stored in the wall" respectively. This implies that the tool works on a partially observable model. To attain reasonable estimates, we can predict these hidden variables—and similarly the future value of observable values to accommodate for the observational delay. Assuming that a full state is known at τ_t and that a control choice has already been made, then the state at τ_{t+15} can be captured by forward simulation of the model. Experiments show that this method of approximating the hidden variables $\tilde{T}_e^i$ and $\tilde{T}_h^i$ allowed a drift of no more than 0.1 C° between the repeated estimates of the variables in the model used for learning and the model used for evaluation.

4.2 Online Synthesis

Given that energy costs are only known 24 h in advance and that weather forecasts are known to have degrading predictive power the further into the future they look, we utilize an online synthesis procedure. At the same time, as our model used for controller synthesis has hidden variables, a rapid recomputation of a strategy allows us to adjust for errors made in the initial state-estimation and potential discrepancies with the real house (or evaluation model in our case).

We thus propose a method where at each 15-min interval, the volatile variables (energy price, weather and measurable variables of the house) are monitored and transferred to the controller. This allows the controller to instantiate the method of Sect. 4.1 with the most recent measurements. We can then let STRATEGO synthesize a controller on. An overview of this flow is given in Fig. 6. Each day has four 6-h periods, and each period has 24 of 15-min intervals. The reuse interval (k) is 24, which means a single strategy is used for k intervals. In the first interval, STRATEGO gets the current *room temperatures, weather forecast* and *day-ahead electricity price*, estimates the initial state and synthesizes a strategy that minimizes the fitness function F by sampling 12-h (learning horizon) ahead in future. The controller saves the first strategy ($S1$). The heat-pump uses $S1$ during intervals 2–25 and makes another strategy during interval 25, which is then used for the next 24 intervals (i.e. from 26–49).

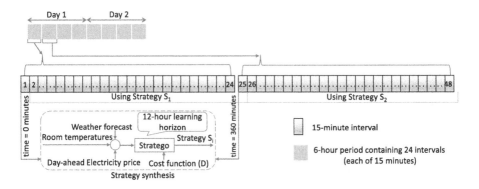

Fig. 6. Online synthesis approach shown on a two day period.

Notice here that it is assumed that the synthesis procedure is *not* instantaneous, implying that a synthesized controller can only be applied in the subsubsequent interval. To overcome this issue, we apply the initial state-estimation as described in Sect. 4.1 to estimate the house state at a time-point $\tau + 15$ from measurements obtained at τ. We set the training horizon of the method to be 12 h, implying that the learning method will only sample the system up to a horizon of 12 h from the starting measurement. This can aptly be done in STRATEGO using the query presented in Eq. 8. We here see that the controller is trained to only react on the observable variables `minute_clock` (tracking real-time), `Ti[i]` (tracking indoor room temperatures) and `Toutdoor_forecast` (tracking weather forecast). The result of the synthesis procedure is a reactive strategy that for an assignment of the input variables yields a (near-)optimal action to take [6,13,18]

```
strategy S = minE (F) [minute_clock <= 12*60)]        (8)
          {} -> {minute_clock, Ti[0], Ti[1], Ti[2], Ti[3],
               Toutdoor_forecast}: <> minute_clock==(12*60)
```

Notice also that Eq. 8 defines a feature vector (observable variables of the state-space) to be only directly measurable variables of the original system. This makes the strategy directly applicable for several intervals (up to the learning horizon) in the actual system under control. We can exploit this to lower the overall computational effort of deploying our approach, which directly impacts the overall energy impact of running the smart heating system. Essentially, by re-using a strategy for several intervals, a single server can act as a controller for a group of houses, i.e. if a strategy only needs to be computed every six intervals, six houses can share the computational resource.

5   Evaluation

To validate our approach, we experiment with controlling the OpSys house for a week with weather conditions matching February 4–10, 2018. As a reference, we use the estimated model presented in Sect. 4. The goal of any controller is to minimize the parameterized cost-criteria defined in Eq. 1 for the period under control. In all experiments, we compare different variations of the online STRATEGO-based controller against a standard bang-bang (BB) controller.

We conduct three series of experiments:

1. a series under realistic assumptions on observability and time,
2. a study of sensitivity to various degrees of measurement noise, and
3. a study of impact of changes in the learning parameters of STRATEGO.

All experiments are conducted on AMD EPYC 7551 limited a single core and 2 GB of memory[1]. We limit the controller to 15-min control intervals which is sufficient for systems with as slow dynamic as floor-heating. For each reported configuration, the experiment is repeated 10 times and the mean value is reported with standard deviation intervals reported in bar-charts. A reproducibility package is available in [12].

In all series, we observe changes to the results when the weights of comfort $(0 \leq W_{comf} \leq 1)$ changes; we modify these values in steps of 0.1. To make this weighting independent of the given week and to allow for this proportional weighting between two units (kWh and squared degrees Celsius), we compute a normalization-factor *norm* based on the BB controller. This normalization-factor is computed by estimating the performance of the BB controller on the week leading up to February 4–10 in terms of *cost* and *comfort*. The normalization-factor is then given directly by $norm = \frac{comfort}{cost}$.

In our plots we report *relative* performance to that of the BB controller; we do so as the behaviour of the BB controller in the model (when replayed with historical weather) is deterministic. We omit to report values for a pure emphasis on cost as this leads the controller to (as expected) turn off all heat.

Realistic Evaluation: In this series, we emulate a realistic setup; this implies that hidden variables are estimated, the weather forecast is stochastic, and the controller only can be applied with a 15 min delay from the variable observation-time, as described in Sect. 4.

We experiment with two configurations and compare them with the standard BB controller. In one, we fix the learning parameters s.t. the wall-clock computation time is not exceeding 15 min on given hardware; namely 600 samples (depicted blue in Fig. 7), and a re-use interval of 24 (6 h) limiting the computation effort—denoted the *realistic* configuration. In a more hypothetical application, we double the training budget to 1200 samples (leading to an approx 30 min computation time) and reduce the re-use interval to 6 (depicted orange in Fig. 7)—named the *best* configuration.

We see that the BB controller is dominated in all ways by any of the two STRATEGO controllers. In particular we see that at $W_{comf} = 0.4$ either STRATEGO controller achieves comparable comfort to the BB controller (Fig. 7b), but at a 33–34% reduction in cost (Fig. 7c). In Fig. 7a, we observe for any setting of

---

[1] Actual memory usage expected to be significantly lower, but not recorded.

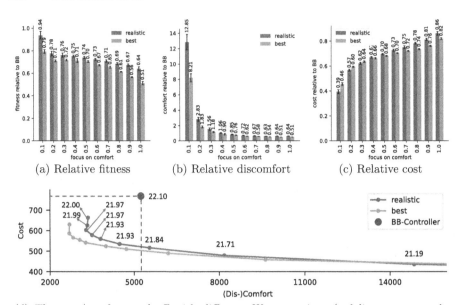

(a) Relative fitness   (b) Relative discomfort   (c) Relative cost

(d) The cost/comfort tradeoff with different W_{comf} settings (red line separates the points on its left side where STRATEGO is outperforming BB w.r.t both comfort and cost)

Fig. 7. February week control under partial observability with 24 reuse intervals and 600 training samples (blue) and 6 reuse intervals and 1200 training samples.

the parameters the STRATEGO-based controllers are dominating in the distance measure and more so with an increased comfort weight. In Fig. 7d we have also annotated the average temperature experienced throughout the week for the *realistic* controller to provide a tangible perspective on the discomfort measure. With a less than $0.16C°$ deviation in the average temperature from the setpoint with $W_{comf} \geq 0.4$, again resulting in a 33% reduction in cost.

As the BB controller is incapable of adjusting to the time-varying cost function, it is expected that the STRATEGO controller can outperform it with a focus on cost. More interesting, the benefit of using STRATEGO grows with an increased focus on comfort. Notice that Eq. 1 penalizes overshooting. We hypothesize that the binary mode of the BB entails periods of large overshooting of the target temperature and others with undershooting due to the 15-min control interval[2]. The STRATEGO controllers can instead compensate gradually and react more subtly.

While the *realistic* controller in general trails the *best* controller, find it to be well-performing in general, trailing with no more than 4% points in comfort for settings with $W_{comf} \geq 0.4$ and a loss in comfort of no more than 13% points in the same range.

---

[2] Due to wear and tear on heat-pumps it is undesirable to change states too often.

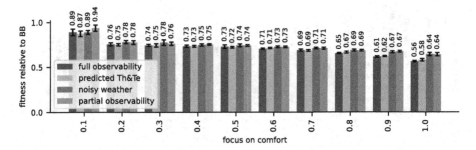

Fig. 8. February week control under different observability situations with 24 reuse intervals and 600 learning runs

Sensitivity Analysis of Impact of Measurement Noise: As our experimental setup is virtual, we can study the impact of stochastic weather-prediction, hidden variables and delayed controller response; this comparison is seen in Fig. 8. The experimental setup is similar to the *Realistic* series apart from the specified changes. We experiment with four configurations: 1. Full observability, allowing for delayed controller response, perfect weather-prediction and direct observation of hidden variables (i.e. an ideal scenario), 2. Predicted $\tilde{T}_e^i$ and $\tilde{T}_h^i$, otherwise as full observability, 3. Noisy weather, otherwise as full observability, and 4. Partial observability, exactly the same setup as in the *Realistic Evaluation* series. In Fig. 8, we observe that while a high emphasis on cost (which is a fully observable variable), the impact of noisy weather prediction and predicted unobservable variables has only a modest effect (2–3%), however with a ≥ 0.8 focus on comfort, we see the uncertainty of the weather significantly impacting the performance (up to 8%), indicating a sensitivity of the controller towards accurate forecasts. We observe an anomaly with a 0.1 emphasis on comfort where the full observability configuration is significantly worse than the predicted scenario.

While the discrepancy appears to be within measurement noise, it still warrants further investigation. We hypothesize that the squaring of the difference of the target and the actual temperature in Eq. 1 leads to rare spikes in the response affecting the partition-refinement scheme deployed of STRATEGO.

Sensitivity Analysis of Learning Parameters: STRATEGO is a sampling-based tool, and the performance (in terms of quality of the controller synthesized) is dependent on the number of samples provided. This is given directly in the number of runs (simulations) the engine is allowed to conduct.

In Fig. 9b we see that an increase in the number of runs (in general) improves the performance. However, with a doubled effort of 1200 runs (approx 30 min of computation pr. strategy), the performance in general improved by 2% and in a rare case by 3%. We can see a similar improvement in performance with an increase from 300 to 600 runs. However, a similar anomaly is observed with an 0.1 emphasis on comfort as was found in the *Measurement Noise*-series of experiments. We conjecture that this effect manifests to a higher degree with an increased learning effort.

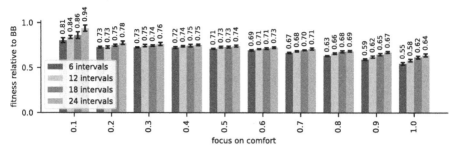

(a) February week with different reuse intervals and 600 learning runs

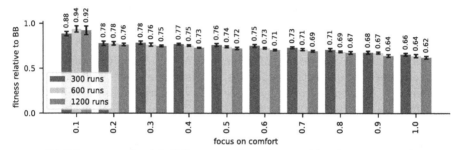

(b) February week with different number of runs with 24 reuse intervals

Fig. 9. Effect of choosing different sets of reuse intervals and number of runs

We here also experiment with reducing the overall computational effort needed for control. In Sect. 4.2 we introduced the *reuse interval* which allows for applying a given control strategy for an extended period. In Fig. 9a we observe that a tighter re-computation cycle of 6 intervals (every $1\frac{1}{2}$ h) allows us to gain 3% performance compared to our *Realistic* series of experiments. Towards a reuse of 24 periods, we observe a drop in performance when the reuse interval is extended.

6 Conclusion

We presented a tool-chain for controlling a heat-pump system in a floor heating case study. The tool-chain offers an end-to-end solution for floor heating applications by establishing an automatic procedure for the identification of house thermodynamics and designing UPPAAL STRATEGO controller. We compare the performance of STRATEGO controller against the traditionally used *bang-bang* controller. Experimental results show that our controller offers significant improvements in both user *comfort* as well as energy *cost*, even when realistic limitations on computation effort are taken into account. In particular, STRATEGO saves 33% energy while preserving the same comfort as the standard bang-bang controller. We also analyse the cost-comfort trade-off paradigm, which shows that we can save energy costs by slightly compromising the comfort. We believe that the results can be further improved by introducing a heat buffer and that the computational effort can be reduced by techniques such as ensemble learning.

Acknowledgements. We would like to thank Simon Thorsteinsson for his extensive help with DYMOLA and acquiring base data for model identification. This research is partly funded by the ERC Advanced Grant LASSO, the Villum Investigator Grant S4OS as well as DIREC: Digital Research Centre Denmark.

References

1. Agesen, M.K., et al.: Toolchain for user-centered intelligent floor heating control. In: IECON 2016–42nd Annual Conference of the IEEE Industrial Electronics Society, pp. 5296–5301 (2016). https://doi.org/10.1109/IECON.2016.7794040
2. Behrmann, G., Cougnard, A., David, A., Fleury, E., Larsen, K.G., Lime, D.: UPPAAL-Tiga: time for playing games! In: Damm, W., Hermanns, H. (eds.) CAV 2007. LNCS, vol. 4590, pp. 121–125. Springer, Heidelberg (2007). https://doi.org/10.1007/978-3-540-73368-3_14
3. Behrmann, G., et al.: UPPAAL 4.0. IEEE Computer Society (2006)
4. Bulychev, P., et al.: UPPAAL-SMC: statistical model checking for priced timed automata. arXiv preprint arXiv:1207.1272 (2012)
5. Carrascal, E., Garrido, I., Garrido, A.J., Sala, J.M.: Optimization of the heating system use in aged public buildings via model predictive control. Energies 9(4), 251 (2016)
6. David, A., et al.: On time with minimal expected cost! In: Cassez, F., Raskin, J.-F. (eds.) ATVA 2014. LNCS, vol. 8837, pp. 129–145. Springer, Cham (2014). https://doi.org/10.1007/978-3-319-11936-6_10
7. David, A., Jensen, P.G., Larsen, K.G., Mikučionis, M., Taankvist, J.H.: UPPAAL STRATEGO. In: Baier, C., Tinelli, C. (eds.) TACAS 2015. LNCS, vol. 9035, pp. 206–211. Springer, Heidelberg (2015). https://doi.org/10.1007/978-3-662-46681-0_16
8. Dixit, M.K., Fernández-Solís, J.L., Lavy, S., Culp, C.H.: Identification of parameters for embodied energy measurement: a literature review. Energy Build. 42(8), 1238–1247 (2010)
9. Ferracuti, F., et al.: Data-driven models for short-term thermal behaviour prediction in real buildings. Appl. Energy 204, 1375–1387 (2017)
10. Fonti, A., Comodi, G., Pizzuti, S., Arteconi, A., Helsen, L.: Low order grey-box models for short-term thermal behavior prediction in buildings. Energy Procedia 105, 2107–2112 (2017)
11. Harasty, S., Lambeck, S., Cavaterra, A.: Model predictive control for preventive conservation using artificial neural networks. In: 12th REHVA World Congress, Aalborg, Denmark (2016)
12. Hasrat, I., Jensen, P., Larsen, K., Srba, J.: Reproducibility package for: end-to-end heat-pump control using continuous time stochastic modelling and uppaal stratego (2022)
13. Jaeger, M., Bacci, G., Bacci, G., Larsen, K.G., Jensen, P.G.: Approximating euclidean by imprecise Markov decision processes. In: Margaria, T., Steffen, B. (eds.) ISoLA 2020. LNCS, vol. 12476, pp. 275–289. Springer, Cham (2020). https://doi.org/10.1007/978-3-030-61362-4_15

14. Jensen, P.G., Larsen, K.G., Legay, A., Nyman, U.: Integrating tools: co-simulation in UPPAAL using FMI-FMU. In: 2017 22nd International Conference on Engineering of Complex Computer Systems (ICECCS), pp. 11–19. IEEE (2017)

15. Østergaard Jensen, S.: OPSYS tools for investigating energy flexibility in houses with heat pumps (2018). https://www.annex67.org/media/1838/report-opsys-flexibilitet.pdf

16. Juhl, R., Kristensen, N.R., Bacher, P., Kloppenborg, J., Madsen, H.: Grey-box modeling of the heat dynamics of a building with CTSM-R (2017). http://ctsm.info/pdfs/examples/building2.pdf

17. Juhl, R., Møller, J.K., Madsen, H.: CTSMR - Continuous Time Stochastic Modeling in R. arXiv (2016). https://doi.org/10.48550/ARXIV.1606.00242

18. Larsen, K.G., Mikučionis, M., Muñiz, M., Srba, J., Taankvist, J.H.: Online and compositional learning of controllers with application to floor heating. In: Chechik, M., Raskin, J.-F. (eds.) TACAS 2016. LNCS, vol. 9636, pp. 244–259. Springer, Heidelberg (2016). https://doi.org/10.1007/978-3-662-49674-9_14

19. Larsen, K.G., Pettersson, P., Yi, W.: UPPAAL in a nutshell. Int. J. Softw. Tools Technol. Transfer **1**(1–2), 134–152 (1997)

20. Ljung, L.: MATLAB system identification toolbox-getting started guide r2016a. Mathworks, Ed., Mathworks (2016)

21. Nassif, N.: Modeling and optimization of HVAC systems using artificial neural network and genetic algorithm. Build. Simul. **7**(3), 237–245 (2013). https://doi.org/10.1007/s12273-013-0138-3

22. Privara, S., Cigler, J., Váňa, Z., Oldewurtel, F., Sagerschnig, C., Žáčeková, E.: Building modeling as a crucial part for building predictive control. Energy Build. **56**, 8–22 (2013)

23. Reynders, G., Diriken, J., Saelens, D.: Quality of grey-box models and identified parameters as function of the accuracy of input and observation signals. Energy Build. **82**, 263–274 (2014)

24. Thilker, C.A., Bergsteinsson, H.G., Bacher, P., Madsen, H., Calì, D., Junker, R.G.: Non-linear model predictive control for smart heating of buildings. In: E3S Web of Conferences, vol. 246, p. 09005. EDP Sciences (2021)

25. Vinther, K., Green, T., Jensen, S.Ø., Bendtsen, J.D.: Predictive control of hydronic floor heating systems using neural networks and genetic algorithms. IFAC-PapersOnLine **50**(1), 7381–7388 (2017)

26. Vogler-Finck, P., Wisniewski, R., Popovski, P.: Reducing the carbon footprint of house heating through model predictive control - a simulation study in Danish conditions. Sustain. Cities Soc. **42**, 558–573 (2018). http://www.sciencedirect.com/science/article/pii/S2210670718301173

27. Yu, X., You, S., Cai, H., Georges, L., Bacher, P.: Data-driven modelling and optimal control of domestic electric water heaters for demand response. In: Wang, Z., Zhu, Y., Wang, F., Wang, P., Shen, C., Liu, J. (eds.) ISHVAC 2019. ESE, pp. 77–86. Springer, Singapore (2020). https://doi.org/10.1007/978-981-13-9528-4_9

Security Vulnerabilities Detection Through Assertion-Based Approach

Salim Yahia Kissi[1]([⊠]) [iD], Rabéa Ameur-Boulifa[2]([⊠]) [iD],
and Yassamin Seladji[1]([⊠]) [iD]

[1] LRIT, University of Abou Bekr Belkaid, Tlemcen, Algeria
{salimyahia.kissi,yassamine.seladji}@univ-tlemcen.dz
[2] LTCI, Télécom ParisTech, Institut Polytechnique de Paris, Palaiseau, France
Rabea.Ameur-Boulifa@telecom-paris.fr

Abstract. Organizations and companies develop very complex software today. Errors and flaws can be introduced at different phases of the software development life cycle and can lead to exploitable vulnerabilities. Furthermore, considering that most systems are exposed to multiple users and environments, such flaws can lead to attacks (or actions) with unpredictable consequences in terms of damage and costs.

Most research that deals with security-related issues of software focuses their efforts on coding errors and flaws, regardless of the infrastructure and platforms that run the software applications. Often, such analyses of software applications vulnerabilities may lack sufficient specification details, thus possibly miss larger systematic flaws, and consequently obscure the existence of serious vulnerabilities. Our research aims at developing a technique capable of discovering the security weaknesses, specifically buffer overflow vulnerabilities in C/C++ programs, through the analysis of source code combined with architecture specifications. The proposed approach relies on the notion of platform assertions that is, a collection of logical relationships used to characterize a platform (execution environment). In this paper, we focus on such assertions and show how vulnerabilities analysis of software applications can be performed with our assertion-based approach. Furthermore, the generation of assertion specifications as well as the construction of an assertion library including various platforms are explored.

Keywords: Assertions · Formal analysis · Vulnerabilities detection · Execution environment

1 Introduction

It is well known that integer errors in software applications, including arithmetic overflow and wraparound can be exploited by malicious actors. Recently, integer errors are classified as one of the most dangerous software weaknesses [5]. One of the reasons is that programmers are not always fully aware about the semantics of integer operations and machine integer types [6].

© Springer Nature Switzerland AG 2022
Y. Aït-Ameur and F. Crăciun (Eds.): TASE 2022, LNCS 13299, pp. 381–387, 2022.
https://doi.org/10.1007/978-3-031-10363-6_25

In our work, we are interested in detecting vulnerabilities resulting from potential flaws in C programs, particularly those related to arithmetic operations. Our focus in this paper is on undefined evaluation within the C standard. To illustrate the problem consider the natural and small C program given in Listing 1.1. We compiled it on different platforms: - X86_64 under ubuntu 18.04 64-bit using gcc7.5.0 compiler; - and X86_64 under windows 64-bit using gcc10.2.0 compiler, without optimization options in both cases. We have noticed that the results of its execution are different. Indeed, we observe that on the windows platform, the read and write service access instruction (line 7) is executed while uid_sid $\neq$ 0. This is due to the sign-magnitude representation of the binary format of uid_sid, the first platform uses 64 bits while the second uses 32 bits.

Listing 1.1. A small program that grants access to services

```
1   void foo(char username[], char password[]){
2       int userId= getUserId(username,password);
3       int serviceId;    // 0 <= userId <= 150*10^6
4       read(serviceId); // 1 <= serviceId <= 64
5       long int uid_sid=(long)userId*serviceId;
6       if (uid_sid==0){
7           readAndWriteService(uid_sid,serviceId);
8       }else{
9           readOnlyService(uid_sid,serviceId);
10      }
11      return;}
```

This situation is not a merely a fringe case, but commonly known. It is specified in the C standard [7] as undefined behaviour: the semantics of the C language does not describe exactly what should happen, but leaves crucial decisions to the implementing compiler and/or the runtime environment. In practice, this usually translates to a wrap of the value, and a change of the sign and value that makes the program produce incorrect results, behave in an unexpected way, or crash. This effect is further amplified from a security perspective, this common software coding mistakes can be used to subvert security services.

We propose an approach that can help programmers prevent such weaknesses, i.e. software vulnerabilities. The advocated approach reduces software vulnerabilities detection to satisfiability problems over logical formulas [10]. The relevance of our approach lies in the fact that it is based on hardware/software co-analysis. We provided a uniform method for software analysis, considering the specifications of its execution environment (CPUs, compilers, operating systems). The main idea is to build a formula based on the path condition of a given target location in conjunction with the formula (assertions) specifying the environment of its execution, and asking an SMT solver for a satisfying solution, to find out whether the unintended solution is possible. Formally speaking, we use symbolic execution to generate program constraint (PC), and get security constraint (SC) from predefined security requirements. In addition, based on a precise knowledge on the execution context of the analysed program (EC), we propose to solve the statement: $EC \vdash PC \land \neg SC$ we seek to find out if there is an assignment of values to program inputs - executed in a certain context - which could satisfy PC but violates SC.

In this paper, we present how we proceed to define the execution context specification, that can be used to uncover and effectively combat possible vulnerabilities. While our motivation for this work is to identify and address security vulnerabilities in a software code, the result can be used to look for any misbehaviour in the code that would be caused by the execution environment.

Related Works. Although integers overflow are a known source of vulnerabilities [6], their systematic detection remains a problem as *"they are perfectly legal in C/C++"* and *"not all overflows are bugs"* [11]. Several works have addressed the issue of integer overflow vulnerability. However, for the analysis most of them focus on either the binary code [1], or on the software code without taking into account the execution environment [9,12]. Nevertheless, there are a number of approaches and tools that explore code paths to track (un)feasible paths via constraint solving, such as KLEE [2] and PREFIX+z3. They are dedicated mainly to find integer errors. Others dedicated to static analysis such as Frama-C [3,4] that is well-known toolkit for analysis of C programs can catch integer overflow, but it accepts only a restrictive subset of C. These tools perform analysis by adding pre and post-conditions as safety properties assertions. Compared to our approach, these assertions doesn't take into account the execution environment.

2 Assertion Construction

Given a programming language, we propose a formalization of the semantics data types through different platforms. The choice of the predicate logic formalism is mainly guided by the tool used for the analysis (we use SMT-z3 solver). We will show how assertions that reflects a calculation can produce an overflow or wraparound. Because of space limitations, we restrict ourselves to arithmetic operations on signed integer.

Integer Arithmetic in C. The C language (as many other languages) provides several standard data types. They consist of basic types (char, int, float and double) attached to modifiers (signed, unsigned, short, and long). We know that computers store data in memory using binary representation; each data type requires different amounts of memory; and operands of different data types can be combined in a single operation. C language provides rules conversion to perform mixed-mode operations on different data types. Such rules refer to the implicit or explicit change of a value from one data type storage format to another e.g. from 16-bit integer to a 32-bit integer. For this, it provides a hierarchy between types that governs the conversion. For the integer data type, is divided into short, int, and long data types that takes different bytes of storage space. The compiler performs always type conversions between any two arithmetic types wherever necessary, without regard to space issue. The conversion preserves the value of an expression if the new type is capable of representing it.

All integer conversion rules are informally defined in C standards [8]. These rules, that determine how compilers handle conversions, include integer promotions, integer conversion rank and the usual arithmetic conversions. Their description relies basically on the range of the types, thus on the execution platform.

Although the problems with type conversions and their unpredictable behaviour are well known, in particular the signed overflow problem and the wrap around behaviour [6], developers don't really know how to detect them due to the semantic subtleties of the language. A precise knowledge of the semantics of arithmetic conversions and their impact on data types through different platforms will doubtlessly enable to predict the behaviour of programs. In the following, we present the formalisation that we propose to model the semantics of data types cross different computer models. To do this, we created a database in which we collected the different known execution platforms identified by their CPU and operating systems associated with the sizes of the supported types (across compilers). An extract of the database is given in Table 1 that yields the size of type `long int` through a variety of platforms. With all types, the database can reach up to 2,000 different sizes by considering the 40 known machines.

Table 1. Size of `long int` across different execution environment

Target platform	OS, Compiler	Compiler options	Size
X86 or X86_64	win10 32, MSVC	No argument	32 bits
	win10 32, gcc		
	ubuntu 14.04 32, gcc		
	ubuntu 14.04 32, Clang		
X86_64	win10 64, MSVC		
	win10 64, gcc		
	ubuntu 18.04 64, gcc	-m32	
	ubuntu 18.04 64, Clang		
	ubuntu 18.04 64, gcc	No argument	64 bits
	ubuntu 18.04 64, Clang		

Formalisation. Almost all modern computers use two's complement signed arithmetic that is well-defined to wrap around. As known the n-bit two's complement notation of an integer belongs to the range $-2^{n-1}, ..., 2^{n-1} - 1$, all values in this interval have a unique representation. If an arithmetic operation produces a result an integer larger than $2^{n-1} - 1$ an overflow will occur because of the limited space. Consequently, a part will be stored in the available range, while the rest will be stored outside. The result will then be incorrect: it "wraps around" subtracting 2^n from, or adding 2^n to, the correct result. Given a signed integer x, let us denote by $\bar{x}$ the value of its two's complement representation. We propose the following equality that gives the direct relation between the two:

$$x = 2^n \times k + \bar{x}$$

such that k is a natural number and n a natural number encoding a bitwidth, i.e. belonging to $\{8, 16, 32, 64\}$ (the set of `size-bit` types). This equation reveals that the value of x can result from several different representations. The base case, when $k = 0$, corresponds to the correct result, while the others correspond to incorrect results. This parameterized formula defines a set assertions that can be used to analyse arithmetic expressions in a program.

To examine the possibility of an overflow of an arithmetic operation, we separate the case where the result of the operation is saved from the case where it is not. Before giving the two cases, let us define a function named `size_max_-rank` (resp. `size_min_rank`), for which the type profile is: `string` $\rightarrow$ `string` $\rightarrow$ `?('a list` $\rightarrow$ `int)` $\rightarrow$ `size-bit`. This function takes as parameters the type of two operands and an optional arithmetic operation (prefixed by `?` in the function type), returns the largest (resp. smallest) value of their size. The size that depends on the computer model will be retrieved from the database.

- **Arithmetic operation.** Given a binary operation on two signed integers $s_1 \diamond s_2$. Let us denote by v the result of its evaluation, i.e. $v = [\![s_1 \diamond s_2]\!]$. The result v satisfies the following formula:

$$(v = 2^n \times k + \bar{v}) \wedge (k \neq 0)$$

where $n = \lambda p.\texttt{size\_max\_rank}(\texttt{type}(s_1), \texttt{type}(s_2), \diamond, p)$ and p is a set of basic parameters of a computer model on which the operation is compiled and will be executed. We derived this formula from the "usual arithmetic conversions" rule. In particular, from the type promotion rule stating that *whenever two operands of different data types are involved in an operation, the operand of lower rank will be converted to a data type of higher rank*. And from the rule stating that arithmetic operators *do not accept types smaller than int* as arguments.

- **Arithmetic operation with assignment.** Given an update statement in the form $x = exp$ and denote by v the result of the evaluation of exp, i.e. $v = [\![exp]\!]$. The variable x satisfies the formula:

$$(x = 2^n \times k + \bar{x}) \wedge (k \neq 0)$$

where $n = \lambda p.\texttt{size\_min\_rank}(\texttt{type}(x), \texttt{type}(v), p)$. This second formula is derived from the rule stating that *if the right-hand operand is of lower rank then it will be promoted to the rank of the left operand*. Note in this case, n is calculated from the type of the result of the expression and the type of the assigned variable.

Illustration. We underline the usefulness of these assertions using our example (given in Listing 1.1). The security requirement is violated when a non-administrator user (`userId` $\neq 0$) accesses privileged services. Thus, the security requirement is defined as $\neg SC \triangleq (\texttt{userId} \neq 0) \wedge (\texttt{uid\_sid} = 0)$. The value of `uid_sid` is obtained by calculating an operation with assignment, we will then use for the analysis of this code the formula of the second case. According to the information from the execution platform stating that the code is compiled by gcc7.5.0 without option and will be run on a x86 64-bit windows. We will then get: EC $\triangleq$ (uid_sid $= 2^{32} \times k + 0$) $\wedge$ ($k > 0$). Indeed, as stated in the code type(uid_sid)= long int and type($[\![$userId $*$ serviceId$]\!]$)=long. And the calculation of size_min_rank(long int, long, {x86 64-bit,gcc7.5.0}) returns the value 32 (after fetching the size of each type from Table 1).

Listing 1.2. Our security problem encoded in Z3-SMT

```
1  ; variables declaration
2  (declare-fun userId () Int)
3  (declare-fun serviceId () Int)
4  (declare-fun uid_sid () Int)
5  (declare-fun k () Int)
6  ; execution context
7  (assert (= (* serviceId userId) (+ (* (^ 2 32) k) 0)))
8  (assert (distinct k 0))
9  (assert (and (>= serviceId 1) (<= serviceId 64)))
10 (assert (and  (>= userId 0) (<= userId 150000000)))
11 ; condition path
12 (assert (= uid_sid 0))
13 ; security constraint
14 (assert (and (distinct  userId 0) (= uid_sid 0)))
```

To analyse our security problem, we used SMT-Z3 solver developed by Microsoft Research (see Listing 1.2). In particular, we see the different formulas involved in our approach, EC (line 7–10) defined by the formula given above that we have completed with the program (user) requirements, PC $\triangleq$ uid_sid $= 0$ (line 10) and SC (line 14). The verification of the satisfiability of this logical code, outputs several models:

```
sat [serviceId=32, userId=134217728, k=1]
sat [serviceId=64, userId=67108864, k=1]
sat [serviceId=64, userId=134217728, k=2]
```

meaning that running our program on this platform may violate the security requirement in certain situations. An example, if the user numbered (userId) 134217728 requests the services numbered (serviceId) 32 or 64, he can get it. This user may then take the role administrator.

3   Conclusion

The buffer overflow can widely affects the security vulnerability of programs. The static analysis of source code aims at automatically detect such bugs but still limited. A lot of studies show that the execution platforms can be a source of bug, in particular for integer overflow. The proposed co-analysis method extends existing methods by exploiting the knowledge about the execution platform specification. A symbolic execution is performed to construct a path execution of a target instruction combined with assertions modelling the execution environment. The proposed assertions are logical formulas that express specification constraints on types and operations. In our current work, we are developing the tool that supports our approach. In parallel, we are extending the assertion library to catch other kind of errors, such as pointers and exception handling.

References

1. Bornebusch, F., Lüth, C., Wille, R., Drechsler, R.: Integer overflow detection in hardware designs at the specification level. In: Proceedings of the 8th International Conference on Model-Driven Engineering and Software Development - MODELSWARD, pp. 41–48. INSTICC, SciTePress (2020). https://doi.org/10.5220/0008960200410048
2. Cadar, C., Nowack, M.: KLEE symbolic execution engine in 2019. Int. J. Softw. Tools Technol. Transf. **23**(6), 867–870 (2021). https://doi.org/10.1007/s10009-020-00570-3
3. Canet, G., Cuoq, P., Monate, B.: A value analysis for C programs. In: 2009 Ninth IEEE International Working Conference on Source Code Analysis and Manipulation, pp. 123–124 (2009). https://doi.org/10.1109/SCAM.2009.22
4. Correnson, L.: Qed. Computing what remains to be proved. In: Badger, J.M., Rozier, K.Y. (eds.) NFM 2014. LNCS, vol. 8430, pp. 215–229. Springer, Cham (2014). https://doi.org/10.1007/978-3-319-06200-6_17
5. CWE: Common weakness enumeration (2021). https://cwe.mitre.org/top25/archive/2021/2021_cwe_top25.html
6. Dietz, W., Li, P., Regehr, J., Adve, V.: Understanding integer overflow in C/C++. ACM Trans. Softw. Eng. Methodol. **25**(1), 1–29 (2015). https://doi.org/10.1145/2743019
7. ISO: ISO C Standard 1999. Technical report (1999). http://www.open-std.org/jtc1/sc22/wg14/www/docs/n1124.pdf. iSO/IEC 9899:1999 draft
8. ISO: ISO/IEC 9899:2011 Information technology – Programming languages – C. International Organization for Standardization, Geneva, Switzerland, December 2011. http://www.iso.org/iso/iso_catalogue/catalogue_tc/catalogue_detail.htm?csnumber=57853
9. Kirchner, F., Kosmatov, N., Prevosto, V., Signoles, J., Yakobowski, B.: Frama-C: a software analysis perspective. Form. Asp. Comput. **27**(3), 573–609 (2015). https://doi.org/10.1007/s00165-014-0326-7
10. Kissi, S., Seladji, Y., Ameur-Boulifa, R.: Detection of security vulnerabilities induced by integer errors. In: Proceedings of the 16th International Conference on Software Technologies - ICSOFT, pp. 177–184. INSTICC, SciTePress (2021). https://doi.org/10.5220/0010551301770184
11. Moy, Y., Bjørner, N., Sielaff, D.: Modular bug-finding for integer overflows in the large: sound, efficient, bit-precise static analysis. Technical report, MSR-TR-2009-57, May 2009. https://www.microsoft.com/en-us/research/publication/modular-bug-finding-for-integer-overflows-in-the-large-sound-efficient-bit-precise-static-analysis/
12. Muntean, P., Monperrus, M., Sun, H., Grossklags, J., Eckert, C.: IntRepair: informed repairing of integer overflows. IEEE Trans. Software Eng. **47**(10), 2225–2241 (2021). https://doi.org/10.1109/TSE.2019.2946148

The Complexity of Evaluating Nfer

Sean Kauffman$^{(\boxtimes)}$ and Martin Zimmermann

Aalborg University, Aalborg, Denmark
{seank,mzi}@cs.aau.dk

Abstract. Nfer is a rule-based language for abstracting event streams into a hierarchy of intervals with data. Nfer has multiple implementations and has been applied in the analysis of spacecraft telemetry and autonomous vehicle logs. This work provides the first complexity analysis of nfer evaluation, i.e., the problem of deciding whether a given interval is generated by applying rules.

We show that the full nfer language is undecidable and that this depends on both recursion in the rules and an infinite data domain. By restricting either or both of those capabilities, we obtain tight decidability results. We also examine the impact on complexity of exclusive rules and minimality. For the most practical case, which is minimality with finite data, we provide a polynomial time algorithm.

Keywords: Interval logic · Complexity · Runtime verification

1 Introduction

Nfer is a rule-based language and tool for event stream analysis, developed with scientists from National Aeronautics and Space Administration (NASA)'s Jet Propulsion Laboratory (JPL) to analyze telemetry from spacecraft [18–20]. Nfer rules calculate data over periods of time called intervals. Nfer compares and combines these intervals to form a hierarchy of abstractions that is easier for humans and machines to comprehend than a trace of discrete events. This differs from traditional Runtime Verification (RV) which computes language inclusion and returns verdicts. The equivalent problem for nfer, called the evaluation problem, is to determine if an interval will be present in nfer's output given a list of rules and an input trace.

The nfer syntax is based on Allen's Temporal Logic (ATL) [2] and is designed for simplicity and brevity in many contexts. When it was originally introduced, nfer was used to find false positives among warning messages from the Mars Science Laboratory (MSL), i.e., the Curiosity rover, at JPL [18]. Researchers found the language to be much more concise than the ad hoc Python scripts in common use. Nfer has also been deployed to capture disagreements between parallel Proportional-Integral-Derivative (PID) controllers in an embedded system ionizing radiation experiment [19, 26] and to locate unstable gear shifts in an autonomous vehicle [17].

This research was partly funded by the ERC Advanced Grant LASSO, the Villum Investigator Grant S4OS and DIREC, Digital Research Center Denmark.

© Springer Nature Switzerland AG 2022
Y. Aït-Ameur and F. Crăciun (Eds.): TASE 2022, LNCS 13299, pp. 388–405, 2022.
https://doi.org/10.1007/978-3-031-10363-6_26

Nfer is expressive enough for many applications and termination of the nfer monitoring algorithm has been conjectured to be undecidable [15]. The intuition for nfer undecidability is that recursion in its rules is possible and the intervals nfer computes may carry data from an infinite domain.

Despite this expressiveness, nfer's implementations have been demonstrated to be fast in practice. Both the C [16] and Scala [11] versions have been compared against tools such as LogFire and Prolog [19], Siddhi [17], MonAmi and DejaVu [12], and TeSSLa [14] and in every case found to be faster than the alternatives performing the same analysis. The question remains if nfer evaluation is indeed undecidable and, if so, if there are useful fragments of nfer with a tractable evaluation problem.

Our Contribution. In this work, we determine the complexity of evaluating different fragments of nfer. We find that any one of several restrictions on the language permit decidable evaluation and we prove tight bounds for most of these fragments.

We begin by defining a natural syntactic fragment of nfer using only inclusive rules called inc-nfer. Full nfer supports a form of negation using what are called exclusive rules, but we show that these are unnecessary to obtain undecidability. The result relies, instead, on recursion between rules and on intervals carrying data from an infinite domain. Thus, we then examine language fragments where either or both of these capabilities are restricted. We prove that, without recursion, inc-nfer evaluation is NExpTime-complete, without infinite data it is ExpTime-complete, and without either it is PSpace-complete.

We then introduce exclusive rules and examine the full nfer language. It has been openly questioned what effect negation has on the expressiveness of nfer [12]. Of note is that recursion in rules must be prohibited when exclusive rules are used. We prove that, without infinite data, adding exclusive rules has no effect and nfer evaluation remains PSpace-complete. With infinite data, however, we prove the problem is in AExpTime(poly).

Finally, we examine the effect of minimality on the complexity of nfer evaluation. Minimality is a so-called meta-constraint on the results of nfer that was a primary motivator of nfer's development, since it was discovered existing tools like Prolog struggled with such meta-constraints [19]. We show that minimality has a substantial effect on the complexity of nfer evaluation. With infinite data, we prove the problem is in ExpTime. The most common method of using nfer is with minimality and finite data, however, and we prove evaluation for this configuration is in PTime.

All proofs omitted due to space restrictions can be found in the full version [21].

Related Work. Nfer is closely related to other classes of declarative programming systems but it differs from them all in several ways. For example, a rule-based programming system modifies a database of facts [4,10]. Unlike these systems, however, nfer is monotonic and can only add intervals, not remove them. Nfer also resembles Complex Event Processing (CEP) systems where declarative rules are applied to compute information from a trace of events [5,22,28]. CEP systems do not usually include explicit notions of time or temporal relationships, though, which are central to `nfer`. In this way, `nfer` more closely resembles stream-RV systems [6–8]. Still, `nfer` is differentiated from these systems by its emphasis on temporal intervals and its ATL-based syntax.

Some research has examined the complexity of logics based on ATL, specifically Halpern and Shoham's modal logic of intervals (HS) [9]. Montanari et al. showed that the satisfiability problem for the subset of HS consisting of only *begins/begun by* and *meets* is EXPSPACE-complete over the natural numbers [25]. Later, they showed that adding the *met by* operator increases the complexity such that the language is only decidable over finite total orders [24]. Aceto et al. identified the expressive power of all fragments of HS over total orders as well as only dense total orders [1]. `Nfer` is not a modal logic, however, and these complexity results are not relevant to its evaluation problem.

2   The Inclusive Nfer Language

The `nfer` language supports two types of rules: inclusive rules and exclusive rules. This section describes the `inclusive-nfer` formalism, subsequently abbreviated `inc-nfer`, that supports only inclusive rules. `Inc-nfer` is sufficiently expressive to obtain an undecidability result and we find that initially omitting exclusive rules simplifies our presentation. `Inc-nfer` is also a natural subset of `nfer` that was first introduced in [18]. It supports many use cases, including the MSL case-study described above. The implementation of `nfer` written in Scala at JPL [11, 19] also supports only inclusive rules. We expand our analysis to include exclusive rules in Sect. 4 while Sect. 5 addresses minimality, an important extension of `nfer` semantics. Note that, to improve comprehensibility and simplify later proofs, the semantics presented here differs slightly from prior work but these changes do not affect the language capabilities.

Preliminary Notation. We denote the set of nonnegative integers as $\mathbb{N}$. The set of Booleans is given as $\mathbb{B} = \{true, false\}$. We fix a finite set $\mathcal{I}$ of identifiers. $\mathbb{M}$ is the type of maps, where a map $M \in \mathbb{M}$ is a partial function $M : \mathcal{I} \nrightarrow \mathbb{N} \cup \mathbb{B}$.

An event represents a named state change in an observed system. An event is a triple (η, t, M) where $\eta \in \mathcal{I}$ is its identifier, $t \in \mathbb{N}$ is the timestamp when it occurred, and $M \in \mathbb{M}$ is its map of data. The type of an event is given by $\mathbb{E} = \mathcal{I} \times \mathbb{N} \times \mathbb{M}$. A sequence of events $\tau \in \mathbb{E}^*$ is called a *trace*.

Intervals represent a named period of state in an observed system. An interval is a 4-tuple (η, s, e, M) where $\eta \in \mathcal{I}$ is its identifier, $s, e \in \mathbb{N}$ are the starting and ending timestamps where $s \leq e$, and $M \in \mathbb{M}$ is its map of data. The type of intervals with data is $\mathbb{I} = \mathcal{I} \times \mathbb{N} \times \mathbb{N} \times \mathbb{M}$. A set of intervals is called a *pool* and its type is given by $\mathbb{P} = 2^{\mathbb{I}}$. We say that an interval $i = (\eta, s, e, M)$ is labeled by η. We define the functions $id(i) = \eta$, $start(i) = s$, $end(i) = e$, and $map(i) = M$.

Syntax. Inclusive rules test for the existence of two intervals matching constraints. When such a pair is found, a new interval is produced with an identifier specified by the rule. The new interval has timestamps and a map derived by applying functions, specified in the rule, to the matched pair of intervals. We define the syntax of these rules, including mathematical functions to simplify the presentation, as follows:

$$\eta \leftarrow \eta_1 \oplus \eta_2 \textbf{ where } \Phi \textbf{ map } \Psi$$

where, $\eta, \eta_1, \eta_2 \in \mathcal{I}$ are identifiers, $\oplus \in \{\textbf{before}, \textbf{meet}, \textbf{during}, \textbf{coincide}, \textbf{start},$ $\textbf{finish}, \textbf{overlap}, \textbf{slice}\}$ is a *clock predicate* on three intervals (one for each of η, η_1, and η_2), $\Phi : \mathbb{M} \times \mathbb{M} \to \mathbb{B}$ is a *map predicate* taking two maps and returning a Boolean representing satisfaction of a constraint, and $\Psi : \mathbb{M} \times \mathbb{M} \to \mathbb{M}$ is a *map update* taking two maps and returning a map.

We omit the precise syntax for specifying map predicates and updates, but we require that these functions are limited to only simple arithmetic operations. This matches what is possible using the C nfer tool [14]. Specifically, map predicates and map updates must be expressible using the standard mathematical operations: addition, subtraction, multiplication, division, modulo, and the comparisons: $<, \leq, >, \geq, =$ on natural numbers, and the Boolean operators: $\wedge, \vee, \neg$. This limitation excludes exponentiation and any form of recursion in the functions. Since we do not support real numbers in the theory, division is limited to integer quotients. These decisions are discussed in Sect. 6.

Semantics. Inc-nfer defines how rules are interpreted to generate pools of intervals from inputs. The semantics utilizes functions, referenced by the rule syntax, that specify the temporal and data relationships between intervals. The semantics of the nfer language is defined in three steps: the semantics R of individual rules on pools, the semantics S of a specification (a list of rules) on pools, and finally the semantics T of a specification on traces of events.

We first define the semantics of inclusive rules with the interpretation function R. Let Δ be the type of rules. Semantic functions are defined using the brackets $[\![\_]\!]$ around syntax being given semantics.

$$R [\![\_]\!] \; : \; \Delta \to \mathbb{P} \to \mathbb{P}$$
$$R [\![\, \eta \leftarrow \eta_1 \oplus \eta_2 \textbf{ where } \Phi \textbf{ map} \Psi \,]\!] \; \pi$$
$$= \{ \, i \in \mathbb{I} \; : \; i_1, i_2 \in \pi \; . $$
$$id(i) = \eta \wedge \; id(i_1) = \eta_1 \wedge \; id(i_2) = \eta_2$$
$$\wedge \; \oplus(i, i_1, i_2) \; \wedge \; \Phi(map(i_1), map(i_2))$$
$$\wedge \; map(i) = \Psi(map(i_1), map(i_2)) \, \}$$

In the definition, a new interval i is produced when two existing intervals in π match the identifiers η_1 and η_2, the temporal constraint $\oplus$, and the map constraint Φ. $\oplus$ defines the start and end timestamps of i and Ψ defines its map.

The possibilities referenced by $\oplus$ are shown in Fig. 1. These clock predicates are based on ATL and described formally in previous definitions of nfer [18,19]. They relate two intervals using the familiar ATL temporal operators and also specify the start and end timestamps of the produced intervals. In the figure, the two matched intervals are shown as dark-gray boxes where time flows from left to right and the light-gray box is the produced interval. For example, given intervals i, i_1, i_2 where $id(i) = A$, $id(i_1) = B$ and $id(i_2) = C$, $A \leftarrow B \textbf{ meet } C$ holds when $end(i_1) = start(i_2)$, $start(i) = start(i_1)$, and $end(i) = end(i_2)$.

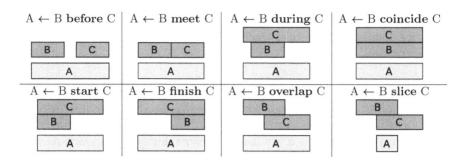

Fig. 1. nfer clock predicates for inclusive rules

The following one-step interpretation function S defines the semantics of a finite list of rules, also called a specification. Given a specification $\delta_1 \cdots \delta_n \in \Delta^*$ and a pool $\pi \in \mathbb{P}$, $S[\![\_]\!]$ returns a new pool obtained by recursively applying $R[\![\_]\!]$ to every rule in $\delta_1 \cdots \delta_n$ in order, where each is called using the union of π with the new intervals returned thus far.

$$S[\![\_]\!] \ : \ \Delta^* \to \mathbb{P} \to \mathbb{P}$$

$$S[\![\, \delta_1 \cdots \delta_n \,]\!] \ \pi \ = \ \begin{cases} S[\![\, \delta_2 \cdots \delta_n \,]\!] \ (\pi \ \cup \ R[\![\, \delta_1 \,]\!] \ \pi\,) & \textbf{if } n > 0 \\ \pi & \textbf{otherwise} \end{cases}$$

Inc-nfer specifications may contain recursion in the rules, so one application of the specification may not be sufficient to produce all of the intervals. The interpretation function $T_{\mathrm{inc}}[\![\_]\!]$ for *inc*lusive nfer defines the semantics of a specification on a pool by applying S until the inflationary fixed point is reached.

$$T_{\mathrm{inc}}[\![\_]\!] \ : \ \Delta^* \to \mathbb{P} \ \to \ \mathbb{P}$$
$$T_{\mathrm{inc}}[\![\delta_1 \cdots \delta_n]\!] \ \pi \ = \ \bigcup_{i>0} \pi_i \ . \ \pi_1 = \pi \ \wedge \ \pi_{i+1} = S[\![\, \delta_1 \ \cdots \delta_n \,]\!] \ (\pi_i)$$

To maintain consistency with prior work and simplify our presentation, we also overload $T_{\mathrm{inc}}[\![\_]\!]$ to operate on a trace of events $\tau \in \mathbb{E}^*$ by first converting τ to the pool $\{init(e) : e \text{ is an element of } \tau\}$ where $init(\eta, t, M) = (\eta, t, t, M)$.

Example 1. Here, we present an example of an inc-nfer specification with rules useful for our complexity analysis. Fix $\mathcal{I} = \{\eta_j : 0 \le j \le n\} \cup \{d\}$ and consider the specification $D_n = \delta_1 \cdots \delta_n$ where δ_j is the rule

$$\eta_{j+1} \leftarrow \eta_j \textbf{ coincide } \eta_j \textbf{ where } m_1, m_2 \mapsto m_1 = m_2 \textbf{ map } m_1, m_2 \mapsto \{d \mapsto m_1(d)^2\}.$$

Here, m_1 and m_2 denote the maps of the intervals matched by the left and right side of the coincide operator and d represents the only element in their domain.

When applying this specification to the trace $\tau = (\eta_0, 0, \{d \mapsto 2\})$ we obtain

$$T_{\mathrm{inc}}[\![D_n]\!] \ \tau = \{(\eta_0, 0, 0, \{d \mapsto 2\}), (\eta_1, 0, 0, \{d \mapsto 4\}), \ldots, (\eta_n, 0, 0, \{d \mapsto 2^{2^n}\})\}.$$

Remark 1. In many of our lower bound proofs, the timestamps of intervals are irrelevant. For the sake of readability, we will therefore often disregard the timestamps and denote intervals by $(\eta, y_0, \ldots, y_k)$ where $\{y_0, \ldots, y_k\}$ is the image of the map function of the interval. Here, we assume a fixed order of the map domain that will be clear from context.

Also, note that the rules δ_j in Example 1 produce an interval i' labeled by η_{j+1} from an interval i such that i and i' have the same timestamps and the map value of i' is obtained by squaring the map value of i. Many of the rules we use in our lower bounds proofs have this format. Again, for the sake of readability, we will not spell out those rules but instead say that the rule produces the interval (η_{j+1}, y^2) from an interval of the form (η_j, y).

We are interested in the `nfer` evaluation problem: Given a specification D, a trace τ of events, and a target identifier η_T, is there an η_T-labeled interval in $T_{inc}[\![D]\!]\tau$? Here, we measure the size of a single rule in D by the sum of the length of its map predicate and map update measured in their number of arithmetic and logical operators, with numbers encoded in binary. The size of an event is the sum of the binary encodings of its timestamps and its map values. We disregard the identifiers, as their number is bounded by the number of events in the input trace and the number of rules.

3   Complexity Results for Inclusive Nfer

In this section, we determine the complexity of the `inc-nfer` evaluation problem. In its most general form it is shown to be undecidable, but we show decidability for three natural fragments.

The undecidability result relies on the recursive nature of `inc-nfer`, i.e., an η-labeled interval can be (directly or indirectly) produced from an another η-labeled interval, and on the fact that the map functions range over the natural numbers, i.e., we have access to an infinite data domain.

Theorem 1. *The evaluation problem for* `inc-nfer` *is undecidable.*

Proof. We show how to simulate a two-counter Minsky machine [23] with `inc-nfer` rules so that the machine terminates iff an interval with a given target identifier can be generated by the rules.

Formally, a two-counter Minsky machine is a sequence

$$(0 : I_0)(1 : I_1) \cdots (k - 2 : I_{k-2})(k - 1 : \texttt{STOP}),$$

of pairs $(\ell : I_\ell)$ where ℓ is a line number and I_ℓ for $0 \leq \ell < k - 1$ is one of `INC(X`$_i$`)`, `DEC(X`$_i$`)`, or `IF X`$_i$`=0 GOTO` ℓ' with $i \in \{0, 1\}$ and $\ell' \in \{0, \cdots, k - 1\}$.

A configuration of the machine is a triple (ℓ, c_0, c_1) consisting of a line number ℓ and the contents $c_i \in \mathbb{N}$ of counter i. The semantics is defined as expected with the convention that a decrement of a zero counter has no effect. The problem of deciding whether the unique run of a given two-counter Minsky machine starting in the initial configuration $(0, 0, 0)$ reaches a stopping configuration (i.e., one of the form $(k - 1, c_0, c_1)$) is undecidable [23].

This problem is captured with `inc-nfer` as follows: We encode a configuration (ℓ, c_0, c_1) by an interval with identifier ℓ and two map values c_0, c_1. These intervals use the same timestamps so we drop them from our notation and also write (ℓ, c_0, c_1) for the interval encoding that configuration.

For every line number $0 \leq \ell < k - 1$ we have one or two rules that are defined as follows (here, we only consider $i = 0$, the rules for $i = 1$ are analogous):

- $I_\ell = \text{INC}(X_0)$: We have a rule producing the interval $(\ell + 1, c_0 + 1, c_1)$ from an interval of the form (ℓ, c_0, c_1)..
- $I_\ell = \text{DEC}(X_0)$: We have two rules, one producing the interval $(\ell + 1, c_0 - 1, c_1)$ from an interval of the form (ℓ, c_0, c_1) with $c_0 > 0$, and one producing the interval $(\ell + 1, c_0, c_1)$ from an interval of the form (ℓ, c_0, c_1) with $c_0 = 0$.
- $I_\ell = \text{IF } X_0\text{=0 GOTO } \ell'$: We have two rules, one producing the interval (ℓ', c_0, c_1) from an interval of the form (ℓ, c_0, c_1) with $c_0 = 0$, and one producing the interval $(\ell + 1, c_0, c_1)$ from an interval of the form (ℓ, c_0, c_1) with $c_0 > 0$.

Then, we have an interval labeled by $k - 1$ in the fixed point iff the machine reaches a stopping configuration.   □

As already discussed, the undecidability relies both on recursion in the rules and on the map functions having an infinite range. In the following, we show that restricting one of these two aspects allows us to recover decidability. In fact, we give tight complexity bounds for all three fragments. We continue by introducing some necessary notation to formalize these two restrictions.

First, recall that a map of an interval is a partial function from $\mathcal{I}$ to $\mathbb{N} \cup \mathbb{B}$, i.e., it has an infinite range. We will consider the evaluation problem restricted to intervals with maps that are partial functions from $\mathcal{I}$ to $\{0, 1, \ldots, k - 1\} \cup \mathbb{B}$ with a *bound* k given in binary and all arithmetic operations performed modulo k. We denote the fixed point resulting from these semantics by $T_{\text{inc}}^k[\![\_]\!]$.

Second, for a rule $\eta \leftarrow \eta_1 \oplus \eta_2$ **where** Φ **map** Ψ we say that η appears on the left-hand side and the η_i appear on the right-hand side. An `inc-nfer` specification $D \in \Delta^*$ forms a directed graph $G(D)$ over the rules in D such that there is an edge from δ to δ' iff there is an identifier η that appears on the left-hand side of δ and the right-hand side of δ'. We say that D contains a cycle if $G(D)$ contains one; otherwise D is cycle-free.

We begin our study of decidable fragments of `inc-nfer` by considering both restrictions at the same time.

Theorem 2. *The cycle-free `inc-nfer` evaluation problem with finite data is* PSPACE-*complete.*

Proof. We only prove the lower bound here, the upper bound is shown for full `nfer` in Theorem 5. We proceed by a reduction from TQBF, the problem of determining whether a formula of quantified propositional logic evaluates to true (see, e.g., [3] for a detailed definition), which is PSPACE-hard. So, fix such a formula φ. Let π_j for $j \geq 1$ denote the j-th prime number. We assume without loss of generality that $\varphi = Q_2 x_2 Q_3 x_3 \cdots Q_{\pi_n} x_{\pi_n} \bigwedge_{i=1}^{m} (\ell_{i,1} \vee \ell_{i,2} \vee \ell_{i,3})$ where each Q_{π_j} is in $\{\exists, \forall\}$, and each $\ell_{i,i'}$ is either x_{π_j} or $\neg x_{\pi_j}$ for some j. As we label variables by prime numbers, we can uniquely identify a variable valuation $V \subseteq \{x_{\pi_j} : 1 \leq j \leq n\}$ by the number $\prod_{x_{\pi_j} \in V} \pi_j$. As the map values we will consider only have to encode valuations, and are therefore bounded by $\prod_{j \leq n} \pi_j$, we can use the bound $1 + \prod_{j \leq n} \pi_j$ on the map values we consider.

We present three types of rules:

1. Rules to *generate* every possible variable valuation (encoded by an interval whose map contains the number representing the valuation).
2. A rule to *check* whether a valuation satisfies $\bigwedge_{i=1}^{n} (\ell_{i,1} \vee \ell_{i,2} \vee \ell_{i,3})$.
3. Rules to simulate the quantifier prefix to check whether the full formula evaluates to true.

Let us explain all steps in detail. As all intervals in this proof will have the same timestamps, we will drop those to simplify our notation. Furthermore, the map of an interval will contain a single integer value. For these reasons, we denote intervals by (η, s) where η is an identifier and s is the map value.

To generate the valuations, we start with the trace containing only a single fixed event that yields the interval $(G_0, 1)$. Further, for $1 \leq j \leq n$ we have rules producing the intervals $(G_j, s \cdot \pi_j)$ and (G_j, s) from an interval of the form (G_{j-1}, s) for some s. The fixed point reached by applying these rules contains the 2^n intervals of the form (G_n, s) where s encodes a variable valuation.

In the valuation encoded by some s, a variable x_{π_j} evaluates to true if $s \bmod \pi_j = 0$ and evaluates to false if $s \bmod \pi_j \neq 0$. Hence, to check whether the valuation encoded by some s satisfies $\bigwedge_{i=1}^{m} (\ell_{i,1} \vee \ell_{i,2} \vee \ell_{i,3})$ we have a rule that produces the interval (C_k, s) from an interval of the form (G_k, s) for some s such that $\bigwedge_{i=1}^{m} (\psi_{i,1} \vee \psi_{i,2} \vee \psi_{i,3})$ evaluates to true, where $\psi_{i,i'}$ is equal to $s \bmod \pi_j = 0$ if $\ell_{i,i'} = x_{\pi_j}$, and where $\psi_{i,i'}$ is equal to $s \bmod \pi_j > 0$ if $\ell_{i,i'} = \neg x_{\pi_j}$.

We now simulate the quantifier prefix. Intuitively, we check whether partial variable valuations cause the formula to hold. We do so by the following rules: If the variable x_{π_j} is existentially quantified, we have a rule producing the interval (C_{j-1}, s) from an interval of the form (C_j, s) with $s \bmod \pi_j > 0$, and a rule producing the interval $(C_{j-1}, s/\pi_j)$ from an interval of the form (C_j, s) with $s \bmod \pi_j = 0$. So, to generate an interval labeled by C_{j-1} at least one interval labeled by C_j has to exist, and their maps must be compatible.

Finally, if the variable x_{π_j} is universally quantified, we have a rule producing the interval (C_{j-1}, s) from two intervals of the form (C_j, s) and $(C_j, s \cdot \pi_j)$ (which can be done using a **coincide**-rule). Thus, to obtain an interval labeled by C_{j-1} both intervals labeled by C_j with corresponding map values have to exist.

An induction shows that a partial valuation $V \subseteq \{x_{\pi_j} : 1 \leq j \leq n'\}$ for some $0 \leq n' \leq n$ satisfies $Q_{\pi_{n'+1}} x_{\pi_{n'+1}} \cdots Q_{\pi_n} x_{\pi_n} \bigwedge_{i=1}^{m} (\ell_{i,1} \vee \ell_{i,2} \vee \ell_{i,3})$ iff the interval $(C_{n'}, \prod_{x_{\pi_j} \in V} \pi_j)$ is generated by applying these rules. So, for $n' = 0$ we obtain the correctness of our reduction: The formula φ evaluates to true iff $(C_0, 1)$ is in the fixed point induced by the rules above.

Furthermore, the rules above are cycle-free, there are linearly many rules in the number n of variables and each rule is of polynomial size in the size of φ.

Finally, as $\pi_j \leq j(\ln j + \ln\ln j)$ for all $j \geq 6$ [27], all numbers appearing in the maps of the intervals are bounded by

$$\prod\nolimits_{j=1}^{n} \pi_j \leq c \cdot \prod\nolimits_{j=1}^{n} j(\ln j + \ln\ln j) \leq c \cdot (n(\ln n + \ln\ln n))^n$$

whose binary representation is polynomial in the size of φ. Here, c is some constant that is independent of n.   □

Now, we turn our attention to the remaining two fragments obtained by considering finite-data with cycles and cycle-free specifications with infinite data. In both cases, we again prove tight complexity bounds. For both upper bounds, we rely on algorithms searching for witnesses for the existence of an interval in the fixed point. As these arguments are used in multiple proofs, we introduce them first in a general format. So, fix some specification D and some trace τ of events. If i is an interval in $T_{\mathrm{inc}}\llbracket D \rrbracket\, \tau$, then either there is an event e in τ such that $init(e) = i$ (we say that i is initial in this case) or there are intervals i_1, i_2 in $T_{\mathrm{inc}}\llbracket D \rrbracket\, \tau$ and a rule $\delta \in D$ such that i is obtained by applying δ to i_1 and i_2. So, for every interval i_0 in $T_{\mathrm{inc}}\llbracket D \rrbracket\, \tau$ there is a binary (witness) tree whose nodes are labeled by intervals in $T_{\mathrm{inc}}\llbracket D \rrbracket\, \tau$, whose root is labeled by i_0, whose leaves are labeled by initial intervals, and where the children of a node labeled by i are labeled by i_1 and i_2 such that there is a rule δ so that i is obtained by applying δ to i_1 and i_2. Further, we can assume without loss of generality that each path in the tree does not contain a repetition of an interval (if it does we can just remove the part of the tree between the repetitions). Hence, the height of the tree is bounded by the number of intervals. Furthermore, if D is cycle-free then the height of a witness tree is also bounded by the number of rules in D. Note that the same arguments also apply to $T_{\mathrm{inc}}^{k}\llbracket D \rrbracket\, \tau$ in case we deal with finite data.

Proposition 1. *An interval is in $T_{\mathrm{inc}}\llbracket D \rrbracket\, \tau$ ($T_{\mathrm{inc}}^{k}\llbracket D \rrbracket\, \tau$) iff it has a witness tree.*

We continue by settling the case of specifications with cycles, but restricted to finite data.

Theorem 3. *The* `inc-nfer` *evaluation problem with finite data is* ExpTime-*complete.*

Proof. We first prove the lower bound by reducing from the word problem for alternating polynomial space Turing machines (see, e.g., [3] for detailed definitions). As ExpTime = APSpace, this yields the desired lower bound. Thus, fix an alternating polynomial space Turing machine $\mathcal{M}$, i.e., there is some polynomial p such that $\mathcal{M}$ uses at most space $p(|w|)$ when started on input w. Let us also fix some input w for $\mathcal{M}$. We construct an instance of `inc-nfer` that simulates a run of $\mathcal{M}$ on w. To simplify our construction, we make some assumptions (all without loss of generality):

– The set Q of states of $\mathcal{M}$ is of the form $\{1, 2, \ldots, q\}$ for some $q \in \mathbb{N}$ and 1 is the initial state.

- The tape alphabet Γ of $\mathcal{M}$ is equal to $\{0, 1, \ldots, 9\}$ and 0 is the blank symbol.
- Every run tree of $\mathcal{M}$ has only finite branches, i.e., $\mathcal{M}$ terminates on every input. To this end, we assume the existence of a set of terminal states, which is split into accepting and rejecting ones.
- Every nonterminal configuration (one with a nonterminal state) has exactly two successor configurations. Such states are either existential or universal.

So, a configuration of $\mathcal{M}$ is of the form $\ell q r$ with $q \in Q$ and $\ell, r \in \Gamma^*$ such that $|\ell| + |r| = p(|w|)$, with the convention that the head is on the first letter of r.

For $c \in \Gamma^*$, let c^R denote the reverse of c. Due to our assumption on Γ we can treat ℓ and r^R as natural numbers encoded in base ten. We uniquely identify a configuration $\ell q r$ by the triple (ℓ, q, r^R) of natural numbers. The initial configuration of $\mathcal{M}$ on w is encoded by the triple $(0, 1, w^R)$ representing that the tape to the left of the head has only blanks, the machine is in the initial state 1, and w is to the right of the head with the remaining cells of the tape being blank.

This encoding allows us to read the tape cell the head is currently pointing to, update the tape cell the head is pointing to, and move the head by simple arithmetic operations. For example, whether the head points to a cell containing a 3 is captured by $r^R \bmod 10$ being 3, and writing a 7 to the cell pointed to by the head is captured by adding $-(r^R \bmod 10) + 7$ to r^R. Finally, moving the head to, say, the right, is captured by multiplying ℓ by 10 and then adding $r^R \bmod 10$ to it, and then dividing r^R by 10 (which is done without remainder and therefore removes the last digit of r^R). In the following, we use intervals of the form (A, ℓ, q, r^R) to encode the configuration $\ell q r$ of $\mathcal{M}$. Here, A is some identifier and we disregard timestamps, as all intervals have the same start and end. Hence, ℓ, q, and r^R are three map values of the interval.

We now describe the rules simulating $\mathcal{M}$ on w. We start with some fixed event that yields the interval $(G, 0, 1, w^R)$ encoding the initial configuration. As described above, the computation of a successor configuration can be implemented using arithmetic operations. Thus, given the interval encoding the initial configuration, one can write rules (one for each transition of $\mathcal{M}$) that generate the set of all configurations, encoded as intervals of the form (G, ℓ, q, r^R). Furthermore, one can write a rule that produces the interval (A, ℓ, q, r^R) from every interval (G, ℓ, q, r^R) with an accepting q.

Now, we describe rules to compute the set of accepting configurations, i.e., the smallest set A of configurations that contains all those with an accepting terminal state, all existential ones that have a successor in A, and all universal ones that have both successors in A. For every transition t from an existential state q, there is a rule to produce the interval (A, ℓ, q, r^R) if the intervals (G, ℓ, q, r^R) and $(A, \ell', q', r^{R'})$ already exist, where $(\ell', q', r^{R'})$ encodes the configuration obtained by applying the transition t to the configuration encoded by (ℓ, q, r^R). Thus, to declare an existential configuration as accepting at least one of its successor configurations has to be already declared as accepting.

Now, let us consider universal configurations. Due to our assumption, for every pair of a state and a tape symbol, there are exactly two transitions t_1 and t_2 that are applicable. There are two rules for this situation. The first one

---

Algorithm 1. Algorithm checking the existence of a witness tree

---

Input: Specification D, trace τ, bound k, target identifier η_T
1: $n := 0$
2: **nondeterministically guess** interval i labeled by η_T
3: **while** $n < b(D, \tau, k)$ **and** i is not initial **do**
4:     $n := n + 1$
5:     **nondeterministically guess** intervals i_1, i_2 and $\delta \in D$ such that i is obtained
        by applying δ to i_1 and i_2
6:     **universally pick** $i := i_j$ for $j \in 1, 2$
7: **if** i is initial **then return** accept
8: **else return** reject

---

produces the interval (B, ℓ, q, r^R) if the intervals (G, ℓ, q, r^R) and $(A, \ell', q', r^{R'})$ already exist, where $(\ell', q', r^{R'})$ encodes the configuration obtained by applying the transition t_1 to the configuration encoded by (ℓ, q, r^R). The second one produces the interval (A, ℓ, q, r^R) if the intervals (B, ℓ, q, r^R) and $(A, \ell', q', r^{R'})$ already exist, where $(\ell', q', r^{R'})$ encodes the configuration obtained by applying the transition t_2 to the configuration encoded by (ℓ, q, r^R). Thus, to declare a universal configuration as accepting both of its successor configurations have to be already declared as accepting.

Finally, there is a rule producing an interval with identifier η_T from the interval $(A, 0, 1, w^R)$, indicating that the initial configuration is accepting. Thus, the fixed point contains an interval labeled by η_T iff $\mathcal{M}$ accepts w.

It remains to show that the specification has the required properties. It is of polynomial size and each rule has polynomial size (both measured in $|\mathcal{M}| + |w|$). Further, all numbers used in the intervals are bounded by $\max\{|Q|, 10^{p(|w|)}\}$, whose binary representation is bounded polynomially in $|\mathcal{M}| + |w|$.

Now, we prove the upper bound. We are given a specification D, an input trace τ of events, a $k \in \mathbb{N}$ (given in binary), and a target label η_T and have to determine whether the fixed point $T_{inc}^k[\![D]\!] \tau$ contains an interval labeled by η_T. We describe an alternating polynomial space Turing machine solving this problem by searching for a witness tree. APSPACE = EXPTIME yields the result.

To this end, we rely on the following properties.

1. Every interval in $T_{inc}^k[\![D]\!] \tau$ can be stored in polynomial space, as every value in its map can be stored using $\log k$ bits, and there are only linearly many such values (measured in $|D| + |\tau|$).
2. There are only exponentially many intervals in $T_{inc}^k[\![D]\!] \tau$, e.g.,

$$b(D, \tau, k) = \iota \cdot t^2 \cdot k^{|D|+|\tau|} \leq \iota \cdot |\tau|^2 \cdot 2^{(\log k)(|D|+|\tau|)}$$

   is a crude upper bound. Here, ι is the number of identifiers appearing in D and τ and t is the number of timestamps in τ (recall that `inc-nfer` does not create new timestamps).
3. Given three intervals i, i_1, i_2 and a rule $\delta \in D$ one can determine in polynomial space whether i is obtained by applying δ to i_1 and i_2.

Using alternation, Algorithm 1 determines whether a witness tree exists whose root is labeled by η_T and whose height is bounded by b. Due to Proposition 1, this is equivalent to an interval labeled by η_T being in $T_{\text{inc}}^k[\![D]\!]\,\tau$. Due to the above properties, one can easily implement the algorithm on an alternating polynomial space Turing machine, yielding the desired upper bound. $\qquad\square$

Finally, we consider the last fragment: cycle-free specifications with infinite data. A crucial aspect here is that cycle-free specifications imply an upper bound on the map values of intervals in the fixed point, as each interval in the fixed point can be generated by applying each rule at most once. For the lower bound, we generate *large* numbers using a set of cycle-free rules and encode configurations using these numbers as before.

Theorem 4. *The cycle-free* `inc-nfer` *evaluation problem with infinite data is* NExpTime-*complete.*

4   The Full Nfer Language

This section introduces the second type of `nfer` rules, called *exclusive rules*, that test for the existence of one interval and the absence of another interval matching constraints. These rules were introduced in [19] and they, together with inclusive rules, complete the `nfer` language. We define the syntax of these rules, including mathematical functions to simplify the presentation, as follows:

$$\eta \leftarrow \eta_1 \textbf{ unless } \ominus \eta_2 \textbf{ where } \Phi \textbf{ map } \Psi$$

where, $\eta, \eta_1, \eta_2 \in \mathcal{I}$ are identifiers, $\ominus \in \{\textbf{after}, \textbf{follow}, \textbf{contain}\}$ is a *clock predicate* on two intervals (one for each of η_1 and η_2), and Φ and Ψ are the same as in inclusive rules. We say that an exclusive rule *includes* η_1 and *excludes* η_2.

Exclusive rules share many features with inclusive rules but they require additions to the `inc-nfer` semantics that were omitted in Sect. 2 for brevity. Notably, these changes to the semantics produce equivalent results when evaluating inclusive rules. The following definition gives semantics to exclusive rules:

$$
\begin{aligned}
R\,[\![\,\eta &\leftarrow \eta_1 \textbf{ unless } \ominus \eta_2 \textbf{ where } \Phi \textbf{ map } \Psi\,]\!]\,\pi \\
&= \{\,i \in \mathbb{I} \;:\; i_1 \in \pi \;.\;\; id(i) = \eta \wedge id(i_1) = \eta_1 \\
&\qquad\quad \wedge\; start(i) = start(i_1) \wedge end(i) = end(i_1) \\
&\qquad\quad \wedge\; map(i) = \Psi(map(i_1),\{\;\}) \\
&\qquad\quad \wedge\; \neg\,(\,\exists\; i_2 \in \pi \;.\;\; id(i_2) = \eta_2 \\
&\qquad\qquad\quad \wedge\; \ominus(i_1, i_2) \wedge \Phi(map(i_1), map(i_2))\,)\,\}
\end{aligned}
$$

Like with inclusive rules, exclusive rules match intervals in the input pool π to produce a pool of new intervals. The difference is that exclusive rules produce new intervals where one existing interval in π matches the identifier η_1 and no intervals exist that match the identifier η_2 such that the clock predicate $\ominus$ and the map predicate Φ hold for the η_1-labeled and the η_2-labeled interval.

The three possibilities referenced by $\ominus$ are shown in Fig. 2. These clock predicates are based on ATL and described formally in a previous definition

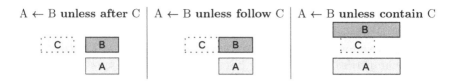

Fig. 2. nfer clock predicates for exclusive rules

of nfer [19]. They relate two intervals using familiar ATL temporal operators while the timestamps of the produced interval are copied from the included interval rather than being defined by the clock predicate. In the figure, the excluded interval labeled C is shown as a rectangle with a dotted outline and the produced interval labeled A is always the same as the included interval labeled B. For example, given intervals i, i_1, i_2 where $id(i) = A$, $id(i_1) = B$ and $id(i_2) = C$, $A \leftarrow B$ **unless follow** C holds when $end(i_2) = start(i_1)$, $start(i) = start(i_1)$, and $end(i) = end(i_1)$.

Exclusive rules are forbidden in specifications with cycles because the intervals they produce depend on the persistent non-existence of other intervals. When cycles exist in a specification, rules are evaluated multiple times and each evaluation may add intervals. Exclusive rules may have non-deterministic behavior in a specification with cycles because the intervals they exclude may be produced either before or after the exclusive rule is evaluated. The order in which rules are evaluated may also affect the result of applying exclusive rules for this reason, which motivates a generalization of the $T_{\mathrm{inc}}[\![\_]\!]$ (resp. $T_{\mathrm{inc}}^k[\![\_]\!]$) function.

$$T_{\mathrm{full}}\,[\![\_]\!] \; : \; \Delta^* \to \mathbb{P} \to \mathbb{P}$$

$$T_{\mathrm{full}}\,[\![\,\delta_1 \cdots \delta_n\,]\!]\,\pi = \begin{cases} S\,[\![\,topsort(\delta_1 \cdots \delta_n)\,]\!]\,(\pi) & \textbf{if } \exists\; topsort(\delta_1 \cdots \delta_n) \\ T_{\mathrm{inc}}\,[\![\,\delta_1 \cdots \delta_n\,]\!]\,(\pi) & \textbf{otherwise} \end{cases}$$

where *topsort* is a topological sort of the directed graph $G(D)$ described in Sect. 3 and $T_{\mathrm{inc}}[\![\_]\!]$ is the interpretation function defined in Sect. 2. A topological sort, which can be computed in linear time [13], only exists in a cycle-free specification. In that case, *topsort* orders the rules such that the fixed-point computation of $T_{\mathrm{inc}}[\![\_]\!]$ can be short-circuited, since one application of $S[\![\_]\!]$ is sufficient to produce the final pool. The results of $T_{\mathrm{full}}[\![\_]\!]$ are independent of the topological sort, as any such ordering will guarantee that all intervals matched by a rule exist before it is applied using $R[\![\_]\!]$.

In the following, we study the complexity of the cycle-free nfer evaluation problem with finite and infinite data, starting with the former.

Theorem 5. *The cycle-free* nfer *evaluation problem with finite data is* PSPACE-*complete.*

Proof. The lower bound already holds for the special case of inc-nfer (see Theorem 2), so we only need to prove the upper bound. To this end, we show how to witness in alternating polynomial time that a given interval is in the fixed point, which yields the desired bound due to APTIME = PSPACE. Note that we cannot just search for a witness tree as for `inc-nfer`, as we also have to handle exclusive rules.

Intuitively, an exclusive rule requires the existence of one interval in the fixed point and the non-existence of other intervals in the fixed point. We have seen how to capture existence of an interval via the existence of a witness tree. Hence, we can capture the non-existence of an interval via the non-existence of a witness tree. As we construct an alternating algorithm, we use duality to capture the non-existence of a witness tree and switch between an existential and a universal mode every time the non-existence of an interval is to be checked.

As in Algorithm 1, the algorithm keeps track of a single interval and applies rules in a backwards fashion. Using alternation, it guesses and verifies a tree structure witnessing the (non-)existence of intervals in the fixed point. To simulate exclusive rules, it uses a Boolean flag f to keep track of the parity of the number of exclusive rules that have been simulated, initialized with zero. If f is zero, then a rule δ is guessed nondeterministically. If this rule is inclusive, two intervals i_1 and i_2 are guessed nondeterministically such that the current interval i is obtained from i_1 and i_2 by applying δ. Then, the current interval is updated by universally picking $i := i_1$ or $i := i_2$, so that both choices are checked. This case is similar to Algorithm 1.

On the other hand, if the rule is exclusive, then a single interval i_1 is guessed nondeterministically and another interval i_2 is picked universally so that δ includes i_1, excludes i_2, and i is the result of applying δ to i_1. Now, the current interval is updated by universally picking $i := i_1$ or $i := i_2$, so that both choices are checked. In the second case, the flag is toggled to signify that another exclusive rule is simulated.

In the case where f is equal to one, the approach is just dual, i.e., we switch existential and universal choices. As the input specification is cycle-free, we need to simulate at most $|D|$ applications of a rule. Finally, acceptance depends on whether the value of the flag, i.e., while the flag is zero the last interval has to be initial (i.e., in the input trace) while it has to be non-initial if the flag is one.

The algorithm runs in alternating polynomial time as each run simulates at most $|D|$ rule applications and each application can be implemented in deterministic polynomial time due to the encodings of the map values and time stamps being bounded by $|D| + |\tau|$.   □

Finally, we consider the case of infinite data. Here, the upper bound we obtain is AEXPTIME(poly), the class of problems decided by alternating exponential-time Turing machines with a polynomial number of alternations between existential and universal states.

Theorem 6. *The cycle-free* `nfer` *evaluation problem with infinite data is* NEXPTIME-*hard and in* AEXPTIME*(poly).*

5   Minimality

This section discusses the *minimality* restriction and its implications on the complexity of the `nfer` evaluation problem. Traditionally, `nfer` supports the concept

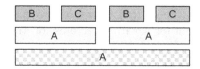

Fig. 3. Minimality discards the checkered interval produced by $A \leftarrow B$ **before** C

of a *selection function* that may modify the results of $R[\![\_]\!]$ [19]. The reason is to support minimality, which filters any intervals that are not minimal in their timestamps. Although minimality was originally introduced for its utility [18], it has positive implications for evaluation complexity as well.

Figure 3 shows the effect of minimality on the evaluation of a single rule. In the figure, time moves from left to right and the dark-gray intervals are the inputs to $R[\![A \leftarrow B \text{ \textbf{before} } C \text{ \textbf{where} } true \text{ \textbf{map} } \{ \ \}]\!]$. This evaluation produces the three intervals labeled A but minimality discards the longer interval with a checkerboard pattern because there are shorter A intervals in the same period.

Given a pool π of existing intervals and a pool π' of intervals to add, the **minimality** function returns only the minimal intervals in π' that do not subsume any interval in π. That is, the intervals where there is not another interval with the same identifier with a shorter duration during the same time. No new intervals will be produced with the same identifier and timestamps when one already exists in π. If there are multiple intervals with the same identifier and the same timestamps in π', the one with the least map is retained (with respect to some fixed ordering of maps). We define minimality as the following:

$$\textbf{minimality} : \mathbb{P} \times \mathbb{P} \to \mathbb{P}$$
$$\textbf{minimality} \, (\pi', \pi)$$
$$= \{(\eta, s, e, M) \in \pi' : \nexists(\eta, s_1, e_1, M_1) \in \pi . \ s \le s_1 \wedge e_1 \le e\}$$
$$\cap \{(\eta, s, e, M) \in \pi' : \nexists(\eta, s_2, e_2, M_2) \in \pi' . \ (s \le s_2 \wedge e_2 < e) \vee (s < s_2 \wedge e_2 \le e)\}$$
$$\cap \{(\eta, s, e, M) \in \pi' : \nexists(\eta, s_3, e_3, M_3) \in \pi' . \ s = s_3 \wedge e = e_3 \wedge M_3 \prec M\}$$

where $\prec$ is a total order over $\mathbb{M}$ used as a tiebreaker when more than one new intervals exist in π' with equal identifiers and timestamps.

For the **nfer** evaluation problem under minimality we replace $R[\![\_]\!]$ in the semantics with an interpretation function that applies **minimality** to the result of $R[\![\_]\!]$.

$$R_{min}[\![\_]\!] : \Delta \to \mathbb{P} \to \mathbb{P}$$
$$R_{min}[\![\delta]\!] \, \pi = \textbf{minimality} \, (R[\![\delta]\!]\pi, \pi)$$

Theorem 7. *The* **nfer** *evaluation problem with finite data and minimality is in* PTIME.

Proof. Consider an instance with specification D, trace τ, and bound k on the map values. Due to minimality, the size of $T_{full}^k[\![D]\!] \tau$ is bounded by $(\iota \cdot t^2) + |\tau|$, where ι is the number of identifiers in D and τ and t is the number of timestamps in τ. Note that this bound is independent of k.

Also, map values and timestamps can be represented with polynomially many bits in the size of D and τ. Hence, we can compute $T_{\text{full}}^{k}[\![D]\!]\,\tau$ and check whether it contains an interval labeled by the target identifier in polynomial time.   □

A similar approach works for infinite data.

Theorem 8. *The* nfer *evaluation problem with infinite data and minimality is in* ExpTime.

6   Discussion and Conclusion

We have studied the complexity of the nfer evaluation problem. It is undecidable in the presence of recursion and infinite data, even without exclusive rules. In contrast, regardless of the presence of exclusive rules, the evaluation problem is decidable for cycle-free specifications or with respect to finite data. Most importantly for applications, the problem is in PTime if we impose the minimality constraint and restrict to finite data. While we only allow natural numbers and Booleans as map values, our upper bounds also hold for more complex data types, i.e., signed numbers, (fixed-precision) floating point numbers, and strings, which were included in the original definitions [18,19].

Most of our complexity bounds are tight, but we leave two gaps. First, the cycle-free nfer evaluation problem with infinite data is NExpTime-hard and in AExpTime(poly). Recall that the lower bound already holds for inc-nfer, i.e., without exclusive rules, while the polynomial number of alternations in the upper bound are used to simulate exclusive rules (our algorithm requires one alternation per exclusive rule). One approach to close this gap is to capture alternations of a Turing machine using exclusive rules.

Secondly, the nfer evaluation problem with infinite data and minimality is in ExpTime while no nontrivial lower bounds are known. The upper bound follows from the fact that the map values may be of doubly-exponential size, i.e., they require exponential time to be computed. However, minimality is a very restrictive constraint that in particular severely limits the ability to simulate nondeterministic computations. Coupled with the fact that minimality implies a polynomial upper bound on the number of intervals in the fixed point, this explains the lack of a nontrivial lower bound.

All our lower bound proofs only use intervals with the same timestamps, i.e., the complexity stems from the manipulation of data instead of temporal reasoning. Similarly, the upper bound proofs are mostly concerned with encoding of data and the temporal reasoning is trivial. One of the reasons is that nfer rules do not create new timestamps for intervals; newly created intervals can only use timestamps that already appear in the input trace. This leaves only a polynomial number of combinations of start points and end points, which is (at least) exponentially smaller than the number of data values. For this reason, we propose to investigate data-free nfer to analyze the complexity of the evaluation problem with respect to the choice of temporal operators. In this case, there are only polynomially many possible intervals in the fixed point. So, a trivial upper bound on the complexity is PTIME, but we expect better results for fragments.

Another interesting fragment is the combination of cycles and exclusive rules. As long as exclusive rules lie outside cycles the deterministic semantics can be defined. In the full version of this paper [21] we show that this fragment has an EXPTIME-complete evaluation problem when restricted to finite data.

References

1. Aceto, L., Della Monica, D., Goranko, V., Ingólfsdóttir, A., Montanari, A., Sciavicco, G.: A complete classification of the expressiveness of interval logics of Allen's relations: the general and the dense cases. Acta Inform. **53**(3), 207–246 (2015). https://doi.org/10.1007/s00236-015-0231-4

2. Allen, J.F.: Maintaining knowledge about temporal intervals. Commun. ACM **26**(11), 832–843 (1983)

3. Arora, S., Barak, B.: Computational Complexity: A Modern Approach, 1st edn. Cambridge University Press, USA (2009)

4. Barringer, H., Havelund, K.: TRACECONTRACT: a scala DSL for trace analysis. In: Butler, M., Schulte, W. (eds.) FM 2011. LNCS, vol. 6664, pp. 57–72. Springer, Heidelberg (2011). https://doi.org/10.1007/978-3-642-21437-0_7

5. Chen, J., DeWitt, D.J., Tian, F., Wang, Y.: NiagaraCQ: a scalable continuous query system for internet databases. In: International Conference on Management of Data (ACM SIGMOD 2000), pp. 379–390. ACM (2000). https://doi.org/10.1145/342009.335432

6. Convent, L., Hungerecker, S., Leucker, M., Scheffel, T., Schmitz, M., Thoma, D.: TeSSLa: temporal stream-based specification language. In: Massoni, T., Mousavi, M.R. (eds.) SBMF 2018. LNCS, vol. 11254, pp. 144–162. Springer, Cham (2018). https://doi.org/10.1007/978-3-030-03044-5_10

7. Faymonville, P., Finkbeiner, B., Schwenger, M., Torfah, H.: Real-time stream-based monitoring (2019)

8. Hallé, S.: When RV meets CEP. In: Falcone, Y., Sánchez, C. (eds.) RV 2016. LNCS, vol. 10012, pp. 68–91. Springer, Cham (2016). https://doi.org/10.1007/978-3-319-46982-9_6

9. Halpern, J.Y., Shoham, Y.: A propositional modal logic of time intervals. J. ACM **38**(4), 935–962 (1991). https://doi.org/10.1145/115234.115351

10. Havelund, K.: Rule-based runtime verification revisited. Int. J. Softw. Tools Technol. Transfer **17**(2), 143–170 (2014). https://doi.org/10.1007/s10009-014-0309-2

11. Havelund, K.: Git repository (2022). `git@github.com:rv-tools/nfer.git`. Accessed January 2022

12. Havelund, K., Omer, M., Peled, D.: Monitoring first-order interval logic. In: Calinescu, R., Păsăreanu, C.S. (eds.) SEFM 2021. LNCS, vol. 13085, pp. 66–83. Springer, Cham (2021). https://doi.org/10.1007/978-3-030-92124-8_4

13. Kahn, A.B.: Topological sorting of large networks. Commun. ACM **5**(11), 558–562 (1962). https://doi.org/10.1145/368996.369025

14. Kauffman, S.: `nfer` – a tool for event stream abstraction. In: Calinescu, R., Păsăreanu, C.S. (eds.) SEFM 2021. LNCS, vol. 13085, pp. 103–109. Springer, Cham (2021). https://doi.org/10.1007/978-3-030-92124-8_6

15. Kauffman, S.: Runtime monitoring for uncertain times. Ph.D. thesis, University of Waterloo, Department of Electrical and Computer Engineering, Waterloo, ON, Canada (2021). http://hdl.handle.net/10012/16853

16. Kauffman, S.: Website (2022). http://nfer.io/. Accessed January 2022

17. Kauffman, S., Dunne, M., Gracioli, G., Khan, W., Benann, N., Fischmeister, S.: Palisade: a framework for anomaly detection in embedded systems. J. Syst. Architect. **113**, 101876 (2021). https://doi.org/10.1016/j.sysarc.2020.101876

18. Kauffman, S., Havelund, K., Joshi, R.: **nfer** – a notation and system for inferring event stream abstractions. In: Falcone, Y., Sánchez, C. (eds.) RV 2016. LNCS, vol. 10012, pp. 235–250. Springer, Cham (2016). https://doi.org/10.1007/978-3-319-46982-9_15

19. Kauffman, S., Havelund, K., Joshi, R., Fischmeister, S.: Inferring event stream abstractions. Formal Methods Syst. Design **53**(1), 54–82 (2018). https://doi.org/10.1007/s10703-018-0317-z

20. Kauffman, S., Joshi, R., Havelund, K.: Towards a logic for inferring properties of event streams. In: Margaria, T., Steffen, B. (eds.) ISoLA 2016. LNCS, vol. 9953, pp. 394–399. Springer, Cham (2016). https://doi.org/10.1007/978-3-319-47169-3_31

21. Kauffman, S., Zimmermann, M.: The complexity of evaluating nfer. arXiv:2202.13677 (2022)

22. Luckham, D.: The power of events: an introduction to complex event processing in distributed enterprise systems. In: Bassiliades, N., Governatori, G., Paschke, A. (eds.) RuleML 2008. LNCS, vol. 5321, p. 3. Springer, Heidelberg (2008). https://doi.org/10.1007/978-3-540-88808-6_2

23. Minsky, M.L.: Computation. Prentice-Hall, Englewood Cliffs (1967)

24. Montanari, A., Puppis, G., Sala, P.: Maximal decidable fragments of Halpern and Shoham's modal logic of intervals. In: Abramsky, S., Gavoille, C., Kirchner, C., Meyer auf der Heide, F., Spirakis, P.G. (eds.) ICALP 2010. LNCS, vol. 6199, pp. 345–356. Springer, Heidelberg (2010). https://doi.org/10.1007/978-3-642-14162-1_29

25. Montanari, A., Puppis, G., Sala, P., Sciavicco, G.: Decidability of the interval temporal logic ABB over the natural numbers. In: Proceedings of STACS 2010. pp. 597–608. Schloss Dagstuhl - Leibniz-Zentrum für Informatik (2010). https://hal.archives-ouvertes.fr/hal-00717798

26. Narayan, A., et al.: System call logs with natural random faults: experimental design and application. In: International Workshop on Silicon Errors in Logic - System Effects (SELSE 2017). SELSE-13, IEEE (2017)

27. Rosser, B.: Explicit bounds for some functions of prime numbers. Am. J. Math. **63**(1), 211–232 (1941). http://www.jstor.org/stable/2371291

28. Suhothayan, S., Gajasinghe, K., Loku Narangoda, I., Chaturanga, S., Perera, S., Nanayakkara, V.: Siddhi: a second look at complex event processing architectures. In: Workshop on Gateway Computing Environments (GCE 2011), pp. 43–50. ACM (2011). https://doi.org/10.1145/2110486.2110493

Supporting Algorithm Analysis with Symbolic Execution in Alk

Alexandru-Ioan Lungu and Dorel Lucanu[(⊠)]

Alexandru Ioan Cuza University, Iaşi, Romania
dlucanu@info.uaic.ro

Abstract. Alk is an educational platform designed for writing, executing, and analyzing algorithms. The platform consists of an algorithmic language, an interpreter able to execute algorithms, and tools to understand, analyse, and evaluate algorithms, and to acquire a rigorous algorithm thinking. In this paper, we present Alk and show how the analysis and evaluation tools are built using symbolic execution and data-flow analysis.

1 Introduction

Alk is an educational platform designed for writing, executing, and analyzing algorithms. To have a taste of Alk, we consider the algorithm described in Fig. 1 using Alk Language [15,16]. This algorithm can be executed as it is using the Alk interpreter (we suppose it is stored in the file fstalg.alk):

```
$ alki -a fstalg.alk -m -i "a |-> [1,2,2,3,3,3] "
a |-> [1, 2, 2, 3, 3, 3]
slp |-> 3
i |-> 6
```

where the value of the option -i describes the initial state of the algorithm execution, which consists of a single variable a having as value the array [1,2,2,3,3,3]. When the initial state is complex, it could be included in a file, given then as the value for the option -i. The option -m is for displaying the final state. In this way we see the execution of the algorithm as a process transforming the initial state into the final state; how the input is encoded in the initial state and the output is extracted from the final state is a different story.

```
slp = 1;
i = 1;
while (i < a.size())
{
  if (a[i] == a[i - slp])
  slp = slp+1;
  i = i + 1;
}
```

Fig. 1. An algorithm in Alk

In this paper we describe the tools included in the Alk platform that help the user in analyzing, evaluating, and understanding algorithms. These tools are based on three main features implemented in Alk:

symbolic execution helped by *data-flow analysis* and *abstract interpretation*.

© Springer Nature Switzerland AG 2022
Y. Aït-Ameur and F. Crăciun (Eds.): TASE 2022, LNCS 13299, pp. 406–423, 2022.
https://doi.org/10.1007/978-3-031-10363-6_27

The analysis of the algorithms raises several challenges that must be addressed.

Perhaps the most important challenge is what analysis mechanisms are suitable for understanding the algorithm behavior and acquiring a rigorous algorithmic thinking. How to discover what an algorithm computes? How to understand loops and what properties a loop preserves? How to reason when an algorithm is used by another one? How to evaluate the execution time of an algorithm?

There are also several language-dependent challenges. As we can see in Fig. 1, the Alk language does not include variable declarations. In order to analyze an algorithm, the types for the variables used in that algorithm must be known and they can be found using data-flow analysis. Another examples where the data-flow analysis is useful include the set of variables modified by a loop statement (e.g., to check loop invariants) and worst case execution time analysis (to find out recurrences). The size of arrays in Alk is dynamic. For instance, given an assignment `a[7] = z;`, the only information about size we know is that it is greater than or equal to 8. This can be easily handled for concrete executions, but becomes problematic when the array is specified as a theory for a SMT solver (see [17] for such a theory). Alk includes also statements for describing non-deterministic or randomized algorithms. If the analysis of the non-deterministic algorithms is similar to that of deterministic ones, the randomized algorithms require other means, which are out of the scope of this paper.

Symbolic execution is used by almost all analysis tools and methods. A symbolic execution interpreter of a language can be obtained from the concrete execution one [2,14]. However, its implementation requires the extension of the language definition with symbolic values, an interface to a external prover (e.g., SMT solver), and a set of annotations, e.g., for algorithm specification, loop invariants, state invariants, initializing some variables with fresh symbolic values, loop upper bounds for the execution time analysis.

Contribution. The main contributions of this paper include:

1. A description of the algorithmic language Alk, including its extension to handle symbolic executions. The symbolic extension is mainly based on the approach presented in [2,14], but taking into account the specificity of the Alk language and its implementation [15].
2. We show how experiments performed using the symbolic execution can help a user to understand what a piece of an algorithm computes. For instance, we may experimentally discover what a loop executes.
3. Once we make a presumption on what a loop computes, we may use invariants to check if the presumption is valid. The verification of the invariant is accomplished by symbolic execution and a SMT solver (Z3, [9]).
4. We use a (pre/post)-condition specification of an algorithm in order to understand how it is used by other algorithms. Usually, this kind of specification is for the problem solved by the algorithm. Here we use it only for understanding some properties of the data computed by an algorithm.
5. We show that a data-flow analysis and symbolic execution (based on an abstract semantics of the language) can be used to derive recurrences helping

to evaluate the execution time of an algorithm. This is work in progress, but the experiments we have done up to now are promising.

Even if some analysis means presented are strongly related to algorithm/program verification, the focus of this paper is not on verification. In order to verify an algorithm, a complete formal specification of the problem is needed, and that depends on the problem domain. In most cases, the annotation language must be extended with statements that express concepts and relations in the problem domain.

Related Work. There are similarities between Alk and Python: both are dynamically typed languages, use similar data structures, and work based on an interpreter. Python is a language created for a more general purpose: web development, software development, mathematics, system scripting, and so on. So, only a kernel of Python has to be used as an algorithmic language, which is fine for simple deterministic algorithms. For non-deterministic algorithms or randomized algorithms, external libraries must be used, and the algorithms must be instrumented in order to compute, e.g., the probability of a computation. The Alk interpreter detects if an execution is randomized and automatically start to compute the probability. Also, for a non-deterministic algorithm it may display all possible results. In order to analyse algorithms in Python, external tools must be used. For instance, for checking invariants for Python programs can be used Nagini [10], which based on the Viper infrastructure [18].

The implementation of the Alk platform follows the methodology and the logical foundation promoted by the K Framework [6,7], including the formal definition of the language and the analysis components. The verification is implemented using reachability logic [14,21] and the annotation language is the usual one used by program verifiers, e.g., Dafny [13], Why3 [5], Frama-C [12], JML [11], Key [1], Verifast [22], etc. However, Alk uses a minimal set annotations since the focus is the algorithm understanding and not full verification. The implementation of the data-flow analysis and abstract interpretation components follows a classic approach [8,19,20]. The time analysis component is inspired from [4] and combined with symbolic computation [3].

Structure of the Paper: Section 2 introduces the Alk language together with its concrete and symbolic semantics. Section 3 shows how the symbolic execution of algorithms can be used to understand what an algorithm computes. Section 4 shows how the invariants can be used to understand the behavior of loops and how this invariants are checked using symbolic execution. The specification of Alk algorithms and the use of these specifications is presented in Sect. 5. Section 6 presents a case study of symbolically estimating the execution time of an algorithm. Finally, Sect. 7 ends the paper with some concluding remarks.

2   Alk - An Educational Algorithmic Language/Framework

What is the best language for writing, testing and analyzing algorithms, and helpful in acquiring an algorithmic thinking? Most of the textbooks use a pseudocode for writing algorithms. A pseudocode is a mix between a set of statements with a precise semantics (code) and text written with a free syntax and intuitive semantics (pseudo). A requirement, which is almost always omitted, is that the text with free syntax must be able to be translated into code, such that we can get a full formal description of the algorithm, if needed. Obviously, the algorithm described in pseudocode cannot be tested/executed and the analysis is semi-formal. Some textbooks are presenting algorithms as programs in a programming language, e.g., Pascal, C, C++, Java, Python, etc. These algorithms can be tested and formally analyzed. A main drawback of such an approach is that the algorithm design techniques (and algorithmic thinking) must be learned at the same time with the use of the programming language, which also could be a strong challenging task. Moreover, many times a big part of the effort is oriented towards the implementation of the needed data structures, their testing, and only after that to the algorithm description in the terms of the implemented data structure. The testing is not always easy, because there are needed routines for reading input data and for writing the output results. The analysis of the algorithms requires the use of additional specialized tools.

What properties should have a suitable algorithmic language? We think that the following features are essential for an algorithmic language (the order is arbitrary).

1. *To have a formal definition for both the syntax and the semantics.* The syntax should be as simple as possible, expressive, and intuitive, including the main algorithmic thinking structures. The semantics of a programming language can be given using various paradigms, e.g., operational, axiomatic, denotational, at different abstraction levels. For an algorithm oriented language, the best choice is an operational semantics at an abstract level that help the algorithmic thinking, the understanding of the execution of the algorithms, and to supply a computation model suitable for analysis.
2. *To be executable such that the algorithms or fragments of them can be tested in an easy and flexible way.* Having a formal definition, it should be easy to implement an interpreter.
3. *To include means for relating an algorithm to the problem solved by it.* This can be achieved, e.g., by suitable data structures and annotations.
4. *To offer support for algorithm analysis and algorithm thinking.* This should also be based on the formal definition and incorporated in a natural way.
5. *To allow to describe various kind of algorithms (e.g., deterministic, non-deterministic, probabilistic).* This feature should be supported by a natural component of the algorithm oriented language, in contrast with using external structures.

The main purpose of this paper is to show how Alk fulfills the requirements 1 (formal definition) and 4 (algorithm analysis and algorithm thinking). In this section we briefly present its syntax and semantics.

```
bubbleSort(out a)
@requires a.size() > 0
{
    last = a.size()-1;
    while (last > 0)
    {
        n1 = last;
        for (i = 0; i < n1; ++i)
        {
            last = askIth(a, i);
        }
    }
}

bubbleSort(b);
```

```
swap(out a, i, j)
@requires 0 <= i && i < a.size() &&
          0 <= j && j < a.size()
{
    temp=a[i]; a[i]=a[j]; a[j]=temp;
}

askIth(out a, i)
@requires a.size() > 1 &&
          0 <= i && i < a.size()-1
{
    if (a[i] > a[i+1]) {
        swap(a, i, i+1);
        return i;
    }
    return 0;
}
```

Fig. 2. Bubble Sort in Alk

2.1 Syntax

The syntax of the Alk language is very simple, similar to the imperative part of C or Java. We do not include its formal definition here, which is intuitive, and we use instead examples to get its flavor. Figure 2 shows a typical description of algorithms in Alk. The algorithm bubbleSort proceeds by asking for inversions (successive element in wrong order) and solving them until no more inversions are found (and the array is sorted). The variable last stores the position of the last inversion. Some operations of the algorithm are described as separated algorithms. The last line is for testing the algorithm. There are no variable declarations, so that the algorithm can be executed as well on integers, floats, or strings:

```
$ alki -a bubblesort.alk -m -i "b |-> [2, 3, 1]"
b |-> [1, 2, 3]
$ alki -a bubblesort.alk -m -i "b |->  [1.2, 1.5, 1.4]"
b |-> [1.2, 1.4, 1.5]
$ alki -a bubblesort.alk -m -i "b |-> [\"ab\", \"ac\", \"aa\"]"
b |-> ["aa", "ab", "ac"]
```

The annotations @requires are only informative here for the concrete executions, but they could be easily transformed into run-time verification assertions (not implemented yet). Later, we show how this kind of annotations are used for static analysis.

Remark 1. In order to save space, we often use mathematical notation in annotations. Examples: $a \wedge b$ instead of a && b, or $a \leq b \leq c$ instead of a <= b && b <= c. We also interchangeably use the notions of algorithm and that of Alk program.

Alk algorithms may process complex data structures without using special definition for them. Here is a directed graph D and its description as an Alk value:

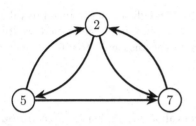

```
D |-> {
         V -> [2, 5, 7]
         adj -> {
                  2 |-> < 5, 7 >
                  5 |-> < 2, 7 >
                  7 |-> < 2 >
                 }
      }
```

The Alk value D is a structure with two fields: $D.\mathsf{V}$ (for vertices) and $D.\mathsf{adj}$ (for arcs given by the external adjacency lists), where $D.\mathsf{V}$ is an array and $D.\mathsf{adj}$ is a map having the elements of $D.\mathsf{V}$ as keys and the corresponding the external adjacency lists as values. Here is the Alk recursive description of the DFS algorithm:

```
dfsRec(out D, i, out S) {
  if (!(i in S)) {
    // visit i
    S = S U {i};
    foreach j from D.adj[i]
      dfsRec(D, j, S);
  }
}
```

2.2   Semantics

A *concrete configuration* is a pair $\langle \kappa \rangle \langle \sigma \rangle$, where κ is the code/algorithm to be executed and σ is the current state. Since we want the algorithms to be described at an abstract level, independent on the value representation, a state σ is modeled as a map from the algorithm variables to their values. The set of possible values for variables includes integers, Booleans, floats, strings, structures (records), arrays, lists, maps, sets, and any combination of these. We write $\langle \kappa \rightsquigarrow \ldots \rangle \langle \ldots \sigma \ldots \rangle$ when we want to emphasize the first piece κ of code to be evaluated/executed in the next step and the part σ of the state that is used in evaluating/executing κ. The semantics is given by rules of the form

$$\langle \kappa \rightsquigarrow \ldots \rangle \langle \ldots \sigma \ldots \rangle \Rightarrow \langle \kappa' \rightsquigarrow \ldots \rangle \langle \ldots \sigma' \ldots \rangle \ \text{ if } \psi$$

where κ and σ may include meta-variables, and ψ is a condition. The syntax of rules is inspired from the K Framework (see, e.g., [6,7]) and the set of such rules completely describes the operational semantics of the language. Here are three examples of rules, describing the semantics of the assignment operator and of the if statement:

$$\langle X = V \rightsquigarrow \kappa \rangle \langle \sigma \rangle \qquad\qquad \Rightarrow \quad \langle V \rightsquigarrow \kappa \rangle \langle \sigma[X \mapsto V] \rangle$$

$$\langle \text{if } true \ S_1 \text{ else } S_2 \rightsquigarrow \kappa \rangle \langle \sigma \rangle \quad \Rightarrow \quad \langle S_1 \rightsquigarrow \kappa \rangle \langle \sigma \rangle$$

$$\langle \text{if } false \ S_1 \text{ else } S_2 \rightsquigarrow \kappa \rangle \langle \sigma \rangle \quad \Rightarrow \quad \langle S_2 \rightsquigarrow \kappa \rangle \langle \sigma \rangle$$

The right-hand side of the assignment and the if condition are reduced to values by similar rules. The meta-variable κ is for the remaining code to be executed. Non-deterministic algorithms are written using the choose X from C statement, having the following semantics:

$$\langle \text{choose } X \text{ from } CV \rightsquigarrow \kappa \rangle \langle \sigma \rangle \quad \Rightarrow \quad \langle \kappa \rangle \langle \sigma[X \mapsto V] \rangle$$

where CV is a "container value" (obtained by evaluating C), V is a value *arbitrarily* chosen from CV, and $\sigma[X \mapsto V]$ is σ but where the new value of X is V. The randomized algorithms are described using various probabilistic distributions, like uniform X from C with the semantics:

$$\langle \text{uniform } X \text{ from } CV \rightsquigarrow \kappa \rangle \langle \sigma \rangle \langle prob \rangle \quad \Rightarrow \quad \langle \kappa \rangle \langle \sigma[X \mapsto V] \rangle \left\langle prob \cdot \frac{1}{CV.size()} \right\rangle$$

where V is a value *uniformly* chosen from CV. Note that for probabilistic algorithms, the configuration is extended with a new "cell" storing the probability of the execution path.

2.3 Concrete and Symbolic Executions

A *concrete execution* is a sequence of execution steps

$$\langle \kappa_0 \rangle \langle \sigma_0 \rangle \Rightarrow \langle \kappa_1 \rangle \langle \sigma_1 \rangle \Rightarrow \langle \kappa_2 \rangle \langle \sigma_2 \rangle \Rightarrow \dots$$

where κ_0 is the initial algorithm and σ_0 is the initial state. An execution step is obtained by applying a semantic rule.

A *symbolic configuration* is a triple $\langle \kappa \rangle \langle \sigma \rangle \langle pc \rangle$[1], where κ is the symbolic code/algorithm to be executed, σ is the current symbolic state, and pc is the path condition. Symbolic code and symbolic states are similar to concrete ones, but where the values can be symbolic expressions built with symbolic logical variables, operators from the definition of Alk, and possible new logical functions. Symbolic code may also include annotations that can declare and/or constraint the use of symbolic values (we will see later some examples). As for concrete configurations, we write $\langle k \rightsquigarrow \dots \rangle \langle \dots \sigma \dots \rangle \langle pc \rangle$ to emphasize only the components involved in the next step. A *symbolic execution* is a sequence of execution steps

$$\langle k_0 \rangle \langle \sigma_0 \rangle \langle pc_0 \rangle \Rightarrow \langle k_1 \rangle \langle \sigma_1 \rangle \langle pc_1 \rangle \Rightarrow \langle k_2 \rangle \langle \sigma_2 \rangle \langle pc_2 \rangle \Rightarrow \dots$$

where all path conditions are satisfiable (this is checked with a SMT solver, e.g., Z3). The semantic execution steps are obtained by applying rules of the form

$$\langle \boldsymbol{\kappa} \rightsquigarrow \dots \rangle \langle \dots \boldsymbol{\sigma} \dots \rangle \langle \mathbf{pc} \rangle \Rightarrow \langle \boldsymbol{\kappa'} \rightsquigarrow \dots \rangle \langle \dots \boldsymbol{\sigma'} \dots \rangle \langle \mathbf{pc'} \rangle \ \text{if } \psi$$

---

[1] The symbolic execution is given only for non-randomized algorithms.

```
@requires ∀i:int•
   0 ≤ i < a.size()-1 → a[i] ≤ a[i+1];
slp = 1;
i = 1;
while (i < a.size())
{
   if (a[i] == a[i - slp])
   slp = slp+1;
   i = i + 1;
}
```

```
@havoc(a: array<int>);
@assume ∀i:int•
   0 ≤ i < a.size()-1 → a[i] ≤ a[i+1];
@assume a.size() == 3;
slp = 1;
i = 1;
while (i < a.size())
{
   if (a[i] == a[i - slp])
   slp = slp+1;
   i = i + 1;
}
```

Plateau1   Plateau2

Fig. 3. Different versions of Plateau

which are automatically obtained from the concrete ones [2,14]. Here the symbolic counterparts of the concrete rules presented in the previous section:

$$\langle X = V \rightsquigarrow \kappa \rangle \langle \sigma \rangle \langle pc \rangle \qquad \Rightarrow \qquad \langle V \rightsquigarrow \kappa \rangle \langle \sigma[X \mapsto V] \rangle \langle pc \rangle$$
$$\langle \text{if } B \; S_1 \text{ else } S_2 \rightsquigarrow \kappa \rangle \langle \sigma \rangle \langle pc \rangle \qquad \Rightarrow \qquad \langle S_1 \rightsquigarrow \kappa \rangle \langle \sigma \rangle \langle pc \wedge B \rangle$$
$$\langle \text{if } B \; S_1 \text{ else } S_2 \rightsquigarrow \kappa \rangle \langle \sigma \rangle \langle pc \rangle \qquad \Rightarrow \qquad \langle S_2 \rightsquigarrow \kappa \rangle \langle \sigma \rangle \langle pc \wedge \neg B \rangle$$
$$\langle \text{choose } X \text{ from } SCV \rightsquigarrow \kappa \rangle \langle \sigma \rangle \langle pc \rangle \qquad \Rightarrow \qquad \langle \kappa \rangle \langle \sigma[X \mapsto ?V] \rangle \langle pc \wedge ?V \in SCV \rangle$$

where B is now a symbolic value (expression), SCV is a symbolic "container value", and $?V$ is a fresh symbolic variable (implicitly considered existentially quantified).

3 Understanding Algorithms by Experimentation

Consider the algorithm Plateau1 in Fig. 3 (left) and assume that we want to find out what is computed in the variable slp. One possibility is to test the algorithm for various inputs. For instance, executing the algorithm with the initial state a $\mapsto [1, 2, 3]$, the final state will include slp $\mapsto 1$. This answer does not say too much to us. Instead, we may use symbolic execution to find out what conditions should satisfy a for a given value of slp. We added to the Alk language two annotations that allows us to symbolically execute algorithms: @havoc$(X:T)$;, which assigns a fresh symbolic value of type T to the variable X, and @assume ϕ;, which adds to the path condition the constraint ϕ. Executing symbolically the algorithm Plateau2 in Fig. 3 (right), with the initial path condition a.size() == 3 stated by the @assume annotation and analyzing the path condition from the final states, we get the following information:

1. slp $\mapsto$ 3 if ($a[1]==$a[0]) $\wedge$ ($a[2]==$a[0]);
2. slp $\mapsto$ 1if !($a[1]==$a[0]) $\wedge$!($a[2]==$a[1]);
3. slp $\mapsto$ 2 if ($a[1]==$a[0]) $\wedge$!($a[2]==$a[0])$\vee$!($a[1]==$a[0]) $\wedge$ $a[2]==$a[1]).

Now it is easy to guess that slp stores the length of the longest array segment of equal elements (plateau).

We explain now how the above information is obtained. The symbolic execution is considering some assumptions stated using @assume by appending them into an initial path condition. Each time the while loop is reached, the i < a.size() condition is evaluated and the execution is split. The first generated branch assumes that the condition does not hold and continues with the code after the while statement, while the second generated branch assumes that the condition holds and executes the statements inside the loop.

The symbolic execution of loops usually leads to infinite executions. This is why, in the previous example, there is a constraint on a.size() to be equal to 3, which bounds the number of executions:

$$
\begin{array}{ccc}
 & !(1 < a.size()) & \\
init & & !(2 < a.size()) \\
 & 1 < a.size() & \\
 & & 2 < a.size() \longrightarrow !3 < a.size()
\end{array}
$$

Furthermore, the execution splitting is also happening on the if statement. One branch assumes the equality of two elements in the array, while the other presumes that two elements are not equal. These assumptions are reflected in the path condition:

$$
\begin{array}{ccc}
 & !(\$a[1] == \$a[2]) \longrightarrow slp \mapsto 1 \\
!(\$a[0] == \$a[1]) & \\
 & \$a[1] == \$a[2] \longrightarrow slp \mapsto 2 \\
init & \\
 & !(\$a[0] == \$a[2]) \longrightarrow slp \mapsto 2 \\
\$a[0] == \$a[1] & \\
 & \$a[0] == \$a[2] \longrightarrow slp \mapsto 3
\end{array}
$$

The user can also add assertions to check if the algorithm is satisfying a post condition. The annotation for an assertion is of the form @assert ψ; and its symbolic execution determines if the provided property ψ is implied by the current path condition.

4   Understanding Loops

The use of invariants can help to check if the intended behavior of an iterative structure is the same to that described in the algorithmic language. Consider again the algorithm from Fig. 3. In Sect. 3 we presumed that slp stores the length of the longest plateau. Now we can check that using an appropriate invariant, as it is suggested in Fig. 4 (left). The invariant explains in fact what kind of value is stored by the variable slp at the beginning and at the end of the body of the while loop, for each iteration.

Alk interpreter is able to check the invariant by symbolic execution of the annotated algorithm and to eliminate the concern of endless symbolic executions due to the lack of constraints over loop conditions. When an invariant is defined,

```
while (i < a.size())
  @invariant ∀k:int ::
    ∀l:int• i <= a.size() ∧
    (0 <= k ∧ k <= l ∧
     l < i ∧ a[k] == a[l]
     ⇒
     (l-k) <= slp);
  @modifies slp, i;
{
  if (a[i] == a[i - slp])
    slp = slp+1;
  i = i + 1;
}
```

```
@havoc(i: int);
@havoc(slp: int);
@assume ψ ∧ i < a.size();
if (a[i] == a[i - slp]) slp = slp+1;
i = i + 1;
@assert ψ;
```

Invariant annotation

Invariant checking by symbolic execution
(the first branch)

Fig. 4. Plateau3

the Alk interpreter simply splits the symbolic execution. The first branch tries to validate the invariant by executing the loop body, while the second one manages the code after the while statement, assuming the invariant and the negated condition. An example of the first branch is In Fig. 4 (right), which includes the algorithm that is symbolically executed to check the invariant, where ψ is the invariant from the left hand side: the execution of the loop body starts from a symbolic state satisfying the invariant and the condition, and at the end the invariant is checked again. If this process ends successfully, Alk considers the invariant as verified. Otherwise, it warns the user that the used invariant couldn't be verified. A description of the second branch, which continues the execution assuming that while loop was executed, is shown in Fig. 5: the execution of while is abstracted by checking that initially the invariant holds, assigning fresh

```
while (i < a.size())
  @invariant ψ;
  @modifies slp, i;
{
  if (a[i] == a[i - slp])
    slp = slp+1;
  i = i + 1;
}
x = slp;
```

```
@assert ψ
@havoc(i: int);
@havoc(slp: int);
@assume ψ ∧ !(i < a.size());
x = lsp;
```

Invariant annotation

Symbolic execution of the while loop
(the second branch)

Fig. 5. Plateau4

symbolic values to the variable modified by the invariant, and assuming the invariant and the negation of the `while` loop.

There is also a data-flow analysis component that at this stage can compute the set of variables changed inside a loop body. This system is built based on the support of data-flow framework inside Alk. Overall, the `modifies` annotation can be generated if none is already specified. This process is taking place in the preprocessing stage, so there is no prior symbolic execution, so no proper context. It takes advantage of the fact that the current configuration is symbolic and tries to inject the `modifies` annotations, while taking care of semantics equivalence.

The steps described above are summarized by the following rules:

$$\left\langle \begin{array}{l} \texttt{while}\ (E) \\ \quad \texttt{@invariant}\psi; \\ \quad S \rightsquigarrow \kappa \end{array} \right\rangle \langle\sigma\rangle \langle pc\rangle \Rightarrow \left\langle \begin{array}{l} \texttt{while}\ (E) \\ \quad \texttt{@invariant}\psi; \\ \quad -\ MV; \\ \quad S \rightsquigarrow \kappa \end{array} \right\rangle \langle\sigma\rangle \langle pc\rangle$$

$$\left\langle \begin{array}{l} \texttt{while}\ (E) \\ \quad \texttt{@invariant}\ \psi; \\ \quad \texttt{@modifies}\ MV; \\ \quad S \rightsquigarrow \kappa \end{array} \right\rangle \langle\sigma\rangle \langle pc\rangle \Rightarrow \left\langle \begin{array}{l} \texttt{@havoc}(MV); \\ \quad \texttt{@assume}\ \psi \wedge E; \\ \quad S; \\ \quad \texttt{@assert}\ \psi; \end{array} \right\rangle \langle\sigma\rangle \langle pc\rangle$$

$$\Rightarrow \left\langle \begin{array}{l} \texttt{@assert}\ \psi; \\ \quad \texttt{@havoc}(MV); \\ \quad \texttt{@assume}\ \psi \wedge \neg E; \rightsquigarrow \kappa \end{array} \right\rangle \langle\sigma\rangle \langle pc\rangle$$

The first rule correspond to the program transformation given by the data-flow analysis component (and therefore we used a different arrow), and the last two rules to the two branches generated: the invariant checking and the symbolic execution of the program that follows after the looping structure.

Writing invariants is not always an easy task. More commonly, one specifies what property is expected after the loop is finished. For instance, for the plateau example, we expect that `slp` to store the length of the longest plateau and this can be specified as in Fig. 6 (left). Then, the symbolic interpreter should automatically derive the invariant and check it as in Fig. 6 (right). Finally, the invariant and the negation of the loop condition should imply the `loopassert` condition:

$$\left\langle \begin{array}{l} \texttt{while}\ (E) \\ \quad S \\ \quad \texttt{@loopassert}\ \phi; \\ \rightsquigarrow \kappa \end{array} \right\rangle \langle\sigma\rangle \langle pc\rangle \Rightarrow \left\langle \begin{array}{l} \texttt{while}\ (E) \\ \quad \texttt{@invariant}\ \psi; \\ \quad \texttt{@modifies}\ MV; \\ \quad S \rightsquigarrow \kappa \end{array} \right\rangle \langle\sigma\rangle \langle pc \wedge (\psi \wedge \neg E) \implies \phi\rangle$$

The idea behind this feature is to allow the interpreter itself to determine the invariant based on an assertion preferred by users non-familiar with invariants. The transformation shows that Alk should find ψ which together with the negated condition imply the provided assertion ϕ.

```
while (i < a.size())
{
  if (a[i] == a[i - lg])
    lg = lg+1;
  i = i + 1;
}
@loopassert (∀k:int ::
  ∀l:int•
    0 <= k∧k <= l∧
    l < a.size∧a[k] == a[l]
    ⇒
    (l-k) <= lg);
```

```
while (i < a.size())
  @invariant (∀k:int ::
  ∀l:int•
    0 <= k∧k <= l∧
    l < i∧a[k] == a[l]
    ⇒
    (l-k) <= lg);
  @modifies lg, i;
{
  if (a[i] == a[i - lg])
    lg = lg+1;
  i = i + 1;
}
```

Loop assert annotation   Invariant annotation

Fig. 6. Loop assertion

5   Understanding the Use of Algorithms

Alk language has support for understanding algorithms as functions from input states that satisfy certain properties (known as precondition) to output states that satisfy certain properties (known as postcondition). Similar to verification languages, Alk includes the annotation @requires for specifying the precondition and the annotation @ensures for postcondition. The pairs of these annotations are also known as *contracts* and they help in a correct use simpler algorithms as "sub-algorithms" in more complex algorithms. In this section we explain how these annotations are handled by the symbolic execution.

Technically, the Alk interpreter parses the whole algorithm and identifies the functions that should be verified. It identifies the ones which have at least one @ensures annotation and it starts the verification process. Once a function is fully verified, the calls will not execute the function body, but they make use of the pre-conditions and post-conditions which were previously validated.

The pre-conditions should hold at the start of the function call, which means that it is safe to assume them before verifying the body statements. Obviously, this step and the ones to come should work on freshly generated symbolic values for each parameter in use. This means that Alk uses a @havoc statement for all parameters (i.e. input, output, global uses and global modifies).

The challenge here is to determine the data type of each parameter, as the path condition should keep track of these details in order to make use of the SMT solver. We extended the annotation language by allowing to express type constraints for some variable. For instance, in Fig. 7, the parameter a of the function askIth is constrained to have the type array<int> by the first @requires annotation. This kind of annotations are not required when a type-inference analysis component can determine the type of parameters from the function

```
askIth(out a, i)
@requires a: array<int>
@requires i: int
@requires a.size() > 0∧0 <= i∧
    i < a.size()-1
@ensures a[i] <= a[i+1]
@ensures \result  > 0 ⇒ \result  == i
@ensures \result : int
{
  if (a[i] > a[i+1]) {
    temp = a[i];
    a[i] = a[i+1];
    a[i+1] = temp;
    return i;
  }
  return 0;
}
```

```
@havoc(a:array<int>);
@assume a.size() > 0∧0 <= i ∧
    i < a.size()-1;
if (a[i] > a[i+1]) {
  temp = a[i];
  a[i] = a[i+1];
  a[i+1] = temp;
  \result  = i;
}
\result  = 0;
@assert a[i] <= a[i+1] ∧
    \result  > 0 ⇒ \result  == i
```

Specification of `askIth()`   Its checking by symbolic execution

Fig. 7. Pre/post-condition specification

body[2]. Similarly, the return type can be specified using ensures annotations for \result, when it cannot be computed by the type inference component. After the type of parameters are known, a new thread with the following initial symbolic configuration is generated in order to check the function body against its specification:

$$
\begin{array}{l}
F(LP, \text{out } OP) \\
\quad \text{uses } IGV \\
\quad \text{modifies } MGV \\
\quad \text{@requires } \phi \\
\quad \text{@ensures } \psi \\
\quad S
\end{array}
\Rightarrow
\left\langle
\begin{array}{l}
\text{@havoc}(MGV, IGV, OP, LP); \\
\text{@havoc}(\backslash\text{result}); \\
\text{@assume } \phi; \\
S[(\backslash\text{result} = R];)/(\text{return } R;);] \\
\text{@assert } \psi;
\end{array}
\right\rangle
\langle \sigma \rangle \langle pc \rangle
$$

LP is the list of the "call-by-value" parameters, OP the list of out parameters defined outside function, IGV the set of the uses global variables that are used in the function body and not modified, and MGV the list of the modifies global variables used that are modified by the function body. The @havoc annotations initialize the parameters with fresh symbolic values. Each return statement is replaced by an assignment of the reserved variable \result. Any loop invariant and/or assertion in the function body S (if any) are validated using the approach presented in the previous sections. Finally, the post-condition should be asserted in order to ensure that the user defined annotations are validated.

---

[2] This is work in progress and it is also data-flow-based.

The function calls are no longer executing the function body statements, but makes use of the validated conditions:

$$\langle F(VS) \rightsquigarrow \kappa \ \rangle \langle \sigma \rangle \langle pc \rangle \Rightarrow \left\langle \begin{array}{l} \texttt{@assert } \phi; \\ \texttt{@havoc}(MGV, IGV, OP, -); \\ \texttt{@assume } \psi; \\ \texttt{\textbackslash result} \rightsquigarrow \kappa \end{array} \right\rangle \langle \sigma \rangle \langle pc \rangle$$

At first, the pre-conditions should be asserted in order to make sure the initial assumptions hold. Afterwards, only the variables which are to be changed in the function body are actually assigned to fresh symbolic values and are constrained by the post-conditions. While evaluating the post-conditions, the returning value of the function is in fact the symbolic value assigned to the special variable \result, in order to consider the right constraints. An example is shown in Fig. 8, where $result_0 is the symbolic value of the variable \result.

```
@symbolic $a : int;
a = $a;
@assume a.size() > 3;
last = askIth(a, 2);
```

```
@assert a.size() > 0 ∧ 0 <= 2 ∧
        2 < a.size() - 1;
@havoc(a:array<int>);
@assume(a[2] <= a[3] ∧
        $result_0 > 0 ⇒ $result_0 == 2);
last = $result_0;
```

Call of askIth()   Using function specifications

Fig. 8. Verified function call

6   Hints for Estimating Execution Time

The Alk interpreter has an internal data-flow framework implemented which helps developing different kind of analysis tools. For instance, it can be successfully executed against Live Variables and Constant Propagation systems, which are used to analyze an algorithm.

A data-flow framework is a mechanism over which analysis tools can be created. Such approach is easy to use as it allows a consistent interface across all analyzers. This framework will also aid the implementation of several static tools required for the previous features like identifying the variables modified in a loop or identifying the data type of a variable.

Worst Case Execution Time (WCET) estimation analysis tool[3] is inspired from [4] and it is based on the data-flow analysis that consists of the following components:

– **CFG:** this is a forward analysis and it uses the original control flow graph.

---

[3] This tool is under development and it reached a state in which it can display recurrence formulas for each variable modified inside a loop statement.

- **Lattice domain:** consists of execution path sets and the inclusion relation. An execution path consists of an environment and a path condition. A set of execution paths is also called a program context.
- **Transfer function:** this function is applied over all execution paths inside a program context. A simple statement is symbolically evaluated, an if statement modifies the path condition and a loop statement *virtualizes* the execution path updating the path condition.
- **Initialization function:** all CFG node states are initialized with the empty program context, excluding the input node which is initialized with a singleton program context containing the initial execution path.

The *virtualization* process, used by the transfer function, means that all variables are reassigned a virtual symbolic value representing the state at the beginning of a generic loop iteration t. For this matter, each loop statement is mapped to an indexed name used by the virtual value. For example, t_{l0} is the index of an iteration of loop l0. This technique is used in order to fit the data-flow constraints. That is, there is no need to generate a new execution path for each loop body execution, otherwise there is no proper fix-point to satisfy the data-flow prerequisites. Even if this tool limits itself to one single execution of a loop body, the information about how the variables are changed is insightful enough.

```
@havoc(n : int);
sum = 0;
i = 1;
while (@count(i <= n))
{
    sum = sum + i;
    i = i + 1;
}
```

Fig. 9. Operation annotation

The @count annotation is pre-processed and it is replaced by an incrementation operation on a fresh variable. This is used in order to identify which operations should be considered when computing the WCET. For the algorithm in Fig. 9, the WCET tool identifies a single loop which captures three variables: sum, i and n. In this example, the while condition evaluation is counted. Because there is only one loop, the recurrence formulae are omitting the l0 quantifier. Here are the computed recurrences:

$$i(t) = \begin{cases} 1, & t = 0 \\ i(t-1) + 1, & (t-1) \leq n(t-1) \end{cases}$$

$$sum(t) = \begin{cases} 0, & t = 0 \\ sum(t-1) + i(t), & i(t-1) \leq n(t-1) \end{cases}$$

$$n(t) = \begin{cases} \$n, & t = 0 \\ n(t-1), & i(t-1) \leq n(t-1) \end{cases}$$

$$@count(t) = \begin{cases} 0, & t = 0 \\ @count(t-1) + 1, & i(t-1) \leq n(t-1) \end{cases}$$

It can be seen that these functions are not defined for all non-negative t. For example, there is no valid definition for the sum variable if i exceeds n.

For execution paths which are considering the negated value of a while condition, the variables inside the program context are *virtualized* into a symbolic value representing the state at iteration ω. Consider that ω_{l0} is the first iteration for which the loop l0 condition is not satisfied. For the algorithm in Fig. 9, the final environment and path condition are displayed below:

$$i \mapsto i(\omega) \qquad\qquad sum \mapsto sum(\omega)$$
$$n \mapsto n(\omega) \qquad\qquad @count \mapsto @count(\omega)$$
$$PC \mapsto \neg(i(\omega) \le n(\omega))$$

At the final stage of this analysis process, Alk identifies the value for @count, which is in fact the number of evaluations of the while condition. Using this metric, an approximation of the WCET can be computed as long as the recurrence formulae can be resolved. Assume that $n = N$ is the size of an instance. By solving the formulae, Alk identifies that $@count = N$, and $\omega = N$. It is easy to notice that the WCET, specified by the chosen @count expression, is $O(N)$. This result helps an algorithm designer to understand how his algorithm works.

7 Conclusion

We presented Alk, a platform dedicated to educational use and showed how the symbolic execution and data-flow&abstract-interpretation-based analysis supply a suitable way to build tools that facilitate the understanding of algorithms.

Starting right from the light-weight syntax and intuitive but formal semantics, the Alk platform focuses on delivering an out-of-the-box solution for the users which are new to algorithm design and analysis. The Alk interpreter is equipped with a symbolic execution engine which can check assertions, invariants and functions against specification or assumptions. All of these were designed to allow experimentation and better understanding, while it also avoids altering the core algorithm structure. As of a greater impact, the WCET tool using data-flow framework is implemented to aid the understanding of algorithm efficiency and display relations helping to approximate the worst case execution time.

The Alk interpreter reached a mature state, which ensures that the concrete and symbolic execution engines are solid, while the verification phase is theoretically correct and efficient due to the Z3 engine. The data-flow framework is well supported and optimized and completely supports several analysis tools.

The WCET mechanism is still under development. The challenges which make the difference between the current system and a real WCET tool is that these recurrence formulae are not yet solved by the Alk interpreter. This means that there are no generated constrains over the ω values. There is future work which targets the implementation of a recurrence formulae solver, which can determine the final values of the variables and eventually the final value of a @count variable, but right now these metrics are useful just to understand the changes inside the program state in regard to loop.

Acknowledgment. We warmly thank the anonymous TASE reviewers for their insightful comments, which helped us to improve the presentation.

References

1. Ahrendt, W., Beckert, B., Bubel, R., Hähnle, R., Schmitt, P.H., Ulbrich, M. (eds.): Deductive Software Verification - The KeY Book - From Theory to Practice. Lecture Notes in Computer Science, vol. 10001. Springer, Heidelberg (2016). https://doi.org/10.1007/978-3-319-49812-6

2. Arusoaie, A., Lucanu, D., Rusu, V.: A generic framework for symbolic execution. In: Erwig, M., Paige, R.F., Van Wyk, E. (eds.) SLE 2013. LNCS, vol. 8225, pp. 281–301. Springer, Cham (2013). https://doi.org/10.1007/978-3-319-02654-1_16

3. Ballabriga, C., Forget, J., Lipari, G.: Symbolic WCET computation. ACM Trans. Embed. Comput. Syst. **17**(2), 39:1–39:26 (2018)

4. Blieberger, J.: Data-flow frameworks for worst-case execution time analysis. Real Time Syst. **22**(3), 183–227 (2002)

5. Bobot, F., Filliâtre, J.-C., Marché, C., Paskevich, A.: Let's verify this with why3. Int. J. Softw. Tools Technol. Transf. **17**(6), 709–727 (2015)

6. Chen, X., Roşu, G.: Matching μ-logic: foundation of K framework. In: Proceedings of the 8th Conference on Algebra and Coalgebra in Computer Science (CALCO 2019). Leibniz International Proceedings in Informatics (LIPIcs), vol. 139, pp. 1–4. Schloss Dagstuhl-Leibniz-Zentrum fuer Informatik (2019)

7. Chen, X., Roşu, G.: $\mathbb{K}$—a semantic framework for programming languages and formal analysis. In: Bowen, J.P., Liu, Z., Zhang, Z. (eds.) SETSS 2019. LNCS, vol. 12154, pp. 122–158. Springer, Cham (2020). https://doi.org/10.1007/978-3-030-55089-9_4

8. Cousot, P.: Principles of Abstract Interpretation. MIT Press, Cambridge (2021)

9. de Moura, L., Bjørner, N.: Z3: an efficient SMT solver. In: Ramakrishnan, C.R., Rehof, J. (eds.) TACAS 2008. LNCS, vol. 4963, pp. 337–340. Springer, Heidelberg (2008). https://doi.org/10.1007/978-3-540-78800-3_24

10. Eilers, M., Müller, P.: Nagini: a static verifier for Python. In: Chockler, H., Weissenbacher, G. (eds.) CAV 2018. LNCS, vol. 10981, pp. 596–603. Springer, Cham (2018). https://doi.org/10.1007/978-3-319-96145-3_33

11. Huisman, M., Ahrendt, W., Grahl, D., Hentschel, M.: Formal specification with the Java modeling language. In: Ahrendt, W., Beckert, B., Bubel, R., Hähnle, R., Schmitt, P., Ulbrich, M. (eds.) Deductive Software Verification – The KeY Book. LNCS, vol. 10001, pp. 193–241. Springer, Cham (2016). https://doi.org/10.1007/978-3-319-49812-6_7

12. Kosmatov, N., Signoles, J.: Frama-C, a collaborative framework for C code verification: tutorial synopsis. In: Falcone, Y., Sánchez, C. (eds.) RV 2016. LNCS, vol. 10012, pp. 92–115. Springer, Cham (2016). https://doi.org/10.1007/978-3-319-46982-9_7

13. Leino, K.R.M.: Dafny: an automatic program verifier for functional correctness. In: Clarke, E.M., Voronkov, A. (eds.) LPAR 2010. LNCS (LNAI), vol. 6355, pp. 348–370. Springer, Heidelberg (2010). https://doi.org/10.1007/978-3-642-17511-4_20

14. Lucanu, D., Rusu, V., Arusoaie, A.: A generic framework for symbolic execution: a coinductive approach. J. Symb. Comput. **80**, 125–163 (2017)

15. Lungu, A., Lucanu, D.: Alk interpreter. https://github.com/alk-language/java-semantics. Accessed 23 Feb 2022

16. Lungu, A., Lucanu, D.: Alk interpreter - reference manual. https://github.com/alk-language/java-semantics/wiki/Reference-Manual. Accessed 27 Feb 2022

17. Lungu, A.-I.: Extended Z3 array. In: 23th International Symposium on Symbolic and Numeric Algorithms for Scientific Computing (FROM Workshop), SYNASC 2021. IEEE (2021, to appear)
18. Müller, P., Schwerhoff, M., Summers, A.J.: Viper: a verification infrastructure for permission-based reasoning. In: Pretschner, A., Peled, D., Hutzelmann, T. (eds.) Dependable Software Systems Engineering. NATO Science for Peace and Security Series - D: Information and Communication Security, vol. 50, pp. 104–125. IOS Press (2017)
19. Nielson, F., Nielson, H.R.: Principles of Program Analysis. Springer, Cham (1999). https://doi.org/10.1007/978-3-662-03811-6
20. Rival, X., Yi, K.: Introduction to Static Analysis: An Abstract Interpretation Perspective. MIT Press, Cambridge (2020)
21. Stefanescu, A., Ciobâcă, Ş., Mereuta, R., Moore, B.M., Serbanuta, T.-F., Rosu, G.: All-path reachability logic. Log. Methods Comput. Sci. **15**(2) (2019)
22. Vogels, F., Jacobs, B., Piessens, F.: Featherweight verifast. Log. Methods Comput. Sci. **11**(3), 1–57 (2015)

Author Index

Printed in the United States
by Baker & Taylor Publisher Services